Labor Economics and Industrial Relations

Wertheim Publications in Industrial Relations

Established in 1923 by the family of the late Jacob Wertheim
"for the support of original research in the field of industrial cooperation"

D1395383

Labor Economics and
and
Industrial Relations

▪──────────▪

Markets and Institutions

Edited by **Clark Kerr** and **Paul D. Staudohar**

Distributed by Harvard University Press
Cambridge, Massachusetts and London, England
1994

10 9 8 7 6 5 4 3 2 1

This book is printed on acid-free paper, and its binding materials
have been chosen for strength and durability.

Library of Congress Cataloging-in-Publication Data

Labor economics and industrial relations : markets and institutions /
    edited by Clark Kerr and Paul D. Staudohar.
        p.   cm.—(Wertheim publications in industrial relations)
    Includes bibliographical references and index.
    ISBN 0-674-50641-3 (acid free)
    1. Labor economics.   2. Industrial relations.   3. Labor market.
4. Trade-unions.   5. Labor policy.   6. Labor economics—United
States.   7. Industrial relations—United States.   8. Labor market—
United States.   9. Trade-unions—United States.   10. Labor policy—
United States.   I. Kerr, Clark, 1911–   . II. Staudohar, Paul D.
III. Series.
HD4901.L117   1994
331—dc20   94-2377
                                                           CIP

To Adam Smith,
the first among unequals

Contents

I. The Provinces of Labor Economics

II. A Central Dispute:
Determinateness vs. Indeterminateness

III. Other Great Issues

IV. Internal Labor Markets: A New Exploration

V. The New Industrial State II: What Form Is It Taking?

Contents

VI. Labor Economics in a Changing World

Acknowledgments

We are grateful to Maureen Kawaoka for her extensive administrative and research assistance throughout the project. Helpful suggestions on the project were made, in particular, by John T. Dunlop, George H. Hildebrand, Bruce E. Kaufman, Richard A. Lester, Jacob Mincer, Daniel J. B. Mitchell, Melvin W. Reder, Lloyd G. Reynolds, George Strauss, and Lloyd Ulman. Library assistance was provided by Terence Huwe, librarian at the Institute of Industrial Relations, University of California, Berkeley, and his assistant, Janice Kimball. Special thanks go to James A. Baker and Gordon Olsen for their early thoughts on the project.

Clark Kerr
Paul D. Staudohar

Foreword

On January 20, 1969, I inherited a strike of longshoremen all along the East and Gulf Coasts of the United States. When the strike had started the previous fall, President Lyndon Johnson had declared that it threatened to cause a national emergency and, under the authority of the Taft-Hartley Act, got an injunction to stop the strike. His action was challenged by the union, and the issue was taken on a fast track to the Supreme Court, where the president's determination was upheld. The 80-day period provided under Taft-Hartley ran its course without a settlement. Then the strike resumed, and when I became secretary of labor, I had on my hands an action that had been declared a national emergency by a president of the United States and by the Supreme Court.

I disagreed. I thought both the president and the Court were wrong in their judgments. As a labor economist I had studied emergency disputes, and discussed how to handle them with thoughtful, experienced people, Clark Kerr being notable among them. I had worked in labor disputes as an arbitrator and mediator, and criticized in writing the Kennedy and Johnson administrations' practice of quick and frequent intervention in labor disputes. All this led me to take a different approach.

"OK, professor," reporters now said to me, "we see what you have written, now what are you going to do?" I went to President Nixon and told him I had a strategy for the longshoremen's dispute that was also a strategy for dealing generally with collective bargaining: the best settlements will come if, with due mediation efforts, we let the parties fight it out and work it out themselves. Nixon agreed. He liked strategies. He also liked the idea of freeing himself from a time-consuming involvement in what would likely be a messy, no-win situation. I warned him that he would get lots of pressure from businesses who were hurting and from politicians pleading their case; I said that now was the time to decide that he would stand firm against pleas to intervene from the White House or to direct me to do so. He stood firm. After about six weeks, the strike was settled on reasonable terms. More important, we had taken a stand for free collective bargaining and for great restraint in government intervention, and for the direct settlement of disputes.

This was a turning point in the collective bargaining process. Government involvement and pressure declined sharply, and the use of the emergency-dispute authority has virtually ceased.

There were plenty of critics of this strategy, but it held up because it had a solidly established intellectual base. The subject had been well worked over in the field of labor economics and industrial relations. The discipline of economics provided a structure for analyzing the impact of a major interruption in the normal flow of business and finance and a means of putting data behind the analysis. Other behavioral disciplines provided insight into political pressure points and the likely reactions of organizations involved. My work with lawyers on this problem gave me a sense of both the limitations and possibilities in actions that could be taken. And experience in mediation and arbitration of labor disputes provided a sense of how the pulling and hauling might go.

So my initiation as a cabinet officer turned out to be an exercise in the use of my training as a labor economist.

I remembered the case studies in the *Causes of Industrial Peace under Collective Bargaining*, having written two of them, and I learned an important lesson in completing that assignment. When the parties start to value their relationship very highly for its own sake, that relationship is likely to deteriorate. A solid and durable relationship emerges when the participants use it to solve important and difficult problems. Preoccupation with the relationship as such can lead a union to neglect grievances so as not to upset management. And on the other hand, it can lead management to go easy on discipline or on necessary change for fear of a negative reaction from the union. The relationship inevitably goes downhill because the parties are not getting what they want out of it.

Later, as secretary of state, I found the same to be true in international relations. Take the United States and China, for example. So long as we saw this relationship primarily as the geostrategic prism of the Soviet-U.S.-China triad, the Chinese calculated that they could use our desire to maintain good U.S.-China relations as a pressure point on us. They were good calculators. They saw that they could extract concessions from us on issues of substance by threatening a deterioration of the relationship. I remembered what I had learned in my labor relations career and, with the full support of President Reagan, changed the conceptual underpinning of our approach to China.

Clark Kerr and labor economics: the man and the field are virtually synonymous. He has taught us to combine a rigorous use of economics with the practical wisdom that emerges from direct engagement with people and organizations struggling to reconcile their diverse interests and pursue their common objectives. I never cease to use what I learned from Clark Kerr.

George P. Shultz

Introduction: Labor in the Course of the Development of Economic Thought

■ ─────────────── ■

Clark Kerr

Labor economics began with Adam Smith in 1776, with his *The Wealth of Nations*. His major themes included the centrality of labor to the economy and the special characteristics of labor as a participant in the economy, and these themes have been in the midst of the discussions ever since. How central are they? How special?

The essays presented here review the course of labor economics over the more than two centuries since Adam Smith's day: the contending theories, the changing environmental contexts, the evolving issues, the differing policies. We are pleased that they have as their authors so many of the leading contributors and participants in the controversies of the past half-century and more. We regret, however, that three or four persons whom we very much wished to participate were unable to do so because of prior obligations.

We greatly appreciate the foreword by George Shultz, who was himself one of the leading participants among the "revisionists," as will be evident later. He makes the point that the understanding that flows from the study of labor economics and industrial relations, and the skills that are enhanced by practical participation in these fields are useful in wider areas of economics and politics, as he has proved so well during his remarkable career of public service on the national and world scenes.

The essays in this volume are divided into six groups. A brief description of the groups and the papers within them follows.

The Provinces of Labor Economics

One central dispute has been over how wide a scope of human activity labor economics should include. Joseph A. Schumpeter, in his *History of Economic Analysis,* distinguished among "economic theory" with its "explanatory hypotheses" that make use of "simplifying schematics or models"; "economic sociology" concerned additionally with "social facts," "institutional frameworks," and "general forms of human behavior"; and "political economy" that further concentrates on the "economy of the state" and on "public policies of an economic nature" within the "historical-political framework."[1] (He also, of course, listed "economic history" and "economic statistics.") This theme of scope runs through the essays that follow. How narrow? How broad?

The first essay, by George H. Hildebrand ("The Labor Factor within the Classical and Neoclassical Systems of Economic Analysis") surveys the field of labor economics from Adam Smith to John R. Hicks. Within the typology of Schumpeter, David Ricardo and the Austrians (and their associates elsewhere) were in the economic theory category; Smith and Alfred Marshall in the economic sociology mode — for example, Adam Smith wrote about the impact of the division of labor on the nature of the worker, and Marshall was concerned with morality as well as with markets; and Karl Marx was clearly in the broader field of political economy. Hicks, in his original edition of *The Theory of Wages,* is usually put in the neoclassical line of Marshall.[2] As I interpret him, however, he was then (in 1932) a deviationist. He deviated in the direction of Ricardo and the Austrians, looking more for simplified "explanatory hypotheses" than for the impacts of "institutional frameworks" and "human behavior." However, in his second edition (1963) Hicks clearly returned to the Marshallian line.

Jack Barbash, in the second essay ("Americanizing the Labor Problem: The Wisconsin School"), discusses one of the two great alternatives within the political economy typology — John R. Commons and the Wisconsin school (the other being quite clearly Marx and Engels and their successors, although the two approaches otherwise were and are in bitter conflict). The Wisconsin school was heavily concerned with the economy of the state and public policies of an economic nature. Markets with competition gave way to institutions with rules. According to the Wisconsin school, labor should not be viewed as a commodity, nor unions as an aberration (see the discussion in Mark Perlman, *Labor Union Theories in America*[3]), nor government interference as an evil — as some of the conservative economists of the day saw it. From World War I to the end of the New Deal the institutionalists dominated the study of labor problems in the United States, and they left a legacy of fundamental social legislation. Barbash points out that the Wisconsin school moved the study of labor economics and industrial relations to an American from a British and often quasi-socialist orientation, as illustrated by Sidney and Beatrice Webb, and by G. D. H. Cole.

The revisionists, increasingly dominant from the middle 1930s to the middle 1960s, are the subject of the third essay ("The Social Economics Revisionists: The 'Real World' Study of Labor Markets and Institutions"). They drew on the institutionalists but they were not neoinstitutionalists. They were more fundamentally neoclassical revisionists or neoclassical incrementalists, going beyond Smith and Marshall but in the same direction of economic sociology or "social economics" — to use another phrase associated with Schumpeter. In particular, they opposed the Austrian deviation of John R. Hicks in 1932. They took the social economics observations of Smith and Marshall (and the exceptions of Hicks in 1932, which Hicks then thought were of little importance — although he acknowledged their existence, which the Austrians did not), made them central to the study of labor economics, and then provided some additional observations of their own. They insisted on calling attention to what Max Weber once termed "inconvenient facts" — inconvenient for preexisting "opinions."[4] In the studies of the revisionists, labor markets became social as well as economic institutions, and unions became not economic monopolies selling labor but political entities participating in the setting of wages — albeit under strong economic constraints; institutional or internal labor markets were placed alongside external markets as highly influential institutions. The revisionists had participants spread across many universities and colleges, but if there could be said to have been a central axis, it was Harvard-Berkeley, as contrasted with Wisconsin.

The next turn was to the Chicago school that took over dominance in the 1960s (actually it might better have been identified as the Chicago-Columbia school). It had two distinguishing characteristics. It used the new methodology of econometrics, a powerful additional tool; and it was restorationist in its orientation — going back to a greater (even almost exclusive) emphasis on the competitive market and on rational behavior within it (markets that clear, and participants that maximize). The method and the orientation went together.

Econometrics works best in analyzing a multitude of individual decisions, and such a multitude of decisions are best found in fully or at least highly competitive markets. Thus the econometric restorationists made their studies mostly on the supply side of labor markets. They were greatly aided by new data sets produced by federal agencies. They added, within the orbits of their studies, great precision to interpretations of the evidence and opened up new areas for statistical exploration, particularly the formation of human capital, and in doing this they also expanded the boundaries of economics to include the family as an economic unit.

The applications of human capital theory to empirical analysis of labor markets is described by Jacob Mincer ("Human Capital: A Review") in an essay that centers on the studies of the formation and consequences of human capital. Mincer was one of the leading architects of the renewed interest in human capital, along with Theodore W. Schultz and Gary Becker. Here again, it was Adam Smith who first emphasized the importance of human capital. Human capital analysis helps greatly to explain wage differentials, since schooling and training are so basic to the determination of occupational wages. Human capital analysis is also central to the explanation of trends in wage rates as they relate to productivity growth, and it contributes in very important ways to analyzing policies for economic growth. Initially human capital related more heavily to the supply side of labor markets. More recently a focus on the demand side addresses two topics: implications of firm-specific human capital for hiring, training, and turnover decisions of firms; and implications of changes in technology for changes in demand for human capital and their effects on the wage structure. As Mincer notes, human capital theory fits in well "with the mainstream of economic theory." Previously, he says, labor economics with a major interest in "labor-management relations" had "coexisted rather marginally and unevenly" on the far edge of economic theory. Human capital analysis has been one of the great triumphs of empirical economic analysis and one of the great illuminations of its uses. The best ore in the econometrician's mine has been human capital, and it has been well exploited.

A separate group consisting of neo-Marxists paralleled the development of the Chicago school, but they were intent instead on restoring Marx. Labor economics split toward conservative "theory" and radical "political economy," and moved away from the more moderate social economics.

The Chicago school may now be in the process of being challenged, although it is too early to say how successfully, by a new group that might be called the new revisionists. They use econometrics but are not solely committed to it — it is one methodology but not the only one. They follow, as did their revisionist predecessors, their curiosity about developments and their concern about problems more than they do their competence in the use of a single technique. Bruce E. Kaufman, in his essay in this volume, calls this the Cambridge group. I refer to it as the Harvard-MIT axis. By whatever name, this group (old and new members) is well represented in this volume of essays, by John T. Dunlop and Robert M. Solow and John Kenneth Galbraith as central personalities, as well as by Richard B. Freeman, Paul S. Osterman, Michael J. Piore, and Thomas A. Kochan as younger participants.

A Central Dispute: Determinateness versus Indeterminateness

Those labor economists more involved in the study of economic theory have been the more attracted by rigor; those in social economics, also by relevance; and those in political economy, more explicitly by visions of reform. Robert Aaron Gordon in his 1975 presidential address to the American Economic Association, "Rigor and Relevance in a Changing Institutional Setting," discussed the contest of rigor versus relevance, and he came out on the side of "relevance with as much rigor as possible," which is the standard social economists' answer; the theorists (and econometricians) say rigor; and the political economists say relevance above all else.[5] Labor economists, and economists more generally, have now been more on one side and then later more on the other, weaving back and

Table I.1 A schematic view of the evolution of labor economics, drawing on Schumpeter's typology

Economic theory	Social economics	Political economy
Ricardo	Smith	Marx
The Austrians (and others)	Marshall	The Wisconsin School
Hicks (1932)	Douglas (1934)	
	The revisionists (including Hicks 1963)	
The Chicago School		The neo-Marxists
	The New Revisionists	

forth. This may be because there is no perfect solution. Hume argued that nothing can be proved, however rigorous the logic, by deduction from unproved premises; Descartes said that nothing of importance can be inducted from confusion, however relevant the presence of surface confusion may be.

This dispute in economics goes back a long way. Aristotle took the position that the understanding of human affairs did not lend itself to mathematical formulas, and Alfred Marshall said that "economic doctrine . . . is not a body of concrete truths." Others, however, have seen "laws" at work as, for example, the "two postulata" of Malthus based on food and sex, and the "laws of motion" of Marx and Engels (analogous to those of Newton). It is a great temptation, as Spinoza said, to try to find an ordered universe with fixed rules that yields to mathematical explanations, that leads to certainty. When one departs from such a universe, as Fritz Machlup said in his 1966 presidential address to the American Economic Association, it becomes "messy"; but in getting closer to reality and to an understanding of individual cases, he acknowledged, it may be necessary to be messy — most regretfully.[6] Which road to take? Labor economics has wavered in its choices between the rigor of the rationalists and the relevance of the empiricists.

Perhaps there is at least one lesson to be learned, and that is the value of some humility in making fully assured policy pronouncements to those who bear the burdens of decisions. Rigor can be too far removed from reality; and relevance is not all that precise — it is messy. Hegel wrote that "to know before we know is absurd" — and we do not always know for sure.

Which is the best model of the labor market? Is it one that yields a "standard rate" as a result of strong competition among firms, high mobility among workers, good information all around, and rational behavior oriented toward calculation of economic costs and benefits; is it a "broadly competitive" market with some imperfections; or is it a market with competition restricted by actions of institutions, among other possibilities? The second model yields wider or narrower bands or ranges of wages for similar workers in similar jobs in the same labor market. The third reflects the varying power and policies of institutions.

Bruce E. Kaufman ("The Evolution of Thought on the Competitive Nature of Labor Markets") reviews the arguments over determinateness versus indeterminateness, from Smith through Marshall to what he calls the post war labor economists, the Chicago school, and finally the Cambridge group. He concludes that we still need to know more about real-world labor markets. The one point of full agreement he finds, however, is that bilateral monopoly, as discussed by Francis Y. Edgeworth[7] and later by A. C. Pigou,[8] yields a range of indeterminateness. Elsewhere there are many "inconvenient facts" that lead to inconsistent conclusions.

Richard A. Lester ("Wage Differentials and Minimum-Wage Effects") argues the case for relatively wide bands for wages. He draws on his own studies made after World War II and on recent studies that confirm his earlier findings. He quotes one recent study as follows: observed patterns "cannot plausibly be rationalized without the introduction of noncompetitive considerations or additional constraints." Labor markets are subject to many noncompetitive and "impeditive" forces, as Lester earlier wrote. They are quite different from the competitive model and do not work nearly as precisely.

Lloyd G. Reynolds ("Modeling Third World Labor Markets"), as in his earlier labor market studies after World War II in the United States, takes a view that labor markets generally are "broadly competitive." His essay here is concerned with situations in Third World nations which show a "distinct family relation to our own." He argues against those who see largely unconnected markets, rural and urban: "dual labor markets do not stand up well in light of the facts." He finds labor markets to be intertwined, as he did in his earlier labor market studies in the United States — not one great big fully competitive labor market, but rather labor markets that have important connections to one another. He finds that labor markets have imperfections but work reasonably well: "market pressures do operate with compelling force."

Albert E. Rees ("Occupational Wage Differentials") looks at occupational wage differentials in the United States. This essay, regrettably, is his last of many contributions to the literature. Occupational wages are presented as the basic building blocks of the total wage structure affecting, in particular, interindustry differentials. Occupational differentials are very heavily influenced by schooling and training, above all other considerations. The study of occupational wage differentials does support the view that there is a basic national wage structure held together by competition and mobility, and based on skill levels. Other factors, however, are also at work, including gender, race, size of establishment, union status, and, it might be added, geographical location. Rees's general view is much like that of Reynolds. A contrary view, long held by John T. Dunlop, is that interindustry differentials vary widely for the same job classifications, carefully defined for job context, largely because of the product market and some local community influences.[9] Interoccupational wage differentials have little influence on or leverage with interindustry differentials. The Rees view puts more emphasis on the supply side, the cost of preparing for occupations in the labor market; Dunlop emphasizes the demand side, conditions in the product market.

Other Great Issues

Melvin W. Reder ("On Labor's Bargaining Disadvantage") takes up another issue that goes back to Adam Smith — the alleged disadvantage of workers versus employers. For Smith, this issue arose because employers could hold out longer than workers and were easier to organize than workers; Marx added the impact of the "reserve army of the unemployed." But, as others pointed out later, workers could (and sometimes do) withhold effort, since the labor contract is "necessarily incomplete." To Reder, the answer is that the outcome of bargaining depends on the circumstances, and circumstances vary.

Unemployment was not a big issue for the classical and neoclassical economists, although it was for Marx. Their model of the labor market led to expected adjustments that cleared the market, and unemployment (except frictional and seasonal) disappeared. With the Great Depression, however, the problems of unemployment had to be faced, and new models of the labor market were proposed, in particular by Keynes. Stagflation, more pronounced after about 1970 with historically high rates of inflation given the levels of unemployment, raised again the issue of appropriate models of the labor market. Robert M. Solow in his essay ("Two [or Three] Ways of Thinking about Unemployment") discusses the possibility that there may not be a single equilibrium rate of unemployment but that "the labor market may admit a whole range of equilibria" and "this allows a point of entry for the institutional factors that have long been the stuff of labor economics." The labor economist revisionists found ranges of wages, not a standard rate, in broadly competitive markets. These ranges opened policy choices to employers. So also would a range of equilibria open policy choices to governments. Solow goes on to explore the public policy implications of such a range of equilibria.

Richard B. Freeman ("American Exceptionalism in the Labor Market: Union-Nonunion Differentials in the United States and Other Countries") turns to a second great issue of more modern origins — the impact of unions on the economy. This essay may be viewed as an addition to his widely known book written with James Medoff,

What Do Unions Do?, and as an expansion of it on a more international basis.[10] Unions do raise wages, and more in the United States than elsewhere. Unions are also declining more in the United States than elsewhere. This raises a question of whether there is a peril point beyond which unions may have to accept high risks for survival. Everywhere unions have a "voice effect," but only in the United States do they have a significant "monopoly wage" effect.

Internal Labor Markets: A New Exploration

The revisionists often served as arbitrators in labor-management disputes during and after World War II. Having studied external labor markets, they then were able to get a close look at the inside of internal labor markets, with their wage structures, their seniority rules, their grievance procedures. This is where most workers live most of the time, and these markets and their rules are usually more important to workers than what is going on in the external markets, about which, in any event, they have imperfect information. What the worker at the next station is paid and how much seniority he or she has are more relevant questions than what is happening in the plant across town. The operations of these internal markets affect the functioning of external markets, levels of unemployment, rates of productivity, adaptations to the changing composition of the labor force, and much else. They are central institutions in the modern economy. These markets began building as firms became larger, as personnel administration became an integral part of management, and as collective bargaining spread.

Paul S. Osterman ("Internal Labor Markets: Theory and Change") discusses the development of the concept of internal labor markets in the literature, the origins of these markets, and their changing natures. Osterman, who has contributed substantially to the literature in this area, explains why internal labor markets are important to the functioning of the economy. He also notes that internal labor markets may, in turn, have submarkets within them, and that internal labor markets are continually changing their structures and operations, partially in response to external pressures.

Sanford M. Jacoby ("Managing the Workplace: From Markets to Manors, and Beyond") develops the history of the rise of internal markets within the firm, from the foreman-dominated relationship to personnel administration to human relations in industry, human resource management, and participative arrangements. Jacoby does for the management side what Sumner Slichter did with his reports on the impact of unions and collective bargaining on industrial management.[11] There has been a transition, in the long run, from greater emphasis on the technical environment to greater emphasis on the human environment.

John T. Dunlop ("Organizations and Human Resources: Internal and External Markets") was a leader in calling attention to internal labor markets with their "seniority districts," their "job families," and their "wage contours." He shows in this essay how the changing structure of the economy led to the building of these markets, and he discusses the several forms they take. He also provides some indication of what proportion of the labor force may be said to be employed within structured internal labor markets: about one-half. He observes that conventional labor market theory "neglected a vast range of activities within the walls of organizations as well as their forms of interaction with external markets."

David Lewin ("Explicit Individual Contracting in the Labor Market") draws attention to a new phenomenon that works in the opposite direction from the development of internal labor markets and their common rules. This is the expansion of individual contracting with workers, person by person. He finds that a higher percentage of the labor force in the private sector is covered by individual contracts (24 percent) than is covered by collective bargaining (13 percent).

The New Industrial State II: What Form Is It Taking?

In *The New Industrial State*, John Kenneth Galbraith set forth his understanding of the new world in which private governments control the large corporations, and of the central role within the corporations of the "technostructure."[12] This new industrial state keeps on evolving.

. One feature of the older industrial state was the growth of "countervailing power" that led to less reliance on competitive markets and more on bilateral monopoly.[13] In his essay in this volume ("Countervailing Power: Memoir and Modern Reality"), Galbraith notes the declining strength of American trade unions that has reduced the bilateral aspect of monopoly. The other essays that follow in the section address aspects of this change as we enter the New

Industrial State II — a state that incorporates many additional transformations, several of which Galbraith notes. And Galbraith is "less than optimistic" about the future.

The shift away from the countervailing power of unions can be a cause for substantial concern. George Shultz has said that "the underlying reality is that there need to be checks and balances governing the work place," and that "free societies and free trade unions go together."[14] Arnold R. Weber has agreed that we "need unions as a balancing force."[15] But how?

Daniel J. B. Mitchell ("A Decade of Concession Bargaining") highlights the decline of union power as he describes and analyzes the "dramatic events in union wage determination." As many as half of all organized workers were affected by concessions in the peak year of 1983. Mitchell explains why this all happened as it did. The period left unions counting their losses after a half-century of counting gains. Mitchell ends up at least flirting with optimism, particularly because we may be more realistic in the future about basic economic forces at work, and because collective bargaining might become more cooperative and less adversarial.

Peter Feuille ("Changing Patterns in Dispute Resolution") documents the great decline in union strike activity as unions have lost economic strength. They have, however, apparently gained political strength and with it expanded coverage in the public sector. Strike activity in private industry has gone down with union strength, but third parties have also become more active in settling disputes peacefully — with private arbitration used to resolve grievances and with public authorities setting by law many important aspects of employment conditions, such as health and safety requirements.

Michael J. Piore ("Unions: A Reorientation to Survive") sets forth a new model of union activity that might reverse the decline of the union movement — the union as "an institution that mediates between the economic and the social structures." Such a union would be concerned with broadly defined "human welfare" both in the place of employment and in the surrounding community. It would be oriented toward the local community and would practice local participatory democracy. It would concentrate particularly on the needs of disadvantaged workers, regardless of craft or industry.

Labor Economics in a Changing World

New problems for study arise, and new combinations of methodologies are needed to address them.

One of these newer problems has been the changing rate of productivity increases. The rates of increase began falling in the United States in the early 1970s, at about the same time that international economic competition began to increase dramatically. Edward F. Denison ("Productivity: Data and Determinants"), out of his long years studying productivity, discusses what has happened and why. He emphasizes the skill levels of the labor force, the creation of new knowledge, the changing composition of the labor force, and the performance of management — which is the factor least subject to proof, but which may be of major importance. He suggests areas for remedial attention.

For Denison, as for Rees on interoccupational wage differentials, this contribution was his final statement of his views on productivity, after having been the leader in this area for so many years.

New energy is being directed at absorbing more minorities and more women into the labor force. Governmental policies have sought to aid this process, as is discussed by Jonathan S. Leonard ("The Specter of Affirmative Action"). He finds basic contradictions in federal policies, ineffectiveness in their application, and modest results. No early solutions are foreseen.

Ray Marshall ("Organizations and Learning Systems for a High-Wage Economy") treats another current problem of great importance and complexity: how workplace skills may be raised in an economy that is undergoing internal technological change and greater external competition than ever before. How may our learning systems be improved, since "ideas, skills and knowledge . . . have been responsible for most human progress"? Learning systems "include families, work, community institutions, media, and political processes, not just formal schools." Marshall makes a series of proposals for improving schools, the school-to-work transition, families as learning systems, and employer investments in training. At stake is whether the United States might become a "second-rate economic power."

Thomas A. Kochan ("Principles for a Post–New Deal Employment Policy") states the belief that once again, as during the Great Depression, the nation needs an activist approach to employment policies in the United States. He emphasizes concentrating on long-term investments in human resources and on "mutual-gains strategies" for management and workers. To assist in this, he calls for a new generation of labor economists to follow in the steps of the institutionalists and what he calls "the post–War Labor Board generation of labor economists and industrial relations specialists." Members of these earlier groups, as he notes, were broadly trained, had practical experience in the field, and had opportunities to be involved in policy-making and analysis. This new generation would "carry on the tradition of prior generations of institutional labor economists." So speaks one of the new revisionists.

Notes

1. Joseph A. Schumpeter, *History of Economic Analysis*, edited (from manuscript) with an introduction by E. Boody Schumpeter (New York: Oxford University Press, 1954).
2. John R. Hicks, *The Theory of Wages* (London: Macmillan, 1932).
3. Mark Perlman, *Labor Union Theories in America*. (White Plains, N.Y.: Row and Peterson, 1952).
4. Max Weber, "Science as a Vocation," in H. H. Gerth and C. W. Mills, trans. and eds., *From Max Weber: Essays in Sociology* (New York: Oxford University Press, 1946).
5. Robert Aaron Gordon, "Rigor and Relevance in a Changing Institutional Setting." *American Economic Review* 66, no. 1 (March 1976): 1–14.
6. Fritz Machlup, "Theories of the Firm." *American Economic Review* 57, no. 1 (March 1967): 1–33.
7. Francis Y. Edgeworth, *Mathematical Physics* (London: Kegan Paul, 1881).
8. A. C. Pigou, *Principles and Methods of Industrial Peace*. London: Macmillan, 1905.
9. See John T. Dunlop, "The Task of Wage Theory," in George Taylor and Frank Pierson, eds., *New Concepts in Wage Theory* (New York: McGraw-Hill, 1957) 117–139.
10. Richard B. Freeman and James Medoff, *What Do Unions Do?* (New York: Basic Books, 1984).
11. Sumner H. Slichter, *Union Policies and Industrial Management* (Washington, D.C.: Brookings Institution, 1941). Sumner H. Slichter, James J. Healy, and E. Robert Livernash, *The Impact of Collective Bargaining on Management* (Washington, D.C.: Brookings Institution, 1960).
12. John Kenneth Galbraith, *The New Industrial State* (Boston: Houghton Mifflin, 1967).

13. John Kenneth Galbraith, *American Capitalism: The Concept of Countervailing Power* (Boston: Houghton Mifflin, 1952).
14. George P. Shultz, unpublished remarks at the National Planning Association Gold Medal Award Dinner, New York City, October 9, 1991.
15. Arnold R. Weber, "Labor Management Relations in a Universe of Paradoxes," unpublished remarks at a conference honoring William Usery, May 20, 1992.

Contributing Authors

Jack Barbash is Bascom Professor of Economics and Industrial Relations (Emeritus) at the University of Wisconsin–Madison. He is a former president of the Industrial Relations Research Association and the Association for Evolutionary Economics. His most recent books are *The Elements of Industrial Relations* (1984) and *Theories and Concepts in Industrial Relations,* with Kate Barbash (1989). He has served as an economist for trade unions and as a civil servant specializing in labor.

Edward F. Denison (1915–1992) was Senior Fellow Emeritus in the Division of Economic Studies of the Brookings Institution. He held a Ph.D. in economics from Brown University and was a graduate of the National War College. Denison analyzed economic growth in advanced countries at Brookings since 1962, and before that at the Committee for Economic Development, where he introduced the concepts and techniques of sources-of-growth analysis. He also made important contributions to the measurement of national income and product, chiefly while employed at the U.S. Department of Commerce from 1941 to 1956 and again from 1979 to 1982. Among his books are *The Sources of Economic Growth and the Alternatives Before Us* (1962) and *Trends in American Economic Growth, 1929–1982* (1985).

John T. Dunlop is Lamont University Professor Emeritus at Harvard University. He was Chairman of the Department of Economics from 1961 to 1966, Dean of the Faculty of Arts and Sciences from 1970 to 1973, and Acting Director of the Center for Business and Government at the Kennedy School of Government from 1987 to 1991. He has been Editor of the Wertheim Series in Industrial Relations since 1945, and from 1975 to 1976 was U.S. Secretary of Labor. Dunlop is the author of *Wage Determination under Trade Unions* (1944); *Industrial Relations Systems* (1958); *Industrialism and Industrial Man,* coauthored with Clark Kerr, Frederick H. Harbison, and Charles A. Myers (1960); *Labor and the American Community,* coauthored with Derek C. Bok (1970); *Dispute Resolution, Negotiation and Consensus Building* (1984); and *The Management of Unions: Decision-Making with Historical Constraints* (1990).

Peter Feuille is a Professor of Labor and Industrial Relations at the University of Illinois. In the years since he received his Ph.D. from the University of California, Berkeley, he has published widely on various industrial relations topics, with a special focus on labor-management dispute resolution in government. He is the coauthor of *Police Unionism* and *Public Sector Labor Relations,* and his articles, chapters, and papers have appeared in a variety of journals, books, and conference proceedings. In addition, he is an active grievance and interest arbitrator.

Richard B. Freeman is Professor of Economics at Harvard University, Program Director of the National Bureau of Economic Research Program in Labor Studies, Executive Programme Director of the Comparative Labour Market Institutions Programme at the London School of Economics Centre for Economic Performance, and is currently serving as Faculty Co-Chair of the Harvard University Trade Union Program. His research in labor-related issues includes trade unionism around the world, labor in transitions to market economies, comparative labor markets, and economic development. He is the author of *Labor Markets in Action: Essays in Empirical Economics, Labor Economics, The Overeducated American, The Black Elite: The New Market for Highly Educated Black Americans,* and *The Market for College Trained Manpower,* and the coauthor of *What Do Unions Do?*

John Kenneth Galbraith is the Paul M. Warburg Professor of Economics Emeritus at Harvard University. He has also taught at the University of California, Berkeley, Princeton University, and Cambridge University. Galbraith was Deputy Administrator of the Office of Price Administration in the early 1940s and was principal organizer of the wartime system of price control, which he oversaw until 1943. In 1945, he was a Director of the U.S. Strategic Bombing Survey. He later was awarded the Medal of Freedom. He is a former editor of *Fortune* magazine. From 1961 to 1963 he was U.S. Ambassador to India. Galbraith's books include many well-remembered titles, such as *The Affluent Society, The Great Crash, The New Industrial State, Economics and the Public Purpose,* and *The Age of Uncertainty.* His most recent book, *The Culture of Contentment,* was published in 1992. Galbraith is a past president of the American Academy and Institute of Arts and Letters and of the American Economic Association.

George H. Hildebrand is Maxwell M. Upson Professor of Economics and Industrial Relations Emeritus at Cornell University. He also served many years as Professor at the University of California, Berkeley, and the University of California, Los Angeles, and was Director of the Institute of Industrial Relations at UCLA from 1956 to 1959. He has been a labor arbitrator for more than 40 years. Among his books are *The Pacific Coast Maritime Shipping Industry,* coauthored with Wytze Gorter (two volumes, 1952 and 1954); *Manufacturing Production Functions, United States, 1957,* coauthored with Ta-Chung Liu (1965); *Growth and Structure in the Economy of Modern Italy* (1965); *American Unionism: An Historical and Analytical Survey* (1979); and *Capital and Labor in American Copper, 1845–1990,* coauthored with Garth Mangum (1992).

Sanford M. Jacoby is Professor of History and Management at the University of California, Los Angeles, and at UCLA's Anderson Graduate School of Management. He also serves as Associate Director of the UCLA Institute of Industrial Relations. He received his A.B. from the University of Pennsylvania and his Ph.D. in economics from the University of California, Berkeley.

He is the author of numerous articles — on industrial relations, labor economics, and economic and labor history — and two books, *Employing Bureaucracy: Managers, Unions and the Transformation of Work in American Industry* (1985) and *Masters to Managers: Historical and Comparative Perspectives on American Employers* (1991).

Bruce E. Kaufman is Professor of Economics and Director of the Beebe Institute of Personnel and Employment Relations at Georgia State University. He received his Ph.D. from the University of Wisconsin–Madison. His numerous articles have appeared in the leading journals. Among his books are *The Economics of Labor Markets and Labor Relations* (1986), *How Labor Markets Work* (1988), and *The Origins and Evolution of the Field of Industrial Relations in the United States* (1992).

Clark Kerr, coeditor of this volume, is President Emeritus of the University of California and Professor Emeritus of Economics and Industrial Relations at the University of California, Berkeley. He received his B.A. degree in 1932 from Swarthmore College, his M.A. degree in 1933 from Stanford University, and his Ph.D. degree in economics in 1939 from the University of California, Berkeley. Kerr is a past president of the Industrial Relations Research Association, and was a founding vice president of the National Academy of Arbitrators. He has served as Chairman of the Board of Trustees, Work in America Institute, from 1975 to the present. His books include *Industrialism and Industrial Man,* coauthored with John T. Dunlop, Frederick H. Harbison, and Charles A. Myers (1960); *Labor and Management in Industrial Society* (1964); *Labor Markets and Wage Determination* (1977); and *The Future of Industrial Societies* (1983).

Thomas A. Kochan is George M. Bunker Professor of Management and a Leaders for Manufacturing Professor at the Sloan School of Management, Massachusetts Institute of Technology. He received his Ph.D. in industrial relations from the University of Wisconsin–Madison in 1973. From 1973 to 1980 he was on the faculty of the School of Industrial and Labor Relations at Cornell University. Kochan has served as a third-party mediator, fact finder, and arbitrator and as a consultant to a variety of government and private-sector organizations and labor-management groups. He has done research on a variety of topics related to industrial relations and human resource management in the public and private sectors. His recent books include *The Transformation of American Industrial Relations* (1986), *An Introduction to Collective Bargaining and Industrial Relations* (1991), and *Transforming Organizations* (1992). In 1992 Kochan was elected President of the International Industrial Relations Association.

Jonathan S. Leonard is Professor of Industrial Relations at the Haas School of Business, University of California, Berkeley. He has served as a Senior Economist on the President's Council of Economic Advisers, and as a consultant to the U.S. Department of Labor, the U.S. Equal Employment Opportunity Commission, the U.S. Department of Education, the U.S. Civil Rights Commission, the Advisory Council on Affirmative Action to the U.S. House of Representatives, the National Academy of Sciences, the Organization for Economic Cooperation and Development, the Canadian Department of Labor and Immigration, and other government agencies, businesses, and unions. Since earning his Ph.D. in economics from Harvard in 1983, he has also been a Research Associate of the National Bureau of Economic Research and an Olin Fellow. He has served as a Coeditor of the *Journal of Human Resources* and as Editor of *Industrial Relations*.

Richard A. Lester is Professor Emeritus of Economics at Princeton University. He received his Ph.D. degree in economics from Princeton in 1936 and was Professor of Economics at Princeton from 1945 to 1974. He was Dean of the Faculty from 1968 to 1973, and since 1945 has been a Research Associate in the Princeton Industrial Relations Section. Other positions he has held include member of the Executive Committee, 1951 to 1953, and Vice President, 1961, of the American Economic Association; President of the Industrial Relations Research Association, 1956; Chairman, Southern Textile Commission, National War Labor Board, 1944 to 1945; Chairman, New Jersey Employment Security Council, 1955 to 1965; and Vice Chairman of the President's Commission on the Status of Women, 1961 to 1963. Among his numerous publications are *Economics of Labor* (1941, 1964); *As Unions Mature* (1958); and "Wages, Benefits, and Company Employment Systems" in *How Labor Markets Work*, edited by Bruce E. Kaufman (1988).

David Lewin is Professor at the Anderson Graduate School of Management, Director of the Institute of Industrial Relations, and Director of the Human Resources Roundtable at the University of California, Los Angeles. Previously he taught for two decades at Columbia University. He has published nine books, including *The Modern Grievance Procedure in the United States* (1988) and *Research Frontiers in Industrial Relations and Human Resources* (1992), and his many articles have appeared in the leading journals. He is a coeditor of *Advances in Industrial and Labor Relations* and is a member of the editorial boards of *Industrial Relations* and *California Management Review*. He has served as a consultant to business, labor, and government organizations, including the U.S. Department of Labor, Organization for Economic Cooperation and Development, National Science Foundation, and the International Labor Organization.

Ray Marshall holds the Audre and Bernard Rapoport Centennial Chair in Economics and Public Affairs at the University of Texas at Austin. He served as U.S. Secretary of Labor from 1977 to 1981. Marshall holds a Ph.D. in economics from the University of California, Berkeley. He has authored or coauthored more than 200 books, monographs, and articles on such topics as the economics of the family, education and the economy, U.S. competitiveness in an internationalized economy, labor in the South, international workers' rights, and minority business development. Among his books are *Employment Discrimination* (1978), *Employment of Blacks in the South* (1978), *Basic Trends Affecting Women's Jobs and Job Opportunities* (1983), *Labor Economics: Wages, Employment and Trade Unionism* (5th edition,

1984), and *Thinking for a Living: Education and the Wealth of Nations* (1992).

Jacob Mincer is Buttenwieser Professor of Economics and Human Relations at Columbia University, where he has taught since 1959. Since 1960 he has been a Research Associate of the National Bureau of Economic Research. Mincer was named Distinguished Fellow of the American Economic Association in 1989, and was awarded an honorary Doctor of Laws by the University of Chicago in 1991. His books include *Economic Forecasts and Expectations* (1969); *Schooling, Experience and Earnings* (1974); *Trends in Women's Work*, edited with R. Layard (1985); *Studies in Human Capital* (1993); and *Studies in Labor Supply* (1993). He is the author of more than 60 articles in the leading journals.

Daniel J. B. Mitchell is Professor at the Anderson Graduate School of Management, University of California, Los Angeles. He was Director of the UCLA Institute of Industrial Relations from 1979 to 1990. During phase two of the Nixon administration's wage and price controls program, Mitchell was Chief Economist of the Pay Board, the agency that administered wage controls. He has twice been associated with the Brookings Institution, most recently as a Senior Fellow in the Economic Studies program. Mitchell has served as a consultant to the Congressional Budget Office, the Federal Reserve Board, the President's Council on Wage and Price Stability, the U.S. Department of Labor, and the International Labour Organisation. His publications have generally been in the areas of wage determination, wage and price controls, concession bargaining, flexible pay plans, and other aspects of labor market analysis. He is the author of the textbook *Human Resource Management: An Economic Approach*.

Paul S. Osterman is Professor of Human Resources and Management at the Sloan School of Management, Massachusetts Institute of Technology. He received his Ph.D. in economics from MIT. He is the author of many articles on topics such as employment policy, internal labor markets, human resources within firms, poverty, and social policy. Osterman's three books are *Getting Started: The Youth Labor Market* (1980), *Internal Labor Markets* (1983), and *Employment Futures: Reorganization, Dislocation, and Public Policy* (1988).

Michael J. Piore is a labor economist and a Professor of Economics at the Massachusetts Institute of Technology. He received his B.A. and Ph.D. degrees from Harvard University. Piore has written extensively on various aspects of industrial relations and employment and training. In contrast with the dominant approach in economics, which tends to treat economic activity as analytically separate from social life, his work is distinguished by its concern with the way in which economic activity is embedded in institutional and social structures. His published works include *Internal Labor Markets and Manpower Adjustment*, with Peter Doeringer (1971); *Unemployment and Inflation: Institutionalist and Structuralist Views*, editor

(1979); *Birds of Passage: Migrant Labor and Industrial Societies* (1979); *Dualism and Discontinuity in Industrial Society,* with Suzanne Berger (1980); and *The Second Industrial Divide,* with Charles Sabel (1984).

Melvin W. Reder is the Isidore Brown and Gladys J. Brown Professor of Urban and Labor Economics Emeritus at the Graduate School of Business at the University of Chicago. He received an A.B. in economics from the University of California, Berkeley, in 1939 and a Ph.D. in economics from Columbia University in 1946. He is the author of numerous articles in professional journals. His books are *Studies in the Theory of Welfare Economics* (1947) and *Labor in a Growing Economy* (1958), and he is coeditor of *Nations and Households and Economic Growth: Essays in Honor of Moses Abramovitz* (1974) and *Behavioral Foundations of Economic Theory* (1987).

Albert E. Rees (1921–1992) had long associations with Princeton University and the University of Chicago where he served as Professor of Economics. He received his Ph.D. in economics from the University of Chicago. Rees served on the President's Council of Economic Advisers and the President's Committee to Appraise Employment and Unemployment Statistics, and was appointed in 1974 by President Ford to head the Council on Wage and Price Stability. In 1979 he became President of the Alfred P. Sloan Foundation. His books include *The Economics of Trade Unions* (1962), *The Economics of Work and Pay* (1973), and *Striking a Balance: Making National Economic Policy* (1984).

Lloyd G. Reynolds is Sterling Professor Emeritus at Yale University. He was Chairman of the Department of Economics and founding Director of the Yale Economic Growth Center. His publications include *The British Immigrant in Canada* (1935); *The Control of Competition in Canada* (1940); *Labor Economics and Labor Relations* (1949); *The Structure of Labor Markets* (1952); *The Evolution of Wage Structure,* with Cynthia H. Taft (1956); *Wages, Productivity, and Industrialization in Puerto Rico,* with Peter Gregory (1965); *The Three Worlds of Economics* (1971); *Image and Reality in Economic Development* (1977); and *Economic Growth in the Third World, 1860–1980* (1984).

George P. Shultz is Professor of International Economics at the Graduate School of Business at Stanford University and is a Distinguished Fellow at the Hoover Institution. He served as the sixtieth U.S. Secretary of State from 1982 to 1989. He received his B.A. degree from Princeton University and his Ph.D. from Massachusetts Institute of Technology. After serving as Professor at MIT and the University of Chicago, and Dean of the Graduate School of Business at Chicago, he became U.S. Secretary of Labor in 1969. He also served the Nixon administration as Director of the Office of Management and Budget and Secretary of the Treasury. From 1974 until his appointment as Secretary of State, Shultz was President of Bechtel Group, Inc. Shultz's publications include *Pressures on Wage Decisions* (1950), *The Dynamics of a Labor Market* (1951), *Labor Problems: Cases and Readings* (1953), *Manage-*

ment *Organization and the Computer* (1960), *Strategies for the Displaced Worker* (1966), *Guidelines, Informal Controls, and the Market Place* (1966), *Workers and Wages in an Urban Labor Market* (1970), and *Economic Policy Beyond the Headlines* (1978). He is a past president of the Industrial Relations Research Association.

Robert M. Solow is Institute Professor of Economics at Massachusetts Institute of Technology. One of the world's leading economists, he was awarded the Alfred Nobel Memorial Prize in Economic Science in 1987. Solow received his Ph.D. from Harvard University in 1951. He is well known for analysis of problems of long-term economic growth, mathematical economic theory, technological change, and unemployment. He is the author or coauthor of more than 100 papers in professional journals. His books include *Linear Programming and Economic Analysis* (1958), *Capital Theory and the Rate of Return* (1963), *The Nature and Causes of Unemployment in the U.S.* (1964), *Growth Theory* (1970), and *Made in America* (1989). Solow is the recipient of numerous honorary degrees from distinguished universities around the world, including Harvard, Yale, Chicago, Paris, and Geneva.

Paul D. Staudohar, coeditor of this volume, is Professor of Business Administration at California State University, Hayward. He received his Ph.D. in economics from the University of Southern California. He is a member of the National Academy of Arbitrators. Among his books are *Personnel Management and Industrial Relations,* coauthored with Dale Yoder (1982); *Labor Relations in Professional Sports,* coauthored with Robert C. Berry and William B. Gould (1986); *The Sports Industry and Collective Bargaining* (1986, 1989); *Industrial Relations in a New Age* (1986) and *Economics of Labor in Industrial Society* (1986), coedited with Clark Kerr; *Deindustrialization and Plant Closure,* coedited with Holly E. Brown (1987); and *The Business of Professional Sports,* coedited with James A. Mangan (1991).

Labor Economics and Industrial Relations

I

The Provinces of Labor Economics

1

The Labor Factor within the Classical and Neoclassical Systems of Economic Analysis

■ ─────────────────── ■
George H. Hildebrand

As a distinct discipline, labor economics today is not quite a century old. Before, it was simply an integral part of the central tradition of theoretical speculation that began with Adam Smith.

When labor economics finally did emerge as a specialized field, the older theories of value and distribution were destined to occupy a subordinate place, because the founders of the new discipline were so strongly oriented to other interests — unions and unionism, labor history, collective bargaining, social and protective labor legislation, and industrial disputes. In consequence, topics such as wage and employment theory were typically considered to be a part of general economics, rather than of labor economics itself. The specialized study of wages, labor markets, and institutions did not begin to occupy a prominent position in the field until the later 1920s.

At that time, Paul H. Douglas (1892–1976) began his quantitative studies of real wages and labor supply and demand. Douglas, in fact, was in the fullest sense a transitional figure, for he brought to the field an uncommon proficiency in neoclassical theory joined with a lively determination to employ "inductive, statistical and quasi-mathematical method" to establish some actual empirical values for the slopes of labor demand and supply functions for the American economy of that time.

Douglas's major departure in labor economics had the benefit of some 150 years of preceding reflections representing the impressive accumulated works of the classical economists and their neoclassical successors. Indeed, without this great intellectual endowment his own studies would have been highly unlikely.

The Period of Classical Economics

For many years the term *classical economics* has been used to designate that group of economists — mainly British — whose "orientation"[1] began with Adam Smith and his *An Inquiry into the Nature and Causes of the Wealth of Nations* (1776), described by Schumpeter as one of the two most influential books ever written (the other being Darwin's *The Origin of Species* [1859]). The other major figures were Thomas R. Malthus, David Ricardo, James Mill, John Stuart Mill, and John Elliott Cairnes.[2] Karl Marx must also be included, for he shared the same conceptual apparatus and was interested in many of the same problems. All of these men were concerned with a set of common ideas that purported to explain how a market-controlled economy worked, and therefore how the prices of goods and productive services were determined. Woven into the texture of this elaborate analytical system were ideas about human nature and economic motivation, the proper relation between the individual and the state, money and its functions, the growth of population, the causes of economic development, and the nature of internal and international trade.

Central to this mass of speculation was labor, viewed as the source of the national income and as a major claimant to that income. Thus the classical economists were concerned with theories of wages and with the relation of labor expended to the prices of commodities.

Derived from these theoretical inquiries are some of the topics that long afterward were to become standard components of the new discipline of labor economics: the demand for labor, the supply of labor, the structure of wages among occupations, human capital, and movements in real wages and earnings.

Adam Smith (1723–1790)

The Wealth of Nations is both a treatise on economic theory and a manual of prescriptions for economic policy. Its argument is backed up by a plethora of practical examples. Its central concern is with the nature and causes of economic development. In the course of presenting his views, Smith has given us a fine account of how the price system works to bring progress without design. At the same time, he has provided us with the first extensive treatment of what later came

4

to be termed the theory of value and distribution. It is within this broad context that Smith's contributions to the recent development of labor economics are to be found.

He opens his long treatise on the market economy by raising the primary question of the whole inquiry, Why have some countries become rich while "the savage nations of hunters and fishers" have remained poor? The answer, Smith contends, lies in the improvement of the productive powers of labor, which in turn is brought about by development of the division of labor.[3] He illustrates the point with examples of the separation and simplification of occupations within a firm, but given the larger context it is clear that he is also thinking of the differentiation of all economic activities through specialization.[4] Thus he attributes the gains in labor productivity to the simplification of jobs, which promotes greater dexterity, saves time by confining the work to one site, and allows access to capital equipment. Elsewhere he points to specialization of activity, which promotes efficiency, the production of surpluses, and thereby, trade (book I, chap. 1, 3–11).

In making extensive comparisons of various parts of the world, Smith was drawn into an attempt to explain what "occasions" the emergence of a division of labor in some lands but not in others. The answer, he says, is the "very slow and gradual" operation of a "propensity to truck, barter, and exchange" — an inborn trait that is unique to the human species. No animal ever made a contract or an exchange with another.[5]

Developing the argument, Smith credits the settlement of America with enlarging the division of labor in Europe by opening a vast new market. Here was a way to export surplus products and bring back other goods for which there was an unfilled demand (book IV, chap. 1, 415–416).

At this point he introduces one of the most subtle arguments in the book. Man in civilized society, he says, requires the cooperation of "multitudes" of people to provide the goods and services to satisfy his wants. It is futile, and indeed impossible, to appeal to friendship or benevolence to obtain such far-reaching cooperation. But there is another way: let the buyer pay the asking price, that is, appeal to the self-love of the butcher and the baker. Thus the gains from trade can be shared. The great insight here was his recognition that the vast market system that allowed the division of labor in his own time was essentially a method of enlisting countless people to engage in tacit cooperation for their mutual benefit — without need for political coercion, military domination, or vain appeals to charitable or benevolent intentions (book I, chap. 2, 13–16).

Smith was adamantly opposed to restrictions against imports. Capital is essential to all production and is always scarce, and obstruction of imports artificially diverts capital to less productive uses. Every owner of capital always has his own best interest in mind, and thus seeks the largest return, which also "leads him to prefer that employment which is most advantageous to society." In this way he is "led by an invisible hand to promote an end which was not part of his intention" (book IV, chap. 2, 421–423).

The real meaning of this famous metaphor is far from obvious, partly because of its unqualified formulation and partly because the object, thing, or condition to which the "invisible hand" refers is not actually indicated. To some it has meant the Deity; to others, a law of nature; and to some moderns, the workings of the principle of unintended consequences. Here it must be said without elaboration that it actually refers to the theoretical rule that where full and unrestricted competition is free to operate (Smith called it the "system of natural liberty"), producers can maximize profits consistently, with the optimum attainment of the consumers' welfare. But Smith was not naive — quite the contrary. He was fully aware of impediments to competition and of the monopolistic inclinations of all producers and traders.

In book I, chapter 6, Smith attacks the value problem by introducing a simple but quite potent model of production in "that early and rude state of society which precedes both the accumulation of stock and the appropriation of land." He then contends that if it takes twice the labor time to kill a beaver than to kill a deer, it is "natural" that in exchange one beaver should be worth two deer. He then observes that this cost ratio may be altered to reflect differences in the arduousness of different kinds of labor and in the time and labor needed to acquire the skills essential to certain occupations. Finally, Smith says that in the primitive society "the whole product of labour belongs to the labourer."

Several important ideas emerge from this discussion. The technical cost ratios that underlie relative prices are measured in labor time.[6] However, the relative rates of production implied for equilibrium actually will reflect the relative marginal utilities of the goods involved. As Frank H. Knight noted many years ago, Smith has given us a simple illustration of his central principle of indirect production through exchange, guided by the opportunity cost of switching production between the two products (the demand side). Moreover, Smith has eliminated the problem of distribution by confining production to one factor only, labor. Thus the national product involved depends solely on the amount and productivity of labor expended —

a fundamental idea that underlies his theory of development, which is that progress rests on the rate of accumulation of capital (viewed by him as saved-up wage goods), the size of the labor force available, and the physical productivity of that labor force in various uses. Finally, note that in Smith's system of natural liberty, property in the form of one's self — the capacity to work — is a primary element, here presented in its starkest form. He even suggests that past investment to acquire a skill brings higher compensation later.

Because Adam Smith's model of the "original" economy and society includes only labor as a factor of production, the pricing of labor services through exchange among producers resolves the problem of value and distribution in one stroke. Put another way, the prices of final goods and those of factor inputs are simultaneously determined, a unified solution that was not to reappear until Léon Walras (1834–1910) published *Éléments d'économie politique pure* in 1874.

In developing his model of the original society, Smith was concerned not with a methodological fiction but with a general theory of the progress of the economy and of the system of natural liberty as a whole. This allowed him to identify the nature and causes of economic advance, and at the same time to demonstrate its effects on the population. This is well illustrated by his first chapter on wages (book I, chap. 8).

The advance begins, he argues, with the appropriation of all usable land for private ownership, which gives rise to rent, and with the accumulation of stock (capital), which he viewed as goods saved up from the previous year for the maintenance of laborers and their families. The size of this capital stock determines the number of workers that can be engaged; it constitutes Smith's conception of the total demand for labor in an economy at a given time. As employment increases with expansion of these savings, national output also increases, and with it the wages fund for the next year. Driving the process is the incentive to save, which is governed by the expected rate of profit, which, like rent and wages, is a cost of production for any commodity. However, Smith treats these input prices as separately determined factors, independent of the demands for final products — all elements of the typical classical view.

Progress itself gives rise to institutional development, which has come to be termed the employment relationship, or the buying and selling of the services of legally free laborers through a market. In his very practical way, Smith argues that both the employing masters and their employed laborers naturally develop an adversarial relationship with each other, because each is now "disposed to combine" against the other. If the laborer tries to bargain alone, he will lose, although his wage cannot be depressed below subsistence level — at least not for long — for the labor force would then not last beyond a single generation. If, then, the laborers combine, they improve their bargaining power, but only within limits.

In Smith's bargaining theory of wages, as in Alfred Marshall's more than a century later, an employer combination within a given trade enjoys a composite advantage because their number are relatively small, making it easier for them to combine; because the law against combination in the mideighteenth century was directed only against workers; and because the masters have the capital to hold out longer in a given dispute.

In this competition between the two combinations, there exists no determinate wage that would be mutually advantageous for both sides to accept. Rather, there is a negotiable range of possible settlements, with the outcome dependent on bargaining strength and skill, or what Smith himself termed "the higgling and bargaining" of the market.[7] Indeed, the situation is essentially the same as that contemplated in labor markets today, under bilateral monopoly with collective bargaining.

Smith moves next to a subsistence theory. "A man," he says, "must always live by his work," both to maintain himself and to bring up a family. The result is an economy-wide average minimum real wage, with the characteristics of an infinitely elastic long-run supply curve. In turn, the demand for labor in this market is simply the stock of wage goods saved up for that year.

At this point Smith's version of the wages fund doctrine makes its appearance. The aggregate demand for labor moves in direct proportion to the increase in funds for the payment of wages. These funds increase with net national output and with savings (accumulation) from that output. Rising wages are thus a symptom of growing national wealth. Because the rate of population (and labor force) growth tends to be lower than the rate of accumulation and of growth in labor demanded, real wages can rise above the subsistence minimum, although the increase of population will act ultimately as a check on the rise of real wages. Thus the short-run advance in real wages can be larger than that for the long-run, when the effect of faster population growth operates as a check.

Smith's general view of average real wages rests decisively upon the rate of accumulation, which is the key factor that differentiates stagnant from progressive economies.

A final point about general real wages involves Smith's advocacy of what would later become the principle of the economy of high wages (book I, chap. 8). He begins with the question, Are higher wages for the "lower ranks" of the working population an advantage for society itself? He answers that "it is but equity" that this development should occur. It will enable the parents in such families to provide better for their children; it will increase marriages and births; and it will permit better personal maintenance for the parents themselves. These effects, in sum, will promote the growth of the population, which in a growing economy leads to more saving, accumulation, and national output.

There remains Adam Smith's remarkably sophisticated analysis of the problem of wage differences (or structure) by occupations, in particular the treatment of equalization of net advantages. Every occupation, Smith says, offers certain advantages and disadvantages to those employed in it. The advantage may be a pleasant location or challenging professional work. A disadvantage might involve difficult or dangerous surroundings, or skills that are expensive to acquire. If the sum of the money values of the disadvantages is deducted from the sum of the money values of the advantages, one obtains the money value of the net advantages of the occupation. Given full freedom of competition and mobility of labor within the occupation in a given labor market area, then its net advantages tend to level out, and with this, the pecuniary reward paid in the occupation.

As Smith was well aware, money wages among occupations differ because of variations in the circumstances or nature of the jobs involved (job utilities and disutilities). Thus a nation or an area will have an occupational wage structure. In a regime of full competition and full labor mobility, this structure will equalize the net advantages of the different occupations. In brief, Smith contends, competition operates to equalize net advantages by bringing about the formation of differentials in money wages. In this way the distribution of the labor force among occupations will be stabilized through the joint action of labor mobility and ensuing induced changes in occupational wages.

To explain this equilibrium wage structure, Smith refers to five factors that give rise to the initial inequalities in the net advantages of different occupations. First, occupations may vary in ease of difficulty, or cleanliness or dirtiness. Thus a tailor's work is easier than a weaver's while a blacksmith's is cleaner and less dangerous than a coal miner's. Second, they may vary in the ease and cheapness, or difficulty and high expense, of acquiring the necessary skills for the trade or profession, including interest on the investment required. Thus skilled labor earns more than unskilled, and those in the arts and professions earn more than skilled workers. Third, occupations vary in the stability or "constancy" of the employment they offer. Artisans in manufacturing have steadier engagements than those in the building trades. An unskilled coal heaver in London may therefore make more than a skilled artisan. Fourth, there is the degree of trust required. The pay of the goldsmith exceeds that of others in comparable activities because of the high value of the materials entrusted to him. Fifth and finally, there are variations in the likelihood of success in different occupations. The failure rate is higher in the liberal professions than in the mechanical trades, and so the pay is also higher.

It should be noted that Smith's approach to net advantages was followed almost exactly by Marshall.[8] Both, moreover, deal with job disutilities as measurable in money. Furthermore, Smith's treatment of the costs of acquiring a skill reorganizes the basic principle of modern human capital theory, that interest on the investment in skill is a cost that directly affects skilled wages and salaries. And Smith's view primarily emphasizes the supply side in the formation of the occupational wage structure, although he allows some influence for demand with respect to regularity of employment and degree of trust. However, Smith's static competitive model does not fully account for actual occupational differentials, because it overlooks various barriers to entry, such as lack of capital to invest in obtaining a skill, licensure in certain trades and professions, and job reservation systems built around racial, ethnic, and other criteria for the inclusion or exclusion of candidates.

No summary can do justice to Adam Smith's impressive early contribution to labor economics. Among the outstanding themes and ideas that must be mentioned is the concept of the division of labor and its effects on productivity and job structure. Another is his recognition of bilateral monopoly and the indeterminacy of wages. Still another is his equally modern view of occupational wage structure and the equalization of net advantages. Finally, there is the role of competition in harnessing self-interest to the public interest.

Thomas R. Malthus (1766–1834)

Malthus is noted for two major contributions in the history of economics: his principle of population (1798) and his insistence on the possibility of general overproduction (1820). Regarding the latter, all one need say here is that Malthus was concerned not with the business cycle as such, but with the economics of depression because of deficient effective demand.

In 1798 Malthus published a brief version of his *An Essay on the Principle of Population, as It Affects the Future Improvement of*

Society, with Remarks on the Speculations of Mr. (William) God-win, M. (the Marquis de) Condorcet, and Other Writers. The purpose and the inspiration of the *Essay* are fully disclosed in its subtitle. Malthus believed that his views on population constituted the definitive explanation for poverty and therewith the decisive refutation of Condorcet's and Godwin's ideas for the perfect society. In the end, Malthus's theory lacked scientific underpinnings hence it properly belongs in the category of ideology rather than good economics, as is also true of the theories of Condorcet and Godwin. Yet his principle of population enjoyed scholarly attention and prestige for almost a century, in the meantime entering the domain of classical economics as one of its foremost building blocks.

In 1793, William Godwin (1756–1836) had published his *Enquiry Concerning Political Justice.* His central contentions were that men are ultimately guided by reason and are thus rational creatures, and that therefore they can live together peacefully, without laws and institutions. By what George Stigler calls "a noncoercive reform," Godwin would have eliminated private property, marriage, and most of law and government.[9] In this way, he believed, humankind could live in perfect harmony and equality. In short, to get better people, design better institutions.

The Marquis de Condorcet (1743–1794) also believed in the perfectibility of humans and society, to be achieved by the operation of the law of the gradual progress of the human mind. The advancement of knowledge, he argued, would root out error and prejudice, and release men and women from bondage to obsolete institutions. Poverty and inequality would ultimately disappear. To support his vision, Condorcet followed a pattern of thinking employed by Smith, Turgot, and others: the construction of a conceptual historical series to depict the law of progress. According to this view, there were ten "epochs," beginning with hunters in the state of nature, and ending with the period then under way (1795) in Western Europe, and in this way one could predict the future. Through inevitable progress, the human race would advance toward infinitely improving happiness.

Both of these writers rely on the conception of laws of nature to support their optimistic visions of the future. By contrast, Malthus puts forward a profoundly pessimistic view, also by appeal to the laws of nature. There exist, he argued initially, two basic constants that underlie a pessimistic view: the passion between the sexes and the finite supply of arable land on the earth. Inevitably there is a gap between the growing population, which reproduces itself more and more through the sheer fact of its own growth, and the quantity of food that this land is capable of producing, which cannot expand through its own growth but must depend upon injections of capital and technical improvements. The gap between population and food supply keeps humankind at the level of subsistence if population grows unchecked.

Malthus attempted to give this gap specious precision by assigning his famous ratios: population will grow "geometrically," he said — at a compound annual rate applied to an ever-expanding base — and food supply only "arithmetically" — at fixed or declining increments to a fixed original base. With the clash of these ratios, certain "checks" to population growth will come into operation: the "positive" (famine, disease, and war, which raise the death rate), and the "preventative" (abortion, infanticide, and birth control, which lower the birth rate). In the 1803 edition of his essay, Malthus added "moral restraint," a preventative check resting on delayed marriage with strict continence, which also reduces the birth rate. As Stigler says, Malthus introduced this new factor to deflect Godwin's attack on the original essay, that there existed historical cases in which the working population had lived above the subsistence level for lengthy periods without visible operation of the original checks.[10]

Perhaps the weakest part of Malthus's argument concerns the potential growth of the food supply. Originally the constraint here was the fixed supply of land, which technical advances could not fully overcome. Behind this notion is the idea, as Mark Blaug points out, that repeated infusions of technical improvements were themselves somehow subject to diminishing returns.[11]

The criticisms of David Ricardo (1772–1823) and Nassau Senior (1790–1864) should also be noted. Ricardo initially accepted the principle that in the long run real wages must equal some subsistence minimum, the so-called Iron Law of Wages. But in a progressive (capital-accumulating) society, Ricardo then argued, the market (short-run) rate of wages will persistently exceed this "natural" (long-run) rate, because the repeated injections of new capital will increase the demand for labor faster than labor supply can respond through expanding population (*Principles of Political Economy and Taxation*, 1817). In *Two Lectures on Population* (1829), Senior went further, holding that — absent disturbing causes — "food has a tendency to increase faster than population . . . in fact, it has generally done so."[12]

During the second half of the nineteenth century and beyond, the Western industrial countries experienced steadily rising levels of per capita real income along with increasing populations, but with falling death rates (better food, medicine, and sanitation) and falling birth rates — the latter being a bourgeoisification effect, that at the margin children are in competition with other consumption goods. Malthus would have had to attribute this phenomenon to increased moral restraint. More recent opinion in economics would hold that the choice of family size has become a factor in the maximization of returns from increasing income, and is supposedly confirmation that the original gloomy Malthusian vision is now obsolete.

But in one fundamental respect Malthus is not obsolete. His basic claim, after all, was that over the long run there would develop a slowly widening gap between the growth of population and that of the food supply. At the present rate of growth in the world population — about 2 percent a year — by the year 3400 each person now alive would have 1 trillion descendants. Even by 2100 this yields a population of 50 billion persons.[13] (These projections of course neglect the intrusion of other major factors such as wars, famines, epidemics, and the deliberate reduction of birth rates.) It is difficult to believe that the growth of the food supply could be sustained at a comparable rate, in which case even 2 percent per annum would ultimately be excessive, and the Malthusian checks would come into play.

Karl Marx (1818–1883)

There is good reason to include Marx among the classical economists; indeed, some would rank him with Smith, Ricardo, and John Stuart Mill for the range and quality of his thought. What kind of a labor economist was he? A quick — but not superficial — judgment would be that he was probably the best for his time, despite the uncompromising dogmatism of his approach.

Marx's view of capitalism starts from the free labor market, where the worker is technically free to sell his labor or withhold it. If he withholds it, he must fall back on his own resources to sustain himself and his family. Since he is without property and there exists no protective network of social insurance, the option of holding out is really illusory. In consequence he will sell his labor for a subsistence wage, while his employer will extract the full value of his labor power for each day he works. This excess value over the wage is what Marx called surplus value. The underlying idea is that labor time is the source of all exchange value for any commodity, including the cost of maintaining the laborer and his family (the subsistence wage). Surplus value is extracted in two ways: by prolonging the working day beyond the average time required to recover the cost of the wage, and by the force of competition among employers, which lowers wage costs by substituting machinery and new processes for the manufacture of wage goods. Either way, surplus value will increase.

The key to capitalism, in Marx's opinion, is the ability of the employer to exploit the difference between the exchange value of labor, as measured by the wage, and the value of labor power, which is the total amount of exchange value extracted from the worker in a given period of time. For Marx's system, surplus value is the true and only source of profit, interest, and rent. More important for the reconversion of surplus value into capital are two associated ideas. One is the *realization* of profit, initially as the money obtained by sale of the commodity produced, where the profit itself normally represents the surplus labor time extracted with its production. The other concept is the subsequent *reconversion* of this profit into additional capital, which can take the form of machinery and raw materials (constant capital) or added workers at the same wage (variable capital).

This leads to Marx's dynamic view of capitalism: it is an economic system that invokes an unceasing effort to expand capital, because it is driven by the endless attempt to extract and realize profit. Other very important consequences also follow, which will be considered after a deeper look at the free labor market. In Marx's conception, the historic consequence of the illusory liberation of serfs and guild craftsmen was to thrust them onto the labor market, without property of any kind and without the guildsman's control over his work, his materials, or his product. Marx called this the *alienation* of the worker from society and, above all, from his work — a kind of isolation and exile from normal society that rendered him a defenseless appendage to the machine.

Contributing to the worker's predicament is the ever-present threat of unemployment as an inevitable consequence of the internal dynamics of the system. Capital accumulation, with its reconversion into machinery, in part, directly displaces labor in the production of wage goods. Moreover, the process of accumulation is unstable: according to Marx it brings about fluctuations ("periodic" cycles) and recurring major crises that rupture the sequence of purchase and sale, and so create unemployment. Thus the instability of capitalism brings with it the reserve army of the unemployed, which is a direct cause of misery and a means by which the free labor market depresses wages to their lowest possible level.[14]

Marx lacked access to later ideas of labor supply and demand schedules, but the implications of his discussion permit the use of these ideas without violence to his argument. In his thinking, the long-run supply of labor is essentially the same as is found in Smith, Malthus, and Ricardo; a minimum of bare subsistence is provided, and then, as the excess supply is fully taken up, the horizontal supply curve finally turns sharply upward.[15] Ordinarily, total labor demanded falls short and to the left of this point. To the right and upward, one is in the range of short-run supply, where the wage is above its long-run "natural" price.

As the accumulation of capital proceeds, the curve of the short-run demand for labor is pushed toward the right as the capitalists extend the process of realization and reconversion of profits. When, ultimately, the wage is pushed above the level of long-run supply, it necessarily contracts the margin of surplus value — "labor ceases to circulate at its value." In short, labor scarcity results in a wage push. Profits fall, and a realization crisis is at hand. Business losses, liquidation, massive unemployment, and a collapse of wages all then follow. In time recovery can occur, Marx argues, through forces that restore the profit rate: the depreciation of existing capital, which lowers the value of existing constant capital, and a fall in wages invoked jointly by overall contraction and further mechanization, which create massive unemployment.[16]

Marx presents two major ideas about economic crisis, depression, and recovery. Both of them are surprisingly modern. One, which is built on Ricardo's work, is the notion that excessive capital accumulation (net investment) can outrun labor supply and thereby force wages up and depress the rate of profit. The other idea, which is both more subtle and more typically Marxian, is that capitalism contains no internal stabilizing mechanism for offsetting crises and slumps. Its central driving force is production for accumulation, not for consumption. Accordingly, the cause of a realization crisis is not an inability of workers to buy back the product — the underconsumption argument. In fact, higher wages and wage income are precisely the cause of the crisis. In short, the root of the trouble is the encroachment of labor demand on labor supply because of overaccumulation.

With the foregoing analysis, Marx undertook a devastating attack on the famous argument by Jean-Baptiste Say (1767–1832) for the impossibility of general overproduction. In 1803, in his *Traité*, Say had put forward his slogan that "goods buy each other" and said that thus total demand can be limited only by total production. Say's model, Marx noted, rested upon an economy of self-employed consumers who produce and exchange use-values–*einfache warenproduktion*.[17] There is no wage labor, no profit, no surplus value, and above all no capital accumulation. Money is only a medium of exchange. There can be no hoarding and no realization crisis. By assuming away capital accumulation, Say had eliminated the problem itself.[18]

Ricardo had approached the issue in a more sophisticated way, with a model that incorporates profit and capital accumulation. In conceding that, in the short run, accumulation could encroach on labor supply, force up wages, and cut profit, Ricardo held that the fall in capital outlay (investment) would be offset automatically by higher final consumption; in other words, the sum of the marginal propensities to invest and to consume supposedly were equal to unity. In objection Marx argued that the fall in the profit rate would cause a flight into money; this would rupture the sequence of purchase and sale and thus invoke a liquidation crisis. Consumption wants may be unlimited, he said, but this will not check contraction, because the demand for capital goods is governed not by consumers' wants but by the profit rate. When the rate falls, a substantial part of total demand is wiped out, and the working class has no purchasing power to fill the gap. Notwithstanding Say's model, the total production outstrips the market. Or, as a modern Keynesian would say, income must fall until saving contracts to equal the lower rate of investment.

Marx's theory of economic crises leads naturally to a brief consideration of his theory of history, because the two are components of an overall view of the origin and inevitable destiny of all human societies. In *The German Ideology*, written with Friedrich Engels (1820–1895), Marx sought to invert the idealist teachings of Hegel by introducing the notion of historical materialism, contending that *work* is the basic human activity from which all ideas, values, beliefs, and institutions are derived. Work is also the source of economic goods. The organization of work, together with its technical base, Marx designated as the "mode of production" in any given social order. Viewed as a cross section of a particular society or stage in history, the mode of production is the "basement" or *unterbau* that determines the character and contents of the superstructure or *überbau*, where the ideas of the state, property and institutions are to be found.[19] The line of causation here is one-way and upward; in short, the mode of production determines how men think and what they think. More important, the ideas and institutions of a given society will reflect the economic interests of the dominant class, whose very existence has been prescribed by the prevailing mode of production.

Through historical time, each nation necessarily passes through a series of developmental stages whose characteristics are determined by the corresponding mode of production. For instance, in each stage there will prevail a particular form of ownership of the means of production: slaveowners and slaves, landowners and serfs, owners of capital and wage workers.

It is of some interest that Marx and Engels designate the first or "original" stage as "tribal communism," and the last one as "final communism." In the first there is said to be common ownership of hunting and fishing grounds. There is no state, no private class of owners, and no money and trade. In the ultimate stage, as well, there is no owning class, no money and trade, and no state — in place of the state there will be only what Engels termed "the administration of things."[20] Moreover, there will exist absolute abundance, that is, no economic scarcity. Abundance without coercion or conflict is the actual Marxian vision.

This brings us to what Marx called the "dictatorship of the proletariat," which he designated as the first phase of the revolutionary socialist overthrow of the "bourgeois" or capitalistic society. In his *Critique of the Gotha Programme* (1875) Marx provides a rather sparse and didactic description of this first phase of final communism, cast in question-and-answer form to attack his adversaries in the German Workers' Party, in particular Ferdinand Lassalle.

Marx begins by questioning the slogan "equitable distribution of the proceeds of labor" as the standard for the advent of socialism. Is everyone included? Is there a remainder to be used otherwise? His answers show his considerable sophistication as an economist: the total social product must contain deductions for the replacement of the means of production consumed in the previous year; for the expansion (net investment) of production in the next period; for insurance reserves against adverse events; for administrative overhead; and for special (public) goods such as schools and health programs. Thus each worker actually gets his or her *average* portion of the final net product, in a coupon conveying his or her share of total consumers' goods, measured by a common standard for the labor contributed. The actual individual shares will not be literally equal but "proportional," to allow for differences in skill and productive capacity and in the duration and intensity of the work performed, and for marital status and number of children. For the dictatorship of the proletariat, then, Marx was stressing the bourgeois principle of rewards in accordance with productive contributions, rather than according to strict equality.

One of the central questions the Marxian scheme raises is, How is the course of continuous change brought about? Here certain difficulties emerge. Recall that Marx insists that change in historical time originates within the mode of production, or *unterbau*. All other socioeconomic phenomena are derivative. Bear in mind that the *unterbau* is a combination of the productive forces (technology, resources, and people) and productive relations, how people are related to each other in performing work at the task of production — in other words, the "work mode." In primitive communism people work as hunters or fishers, acting along but in voluntary endeavor in the service of the clan or tribe. There is neither supervision nor a state, nor is there private ownership of the means of production. Accordingly, in Marx's conception of the Beginning there is no ruling class.

How, then, is the revolutionary change brought about that occasions the Fall of Man — that effects the transition to the several successive phases of class society? Marx does not appeal to class conflict here because it cannot exist under primitive communism. Nor does he contend that the change originates from the development of the productive forces, because there is no development at this stage. All that he offers is the casual suggestion that private property and a class interest might have been introduced with slaves taken as prisoners of war or through sporadic seizures of common lands for private use with serfs. In short, the formation of economic classes begins not with the operation of a systematic law but with a random event. From that point on, the class struggle emerges and determinism takes over.

In Marx's conception, the definition of an economic class turns on the ownership and control of the means of production.[21] All human history, he contends repeatedly, is governed by the conflict between the owning class and the propertyless class. What is decisive for the evolutionary series is the form taken by the property owned. For the earlier periods, it is slaves, then serfs on the land. In bourgeois society, capital is the dominant form: the ownership of capital permits the exploitation of wage labor to extract the surplus value that both sustains and permits the expansion of the capitalistic system. The possession of capital enables the owning class to control the state and thus to dominate wage labor. Because the interests of the employing class and the working class are completely opposed, class struggle is the preponderant condition of social life.

As R. N. Hunt has observed, all members of society are caught in the net of production relations imposed by the prevailing mode of production. There can be no possibility for an ameliorative labor policy, for class interests prevent it. The only choice for the proletariat and its vanguard is to heighten class consciousness and thereby to intensify the struggle until the opportunity ultimately comes to seize the state power.

Thus the real message of *The Critique of the Gotha Programme* is Marx's insistence on the principle that the transition to final communism must be preceded by a proletarian dictatorship. One of his reasons is that the defeat of the bourgeoisie requires that it be stripped of its capital, and with it, its power. Another involves an argument from cultural lag: values and institutions die hard. Workers will continue for a time to insist on wages in accordance with productivity as the incentive for output.[22] In other words, the egalitarian group incentives of a communist society apparently are more a matter of nurture than nature. They can be acquired only through teaching and experience.

A certain ambiguity runs through Marx's views on democracy. On the one side, he protests long and bitterly against the injustice of class rule and promises a future society without coercion or economic scarcity, in which every person for the first time will be completely free to pursue his or her own real interests. On the other, he insists on the necessity of the intervening phase of proletarian dictatorship — yet another form of minority class rule in which there can be no freedom of choice and no competition among political parties — all in the service of a utopian vision of an earthly paradise. Moreover, he concedes at one point that perhaps the intervening period of dictatorship may not be necessary in a few countries, such as the United Kingdom, Holland, and the United States. His underlying problem derives from an insoluble conflict between a deterministic view of history and a strong belief in the freedom of will.

To sum up, among Marx's major ideas for labor economics must be included his views of the free labor market, the inherent instability of capitalism, the alienation of the worker, the industrial reserve army of the unemployed, and his theory of history and the role of labor in the future.

Neoclassical Economics

Apparently Thorstein Veblen (1857–1929) was the economist who devised the term *neoclassical economics,* in a notable iconoclastic paper, "The Preconceptions of Economic Science," published in two parts in 1899–1900 in the *Quarterly Journal of Economics.*[23] Veblen's purpose in bestowing the adjective was twofold. He wished to emphasize the continuity between the more recent (post-1870) price and distribution theory and its older classical antecedents. And he wanted to impeach the position of the newer price theorists by attempting to show that recent thinking was weakened by an asserted dependence on the same assumptions and preconceptions that were central to the classical system.[24]

There was, of course, some continuity involved. Smith and

Ricardo had viewed the emerging market economy as a stable and permanent system driven by the forces of self-interest and competition. Normal price and equilibrium were the ruling ideas in this view. Because the same concepts and terminology were retained by the price theorists emerging after 1870, clearly there was a link.

However, Veblen's larger objective was a reconstruction of economic theory itself that was intended to supplant the notions of system, interdependence, and permanence with a theory of process and change involving what he called cumulative causation. The ultimate goal was a developmental-stage theory that stressed the transitory nature of institutions such as property, competition, and business enterprise. From this standpoint, all price theory — new and old — was inappropriate to the task and hopelessly burdened, anyway, by obsolete underlying assumptions.

The continuity noted by Veblen, although a fact, tended to obscure a much more fundamental point: that the price theory that appeared after 1870 was the product of a genuine revolution in thought. The core of that revolution concerned the introduction in 1871 of the principle of marginal utility, which was followed several years later by the principle of marginal productivity, with both being seen as decreasing functions of the relevant increasing quantities. Adoption of the concept of marginal utility by William Stanley Jevons and Carl Menger in 1871, and, in more general form, by Léon Walras in 1874 and 1877, tied use value to exchange value for the first time, and provided the negatively sloped final demand curves that could explain price where supply was given, without recourse to the cost of production.[25] Still to come was a theory of longer-run supply, to account for the valuation of the factors of production — in other words, a theory of distribution that would be unified with the utility theory of value.[26]

This need was met by Alfred Marshall in 1890, who showed that (1) the prices of final goods were determined by diminishing marginal utility; while (2) the prices of factor inputs were set by diminishing marginal productivity, given conditions of factor supply. Both ideas were components of what Marshall referred to as the "general relations of demand and supply" that composed the competitive theory of value and distribution as he saw it at that time, a theory that was to enjoy its intellectual ascendancy among the next two generations of economists.

Alfred Marshall (1842–1924)

As an undergraduate at St. John's College, Cambridge, Marshall got the opportunity to undertake an extensive study of mathematics and is said to have shown great ability, sufficient, eventually, to take him beyond the preparation even of Walras. During those years he came under the influence of some dons who were interested in the social problems of British industrialism. This led him into a lifelong concern with poverty that in turn took him into economics. After marrying Mary Paley in 1877, he moved to University College, Bristol, and then to Balliol for a year. In 1884 he succeeded Henry Fawcett as Professor of Political Economy at Cambridge, holding this chair until his retirement in 1908.[27]

Although Marshall fully understood and appreciated Walras's work, he once admitted rather wryly that he did not find much interest in the principle that everything depends on everything else. Instead Marshall preferred to examine the approach to equilibrium as a problem mainly of microeconomics or partial equilibrium analysis. He developed his apparatus of markets, competition, substitution, and demand and supply to deal with most of the main problems of the theory of price and distribution extant around 1890 to 1900.

At the same time, Marshall became keenly interested in questions of poverty, wages, and unemployment. As a careful reading of books V and VI of his *Principles of Economics* will quickly show, he also became a labor economist, and a very able one as well. Two examples will demonstrate this.[28] To account for the demand for labor, Marshall used the marginal (net) productivity principle, which in essence says that the schedule of demand prices for any type of labor will reflect, for each wage, the differential product attributable to the marginal worker (strictly, any one of a homogeneous group), multiplied by its price, less the expense of materials specifically provided to that worker. But for very short periods Marshall recognized that marginal variation of all inputs was so limited that one could view the case as one of fixed technical coefficients among the inputs for production.[29] This led him to his well-known theory of derived demand, which states that, given the schedule of final demand (in this case, houses), deduct the total supply price for all other cooperating factors of production (whose quantities are given and unchanged) from each final demand price; the net residuals will be the derived demand prices for the remaining factor, in this case the wage space or margin possible for plasterers, who have gone on strike. This subtraction can be made for each final demand price and quantity, to yield a derived demand schedule (wages and quantities) for the labor of plasterers. Obviously this would be a very short-run demand curve.

Marshall then raises a very interesting problem. When will a strike, as among the plasterers, drive up wages by a "very great amount"? In fact the question is, What influences will aid a union on strike by providing a very low elasticity of demand for its services, hence little prospective loss of jobs with a higher wage? His answer is fourfold. First, the services of the labor group must be "essential, or nearly essential"; in short, there must be no good substitutes for plasterers available. Second, the demand for the final product must be "stiff and inelastic," as here, because there are no close substitutes for houses. Hence a rise in supply price will occasion only a very small loss in sales. Third, the cost of the input — the services of plasterers — is but a small part of total costs of production; thus, with a wage increase there will be little upward displacement of the supply curve for houses. And fourth, the small decline in the quantity of houses that would be demanded at higher prices will cause a large drop in the supply prices of the cooperating inputs, whose supply curves are virtually vertical; in consequence there will be an even larger margin for raising the wages of plasterers.[30] Lack of mobility underlies these vertical supply curves for the cooperating factors.

Marshall's case yields some other interesting questions as well. Will the highly favorable circumstances for the plasterers change over a longer period of time, when the fixed factors could be withdrawn or houses could be redesigned to eliminate plaster altogether? Or suppose that, instead of a craft union, the plasterers and other trades formed an industrial (all-grades) union; how would this change affect bargaining power for plasterers and for the others? And finally, would it make any difference if the separate building crafts chose to bargain as a coalition and thus to undertake a joint strike?

In Marshall's second extraordinary case of collective bargaining, the employers in a trade act together in a coalition, while the employees similarly form a concerted group for bargaining over wage rates and working conditions. His conclusion, which leads straight back to Smith, is that wages are indeterminate. Only bargaining can determine the division of shares between wages and profit. However, the range for settlement does not lie between zero and infinity: wages cannot be driven down permanently because the skilled workers will leave the trade and cannot be replaced. Further, wages must be high enough in an average year to attract new young people to the trade. At the same time, wages cannot be pushed so high as to curtail profits and induce the withdrawal of capital and enterprise. Accordingly, there are limits to the range of practicable settlements. Within this range, higgling and bargaining would prevail, perhaps tempered further if the matter were to be taken to conciliation and mediation, or arbitration.[31]

Marshall also perceptively notes a variant of this case in which several crafts (trades) in the industry organize separately, bringing about multiple-union bargaining, with each organization acting independently on an industry-wide basis. In his view, the ensuing strife would be even greater in this situation, with larger losses on both sides.

At the time Marshall was writing, only about 10 percent of the British work force belonged to unions. He adds that although the unions get much attention, the result is to conceal "the deep silent strong stream" of the normal forces of demand, supply, and substitution, which are "not seen" but which "control the course of those episodes which are seen." In short, Marshall's world was predominantly decentralized, and was composed of many small firms and strong competitive forces. Union bargaining was comparatively uncommon; the cases of bilateral monopoly were indeed rare enough to support his view that they were unimportant.

Like Adam Smith before him, Marshall had an interest in investment in human capital. Noting that in a regime of free labor the worker owns his capacity to provide labor services to others for wages, he recognized that the rearing, educating, and training of a worker is a type of investment for future returns. In the United Kingdom of those days, such investing depended on parental resources, the ability to make good forecasts, and the willingness to sacrifice. For the low-income working people, these factors were all unfavorable. As a result, Marshall believed, a large potential in undeveloped abilities was lost, with effects perpetuated across the generations. By contrast, the children of artisans had a far better chance, all the more so because they were better acculturated for skilled work and had superior access to such jobs. In Marshall's cautious judgment, "the most valuable of all capital is that invested in human beings."[32] Unfortunately for the parental investors, he concedes, the only returns they can reap are the rewards of virtue.

Turning to wage theory, it is well known that Marshall always insisted that the marginal productivity theory was not, strictly, a theory of wages. Rather, it explained only the demand for labor. As in all matters of price determination, supply must also be considered — in particular, as regards labor, the long-run supply of labor. As he put it, "Wages tend to retain a close though indirect and intricate relation with the cost of rearing, training and sustaining the energy of efficient labor" (book VI, chap. ii, 532). This says that the supply of labor, as with any factor of production, rests in the long run on its cost of production — incidentally a quite classical position. As he summed it up, "Wages are not governed by demand-price nor by supply-price, but by the whole set of causes which govern demand and supply" (book VI, chap. vi, 532). This is a good example of Marshall's tendency to bring classical and neoclassical thinking together to produce a theory of wages that, whatever its weaknesses, was more complete than the one-factor demand explanation favored by the Austrian school.

In the area of relative wages, Marshall showed little interest in the problem of internal wage structure, possibly because British industry in his time was largely composed of small firms with personalized employment policies. However, he was well aware that even these businesses typically paid more than a single rate. Thus he spoke habitually of "grades" or "ranks" of occupations, essentially in the three-tier system of unskilled through semiskilled to skilled jobs.

This mode of thinking also led him to the problem of wage structure within and among occupations. Thus Marshall argues that the work done by the "various classes of operatives" in a shoe factory "is not all of the same difficulty." However, the mobility of labor is great enough that "the wages of labour of the same industrial grade or rank tend to equality in different occupations throughout the same western country" (book VI, chap. ii, 539). Therefore each worker in a given grade can, with the wages earned over 100 days, buy the net product of 100 days' labor of any other worker of the same grade. Competition, substitution, and labor mobility together will bring about this normal outcome.

This line of reasoning took Marshall into the consideration of a related problem: suppose that there is an increase in the net efficiency of workers in some other trade whose product is bought by boot and shoe operatives. What will be the economic effect for the latter workers? It will raise their real wages in proportion to the percentage share they spend on the improved product. More generally, the level of the operatives' real wages "depends directly on, and varies directly with, the average efficiency of the trades ... which produce those things on which they spend their wages" (book VI, chap. ii, 540). If, then, the workers in another trade block an improvement that would raise efficiency 10 percent, the loss to the shoe operatives will be 10 percent of the share they spend on this product. Further, if efficiency increases 10 percent in a trade that competes with boots and shoes, the latter operatives will have at least a temporary fall of real wages, all the more if they do not buy this substitute.

In general, capital competes with labor in certain trades. But capital instruments embody both labor and savings ("waiting"); the real competition here is between low-capital-intensive and high-capital-intensive modes of producing a commodity, while the effects for labor involve direct versus indirect uses for capital in the production of more capital goods, and less direct uses of it in making final goods, or the reverse. In the main, competition between labor and capital is not the predominant relationship; labor gains from cheap capital because greater use of the latter in industry increases labor productivity, real wages, and employment opportunities. In turn, increased saving lowers the interest rate, pushes out the margins of use for capital, raises national product, and increases employment more than enough to offset the displacement of labor in local situations (book VI, chap. ii, 541–542).

Marshall did not have much to say about unemployment in *Principles of Economics*, probably because he had planned a later book on the trade cycle, which he never completed. Thus, in *Principles*, he reaches no settled conclusions. However, he does touch on the idea of structural unemployment, at least in the sense of pools of unemployment that persist even when general business conditions are good. As an example he cites the boom and collapse in British coal in 1873. During the expansion, many inexperienced men had migrated to the industry in response to many openings at very high wages. After the collapse many were left without jobs, even including some skilled miners; wages fell sharply with the persistent excess supply of labor (book VI, chap. v, 575).

Regarding low wages, Marshall argues that poor educational and technical preparation are the primary reason for low labor efficiency. In turn these deficiencies give rise to a section of the labor force whose abilities are "of a very low order." These workers have an urgent need for wages and, for the same reason, a very high marginal utility of money. Their lack of adequate vocational preparation, furthermore, denies them many choices. Accordingly, they are congested in the dirtiest and most disagreeable jobs. As a remedy Marshall observed simply that workers of this kind "should be made scarce and therefore dear" (book VI, chap. iii, 558).

This idea raises questions about Marshall's view of human nature and his philosophy of progress, as well as the relation of both to questions of policy. Robin Matthews has shown that Marshall believed strongly in the malleability of human nature.[33] Rising real wages change peoples' nature through improved skills, better patterns of consumption, and improved personal productivity. Even more, they contribute to the formation of "better" moral character. Rising income leads to greater parental concern for the education and training of children. It fosters the habit of looking ahead in personal planning; it promotes a greater sense of responsibility in expenditures and in use of time. The large result, Marshall believed, was better moral character.[34]

But what about the "residuum," those parents whose personal

weaknesses lead to low wages and poorly prepared children? Here there is a clear need for intervention, in the main but not entirely by the state — education, technical training, improved public health, and town planning. If the beneficial effects of raising wages were immediate, employers would do it in their own interest, at least most of them would. But these results take time. Hence the problem is one of creating external economies, through redistributive taxation and public spending, so long as it does not damage capital formation, for then such policies would prove self-defeating.[35] Because progress improves both the moral character and the productive efficiency of workers, it should consistently be promoted.

Marshall's contributions to later labor economics were both extensive and diverse. He did much to develop marginal productivity theory, which he linked to the principle of substitution. He provided an interesting view of the short-run elasticity of demand for labor. He turned Smith's bargaining theory of wages into a theory of bilateral monopoly with indeterminacy of wages. He undertook important explorations of the link between real wages and labor efficiency, and he emphasized the tie between economic progress and changes in human nature.

Arthur Cecil Pigou (1877–1959)

A distinguished economist once declared that A. C. Pigou's *Economics of Welfare* was the best book on labor economics ever written. In considerable part this claim stands up. Unfortunately it deflects attention from Pigou's many other accomplishments, from his systematic reformulation of the theory of economic welfare to his contributions to macroeconomics, in particular the theory of unemployment. Beyond these, he was a prolific writer on a large variety of other important topics, ranging from tariff reform and business cycles through public finance to socialism and capitalism as theories of economic organization.

Pigou came to King's College, Cambridge, from Harrow, where he had been a contemporary of Winston Churchill's. With Marshall's own support he succeeded him as University Professor of Political Economy, in 1908. *Wealth and Welfare* appeared in 1912, becoming, after revision, *The Economics of Welfare* in 1920.[36] In method and conception Pigou was Marshallian throughout his career, as a review of his writings will readily show.

When Pigou published *The Theory of Unemployment* in 1933, he could not have known that his colleague and friend John Maynard Keynes would use it as the examplar of the classical theory of employment and unemployment that Keynes would attack vigorously in his *General Theory of Employment, Interest and Money,* which was to appear only three years later. Of equal interest, as de Graaff has noted, Pigou responded in his own defense in the same year with a savage review of Keynes's new book (in *Economica,* May 1936). Yet by 1950, in *Keynes's General Theory: A Retrospective View,* Pigou conceded with complete professional honesty that the Keynesian short-run underemployment equilibrium was in fact possible, although this view had been denied throughout the history of classical theory.[37]

To view Pigou as a labor economist, the most convenient place to begin is with his "An Analytical View of Industrial Peace" in *The Economics of Welfare* (1950).[38] Marshall had shown that when bilateral monopoly is present in a labor market, the wage rate will be indeterminate, because there is no unique equilibrium point at which the objective rate of exchange (the wage rate) will equal the preferred technical rates of substitution of the two bargaining parties, the union and the employers' association. By contrast, where full freedom of competition prevails, single-rate equilibrium will be established. With collective bargaining there will exist a "range of indeterminacy" within which the union will want more than the competitive rate and the employers' association, less. But the higher the rate the fewer the jobs, so there is an upper limit beyond which the union will not go. Also, the lower the rate the smaller the number of workers that can be retained or recruited. Accordingly, the employers have a lower limit below which it will be against their interest to go. Thus for any wage *outside* these limits it will be in the interests of both parties to move in the *same* direction. Further, the less elastic the employers' demand for labor and the employees' demand for jobs, the wider the range will be.

Within the range, the union must choose a minimum rate that, given the costs of a strike, would be preferable to striking. The location of this "sticking point" will depend on the estimate of costs and possibly the need for a strike for political reasons. Following the same reasoning, the employers will have a similar point. If the union's point lies below this one, then there exists a "range of practicable bargains" within which negotiations can produce a settlement. If not, there is no range and a strike or lockout will follow. If both parties have the same expectations about how a strike would end and at what wage, and that a strike involves positive costs, then a bargaining range will exist.

Here Pigou introduces the concept of "negative" costs — offsets that reduce the positive costs of a strike. Coal producers with large inventories and inelastic demand may find a strike a welcome interruption to production because the context lowers its true costs to an acceptable level. For a union, negative costs that may lower the positive costs of a strike come into play when a strike might earn greater respect from an employer, aid an organizing drive, or consolidate a divided rank and file.

An increase in the union's strength alone would probably raise both sticking points by lowering the union's expected costs of a strike and raising the employers'. Conversely, if the employers alone gain strength, both sticking points would be lowered. If both sides become stronger, the range of practicable bargains will widen, but the amount cannot be predicted.

Pigou also had some important insights into arbitration. An agreement by two parties to arbitrate creates an added positive cost for striking — the risk of loss of public support for the side that breaks the arbitration agreement. There is also the risk that in accepting arbitration a party may be awarded less than it could have had by negotiations without a strike. Beyond these risks, those who are tempted to limit an arbitration to an award within the practicable range face the reluctance of both sides to reveal their sticking points at the start. Indeed, this problem lies behind the reluctance to arbitrate major wage issues at all. Governments have tried to reduce reluctance by intervening with the power to recommend terms of settlement but without compelling acceptance. Here the underlying idea is to add the risk of hostile public opinion as a cost for refusing a recommended settlement.

One of Pigou's primary concerns in the field of economic policy involved wages, in particular the welfare implications of state intervention affecting wages. Wage subsidy was an area of policy to which he made an important contribution (see Pigou part IV, chap. vii). His interest here was inspired by his long-standing belief that the advent of strong and widespread unionism, together with the introduction of unemployment benefits, had brought about what he called "uneconomically high wage rates." The results were wage-distortion unemployment in certain industries and associated "material and moral waste." Market forces could not be expected to correct these departures from demand and supply equilibrium in labor markets. Thus the question was whether subsidies to the prevailing wage — which lower the cost of hiring additional workers — could increase employment and possibly the national product. After extensive technical exploration, Pigou concludes that although a wage-subsidy policy could relieve wage-distortion unemployment and, under the right conditions, add to national income, in practice it "would be bungled" and the nation "would lose more than it gained."

Pigou was probably the first economist to recognize that the distribution of the labor force over occupations and locations carried major implications for maximizing the national income and thereby economic welfare. As usual, his approach is subtle, very analytical, and highly enlightening when followed with care. He begins with Smith's and Marshall's distinction between the incidental advantages and disadvantages of a job and the wage rate (part III, chap. ix). If these are fully known to a group of workers, they will wish to migrate more to jobs with higher net advantages and less to those with lower ones. There will thus emerge differences in the net advantages among a group of jobs; these in turn will influence relative labor supplies; in competitive equilibrium the associated marginal net products will differ also; and these will equal their respective wage rates, which will be unequal. In short, the relevant inequalities will make for a larger national product than otherwise. To the extent that the distribution of labor falls short of this ideal — and accordingly marginal net products are closer to equality — the national product will be lower. This can occur, for example, when workers underestimate the negative aspects of dangerous or unstable trades.

Other factors also adversely affect the mobility of labor. *Ignorance* of opportunities will impair or misdirect the flow of new entrants. *Costs of movement* pose another obstacle. These involve money costs, which can be unequal because of variations in family size, ages of members, or number of employed members. Other costs are intangible, such as attachment to a location or goodwill enjoyed in a working establishment. Finally, migration is affected by *artificial barriers or restrictions,* such as differences in religion or language; barriers against women; or job restriction practices of unions and public authorities.

The reduction of obstacles to the mobility of labor can be achieved by dissolution from within, for instance by better labor market information and lower costs of transfer to new locations. It can be cut further at public expense, through labor exchanges and, as in the United States, by statutory bans against discrimination in hiring and employment according to race, ethnicity, sex, or age. In turn, the increased mobility of labor can lead directly to larger national output and improved economic welfare.

Pigou also examines the problem of the low-wage worker (part XIII, chap. ix). Unlike his teacher, Marshall, however, he is much less concerned with universally available general education and technical training than he is with direct supplementation of incomes. At the start he notes the commonly advanced contention that jobs that pay less than a "living wage" should have their rates forced up irrespective of any ensuing unemployment. This policy, he argues, would injure the national income; indeed, it would injure the very people it is intended somehow to benefit. There is one exception, however: when wages are low because of employer exploitation (by which Pigou means a forward-rising supply curve of labor). In this case, he says, the increase of the wage to a statutory minimum would drive out inefficient firms, which would raise the national income and also improve the productive capacity of the group affected.

But the main effect would be to expel many low-wage workers from all employment, and in that event the nation would require a well-conceived public welfare policy. Pigou therefore avoided any approach through the minimum wage, and preferred instead to introduce "adequate supplementary welfare" to bring such incomes up to a designated minimum.

This leads to Pigou's evaluation of policy to guarantee a national minimum standard of real income (part IV, chap. xiii). He begins with a question: Will a transfer of income from the "relatively rich" to the "relatively poor" increase the national income? His answer is unequivocally affirmative and includes the claim that such a transfer must increase national income "in a wholly unambiguous way." (The increase in welfare derives from Pigou's special view of the measurability of the marginal utility of money, which follows Marshall.) However, everything depends on the design of the chosen plan. The wrong approach can reduce national income and economic welfare, and even cut the real incomes of the poor below what they could earn from work alone. The correct policy would be to adopt a "guaranteed minimum standard." It must be objective in content, to include standardized housing, medical care, education, food, leisure, sanitary conveniences, and workplace safety. And it must be absolute — freedom of choice must be highly circumscribed. The chosen level must avoid extreme want, irrespective of any adverse effect on the national income. In principle the level is that point at which "the direct good resulting from the transference of the marginal pound . . . to the poor just balances the indirect evil" occasioned by the consequent reduction of the national income.

Pigou recognized that the guarantee might cause a flight of capital, hence he leaned toward an international standard, which would require a level below those set by the richer countries. Whatever the level adopted, if it were scaled to size of family, it could raise the birth rate. The larger problem would be the attraction the guarantee would have for drawing in poor immigrants, whose consumption would exceed their production. The result would be a growing burden on the other inhabitants, which in his judgment suggested that the immigration of such persons should be prohibited.

Among Pigou's important contributions to labor economics was his further development of the theory of bilateral monopoly, in particular the concept of sticking points. He also explored the possibility for subsidies to wages and the relationship between labor mobility and economic welfare. He provided reasoned objections to the minimum wage and offered a sophisticated case for a minimum guarantee of real incomes.

Sir John Richard Hicks (1904–1989)

J. R. Hicks followed the three great Cambridge economists — Marshall, Pigou, and Keynes — to become probably the ablest general economic theorist of his own time. He began his study of economics at Oxford, taught for nine years at the London School of Economics, and then spent a decade at Manchester. In 1946 he became a fellow of Nuffield College, Oxford, advancing in 1952 to become Drummond Professor of Political Economy and Fellow of All Souls.[39]

Hicks himself said in 1963 that "at first I regarded myself as a labour economist and not a theoretical economist at all." He credits Lionel Robbins, his colleague at the London School of Economics, with turning his interest to theory, and in particular to the work of Walras, Pareto, Edgeworth, Wicksell, and the Austrians, "with all of whom I was more at home at that stage than I was with Marshall and Pigou."[40]

It was in this opening phase as a labor economist that Hicks published his first major paper, "Edgeworth, Marshall, and the Indeterminateness of Wages" (*Economic Journal*, 1930), following this with *The Theory of Wages* in 1932 (second edition, 1963). It would be well to emphasize, however, that despite the orientation of both of these studies to matters of "labor," they are replete with economic theory. Indeed, they both underscore the point that Hicks consistently took conventional equilibrium analysis as his point of departure for considering all of his chosen topics in the labor field — from the wage premium acquired by labor unions to the consequential effects of an international limitation below optimum for weekly working hours. In addition to his own generous acknowledgment of Robbins's early influence, it is of some significance that Hicks credits Eugen von Böhm-Bawerk, the eminent Austrian economist, as the primary source for his analysis of the effects of a general rise in wages, specifically Böhm's "Macht oder ökonomisches Gesetz" ("Power or Economic Law").[41]

Hicks's *The Theory of Wages* begins with a section on the free market in which the entire discussion is directed to an analysis of the forces of demand, supply, wages, and competition, and how these forces work toward equilibrium — entirely in the spirit and context developed by Marshall and Pigou. Hicks's goal, in short, is to develop a conceptual model for handling the behavior of a fully competitive labor market. With this model — or paradigm — he then turns to the second section, which concerns the impacts flowing from the regulation of the labor market by unions and the state. Put a little differently, Hicks's procedure is first to construct a theoretical model of the processes that bring about equilibrium and then to change the ruling conditions or parameters to determine what the effects are likely to be in a labor market in which the agencies initiating change — unions and the state — are seen as imposing interferences on or distortions of the workings of competition. As Hicks says himself, "One of the principal objects of this book" is to set forth "the possibilities and probable consequences of interference with the competitive course of wages."[42]

In a competitive labor market, where labor demand equals labor supply, there will be a definite wage and no wage-affecting unemployment. If demand exceeds supply, there will be a shortage of labor and the wage will rise. If demand falls short of supply, unemployment will occur and the wage will fall until unemployment disappears. In equilibrium every person gets the same wage; differences in net job advantages, along with costs of movement, may be ignored. Further, the wage will equal the value of the marginal product. An increase in labor input, with cooperating factors fixed, will lower marginal product. Finally, this is a drastically oversimplified market: there is only one grade of homogeneous labor; there is only one wage rate; there is neither an internal nor an external wage structure; and "capital" is a label that designates many different components treated as a unified bundle. Also, there are no structural rules to control access to, exit from, or movement within this market. What we have, therefore, is what Dunlop has termed the bourse model.

The initial presentation is simply the short-run marginal productivity theory, which rests upon one variable factor and the principle of nonproportional outputs. At this point Hicks introduces the possibility of a change of production methods, initially with all factors now variable but only together in fixed proportions. Later he looks into changes in these fixed input ratios induced by a change in relative factor prices.

To convey the idea, consider a simple production surface with two input factors and a given ratio of prices for units of each. For a chosen output, the tangency between the price line and the designated isoquant will determine the least-cost mode, because the ratio of prices will equal the technical ratio of substitution between the two inputs, of which each has a marginal product at this point. This same point of tangency also indicates the maximum output for a given expenditure, given also the existing method. Now if the method is retained but the expenditure varied, one gets a series of tangency points that together provide a locus function that represents the expansion path or scale line for this method at the prevailing ratio of factor prices. With a change in the price ratio, a new scale line will be created, with new factor proportions.

According to Hicks, the rule of proportionality will determine the choice of the least-cost method; this rule says that the ratio of the marginal product of each input to its price must equal the same ratio for the other input. But the choice of the optimum output will be determined by a second rule: that the marginal products of each factor must *equal* their respective prices. At this point nothing can be gained by changes of scale or in factor proportions. Long-run average and marginal costs of product will be equal to the product's competitive selling price. Thus output, inputs, and method are all determined at the firm's optimal position, the Wicksellian case.

Following Walras, Hicks now asks, Given that all production methods in all industries are fixed, but that some are capital-intensive and some labor-intensive, will any unemployment appear with an increase in the general level of wages? Instinct says no, because all prices will rise proportionately. But this is wrong: the higher wage costs will hurt the profits of labor-intensive industries more, while the capital-intensive group will become relatively more profitable. Some labor will be added there, while the first group will undergo contraction and will let more workers go than can be absorbed. Net unemployment will follow.

A different process of adjustment will occur if the level of wages is increased and proportionality prevails at the start. If time is ample to permit full adaptations of capital as well as changes in method, the rise in wages will induce a shift to more capital-intensive methods. Accordingly, there will be a shift against labor across industries, and net unemployment will follow. In the end equilibrium will be restored at the least-cost level.

Regarding these disturbances and the subsequent adjustments they invoke, Hicks insists that the return to equilibrium has to be a slow process, mainly because most capital is fixed and long-lived, hence must be worked down before it is replaced.

Hicks's views on the economics of inventions are of some interest.[43] Under full competition, he contends, an invention will be adopted only if it raises national income, because it must lower production cost; either output will be increased or, at the same output, resources will be set free to be used elsewhere. When an invention is introduced, it raises the marginal products of all inputs, although not necessarily in the same proportion. Thus innovations may be classified in three ways: (1) those that raise the marginal product of capital relatively more than that of labor and hence are *laborsaving;* (2) those that lower the marginal product of capital relative to that for labor and hence are *capital-saving;* and (3) those that leave the relative marginal products intact and hence are *neutral.*[44]

Noting that laborsaving inventions seem to have predominated in industrial history, Hicks thinks that this is not illusory and does not derive from a preoccupation with the contributions of the mechanical and physical sciences to the development of fixed capital. Rather, he prefers the economist's explanation: changes in relative factor prices spur innovations to substitute for the dearer factor. Because the rate of capital formation has consistently outrun the rate of growth in the labor force, labor has been the ever-scarcer factor. Hence its relative price has been increasing for many decades. This, Hicks believes, explains the laborsaving bias of induced inventions, and through this, the same bias in all inventions, because the autonomous ones will be random, with no bias either way.

Returning now to Hicks's belief that unionism — at least in the United Kingdom — introduced a downward rigidity in wage rates and, in addition, a substantial wage premium above the competitive level after World War I, there arises an obvious need to explain how these developments came about. Part of the answer, he suggests, derives from the formation of highly centralized national bodies negotiating on behalf of labor and management across a broad range of industries. Another influence involves the role of the state, both through wage boards that set wages and with the advent of unemployment insurance, which carries the decisive provision that wages on offer for job vacancies that are below prevailing rates "shall not be regarded as suitable employment, refusal of which disqualifies for benefit."[45] The effect of these developments was to shore up union scales despite heavy unemployment at certain times in the 1920s. Finally, unemployment was made worse by the return to the gold standard in April 1925, at the prewar par of exchange. This seriously overvalued sterling for the rest of the decade.[46]

Hicks's early interest in the theory of collective bargaining drew his attention to a little known but still important book, *Mathematical Psychics* (1881), written by Francis Ysidro Edgeworth, who was one of Hicks's predecessors as Drummond Professor of Political Economy at Oxford. Although Edgeworth's distinguished talents lay primarily in mathematics and statistical theory, in this work he addressed the problem of the indeterminacy of equilibrium under bilateral bargaining.[47]

By "indeterminacy" Edgeworth meant the very problem that Smith had glimpsed in his bargaining theory of wages and that had also interested Marshall: situations in which full freedom of exchange fails to set the price and terms of a contract between two trading parties. In bilateral bargaining, Edgeworth contended, there is no uniquely determined point of stable equilibrium. Instead the outcome depends on bargaining skills and strength. To illustrate the case, he devised a box diagram in which two traders' systems of indifference curves are superimposed on each other. At the point of tangency for each pair of opposing curves, the two private rates of substitution will equal each other and also a common potential rate of exchange. The result is a locus function that Edgeworth called the contract curve. The final settlement can be any point along this curve within the trading zone; both parties will gain from trade, or only one will gain while the other will be no worse off. For any trade there is no unique point of equilibrium.

In an attempt to find a determinate solution to the problem, Hicks developed his own diagram in which he introduces an employer's concession curve and a union's resistance curve (see Fig. 1.1). Note, first, that the employer's concession curve rises with the expected

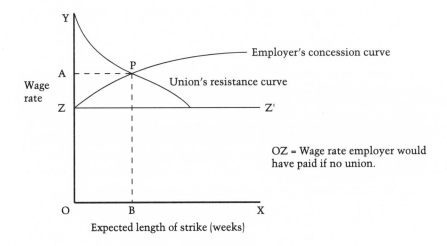

OZ = Wage rate employer would have paid if no union.

Expected length of strike (weeks)

length of the strike, but at a decreasing rate. Any point on this curve is the highest wage rate the employer would be willing to pay to avoid a strike of corresponding length.

Second, note the union's resistance curve, which at each point is the minimum increase it will accept to avoid a strike of that length. Also, initially the curve drops at a decreasing rate as it moves to the right. Beyond the interception point at P it begins to fall at an increasing rate, reflecting the union's increasing weakness in holding out with a strike of longer expected length.

At P the union has the highest rate it can get from the employer without a strike or with a strike of unacceptable length. Astute bargaining should bring both parties to a settlement at P. If a strike should occur, both bargaining curves may shift during its course. Much more could be said, but here one needs only observe that Hicks did succeed in showing that a determinate solution could occur.

Hicks believed that the ability of a union to extract a wage premium — or even a premium over the previous one — is stronger in good times, when the costs of a strike are higher for an employer and the morale of the members is stronger.

Although Hicks's pioneering study contains no econometrics or systematic quantitative evidence, he was nonetheless convinced by the principles of equilibrium theory that the extraction of wage premiums by unions had to create unemployment and compel the introduction of ever more capitalistic production functions by employers driven by the need for substitution. He was somber in his conclusions, but he proposed no reforms. Instead *The Theory of Wages* ends rather surprisingly with a quite elegant analysis of the adding-up problem, followed by a careful and definitive presentation of the mathematical foundations of Marshall's four rules affecting the elasticity of derived demand.

From the standpoint of labor economics it is unfortunate that Hicks turned at this point — save for the 1963 revision of *The Theory of Wages* — to a large array of other important problems: the theory of value, the Keynesian short-run theory of unemployment equilibrium, capital theory, and the theory of economic history. Although all this indirectly represented a loss to labor economics, there can be no doubt that the discipline of economics itself is all the richer from this impressive demonstration of Professor Hicks's great range and depth of intellectual interests.

Notes

1. Diehl, 351.
2. According to Blaug, the term *classical economics* was devised by Marx to identify the group of economists from Petty to Ricardo in Britain and from Boisguilbert to Sismondi in France, all of whom studied "the real relations" of production in capitalistic society. Later Keynes applied the term to those economists from Smith to Pigou who accepted Say's law of markets. Blaug, 162 n. 1.
3. According to Edwin Cannan, the phrase "division of labor" was not in familiar use in 1776. He attributes it to Bernard de Mandeville, *Fable of the Bees* (1729), part 2, dialogue 6. (See *Wealth of Nations*, book I, chap. 1, 3 n. 1).
4. Smith's examples, which are now well known, involve the manufacture of pins and nails. Less known is his opinion that the simplification and routinization of jobs in modern industrialism is a source of stupifying boredom.
5. Smith believed that the propensity to truck, barter, and exchange was part of human nature. But within a division of labor, the choice of a particular trade derives from nurture, which is the main difference between a philosopher and a street porter.
6. This is a version of the labor theory of value, but it could just as well be marginal utility theory, since relative marginal utilities also equal relative prices.
7. Smith had glimpsed here the indeterminacy of wages under bilateral monopoly, as later developed by Edgeworth, Marshall, Pigou, and Hicks.
8. Marshall, book VI, chap. iii, 8.
9. Stigler, 157.
10. Ibid., 165.
11. Blaug, 550. Nonproportional returns are also involved, because the usual notion is a finite area of arable land to which successive doses of capital are applied.
12. Stigler, 172.
13. As calculated by Professor Ben Zuckerman.
14. Marx, *Capital*, vol. 1, 693–694.
15. This curve of total labor supply is identical in form to that used to show Keynes's case of the downward rigidity of wages.
16. Hildebrand, *Theory of Markets*, 439–443; Marx, *Theorien*, vol. 1, 299, 309.
17. Marx, *Theorien*, vol. 1, 264. In essentials this case is identical to Smith's "original state."
18. Hildebrand, *Theory of Markets*, 405–422.
19. Hunt, 37–38.

20. Engels is the primary source for details about "final communism"; see *Anti-Dühring*.
21. Hunt, 41; Dahrendorf, 13.
22. This point is developed in *Anti-Dühring*.
23. See Aspromourgos.
24. Teggart, 49–55.
25. See Campus.
26. Walras may have resolved the problem, but his disclosure was too obscure for many.
27. See Corry.
28. Marshall, book V, chap. viii, 406–407. All references are to the 8th ed. (1920).
29. Ibid., chap. vi, 381–386.
30. Ibid., book VI, chap. viii, 627–628. See also Kerr and Hicks.
31. Within this range, at any point the agreed-upon objective rate of substitution through exchange will equal the private rates of substitution of the bargaining parties.
32. Marshall, book VI, chap. iv, 560–564. Hereafter cited in text.
33. Matthews, 20–30.
34. Ibid., 22.
35. Ibid., 25–30.
36. See de Graaff.
37. Strictly speaking, the classical view was not "wrong," as Pigou himself observed. It was simply not applicable when the necessary conditions were not present. If money wages, the price level, and the money rate of interest are all rigid and downward, then the classical mechanisms of adjustment to full employment cannot operate.
38. *The Economics of Welfare*, 4th ed. (part III, chap. vi). Hereafter cited in text.
39. See Bliss.
40. Hicks, cited in Bliss.
41. In *Gesammelte Schriften*, vol. 1. See Hicks, 190 n. 1.
42. Ibid., 24.
43. Hicks introduces the elasticity of substitution to predict the response of relative income shares to an innovation that affects relative marginal productivities. Space is lacking for adequate examination here.
44. Hicks, 121.
45. Ibid., 177.
46. Ibid., 175–176.
47. Ibid., 141–143. See also Hicks, "Edgeworth, Marshall, and the Indeterminateness of Wages," *Economic Journal*, 40:158 (June 1930), 216–221.

References

Aspromourgos, Tony. "Neoclassical," *The New Palgrave,* vol. 3 (1987), 625.

Blaug, Mark. *Economic Theory in Retrospect,* 3rd ed. (Cambridge: Cambridge University Press, 1978).

Bliss, Christopher. "John R. Hicks," *The New Palgrave,* vol. 2 (1987), 641–646.

Campus, Antonietta. "Marginalist Economics," *The New Palgrave,* vol. 3 (1987), 320–322.

Cain, Glen G. "Paul H. Douglas (1892–1976)," *International Encyclopedia of the Social Sciences,* vol. 18 (1979), 153–157.

Clark, Colin G. "Paul Howard Douglas (1892–1976)," *The New Palgrave,* vol. 1 (1987), 920–921.

Condorcet, Marquis de. *Outline of the Historical Picture of the Progress of the Human Mind,* trans. Leona M. Fassett, in George H. Hildebrand, *The Idea of Progress: A Collection of Readings* (Berkeley: University of California Press, 1949), 321–358.

Corry, Bernard. "Alfred Marshall," *International Encyclopedia of the Social Sciences,* vol. 10 (1979), 25–33.

Dahrendorf, Ralf. *Class and Class Conflict in Industrial Society* (Stanford, Calif.: Stanford University Press, 1959).

Diehl, Karl. "The Classical School," *Encyclopedia of the Social Sciences* (1937), 351–357.

Douglas, Paul H. *Real Wages in the United States, 1890–1926* (Boston: Houghton Mifflin, 1930).

————.*The Theory of Wages* (New York: Macmillan, 1934).

Dunlop, John T. "Labor Markets and Wage-Determination: Then and Now," in Bruce E. Kaufman, ed., *How Labor Markets Work* (Lexington, Mass.: Lexington Books, 1988), 47–87.

Ekelund, Robert B Jr., and Robert F. Hebert. *A History of Economic Theory and Method,* 2nd ed., (New York: McGraw-Hill, 1983).

Engels, Friedrich. *Anti-Dühring: Herr Eugen Dühring's Revolution in Science* (1875).

Godwin, William. *Enquiry Concerning Political Justice* (1793).

de Graaff, J. V. "Arthur Cecil Pigou," *The New Palgrave,* vol. 3 (1987), 876–879.

Hicks, John R. *The Theory of Wages* (London: Macmillan, 1932; New York: Peter Smith, 1948).

Hildebrand, George H. "The Theory of Markets and the Problem of Economic Crises, from Quesnay to Marx: A Study in the History of Economic Thought" (Ph.D. diss., Cornell University, 1942).

Hildebrand, George H., and Ta-Chung Liu. *Manufacturing Production*

Functions in the United States, 1957 (Ithaca, N.Y.: Cornell University, 1965).

Hunt, R. N. Carew. *Theory and Practice of Communism: An Introduction,* 5th ed., revised (New York: Macmillan, 1957).

Kaldor, N. "The Equilibrium of the Firm," *Economic Journal,* 44:173 (March 1934), 60–76.

Kaufman, Bruce E., ed. *How Labor Markets Work* (Lexington, Mass.: Lexington Books, 1988).

Kerr, Clark. "The Neoclassical Revisionists in Labor Economics," in Bruce E. Kaufman, ed., *How Labor Markets Work,* 1–46.

Malthus, Thomas Robert. *An Essay on the Principle of Population . . .* (1798; 3rd ed. 1803).

Marshall, Alfred. *Principles of Economics: An Introductory Volume,* 8th ed. (1920; London: Macmillan, 1930).

Marx, Karl. *Capital,* Kerr Edition, 3 vols., (Chicago: University of Chicago Press, 1906).

——.*Critique of the Gotha Programme* (1875).

——.*Theorien über den Mehrwert,* ed. Karl Kautsky, vol. 2 (Stuttgart, 1905); vol. 4 (Stuttgart, 1910).

Marx, Karl, and Friedrich Engels. *The German Ideology* (1845–1846).

Matthews, Robin C. O. "Marshall and the Labour Market," in John K. Whitaker, ed., *Centenary Essays on Alfred Marshall* (Cambridge: Cambridge University Press, 1990), 14–43.

Pigou, Arthur C. *The Economics of Welfare,* 4th ed. (London: Macmillan, 1950).

Schultz, Henry. "Marginal Productivity and the General Pricing Process," *Journal of Political Economy,* 37:5 (October 1929), 505–551.

Smith, Adam. *An Inquiry into the Nature and Causes of the Wealth of Nations,* ed. with an introduction by Edwin Cannan, Modern Library (New York: Random House, 1937).

Stigler, George J. "The Ricardian Theory of Value and Distribution," in George J. Stigler, *Essays in the History of Economics* (Chicago: University of Chicago Press, 1965), 156–197.

Teggart, Richard Victor. *Thorstein Veblen: A Chapter in American Economic Thought* (Berkeley: University of California Press, 1932).

Zuckerman, Ben (Professor of Astronomy, University of California, Los Angeles). Letter, *National Review* (April 27, 1992), 19–20.

2

Americanizing the Labor Problem: The Wisconsin School

Jack Barbash

There is enough coherence to the Wisconsin approach to labor problems to call it a school, as many have. The Wisconsin School in full flower — which is this chapter's focus — was a group of men and women who came to the University of Wisconsin in Madison in the early decades of the twentieth century. Richard T. Ely founded the group in 1892 but it was John R. Commons, recruited by Ely in 1904, who gave the school its coherence.

In this chapter I will try to define what the Wisconsin School stood for, to situate it in its diverse contexts, and briefly to look at several representative figures, including Commons, Selig Perlman, Edwin E. Witte, Sumner H. Slichter, Arthur J. Altmeyer, William M. Leiserson, David J. Saposs, Philip Taft, and the American Association for Labor Legislation (AALL). Although members of the School, including Commons, ranged over the whole field of economics, the emphasis here is on the labor problem.

I have chosen this particular company of economists to write about, out of dozens of others, because I think they are central to the Wisconsin labor tradition. My knowledge of their work is reinforced by a personal association with most of them, and their careers are well documented. Perlman, Saposs, and Taft will be discussed as representative of trade union scholarship; Slichter reflects interests in collective bargaining and personnel administration; Leiserson is included here for his interest in arbitration; and Witte, Altmeyer, and AALL are included for their work in public policy and its administration.

The Wisconsin School took as its mission, in Saposs's words, that "learning empirically derived should be devoted to the solution and remedial treatment of vital social problems" (Saposs 1960a, 7–8).

Turn-of-the-century Wisconsin might not at first impression appear to be the most natural site for such an enterprise, but several circumstances joined to make it so. The Progressive Era — "that impulse toward criticism and change that was everywhere so conspicuous after 1900" (Hofstader 1955, 5) — shaped the national mood. "The intellectual tempo" of the University of Wisconsin, Saposs remembered, "was set by the imaginative and social crusading La Follette Progressive movement, complemented by the brilliantly led Victor L. Berger practical Milwaukee reform socialists. Joining in this exhilarating social crusade was the State University headed by the socially farseeing and adventuresome geologist Charles S. Van Hise. He gave impetus and guidance to the ideal that the University was truly a handmaiden of the State. Associated with him was a galaxy of dedicated and profound scholars" (Saposs 1960a, 7–8).

John R. Commons (1862–1945)

The Wisconsin School — to summarize it in a phrase out of Commons's *Legal Foundations of Capitalism* — sought "a new equity that will protect the job as the older equity protected the business" (Commons [1924] 1959, 307). Modern democracy's "first great problem" was "how to get a fair living by reasonable hours of work, leaving enough leisure for both childhood and manhood" (Commons 1913, 3–4).

The idea of equity for labor goes back to Adam Smith. "It is but equity that they who feed, clothe and lodge the whole body of the people should have such a share of the produce of their own labor as to be themselves tolerably well fed, clothed and lodged" (Smith [1776] 1901, 193). Mainstream economists voiced similar sentiments occasionally, but the genius of Commons and his company was to build a whole school of thought on "the one foundation of labor" (Commons [1934] 1964, 131).

Theory and practice were one for Commons. "A theory is only a tool for investigating practice, like a spade for digging up facts and converting them into an understandable system" (Commons 1934, 722). Commons wasn't all that adept at theory making, as he acknowledged, and, Selig Perlman excepted, neither were the other members of the Wisconsin School. They preferred problem solving to science building (see Barbash 1991). But it is, nonetheless, possible to derive a conceptual framework from their works that is true to the Wisconsin purpose.

Commons began from the moral standpoint that equity was labor's due as the human factor of production. The market, while it served conventional commodities passably well, was unsuited to the complexities of buying and selling labor.

Labor's inherent bargaining weakness in the employment relationship rendered it incapable of negotiating equity on its own power. Public policy, including the legalization of trade unionism and collective bargaining was, therefore, necessary and justifiable to maintain equity in the employment relationship in ways compatible with American values. Equity was not only morally right for Commons, it was also essential to labor efficiency. Employers had to treat employees fairly to get the most out of them.

Commons and his associates directed their reform efforts across the entire range of labor problems including vocational education, worker education, apprenticeship, workers' compensation, job safety, factory inspection, social security, unemployment compensation, employment offices, trade unionism, collective bargaining, civil service, and the professional administration of the labor law. They not only researched these problems but they also used the research products in the arguments for enactment. Then, to top it off, they helped handle the administration of the legislation. The broad scope of operation by these scholars, and the versatility of their skills, constitute a remarkable accomplishment.

Commons was concerned with finding American ways of achieving labor equity so as to allay fears that European socialism and class struggle were being imported into the United States. America was different from Europe, the extensive historical researches of Commons and his colleagues revealed. Free land, free political institutions, public education, and indigenous idealism encouraged a more open society. At the same time the federal-state system, the conservatism of the American character, a conservative judiciary, and mass immigration made labor reform more difficult (Commons 1918, 3).

The Wisconsin School's scheme of labor reform had to reckon also with the conservative drift of received economics, which generally treated government intervention, trade unionism, and collective bargaining as obstructions to the free market ideal-type and to natural-law individualism. Wisconsin's institutional analysis sought to demonstrate that the individual "propertyless" worker (Commons and Andrews 1916, 2) was powerless to bargain with corporate employers on anything like an equal plane and that union collective action and collective bargaining were necessary to create a "countervailing power," as John Kenneth Galbraith later termed it.

Radical change by conservative means fairly characterizes the

Commons and Wisconsin style. The notion, radical for the time — and maybe even yet in the United States — was that government had a positive and continuing function to perform in ameliorating injustice in the employment relationship for which the market alone was ill suited.

Commons's brand of conservatism consisted of a strategic judgment that equity in the employment relationship was achievable under capitalism. This notion set him apart from many if not most of his intellectual contemporaries who were concerned with the labor problem. Marx, whom Commons and Perlman frequently took as a point of reference, didn't foresee that trade unionism, might, as Commons put it, "make an agreement with the capitalists and divide the product between them" (Commons 1919, 194). But Commons's acceptance of capitalism was far from unbounded. "Understanding the human element in industry is the acid test of capitalism today" (Commons 1921, 121).

Commons added American pragmatism to labor's methods (see Barbash 1967). The strike was like "withholding your property until you can agree on the terms of exchange" (Commons 1921, 1). He called conflict of interest a "natural and necessary ingredient . . . of the social process"; but in collective bargaining he saw conflict as fusing "into dependence on each other" (Commons 1934, 4). "Legislation goes beyond the legal face of things and looks" at the real bargaining relationship. The elected legislators are able to recognize that the labor bargain is not only about wages but "about life itself" (Commons [1924] 1959, 307).

Commons was careful to differentiate his mode of government involvement from the European model of centralized bureaucratic administration. The Wisconsin School favored instead the diffusion of state power by such means as federalism, consensus and involvement of the affected parties, expert administration, voluntary collective bargaining, incentive instead of coercion, due process including objective investigation of the facts, and, finally, incremental, step-by-step change rather than wholesale change. All of these precepts Commons had learned from his own experience with regulation, mostly in Wisconsin; until the 1930s there was not much to learn about progressive labor legislation from the federal experience.

The Wisconsin School

Commons was not, by the usual standard, a great platform teacher. His teaching genius lay in his ability to come up with challenging hypotheses and then engage his students as coventurers in testing them with field research and investigation.

Commons had no faith in "ideal solutions." The spirit of true democracy "investigates, takes into account all of the facts, gives due weight to each and works out, not an ideal but a reasonable solution day-by-day" (Commons 1919, 185). His extraordinary ability to instill a spirit of discipleship in his students is probably unequalled in academic social science. (See Harter 1962, 30, and Saposs 1960a, 11–13, for lists of his students who rose to prominence.)

Edwin E. Witte remembered how students in Commons's classes came in as rebels but went out into the world "to improve what . . . was wrong . . . without destroying our political, economic and social structure," to "know the facts, . . . to think in terms of remedies rather than criticisms and to learn from the people directly interested" (Witte in Harter 1962, 77–78). When the U.S. Supreme Court nullified the District of Columbia's minimum wage law (William Haber recalled) Commons made it a class assignment to prepare a "minimum wage law which could be accommodated to the Court's philosophy" (University of Wisconsin 1966, 51).

Many years later Saposs recalled how Commons "aroused our curiosity and broadened our horizons through his analytical mind and provocative ideas" (Saposs 1960a, 10–11). To Selig Perlman, Commons was an "intellectual democrat." He asked "genuinely groping questions without any definite goal — a mere stabbing in this direction and that . . . and then . . . a question or a series of questions would come forth which . . . touched the nerve of the situation" (Perlman 1950, 5).

Selig Perlman (1888–1959)

Perlman more than anybody else in the Wisconsin School, grasped the nettle of the debate over union purposes (see M. Perlman 1958). The reputation of Commons's "beloved" and "brilliant" student and later colleague (Commons [1934] 1964, 81) rests mainly on *A Theory of the Labor Movement* (1928). He was also a teacher with "great power for pithy and epigrammatic expression," "sharp and rapier-like" humor and "a great talent for generalizing" (Taft 1960, 17; Taft 1976, 256).

Like his mentor, Perlman rejected socialism as the necessary historical mission of the working class and the trade union movement, and made this the continuing thrust of his analysis. Closer to the manual worker's interest than socialism are — and here Perlman gave his own twist to Commons's distinction between the "higher" and "lower" idealism — (Commons 1913, Ch. 14) " 'shop rights' which to the workingman at the bench are identical with 'liberty' itself — since, thanks to them, he has no need to kowtow to foreman or boss, as the price of holding his job and, after all, is not this sort of liberty the only sort which reaches the workman directly and with certainty and that can never get lost en route, like the 'broader' liberty promised by socialism?" (Perlman [1928] 1949, 275).

Scarcity consciousness and job control are the key Perlman concepts. The manual worker is viewed as primarily motivated by a "fundamental scarcity consciousness... which rules unionism today as it ruled the gilds of the past.... [Manualists also include] peasants in Russia, modern wage earners or medieval master workmen.... Their basic economic attitudes [are] determined by a consciousness of scarcity of opportunity ... and stand out in contrast with the businessman's abundance consciousness or consciousness of unlimited opportunity.... Job control, mastery of job opportunities [are the real roots of the manualist] social group psychology" (Perlman [1928] 1949, 278 passim). Trade unions come to capitalism, Perlman said, "as bargainers, desiring to strike the best wage bargain possible. What impresses them is not so much the fact that the employer owns the means of production but that he possesses a high degree of advantage over them" (Perlman 1922, 266–276). American unions have learned "the lesson that under no circumstances can labor here afford to arouse the fear of the great middle class for the safety of private property as a basic institution" (Perlman [1928] 1949, 160).

Samuel Gompers's American Federation of Labor (AFL) and its constituent unions provided the best "fit to the conditions imposed by the external environment and the American workingman's psychology" (Perlman [1928] 1949, 201). He specified the Gompers model as follows:

First, labor must organize *separately* from the other producing classes.

Second, the capitalist system had come to stay, and there was no desirable escape from it, by way of either producers' co-operatives or state socialism.

Third, labor parties merely expose labor's weakness as a vote-getter and cause internal dissension. It is, however, important for labor to have a "collective bargaining arrangement" with one of the existing parties during any particular election.

Fourth, it is safest to build unions around the job-interest common to all wage earners, whatever their politics, religion, or ethnic origin, since the American working class is notably divided into such vertical groups.

Fifth, the strongest unity comes when those whose jobs come out of the same "job reservoir," due to a common trade skill, are joined in one organization.

Finally, labor must strive, by all means of economic coercion or persuasion, to bring employers around to recognizing unions as co-administrators with themselves of the available jobs. But Gompers insisted that labor should never run the risk of being called subversive by advocating any sort of "worker's control," socialism, or nationalization of industry (Perlman 1957, 224; emphasis in original).

David J. Saposs (1886–1968)

Unlike most other members of the Wisconsin School who operated from a permanent university or government base, Saposs moved from job to job, to where the labor action was. His career included service with the U.S. Commission on Industrial Relations (1913), the University of Wisconsin (1914–1917), the Immigrant Workers Study (1918), the Steel Strike Investigation (1919–1920), Brookwood Labor College (1922–1933), company unionism studies (1934–1935), the National Labor Relations Board (1942–1945), the Office of Military Government for Germany and the Mutual Security Administration (1946–1952) (see Barbash 1966, 156–157).

The niches of the labor problem which David J. Saposs carved out for himself and illuminated include left-wing unionism, industrial unionism, immigration, and comparative labor movements and ideologies (see Barbash 1966, 158–162, for a bibliography).

Saposs never fully shared Commons's and Perlman's high appreciation of Gompers, craft unionism, the early American Federation of Labor and voluntarism. His approach to union radicalism was more matter-of-fact. His book *Left-Wing Unionism* (1926) is subtitled *A Study of Radical Policies and Tactics*. Saposs refers to another of his books, *The Labor Movement of Post-War France* (1931), as a "more comprehensive treatment of practices and activities," in contrast to the earlier literature with its emphasis on "the theoretical and philosophic phases of the French labor movement" (Saposs 1931, x). Saposs's work on immigration, the ascendant industrial union interest, and the decline of traditional antistate voluntarism suggest a more positive viewpoint, however.

Saposs's interests came into sharper focus with the coming of the New Deal and with the investigations of company unions for the Twentieth Century Fund (Saposs 1936). He moved soon after to the newly created National Labor Relations Board as chief economist, and his research there was shaped by the practical tasks of shielding the new law from a massive employer onslaught. He framed the economic analysis for the Wagner Act's constitutional argument (Saposs 1937). Saposs then fleshed out the bare bones of the collective bargaining provision in the act by putting it in empirical contexts (Saposs 1940).

As communist influence became important in the labor movement, bearing out Saposs's final words in *Left-Wing Unionism* ("Unless the communists demonstrate the knack of coordinating the idealistic with the practical their efforts at organizing separate unions are certainly doomed to failure" [Saposs 1926, 190]), he became the first, and for a time one of the few responsible critical analysts of communist unionism. The main body of his work in this area is represented by two books on communist influence in the unions and political parties (Saposs 1959; Saposs 1960b). Toward the end of his career Saposs studied the varying patterns of ideology and practice in the international labor movement (Saposs 1962).

Saposs's career over the long term has been more outspokenly pro-union, one might say, than that of his Wisconsin contemporaries. His public or quasi-public posts represented efforts to affirm and protect worker and union rights. There was also that phase of his career in the direct service of unions or union interests (Labor Bureau, Inc.; Brookwood Labor College; and the Amalgamated Clothing Workers). Saposs's work was never far from the clamor of labor conflict.

Philip Taft (1902–1976)

Taft is the transition figure between the older Wisconsin tradition and the labor revolution of the 1930s and after. He was steeped in labor's early struggles, and he also worked assiduously at understanding the new unionism.

Philip Taft was the premier labor historian of his time. No other scholar ranged as broadly over the trade union terrain nor penetrated as deeply into the workings of unions (see bibliography in *Labor History: Philip Taft* 1978, 130–136). Taft was, therefore, not only a historian of labor, he was also the leading student of union governance (Taft 1954; Taft, Estey, and Wagner 1964) — or, as John R. Commons might have said, of the union as a going concern.

Taft was rare among scholars in bringing to his scholarship real-world experience as a newsboy, casual laborer, harvest field hand, factory operative, seaman, coal "passer," oil pipeline layer, and Industrial Workers of the World (IWW) activist (see "Autobiography" in *Labor History: Philip Taft* 1978, 39–71). He was 26 years old when he arrived in Madison as a freshman.

Taft shared with his Wisconsin forbears a belief in the fitness of American unionism to the American environment. He neither attempted nor offered a "theory" except for reaffirming the general validity of the Wisconsin perspective. "My approach has been empirical and avoidance of grand theorizing" (Taft in Brody 1978, 11). The Wisconsin School, he posited, "shared a belief approaching, but some distance from, a faith that the trade unions would survive and prosper in the American economy, and this prospect was desirable. They believed that unions had an important role, not to train the working class to accept the leadership of a revolutionary intelligentsia, but in enlarging the rights of individuals at the place of work. They recognized the conservative character of the trade union, but did not despair of its eventual ability to adapt itself to a changing technology" (Taft 1966, 69–70).

With some modernization Taft held to the Perlman theory that "the essence of unionism is to seek a voice in the determination of the terms of employment" (Taft 1976, 256). Business unionism, in fact, has been the goal of American trade unionism throughout its history. It is still "highly suitable for enlarging the rights and liberties of the individual and for protecting him against changes in the supply of and demand for labor" (Taft 1964, xvi). Contrary to the conventional wisdom, business unionism was capable of sacrifice and idealism.

Taft tried to understand American labor on its own terms. "The American Federation of Labor's voluntarism partakes less of Herbert Spencer and more of a fear of the injuries inflicted by strong government on the unions" (Perlman and Taft 1935, 6). He later stated, "Government has in the past been as effective in inhibiting labor organization and collective bargaining as the New Deal labor laws have been in protecting the right to organize" (Taft 1964, xvii). Taft thought that the radical influence on the labor movement needed to be distinguished as between socialist and communist. "Socialists and syndicalists acted as individuals with a common philosophy and specifically did not agree on specific trade union problems. The Communists acted . . . as a bloc" directed by "non-union political commissars" who took their orders from outside communist organs of power (Taft 1954, 15). The hard critics of business unionism's democracy, honesty, and responsibility found Taft their most redoubtable antagonist. There was little in the critics' intellectual analysis to make their position necessarily superior to the paths that trade unions have historically hacked out for themselves.

Taft was not, however, an uncritical observer and recorder of the trade union performance. He noted (with Perlman) the "strategic blunders" of the AFL in the steel industry, first in 1901 and again during World War I, when broader labor movement solidarity might have breached the antiunion fortress that the steel industry presented up through the first third of the twentieth century. He dismissed union autonomy — as grounds for "overrid[ing] moral considerations in instances of graft and dishonesty" — and the "surrender to business philosophy during the Coolidge period" (Perlman and Taft 1935, 635–636).

Contrary to the notion that he was pro-AFL, Taft wrote the first article on the Congress of Industrial Organizations (CIO) to appear in an academic journal (Taft 1937). According to Taft, the AFL leadership brought the "great crisis" of the 1930s on itself, through a series of errors and an "ignoring of the spirit, practice, and constitutions of the AFL" (Taft 1964, xx).

Selig Perlman was Taft's great intellectual influence, but over time Taft evolved a critical standpoint toward his teacher. Perlman had exaggerated the relationship between ideology and behavior, he believed. It was not clear to Taft why middle-class commitment to antimonopoly sentiment or cheap money were necessarily antithetical to unionism. Nor was it clear why commitment to socialism as an ideology necessarily affected the *practice* of unionism. So long as workers have a "common interest" in job protection, their antecedent origins need not affect their unionism. Perlman's economic group psychology was found by Taft to be "a separation between those who prefer a secure, though modest return . . . and those who play for big stakes — a dubious proposition"; Perlman's definition of intellectual was almost "meaningless." But Taft thought that Perlman's basic proposition "that the essence of unionism is to seek a voice in the determination of the terms of employment" had stood the test of time (Taft 1976, 254–256 passim).

Sumner H. Slichter (1892–1959)

Slichter's formal relationship with the Wisconsin School ended in 1914, the year he received his Master's degree from the University of Wisconsin and also the year he served with Commons and several others in his circle at the U.S. Commission on Industrial Relations. Afterward Slichter went on to Chicago for his Ph.D. and then to a teaching post at Cornell. He was most closely associated with the Harvard Business School during his career, but he continued to maintain close personal ties with Madison (Dunlop in Slichter 1961, xi–xxiv).

Slichter was more critical of unions in their maturer stages than were his Wisconsin contemporaries, questioning whether business unionism was good enough for modern conditions. He had fewer qualms about public regulation. "Trade unions have attained such power that public policy should endeavor to regulate the use of these powers" (Slichter [1952] 1961, xvi). Interestingly, a law to that general effect, known as the Slichter Law, was later passed in Massachusetts.

Much of Slichter's earlier work is in the Wisconsin mold. A young Slichter put the labor problem more incisively than anybody else: it "exists because man is not only the end but also a means of production" causing "a clash between life and work" (Slichter 1928, 287).

Slichter was severely critical of management's "handling of men" in the 1920s. "The present form of organization, which leaves labor on the outside as regards share in control and direct participation in prosperity renders it inevitable that, barring the employees of a few altruistic employers, the workmen shall feel that they are simply outsiders used for the benefit of industry" (Slichter [1920] 1961, 182–183).

Commons, in his introduction to the published version of Slichter's master's thesis, wrote that Slichter connects high turnover with "the lack of good will of labor as a whole" (quoted in Dorfman 1959, 539). This anticipates an interest, according to Slichter, in "specialized personnel administration [which] is undoubtedly the most significant development in industrial relations . . . in several decades." The end of large labor surpluses has confronted American management with the need for enhancing "the good will of their workers" which they "have set about getting . . . with the same determination and lavish expenditure which they use in capturing the good will of the consumer" (Slichter quoted in Dorfman 1959, 540).

Slichter's detailed investigations of collective bargaining led to such fruitful concepts as industrial jurisprudence, civil rights in industry, and management by rule rather than by arbitrary decision (Slichter 1941, 2; see also Slichter, Healy, and Livernash 1960). It was Slichter, finally, who took note of the high point of equity in the "laboristic state," which he defined as "the gradual shift from a capitalistic community ... to a community in which employees rather than businessmen are the strongest single influence." And with the laboristic state came new problems for the community: individual rights in the unions, power versus "principle and reason," strikes that "jeopardize the public health, safety and economic welfare," and collective bargaining's effect on prices (Slichter [1948] 1961, 255–260).

William M. Leiserson (1883–1957)

William M. Leiserson was representative of the jointly-agreed-to third party in collective bargaining, the private arbitrator — a system unique to North American industrial relations (see Eisner 1967). Leiserson was more than a judge in industrial disputes. He sought to create a psychological atmosphere of accommodation among the parties. In acts and words, he gave voice to highly prized Wisconsin values: pragmatism, common sense, problem solving, anti-ideology. He brought to arbitration a philosophic commitment to free collective bargaining and voluntarism, a view of arbitratorship as a calling, successful experience as "impartial chairman," and an ability to turn a resonant phrase.

Leiserson started out as a student socialist but immersion in the Wisconsin Idea, notably in setting up an employment-office system, apparently converted him. He became one of the classic arbitrators and an influential member variously of the National Mediation Board and the National Labor Relations Board. He advised, counseled, dispensed good sense for the asking, and wrote a good deal.

Leiserson once wrote about another arbitrator in words that fit Leiserson as well:

> He would not decide cases merely on the merits of the briefs or arguments of the parties, for it would not help the industry or either party to have the other party lose a case if it was right but happened to present its case poorly or had its arguments wrong. He would make investigations on his own initiative, get all the facts in the situation, and then decide on the basis of those facts

regardless of what might have been presented or omitted in the argument of the case. In making these investigations he often consulted each party separately and in confidence. He found it necessary to do this to get the real truth in industrial cases, which as in ordinary law cases are often hidden by the trial. But it was also necessary at the same time to retain the confidence of both parties in his honesty and impartiality. He was able to accomplish both these things; and thus he laid the basis for a successful industrial jurisprudence (Leiserson 1964, 58).

Leiserson didn't "listen much to what you fellows say to me. What I really do is try to find out what is on your mind while you are speaking all those words." Arbitrators "must find a way of making the provisions of the agreement appeal to the sense of justice of those who lose as well as those who win the cases." As to experts, "When we have decided what we want, we say to the expert, 'You show us how to do this.' But we ourselves have to make the policy decision" (Leiserson 1957, 93–94).

Late in life Leiserson embarked on a Webbian treatise on trade union government. Unfortunately, he did not live to complete it. Leiserson viewed with considerable alarm "the threat to freedom" that existed in some union governments. The problem was how to find a middle ground between "security, discipline and administrative efficiency, and individual freedom, and popular control." He located the source of authoritarian rule in a leadership "haunted by anxiety for [the union's] safety" (Leiserson 1959, 68, 77, 81).

American Association for Labor Legislation (1906–1942)

Nowhere was Commons's capacity for discipleship more in evidence than in his ability to train a corps of students for public service who were committed to professionalism, interest group concerns, and professional labor law administration. Representative of Commons's influence on labor law here are Arthur J. Altmeyer, Edwin E. Witte, and the American Association for Labor Legislation.

According to historian Kenneth Davis, the United States began to catch up with Western Europe in social insurance in "the second decade of the present century . . . largely through the activities of the American Association for Labor Legislation" (Davis 1986, 438). Commons was one of the principal founders of the association, along with Ely and other reform-minded economists, "to encourage the study of labor conditions with a view to promoting desirable labor legislation" (Fitch 1949, 83). "Most of the founders . . . were practical minded men of goodwill, inclined to deal with specific immediate problems in their own specific immediate terms, without great concern for 'underlying' purposes or 'overall' ideals" (Davis 1986, 438). Led by John B. Andrews, one of Commons's doctoral students and a coauthor with him of *The History of Labour in the United States* and *The Principles of Labor Legislation*, the AALL focused on workmen's compensation and industrial safety, unemployment, and social insurance (Lubove 1968, 30). But "its work for compensation for industrial accidents overtopped all others" (Fitch 1949, 88).

The AALL was hailed as "the opening of a new era in scientific social betterment" (Lubove 1968, 31–32). Commons stated that the "trained expert" rather than the amateur and "narrow interest groups" would "apply to legislation the same study of causes, of processing, and of effects, that lies at the bottom of our science" (Commons in Lubove 1968, 32). Nearly all of the AALL agenda was enacted by the first third of the twentieth century (Moynihan 1973, 239). The AALL brought about "a revolution in the manner and practice of administering labor law" (Fitch 1949, 93).

Commons believed that incentive rather than coercion should be used to get employers to achieve the objectives of law. For example, workmen's compensation should not be merely a new kind of employers' liability but should be an additional means of preventing accidents (Commons 1913, 401). The AALL favored a preventive approach to workmen's compensation by scaling employer contributions according to their effectiveness in cutting accidents and injuries.

Arthur J. Altmeyer (1891–1972)

Commons seems to have been proudest of his role in setting up the Industrial Commission of Wisconsin, the labor regulatory agency. "Instead of specifying the many details of factory inspection [for example] the legislature boiled them down into one paragraph". The commission, taking on the function of a "fourth branch of government" relied on investigation and research, and made case-by-case law. (Commons 1913, 395–396).

Arthur Altmeyer, another Commons Ph.D. and later Social Security administrator, wrote his dissertation on the Industrial Commission of Wisconsin, which he served as secretary. He noted several principles which commission experience validated, including the ideas that investigation and research do not exist in isolation but are "an integral part of the administrative process or a by-product of that process" (Altmeyer 1932, 316), and that without participation of the affected interest groups "there can be no assurance that the administrative definitions will be reasonable, that is, take account of all the facts" (Altmeyer 1932, 318). Commons, reflecting on the matter later, thought of the commission as a sort of collective bargaining board which extended the collective bargaining process from the "industrial government of the workplace to the regulatory agency" (Commons [1934] 1964, 173).

As one of the founders of the social security system, Altmeyer had cause to remember Commons's dictum, "Administration is legislation in action," and he came to regard the administration of the act as important as the act itself (Altmeyer 1966, vi).

Edwin E. Witte (1887–1960)

Edwin E. Witte was an authentic product of the Wisconsin School and a protagonist of the Wisconsin Idea. He was born and bred in Wisconsin. He served in various Wisconsin agencies: the Industrial Commission, the Legislative Reference Bureau, and the University of Wisconsin. Although he also served several tours of duty outside of Wisconsin, he always returned to his roots. Witte's standpoint was Wisconsin progressivism, which meant, as his biographer summarized it, "government for the protection and welfare of the common man, especially the industrial laborer; and personal devotion to public affairs according to the Wisconsin Idea of the intellectual committed to the service of the state" (Schlabach 1969, 9).

His devotion to John R. Commons was characteristic of the Wisconsin School circle. Commons "was the most lovable man I have ever known," he said. "I owe to Commons my entire outlook on life and a great many of my ideas" (Witte in Schlabach 1969, 19).

Witte did not partake of Commons's broad theoretical interests except as they impinged on particular investigations and undertakings, which included the labor injunction, mediation, arbitration and regulation of labor affairs, the administration of labor legislation, and Witte's greatest project, the making of the American social security system. He wrote only one book during his lifetime, *The Government in Labor Disputes* (1932), which was a reworking of his 1927 doctoral dissertation. Institutionalism's works, Witte used to say, were to be found not only in books and journal articles but (as Witte himself exemplified to a high degree) in the laws, administrative regulations, litigation, collective agreements, and arbitration awards.

Institutionalism was not a body of formal theory for Witte but a method for investigating facts leading to policy. He believed that criticism is less important than constructive involvement in the policy process. "It is not the critic who counts," Witte once quoted Theodore Roosevelt as saying, "not the man who points out how the strong man stumbled. . . . The credit belongs to the man who is actually in the arena . . . that his place shall never be with those cold and timid souls who know neither defeat nor victory" (Witte in Lampman 1962, xiii).

Witte was universally admired by those who knew him for qualities of character, mind, investigative method and attention to detail. "His ideas were not so bold as they were commonsensical. He did not offer brilliant new conceptualizations of human problems and their solutions but he did analyze ideas carefully and apply them creatively to the realities of life. Sometimes he underrated the possibilities for political and constitutional changes in American development. But he entered the process of historical change with ideas that helped form a link of continuity between older, individualistic concepts and newer, more social approaches" (Schlabach 1969, 203).

The Wisconsin Model

The "Wisconsin model" may be conceptualized as a species of bargaining wherein government negotiates the terms of labor equity with job-conscious, job-control trade unionism and with efficiency-driven human relations management. As to method: Wisconsin institutionalism, "generalizing from the habits and customs of social life" (Commons [1924] 1959, vii), moves freely and unselfconsciously across disciplines to bring together theory and practice for the purpose of problem-solving.

"I have no system. I have an administrative process," Commons once said (Dorfman 1959, 391). I think he meant that effective policy partook more of process — that is, due process, reasonable value — than of specified content. Commons reflected the Wisconsin School faith in the therapeutic power of bargaining to bring reasonable people to agreement and the importance of countervailing force to moderate excess (Bronfenbrenner 1985, 24).

The question properly arises as to whether Wisconsin-type problem solving actually solved any problems. "Through his students Commons was the intellectual origin of the New Deal, of labor legislation, of social security, of the whole movement toward a welfare state" (Boulding 1956, 7). According to Joseph Dorfman, Commons "more than any other economist was responsible for the conversion into public policy of reform proposals designed to alleviate the defects in the industrial system" (Dorfman 1959, 377). Paul McNulty notes that the Wisconsin School was "not simply . . . the leading center for labor studies, the temper of the Wisconsin approach attracted and was characteristic of many other leading students of labor" (McNulty 1980, 171).

It is only possible to speak tentatively — and at this point cursorily — of a third generation of the Wisconsin School, counting Commons and Ely as the first and Perlman and his colleagues as the second. The third generation shares a common tradition but changing times and circumstances make it necessarily a more diffuse movement. The Industrial Relations Research Association (IRRA) presidents of the midsixties and later who have Wisconsin School ties can serve as a sample of those from this generation who have attained national recognition in the field: Edwin Young (1965), Douglas H. Soutar (1973), Gerald G. Somers (1975), Charles C. Killingsworth (1978), Jack Barbash (1980), Rudolph A. Oswald (1981) Everett M. Kassalow (1985), Lloyd Ulman (1986), James L. Stern (1991). (Brief biographical items on each can be found in the IRRA directories.)

This third generation basically shares with its forerunners the view of the labor problem as a moral question, the research method of "go and see," and a preference for problem solving over theory making. Also like their antecedents, they accept the essentiality of trade unionism, collective bargaining, human relations management, and the positive but restricted role of the state in a viable industrial relations order.

Being further along in the maturing of the labor problem, the third generation of the Wisconsin School dwells more on particulars and excesses than on the larger generalities. Their specializations include trade unionism, collective bargaining, public-sector employment relations, incomes policies, labor history, labor theory, labor markets, comparative movements, economic development, public policy and its administration, personnel administration, and university administration.

This generation is not bound by the close collegial ties of the past generations. To begin with, there is no father figure like Commons to gather around, although Perlman and Witte came close to it for some. Nor have there been grand projects like the labor history or documentary history to enlist their collaboration (Commons 1910; Commons 1918), although several in the group have collaborated on more limited undertakings in labor history and industrial relations (Somers 1963; Derber and Young 1957; Somers 1969).

The Wisconsin School in the Broader Realm of Ideas

The Wisconsin School intersects with several streams of thought and practice. The intellectual history of labor and industrial relations begins with Marx, not because he said the last word but because he raised the enduring questions. Marx was the first to treat capitalism and its labor process as a system and to derive exploitation and alienation as the durable issues of the labor reform agenda. The theory and practice of western industrial relations may be viewed in its essence as an undertaking in the amelioration of exploitation and alienation under capitalism.

Max Weber rendered capitalism's essence as management rationality, thereby imputing the kind of value creation to capitalist management that Marx denied it. Frederick Taylor made a science of applying rationality to the labor input to replace "the arbitrary judgment" of capitalist management and unions with one equitable "code of law," scientifically determined (Taylor 1947, 189). Elton Mayo relied on management itself, armed with his science of "human relations," to put an end to the consequences of rationality, namely workplace "anomie." The socialists Beatrice and Sidney Webb were the first to make the scholarly case for trade unionism and collective bargaining as a necessary counterbalance to management power, not only under capitalism but also under socialism.

Commons and the Wisconsin School were not content only to argue that trade unionism, collective bargaining, employer personnel policy, and public policy could achieve a measure of equity in the capitalistic workplace. They became activist advocates and administrators in behalf of their case.

It is usual to group Thorstein Veblen, Wesley C. Mitchell, and John R. Commons as the eminent institutional economists. According to

Dorfman, Veblen "furnished the theoretical stimulus for the development of the thirties, . . . Mitchell supplied the statistics [but] it was . . . Commons and his group in Wisconsin who provided the New Dealers with . . . practical instrumentalities and . . . experienced personnel to direct the new agencies. . . ." (Dorfman 1959, 398). "Of the three," Boulding judged that Commons "[is] probably the most important" (Boulding 1956, 6). Mitchell once observed that Commons invented institutions while Veblen stood "on the sidelines and watched them develop" (in Dorfman 1964, 44).

The University of Wisconsin was not alone among the pioneering American universities in the study of labor problems. Robert F. Hoxie, Harry Millis, and Paul H. Douglas at Chicago; Sumner H. Slichter and Benjamin Selekman at Harvard; and George E. Barnett and Jacob Hollander at Johns Hopkins were all important pioneers. But, as noted by Adolf Sturmthal, Wisconsin "undoubtedly represent[ed] the largest and in many ways the most significant single contingent among students of labor" (Sturmthal 1951, 483).

An additional word on Johns Hopkins: more than any of the other academic programs in labor studies, it represented in its time something comparable to Wisconsin, even if more restricted in scope and underlying philosophy. The fathers of this second coming — Ely's program at Hopkins was the first — were Hollander (1871–1940) and Barnett (1873–1938), principally Barnett. In 1903 they initiated a "seminary" in the Department of Political Economy to investigate the governing of American trade unions, in the manner of Beatrice and Sidney Webb who, just a few years earlier, had published their monumental *Industrial Democracy* (see McNulty 1980, 169ff.; M. Perlman 1958, 25ff., 144ff.; and Dorfman 1959, 518–524.)

Piece by piece the Hopkins seminarians put together a sort of political science of trade unionism in the early years of the twentieth century. Many of the papers were later incorporated into monographs published by the Johns Hopkins University Press from 1904 on as *Studies in Historical and Political Science*. However, neither the Johns Hopkins group nor, for that matter, Wisconsin ever produced the Webbs' kind of grand design, as seen in *Industrial Democracy* ([1897] 1914) and *History of Trade Unionism* ([1896] 1920).

No significant aspect of trade union government and functioning was left untouched by the Hopkins group. The themes they covered included finance, organizing, welfare, wage policies, work rules, local and national bodies, jurisdiction, apprenticeship, regulation of entry, union labels, and strikes and boycotts.

Barnett took the printers' union as his personal domain (1909).

Other leading unions that were studied included the molders, cigar makers, building trades, railroad brotherhoods, meat cutters, shoe workers, bricklayers, and steelworkers.

Barnett came closest to the development of an evolutionary theory of trade union government in his classic essay, "The Dominance of the National Trade Union in American Labor Organization."

> In the earliest period — from the end of the eighteenth century to about 1815 — the local union was the only form of trade-union grouping. . . . The second period extending from 1821–1838, was marked by the rise of the city federation, or, as it was then called, the trades' union. [The third period] from 1865 to 1888 marked the formation of national federations. . . . The fourth period in the structural history of American trade unionism, from 1897 to the present — has been distinguished by the increasing control exercised by the national trade union over the other forms of grouping." (Barnett 1913).

Barnett saw little future for unionism. There was "no reason to believe," he said (in his 1932 American Economic Association presidential address) "that American trade unionism will so revolutionize itself within a short period of time as to become a more potent social influence than it has become in the last decade" (Barnett 1933). He spoke these words on December 29, 1932. Within months Franklin D. Roosevelt was elected president and John L. Lewis started the Committee for Industrial Organization.

The members of the Hopkins group were primarily scholars, not scholar-advocates like Commons and the Wisconsin group. Barnett and Hollander wanted nothing much more than to enlarge the empirical base of economics to include the facts of unionism. Hollander was mostly interested in the history of economic thought. Barnett's interest in labor was only intermittent. Neither man had Commons's interest in reforming the theory and practice of labor, although some of the Hopkins progeny — such as Solomon Blum on labor economics, David McCabe on the standard rate, P. J. Kennedy on union benefits, Leo Wolman on union membership tendencies, and Joel Seidman on union democracy — went on to make important contributions to the field. (A comprehensive bibliography of the considerable Hopkins output can be found in the *U.S. Dept. of Labor Library Catalog* 1975.)

The Wisconsin School arose in the era when labor was the underdog and when a system of formal economic analysis seemed to justify this by discouraging equitable remedies to the labor problem. The Wisconsin School's eclipse began with the ascendancy of what Slichter called "the laboristic state." Methodologically, the freewheeling, case-by-case, problem-solving, antitheory style of the Wisconsin school, and of industrial relations generally, increasingly lost ground to the more rigorous, econometric model building and science building of labor economics, which is more economics than labor.

The labor union's fall from power in the 1980s and afterward has caused the preemption of collective-bargaining-oriented industrial relations in the Wisconsin mode by human resources management, which is closer to the unilateralism of the "new" industrial relations (see Barbash 1988, 32). To put it another way, the Wisconsin School's multifactor model, with employees, unions, management, and state as independent variables, has been increasingly displaced by the univariable model, which proceeds out of management efficiency.

The Wisconsin School has stood for more than how-to-do-it practicality, as high as that has always been in its priorities. Although its core subject matter is the employment relationship, the Wisconsin School connects this with the broader realm of social ideas, imparting insights into all sorts of human relationships in conflict and its resolution. Concepts like administration, equity, institutions, bargaining, reasonableness, goodwill, class, intellectualism, unionism, labor movement, job consciousness, due process, idealism, and industrial government have been given substance, history, and operational forms. In this way the process of studying and investigating labor problems has taken on the qualities of a genuine liberal education. In the words of Friedrich Hayek, "In most of our tasks we need not only be competent scientists and scholars but . . . also . . . experienced men of the world and, in some measure, philosophers" (Hayek 1967, 126).

References

Altmeyer, Arthur J. 1932. *The Industrial Commission of Wisconsin.* Studies in the Social Sciences and History, no. 17. Madison: University of Wisconsin.

——. 1966. *The Formative Years of Social Security.* Madison: University of Wisconsin Press.

Barbash, Jack. 1966. "David J. Saposs and the Wisconsin School," in *The Labor Movement: A Re-examination.* A Conference in Honor of David J. Saposs, Ed. Jack Barbash. January 14–15. Madison: University of Wisconsin Industrial Relations Research Institute.

——. 1967. "John R. Commons and the Americanization of the Labor Problem," *Journal of Economic Issues*, vol. 1, no. 3.

——. 1988. "The New Industrial Relations in the US, Phase II," *Relations Industrielles*, vol. 43, no. 1.

————. 1991. "Industrial Relations Concepts in the USA," *Relations Industrielles,* vol. 46, no. 1.

Barnett, George E. 1909. *The Printers: A Study in American Trade Unionism.* Publications of the American Economic Association, series 3, vol. 10, October.

————. 1913. "The Dominance of the National Trade Union in American Labor Organization," *Quarterly Journal of Economics,* vol. 27.

————. 1933. "American Trade Unionism and Social Insurance," *American Economic Review,* March.

Boulding, Kenneth. 1956. "A New Look at Institutionalism," *American Economic Review, Papers and Proceedings.*

Brody, David. 1978. "Philip Taft, Labor Scholar," in *Labor History: Philip Taft,* vol. 19, no. 1, Winter.

Bronfenbrenner, Martin. 1985. "Early American Leaders — Institutional and Critical Traditions," *American Economic Review,* December.

Commons, John R., et al. 1910. *Documentary History of American Industrial Society.* 10 vols. Cleveland, Ohio: Arthur Clark Co.

————. 1913. *Labor and Administration.* New York: Macmillan.

————. 1919. *Industrial Goodwill.* New York: McGraw-Hill.

————. 1921. *Industrial Government.* New York: Macmillan.

————. [1924] 1959. *Legal Foundations of Capitalism.* Madison: University of Wisconsin Press.

————. 1934. *Institutional Economics.* New York: Macmillan.

————. [1934] 1964. *Myself.* Madison: University of Wisconsin Press.

———— and associates. 1918. *The History of Labour in the United States.* New York: Macmillan.

Commons, John R, and John B. Andrews. 1916. *The Principles of Labor Legislation.* New York: Harper & Bros.

Davis, Kenneth. 1986. *FDR: The New Deal Years.* New York: Random House.

Derber, Milton, and Edwin Young, eds. 1957. *Labor and the New Deal.* Madison: University of Wisconsin Press.

Dorfman, Joseph. 1959. *The Economic Mind in America, 1918–1933.* New York: Viking Press.

————. 1964. *Institutional Economics.* Berkeley: University of California Press.

Dunlop, John T. 1961. "Sumner Huber Slichter," in Sumner H. Slichter, *Potentials of the American Economy.* Cambridge, Mass.: Harvard University Press.

Eisner, J. Michael. 1967. *William Morris Leiserson.* Madison: University of Wisconsin Press.

Fitch, John R. 1949. "Labor Legislation and Social Security," in *John B. Andrews Memorial Symposium* (November 4–5). Madison: University of Wisconsin Industrial Relations Center.

Harter, L. B. 1962. *John R. Commons.* Corvallis: Oregon State University Press.

Hayek, Friedrich A. 1967. *Studies in Philosophy, Politics and Economics.* New York: Simon & Schuster, Clarion Book.

Hofstader, Richard, 1955 *The Age of Reform.* New York: Knopf.

Labor History: Philip Taft. 1978. Vol. 19, no. 1, Winter.

Lampman, Robert J., ed. 1962. *Social Security Perspectives: Essays by Edwin E. Witte.* Madison: University of Wisconsin Press.

Leiserson, William M. 1957. Quoted in Memorial Session, *Proceedings of Industrial Relations Research Association Annual Meeting.* New York: Industrial Relations Research Association.

————. 1959. *American Trade Union Democracy.* New York: Columbia University Press.

————. 1964. Quoted in *Labor Arbitration — Perspectives and Problems, Proceedings of National Academy of Arbitrators Meeting.* Washington, D.C.: Bureau of National Affairs.

Lubove, Roy. 1968. *The Struggle for Social Security, 1900–1935.* Cambridge, Mass.: Harvard University Press.

McNulty, Paul J. 1980. *The Origins and Development of Labor Economics.* Cambridge, Mass.: MIT Press.

Moynihan, Daniel P. 1973. *The Politics of Guaranteed Income.* New York: Random House, Vintage.

Perlman, Mark. 1958. *Labor Union Theories in America.* Evanston, Ill.: Row Peterson & Co.

Perlman, Selig. 1922. *A History of Trade Unionism in the United States.* New York: Macmillan.

————. [1928] 1949. *A Theory of the Labor Movement.* New York: Augustus Kelley.

————. 1950. "John Rogers Commons, 1862–1945," in John R. Commons, *Economics of Collective Action.* New York: Macmillan.

————. 1957. "America and the Jewish Labor Movement: A Case of Mutual Illumination," *Publications of the American Jewish Historical Society,* March. New York: American Jewish Historical Society.

Perlman, Selig, and Philip Taft. 1935. *The History of Labor in the United States, 1896–1932.* New York: Macmillan.

Saposs, David J. 1926. *Left-Wing Unionism: A Study of Radical Policies and Tactics.* New York: International Publishers.

————. 1931. *The Labor Movement of Post-War France.* New York: Columbia University Press.

————. 1936. *Labor and the Government.* New York: Twentieth Century Fund–McGraw.

————. 1937. *Governmental Protection of Labor's Right to Organize.* Bulletin no. 4. Washington, D.C.: National Labor Relations Board.

————. 1940. *Written Trade Agreements in Collective Bargaining.* Bulletin no. 4. Washington, D.C.: National Labor Relations Board.

————. 1959. *Communism in American Unions.* New York: McGraw-Hill.

————. 1960a "The Wisconsin Heritage and the Study of Labor: Works and

Deeds of John R. Commons," *School for Workers 35th Anniversary Papers*. Madison: University of Wisconsin School for Workers.

———. 1960b *Communism in American Politics*. Washington, D.C.: Public Affairs Press.

———. 1962. *Labor Ideology Impact on Industrial Relations*. Honolulu: University of Hawaii Industrial Relations Center.

Schlabach, Theron F. 1969. *Edwin E. Witte: Cautious Reformer*. Madison: Wisconsin State Historical Society.

Slichter, Sumner H. [1920] 1961. "Industrial Morale," in Sumner H. Slichter, *Potentials of the American Economy*. Cambridge, Mass.: Harvard University Press.

———. 1928. "What Is the Labor Problem?" in J. B. S. Hardman, *American Labor Dynamics*. New York: Harcourt Brace.

———. 1941. *Union Policies and Industrial Management*. Washington, D.C.: Brookings Institution.

———. [1948] 1961. "Are We Becoming a 'Laboristic' State?" in Slichter, *Potentials*.

———. [1952] 1961. "Some Things That I Think and How I Got That Way," in Slichter, *Potentials*.

Slichter, Sumner H., James J. Healy, and E. Robert Livernash. 1960. *The Impact of Collective Bargaining on Management*. Washington, D.C.: Brookings Institution.

Smith, Adam. [1776] 1901. *The Wealth of Nations*. Library of Universal Literature. New York: Collier.

Somers, Gerald G., ed. 1963. *Labor, Management and Social Policy: Essays in the John R. Commons Tradition*. Madison: University of Wisconsin Press.

———. 1969. *Essays in Industrial Relations Theory*. Ames: Iowa State University Press.

Sturmthal, Adolf. 1951. "Comments on Selig Perlman's *A Theory of the Labor Movement*," *Industrial and Labor Relations Review*, vol. 4, no. 4, July.

Taft, Philip. 1937. "The Problem of Structure in American Labor," *American Economic Review*, vol. 27, no. 1, March.

———. 1954. *The Structure and Government of Labor Unions*. Cambridge, Mass.: Harvard University Press.

———. 1960. "Professor Perlman's Ideas and Activities," in *School for Workers 35th Anniversary Papers*. Madison: University of Wisconsin School for Workers.

———. 1964. *Organized Labor in American History*. New York: Harper & Row.

———. 1966. "American Labor's Origins and Ideology," in Barbash, ed., *The Labor Movement: A Re-examination*.

———. 1976. "Reflections on Selig Perlman as Teacher and Writer," *Industrial and Labor Relations Review*, January.

Taft, Philip, Martin Estey, and Martin Wagner, eds 1964. *Regulating Union Government*. New York: Harper & Row.

Taylor, Frederick W. [1911] 1947. *Scientific Management.* New York: Harper.

U.S. Department of Labor Library Catalog. 1975. Boston: G. C. Hall and Co., vol. 17, pp. 284ff.

Webb, Sidney and Beatrice. [1896] 1920. *History of Trade Unionism.* London: Longmans, Green.

———. *Industrial Democracy.* [1897] 1914. London: Longmans, Green.

Witte, Edwin E. 1932. *The Government in Labor Disputes.* New York: McGraw-Hill.

———. 1957. "Economics and Public Policy," *American Economic Review,* March.

3

The Social Economics Revisionists: The "Real World" Study of Labor Markets and Institutions

Clark Kerr

Paul Douglas in 1934 wrote that "the marginal productivity school . . . has described a portion of reality"; but "it is dangerous to assume that the neat tidy world [of marginal productivity analysis] is in fact a picture of the *real world*" (Douglas 1934, 95–96; emphasis added). This from an economist who had contributed significantly to the advancement of the use of marginal productivity analysis, particularly with the Cobb-Douglas function, but who knew that there was much still open to further exploration and explanation. Douglas, significantly, was among the first to make an extensive study of unemployment and its "tragic consequences" (Douglas and Director 1931).

It was to this "real world" that my generation in labor economics — we who came of age in graduate school in the 1930s (and to a lesser extent in the 1940s) and with practical experience in World War II — turned our attention. Like Douglas, we agreed that the "neo-classical school has constructed a valuable theoretical scaffolding" (Douglas 1934, xii). Another *Theory of Wages*, this one by John R. Hicks in 1932, provided that theoretical scaffolding. (I shall refer to it here as Hicks I, and to its 1963 revision as Hicks II.)

Hicks, Douglas, and Other
Predecessors

What I have elsewhere called the "neoclassical revisionists" in labor economics (Kerr 1988) were the dominant group in the United States for three decades after Douglas in 1934, until Hicks (as a convert to social economics revisionism) in 1963. We were in substantial part engaged during those 30 years in a criticism and revision of Hicks I and a reaffirmation and elaboration of Douglas (especially chapter 3 of *The Theory of Wages*), although we were more concerned with the former than the latter, because Douglas was relatively ignored in the earlier years after the publication of his book. Over time, however, he has gained greatly in stature. Cain wrote of Douglas as "the greatest labor economist in the first 50 years of this century" (Cain 1977, 2). I shall present him here as the first revisionist, although I realize that he may also be viewed (except for chapter 3 of his *Theory of Wages*) as a hard-line neoclassical traditionalist, as Albert Rees has described him: "Douglas's wage theory is grounded firmly in marginal productivity theory" which "was unusual for labor economists of his generation, most of whom were institutionalists." (Rees 1979, 915). Douglas was both a revisionist and a traditionalist — a great transitional figure in labor economics as both a true believer in and a doubter of fundamentals. Douglas was at first relatively ignored, partly because of this inconsistency but also partly because he became more and more involved in politics and did not follow up on his revisionist views.

I choose 1963 as the terminal year for the revisionists in part because Hicks in that year published the second edition of his *Theory of Wages* (Hicks II), which repudiated much of the first edition. He wrote that "my views ... had changed so much that I no longer desired to be represented by" that first edition (Hicks II, v). It was a "thoroughly bad book" which "I should have been very happy if it could have been forgotten" (Hicks II, 311). He later called the book "a piece of rubbish" (Klamer 1989, 173). Hicks did note, however, that "several parts ... are still alive in the sense that they provide convenient starting-points for much more modern discussion" (Hicks II, v).

Hicks in my judgment was far too critical of his original book. It was a thoroughly good book — perhaps the best after Marshall — as an explanation of how a largely structureless labor market would operate. It was then possible for others to note the differences from that model that social behavior, both formal and informal, could and did make as one came closer and closer to an understanding of the real world. The real world made more sense approached this way than if one were to start with all the details of its surface confusions. My Berkeley colleague Lloyd Fisher had an oft-repeated phrase: "Truth is more likely to emerge from error than from confusion." My addition to that is: Hicks was never confused. He wrote about a world of competitive firms, of largely frictionless markets for workers, of adequate information for making decisions, of decisions made to maximize net economic benefit. He aimed at fully determinate solutions, and mostly found them. His first approximation to reality made possible second and third and fourth aproximations, as earlier assumptions were modified and new ones added. Determinacy was the loser.

The revisionists spent 30 years analyzing the impacts of social structures and social behavior on economic structures and economic behavior, including those originated by formal institutions; thus we were sometimes called neoinstitutionalists. We were adding the "social forces" that Hicks came to acknowledge must be considered along with "economic forces" (Hicks 1955; this article was actually the first but less complete statement of his conversion to our point of view[1]). Hicks II notes that Hicks I had recognized that labor markets were special kinds of markets that require a "special theory of wages"; that "justice" is important in the relative treatment of employees and so is "fairness" in treatment of all workers over time — that employees are not just another commodity, even if they are unorganized (Hicks II, 316–317). This is true, but Hicks I also said (p. 80) that "these rules of fairness and justice are simply rough-and-ready guides whereby the working of supply and demand is anticipated." They should be acknowledged but then ignored. We did not agree. Had Hicks defined his qualifications more broadly in Hicks I (for example, the "costs of transference" of workers) and given them far more weight (for example, the influence of concepts of fairness and justice) the history of labor economics would have taken a different course.

The long and fruitful battle with Hicks was over by 1963. "Social forces," he then fully acknowledged, play an essential role, not just a marginal one. This reversal by one of the world's foremost economists demonstrated the greatness of his spirit as well as his mind. Hicks II responded most favorably to the findings of the revisionists, and for us, this was our greatest victory.

In his conversion from an Austrian to a revisionist point of view,

Hicks wrote that he had felt, when writing Hicks I, "much more at home" with "the Austrians" (and also with Cassel, Walras, Pareto, Edgeworth, Taussig, and Wicksell) than with Marshall and Pigou (Hicks II, 306). He noted the influence in his changed views of Paul Douglas, J. M. Keynes, Joan Robinson, William Beveridge, and Henry Clay, but also of our British revisionist friends and colleagues and, in particular, Kenneth Knowles, Henry Phelps Brown, and Barbara Wooten. He might also have noted that he had returned to the tradition of Smith, Marshall, and Pigou — the tradition out of which he had originally come.

By 1963, in addition to Hicks II a new methodology (econometrics) and a new effort at neoclassical restoration (the Chicago school) were taking over. Also, most of the once-young revisionists had moved on to other endeavors.

Our revisionist group had concentrated much more on challenging Hicks I than on supporting Douglas. Hicks was the "big book" of the time, and it is what was taught in graduate school, much more than Douglas. It would have helped if we had then also known about Joseph Schumpeter, but his work had not by that time appeared in English and was not widely taught in our seminars. In his early "European period" (to 1931), Schumpeter had already been advancing the cause of "social economics." "By this term Schumpeter essentially meant an analysis of economics as a social phenomenon as opposed to an exclusively economic phenomenon. The classical economists had made several assumptions about socio-economic reality, which they then mistakenly treated as if they were true pictures of reality. They thought, for example, that individuals maximize; that there is perfect competition; and so on. To Schumpeter, this was clearly wrong. One could indeed make assumptions about reality; that was the proper way to proceed in economic theory. But it was naive to believe that an assumption is the same as reality" (Swedberg 1991, 36–37). This also became a central theme of the revisionists — economic activity in a social environment; but Schumpeter was then largely unknown to us (although Richard Lester did attend one of his seminars in Bonn in 1930–1931). We were anticipatory Schumpeterians.

Paul Douglas in 1934 was not our only known "real world" predecessor within the mainstream of economics. Adam Smith — the first and greatest of all labor economists — lived in the real world of the division of labor, the anticompetitive inclinations of employers, the degradation of laborers by repetitive work. And he set the central themes for the study of labor economics ever since: that (1) "the annual labor of every nation is the fund which originally supplies it with all the necessaries and conveniences of life which it annually consumes," and labor is, thus, the most important factor of production: it is the "skill, dexterity, and judgment with which its labor is generally applied" that basically determines the wealth of nations; and (2) that it is a very complex factor to understand (Smith 1776, Introduction). Karl Marx had seen the importance of depressions, of the "reserve army of the unemployed," and of the alienation of labor. Alfred Marshall knew intimately the wage structure of England and had given helpful explanations of it. Pigou had elucidated bargaining "ranges."

But there was also the tradition of Newton and, in economics, Ricardo: to find the great central principles from which so much else could be deduced. Immanuel Kant later observed that theory without facts is often nonsense and, equally, that facts without theory are devoid of meaning — and as revisionists, we were Kantians. Hicks I was strong on theory. By 1963, Hicks, like Douglas in 1934, had also made contact more fully with the facts without ignoring theory. It was to this development of facts in relation to theory that our revisionist group was devoted. We chose that point on "Hume's fork" where empirical reasoning makes contact with abstract reasoning, while conducting our studies on the tine marked "empiricism." The revisionists had an in-between approach — in between a priori models and a posteriori facts, with an interest in both. Thus we chose not to follow the ancient advice of Scholasticus: not to enter the water until we had actually learned to swim. We learned in the water.

The theory to which we most related was Marshall's neoclassical theory, particularly as set forth, with fewer ambiguities, by Hicks I. We could have responded mostly to Karl Marx, but we did not choose to do so. History had already proved him to be wrong (except to the true believers) in his basic analyses — as, for example, in his labor theory of value and the inherently revolutionary inclinations of the working class. We also could have chosen to respond mostly to John R. Commons. The institutionalists largely ignored the market except to condemn it as exploitive, and they were too single-mindedly concerned with the "working rules" of institutions without acknowledging the powerful impacts of surrounding economic forces. Kenneth Boulding once wrote that institutionalism in economics was "an attempt to synthesize the social sciences, an attempt to synthesize bad economics, bad sociology and bad anthropology" (Boulding 1950, 5). This it was not. It was a successful attempt at a good history of the American labor movement, a path-breaking effort to understand the roles and the operations of institutions and to create fruitful initiatives that would change national economic policy.

We also rejected as our model the historians and statisticians of the day as being too interested in specifics, and too often interested just in the isolated details among all those historical episodes and all those statistics.

We were, it might be said, neoclassical revisionists when we studied labor markets, institutionalist revisionists when we studied collective bargaining, and Marxist revisionists when we studied the role of workers in the flow of economic history. We were not, as John Dunlop wrote, just an "institutional side-show"; we were more nearly in the "mainstream of economics" (Dunlop 1988; 80). But, I would add, we were in the current of the mainstream called social economics. Our method was what Keynes once called the "vigilant observation" of all relevant developments using all relevant available information, while drawing on and reacting to preexisting theories.

The revisionists stood, historically, between labor economics as a part of general economics (as seen by Smith, Marshall, Pigou, Hicks, and Douglas) and labor economics as a specialty with a life of its own and with, as it turned out, many costs and only some benefits as the specialization gradually took over. In 1930 there were at most one hundred persons in American universities and colleges devoted more or less exclusively to the study of labor markets and institutions. In 1960 there were at least one thousand, and by then they were organized through the Industrial Relations Research Association, rather than existing as sometimes lonely members of the American Economic Association, finding an occasional article to read and an occasional session to attend in their area of major interest. In 1930 there was no single journal devoted to labor economics or industrial relations. Today there are at least ten in the United States, Britain, Canada, and Australia, and the more general journals of economics carry more articles on labor economics as well. In 1930 there was only one institute in the field (at Princeton). Today, there are more than 50 in the United States and Canada, though they are now mostly fading in significance. The period of expansion from 1930 to 1960 has been called a golden age (Strauss and Feuille 1981). This it was, but I now think that inherent in it was an inevitable decline, as it became too separated — externally from mainstream economics, and internally into subspecialties — and as a chasm opened between labor economics and industrial relations. Labor economists, specialty by specialty, came to write nearly exclusively for each other. Forgotten were other social scientists and forgotten were the

practitioners out in the field. The market came to be the labor economists themselves. Adam Smith's division of labor had come to divide
labor economists, even from each other.

The most proximate starting points in the literature for the revisionists were Hicks I and Douglas. Hicks set forth the best outline
of the workings of unstructured labor markets (while noting minor
exceptions to the central tendencies). Douglas, while using neoclassical "scaffolding," looked at the exceptions and qualifications
and found them to be important (except as noted, quotations are from
chapter 3 of *The Theory of Wages*):

- "There is much in life and even in the economic phases of life
which does not spring from a rational pursuit of individual or group
ends" (Douglas 1934, xv). (Adam Smith in *The Theory of Moral
Sentiments* [1759] had set forth "benevolence," "justice," and "prudence" as motivating people in the conduct of their daily lives including within prudence "self-love." His central concern in *The
Wealth of Nations* [1776] came to be how to channel self-love to
serve society.)
- There is no "uniformity of wages," only a "tendency" in that
direction. "Wages in specific occupations tend to be fixed by custom
and pressures" (Douglas 1934, 66).
- "Labor is far from being completely mobile." There exist "attachment to localities" and "reluctance to change." And some occupations require "long and costly training."
- "Not all labor is successful in finding employment." (He found
unemployment rates of 8 to 11 percent in six European countries in
1929, before the depression started — about the same rates as in the
early 1990s in the same countries.) Workers are "very loath" to see a
cut in their rates and will resist (this before Keynes).
- "The bargaining powers of capital and labor are not equal" (as
Adam Smith had noted).
- There is limited "competition among laborers for work" (the
insider-outsider problem).
- "The state . . . frequently intervenes."

Thus the neoclassical analysis for Douglas described only "a portion of reality" and, consequently, there is a "need for inductive
studies." Nevertheless, Douglas seemed to be convinced that the
portion subject to marginal productivity analysis under conditions of
unrestricted competition was very substantial, as demonstrated in
his study of the Cobb-Douglas function and of supply and demand
curves. Subsequently, the revisionists generally took a much more

skeptical view, as did Richard Lester in the course of the Lester-Machlup debate, and as did Lloyd Fisher in his *The Harvest Labor Market in California* (1953). Fisher really was saying that the "structureless labor market" is a small portion of reality — even a rarity, a very special case. Lester, as I shall note shortly, advanced a range theory of wage differentials that even more broadly challenged the neoclassical model as the basic model (Lester 1952).

The Revisionist Revolution

The 1930s witnessed a revolution in economic theory (Hicks II, 305). Joan Robinson and Edward Chamberlin opened up the whole complex and enormous world of "imperfect competition" that lay between perfect competition and perfect monopoly. John Maynard Keynes challenged the doctrine that depressions would automatically cure themselves. Keynes had two major impacts on labor economists of the time. In general, he challenged orthodoxy. More specifically, he opened up the need for explanations of wage levels beyond marginal productivity in highly competitive and frictionless markets, and thus reserved an area for the impact of institutional and other social factors; and he proclaimed a role for exogenous forces at work on wages outside the system. A. A. Berle and Gardiner Means showed that corporations could not be presumed to act like individuals — unless, perhaps, they were like individuals with split personalities. John Maurice Clark, among others, was engaged in exploring the relationships between theory and reality, rejecting simplistic models, and writing about "workable competition" and the important roles for "social control." The young revisionists were exposed to these then-new views in their classroom studies.

Outside the classroom, reality was changing equally rapidly. E. Wight Bakke wrote *The Unemployed Man* (1933), which was a model of fieldwork exploration, looking as it did at so many aspects of the lives of the unemployed. My own dissertation was entitled *Productive Enterprises of the Unemployed* (1939). Neither Bakke nor I ever met an unemployed person who had voluntarily chosen the Great Depression as an excellent time to enjoy more leisure or to search for a better job. (The Chicago school later argued that all unemployment was voluntary.) World War II was also a definitive experience for several of us. In wage stabilization, we looked for the "going wage" and found "going wages," often with two or more modal clusters when there should be, we had been told, only one. In dispute settlement, we found many factors at work in addition to the dispassionate calculation of economic costs and benefits, and we saw the internal divisions within labor and within capital that made a mockery of concepts of *the* union and *the* employer. In manpower administration, we found slower adjustments to the new demands than we had expected from our classroom studies. One early study for the War Manpower Commission said that there was no manpower problem — supply and demand balanced each other nationwide. That might have been true when viewed nationwide, but it was not the case in Seattle, where I had come from. There was no single national labor market. After the war, several of us were active arbitrators, and we got right-in-the-face views of the complexities of relationships inside the life of the workplace. There were more things than had been dreamt of in our textbooks; economic life was three-dimensional and very exciting to explore firsthand.

We saw not equilibrium but disequilibria. We saw not determinate solutions but indeterminate ranges for solutions. We saw not a market for labor but many markets with distinguishing characteristics. We saw collective action as well as atomistic decision making. We saw systems of beliefs, including justice and benevolence, affecting people, as well as self-love. We were highly conscious of social change as well as timeless truths. We were more concerned with what was barely workable than with what was optimal under optimal conditions.

Never before in American history had American labor markets been in such drastic contraction and then in such drastic expansion within such a short period of time. It was like a series of earthquakes to geologists, for we could see the workings of underlying strata not so obvious in more normal times. We saw more of the total of reality than statistics by themselves could ever show. Our minds were opened by Keynes and the other innovators of thought, and our eyes by the operations of an economy in turmoil and fast transition. The union movement was advancing, the New Deal was introducing the welfare state, the industrial labor force was being better educated and beginning to change in its composition, strikes were spreading across the nation, the Marxists were mounting their greatest intellectual and political challenge and losing, the institutionalists were supplying the New Deal with essential ideas and then fading into history. It was an exciting time to be around as participant-observers. We had little choice but to become revisionists facing the new theories and the new practices. We were, like the antihero in the French farce *Gangster Malgré Lui*, revisionists in spite of ourselves.

The fact is that we did not start out to be revisionists. We started out to be "real world" labor economists exploring aspects of the then fast-changing economic scene. We found many differences between what we had been told to expect and what we observed. This led us to propose revisions of what we had learned. Our goal was to understand reality, and one result was to propose revsions of received doctrines.

If the young revisionists can be said to have had a personal guru, it was Sumner H. Slichter. In age, he was a generation ahead of us — he received his bachelor's degree at Wisconsin in 1913 and his Ph.D. at Chicago in 1918 — but his major writings in labor economics came during the revisionist period, beginning about 1940. Slichter had, however, written *Modern Economic Society* in 1931, in which he introduced two possibilities that were unusual for that time: (1) that unions could have the impact of raising productivity, and (2) that higher wages may conduce to higher productivity (chap. 24).

Another member of the older generation of revisionists, who also did his major writing first around 1940, was Harry A. Millis. He had actually been a teacher of Slichter's at Chicago. He edited *How Collective Bargaining Works* (1942), which was the first extensive exploration of the subject, industry by industry, and which introduced studies by several of the young revisionists. His three-volume textbook, however, written with Royal E. Montgomery in 1938, *The Economics of Labor*, follows an older "problems" approach. Nevertheless, the chapter entitled "A Survey of Wage Theory" is essentially a restatement of Douglas in his *Theory of Wages:* the marginal productivity theory does not work with "mathematical precision"; it is, instead, an explanation of "tendencies."

But it was Slichter in particular among the elder revisionists whom we all knew and admired, and several of us had studied under him. He was the president of the American Economic Association in 1941, and the second president of the Industrial Relations Research Association in 1949. While he had studied under Commons at Wisconsin, "it would be a mistake to classify Slichter as an institutionalist" (Dunlop 1961, xx), yet he produced two famous volumes in the Wisconsin spirit of studying working rules of institutions and their impacts: *Union Policies and Industrial Management* (1941) and *The Impact of Collective Bargaining on Management* (1960), the latter coauthored with James J. Healy and E. Robert Livernash. During his doctoral studies at Chicago, in part under J. M. Clark, he developed what Dunlop called "keen theoretical interests"; but "neither 'institutionalist' nor 'theorist' describes his interests and methods." "He was distrustful of formal models and closed systems" but was "concerned to apply economic principles to a specific problem" (Dunlop

1961, xix, xx). Slichter's "Notes on the Structure of Wages" (Slichter 1950) is an illustration of this. He believed deeply in fieldwork to make direct contact with reality. He lived in the labor economist's netherworld located between high theory and low practice, and was one of the first to explore it.

If the young revisionists can be said to have had a call to action, it was made by John Dunlop (Dunlop 1938, 413). Dunlop wanted to see an effort "to bring theory and observation closer together." In the same journal article, he challenged John Maynard Keynes and won: he showed that money and real wages generally rise together. If the young revisionists can be said to have had a mantra, it was "theory and practice," said and written over and over again.

If the young revisionists can be said to have had an agenda laid out for them, it was provided by Richard Lester in his *Economics of Labor* (1941); for example: the study of labor markets as "some of our most imperfect markets" (p. 43).

The young revisionists were united by their desire "to bring theory and observation closer together." Beyond that, they were divided. Some were more critical and others more supportive of the neoclassical approach; some gave more attention to the nature and impacts of institutions, and others less; some were more clearly economists and others more inclined to a broader social science orientation; some were more interested in policy and others less; some were more attracted to the study of management in general, and to personnel administration in particular, and others more to trade unions; some were more attentive to the flow of history and others less; and there were other distinctions among them in their areas of interest and their intellectual sympathies. In particular, some were all-out revisionists and others were, at least in substantial part, reluctant critics of standard economic theory who accepted some aspects of "social economics." From the outside, it might appear that we all had much in common; from the inside, we were all different in important respects. Generally, however, when writing about labor markets and wage structures we were more neoclassical, while emphasizing "social factors"; and when writing about unions and collective bargaining we were more institutionalist while emphasizing the strong role of economic constraints.

Beyond our own group we felt kinship at the time with many people, including John Kenneth Galbraith (with his *American Capitalism: The Concept of Countervailing Power* [1952] and *The New Industrial State* [1967]), with Edward Mason and Robert Aaron Gordon on theories of the firm; with Robert L. Hall and Charles J. Hitch on full cost pricing (1939); with Herbert Simon, James March, and

Richard Cyert on organizational behavior (although strangely enough we made little contact with the members of this group, which came on about a decade later than we did). However, when their studies did appear, we were sympathetic with the idea of "satisficing" as explaining some individual decision making better than maximizing, such as when workers take the first available job that meets their minimum expectations, as our labor market studies showed; with the idea of "bounded rationality," for "even voluntary movement fails to show any strong drift toward better jobs" (Reynolds 1951, 215); with the importance of trial and error in reaching solutions; with the observation of how difficult it can be to get good information, as we found it to be for workers in external labor markets; with the analysis of how hard it is to calculate "welfare" within complex organizations, as we found for trade unions. (See March and Sevon 1984 for the major themes of this group.) Herbert Simon, James March, and Richard Cyert were our closest counterparts as revisionists in all of economics at that time.

Following are discussions of some of the revisionists' areas of concentration.

The Study of Labor Markets and the Bounded Mobility of Workers

The Social Science Research Council (SSRC) initiated the first study of actual labor markets. I never knew why it chose to look at labor markets, although I later served on its influential Labor Market Study Committee. J. Douglas Brown of Princeton was chairman and Paul Webbink was the staff representative in charge. I was selected by the SSRC to make the first study under its auspices. Again, I never knew why. I had studied the labor market for seasonal farm workers in California and found a backward sloping supply curve in part of its range, which gave rise to my first footnote to J. R. Hicks; but this was a mostly unknown paper presented before the mostly neglected Pacific Coast Economic Association (Kerr 1941).

My study for the SSRC was a very crude and primitive one compared with those that followed later. It was entitled *Migration to the Seattle Labor Market Area, 1940–1942* (Kerr 1942). This experience led me to my first realization that Hicks I and reality could be very far apart. I had learned from Hicks that workers would move if their "costs of transference" would be more than just recovered and that, spread over time, such costs were very frequently "negligible" (Hicks

I, 59). I should have remembered that Adam Smith, on the contrary, had noted that "man is of all sorts of luggage the most difficult to be transported" (Smith 1776, book 1, chap. 8). Costs of transference to the Seattle labor market, in monetary calculations, were negligible. Income differentials, however, were substantial for most workers: for one-third of those that moved, they were 50 percent or more. There were also potential draft deferments for men of draft age, and most migrants got what they considered "better jobs." In addition, these changes for betterment came after more than ten years of the deepest depression in American economic history. Yet only a small number of workers moved. I was impressed by the following:

• The role of inertia in the making of decisions. (Inertia was a major consideration for Joseph Schumpeter; thus his emphasis on the importance of the innovator in economic activity and his fear of bureaucratic socialism.)
• The fact that the push of unemployment was so much more important than the pull of the prospect of "better jobs" in getting people to move.
• The strength of the attachments to familiar localities, and to relatives and friends.
• The hesitation to enter a new cultural environment in a big city with a different ethnic mix, new occupations, and, particularly, with unfamiliar (and very crowded) housing arrangements.
• The reliance, almost alone, on information from relatives and friends rather than from employer and government sources, who supplied inadequate information and were not trusted.

Thus it was mostly the young, those unattached to spouse and children, the unemployed, and those from nearby locations (close enough for a weekend visit home) who moved. The Seattle labor market was not flooded with migrants as it should have been according to Hicks I. The workers had to be recruited, and they came on a trial-and-error basis. The puzzle of the long-term persistence of geographical wage differentials in the United States now seemed to me to be less of a puzzle; it seemed to be more fully understandable.

The second SSRC study, by Charles Myers and W. Rupert Maclaurin (*The Movement of Factory Workers*, 1943), was much more sophisticated, and it confirmed some of the observations from the Seattle survey: most movement was "forced"; attachments to even local neighborhoods were very strong. Myers and Maclaurin additionally found that movement was "largely ineffective" in reducing wage differentials.

A later labor market study conducted by Myers with George P. Shultz (*The Dynamics of a Labor Market*, 1951) followed a plant shutdown. Among other findings they learned that (1) a majority of the displaced workers (three-fifths) did not shop around for the best opportunity but took the first job they could get — they did not make "a systematic search for alternative job opportunities"; and (2) "economic forces" did not explain everything, but that little could be understood without reference to them (Myers and Shultz 1951, 72, 204).

The third study chronologically (and the most influential one) was by Lloyd Reynolds and Joseph Shister (*Job Horizons*, 1949). They found much more at work than "monetary incentives" and noted the "importance of non-wage factors." They reported:

- "A strong aversion to change" including in "one's way of life" (Reynolds and Shister 1949, 87–88).
- A great attachment to "seniority" rights.
- The substantial importance of wages, fringe benefits, and steadiness of employment in job satisfaction, but also of the "physical characteristics of the job," the degree of "independence and control" associated with the job, the "fairness of treatment," the quality of "relationships with fellow workers," and the degree of "job interest" (Reynolds and Shister 1949, chap. 2).
- A great lack of knowledge of alternative opportunities. (Here is the one major point on which "modern work disagrees" [Freeman 1988, 218].)

This third study, in particular, led to the conclusion that there was much more to maximize (or to be satisfied about) than easily compared wage rates, fringe benefits, and potential steadiness of work. Workers were seeking to maximize their entire life (or at least to be satisfied with it — for there were the factors of inertia, low aspirations, lack of adequate information, and uncertainty that limited the efforts of some to maximize). Actual calculations were about the total job and the total life; monetary "costs of transference" were a minor consideration.

Herbert Parnes (*Research on Labor Mobility*, 1954), again under the auspices of the SSRC, and Gladys Palmer (*Labor Mobility in Six Cities*, 1954 — the six cities were Chicago, Los Angeles, New Haven, Philadelphia, St. Paul, and San Francisco), also sponsored by the SSRC, sought to draw together what they thought was then known about the operation of labor markets. Their work may be briefly summarized as follows:

- "Only a very small minority of the labor force is at any one time realistically in the labor market" (Parnes 1954, 188). Those in the market tend to be those with the fewest attachments. Those in the market are more pushed there than pulled.
- Workers have limited knowledge of alternative job opportunities. For information they rely mostly on relatives and friends.
- The worker takes the first job that meets "the standards he has subjectively established for a desirable job" (Parnes 1954, 188). This suggests a "satisficing" model.
- There is great attachment to localities, to friends and relatives, and to occupation.
- Union membership reduces mobility.
- Wages are only one of several important factors in job choice.

A fourth SSRC study, by Richard Lester (1954), put great emphasis on "strong company attachments."

The last of the specific labor market studies to which I shall refer here was by Albert Rees and George Shultz (*Workers and Wages in an Urban Labor Market*, 1970). They demonstrated how "complex" are the operations of labor markets, subject as they are to "economic, institutional, locational and personal" forces. "The employment of a worker is a much more complicated transaction, and one with many more dimensions, than the purchase of a contract in the wheat futures market" (Rees and Shultz 1970, 222). They emphasized the importance, in understanding conditions of supply and demand and their interactions, of: seniority and experience, unionism, schooling, race, sex, specific location of the individual establishment, search costs, and informal sources of information.

They concluded that "actors in the market behave on the whole in rational ways," that they "pursue reasonable goals in appropriate ways" (Rees and Shultz 1970, 222). They demonstrate that the more factors you consider, the more you can understand how people behave, and they make it clear that it takes more than a simplistic economic model of "costs of transference" to explain movement.

Search theory, a concept inspired by George Stigler, generally validated the results of the earlier labor market studies (for a summary, see Kiefer and Neumann 1989.) In particular, search theory elaborated on the importance of information, uncertainties, costs of search, "reservation wages," nonmaterialistic and non-measurable considerations, and implicit and incomplete contracts.

We would have benefited in our studies if we had been able at an earlier date to make contact with the concept of "transaction costs." (See, for example, Williamson 1975). Sumner Slichter, however, in his *Turnover of Factory Labor* (1919), had already set forth the high cost of turnover to both employers and workers.

It came to be accepted that the labor market was not only an economic institution but also a social one. As Robert M. Solow wrote recently, "There is something special about labor as a commodity, and therefore about the labor market too" (Solow 1990, 3). The labor market is, in substantial part, as Solow says, a "social institution." Consequently, it takes several models of labor markets to explain reality, not just one (Kerr 1950).

The Indeterminateness of Wages versus the Standard Rate

During World War II, the basic wage-stabilization policy in the United States was to find the "sound and tested rate," with the help of the Bureau of Labor Statistics, and then to set that as the maximum rate above which wages would not be allowed to go. That seemed like an easy assignment. My baptism by fire was as the first wage stabilization director for the West Coast, Alaska, and Hawaii. The trouble was that we could only find such a rate where it was set by a union (as by the Teamsters in the Northwest) or by an employers association (as in California agriculture) or by collective agreement or governmental action; never where it was established by "competitive" markets. We could find two, three, four, or five modal points and scattered rates above, below, and in between. Seldom did we find situations where the highest and lowest rates were less than 10 percent above and 10 percent below the central modal point. Part of this was, of course, because the jobs and the workers were not identical, but there were many more factors.

We had not expected this. Hicks I had told us that workers would not work for less and employers would not pay more than the standard rate. Hicks acknowledged that there might be a "range of indeterminateness" but that "no one would . . . suggest that the range is a very wide one, so that the practical significance of this contention, even if it is accepted, is small" (Hicks I, 24). The "range of indeterminateness" for the "average worker" is "so narrow that it is not worth considering" (p. 33). He made exceptions for the "exceptional man" and the employer of "superior ability," but they did "not bear generalization" (p. 36). "A 'standard rate' will naturally emerge" (p. 37), and there is "no reason to suppose that standard rates are in any way a particular product of Trade Unionism" (p. 39). "From our point

of view," Hicks wrote, indeterminateness "is supremely uninterest-
ing and unimportant" (p. 63). There are, he acknowledged, conditions which could result in indeterminateness, but "there is no need
to enlarge upon the absurdity and improbability of those conditions"
(p. 64). Had Hicks been correct, there would have been little need for
so much of the agony of decision making for the War Labor Board, or
for the labor economics research that followed.

There is, contrary to Hicks I, an urgent need to examine the certainty and the nature of indeterminateness under broadly competitive market conditions, as the World War II experience made clear
and as many scholarly studies later verified. Rees and Shultz found
that most firms had "some control" over the wages they paid, that
many had "wide latitude" in wage policy, and that few had "no
control" (Rees and Shultz 1970, 36–37). Indeterminateness was a
natural result of the actual labor markets that they and others studied. Why should this be?

Richard Lester in his article "Wage Diversity and Its Theoretical
Implications" (1946b), using Bureau of Labor Statistics data, showed
that high-wage plants paid about one-third more than low-wage
plants and concluded that "uniformity of rates in the same labor
market for the same grade of labor is rare." Usually there was a band
of wage rates for a certain kind of work in manufacturing plants in an
urban area.

In a subsequent paper entitled "A Range Theory of Wage Differentials" (1952), Lester discussed the various factors that can influence
the band of wage rates in particular cases. These factors include
differences in company wage policies, industrial relations programs,
and product markets and profitability. Certain company industrial
relations practices may influence the extent of competition for job
openings and the mobility of labor. Practices that tend to tie a firm's
employees to it include employee benefits, vacation rights, and other
job advantages based on length of service with the firm. The policy of
filling a company's job openings above the entry level by promotion
from within can serve to exclude outside competition from all
jobs above the entry level. Lester also considered other factors —
managerial, psychological, historical — that affect wage differentials
among firms in particular labor markets. He set forth what he called
anticompetitive factors in labor markets and included the impacts of
unions, government policy, seniority rules, practices of promotion
from within and against "pirating" workers from another employer,
internal job evaluation plans, the nonvesting of employee benefits —
an impressive list. Other factors he called "impeditive," and here he
included the impacts of friendships and familiar routines, risk and

uncertainty, and inadequate information, among other factors —
another impressive list.

Lloyd Reynolds dealt with the same subject area as Lester and
came to the same conclusion: that there is a "range or band of feasible
wage levels at which a firm may operate" (Reynolds 1951, 233). An
earlier paper by Reynolds, "Wage Differentials in Local Labor Markets," had appeared in 1946.

Lester joined in a debate with Fritz Machlup that was the main
direct confrontation between the revisionists and the traditionalists.
Machlup ("Marginal Analysis and Empirical Research," 1946), in
reply to an article by Lester on the shortcomings of marginal analysis
(Lester 1946a), challenged what he called bad research and said that
the case for the shortcomings was "not proved."

However, Machlup voiced second thoughts in his presidential address to the American Economic Association in 1966 (Machlup
1967). Marginal analysis, he said, gave the best "first approximation"
to an explanation of wage differentials, and it best fitted situations in
which there were "many firms" and they were "under heavy competition." He acknowledged that to explain individual cases, more
considerations, including both "behavioral" and "managerial," were
necessary. He noted that firms might consider other goals "besides
money profits" — what he called "total utility." However, bringing
in these broader considerations was "messy," he said — and it clearly
is. He further accepted that there were situations in which owners
and managers might have different goals. He also agreed that there
were many conditions of imperfect competition, and he noted that
there were many problems with the quality of available information
in decision making. In general, he said it was a "fallacy of misplaced
concreteness" to use a general model to explain specific cases.

Machlup concluded: "The simple marginal formula based on profit
maximization is suitable where (1) *large groups* of firms are involved
and nothing has to be predicted about particular firms, (2) the effects
of a *specific change* in conditions upon prices, inputs, and outputs are
to be explained or predicted rather than the values of these magnitudes before or after the change, and nothing has to be said about the
'total situation' or general developments, and (3) only *qualitative
answers*, that is, answers about directions of change, are sought
rather than precise numerical results" (Machlup 1967, 31). George
Stigler, who had earlier joined the argument, had already conceded,
"Everyone will agree with him [Lester] that economists have more
often made errors — of omission as well as commission — in observation than in logical analysis, and that incalculable amounts of good
empirical work are still needed" (Stigler 1947, 155).

This is what the revisionists, led by Lester and Reynolds, had been saying: that the theoretical model explained a "portion of reality," such as Lloyd Fisher's harvest labor market, but not the many or even most specific cases that were different from a model that assumed many firms under heavy competition, and that these cases, in their totality, comprised by far the greatest portion of reality. The traditionalists could have their general model as a "first approximation," but the revisionists were needed to explain all the differences from that model that led to closer and closer approximations to reality; that lent concreteness to the theoretical model.

We all might have gotten closer to reality faster if there had been a greater willingness to take a look also at Kenneth Boulding's model: "You must realize that the labor market is like the marriage market" (Boulding 1956, 254). There are, however, many — even many more — qualifications to the marriage model that one encounters in approaching closer to reality.

I conclude that Lester won most of the territory of actual economic life with his revisionist "range theory" analysis, while Machlup was relegated to one small corner of economics, where he could provide a 100 percent explanation. (For the contrary view that Lester "lost the battle," but "not due to new empirical evidence that contradicts Lester's criticisms," see Kaufman 1988, 179). I think Lester won in the end, and that this was another triumph for the revisionists.

Unemployment: Elaborations on Keynes

The then-young revisionists of the 1940s and 1950s were all Keynesians. In fact, Keynes — the greatest of the revisionists — was an inspiration for those of us working at the more micro levels of labor economics. Keynes, we thought, had the proper explanations for and the policy answers to prolonged, non–self-correcting depressions. The revisionists mostly supported and added to his reasons that money wage reductions come hard:

• It is difficult to reduce money wages because of union contracts in general, and thanks to the then-increasing tendency toward longer term contracts in particular.

• Employers, in the absence of unions, often recognized implicit contracts not to reduce money wages they have already established.

• In the absence of such explicit or implicit contracts, unorganized workers can penalize employers for cutting wages by withholding effort and even sabotaging production. Stanley Mathewson had shown their capacities in dramatic terms (Mathewson 1931). We all knew of such actions. Lloyd Reynolds noted how "difficult and unpleasant" can be "the transition to a lower wage" (Reynolds 1951, 233).

• Even Hicks I (p. 65) had noted that the "undercutting" of employed workers by other workers is hindered by its probably "unpleasant personal consequences"; our labor market studies had shown no practices of undercutting — workers went after only already open jobs.

• Hicks I (p. 57) also noted that "the desire of employers to maintain good relations and safeguard the future" will impede a reduction of wages. Many employers want to be "fair" — it pays in the long run. Reynolds, among others, also argued this from his labor market studies (Reynolds 1951, 237).

Overall, however, the revisionists in labor economics made only supplementary contributions to an understanding of unemployment and depressions. They had been preempted by the earlier Keynesian attacks on the traditionalists: a "flexible wage policy" to cure depressions is not possible, even if it were desirable. Stagflation, which is even harder to explain with wages rising under conditions of economic stagnation, did not become a big issue until the 1970s. Several of the explanations then offered, however, were already in the earlier literature, although often they were treated as though they were new discoveries. In particular, the partial separation of job markets from wage markets makes stagflation endemic in modern economies.

Wage Structures

The revisionists, greatly aided by new statistical information, undertook a substantial number of studies of wage structures, and by and large, their conclusions have stood the test of time. I summarize them as follows:

• Interfirm differentials, as noted earlier, for the same jobs in the same labor market, in the absence of organized policies, are substantial. The differentials paid by large firms over small firms still remain, however, something of a mystery.
• Interoccupational differentials are heavily based on skills —

which reflect the impacts of schooling, experience, and training — and also, among closely related occupations, on customary relationships; in both regards, much more so than Adam Smith had supposed. In particular, contrary to Smith, the "disagreeableness of the employments" is not generally positively associated with "pecuniary gains," and certainly particularly not in American labor markets. (For a discussion of "skill margins," see Reder 1955.)

• Interindustry differentials are heavily based on interoccupational differentials, but with high-paying industries paying higher rates for normally lower-paid occupations, and vice versa. Product market conditions are also highly influential.

• Interregional differentials in the United States are very persistent and significant, only subject to gradual narrowing.

Contrary to Adam Smith's expectations for an "equality in the whole of the advantages and disadvantages of different employments of laborer," there is no evidence in the United States that this is occurring — rather the contrary. It has never been the case that, "when the inconstancy of employment is combined with the hardship, the disagreeableness, and dirtiness of the work, it sometimes raises the wages of the most common laborer above those of the most skilful artificers" (Smith 1776, book 1, chap. 10). There is little tendency to equalize net advantages even in the "same neighborhood." The revisionists in their labor market studies helped to show why this is so. Labor economists, in more recent times, have looked more selectively at some of the relevant circumstances as related to gender, race, and "secondary" jobs.

For a good summary of what the revisionists knew about wage structures, see Reynolds (1951) and Reder (1958).

The revisionists' basic findings were (1) that skill is central to explaining wage structures, as the human capital school later showed in much greater detail; (2) that "a full understanding of wage structure involves both markets and non-market institutions" (Rees 1975, 349); and (3) that product market conditions are highly influential.

Union Impacts

The union movement during the period of the revisionists was the strongest in all of American history. The revisionists studied union impacts under these conditions. They found that unions:

• Greatly added to the introduction of "industrial jurisprudence" into American industry, with stronger and more explicit rules governing employment relationships, particularly the role of seniority and the introduction of a judicial system of grievance handling, both aided by the War Labor Board during World War II. Slichter (1941 and 1960, the latter with Healy and Livernash) made the definitive studies of these developments.

• Had a moderating influence on national politics. On the left, they drove communists out of the leadership of the union movement. On the right, they reduced the power of the conservative forces as they supported the New Deal, the New Frontier, the Great Society. In particular, unions helped to ease the introduction of affirmative action, despite the resistance of many of their members.

• Shifted the composition of earnings in the direction of fringe benefits.

• Greatly reduced interpersonal differentials on the same job, thus reducing "job selling" by foremen where it still existed. (In meat packing, as late as 1945, one-third of all workers had higher "red circle" rates set by foremen in return for favors of one sort or another.) Unions set standard rates that reduced or eliminated interfirm differentials among those firms covered by the same contract. Unions, however, had little impact on interoccupational and interindustry differentials, which lay outside their contracts' areas of influence. Unions reduced geographical wage differentials only in those industries with a national scale of union wages (see the discussion in Kerr, 1957b).

• Put direct upward pressure on money wages by raising union wages substantially above nonunion rates (see Lewis 1963; also 1986). But unions have a small impact (if any) on labor's share of national income under American conditions (Kerr 1957a), thus they redistribute labor's share as between the union and nonunion segments of the labor force.

The revisionists generally favored unions as a countervailing force against large corporations and for their role in introducing a system of industrial jurisprudence, but they were critical of unions' inflationary wage pressures and restrictions on output. In any event, they supported workers' right to organize. And the revisionists did not view unions as monopolies selling labor, as so many of the traditionalists did (see the discussions by Milton Friedman and Edward H. Chamberlin, in particular, in Wright 1956). Simons wrote of "the hard monopoly problem in labor organization" (Simons 1948, 35).

For a more modern and sophisticated presentation of views similar to those of the revisionists on the impact of unions, see Freeman and Medoff 1984.

Models of the Trade Union: The Grand Opening of a Non debate

The idea that firms and unions are unified entities, each with one single goal for their efforts, was never an attractive proposition to the revisionists. In the course of participating in disputes presented before the War Labor Board, and in arbitration after World War II (if not before), we saw splits within unions, individual employers, and employer organizations. My first contact with this commonplace of institutional dynamics came during the cotton pickers' strike in California in the fall of 1933 — small growers versus large growers, "Okies" under the leadership of Protestant ministers versus "Mexicans" under communist leaders (Taylor and Kerr 1940). John Dunlop later wrote that all disputes between labor and management really had three aspects — disputes within labor, disputes within management, and disputes between the two against each other. He identified the central importance of "diverse internal interests" and stated that thus "it takes three agreements to make one" (Dunlop 1984, chap. 1). On the union side, there were rivalries among unions, among leaders of individual unions, among internal group interests, among adherents to ideologies. On the employer's side there were rivalries, for example, between the "soft-line" officials in personnel administration, industrial relations, and marketing and the "hard-liners" in finance and engineering.

Berle and Means (1932) had opened up the modern study of the firm with the identification of the separate interests of owners and managers, but they did not see how management could also be split. In fact, however, there is no unity of command with a single goal: *the firm maximizing only monetary profit*. Working-class movements divided between the interests of the workers and their leaders had earlier been presented by Robert Michels (1915). The leaders in the communist nations later became the "new class" after they had seized power, distinct from the proletariat.

John Dunlop proposed what was viewed as an economic model of the trade union in his *Wage Determination under Trade Unions* (1950 [1944]). Or did he? To my reading, he showed how difficult it was to set forth a single and simple economic goal with any precision. He identified half a dozen plausible bottom lines for the union. Which to choose? That is a political issue.

In his preface to the 1950 edition of *Wage Determination under Trade Unions*, Dunlop does say that the "thesis must be rejected that wage determination under collective bargaining is to be explained most fundamentally or fruitfully in terms of a political process" (p. iii). However, this is because the economic environment of collective bargaining is usually so much more decisive a factor and not because the union is not essentially a political entity. What Dunlop rejects is "political wage setting," not the political model of the union per se. He quotes with approval D. H. Robertson's concept of "islands of conscious power" in a sea of economic constraints (Dunlop 1950 [1944], 8), and these constraints are all the more determining; but the conscious power is there too, and the power is political.

In any event, few persons in American history have ever known more about the political infighting within unions and within the union movement than John Dunlop, and by 1944 he already knew enough. Telling him that unions have a political life would be like telling Freud that there is such a thing as sex. All institutions have an internal political life with struggles over power and influence. His economic model was a tour-de-force intellectual effort to set forth the influence of economic constraints and the possible definitions of goals of economic maximization by unions in the process of wage determination.

Arthur Ross argued for a political model of unions in his *Trade Union Wage Policy* (1948). This was at a time of intense rivalry both among unions and among leaders within unions, particularly on the West Coast, where Ross was then located. The Ross presentation was the best statement of what came to be known as the California school of Ross, Lloyd Fisher, and myself — a view of political institutions operating within an economic context. Fisher introduced the idea of the separation of union members' interests and those of union leaders (he had earlier been research director for a major union). I proposed the concept of the union as a wage-setting institution, based first on my observations in Germany, where the government extended union contract wages as minimum wages for an industry, and thus the union fixed wages rather than "sold" labor (Kerr 1948). Ross was a proponent of the importance of "orbits of coercive comparison" and of the effective combinations of our three central ideas.

My own particular view was (and is) that there might possibly be pure economic models of the trade union as a monopoly "selling labor" in operation somewhere, but that there certainly were political models almost everywhere; and that the most common political model was that of the one-party union government acting like a bureaucracy, doing enough to maximize its own survival and that of its current leaders by satisfying the members. This might be called the bureaucratic political model, as against the more hyperactive political model proposed by Ross. Lloyd Reynolds noted that union leaders seek "the minimum [wage] which they judge necessary to keep their members satisfied" (Reynolds 1951, 236). Lloyd Ulman later seemed to agree when he wrote that the union may be "regarded as a 'satisficing' institution" (Ulman 1990, 290).

Ross and Dunlop were both correct. They were talking about separate subjects — Ross was saying that unions were political institutions; Dunlop, that wage determination under trade unions was basically determined by economic considerations. (For an independent view of the controversy, see Reder 1952 and Rees 1952.)

Coincident with the interest in union models was a renewed interest in union histories, resulting in such classics as Lloyd Ulman's *The Rise of the National Trade Union* (1955), Walter Galenson's *Rival Unionism in the United States* (1940) and *The CIO Challenge to the AFL* (1960), and Richard Lester's *As Unions Mature* (1958). Irving Bernstein wrote the best history of the ambience of the times affecting the development of unions during the New Deal period (Bernstein 1970).

Internal Labor Markets: A New Exploration

I first became deeply impressed with the quite separate lives employees live within internal job markets when I was impartial chairman of the contract negotiations between Boeing and the machinists' union during World War II. We had a job evaluation plan which made almost no specific contacts with external labor markets; it had a logic of its own, mostly structured by industrial engineers. We also had a strong seniority plan covering promotions and lateral transfers. There were many grievances in connection with both of these plans, particularly because the national office of the International Association of Machinists (IAM) had seized control from local communist leaders, and the former leaders kept up guerilla warfare via the grievance system. Otherwise we could have been located on the moon. I remember only one brief reference to what was going on in external labor markets, and that was to the local pay rate for nurses. "Voice" was everywhere and "exit" hardly existed, to borrow terms later used by Albert Hirschman (1970). Then, as I looked around, I saw that more people in more places were coming to live more of their lives within internal labor markets and only occasionally in external markets; that there were more transactions going on inside than outside those "black boxes"; that there was a world of internal rules rising alongside the world of external markets; that job markets and wage markets were becoming more separated.

I set forth my views on the importance of major forms of institutional labor markets in "The Balkanization of Labor Markets" (1954). John Dunlop followed along this same line of argument with his discussion of the role of "job families" and "wage contours" and "seniority districts" in 1966. (For an earlier discussion, see Dunlop 1957.) Peter Doeringer and Michael Piore produced their basic book, *Internal Labor Markets and Manpower Analysis,* in 1971. A huge body of literature has followed. Some of it has taken on a normative approach — "good" versus "bad" jobs in "primary" and "secondary" labor markets — rather than the more analytical approach that I had first favored, with primary markets composed of the more structured internal markets and secondary markets composed of the less structured and the nonstructured.

The development of internal labor markets was inherent in the rise of industrial society and larger scale enterprises. Hicks I had distinguished between the "casual" laborers in "a highly competitive market," and those in the "regular trades" who became "more useful to the employer" as mutual attachments developed between them (pp. 66–74). But he in no way saw that the whole process of labor utilization could be greatly changed by the rise of the numbers in the regular trades within the new industrial society, which took on aspects of the "guild" and the "manor," as I noted. Reinforcing the rise of the regular trades was the development of professional personnel managers setting rules for "regular workers," as against the foreman working with more nearly casual laborers as described by Sanford M. Jacoby (1985). Unions were an additional source for the establishment of internal labor markets, with their own rules of behavior as distinct from those of external markets, as Slichter had shown in his *Union Policies and Industrial Management* (1941).

The study of internal labor markets relates to many aspects of labor economics, including the mobility of labor, the setting of wages by employers, the sources of Keynesian unemployment, the location of influence in the power structures of industrial life, the distribution of opportunity within the labor force, the development of job-specific training, the importance of transaction analysis, and the analysis of labor efficiencies in production.

Collective Bargaining and the Causes of Industrial Peace

Collective bargaining was one of the big games in town after World War II, and it drew headlines in its exciting moments. Many studies were made of it, mostly in the institutionalist tradition of concentrating on individual cases and within them on the development of new rules and new processes. Game theory was not as highly developed then as it is today, and, in any event, the exponents of game theory and the students of collective bargaining made no contact with each other. To the students of collective bargaining, game theory dealt with very simplistic models that bore no relation to the complexities that they knew existed; and to those who employed game theory, collective bargaining dealt only with episodes. Had contact been made, game theory might earlier have become more relevant to reality, and collective bargaining studies, particularly as they related to negotiations, more analytical and rigorous. A great opportunity to learn from each other was lost; the mentalities of the builders of universal models and the journalists of today's and yesterday's occurrences were too far apart.

The first comprehensive book covering case studies of collective bargaining was edited by Harry Millis (*How Collective Bargaining Works*, 1942). A continuing interest in the field has been maintained by the Wertheim Series published at Harvard, under the guidance of John Dunlop. The most recent work in the series (prior to this volume), George H. Hildebrand and Garth L. Mangum's *Capital and Labor in American Copper, 1845–1990* (1992), is an example of how such studies should best be done.

There were efforts to create a typology of collective bargaining situations, particularly by Frederick H. Harbison and John R. Coleman (1951). They set forth three types: "armed truce," "working harmony," and "union-management cooperation." E. Wight Bakke had earlier identified what he thought was, and what came to be, the standard type (see his *Mutual Survival*, 1946). (See also Selekman 1949.)

The most coordinated series of studies, conducted after World War II when industrial conflict was at a peak, was led by Clinton Golden for the National Planning Association. Thirteen studies were made, and summary analyses were prepared by John Dunlop, Frederick Harbison with John Coleman, Clark Kerr, Douglas McGregor, and

Charles Myers.[2] It all added up to the conclusion that everything affects everything else — which has a large element of truth to it. Herbert R. Northrup and Harvey A. Young, in a retrospective review ("The Causes of Industrial Peace Revisited," 1968), were correct in concluding, however, that those of us who had conducted the studies had paid too little attention to economic factors, but they, in turn, paid too little attention to their own spelling out of those economic factors and their impacts. We had a lot of content but little form, which is one of the troubles with the institutionalist approach. It may be noted, however, that a favorable view of collective bargaining in a cooperative mode had developed in the minds of those revisionists who worked with the War Labor Board. We had seen how labor and management, working together, had helped to win World War II.

The revisionists did better when they could work within a theoretical "scaffolding," and such a scaffolding was later supplied by John Dunlop in his *Industrial Relations Systems* (1958). It set forth an ordered analysis of such systems, including their major variations, with which others could and have agreed and disagreed ever since. It concentrated on the "actors," the "contexts," the "rules," and the "ideologies," and it quickly became the standard point of reference. (See, for example, the discussion in Reynaud et al. 1990.) A reissue with an added commentary has now been prepared (1993).

Policy: Bits and Pieces

The earlier institutionalists made enormous contributions to policy formation — to the New Deal in general, and to the welfare state and the legal acceptance of trade unions in particular.

By comparison, the revisionists were minor players, although they did affect policies during World War II. Sumner Slichter was the author of the "Slichter Law" in Massachusetts on the handling of labor disputes that greatly affect the public. A totally disowned report for the Committee on Economic Development (CED), written by George Shultz, CED director, and Abraham Siegel, associate director, on behalf of a study group that I chaired and of which John Dunlop, Albert Rees, and Robert M. Solow were members, attempted a comprehensive review entitled *The Public Interest in National Policy* (Independent Study Group 1961). The report was disowned by the CED because it opposed "right to work laws." We supported "collective bargaining as a positive force on the economy" (p. 63); we cautioned that the government should limit itself to broad policies; and we argued strongly for "the protection of individual rights and freedoms in a world of powerful organizations" (p. 66), including "fair employment" practices. This report nevertheless became the background for the policies of two of its members when each later became U.S. secretary of labor — John Dunlop and George Shultz. Lloyd Ulman and his colleagues studied "incomes policies" in nine countries (Flanagan, Soskice, and Ulman 1983). Harold W. Watts and Albert Rees participated in and wrote *The New Jersey Income-Maintenance Experiment* (1977). Any results of these and other studies were of marginal importance as compared with those of the institutionalists, however.

Revisionists also participated in making and administering private policy. One illustration is the pioneering program for assisting displaced workers in the meat packing industry; George Shultz, Arnold R. Weber, and I were all involved (Shultz and Weber 1966). John Dunlop has been the founder and leader of one tripartite policy group, what is now called the Labor-Management Group, which he started in 1975 when he was secretary of labor, and since 1975 I have been the chairman of another, the Work in America Institute organized and led by Jerome M. Rosow.

Strikes: Their Likely Historical Course

A major result of the rising trade union movement was that the number of strikes greatly increased. Hicks wrote that most strikes were due to "faulty negotiations," because they cost both parties more than they gained except for an occasional strike to "burnish" the weapon. Faulty negotiations could occur when employers, unions, or both were guilty of "ignorance" of each other's "dispositions," or when there was a "difference of opinion between the leaders and their rank and file" (Hicks I, 146, 147). But this assumes that each side and, on the union side, both leaders and rank and file, are calculating costs and benefits only in economic terms. The revisionists saw noneconomic calculations, mostly of a political nature, also at work. They saw strikes used for organizing, strikes caused by rival unions or by contests between union leaders, strikes used by leaders to demonstrate the integrity of their efforts or the costs of strikes to their members, and strikes to get government participation in settlements. Hicks did note one politically motivated type of strike, where "socialists can threaten the overthrow of capitalism" (Hicks I, 140). It is inherent in the political model of the union that strikes should result from political as well as economic considerations.

Many studies were made of strike activity as it related to phases of the business cycle, to the season of the year, to their ostensible causes, and much else. (For the British experience, see Knowles 1952; for the United States, see Ross and Hartman 1960.)

The most controversial strike study was conducted by Abraham Siegel and myself ("The Inter-Industry Propensity to Strike: An International Comparison," 1954). We found that in many nations certain industries were more subject to strikes than others. We explained this as a result of their circumstances — "the isolated mass" versus "the integrated community." This idea aroused the opposition of the Marxists and neo-Marxists, first because they thought all workers were more or less equally on their way to the revolution, and second because isolated masses were generally giving way to integrated communities, and this suggested a dying out of the strike (and of the revolution).

The major attack against our findings was made by Edward Shorter and Charles Tilly (1974). They concluded their study by saying that they have "relegated to the domain of fantasy" what they called the "seriously inadequate effort to explain conflict in terms of industrial change." (Shorter and Tilly 1974, 249). In contrast they found that "old Marx" has come out "not badly at all." "We have rediscovered . . . some of the truths about economics and militancy that Marx described so passionately a hundred years ago." Thus they found themselves "firmly within a major intellectual tradition." Their thesis was that the "genuine proletarians" are in the big "urban centers" and not in what they call "mono-industrial" towns (Shorter and Tilly, 294). Yet they found, as we did, comparatively heavy industrial conflict in mono-industrial centers: mining, textile, and maritime centers. And to arrive at their conclusions about France, they ignored Lyon and Lille, which they conceded were mono-industrial, and also the "red-belt" cities around Paris. In any event, historical developments have not validated their neo-Marxist analysis.

Knowles in his study of Great Britain came to much the same conclusion that Siegel and I had reached.

Interpretations of the Flow of History

The most influential efforts to set forth the "laws of motion" of industrial society were made by Adam Smith and by Marx and Engels. By comparison, Saint-Simon's effort was almost totally neglected, but it was more prescient — he had seen a strong tendency toward the development of what would now be identified as a social democratic society. Max Weber had seen movement toward societies run by large bureaucracies; Veblen had seen societies run by engineers. These were among the more influential visions at the time the revisionists came along. The issue was still open, however — more open than ever before. One-third of the world's population was under the domination of communist-run governments. The new nations were trying out the roads they wished to follow. The cold war was at its peak. Friedrich von Hayek was writing and talking about the *Road to Serfdom* (1944). Joseph Schumpeter (1942) was predicting a mild form of creeping socialism bereft of the innovators. The Wisconsin institutionalists still envisioned a highly organized society directed toward effective service to and protection of the workers (similar to Saint-Simon). Keynes argued for a guided capitalism. John Kenneth Galbraith described and analyzed the *New Industrial State* (1967) with its "technostructure." John R. Hicks, still later, wrote his *A Theory of Economic History* (1969) around the expansion of markets.

The revisionists generally were concerned more with current developments (they were satisfied New Dealers) than with long-trend tendencies, and with microaspects rather than overarching developments. There were, however, at least two exceptions. Sumner Slichter set forth his view of the "laboristic" state — "a community in which employees rather than business men are the strongest single influence" — and thought that "the rise of trade unions means that the United States stands on the threshold of major changes in its economic and political institutions" (Slichter 1948).

A second revisionist view was presented in *Industrialism and Industrial Man* (Kerr, Dunlop, Harbison, and Myers 1960) and in *The Future of Industrial Societies* (Kerr 1983). Dunlop's *Industrial Relations Systems* (1958) was written within the same context of social analysis. We saw a gradual and incomplete convergence in the general direction of "pluralistic industrialism." As compared with Slichter, we saw a more nearly "tripartite" industrial society, with roles for organized labor, management, and government roughly balancing each other, and with workers and consumers making their individual decisions. Dennis Robertson, in chapter 11 of *Control of Industry* (1923) had earlier seen the emergence of a system of "joint control" by organized labor and industry. He left open whether this joint control would be exercised in a "negative" or a "constructive" mode. Joint control, in more modern times, would be called the "corporative state."

We thought that pluralistic industrialism would emerge triumphant against its several competitors, particularly communism. John W. Goldthorpe called our analysis the "most ambitious and influential attempt at a non-Marxist understanding of the emerging pattern of global social development" (Goldthorpe 1984, 315). With the collapse of communism, pluralistic industrialism does now stand without major competitors; and pluralism is a major theme of those who are seeking to reform communist societies. We set forth our reasons why we thought this was the dominant trend line of industrial society — essentially because it worked best. This was also a theme followed by Jan Tinbergen (see, for example, "The Theory of the Optimum Regime," 1959). We put heavy stress on the importance of the changing technological base for the evolution of society. This led some to view us as neo-Marxist. We did see technology as central to the changing "base structure" of production, as did Marx, but contrary to Marx, we did not see it as controlling the "superstructure" of thought and action in how to manage the new technology.

David Montgomery has written that *Industrialism and Industrial Man* was "the most influential clarion call to liberate the study of history from both Marxism and the Commons-Perlman school." It made "not the handling of protest, but the structuring of the labor force . . . *the* labor problem in economic development" (Montgomery 1991, 114).

In Retrospect

The revisionists were replaced in their leadership role by the Chicago school in the early 1960s. The Chicago school made excellent use of econometric methodology to explore, in much more depth, the supply side of labor markets, concentrating particularly effectively on individual decisions in building human capital, and also on family decisions in what has been called "the new home economics" (Reynolds 1988, 128). The revisionists had been more interested in the demand side, and in organized wage fixing. The supply side lends itself better than the demand side to explanations not only via econometrics but also via the traditional neoclassical economic activity. The Chicago school had going for it both a powerful technology and new data to which to apply it, and an area of economic analysis still open to detailed exploration that lent itself exceptionally well to explanations provided by traditional mainstream economic theory. The Chicago school was clearly far better at quantification in areas subject to quantification — so long as it did not run out of data sets. And econometric techniques were very cost-effective for their practitioners. Individually, members of the Chicago school could produce more articles faster than the revisionists ever could. It took a data set and a methodology, and care and ingenuity in using both. The revisionists, so measured, were not cost-effective. They required a much more substantial investment in knowledge of history, of the other social sciences, of the use of nonstatistical evidence. They also needed to make their own direct and intensive contact with reality via case studies and participation in the action. They could not just sit in their cubicles.

Together, however, the revisionists on the demand and wage-fixing sides and the neoclassical econometricians on the supply side provided a more rounded picture of labor economics than ever existed before. I would argue, though, that the demand side is the more important of the two — with supply following demand more than the other way around; and also that wage fixing deserves major attention because of its actual significance. I would argue, also, that the demand side and wage fixing are much more complex than supply side adjustments and thus more interesting to study; that they require more contact with reality than does the use of other people's statistics; and that their study is a better background for both teaching and public service. However, I would also argue that the two approaches add greatly to each other in advancing our understanding of labor markets and institutions.

Scholars, too, have their love affairs, and love is a matter of taste. The labor econometricians have a fascination with their computers and their data sets, just as the young revisionists had with direct contact with flesh-and-blood reality.

Now there is developing the school of the new revisionists who use econometrics but also other sources of knowledge, and who look at the totality of labor economics and industrial relations more than the supply side of labor markets. Looking back on the revisionists, Bruce Kaufman has written: "These economists turned labor economics away from a historical, descriptive analysis of labor problems and toward an analytical study of labor markets" (Kaufman 1993, 85). Richard Freeman has written (with specific reference to *The Structure of Labor Markets* by Lloyd Reynolds) that the work was "on target" at least "more often than not," and he added: "May our own work look as good thirty years hence" (Freeman 1984, 219). In evaluating the work of what he calls DKLR (Dunlop, Kerr, Lester, Reynolds), Freeman says:

> On the issues of wage determination, collective bargaining, and the interrelation among employment, wages, and unemployment, which were the principal concerns of the older generation of labor economists, their empirical findings have, with rare exception, been corroborated by modern analysts using sophisticated econometric tools. In one sense, modern human capital earnings models have turned out to be largely "orthogonal" to the older analyses, adding a supply dimension to our view of labor markets without rejecting the older demand results. Moreover, modern efforts to explain away the key findings of the older generation in terms of competitive market behavior have not succeeded, even in the eyes of some of those offering such explanations. [See Krueger and Summers 1986a, 1986b; Dickens and Katz 1986, 1987.] With respect to supply-side issues, which were of less concern to the older generation (save for Reynolds), the basic finding that labor supply has a largely passive effect on wage determination has been accepted in most respects, although observed job search and labor mobility has been interpreted as reflecting a more rational form of behavior. Only in issues which attracted little attention from the older generation — investment in human capital, economics of discrimination, dynamics of unemployment, to name a few topics — have we clearly surpassed our elders. (Freeman 1988, 221)

From the point of view of a revisionist, may I suggest that we left a few traces in the long history of labor economics since 1776.

• We combined what we thought were the best values of both the neoclassical and the institutional approaches, while responding to the new developments in economic society.

• For a time, we held together the inherently mutually explanatory fields of labor economics and industrial relations.

• We recorded and analyzed many important historical developments of our times, particularly in the areas of collective bargaining, and union and management governance.

We made and developed the following observations:

- Labor markets are "social" as well as "economic" institutions.
- Labor markets are mostly "broadly" (not perfectly) competitive, giving rise to a range of wage rates and nonwage benefits instead of a determinate standard rate.
- Given the imperfection of markets, "there is room for collective bargaining and government intervention to do good as well as bad" (Kaufman 1988, 193); room to affect wage policy and employment policy.
- Jobs are multidimensional in their characteristics and are inadequately described and compared by reference to their wage rates alone.
- Internal labor markets have come to take their place along with external markets in influencing economic behavior (black box I).
- Trade unions are political organizations operating within strong economic constraints, not single-minded economic monopolies (black box II). (The traditionalists tended to put aside black boxes as being both not subject to penetration and not important because they just respond to market pressures like an amoeba. Black boxes, as it turns out, affect markets as well as react to them, and they can be penetrated to a degree.)
- Industrial relations can be analyzed as "systems."
- Trade unions have important, but restricted, impacts on wage structures and levels.
- Skill or "learning" (among the five factors of Adam Smith — the others were the "agreeableness or disagreeableness" of the jobs, the "constancy or inconstancy" of employment, the "small or great trust," and the "probability or improbability of success" [Smith 1776, book 1, chap. 10]) is all important as the central building block in wage structures. The second most important building block is the industry-by-industry impact of product market configurations.
- Industrial society is moving mainly in the direction of pluralistic industrialism, not toward the "dictatorship of the proletariat."

We observed the following — but did not develop these observations:

- The importance of transaction costs.
- The phenomenon of efficiency wages.
- The existence of implicit and incomplete contracts.
- The dichotomy of power positions and influence between "insiders" and "outsiders."

- The possibility of stagflation in the partial separation of internal job markets and external wage markets.

We played a supporting role to:

- Keynes in his assertion that wages are "steady" in a downward direction.
- Simon, March, and Cyert on "bounded rationality," "satisficing" decision making, the difficulty of defining welfare in complex and changing institutions, the importance of the quality of available information, the use of trial and error.
- Commons and the institutionalists on the increasingly central roles played by institutions and their rules.
- Schumpeter in asserting that "social economics" can add an important dimension to the study of economics.
- Hicks in his conversion to the significance of "social forces."
- Douglas in that the "real world" warrants direct study, as do more theoretical models of it; and that scholarly studies can contribute to more effective policy development.
- Heraclitus in that "all is flux," including the study of labor economics.

Solow ends his contribution to this volume with reference to the revisionists, and I wish to quote him here: "I hope I am right in thinking that there is a revival."

Notes

1. Hicks once wrote me (October 21, 1983): "Thank you so much for your charming paper, and for writing on it to make sure I should read it. It was indeed a pleasure to find that my work, both my earlier and later work on problems, has been of such special use to a real labour economist like yourself. Especially to find that it is my 1955 paper, which I see you put first of my works in your bibliography, which represents to you my most considered opinion, as I should like it to be regarded."
2. National Planning Association case studies on Causes of Industrial Peace under Collective Bargaining:
   1. Clark Kerr and Roger Randall, *Crown Zellerbach and the Pacific Coast Pulp and Paper Industry*, 1948
   2. Frederick H. Harbison and King Carr, *The Libbey-Owens-Ford Glass Company and the Federation of Glass, Ceramics and Silica Sand Workers of America*, 1948

3. Douglas MacGregor and Joseph N. Scanlon, *The Dewey and Almy Chemical Company and the International Chemical Workers Union,* 1948
4. Donald B. Straus, *Hickey-Freeman Company and Amalgamated Clothing Workers of America,* 1949
5. J. Wade Miller, Jr., *Sharon Steel Corporation and United Steel Workers of America,* 1949
6. Clark Kerr and George Halverson, *Lockheed Aircraft Corporation and International Association of Machinists,* 1949
7. Charles A. Myers and George P. Shultz, *Nashua Gummed and Coated Paper Company and Seven AFL Unions,* 1950
8. R. W. Fleming and Edwin E. Witte, *Marathon Corporation and Seven Labor Unions,* 1950
9. George W. Zinke, *Minnequa Plant of Colorado Fuel and Iron Corporation and Two Locals of United Steelworkers of America,* 1952
10. George P. Shultz and Robert P. Crisara, *The Lapointe Machine Tool Company and United Steelworkers of America,* 1952
11. George S. Paul, *American Velvet Company and Textile Workers Union of America,* 1953
12. Glenn W. Gilman and James W. Sweeney, *Atlantic Steel Company and United Steelworkers of America,* 1953
13. Frederick H. Harbison and John R. Coleman, *Working Harmony: A Summary of the Collective Bargaining Relationships in 18 Companies,* 1953

References

Bakke, E. Wight. 1933. *The Unemployed Man: A Social Study.* London: Nisbet.

———. 1946. *Mutual Survival.* New York: Harper.

Berle, Adolph A., Jr., and Gardiner C. Means. 1932. *The Modern Corporation and Private Property.* New York: Macmillan.

Bernstein, Irving. 1970. *Turbulent Years: A History of the American Worker, 1933–1941.* Boston: Houghton Mifflin.

Boulding, Kenneth E. 1950. *A Reconstruction of Economics.* New York: John Wiley.

———. 1956. "Selections from the Discussion of Friedman's Paper," in David McCord Wright, ed., *The Impact of the Union: Eight Economic Theorists Evaluate the Labor Union Movement.* New York: Kelley & Millman.

Cain, Glen G. 1977. "A Tribute to Paul H. Douglas, 1892–1976, Land Economist and Senator." *Notes and Comments,* presentation to the Labor Economics Workshop, University of Wisconsin, October 11, 1977. Madison: Institute for Research on Poverty, University of Wisconsin.

Dickens, William, and L. F. Katz. 1986. "Interindustry Wage Differences and Theories of Wage Determination." Working Paper 2014. Cambridge, Mass.: National Bureau of Economic Research.

———. 1987. "Interindustry Wage Differences and Industry Characteristics," in K. Lang and J. Leonard, eds., *Unemployment and the Structure of Labor Markets*. London: Basil Blackwell.

Doeringer, Peter B., and Michael J. Piore. 1971. *Internal Labor Markets and Manpower Analysis*. Lexington, Mass.: D. C. Heath.

Douglas, Paul H. 1934. *The Theory of Wages*. New York: Macmillan.

Douglas, Paul H., and Aaron Director. 1931. *The Problem of Unemployment*. New York: Macmillan.

Dunlop, John T. 1938. "The Movement of Real and Money Wage Rates." *The Economic Journal* 48, no. 191 (Sept.): 413–434.

———. 1950 [1944]. *Wage Determination under Trade Unions*. New York: Augustus M. Kelley.

———. 1957. "The Task of Contemporary Wage Theory," in George W. Taylor and Frank C. Pierson, eds., *New Concepts in Wage Determination*. New York: McGraw-Hill. pp. 117–139.

———. 1958. *Industrial Relations Systems*. New York: Holt. Revised ed., 1993, Boston: Harvard Business School Press.

———, ed. 1961. *Potentials of the American Economy: Selected Essays of Sumner H. Slichter*. Cambridge, Mass.: Harvard University Press.

———. 1966. "Job Vacancy Measures and Economic Analysis," in National Bureau of Economic Research, *The Measurement and Interpretation of Job Vacancies*. New York: Columbia University Press. pp. 27–47.

———. 1984. *Dispute Resolution: Negotiation and Consensus Building*. Dover, Mass.: Auburn House.

———. 1988. "Labor Markets and Wage Determination: Then and Now," in Bruce E. Kaufman, ed., *How Labor Markets Work: Reflections on Theory and Practice by John Dunlop, Clark Kerr, Richard Lester and Lloyd Reynolds*. Lexington, Mass.: Lexington Books. pp. 47–87.

Fisher, Lloyd H. 1953. *The Harvest Labor Market in California*. Cambridge, Mass.: Harvard University Press.

Flanagan, Robert J., David W. Soskice, and Lloyd Ulman. 1983. *Unionism, Economic Stabilization, and Incomes Policies: European Experience*. Washington, D.C.: Brookings Institution.

Freeman, Richard. 1984. "The Structure of Labor Markets: A Book Review Three Decades Later," in Gustav Ranis et al., eds., *Comparative Development Perspectives: Essays in Honor of Lloyd G. Reynolds*. Boulder: Westview Press. pp. 201–221.

———. 1988. "Does the New Generation of Labor Economists Know More Than the Old Generation?" in Bruce E. Kaufman, ed., *How Labor Markets Work: Reflections on Theory and Practice by John Dunlop, Clark Kerr, Richard Lester, and Lloyd Reynolds*. Lexington, Mass.: Lexington Books. pp. 205–232.

Freeman, Richard B., and James L. Medoff. 1984. *What Do Unions Do?* New York: Basic Books.

Galbraith, John Kenneth. 1956 [1952]. *American Capitalism: The Concept of Countervailing Power.* Boston: Houghton Mifflin.

———. 1967. *The New Industrial State.* Boston: Houghton Mifflin.

Galenson, Walter. 1940. *Rival Unionism in the United States.* New York: American Council of Public Affairs.

———. 1960. *The CIO Challenge to the AFL: A History of the American Labor Movement, 1935–1941.* Cambridge, Mass.: Harvard University Press.

Goldthorpe, John H. 1984. *Order and Conflict in Contemporary Capitalism.* Oxford: Oxford University Press.

Hall, Robert L., and Charles J. Hitch. 1939. "Price Theory and Business Behavior." *Oxford Economic Papers* no. 2 (May): 12–45.

Harbison, Frederick H., and John R. Coleman. 1951. *Goals and Strategy in Collective Bargaining.* New York: Harper & Bros.

Hayek, Friedrich A. von. 1944. *The Road to Serfdom.* London: Routledge.

Hicks, John R. 1932. *The Theory of Wages.* London: Macmillan.

———. 1955. "Economic Foundations of Wage Policy." *The Economic Journal* 65, no. 259 (Sept.): 389–404.

———. 1963 [1932]. *The Theory of Wages.* London: Macmillan. (The 1932 and 1963 editions are referred to in text as Hicks I and Hicks II, respectively. All page citations are to the 1963 edition.)

———. 1969. *A Theory of Economic History.* Oxford: Clarendon Press.

Hildebrand, George H., and Garth L. Mangum. 1992. *Capital and Labor in American Copper: 1845–1990.* Cambridge, Mass.: Harvard University Press.

Hirschman, Albert O. 1970. *Exit, Voice and Loyalty: Responses to Decline in Firms, Organizations and States.* Cambridge, Mass.: Harvard University Press.

Independent Study Group (Clark Kerr, Chairman). 1961. *The Public Interest in National Labor Policy.* New York: Committee for Economic Development.

Jacoby, Sanford M. 1985. *Employing Bureaucracy: Managers, Unions and the Transformation of Work in American Industry.* New York: Columbia University Press.

Kaufman, Bruce E. 1988. "The Postwar View of Labor and Wage Determination," in Bruce E. Kaufman, ed., *How Labor Markets Work: Reflections on Theory and Practice by John Dunlop, Clark Kerr, Richard Lester, and Lloyd Reynolds.* Lexington, Mass.: Lexington Books. pp. 145–203.

———. 1993. *The Origins and Evolution of the Field of Industrial Relations.* Ithaca, N.Y.: ILR Press.

Kerr, Clark. 1939. *Productive Enterprises of the Unemployed, 1931–1938.* Ph.D. dissertation, University of California, Berkeley.

———. 1941. "Industrial Relations in Large-Scale Cotton Farming," in Pacific Coast Economic Association, *Proceedings of the Nineteenth Annual Conference, 1940.* Eugene, Ore.: Koke-Chapman. pp. 62–69.

———. 1942. *Migration to the Seattle Labor Market Area, 1940–1942.* Seattle: University of Washington Press.

———. 1948. "Economic Analysis and the Study of Industrial Relations," in *Proceedings of the Third Annual Conference on Research and Training in Industrial Relations*, University of Minnesota. Minneapolis: University of Minnesota Press. pp. 12–16.

———. 1950. "Labor Markets: Their Character and Consequences." *American Economic Review* 40, no. 2 (May): 278–291.

———. 1954. "The Balkanization of Labor Markets," in Social Science Research Council, *Labor Mobility and Economic Opportunity*. New York: John Wiley & Sons.

———. 1957a. "Labor's Income Share and the Labor Movement," in George W. Taylor and Frank C. Pierson, eds., *New Concepts in Wage Determination*. New York: McGraw-Hill. pp. 260–298.

———. 1957b. "Wage Relationships: The Comparative Impact of Market and Power Forces," in John T. Dunlop, ed., *The Theory of Wage Determination: Proceedings of a Conference Held by the International Economic Association*. New York: Macmillan. pp. 173–193.

———. 1983. *The Future of Industrial Societies: Convergence or Continuing Diversity?* Cambridge, Mass.: Harvard University Press.

———. 1988. "The Neoclassical Revisionists in Labor Economics (1940–1960): R.I.P.," in Bruce E. Kaufman, ed., *How Labor Markets Work: Reflections on Theory and Practice by John Dunlop, Clark Kerr, Richard Lester, and Lloyd Reynolds*. Lexington, Mass.: Lexington Books. pp. 1–46.

Kerr, Clark, and Abraham Siegel. 1954. "The Inter-Industry Propensity to Strike: An International Comparison," in Arthur M. Kornhauser, Robert Dubin, and Arthur M. Ross, eds., *Industrial Conflict*. New York: McGraw-Hill. pp. 189–212.

Kerr, Clark, John T. Dunlop, Frederick Harbison, and Charles A. Myers. 1960. *Industrialism and Industrial Man: The Problems of Labor and Management in Economic Growth*. Cambridge, Mass.: Harvard University Press.

Kiefer, Nicholas M., and George R. Neumann. 1989. *Search Models and Applied Labor Economics*. New York: Cambridge University Press.

Klamer, Arjo. 1989. "An Accountant among Economists: Conversations with Sir John R. Hicks." *Journal of Economic Perspectives* 4, no. 5 (Fall): 167–180.

Knowles, Kenneth G. J. C. 1952. *Strikes: A Study in Industrial Conflict, with Special Reference to British Experience between 1911 and 1947*. Oxford: Basil Blackwell.

Krueger, Alan, and Lawrence Summers. 1986a. "Efficiency Wages and the Interindustry Wage Structure." Discussion Paper 1247. Cambridge, Mass.: Harvard Institute of Economic Research.

———. 1986b. "Reflections on the Interindustry Wage Structure." Working Paper 1968. Cambridge, Mass.: Harvard University.

Lester, Richard A. 1941. *Economics of Labor*. New York: Macmillan.

———. 1946a. "Shortcomings of Marginal Analysis for Wage Employment Problems." *American Economic Review* 36, no. 1 (Mar.): 63–82.

———. 1946b. "Wage Diversity and Its Theoretical Implications." *Review of Economics and Statistics* (Aug.): 152–159.

———. 1952. "A Range Theory of Wage Differentials." *Industrial and Labor Relations Review* 5, no. 4 (July): 483–500.

———. 1954. *Hiring Practices and Labor Competition.* Research Report Series no. 88. Princeton: Industrial Relations Section, Princeton University.

———. 1958. *As Unions Mature: An Analysis of the Evolution of American Unionism.* Princeton: Princeton University Press.

Lewis, H. Gregg. 1963. *Unionism and Relative Wages in the United States.* Chicago: University of Chicago Press.

———. 1986. *Union Relative Wage Effects.* Chicago: University of Chicago Press.

Machlup, Fritz. 1946. "Marginal Analysis and Empirical Research." *American Economic Review* 36, no. 4, part 1 (Sept.): 519–554.

———. 1967. "Theories of the Firm." *American Economic Review* 57, no. 1 (Mar.): 1–33.

March, James G., and Guje Sevon. 1984. "Behavioral Perspectives on Theories of the Firm." Unpublished paper.

Mathewson, Stanley B. 1931. *Restriction of Output Among Unorganized Workers.* New York: Viking.

Michels, Robert. 1915. *Political Parties: A Sociological Study of the Oligarchical Tendencies of Modern Democracy.* New York: Hearst's International Library.

Millis, Harry A., ed. 1942. *How Collective Bargaining Works.* New York: Twentieth Century Fund.

Millis, Harry A., and Royal E. Montgomery. 1938. *The Economics of Labor.* 3 vols. New York: McGraw-Hill.

Montgomery, David. 1991. "The Limits of Union-Centered History: Responses to Howard Kimeldorf." *Labor History* 32, no. 1 (Winter): 110–116.

Myers, Charles A., and W. Rupert Maclaurin. 1943. *The Movement of Factory Workers.* New York: John Wiley & Sons.

Myers, Charles A., and George P. Shultz. 1951. *The Dynamics of a Labor Market: A Study of the Impact of Employment Changes on Labor Mobility, Job Satisfactions, and Company and Union Policies.* New York: Prentice-Hall.

Northrup, Herbert R., and Harvey A. Young. 1968. "The Causes of Industrial Peace Revisited." *Industrial and Labor Relations Review* 22, no. 1 (Oct.): 31–47.

Palmer, Gladys L. 1954. *Labor Mobility in Six Cities.* New York: Social Science Research Council.

Parnes, Herbert S. 1954. *Research on Labor Mobility: An Appraisal of Research Findings in the United States.* New York: Social Science Research Council.

Reder, Melvin W. 1952. "The Theory of Union Wage Policy." *The Review of Economics and Statistics* 34, no. 1 (Feb.): 34–45.

———. 1955. "The Theory of Occupational Wage Differentials." *American Economic Review* 45, no. 5 (Dec.): 833–852.

———. 1958. "Wage Determination in Theory and Practice," in Neil W.

Chamberlain, Frank C. Pierson and Theresa Wolfson, eds., *A Decade of Industrial Relations Research, 1946–1956*. New York: Harper. pp. 64–97.

Rees, Albert. 1952. "Union Wage Policies," in George W. Brooks, Milton Derber, David A. McCabe and Philip Taft, ed. bd., *Interpreting the Labor Movement*. Champaign: Industrial Relations Research Association. pp. 130–148.

―――. 1975. "Compensating Wage Differentials," In A. J. Skinner and Thomas Wilson, eds., *Essays on Adam Smith*. Oxford: Clarendon. pp. 336–349.

―――. 1979. "Douglas on Wages and the Supply of Labor." *Journal of Political Economy* 87, no. 5, part 1 (Oct.): 915–922.

Rees, Albert, and George P. Shultz. 1970. *Workers and Wages in an Urban Labor Market*. Chicago: University of Chicago Press.

Reynaud, Jean-Daniel, Francois Eyraud, Catherine Paradiese, and Jean Saglio. 1990. *Les systèmes de relations professionnelles: Examen critique d'une théorie*. Paris: Éditions du Centre National de la Recherche Scientifique.

Reynolds, Lloyd G. 1946. "Wage Differentials in Local Labor Markets." *American Economic Review* 36, no. 3 (June): 366–375.

―――. 1951. *The Structure of Labor Markets: Wages and Labor Mobility in Theory and Practice*. New York: Harper & Bros.

―――. 1988. "Labor Economics Then and Now," in Bruce E. Kaufman, ed., *How Labor Markets Work: Reflections on Theory and Practice by John Dunlop, Clark Kerr, Richard Lester, and Lloyd Reynolds*. Lexington, Mass.: Lexington Books. pp. 117–143.

Reynolds, Lloyd G., and Joseph Shister. 1949. *Job Horizons*. New York: Harper.

Robertson, Dennis H. 1923. *The Control of Industry*. London: Nisbet.

Ross, Arthur M. 1948. *Trade Union Wage Policy*. Berkeley: University of California Press.

Ross, Arthur M., and Paul T. Hartman. 1960. *Changing Patterns of Industrial Conflict*. New York: Wiley.

Schumpeter, Joseph A. 1942. *Capitalism, Socialism and Democracy*. New York: Harper & Bros.

Selekman, Benjamin M. 1949. "Varieties of Labor Relations." *Harvard Business Review* 27, no. 2 (Mar.): 175–199.

Shorter, Edward, and Charles Tilly. 1974. *Strikes in France, 1830–1968*. New York: Cambridge University Press.

Shultz, George P., and Arnold P. Weber. 1966. *Strategies for the Displaced Worker*. New York: Harper & Row.

Simons, Henry C. 1948. *Economic Policy for a Free Society*. Chicago: University of Chicago Press.

Slichter, Sumner H. 1919. *The Turnover of Factory Labor*. New York: Appleton.

―――. 1931. *Modern Economic Society*. New York: Henry Holt.

———. 1941. *Union Policies and Industrial Management.* Washington, D.C.: Brookings Institution.

———. 1948. "Are We Becoming a 'Laboristic' State?" *New York Times* (May 16).

———. 1950. "Notes on the Structure of Wages." *Review of Economics and Statistics* 32, no. 1 (Feb.): 80–91.

Slichter, Sumner H., James J. Healy, and E. Robert Livernash. 1960. *The Impact of Collective Bargaining on Management.* Washington, D.C.: Brookings Institution.

Smith, Adam. 1759. *The Theory of Moral Sentiments.* (Indianapolis: Library Classics, 1976.)

———. 1776. *An Inquiry into the Nature and Causes of the Wealth of Nations.* London: W. Straham and T. Cadell.

Solow, Robert M. 1990. *The Labor Market as Social Institution.* Cambridge, Mass.: Basil Blackwell

Stigler, George J. 1947. "Professor Lester and the Marginalists." *American Economic Review* 37, no. 1 (Mar.): 154–157.

Strauss, George, and Peter Feuille. 1981. "Industrial Relations Research in the United States," in Peter B. Doeringer, ed., *Industrial Relations in International Perspective.* London: Macmillan.

Swedberg, Richard, ed. 1991. *Joseph A. Schumpeter: The Economics and Sociology of Capitalism.* Princeton: Princeton University Press.

Taylor, Paul S., and Clark Kerr. 1940. "Documentary History of the Strike of Cotton Pickers in California, 1933" in *Violations of Free Speech and Rights of Labor.* Hearings before a Subcommittee of the Committee on Education and Labor, United States Senate, 76th Congress, 3d Session, Pursuant to S. Res. 266 (74th Congress, Part 54). Washington, D.C.: U.S. Government Printing Office.

Tinbergen, Jan. 1959. "The Theory of the Optimum Regime," in L. H. Klaassen, L. M. Koyck and H. J. Witteveen, eds., *Selected Papers.* Amsterdam: North Holland.

Ulman, Lloyd. 1955. *The Rise of the National Trade Union: The Development and Significance of Its Structure, Governing Institutions, and Economic Policies.* Cambridge, Mass.: Harvard University Press.

———. 1990. "Labor Market Analysis and Concerted Behavior." *Industrial Relations* 29, no. 2 (Spring): 281–299.

Watts, Harold W., and Albert Rees, eds. 1977. *The New Jersey Income-Maintenance Experiment.* New York: Academic Press.

Williamson, Oliver E. 1975. *Markets and Hierarchies: Analysis and Antitrust Implications: A Study in the Economics of Internal Organizations.* New York: Free Press.

Wright, David McCord, ed. 1956. *The Impact of the Union: Eight Economic Theorists Evaluate the Labor Union Movement.* New York: Kelley & Millman.

4

Human Capital: A Review

■ —————————————— ■

Jacob Mincer

The following is, in large part, a review of the contributions of human capital analysis to labor economics. Much of it covers my own research. Fortunately, as the evolution of my research in this field was not atypical, it serves easily as an organizing principle for a review. An emphasis on empirical work and on its connection with theory is another feature of this review. More space is given here to work done after the 1970s than before, partly because the earlier period has already been described in several surveys.[1]

Among the various fields of economics that experienced a great flowering in the second half of the twentieth century, there are few in which the transformation has been as profound as in labor economics. In its major, though not exclusive, concern with labor-management relations, seen in the broader context of sociopolitical institutions, earlier labor economics coexisted rather marginally and uneasily with the mainstream of economic theory. Indeed, in the earlier literature a rejection of price theory as applied to labor services was more in evidence than were attempts to utilize it.

This attitude was, in retrospect, perhaps not surprising. The emphasis on the subject matter of industrial relations is properly interdisciplinary and does have a great deal to do with sociology, politics, and organizational analysis. The abundance of data on a great many aspects of individual characteristics and labor market behavior, the electronic means of processing the massive amount of information, and the econometric methodology all are phenomena of the second half of the century. Before this explosion of information there was little scope for systematic analysis of topics in labor economics, where the facts and even the questions were only dimly discernible.

With the incipient developments at midcentury came a recognition of the differences between industrial relations and labor economics: the former deals with labor-management relations and trains future practitioners (and analysts) mainly in schools of business, while the latter is a branch of economic analysis applied to the study of supply and demand in labor markets. Interestingly, this functional division of labor between industrial relations and labor economics represents less of an intellectual separation today than it did only two decades ago. With economic theory evolving to encompass political economy, including the economic rationale and evolution of institutions, the integration or at least interpenetration of the two branches of labor studies is a wave of the future already in progress.

Returning to the midcentury and before, the tumultuous labor market developments after the upheavals of the Great Depression and the Second World War led to a renewed interest in economic theory as a tool for analyzing labor markets. But there were problems with wielding the tool, aside from the lack of proper data and sophisticated econometric methodologies. Two major misconceptions blunted the potential applicability of economic theory: the assumption of labor homogeneity, which made labor input measurable in time units (man-hours), and the perceived absence of capital markets in agents who produce labor services, that is, in people. The absence of markets in workers obscured the existence of investments in people, hence of the all-important time dimension both in worker and employer decisions, as well as in processes of market equilibria.

These misconceptions could be laid at the door of received classical economics, with its trinity of factors of production: land, labor, and capital. Capital together with land and labor produced goods, but it did not produce or augment land and labor. Ricardo explicitly defined land, and implicitly labor, in terms of its "original and indestructible" characteristics. This implied a "raw," unskilled notion of labor whose homogeneity was not much in dispute.

The concepts of a trinity of productive factors and the implied homogeneity of labor were the basis of the functional, or factor-share, approach to income distribution, dating back to Ricardo. The approach was motivated by an identification of three factors of production with corresponding distinct social classes. The growing attention to personal (or "income size") distribution rather than to functional distribution owes a great deal to the blurring of social class identifications in modern industrial democracies. This shift has also been spurred by the recognition that under present conditions the variance of labor incomes is the dominant component of the aggregate income variance or inequality. By its power to illuminate the distribution of labor incomes,[2] human capital analysis played an important, constructive role in the shift of emphasis from functional to personal income distribution.

To be fair to the classical writers, the heterogeneity of rewards to individual workers did not escape their attention. Their comments can be summed up in two famous principles. The first, Smith's compensatory principle, is conditioned on the strength of competitive forces in the labor market. Under such conditions, labor mobility produces earnings differentials that tend to equalize the "net advantages and disadvantages" of work. The second, Mill and Cairnes's doctrine of "noncompeting groups," in effect proclaims the absence of sufficient labor mobility, which results in real wage differences produced and perpetuated by socially, legally, and culturally imposed and inherited stratifications.

A great deal of labor market research was and continues to be directed toward the assessment of the relative validity of these two principles. One of the compensatory principles suggested by Smith applies to wage differentials due to occupational training. This became the basis for human capital analysis (Mincer 1957 and 1958, Becker 1964). Because it originated from the compensatory principle, human capital theory has been misperceived as asserting "perfectly competitive" labor markets. In fact, however, human capital analysis can be used to detect the existence and strength of barriers to labor mobility. This can be judged by the margin by which the rate of return to human capital investment exceeds the return on alternative investments in competitive markets (Friedman and Kuznets 1945).

The basic merit of human capital theory for labor economics is its ability to handle analytically the heterogeneity (the quality) of labor and the time-bound investment processes that play a major role in creating it. Human capital theory sharpened a previously blunt tool of analysis and produced far-reaching insights. From being a marginal branch of applied economics, labor economics has moved to the forefront of applied fields, where a sophisticated interplay of theory and fact — by no means restricted to human capital topics or approaches — keeps widening our understanding of labor markets.

The contributions of human capital analysis to labor economics are conspicuous in three major areas of study: (1) wage structure and, more generally, the distribution of labor income, (2) labor mobility and related wage and unemployment consequences, and (3) effects of technological changes in labor markets. These are not the only topics that have been illuminated by human capital analysis. Nor is the applicability of human capital analysis restricted to labor economics. Indeed, a major motivation for the modern use of the human capital concept is its role in economic growth.[3] New fields, such as the economics of education, health economics, and demographic economics, have been strongly influenced by human capital theory. Through this link they are often included in the more general field of labor economics.

Another way to explore the natural connection between these fields is to note that the various categories of human capital investments can be described in a life-cycle chronology: resources in child care and child development represent preschool investment.[4] These overlap and are followed by investments in formal school education. Investments in job training and learning, job search and labor mobility, and in work effort occur during the working life, while investments in health and other maintenance activities continue throughout life.[5] The reference to maintenance activities recalls the concept of depreciation, the distinction between gross and net investment which is relevant in human capital as in other capital theory applications.

In the ensuing pages I review the human capital approach and the findings it produced in the three major areas of labor economics I have just listed. As these developments were consecutive both in the labor literature and in my own research, I will present them as evolutions of thought and findings, from the perspective of my own work. This perspective unavoidably omits other approaches and insights within the larger field of labor economics, but it is not idiosyncratic within the human capital "tradition."

The Concept and Fundamentals of Human Capital

The terms *skill*, *labor quality*, and *human capital* are often used interchangeably. Accumulated skill is, indeed, a commonly used definition of human capital. Irving Fisher (1930) defined capital as any asset that gives rise to an income stream. Accumulated human work capacity qualifies as a capital asset in the same sense that physical capital does, even if it cannot be bought and sold (it is, of course, rented), and even though investments in such capital often involve nonmarket activities, such as education.

When wages are viewed as the rental price of a unit of human capital, personal differences in accumulated human capital can account for a great deal of wage heterogeneity. The traditional measurement of labor input in terms of man-hours is clearly inadequate. The shift of focus from homogeneity to labor heterogeneity, and from short-run wage and employment decisions to long-run investment decisions are the major contributions of human capital theory to labor economics.

Human capital analysis extends capital theory to human agents, and it is a major redirection in labor economics and related fields. The concept of human capital is ancient and has been eloquently stated and elucidated by Adam Smith. However, its analytical power becomes implicit in Fisher's definition of capital, and explicit in the rigorous and elegant treatment of Gary Becker (1964). Individual acquisitions of earning power (human capital) are subject to optimization, given costs of and returns on such investments. As returns accrue over long periods, theoretical present values and rates of return become the decision variables. Costs of and gains from these investments are, in large measure, implicit in the wage structure. Responses of individuals to these incentives generate tendencies toward market equilibria both in the distribution of human capital across persons and in the wage distributions. These distributions, in turn, change in response to shifts in demands for and supplies of human capital. Becker's theoretical framework and the methodology of research centering around the rate of return on investments in human capital, has been followed and elaborated in the exploding subsequent literature.

Earlier, my own work (Mincer 1957 and 1958) was an initial attempt to analyze the distribution of labor incomes by a single model of economic choice, in contrast to proliferating sociological models emphasizing "class," biological models emphasizing "ability," and probabilistic models emphasizing "chance." The economic model of occupational choice refers to the choice of the length of training, the cost of which is the postponement of earnings. This direct application of Smith's principle was shown to imply some of the observed patterns of wage differentials, at least in a qualitative fashion. The parametric approach that I later adopted in developing and applying the earnings function (1974) was facilitated by Becker's rate-of-return framework and Ben-Porath's analysis of optimal allocation of investments over time (1967).

In a sense, the distinction between human capital as a factor in economic growth and as a factor in the structure or distribution of labor earnings is a distinction between macro and micro levels. At the micro level, individual investments in human capital produce individual economic growth. The worker's "earnings profile" describes this growth over the working life, and the distribution of earnings is basically seen as a distribution of earnings profiles across workers.

The earnings profile is affected by prior investments in school education.[6] Growth of earnings over the working life is due largely to subsequent labor market investments in formal and informal job training and in labor mobility. These are the forms of human capital investments that are of major concerns to labor economists.

School Education and Earnings

Initially, investment in school education received almost exclusive attention from human capital analysts. While economists since Smith have recognized the importance of education as a type of private and social investment, only in the past few decades have economists undertaken rigorous conceptual and statistical examinations of the evidence on costs, benefits, and rates of return of education. Briefly, the analysis proceeds as follows.

The costs of education borne by the student or student's parents consist not merely of tuition and other school expenditures but also of forgone earnings — the loss of what the student could have earned if he or she had spent the school years in gainful employment. Beyond early schooling, forgone earnings are the largest component (accounting for over one-half) of schooling costs.

Investors in schooling envisage flows of earnings in the labor market that correspond to each schooling level. The discounted difference between the future earnings with and without additional schooling — namely, the present value of the return on the additional investment in schooling — represents the gain or loss on the investment. Gains induce further schooling, and losses discourage it. Of course, the discounted difference between the two future earnings flows (the gain and the loss) depends on the size of the discount rate, or the interest rate at which the individual can borrow, or what he can earn elsewhere on the funds he would invest in education. Unfortunately, individual discount rates are not observable.

An alternative way to represent this decision-making process is to calculate the internal rate of return on the investment — that hypothetical rate of interest which will make the profit equal to zero and, thus, the investment just about worthwhile. Further schooling is encouraged if the internal rate of return on schooling exceeds the rate on alternative investments. This method is more useful, since internal rates of return can be calculated given estimates of costs and of earnings streams.

Comparisons of rates of return on education with rates of return on other investments (say, in business or financial capital) can explain flows into the respective fields. They can also indicate the desirability of existing allocations or of changes in relative allocations of investments from society's point of view — if estimates of social costs and social returns can be formed.

It is understood, of course, that relevant concepts of costs and benefits are real — that is, not restricted to pecuniary terms. Education itself may be desirable for its own sake, and it may enhance future enjoyment of life, apart from the monetary gain. Since people differ in these attitudes and perceptions, different monetary gains (or losses) for different individuals may correspond to the same real rate of return.

More generally, variation in observed individual monetary returns on educational investments is partly due to individual differences not only in nonpecuniary aspects of education (consumption components) but also in efficiency in absorbing education, and to individual differences in discount rates. These in turn result from differences in preferences between the present and the future and from differential access to financing of such investments.

But why do employers pay higher wages to the more educated workers, on average? Evidently the marginal value productivity of the better educated worker is seen and experienced as higher than that of the less educated worker. An increased supply of educated workers reduces the marginal value product, while increased wage differentials induce a greater supply. Hence, in a competitive equilibrium, relative supplies are stabilized at levels at which the wage differential translates into rates of return comparable to those on alternative human or nonhuman investments. Increases in demand favoring more educated workers raise the rate of return on schooling, inducing growth of enrollment until the increased return has been eliminated by the increased supply of more educated workers.

Initially, analyses of effects of education on earnings were carried out by estimating direct and forgone costs of a given increment of schooling and discounting the differentials between earnings profiles of workers with higher and lower levels of schooling. These procedures, which utilized data on annual earnings, produced a variety of estimates. Most estimates showed rates of return comparable to rates on business investments, though they were higher at lower levels of schooling. The rates were permanently higher prior to World War II; they declined temporarily in the 1970s (Freeman 1976) and rose again in the 1980s (Murphy and Welch 1989).

The calculations that are available do not include nonpecuniary or consumption components of costs or returns. To the extent that these are positive and important in the benefits of schooling, the rates are underestimated, though the pattern of their historical changes need not be affected. Distinctions are also made between private and social rates. In calculating private rates, costs and returns to students and their families are computed from after-tax data, and schooling costs do not include public financing of schools. In contrast, the calculation of social costs is based on before-tax earnings and the costs of the relevant school system (per student) regardless of the source of financing. The difficulty in calculating true social rates of return rests with the problem of measuring externalities. To the extent that the gain to society exceeds the sum of gains to students, social returns are underestimated. A public policy assumption dear to educators is that such educational externalities are substantial and positive. This is an important, if almost unverifiable, economic justification of public support for education, though it is not an explanation of the public ownership of schools.

Positive differences in wage levels associated with differences in schooling, or in occupations that differ in levels of required schooling, are the returns on investments in education. Their size depends on the costs of investment and on its profitability. Returns change with changes in costs and in demands for education. However, neither the skill differentials in wages nor level of wages corresponding to a given educational or occupational level, are fixed over the working life.

An analysis of wage changes over the worker's life — the "wage profile" — is required for a more complete understanding of skill differentials as they vary by education and by age.

Earnings Profiles, Earnings Functions, and Wage Distributions

Investments in human capital do not terminate with the completion of schooling: they continue at a diminishing rate between entry in the labor market and retirement. This sequence is represented as an optimal allocation of human capital investments over the life cycle, according to the theoretical analyses pioneered by Becker (1967) and by Ben-Porath (1967). It is the diminishing sequence of investments that gives rise to the typical growth pattern of the wage profile: wages rise at a decelerating pace, reaching a peak or a plateau in about the third decade of working life. Of course the rate of growth, that is the slope of the wage profile, differs among individuals. Growth is steeper the larger the volume of investment. It was understood that the major categories for these postschool investments were job training or learning, and labor mobility. But while data on costs and returns on investments in schooling permitted a direct empirical analysis of the economics of education, the virtual absence of job training data left it a latent, background variable that generated the shapes of earnings profiles as returns on investments in the labor market.

As usual, the absence of direct information led to a proliferation of theories. A common interpretation of the earnings profile is that it is an intrinsic age phenomenon: initial productivity growth of young workers corresponds to inherent biological and psychological maturation, while later stability and decline are due first to stable then to declining physical and intellectual vigor. In the perspective of human capital theory this view is incomplete, as it explains the earnings profile solely by a life-cycle pattern of human capital depreciation, seen as positive (appreciation) in early working life, absent in middle life, and negative in later years. There is evidence that this inherent age-depreciation factor affects earnings only to a minor degree, except during the teen years and in the near- or postretirement years. In data in which age and length of work experience are statistically separable, levels and shapes of earnings curves are mainly a function of experience rather than age (Mincer 1974). In addition, earnings profiles differ by occupation, sex, and other characteristics in systematic ways that cannot be attributed to aging.

One may also interpret the shape of the earnings profile as a learning curve, or a reflection of the growth of skills with age and experience known as "learning by doing." This view is not at all inconsistent with the human capital investment interpretation, so long as opportunities for learning are not costless. If more learning, and hence a more steeply rising wage, is available in some jobs as compared with others, all qualified workers would gravitate to such jobs if learning were thought to be costless. In consequence, entry-level wages in such jobs would be reduced relative to entry wages elsewhere for workers of the same quality, thereby creating opportunity investment costs in moving to such jobs. Thus it is not merely training on the job (formal or informal) but also the processes of occupational choice that give rise to investments in human capital on the job.

The human capital earnings function is an algebraic expression and econometric specification of the earnings profile (Mincer 1974). Its derivation is well known and will not be repeated here. In it, postschool investments are latent variables indexed by time spent working, or work experience (x). The function relates accumulated human capital by schooling (s) and postschooling investments to earnings at each working age. Under plausible conditions, the coefficients of the human capital variable (at s and x) contain rates of return on these investments, which can be estimated.[7]

In more recent formulations, the experience variable is segmented to register intervals of labor force participation and nonparticipation (Mincer and Polachek 1974, Mincer and Ofek 1982), or to take account of interfirm labor mobility (Mincer and Jovanovic 1981). In the latter case, a term T (firm tenure) is added following the experience term (x) in the function. Its coefficients may gauge workers' returns on firm-specific investments (see Human Capital and Labor Mobility later in this chapter).

In Becker's theoretical treatment, the personal income (wage) distribution is determined by individual *abilities* or marginal efficiencies of investment in human capital and *opportunities* that depend on marginal costs of investment (Becker 1967, 1975). The former determine individual demands, the latter individual supply curves. At any given time, the intersections of individual demand and supply curves determine the interpersonal distribution of earnings and the distribution of marginal rates of return on investments in human capital.

This approach shows not only how the distribution of human capital relates to earnings, but also how the distribution of human capital across persons is determined. Several important positive and normative implications follow from the analysis. In principle, it is possible to detect whether inequality of opportunity or ability dominates the observed inequality in wages. The former would produce a downward sloping scatter of intersections, that is, marginal rates of return would tend to be lower for larger investors in human capital. The opposite would occur if inequalities in ability dominated. If inequalities in opportunities and abilities were equally important, there would be no correlation between rates of return and volumes of human capital investment.

The same lack of correlation would hold in the case of equality of opportunity, which is defined by a single, common, horizontal supply curve. Note, incidentally, that equality of opportunity does not imply equality of wages, so long as individual abilities (demand curves) differ. Note also that an optimal interpersonal distribution of wages, in the sense of maximal total output, requires equality of marginal rates of return on investments across persons.[8] In a policy sense, optimization is achieved by equalization of opportunities and not by equalization of incomes (here, wages).

Despite its "reduced form" nature, the earnings function has remained robust as a working tool and an interpretation in the voluminous international research literature.[9] The form of the earnings function is of interest both for theoretical and econometric reasons. It is subject to choice in two respects. First, it can be fitted either to dollar earnings or to the natural logarithms of earnings. In part, this choice depends on whether the focus of interest is on absolute or relative wage differentials. If dollar earnings are analyzed, investment variables (schooling and experience) must also be expressed in dollar cost values. If investments are recorded in units of time — years of schooling and years of experience, clearly a more convenient formulation — the dependent variable, earnings, must be expressed in logarithms. Second, the form of the experience term (working age), x, in the function depends on the assumed time pattern of postschool investments. There is no guidance from theory here, except that the successive installments of investment must decline after full-time entry into continuous employment. A given form of the investment time profile implies a particular form of the earnings profile. To take the two simplest forms, a linear investment decline implies a parabolic experience function, while an exponential decline of investments gives rise to a Gompertz function. It should be clear that neither the semilog form of the function nor the quadratic form of the experience term are inherent in the human capital earnings function. Their general use is simply a matter of convenience and consistency, bolstered by the finding that the statistical fit these forms exhibit is not inferior to alternative forms.[10]

Prior to the appearance of the earnings function, rates of return on education were calculated by equating the present values of the earnings profiles for homogeneous, or otherwise statistically "standardized" workers who differed in education. This procedure assumed that both the level of the earnings profile and its shape were determined by education. The assumption is incorrect if job training (or, more generally, postschool investment) is not rigidly tied to schooling, and if the rate of return on training differs from the rate of return on schooling. The regression procedure for the earnings function relaxes these assumptions and separates the estimates of rates of return on schooling from rates of return on other investments. The coefficients of the schooling variables estimate the rate of return on schooling without further correction, if opportunity costs are the only costs of schooling or if direct costs (tuition) roughly equal student earnings and subsidies. Otherwise, the length of schooling must be corrected by a multiplicative factor $(1 + k)$, where k is the ratio of direct (tuition) costs minus student earnings and subsidies to forgone earnings.

Another distinction that was only briefly discussed in my book (Mincer 1974) is that between earnings and wage rates. Which of these does human capital analysis illuminate most directly? Wage rates represent a payoff to human capital per unit of time. However, earnings are a product of wage rates and time spent in employment (hours per week, weeks per year). Employment periods (hours of work) are outcomes of workers' labor supply and of demand preferences of employers, both being related to wage rates and human capital investments. Still, the connection is not rigid, so that the earnings function is best handled as a wage function, while earnings analyses require an additional analysis of the effects of human capital on labor supply and labor demand. These effects are positive for the following reasons. First, an increase in human capital increases the wage rate, but it need not increase wealth, or not nearly as much, if the rate of return is not exorbitantly high (relative to returns on alternative investments); with no effect or only a minor wealth effect, increased wages induce an increased labor supply as leisure becomes more costly. Second, if human capital investments on the job are shared by employers and workers, both prefer stable employment to turnover. As a result, full-time schedules and continuity of work are typical for skilled workers. Thus both employment and wage rates increase with levels of human capital, and rates of return appear to be somewhat larger in earnings than in wage rates.

Job Training as Observable

A number of alternative theories attempt to explain the upward slopes of wage profiles as devices for economizing on costs of supervision (Becker and Stigler 1974, Lazear 1979), on costs of turnover (Salop and Salop, 1976), and as a consequence of job sorting or job matching for new hires (Jovanovic 1979). These theories and human capital theory are not mutually exclusive; the question is rather one of empirical relevance, validity, and relative importance. As untested hypotheses, they are certainly not more compelling than the job training hypothesis. Fortunately, some progress has been made in directly testing the human capital (job training) hypothesis as information on the incidence of job training and wage consequences has grown in the past decade.

As predicted by investment theory, a positive relation between measured (volumes of) training and slopes of wage profiles was observed by Duncan and Hoffman (1978), Parsons (1986), Lillard and

Tan (1986), Lynch (1988), Gronau (1982), Barron and Lowenstein (1989), and Brown (1989). The effects are found in a variety of micro-data sets (CPS, NLS, PSID, and EOPP). The effects show up both in cross sections, where prior job training corresponds to a subsequently higher wage level, and in time series, where faster wage growth is observed paralleling the incidence and duration of training for individual workers.

In my own study of PSID data, a year with training increased wage growth by an average of 4 to 5 percent (Mincer 1987). The effect of training on wage growth is greater at younger ages (an average of 9 to 10 percent in the first dozen years of working life, a bit over 3 percent subsequently); this difference reflects the greater intensity of training, measured in hours per week, among younger workers. The decline of job training intensity with age, predicted by the theory, is indeed responsible for the decelerating pattern of wage growth.

The same conclusion is reached in a study by H. Rosen (1982). Using the 1976 PSID data, Rosen divided the sample into two groups: workers who had received training during the year and those who had not. Cross-sectional wage profiles were steep and concave in the first group and flat in the second. This suggests, once again, the importance of training and learning in creating the typical shapes of wage profiles.

In panels covering two decades for PSID males I found that workers' training tends to continue as they move from one firm to another. Consequently, trainees tend to have steeper wage trajectories over their working lives, and not merely within a particular firm. Over the observed two decades, wages of all workers increased an average of 62 percent, a part of which (9 percent) was due to mobility.[11]

Another observation of interest is the positive correlation between school education and training. One interpretation of this correlation is persistence of human capital investment. The individual factors of ability and opportunity that induce some persons to invest more in schooling also induce them to continue with larger investments while in the labor market (for example, in job training). An additional, quite plausible interpretation is that training is complementary with education, that better educated workers are more efficient in learning on the job, as they were at school. An implication of this conclusion is that training cannot be viewed simply as an alternative to schooling. Without appropriate schooling the training process is inefficient — the existence of and complaints about remedial education on the job offers a case in point.

The availability of direct information on job training in recent microdata sets makes it feasible to attempt an estimation of national magnitudes of investment in job training, as well as to calculate the profitability in terms of rates of return. Empirically grounded direct estimates are clearly preferable to estimates obtained in a highly indirect procedure I utilized 30 years ago (Mincer 1962). In my new attempt (Mincer 1991d), costs of job training in the economy were estimated for 1976 and 1987 using three entirely different methods:

1. In the "direct" method, time (hours) spent in training per year is valued at wage rates prior to training, or at wage rates of comparable nontrainees.
2. A second direct method uses information on costs of formal training programs and on time spent in these programs and in all training — including informal training, which is the bulk.
3. The third method is an "indirect" one, using wage profiles as in the old paper (Mincer 1962), but with wage gains due to mobility netted out.

The two direct estimates are rather close and add up to over one-half of the total costs of schooling. The third, indirect estimate exceeds the other two by about one-third. This suggests that human capital investments can account for about 75 percent of the growth of the (cross-sectional) wage profiles, leaving a minor role to other, not mutually exclusive explanations.

Another objective of this study was to estimate profitabilities of job training. With estimates of costs of training and associated wage growth over the duration of training, rates of return can be computed. Since estimates of costs and returns differ in the several available data sets, a range of estimates was used. This range of estimates seems to exceed the magnitude of rates of return usually observed for schooling investments. Given the data on workers' tenure at a firm, it also appears that investment in training remains profitable for firms, even in the face of average worker mobility.

The estimated rates of return may suggest underinvestment in training relative to that in schooling. However, the lower rates of return on schooling may in part represent a compensation for lifetime consumption benefits of education. Other qualifications, such as the trade-off between training and mobility, need to be investigated before one can conclude that there is a significant underinvestment in training in the United States. On the other hand, the complementarity between schooling and training may well imply such a potential underinvestment in training. If school quality in the United States has indeed become deficient at least at the precollege level, as the clamor for reform asserts, improvements in the quality of schooling could increase the profitability and the utilization of training.

Human Capital and Labor Mobility

Although there was no lack of valiant effort in the past, research in labor mobility, a major topic in labor economics, was hampered by the paucity of longitudinal data. As a result, the early literature contained mixed, ambiguous findings (Parnes 1970). Wage gains as well as losses appeared to be associated with mobility, and even where gains were likely, immobility appeared to persist. Economic rationality did not seem to fit mobility behavior. The apparent ambiguity in these findings is reconcilable in the human capital approach: as a response to perceived gains in wages, mobility promotes individual wage growth, but to the extent that on-the-job investments contain elements of specificity, wage growth is associated with attachment to the firm rather than with mobility.

Geographic migration

Geographic migrations of labor are an important aspect of labor market behavior that can be analyzed as an investment in human capital. A pioneering analysis of this sort was provided by Sjaastad (1962), and followed by a growing literature (Greenwood 1975, Polachek and Horvath 1977, Da Vanzo 1983).

The workers' migration decisions are a prototypical example of self-investment decisions. The worker considers two (or more) future streams of income depending on location, one of which is his current location. Direct costs of moving and forgone earnings are included (with a negative sign) in the income stream at the new location to which he might move. Movement takes place if the present value of the income stream at the destination exceeds that at the origin.[12] An equivalent rule: workers decide to move if the internal rate of return on the costs of migration exceeds the highest rate on alternative investments (in financial or other human capital).

As with human capital in general, this formulation emphasizes the workers' orientation toward the future in their decisions, an important correction of past thinking in which only current wage differentials were used as incentives for migration. In part, this change was forced on the older labor analysts by the lack of appropriate data.

The investment formulation is rich in empirical implications for migrant selectivity and for the regional wage structure. Thus, younger people are more likely to migrate because their gains are increased by the longer expected payoff period. Migrants are attracted to areas with greatest expected earnings and employment opportunities. High discount rates or high financing costs discourage migration, one reason the more skilled and better educated workers are more likely to migrate: the fact that they previously invested in education and skills training suggests that their discount rates are lower — that is, that they take or can afford to take the long view. For the same reason, and because of the national scope of markets for skilled and educated workers, they tend to invest more in information about distant markets. This is evidenced by a greater skill and education selectivity of migrants in longer distance migration, as well as in the much less frequent return migration of the more skilled compared with less skilled migrants (Da Vanzo 1983).

When the probability of gains from migration is included in the calculation of returns, it is clear why migration waxes and wanes with the business cycle. The expected gains decline in recessions while costs remain largely the same.[13]

Migration affects the regional wage structure. The tendency to narrow wage differentials is implicit in the larger stream of migration to higher income areas. But because of migration costs, gains must remain positive to yield a rate of return no less than normal. In other words, unless differential economic growth reranks the regional wage structure, migration does not eliminate wage differentials. Indeed, under plausible conditions, Becker (1975) has shown that migration flows tend to narrow but not eliminate relative (percentage) wage differentials, while they actually widen the dollar differentials among regional wage levels.

Interfirm labor mobility

Geographic migrations — moves across labor markets — are a relatively small part (perhaps one-fourth) of total labor mobility. Most labor mobility takes place within local markets, usually without necessitating a residential move. Although costs of local mobility are lower than those of geographic mobility, they are not zero. Costs of job search are not negligible, and the potential loss of returns on investments in the present firm can be significant. While investment in information or job search is legitimately an application of human capital investment theory (Stigler 1962), it is now a vast field in economics. I will focus, therefore, on implications of firm-specific human capital investments for labor mobility or labor turnover.

A connection between on-the-job human capital investments and labor mobility or turnover was suggested in Becker's landmark analysis (1964). In it, a distinction is made between general and firm-specific skills acquired in training on the job. Training is general if the resulting increase in productivity is equally valuable in a number of firms which employ similar labor. It is (partly) specific if the increased skill is more effective, as it increases productivity in the firm in which training was acquired more than elsewhere. The implication of this distinction is that in principle, general training, being perfectly transferable, does not inhibit labor mobility.[14] As a result the training investment is financed by workers and not by employers: the latter are not likely to invest, as they risk a capital loss when workers leave. In the specific capital case, however, workers are reluctant to leave, because their skills acquired by training would be of less value elsewhere. In this case, workers would be reluctant to invest in the training themselves because of the risk of layoff, which would inflict a capital loss on them. A solution that reduces the risk of layoffs for workers and of quitting for employers is for both parties to share in the costs of training investments when the acquired skills are firm-specific.

There are problems in identifying empirical counterparts to the concepts of general and specific training, and in identifying whether and how much of costs are borne by workers and by employers. As a result it is more meaningful to think of training processes as mixed in their degree of transferability, rather than in dichotomous terms.

Although one can only observe worker mobility and, only recently, training experience, the theory can be adapted for empirical purposes if one is willing to add a simplifying, rather plausible assumption (Mincer and Jovanovic 1981). The working assumption is that training acquired in firms (as distinguished from classrooms outside the firm) necessarily contains some elements of firm specificity. This is because opportunities for training are likely to exist mainly in firms in which training processes are closely related to and integrated with their production processes. One may, therefore, infer that workers who receive more training are likely to receive more of both components of training (general and specific), without assuming a fixed ratio between the two. Consequently, the scale of training is on average an indicator of the amount of specific training, and so predictions of mobility behavior can be made, within limits, from information on the scale or frequency of training.

Empirical panel data (Mincer 1987, Lillard and Tan 1986, Lynch 1988) confirm that training in the firm reduces subsequent mobility. This is observable in the reduction of the probability of separation at given levels of tenure when workers with more (longer or more intense) training are compared with workers with less training. Equivalently, completed tenure in the firm is longer for the more substantially trained. Moreover, the inhibiting effect of training shows up both in quits and in layoffs, consistent with the theoretical proposition that investment costs of training which to some degree is specific are shared by workers and employers.

The turnover effects of training are observed net of effects of other factors, such as working age (experience), marital status, education, and union status, all of which also affect the frequency of firm separations. As might be expected, union status reduces quitting but not layoffs. Education reduces turnover partly because it is associated with more training, as already explained, but partly because of the greater intensity and efficiency of the search behavior of educated workers and of employers who hire them. Age (experience) patterns show a decline in mobility, as might be expected if costs of mobility increase with age. But the fact, theoretical and observed, that volumes of training decline over age would predict the opposite age pattern for mobility. The theoretical resolution of this puzzle lies in the optimization of training, given that some mobility, not directly connected with training, also tends to diminish with age. Thus, the high turnover of young workers is a function of a search or matching process whereby they ultimately settle in more fitting and hence longer lasting jobs, while at older ages higher family opportunity costs and greater employer reluctance to hire older workers reduce mobility further. Of consequence for training is an expected (and observed) lengthening of the duration of tenure as age advances. Note now that the payoff period (horizon) for general (transferable) investments in training is the remaining working life, while for firm-specific training it is the expected length of tenure in the firm. This implies a rate of investment in general training that declines with age, but an increasingly specific component of training over the working life. Declining turnover with age is thus reinforced.

Training, Turnover, and Unemployment

In addition to higher wages, a major benefit of education is its associated lower risk of unemployment. To understand this relation I analyzed several aspects of unemployment that combine to produce the usually reported unemployment rates (Mincer 1991a). These aspects or components of unemployment are: incidence, that is, the probability of experiencing unemployment (say, during the year) $P(u)$; and duration of the unemployment experience (measured in fractions of the year) $d(u)$. The unemployment rate (u) is the product of the two. In the available microdata sets (PSID, NLS), it appears that the sizable reduction in incidence at higher education levels is far more important than the reduced duration of unemployment in creating the educational differentials in unemployment rates.[15]

Incidence is a product of the probability of separation (turnover) and the probability of unemployment when separated: $P(u) = P(s) \cdot P(u/s)$. The empirical analysis of samples of PSID males shows that differences in turnover account for at least a half of the differences in the incidence of unemployment. The differences in turnover arise, in part, from the greater prevalence of training among the more educated workers. As mentioned before, this observed positive correlation is likely to reflect a complementarity between prior education and subsequent training that in turn shows up both in steeper wage profiles of the more educated and in their less frequent job turnover.

The lower incidence of unemployment of educated workers is due not only to their less frequent job changes, but also to a less frequent encountering of unemployment when they change jobs. Greater acquisition of information, more efficient searches — especially on the job — and a more intensive search by employers to fill the more costly skilled vacancies are the likely reasons for this. Greater efficiency in searching off-the-job, as well, appears to be responsible for the somewhat shorter duration of spells of unemployment experienced by more educated workers.

Just as differential unemployment by education is, in large part, attributable to less turnover at higher levels of education, the decline of unemployment with advancing age (experience) is explained by declining turnover rates over the working life. As described before, the increased specialization and specificity in job progressions as well as increasing costs of and declining returns on moving are responsible for the declining quit rate over the working life. Smaller wage gains in moving (Mincer 1986) and longer duration of unemployment for older workers reflect in part losses due to the specificity of the old job (Topel 1990) and the difficulties of finding a new one. However, the decline in the incidence of unemployment dominates the increase in the duration of unemployment for most of the working life. Consequently, the unemployment rates decline as workers age (Leighton and Mincer 1982).

The family context for women in the labor market results in sporadic intervals of nonparticipation — that is, of labor force withdrawals and reentries. This kind of turnover may be termed inter–labor force mobility, in contrast to job change while in the labor force, or intra–labor force mobility. Because of the former, the total labor turnover for women exceeds turnover for men, although the difference has declined in recent years.

Among the major reasons for women's inter–labor force mobility are family demands involving childbearing and child care, major changes in family income, and geographic migration requiring often prolonged family readjustments. Even when these contingencies do not result in women withdrawing from the labor force, they often involve unemployment and less than optimal job changes. This is a frequent occurrence in migration (Mincer 1978).

Women's shorter job tenure and exogenous, family-motivated turnover result in fewer incentives to provide or to acquire on-the-job training. However, women who invest in school education have incentives to maximize the payoff period, that is, to minimize the number and duration of interruptions in market work. Correspondingly, they also acquire somewhat more job training than the less educated women. The human capital implications are visible in the NLS samples of young and mature women covering a period of 16 years (Mincer 1991c). Women receive much less employer-provided job training than men. Most of it is off the job. Consequently, their intra–labor force turnover is not very sensitive to training. However, because of the greater continuity of work exhibited by the more educated women, turnover and therefore unemployment declines at higher levels of education almost as steeply as unemployment does for men.

Consistent with this analysis, acceleration in education and in labor force continuity of women workers since the late 1970s has reduced the sex differential in unemployment in recent years.

Economic Growth, Technology, and the Demand for Human Capital

At any given time individual demands for human capital investments are determined by individual abilities (marginal efficiencies of investments) and individual supplies by marginal costs of investments, which also differ among people. Together these sets of demand and supply curves determine the distribution of human capital and rates of return on it (Becker 1975). Over historical time (as distinguished from aging) both the demand curves and the supply curves shift as human capital productivities and costs of investments in human capital change. In particular, the changing content and techniques of learning, public policies, and the growth of family incomes affect the supplies (marginal costs) of human capital.[16] On the demand side, industry demands for skilled, educated labor increases either because demand for its services and products increases or because its productivity grows as a result of physical capital accumulation or technological change. This is not to deny the major role of human capital as a source or *cause* of economic growth. It is the demand for human capital as an *effect* of growth that is of primary interest to labor economists.

When human capital is viewed as a factor of production, in addition to physical capital and "raw" or unskilled labor, a hypothesis of complementarity between physical and human capital produces growth of demand for human capital as a consequence of physical capital accumulation (Griliches 1969). Physical capital accumulation raises the marginal product of human capital more than that of raw labor, producing wage (profitability) incentives for the conversion of labor into human capital by means of education and training.

The accumulation of physical capital is not exogenous, however. Indeed, the demand for both physical and human capital responds to opportunities for profit that emerge from cost-reducing and product-innovating changes in technology, to the extent that they are capital- rather than labor-using changes.

Secular growth of demand for human capital, resulting from skill-biased technological change (Nelson and Phelps 1966) or from physical-human capital complementarities, offers a plausible answer to the apparent puzzle of observed small secular changes (if any) in rates of return on education in the face of continuous upward trends in education. Except for the agricultural context (Griliches, Welch, Schultz) these hypotheses were not subjected to empirical verification until quite recently.

Thanks to the availability of rich microdata sets and some indexes of technological change *at the sectoral level*, it has become possible to test the hypothesis that the pace of technology affects the demand for human capital, using U.S. data covering the past two or three decades.

Using a variety of microdata sets, Lillard and Tan (1986) found a greater incidence of training in industries whose pace of productivity growth was faster. Bartel and Lichtenberg (1987) report that, based on census data, relatively more educated workers were employed in those manufacturing industries (in 1960, 1970, and 1980) where capital equipment was newer and research and development (R & D) expenditures were more intensive.

Extending the census data to all broadly defined industries (18 sectors), Gill (1989) observed greater utilization of educated workers and steeper wage profiles in sectors with more rapid decade-long productivity growth.

I tested the hypothesis that recent technological change is biased toward human capital (Mincer 1989). I looked at the same 18 U.S. industrial sectors, using annual PSID data on the male labor force in 1968 through 1987, and Jorgenson-Fraumeni productivity growth (PG) indexes for the period 1960 through 1985.[17] The use of decade-long averages for the intersectoral cross sections of these indexes reduces much of the year-to-year error typical of such residuals.

Consistent with the skill-bias hypothesis, the PSID data show that a more rapid pace of technological change in a sector (indexed by PG) generates a greater demand for education and training of the sectoral work force:

1. The share of educated workers in the sector is greater concurrently, without much of an initial effect on training. In the long run, the use of training increases.
2. Relative wages are higher for more educated workers within sectors with rapid productivity growth concurrently.
3. Mobility of educated and, especially, young workers into these sectors is observable and appears to erode much of the educational wage gains over the course of a decade.
4. Wage profiles are steeper in progressive sectors as profitability of training and of experience is greater.
5. Separation rates increase slightly in the short run. They decline in the long run, presumably because training intensifies.
6. The incidence of unemployment and unemployment rates are unaffected in the short run, but decline rather soon.

All these findings can be viewed as responses of firms and workers to skill-biased technological change. This is true of the utilization and wage effects and, with an additional assumption, of the turnover and unemployment effects. That additional assumption is a degree of firm specificity in training investments necessitated by changing technology, or more precisely, significant employer investments in such training.

Attempts to explore effects of capital-skill complementarity, given the rate of productivity growth, yielded some positive and some ambiguous results. Growth of capital intensity was measured by the growth of the sectoral capital-labor ratio. It showed positive effects on utilization of educated labor, but effects on training and on wages were not visible. Effects on turnover and unemployment were negative. It is, in any case, problematic whether the capital-skill complementarity reflects the technological bias or not, as new capital is likely to embody new technology.

In a previous study (Mincer and Higuchi 1988) it was shown that differences between the United States and Japan in rates of technological change (measured by sectoral and national Jorgenson-type total productivity indexes) can explain why wage structures and turnover rates differ across sectors and between the two countries. The remarkably low turnover rate in Japan viewed as "lifetime employment" is frequently described as a reflection of a culture that puts great emphasis on group loyalty. Yet in the same culture, turnover rates were a great deal higher prior to the Second World War. The difference appears to be an effect of the remarkably rapid technological progress in Japan since 1950. This technological catch-up required sizable investments in human capital in schools and in enterprises. The phenomenal growth of educational attainment in Japan in recent decades is well known. The even more intense effort to adapt, train, and retrain workers for continuous rapid technological changes is not directly visible in available data. However, effects of training on wage growth and turnover are visible in the negative relationship between the two within industrial sectors observed in Japan and in the United States. In both countries, industries with more rapid productivity growth had both steeper individual wage profiles and lower turnover rates. Indeed, using the parameters of those relations, a rate of productivity growth in Japan that was four times that in the United States in the period from 1960 to 1980 predicted rather well the over threefold steeper wage profiles and the less than one-third frequency of firm separations in Japan. Somewhat weaker but quite pronounced differences of the same sort were observed in a comparison of American and Japanese plants in the United States, that is, in the same cultural environment. Here the much larger investments in training and screening of workers in the Japanese plants was directly observable.

Positive associations between the pace of technological change in a sector and indexes of relative demand for human capital do not, by themselves, establish a causal relationship nor the direction of causality, as articulated in the hypothesis of skill-biased technology. One should note also that the sectoral effects are relative to other sectors, and do not imply similar aggregate effects. Thus higher wages or lower unemployment in progressive sectors are observed relative to wages and unemployment in lagging sectors, and the latter may dominate the aggregate. But this is surely not the sense in which "the specter of technological unemployment" has usually been perceived or analyzed. Indeed, with the growth of the "open" economy, that is, of world trade, these perceptions are changing, and the specter of technological unemployment is now more likely to be seen to threaten technologically lagging rather than leading sectors or countries. To resolve the reasonable doubts that may attach to the interpretation based on cross sections, a companion time-series analysis was undertaken as the next step.

The time-series analysis of annual aggregates over a recent 25-year period is provided in my paper "Human Capital, Technology, and the Wage Structure" (Mincer 1991b). This study focuses on rather dramatic changes in wage differentials by education and by experience during the period from 1963 through 1987. Both sets of differentials are, in part, indicators of the payoffs for skill, or of rates of return on human capital investments. Fluctuations in them are the outcome of changes in relative supplies of educated and experienced workers, and relative demands for them. Both relative supply and relative demand variables are brought to bear in equations which "explain" the series of wage differentials. The findings substantially confirm the cross-sectional result:

1. The year-to-year educational wage differentials (between college and high school) are very closely tracked by relative supplies of graduates in (roughly) their first decade of work experience, and by changes in relative demand for more educated workers. The latter is indexed by research and development expenditures per employee (RDE), as well as by relative trends in service employment (RSG). Of these, RDE accounts for most of the explanatory power.

2. With the decline of average productivity growth and the near cessation of average real wage growth, the skill-biased changes in demand take the form of increases in demand for workers with post-secondary education and decreases in demand for workers at lower education levels. The decline in demand for workers at lower educational levels is attributed by Murphy and Welch (1989) to the growth of world trade: imports and exports in U.S. trade more than doubled as a percentage of GNP between 1960 and 1990. That this led to a reduction in wages of less skilled males is a plausible proposition. It is consistent with my regression findings in which both the net balance of merchandise trade (as percent of GNP) and productivity growth indexes are substituted for the research and development variable, although the explanatory power is weaker here. However, when this decline in international competitiveness is attributed to difficulties that the less skilled workers have in handling the newer information technologies, these findings may also reflect the growing skill bias of new technologies. An important question, outside of the present analysis, is to what extent these disadvantages on the supply side are due to inadequate schooling and to deteriorated family life in the United States.

3. Changes in age distributions (cohort effects) account, in part, for

the observed steepening of experience profiles of wages. They do not account for the steepening of the high school profile in the 1980s or for the stabilization of the slope of the college profile between the 1970s and 1980s. A more complete explanation for the steepened profiles is provided by additional variables that reflect the growing profitability of human capital.

4. Capital-skill complementarity appears to be at work alongside skill-biased technology when expenditures on new equipment per worker represent the relevant capital intensity. It is not clear, however, whether the skill bias of new equipment represents anything different than the effect of new technology.

The importance of skill-biased technological change in affecting relative demands for human capital is invoked in an indirect manner in a number of recent micro-level studies that attempt to shed light on the dramatic changes in the U.S. wage structure in the past two decades.[18] In these studies skill-biased technology is suggested as a hypothesis consistent with a variety of observed changes at the industry or plant level. However, no study utilizes explicit indicators of technological change, with the exception of a micro-level study by Krueger of the wage effects of growth of computer use in the 1980s (Krueger 1991).

A natural corollary of the dramatic changes in the skill structure of wages in the 1970s and 1980s is the substantial growth in wage (and income) inequality, especially in the latter period. The widening inequality is viewed by some—perhaps many—observers as an ominous reflection of a deteriorating economy and society. It has stimulated research by economists and sociologists.

The sense in which changes in wage inequality are a corollary of changes in skill differentials in wages (by education and age) is obvious: when these differentials change, total inequality changes in the same direction, unless within-group differences move in an opposite fashion. This proviso is intuitively implausible, yet it did emerge in the 1970s, as some observers report[19]: residual (within education and age groups) inequality did not narrow, when educational differentials shrank. Since residual inequality is the larger part of total inequality,[20] resolutions of puzzles about changes in residual inequality are a matter of some importance in the developing research effort.

A rather clear interpretation of the components of wage inequality between *and* within groups is provided by the human capital model. This has not as yet been exploited in the current literature, despite some precedents: in Chiswick and Mincer (1972) the model was used to document and analyze the long-run stability in wage inequality between 1948 and 1970; Plotnick (1982) extended the analyses to

1977, and so did Dooley and Gottschalk (1984). However, rates of returns on human capital investments were not explicitly used in these analyses, partly because they were not available, and the resulting interpretations may well be insecure. With the superior data currently available, updated analyses are in progress.

Human Capital Supply Responses to Growth in Demand

A question of great interest is whether the growth in inequality, now seen over more than a decade, can be expected to reverse itself, and if so, how fast. To the extent that changes in the age distribution are exogenous and the "baby boom" that steepened the wage profile was followed by a "baby bust," a flattening of age profiles might have been expected, and this in turn would have contributed to a reduction in inequality. But this did not happen, because the age profile of wages is affected not only by demographic change but also by skill premiums, which rose in the 1980s. The major question, therefore, is whether the supply of human capital can be expected to grow sufficiently to eventually reduce the rates of return to a normal level, and so reduce inequality as well.

To answer this question a study of factors affecting the supply of human capital is required. Fragmentary studies of this problem are available. Basically, supply responds to a comparison of expected rates of return on human capital investments with rates on alternative investments. Distinguishing between current costs of and future returns on investments may also be helpful, especially as direct outlays may be especially discouraging to capital-rationed students from middle- and low-income families. As is well known, real tuition costs increased significantly at the post-secondary level of schooling in the 1980s, a possible factor in the widening education wage differential, hence also in wage inequality. But the effect of this factor on the observed differential is not likely to be major. This is because student subsidies reduce the net magnitude of direct costs, so the net amount is not likely to be large as a proportion of total educational costs, which include opportunity costs. However, it may well be of some importance in supply responses.

Though supply can be expected to respond to increased demand for human capital, the response may be slow, as it flows through a long schooling and early-experience pipeline before it affects the relative wage. Judging by past behavior, a decade-long adjustment may well be in prospect,[21] both for rates of return and for inequality, with two qualifications: (1) increases in skill-biased demand at the same or accelerated pace would slow the adjustments further and might continue to augment rates of return and inequality for a while; (2) whether the usual pace of supply adjustments can be relied on in the near future may also be in question. If the current growth of demand for human capital is based on skill-biased technology, and skills acquired at school and on the job are a function of the quality of learning and not merely of the time spent in it, a bottleneck in the expansion of human capital supplies may lie in the inadequate quality of learning absorbed by the work force, especially at the elementary and secondary levels of schooling.

If this quality deteriorated or remained inadequate in the face of growing technological demands in the past decade or two, it may have been a factor in the widening and persistence of educational differentials and in inequality more generally. Evidence on trends in quality of learning is difficult to come by, but apprehension about quality levels appears to be justified by a variety of tests and international comparisons.[22] I should note, incidentally, that quality problems are not restricted to schooling. They start with childhood development before entering school, and they are likely to affect the efficiency of job training. In other words, quality bottlenecks are not effectively overcome by the substitution of training for schooling; they are likely to reduce job training as well.[23]

I hope that the developments in human capital research that I describe here show the wide-ranging scope and power of its applications to labor economics. There are, of course, rival theories for each particular application, but none appears to be as comprehensive, nor are they necessarily mutually exclusive. Partly because of the focus on my own work, a number of topics are not covered: information, discrimination, demographic effects, and macroeconomic implications are some of the important ones. It is the mark of the fruitfulness of the approach that each of the applications grows quickly into a field of its own.

Author's Note

Over the years covered in this chapter, my research was supported by the National Science Foundation, the Sloan Foundation, the Spencer Foundation, the Bradley Foundation, the U.S. Department of Labor, and the U.S. Department of Education.

Notes

1. See Rosen 1977, Sahota 1978, Mincer 1979, Willis 1986.
2. See Sahota 1978.
3. T. W. Schultz was the first effective proponent of this view. The focus on human capital in growth theory has gained momentum in recent years (as, for example, in the work of Lucas, Romer, Becker).
4. See Leibowitz 1974.
5. See Grossman 1972.
6. As well as by preschool investments in child rearing.
7. Estimation of rates on postschool investments is not robust, partly because it depends on the polynomial form in experience and on non-linear techniques. An outside estimate of rates of return on job training may be preferred.
8. Optimization in the sense of maximizing total output also requires an intersectoral equality of marginal rates of return. Thus marginal rates on human capital investments should not diverge from rates on physical capital investments (after adjustments for compensatory factors).
9. For a fine survey and interesting speculations concerning this robustness, see Willis 1986.
10. The semilog form appears to be superior to the arithmetic form, according to Heckman and Polachek (1972). The Gompertz experience function fits somewhat better than the quadratic in the 1960 census data analyzed in my book (1974), and a quartic polynomial fits better the more recent data analyzed by Murphy and Welch (1991). These forms do not apply to earnings of intermittent workers. See Mincer and Polachek 1974.
11. It is worth noting, incidentally, that as wage gains due to interfirm mobility account for no more than 15 percent of wage growth over the working life, another theory of the wage profile can be given minor importance and may contribute in part to its shape. The conclusion (Burdett 1973) is based on search theory: on-the-job searches that result in quitting produce upward moves in a fixed wage-offer distribution. Successive moves result in declining probabilities of incremental wage gains with each move. Hence, both the frequency of moves and the size of wage gains decline, producing an upward sloping and decelerating wage profile.
12. More precisely, utility streams rather than income streams enter the calculation. This distinction is a reminder to empirical analysts not to omit nonpecuniary factors that might compensate for or augment net gains (or losses) in income.
13. An exception to this is the unemployed, whose opportunity costs decline especially if they are not tied to local unemployment compensation.

14. It may actually increase mobility, for the increased productivity may provide a bigger payoff elsewhere than in the firm in which the skill was acquired.
15. To illustrate: in 1979, the incidence of unemployment among white men age 25–54 with less than 12 years of schooling was three times higher than that among white male college graduates.
16. The growth of family incomes reduces financial constraints and increases the family demand for education as a consumption good and as a substitution of "quality" for quantity of children (Becker 1976). Note that family demands affect the supply of human capital to the market.
17. A major advantage in using the Jorgenson-Fraumeni total-factor productivity indexes (1987, updated 1990) was their construction as residuals from quality-adjusted changes in capital and labor inputs. These adjustments eliminate (or at least minimize) a spurious correlation that would otherwise contaminate the observed effects of residuals on human capital inputs.
18. See Bound and Johnson 1991, Davis and Haltiwanger 1990, and various papers in Burtless 1991, and Kosters 1992.
19. See Levy and Murnane 1990; Juhn, Murphy, and Pierce 1989.
20. Wage functions rarely report an R^2 exceeding .30.
21. The adjustment is faster for particular occupations, as might be expected. Freeman 1986 provides a review of a number of studies.
22. See, especially, Bishop 1991.
23. Though remedial job training, which is already a significant part of job training, may increase.

References

Barron, J., D. Black, and M. Lowenstein. 1989. "Job Matching and On-The Job Training," *Journal of Labor Economics*, vol. 7, pp. 1–19.

Bartel, A., and F. Lichtenberg. 1987. "The Comparative Advantage of Educated Workers in Implementing New Technologies," *Review of Economics and Statistics 69*, pp. 1–11.

Becker, G. S. 1964. *Human Capital*, New York: Columbia University Press; Chicago: University of Chicago Press, 1975 (2nd. ed.).

———. 1967. "Human Capital and the Distribution of Personal Income," *W.S. Woytinsky Lecture No. 1*, University of Michigan.

Becker, G. S., K. M. Murphy, and R. Tamura. 1990. "Human Capital, Fertility, and Economic Growth," *Journal of Political Economy* pp. 12–37.

Becker, G. S., and G. Stigler. 1974. "Law Enforcement, Malfeasance, and Compensation of Enforcers," *Journal of Legal Studies*, pp. 1–18.

Becker, G. S., and N. Tomes. 1976. "Child Endowments and the Quantity and Quality of Children," *Journal of Political Economy* 84, S143–S162.

Ben-Porath, Y. 1967. "The Production of Human Capital and the Life-Cycle of Earning," *Journal of Political Economy* 75, 352–365.

Bishop, J. 1991. "Achievement, Test Scores, and Relative Wages," in M. Kosters, ed., *Workers and Their Wages.* Washington, D.C.: American Enterprise Institute.

Blackburn, M. L., D. E. Bloom, and R. B. Freeman. 1990. "The Declining Economic Position of Less Skilled American Men," in G. Burtless, ed., *A Future of Lousy Jobs?* Washington, D.C.: Brookings Institution. pp. 31–76.

Bound, J., and G. Johnson. 1991. "Changes in the Structure of Wages in the 1980's: An Evaluation of Alternative Explanations," *NBER Working Paper* 2983, revised.

Brown, J. 1989. "Why Do Wages Increase With Tenure?" *American Economic Review* 79, 971–991.

Burdett, K. 1973. "On the Job Search." Ph.D. dissertation, Northwestern University.

Burtless, G., ed. 1991. *A Future of Lousy Jobs?*, Washington, D.C.: Brookings Institution.

Chiswick, B. R., and J. Mincer. 1972. "Time Series Changes in Personal Income Inequality in the U.S. Since 1939" *Journal of Political Economy* 80, Part 2, S34–S66.

Da Vanzo, J. 1983. "Repeat Migration in the U.S.," *Review of Economics and Statistics* 65, 552–559.

Davis, S., and J. Haltiwanger. 1990. "Wage Dispersion between and within U.S. Manufacturing Plants, 1963–1987." Paper presented at Brookings Conference.

Dooley, M., and P. Gottschalk. 1984. "Earnings Inequality Among Males in the United States," *Journal of Political Economy* 92, 59–89.

Duncan, G., and S. Hoffman. 1978. "Training and Earnings," in G. Duncan and Morgan, eds., *Five Thousand American Families.* Ann Arbor: ISR, University of Michigan.

Fisher, I. 1930. *The Theory of Interest.* New York: Macmillan.

Freeman, R. B. 1976. *The Overeducated American.* New York: Academic Press.

———. 1986. "Demand for Education," in O. Ashenfelter and R. Layard, eds., *Handbook of Labor Economics,* vol. 1, Amsterdam: North Holland. pp. 357–386.

Friedman, M., and S. Kuznets. 1945. *Incomes from Independent Professional Practice,* New York: Columbia University Press.

Gill, I. 1989. "Technological Change, Education, and Obsolescence of Human Capital." Ph.D. dissertation, University of Chicago.

Greenwood, M. 1975. "Research on Internal Migration in the U.S.," *Journal of Economic Literature* 13, (June), 397–433.

Griliches, Z. 1969. "Capital-Skill Complementarity," *The Review of Economics and Statistics* 51, 465–468.

Gronau, R. 1982. "Sex Related Wage Differentials," *NBER Working Paper* 1002, October.

Grossman, M. 1972. "On the Concept of Health Capital and the Demand for Health," *Journal of Political Economy* 80 (March), 223–255.

Heckman, J., and S. Polachek. 1974. "The Functional Form of the Income-Schooling Relation," *Journal of the American Statistical Association* 69 (June), 350–354.

Jorgenson, D., and B. Fraumeni. 1990. "Investment in Education and U.S. Economic Growth, in *The U.S. Savings Challenge*. Boulder, Colo.: Westview Press.

Jorgenson, D., F. Gollop, and B. Fraumeni. 1987. *Productivity and U.S. Economic Growth*. Cambridge, Mass.: Harvard University Press. Updated series, 1990.

Jorgenson, D., M. Kurado, and M. Nishimizu. 1986. "Japan-US Industry Level Comparisons 1960–1979," Economics Department, Harvard University. Discussion Paper 1254.

Jovanovic, B. 1979. "Job Matching and the Theory of Turnover," *Journal of Political Economy* 87 (October), 972–990.

———. 1979. "Firm Specific Capital and Turnover," *Journal of Political Economy* 87 (December), 1246–1260.

Juhn, C., K. Murphy, and B. Pierce. 1989. "Wage Inequality and the Rise in Returns to Skill." Department of Economics, University of Chicago. Photocopy.

Kosters, M., ed. 1992. *Workers and Their Wages*. Washington, D.C.: American Enterprise Institute.

Krueger, A. 1991. "How Computers Have Changed the Wage Structure," NBER Working Paper 3858.

Lazear, E. 1979. "Why Is There Mandatory Retirement?" *Journal of Political Economy* 87, 261–284.

Leibowitz, A. 1974. "Home Investments in Children," *Journal of Political Economy* 82, Part 2, S111–S131.

Leighton, L., and J. Mincer. 1982. "Labor Turnover and Youth Unemployment," in R. B. Freeman and D. A. Wise, eds., *The Youth Labor Market Problem*. Chicago: University of Chicago Press. pp. 235–275.

Levy, F., and R. Murnane. 1990. "Earnings Levels and Earnings Inequality." University of Maryland. Photocopy.

Lillard, L., and H. Tan. 1986. *Private Sector Training*. Santa Monica, CA: Rand Corporation. R-3331.

Lucas, R. E. 1988. "On the Mechanics of Economic Development," *Journal of Monetary Economics* 22, 3–22.

Lynch, L. 1988. "Private Sector Training and the Impact." Department of Economics, MIT. Draft (October).

Mincer, J. 1957. "A Study of Personal Income Distribution." Ph.D. dissertation, Columbia University.

———. 1958. "Investment in Human Capital and Personal Income Distribution," *Journal of Political Economy* 66, 1–32.

———. 1962. "On the Job Training: Costs, Returns, and Implications," *Journal of Political Economy* 70 (Supplement) 50–79.

———. 1974. *Schooling, Experience and Earnings.* New York: Columbia University Press, NBER.

———. 1978. "Family Migration Decisions," *Journal of Political Economy* 86 (October), 749–773.

———. 1979. "Human Capital and Earnings," in *Economic Dimensions of Education,* Report of the National Academy of Education. (Reprinted in Atkinson, ed. 1980. *Wealth, Income and Inequality.* pp. 103–128.)

———. 1984. "Human Capital and Economic Growth," *Economics of Education Review* 3, no. 3.

———. 1986. "Wage Changes in Job Changes," *Research in Labor Economics,* 8A, 171–197.

———. 1991. "Job Training, Costs, Returns, and Wage Profiles," in D. Stern and J. M. M. Ritzen, eds., *Market Failure in Training?* New York: Springer-Verlag.

———. 1993. "Human Capital and Earnings," "Human Capital, Wage Growth, Labor Turnover, and Unemployment," and "Technology and the Demand for Human Capital." In *Studies in Human Capital,* vol. 1. Brookfield, Vermont: Edward Elgar Publishing Company.

———. 1993. "Labor Supply in the Family Context," "Labor Supply, Human Capital, and the Gender Wage Gap," and "Labor Supply with Wage Floors." In *Studies in Human Capital,* vol. 2. Brookfield, Vermont: Edward Elgar Publishing Company.

Mincer, J., and Y. Higuchi. 1988. "Wage Structures and Labor Turnover in the U.S. and in Japan," *Journal of Japanese and International Economies,* June.

Mincer, J., and B. Jovanovic. 1981. "Labor Mobility and Wages," in S. Rosen, ed., *Studies in Labor Markets,* Chicago: University of Chicago Press. pp. 21–64.

Mincer, J., and H. Ofek. 1982. "Interrupted Work Careers," *Journal of Human Resources* 17, 1–23.

Mincer, J., and S. Polachek. 1974. "Family Investment in Human Capital: Earnings of Women," *Journal of Political Economy* 82, Part 2, S76–S108.

Murphy, K., and F. Welch. 1989. "Wage Premiums for College Graduates," *Educational Researcher,* May.

———. 1991. "Empirical Earnings Profiles," *Journal of Labor Economics* 9 (January).

Nelson, R., and E. Phelps. 1966. "Investment in Humans, Technological Diffusion, and Economic Growth," *American Economic Review* 56 (May), 69–75.

Parnes, H. 1970. "Labor Force Participation and Labor Mobility," in *A Review of Industrial Relations Research,* vol. 1.

Parsons, D. 1986. "Job Training in the Post-Schooling Period." Discussion paper. Ohio State University.

Plotnick, R. 1982. "Trends in Male Earnings Inequality," *Southern Economic Journal* 48, 724–732.

Polachek, S., and F. Horvath. 1977. "A Life Cycle Approach to Migration," in R. G. Ehrenberg, ed., *Research in Labor Economics,* vol. 1. Greenwich, Conn.: JAI Press.

Romer, P. M. 1990. "Endogenous Technological Change, *Journal of Political Economy,* S71–S102.

Rosen, H. 1982. "Taxation and On-the-Job Training Decisions," *Review of Economics and Statistics* 64 (August), 442–449.

Rosen, S. 1977. "Human Capital: A Survey of Empirical Research," in R. G. Ehrenberg, ed., *Research in Labor Economics,* vol. 1. Greenwich, Conn.: JAI Press.

Sahota, G. 1978. "Theories of Personal Income Distribution," *Journal of Economic Literature* 16, 1–55.

Salop, J., and S. Salop. 1976. "Self-Selection and Turnover in the Labor Market," *Quarterly Journal of Economics* 90 (November), 619–627.

Schultz, T. W. 1960. "Capital Formation in Education," *Journal of Political Economy* 68 (December), 571–583.

———. 1961. "Investment in Human Capital," *American Economic Review* 52, 1–17.

Sjastaad, L. 1962. "Costs and Returns of Human Migration," *Journal of Political Economy* 70, Part 2 (October) 80–93.

Stigler, G. J. 1961. "Economics of Information," *Journal of Political Economy* 69 (June), 213–225.

———. 1962. "Information in the Labor Market," *Journal of Political Economy* 70 (Supplement), 94–105.

Topel, R. 1987. "Wages Grow with Tenure," *Journal of Labor Economics* 5.

———. 1990. "Specific Capital, Mobility, and Wages," NBER Working Paper 3294, March.

Welch, F. 1970. "Education in Production," *Journal of Political Economy* 78, 35–59.

Willis, R. 1986. "Wage Determinants: Human Capital Earnings Functions," in O. Ashenfelter and R. Layard, eds., *Handbook of Labor Economics,* vol. 1. Amsterdam: North Holland. pp. 525–602.

II

A Central Dispute: Determinateness versus Indeterminateness

5

The Evolution of Thought on the Competitive Nature of Labor Markets

■ ─────────────── ■

Bruce E. Kaufman

Labor economics focuses on the operation of labor markets and the determination of market outcomes such as wages rates, employment levels, and the distribution of income. The starting point for this chapter is the observation that the outcomes of labor markets, and the economic and social merits of those outcomes, are critically affected by the degree to which labor markets are competitive. The veracity of this statement is amply illustrated by a consideration of the major positive and normative debates that currently divide labor economists.

For example, do wage differentials among occupations and firms compensate workers for additional risks of workplace injury? Do union wage gains cause an inefficient allocation of resources? Is it lower individual productivity, rather than discrimination, that accounts for the reduced earnings of women and minority workers relative to white males? If labor markets are highly competitive, economic theory predicts a "yes" answer to all three questions. On the other hand, the greater the degree of noncompetitive elements in labor markets, the greater the likelihood that the answer to these questions is "no." The implications for public policy, in turn, are clear cut. If labor markets are highly competitive, laws regulating occupational safety and health conditions, protecting and encouraging collective bargaining, and mandating affirmative action in hiring and promotion are likely to be both unnecessary and undesirable. Quite the opposite conclusions emerge, however, in situations where employers do not face effective competition for labor.

Viewed from this perspective, it is arguably the case that the single most important empirical issue in labor economics is the degree to which labor markets are competitive. What is the evidence? Although a great body of empirical research on labor market phenomena has been published in recent years, surprisingly few attempts have been made either to assess the competitive nature of labor markets directly through case study investigation or to reach such a conclusion indirectly through a weighing and sifting of evidence from studies of specific aspects of labor market behavior (for example, wage determination, labor mobility). Perhaps the clearest illustration of this lacuna in the literature is the *Handbook of Labor Economics* (Ashenfelter and Layard 1986), a recently published two-volume set that purports to provide a comprehensive survey of research in modern labor economics. Although the *Handbook* provides exhaustive coverage of both theoretical and empirical work on individual aspects of labor markets and contains numerous *assumptions* about the extent of competition in labor markets, nowhere in it is empirical evidence either presented or interpreted as to the degree to which real world labor markets do or do not operate in a competitive manner.

Given the importance of the topic and the neglect which it has suffered in recent years, a fresh look at the competitive nature of labor markets seems warranted. Ideally, this investigation would include a comprehensive review of observed trends and developments in labor markets since the turn of the century; the various models of perfect and imperfect competition developed by economists; and the implications of these models for labor market outcomes such as wages, employment, and turnover; as well as an assessment of the degree to which labor markets appear to be competitive based on the findings of the empirical literature. Such an undertaking, while greatly needed, is too expansive in scope and size for this chapter. What follows, therefore, is a modest introduction to the subject.

In particular, this chapter provides a brief account of the evolution of thought among economists with regard to both the degree of competitiveness of labor markets and the relevance of competitive theory to the study of the operation and outcomes of labor markets. This account begins with Adam Smith, skips a century to the writings of Alfred Marshall, and then follows the development of labor economics in America from the turn of the twentieth century to the present day, as reflected in the works of major economists such as John R. Commons, Paul Douglas, Clark Kerr, Milton Friedman, Gary Becker, Robert Solow, and Richard Freeman, concluding with some critical remarks concerning the current state of knowledge and research on the competitive nature of labor markets.

Adam Smith

Adam Smith is widely credited with being the "father of economics," and his masterpiece, *An Inquiry into the Nature and Causes of the Wealth of Nations* (1776), is regarded as one of the most influential works ever written on the subject. Although labor markets were still in their formative years of development in the late eighteenth century, Smith nevertheless devoted two chapters of the book to the topic of wage determination. These chapters are of interest not only for the keen insight that Smith brought to the issue but also for the seemingly contradictory views he held concerning the degree to which labor markets are competitive.

Chapter 8 of book I discusses the general level of wages. While Smith portrays the determination of wages as the outcome of demand and supply forces in the labor market, the general thrust of the discussion in this chapter is to suggest that the resulting level of wage rates departs significantly from competitive levels due to the influence of various market imperfections. Smith frames the wage determination process as the outcome of a bargaining process in which the individual worker is most often in a disadvantageous position vis-à-vis the employer. Thus, he states: "What are the common wages of labour, depends everywhere upon the contract usually made between those two parties, whose interests are by no means the same. The workmen desire to get as much, the masters to give as little as possible." He goes on to say, "It is not, however, difficult to foresee which of the two parties must, upon all ordinary occasions, have the advantage in the dispute . . . . masters must generally have the advantage" (book I, chap. 8, 66–67).

What accounts for the superior bargaining power of the employer? Smith cites two major factors. The first is that the worker, having a smaller financial reserve than the employer, has a more pressing need to reach an agreement and begin work. ("In the long-run the workman may be as necessary to his master as his master is to him, but the necessity is not so immediate.") The impact of this inequality in resources is to cause workers to lower their supply price of labor, thus shifting the supply curve of labor to the right and resulting in a lower equilibrium wage than would exist if both parties had equal staying power in the market. The second factor is that collusive wage agreements among employers are easier to effectuate and are regarded with less hostility by public officials than are similar agreements among employees. ("The masters, being fewer in number, can combine much more easily; and the law, besides, authorises, or at least does not prohibit their combinations, while it prohibits those of the workmen.") The result, according to Smith, is that employers possess significantly greater market power over wages than do workers, causing the wage rate to be depressed below the competitive level.

Chapter 8 provides other evidence that Smith saw the wage determination process as significantly affected by market imperfections. An example is his observation that competition among employers is limited by worker costs of mobility ("A man is of all sorts of luggage the most difficult to be transported"); another is his observation that while product prices rise and fall in response to short-run shifts in demand and supply, wage rates exhibit a marked stability ("The money price of labour remains uniformly the same sometimes for half a century together"). It is also useful to point out that Smith saw a full employment economy as a significant antidote to labor's inequality of bargaining power. ("The scarcity of hands occasions a competition among masters, who bid against one another, in order to get workmen, and thus voluntarily break through the natural combination of masters not to raise wages.") Another antidote was the exercise of countervailing market power through combination on the part of workers (that is, collective bargaining), although such power was itself subject to abuse, Smith thought, if not exercised with restraint. Finally, Smith notes that while individual employers seek to hold down wages lest they be placed at a competitive disadvantage, when viewed from a long-run, economy-wide perspective, an on-going, moderate increase in wages is a benefit both to firms and the nation because it stimulates increased work effort, better employee health and productivity, and a growing population.

Smith turns from consideration of the general level of wages in chapter 8 to the pattern of wage differentials among workers and occupations in chapter 10. Here a markedly different view of the labor market emerges. To explain the causes of wage differentials among the different employments of labor, Smith used what today would be called a model of a perfectly competitive labor market. In one of the most famous passages in the book, he states:

> The whole of the advantages and disadvantages of the different employments of labour and stock must, in the same neighborhood, be either perfectly equal or continually tending to equal-

ity. If in the same neighborhood, there was any employment evidently either more or less advantageous than the rest, so many people would crowd into it in the one case, and so many would desert it in the other, that its advantages would soon return to the level of other employments. This would at least be the case in a society where things were left to follow their natural course, where there was perfect liberty, and where every man was perfectly free both to choose what occupation he thought proper, and to change it as often as he thought proper (book I, chap. 10, 99).

Smith then goes on to explain in detail how the balancing of advantages and disadvantages gives rise to a distinct pattern of wage differentials in the market. Jobs that have disagreeable working conditions, for example, must pay a higher wage than otherwise identical jobs, if people are to be induced to accept them. ("The trade of a butcher is a brutal and an odious business; but in most places more profitable than the greater part of common trades.") Likewise, Smith deduced that wages vary directly with the cost of learning a particular skill or trade, the inconstancy of employment, the degree of trust reposed in the workman, and the difficulty of success in the trade.

Do wage rates in the labor market actually differ among workers as predicted by the competitive model? Smith states that they often do not, but he points the finger of blame primarily at the "policies of Europe," which interfere with the workings of the labor market, rather than at any inherent defect of the market itself. With regard to the operation of supply and demand, Smith cites three reasons that the predictions of the competitive model may not hold: newly established firms sometimes have to pay higher than equilibrium wages initially to attract labor; a short-run disequilibrium in wages may occur due to a sudden shift in labor demand or supply; and some people are willing to work for less if the job is not their principal source of income.

While these factors cause wage differentials in the labor market to diverge from those predicted by competitive theory, the divergence is of a short-run nature and of secondary importance relative to the influence of the policy of Europe, which, Smith states, "by not leaving things at perfect liberty, occasions other inequalities of much greater significance" (book I, chap. 10, 118). Smith cites three examples of such policies: the requirement of long apprenticeships that have the effect of discouraging the entrance of new people into a trade, the provision of government subsidies to certain occupations (for example, the clergy) that result in a glut of job seekers, and various laws (such as the poor laws) that restrict the mobility of labor from one geographic area to another. In all three cases, Smith takes a critical view of these interventions in the labor market and suggests that their net result is an inefficient allocation of resources.

What is Smith's conclusion, then, as to the competitive nature of labor markets? On the surface he appears to take a contradictory stance on the issue. In chapter 8, he cites a variety of reasons that competition either works to the disadvantage of labor or fails to adequately protect labor's interest. In chapter 10, on the other hand, Smith portrays the workings of a competitive labor market in a relatively favorable light and seems to suggest that, absent short-run frictions and misguided government policies, supply and demand will give rise to a series of wage differentials that promote an efficient allocation of labor resources.

When confronted with this paradox, most economists have attempted to resolve it by focusing on one chapter and minimizing the significance of the other (see, for example, Rottenberg 1956). An alternative interpretation is that Smith believed there were two different dimensions or "faces" of labor markets, one imperfectly competitive and the other approximately competitive. The imperfect face was associated with the determination of the general *level* of wages; the approximately competitive face, on the other hand, involved *differences* in wage rates among individual workers and occupations. The next two hundred years saw a continuous debate among economists over these issues, with opinions ranging on all sides and fluctuating with the tide of economic developments.

Alfred Marshall

I now jump one hundred years to the great English economist Alfred Marshall. Marshall had the greatest influence on the development and shape of economic science of anyone who wrote on the subject in the one hundred years that followed Adam Smith. (Karl Marx would be the closest challenger.) Marshall lived from 1842 to 1924 and wrote his most influential work — *Principles of Economics* (first edition 1890) — while a professor at Cambridge University. More than any other person, Marshall was responsible for the elaboration and development of the new neoclassical theory of economics that emerged in the late 1800s. Prior to Marshall, the labor theory of value and the wage fund theory were central elements of the classical explanation of the determination of prices and wages. In *Principles*, Marshall reoriented the discussion of these subjects toward an analytic study of demand and supply in product and labor markets, clearly distinguished between competitive versus monopoly market structures, and applied in a thorough-going way the newly emergent theories of marginal utility and marginal productivity.

Marshall's analysis of labor markets and the process of wage determination proceeds in several steps. To start, he makes it clear that wage determination is but a special case of the determination of value by the market forces of supply and demand. He states: "The normal value of everything, whether it be a particular kind of labour or capital or anything else, rests, like the keystone of an arch, balanced in equilibrium between the contending pressures of its two opposing sides; the forces of demand press on the one side, and those of supply on the other" (Marshall 1961, 526). That his study of demand and supply is to be grounded in marginal analysis is then attested to several pages later when he states, "Wages tend to equal the net product of labor; its marginal productivity rules the demand-price for it; and, on the other side, wages tend to retain a close though indirect and intricate relation with the cost of rearing, training, and sustaining the energy of efficient labour" (p. 532).

Although Marshall treats the determination of wage rates as no different in concept from the determination of the price of any other good, he is clearly cognizant that as a practical matter labor markets differ in certain important respects from commodity markets and that these peculiarities affect the wage determination process. Following Adam Smith, Marshall maintained that certain workers suffer from an inequality of bargaining power vis-à-vis employers. He thus states that "while the advantage in bargaining is likely to be pretty well distributed between the two sides of a market for commodities, it is more often on the side of the buyers than on that of the sellers in a market for labour" (Marshall 1961, 335–336). Factors that he cites as being responsible for this inferior bargaining position include: the lack of a reserve fund, workers' difficulty in obtaining financial capital to invest in additional skills and training, the fact that the provision of labor cannot be separated from the person selling it (thus restricting the geographic area over which labor can be traded relative to commodities such as coal or wheat), and the fact that the services of labor are perishable (labor can not be inventoried and sold later, as can commodities).

Although Marshall claimed that these disadvantages in bargaining tilt the wage determination process against employees, he qualified this assertion in several respects. Not all classes of workers suffer from these disadvantages, for example. According to Marshall, manual workers are the group most likely to be paid less than their "real value" (marginal revenue product), while the scarce skills and superior education of professional workers generally provides them with sufficient leverage in the market to obtain competitive rates of pay. Even among manual workers, however, the bargaining disadvantage relative to employers is mitigated by several considerations. One is that in times of "good trade" the keen competition among employers for labor causes a breakdown of collusive practices, and wages go up. Another consideration is the "fluidity of labor," which, according to Marshall, responds with considerable elasticity to inequalities in net advantages among different employments.

What does Marshall conclude, then, about the competitive nature of labor markets? In the short run, it is fair to say, Marshall recognized that the wage structure departs in certain important respects from that which would prevail in a situation of perfect competition, due both to various noncompetitive elements (which most adversely affect the lower grades of labor) and to the slow adjustment of labor supply to demand shifts (a problem most severe for skilled workers). In the long run, however, it is clearly his view that labor markets are approximately competitive — not perfectly so but reasonably close. He states, for example, "There is a constant tendency towards a position of normal equilibrium, in which supply of each of these agents shall stand in such a relation to the demand for its services, as to give to those who have provided the supply a sufficient reward for their efforts and sacrifices. If the economic conditions of the country remained stationary sufficiently long, this tendency would realize itself in such an adjustment of supply to demand, that both machines and human beings would earn generally an amount that corresponded fairly with their cost" (Marshall 1961, 577).

In ending this discussion of Marshall, it is useful to consider briefly his views on the economic and social merits of trade unions, an institution that was rapidly growing in late-nineteenth-century England. Given the strong antiunion sentiments of most economists of his era, plus his contention that in the long run most labor markets are reasonably competitive, it is somewhat surprising that Marshall was supportive, albeit guardedly so, of unions and collective bargaining. Unions arose, Marshall believed, from "the unfairness of bad masters" and, therefore, were best seen as a response to inequitable conditions, rather than as an originating market imperfection. His support of trade unions was based on both economic and social grounds. The economic justification for unions, according to Marshall, was that they level the competitive playing field by providing workers with a countervailing form of power to offset the market power given to employers by short-run barriers to competition. On social grounds, Marshall approved of unions because they improve the "moral character" of the workers through the introduction of self-government into the workplace and the inculcation of self-respect.

Marshall's support of unions was conditional, for he regarded a number of specific union practices (for example, make-work rules, deliberate restriction of output) as clearly injurious to efficiency and the public welfare. He was also critical of certain unions, such as the bricklayers' union, for having raised wage rates considerably above competitive levels. His concerns on this matter were muted, however, by his perception that unions generally have only modest power to raise wages and that the organized actions of both employers and workers are a "succession of picturesque incidents and romantic transformations" that are "apt to be exaggerated" (Marshall 1961, 628).

The Institutionalists

The first American labor economists were the institutionalists, and the foremost figure among this group was John R. Commons, considered by many to be the founder of American labor economics and industrial relations. The center of institutionalism in labor economics was the University of Wisconsin, where Commons taught and where a number of his colleagues and proteges (Selig Perlman, Edwin Witte, Don Lescohier) together defined the "Wisconsin school" of labor economics. For roughly a 30-year period spanning 1905 to 1935 the study of labor economics in America was dominated and defined by the institutional point of view.

Although institutionalism was largely an American development, it drew its early inspiration from two foreign sources: the economists of the German historical school and the English economists/sociologists Sydney and Beatrice Webb (Dorfman 1963; Kaufman 1993). With regard to the operation and outcomes of labor markets, it was the writings of the Webbs, and most particularly their landmark book *Industrial Democracy* (1897), that had the greatest influence on Commons and his associates.

The clearest statement by the Webbs concerning the competitive nature of labor markets is in the chapter "The Higgling of the Market." The basic thrust of the discussion is to suggest that unrestrained competition in product and labor markets will in the normal case result in terms and conditions of labor that are injurious to the economic and social welfare of workers and of the country. The reason, the Webbs state, is that individual workers are generally in the weakest bargaining position of all the parties that buy and sell in the "chain of bargains" that stretches from the customer and retailer at the one end to the manufacturer and worker at the other.

The chain of bargains starts with consumers and extends backward through the various stages of production to the individual worker hired by the manufacturer. As the Webbs portray the process, consumers search among retailers for the lowest priced goods which, in turn, causes similar price competition among wholesalers and then manufacturers. Since the largest component of production cost for many manufacturers is labor, the pressure on manufacturers for lower priced goods necessarily leads them to seek ways to lower labor cost wherever possible. It is at this point, the Webbs say, that the competitive pressure for lower prices from consumers at the retail stage collides with the desire of workers at the production stage for high wages and good working conditions.

What will be the outcome? The Webbs contend that the plane of competition in a free market system is tilted against workers (most particularly manual, unskilled workers), and thus the wage bargain will go against them. Even in a situation of full employment, they say, this will be the case because of certain peculiarities of labor. These include the perishability of labor, workers' lack of a financial reserve, imperfect information about the conditions on the job, and the superior ability of employers at higgling (bargaining). As was true of Adam Smith, the Webbs believe these factors lower the supply price of labor, thus shifting the supply curve of labor rightward and resulting in a lower market price for labor.

The actual situation is far worse, say the Webbs, because most often an excess supply of unemployed job seekers is present in the labor market, a fact that greatly undercuts the individual worker's bargaining power. The pernicious impact such unemployment has on wages and working conditions is vividly described in the following passage:

> When the unemployed are crowding around the factory gates every morning, it is plain to each man that, unless he can induce the foreman to select him rather than another, his chance of subsistence for weeks to come may be irretrievably lost. Under these circumstances bargaining, in the case of the isolated individual workman, becomes absolutely impossible. The foreman has only to pick his man, and tell him the terms. Once inside the gates, the lucky workman knows that if he grumbles at any of the surroundings, however intolerable; if he

demurs to any speeding-up, lengthening of the hours, or deductions; or if he hesitates to obey the order, however unreasonable, he condemns himself once more to the semi-starvation and misery of unemployment. For the alternative to the foreman is merely to pick another man from the eager crowd, whilst the difference to the employer becomes incalculably infinitesimal (Webb and Webb 1897, 658).

Because competition becomes socially destructive in such situations, the Webbs advocate establishing a floor or "standard rate" for wages and working conditions below which no employer can pay. This floor can be established through legislation, such as minimum wage or child labor laws, or through collective bargaining (what they call the "method of legal enactment" and "method of collective bargaining"). The Webbs advocate setting the standard rate at the level that would prevail *if* the labor market were truly competitive, thus maximizing economic efficiency and social welfare.

The imperfect nature of labor markets contained in the Webbs' account is mirrored in the writings of the American institutionalists. The institutionalists were generally quite critical of the social and economic outcomes generated by free, unregulated labor markets. One revealing piece of evidence for this orientation is the fact that they referred to the study of labor not as labor economics, but as the study of *labor problems* (McNulty 1980; Kaufman 1993). The focus of their research and teaching in the labor area was thus not on the operation of the labor market per se but, rather, on the undesirable outcomes or "evils" that emanate from the market, such as insecurity of employment, low pay, and industrial accidents, and on various institutional interventions, such as trade unions, protective labor legislation, and progressive management practices, that can prevent or alleviate these problems. Their comments on labor markets offer further evidence of their view. Representative of these are statements by Solomon Blum that "of all markets the labor market is the poorest," that is, least efficient in operation (Blum 1925, 128), and by Commons and Andrews that a nonunion labor market "tends to result in terms of employment highly oppressive to the worker and injurious to society in general" (Commons and Andrews 1936, 373).

Why do labor markets lead to outcomes that are oppressive and injurious? The institutionalists cite a number of reasons. Following the Webbs, the factor given most importance is the inferior bargaining position of the individual worker. The root cause of the worker's inferior bargaining position is, in turn, twofold. First, the worker's mobility and range of opportunities in the market are restricted due to things such as one-company towns, collusive arrangements among employers, and impediments to mobility (lack of savings, loss of seniority rights). More important, however, is the pervasive, enduring excess supply of labor in most markets and the resulting downward pressure on wages and working conditions. According to Commons (1921), demand-deficient involuntary unemployment is the single greatest source of excess labor supply and the most important cause of labor problems, but immigration, convict labor, and female and child labor are also responsible. The effect of these is to initiate a downgrading of wages and working conditions, as the least profitable or most grasping of employers bring in ever lower forms of competition. Commons and Andrews (1936, 48) describe the process thus: "Another reason for the low wage scale [in industry] . . . is the cutthroat competition of workers for work. Among the unskilled, unorganized workers, the wage that the cheapest laborer — such as the partially supported woman, the immigrant with low standards of living, or the workman oppressed by extreme need — is willing to take, very largely fixes the wage level for the whole group."

Also like the Webbs, the institutionalists advocate using government legislation and collective bargaining to offset the individual worker's inequality of bargaining power. The result, they thought, would be to prevent less than competitive wages and working conditions and a destabilizing downward spiral of wages and purchasing power during a recession. (This perspective, it should be noted, provided much of the intellectual rationale for various pieces of New Deal legislation in the 1930s, such as the National Industrial Recovery Act, National Labor Relations Act [Wagner Act], and Fair Labor Standards Act.) These interventions in the labor market are also beneficial, according to the institutionalists, because they transfer the forces of competition from the wage bargain to other areas of business, such as management efficiency and product quality, and thereby provide a spur to productivity and innovation. In this vein Commons and Andrews (1936, 48) say of minimum wage laws: "Minimum wage legislation, therefore, is designed to answer the demands of social policy in two ways. By setting a barrier below which wages may not fall, it lightens the pitiful poverty and prevents the degeneration in body and spirit of those forced to live on a wage too small to supply the necessities of life. . . . At the same time, employers are forced to compete in efficiency of management, thus securing for society at large the many advantages of constantly improved methods of production."

A second defect of labor markets, and one that Commons emphasizes more than the Webbs do, is the existence of externalities and public goods in the workplace. According to Commons, free labor markets result in excessive numbers of injuries and layoffs, and in undesirable working conditions (for example, long hours, too much heat and noise). As first expounded by Adam Smith in his theory of compensating wage differentials, free markets penalize employers who provide unsafe or unpleasant work environments, because workers will remain there only if they are paid a wage increment that compensates for the additional risk of injury, inconstancy of employment, or unpleasant nature of the work. It is these prospective wage penalties that lead employers "as if by an invisible hand" to provide the type of working conditions that maximize economic efficiency and worker satisfaction.

Commons accepts this conclusion on the level of theory but denies that it applies to the imperfect markets of the real world. The existence of numerous unemployed job seekers, for example, means that employers who have the worst records for safety or layoffs can still attract a work force without paying the penalty of higher wages. The costs of injuries and layoffs, therefore, are largely borne by the affected workers, and as a consequence, firms have little reason to reduce their occurrence (as is true of other production externalities, such as water pollution). He also saw that few workers are willing to voice complaints to management about unsafe or unsanitary working conditions, because they fear being discriminated against or fired (thus leading to a "free rider" problem and an underproduction of desired working conditions, as is the case with public goods). The solution Commons advocates is again various forms of institutional intervention in labor markets, such as worker compensation laws, unemployment insurance laws, and trade unions. The intended effect of these interventions is to supplement market forces, thus moving the performance of the labor market closer to the competitive ideal.

Douglas, Millis, and Slichter

Labor economics in America entered a new phase in the 1930s. The influence of the Wisconsin school began to wane and a new, more analytic group of labor economists emerged as the dominant intellectual force in the field. The leading members of this new group were Paul Douglas, Harry Millis, and Sumner Slichter. Douglas and Millis were both at the University of Chicago, while Slichter was at Harvard University.

Commons and the other members of the Wisconsin school had

largely shied away from the development of economic theory per se, a fact explained by their antipathy to neoclassical economics, their desire to bring an interdisciplinary perspective to the analysis of labor issues, and their lifelong interest and involvement in social reform. Although Douglas, Millis, and Slichter were sympathetic to the institutional point of view and subscribed to some of its major tenets (particularly Millis and Slichter, who were students of Commons's), they nevertheless approached the subject of labor with a perspective that was more nearly that of a professionally trained economist conversant in, and able to apply, economic theory to the analysis of labor markets. The multifaceted nature of these three economists is best seen in Douglas, who in the course of his career wrote influential works on personnel management, industrial relations, and economic theory, pioneered the statistical estimation of economic relationships (he coinvented the Cobb-Douglas production function and was coauthor of the first study to use linear regression to estimate a supply curve of labor), and later in life was elected to the U.S. Senate.

How did these economists view the competitive nature of labor markets? First consider Douglas. In 1934 Douglas published a major research monograph entitled *The Theory of Wages.* In part I of the book he assesses the development and status of the marginal productivity theory of production and distribution, a discussion that necessarily leads him to consider the extent of competition in labor markets. The most revealing evidence of his thoughts on this matter are contained in chapter 3 where, after lengthy discussion and weighing of the evidence, he summarizes the validity of the major assumptions of the theory. Reproduced below are his conclusions:

1. Largely valid but not wholly so
   A. Knowledge by business men of relative productiveness of labor and capital.
   B. Mobility of capital.
   C. (Prior to the passage of the National Industrial Recovery Act.) Non-interference by the government in terms of the wage contract.

2. Primarily valid but with a strong opposing tendency
   A. Competition between laborers for work.
   B. Mobility of labor.
   C. Competition between employers for labor.

3. Partially true but on the whole not true
   A. All capital is employed.

B. All labor is employed.

C. Laborers know their productivity.

D. The bargaining powers of labor and capital are equal.

E. (Since the passage of the National Industrial Recovery Act.) Non-interference by the government in the terms of the wage contract. (Douglas 1934, 94)

Douglas goes on to say:

> It will be seen from the above classification that the assumptions which depart most from reality are those which ascribe more power to the workers than they actually possess. The assumptions which serve to increase the bargaining power of the employers, such as the mobility of capital, and the knowledge of relative productiveness, are far more valid than are the similar assumptions which have been made in the case of labor. Moreover, in the case of those assumptions which are less valid, such as the supposed absence of combination between workers and capitalists, and that of full employment of the factors, the real situation is one which further weakens labor's bargaining power. . . . It can thus be said that up until the summer of 1933 the forces which operated against labor's receiving its marginal product were stronger than those which tend to prevent capital from securing its margin. An increased activity by the state in behalf of labor, or further unionization on the part of the wage-earners themselves, would have helped to redress this balance (Douglas 1934, 94–95).

It is apparent from these excerpts that Douglas saw labor markets as imperfectly competitive — competition was present but it was tipped against workers and was too weak to fully protect their interests. He did not claim that the marginal productivity theory was false, but that the violation of assumptions noted above meant that it at best described a portion of reality. He also clearly perceived that labor unions and labor legislation, rather than being inimical to economic efficiency, had a potentially beneficial effect on the level of wages and working conditions.

Next consider the views of Millis on this subject. Millis was a professor of economics at Chicago, one of the nation's leading labor arbitrators, and chair of the National Labor Relations Board in the early 1940s. Millis, in conjunction with Royal Montgomery of Cornell University, authored a three-volume text on labor economics, the first two volumes of which were published in 1938 (*Labor's Progress and Problems* and *Labor's Risks and Social Insurance*) and the third in 1945 (*Organized Labor*).

In chapter 4 of the first volume, Millis and Montgomery present a survey of wage theory. They state: "The only truthful statement that can be made, so far as the assumption of free and complete competition among employers for labor is concerned, is that in many cases such competition simply does not obtain" (Millis and Montgomery 1938, 192–193). They go on to say (p. 194), "There can be little doubt that on the whole competition among laborers for work is keener than is competition among employers for the services of laborers, and to the extent that it is keener the workers are in a position of relative disadvantage." A more extensive discussion of competition in labor markets is then offered in chapter 8 of volume 3, which examines the union in industry. Summarizing their position, they say (pp. 364–365): "Industry affords an abundance of evidence that a competitive demand for labor does not go far to protect the workers against long hours, excessive overtime, fines, discharge without sufficient cause, and objectionable working conditions." They further state (p. 366), "If there is monopoly control and keen competition is not present in the labor market, the workers may be exploited for the sake of more profit, as illustrated by the former policy of the steel trust with respect to the twelve-hour day and seven-day week so long maintained in the face of strong adverse public opinion. Experience shows that, in the interest of labor and the general social welfare, control must be exercised at many points by law or otherwise [such as by labor unions]."

Millis and Montgomery clearly believe that labor markets contain a number of noncompetitive elements. Like Douglas, however, they do not conclude from this that orthodox wage theory (marginal productivity theory, the theory of competitive markets) should be discarded. In this regard, they state in volume 3 (p. 369): "it is true that, while imperfect, a competition for labor exists. And, of course, the elements of truth of the productivity theory of wages . . . are too real and powerful to be ignored." Their position, then, is that the theory of competitive markets is a useful guide to long-run tendencies, but that in the short run the wage determination process is heavily influenced in most labor markets by a variety of "frictions" and imperfections that, on net, work against the interests of labor. Collective bargaining and labor legislation, therefore, are seen as useful supplements to competitive forces, at least when utilized in a balanced, reasonable manner.

I next come to Sumner Slichter, a professor at Harvard and president of both the American Economic Association and the Industrial Relations Research Association. Slichter had studied under Commons at Wisconsin and then went on to finish his doctoral degree at Chicago in 1918 on the subject of labor turnover in American industry. As part of the research for his dissertation, and in keeping with the "go and see" case study methodology advocated by the institutionalists, he spent a summer as a machine hand in a factory of the International Harvester Company. A close familiarity with the facts of working life was to characterize the remainder of Slichter's 40-year academic career, as most vividly illustrated by his several pathbreaking books on the influence of collective bargaining on management. Slichter was also well versed in economic theory, however, and wrote a number of articles related to macroeconomic issues of stability and noninflationary growth (see Dunlop 1961).

Slichter was less explicit than Douglas and Millis on his views about the competitive nature of labor markets. A review of his writings, however, finds several points relevant to the subject. First, he argues that workers often are not paid the full value of their marginal revenue product (which is to say, they are paid less than competitive wages), but the persons most likely to be affected are inframarginal workers in the firm who for various reasons face significant constraints on mobility (Slichter 1931, 617).

Second, while nonunion workers might not always receive competitive wages, Slichter was dubious that collective bargaining leads to a more efficient wage structure (Slichter 1947, 74–75). The basic problem, as he saw it, is that collective bargaining produces a wage structure that reflects the relative bargaining power of each union-company negotiating pair, with the result that in some cases the wage rate is considerably above the competitive level while in others it is below it.

Third, Slichter thought the biggest defect of nonunion labor markets is that competitive forces inadequately protect workers' interests with respect to working conditions (for example competitive levels of safety and health, fair application of discipline and discharge standards), due to factors such as workers' imperfect information about a firm's internal work practices and the sluggish mobility response of employees to such practices (Slichter 1931, 653–659). It is in this area that Slichter thought collective bargaining could make its most valuable contribution.

Finally, Slichter emphasizes that competitive theory is unrealistic because it assumes labor markets behave much as commodity markets when, in fact, the differences are pronounced (Slichter 1931, 636–650). As an example, he argues that wage rates decline far more sluggishly in labor markets in response to a situation of excess supply than do prices in commodity markets, because wage cuts demoralize workers and result in lower productivity for firms, while price cuts for commodities have no such effect. Another example that he gives great stress to is that a modest boost in the wage rate often does not result in reduced employment, because managers are motivated by the threat to profits to operate the firm in a more vigorous and efficient manner (what has become known as the "shock effect").

The Postwar Labor Economists

In the evolution of thought in American labor economics, next comes a group that, for lack of a better term, I call the postwar labor economists (Kaufman 1988). Others have labeled them neoinstitutionalists (Cain 1976) and neoclassical revisionists (Kerr 1988). The major figures in this group include John Dunlop, Clark Kerr, Richard Lester, and Lloyd Reynolds (DKLR). Several other economists, such as Charles Myers and Arthur Ross, also made significant contributions.

The postwar labor economists dominated the field of labor economics for roughly a 15-year period beginning shortly before the end of World War II and extending to the late 1950s. Their perspective on labor markets was significantly shaped by five factors: a more extensive training in economic theory in graduate school, the publication of several important theoretical works on labor markets by English economists (Keynes, Hicks, Robinson), the events of the Great Depression, the rise of organized labor during the New Deal years, and their experience as arbitrators and administrators for the War Labor Board and related government agencies during World War II.

More so than the previous generation of labor economists, most particularly the institutionalists, DKLR received in their Ph.D. programs in the 1930s a thorough training in neoclassical economic theory. Their interest in theory was further stimulated by the appearance of three highly influential theoretical treatises by English economists: *The Theory of Wages* by John Hicks (1932), *The Economics of Imperfect Competition* by Joan Robinson (1933), and most important, *The General Theory of Employment, Interest, and Money* by John M. Keynes (1936). Hicks and Keynes, in particular, were influential because their perspective on labor markets represented polar opposites — Hicks made the case that labor markets function much as predicted by competitive theory while Keynes's theory of underemployment equilibrium rested, in part, on the failure of wages to clear the labor market. The perspective of DKLR on these theoretical issues was heavily influenced, in turn, by the events of the Depression, which seemed to support Keynes over Hicks; the meteoric growth of trade unionism in the late 1930s, which suggested that institutional forces were well on their way to supplanting market forces as the major determinant of wages and working conditions; and their involvement in the wartime wage-price controls program, an experience that impressed upon them the quantitative importance in wage determination of market frictions (equity concerns, restraints on labor mobility) and the constructive role that collective bargaining can play in promoting efficiency and equity.

When World War II ended and DKLR resumed their academic careers, their central research focus was on the operation of local labor markets, the process of wage determination, and the impact of collective bargaining on the wage structure. The major thrust of this research was to compare the predictions of competitive price theory with the actual outcomes generated by labor markets and, where necessary, to revise the theory so that its predictions were more congruent with reality.

What did these economists conclude about the competitive nature of labor markets? One of the most detailed statements is provided by Clark Kerr in an article entitled "Labor Markets: Their Character and Consequences" (1950). Kerr distinguishes between five types or "models" of labor markets: perfect, neoclassical, natural, institutional, and managed.

The perfect market is the market of perfectly competitive theory. Firms maximize profits, workers maximize net advantages, information and mobility are costless, workers and jobs are homogeneous, and neither unions nor employer associations exist. The labor market thus represents a bourse where firms continually shop for the lowest priced labor and workers stand ready to quit one firm and move to another in pursuit of their highest advantage. The result of the twin forces of profit maximization on the demand side and labor mobility on the supply side is to grind away all wage differentials until one and only one wage prevails in the market for any given type of labor.

The neoclassical market model, according to Kerr, corresponds closely to that envisioned by Alfred Marshall. The perfect market model serves as the basic frame of reference, but a number of qualifications are made with respect to the assumptions. It is recognized, for example, that noncompensating wage differentials for skilled labor will temporarily arise due to unanticipated shifts in demand and the lagged response of supply (due to the time needed to acquire the training), that unskilled workers may be at a bargaining disadvantage due to the perishability of their labor, that unions raise wages above competitive levels in some industries and trades, and that differentiation among workers and jobs exists. Nevertheless, these factors are seen as causing modest-size short-run perturbations to the wage determination process that largely work themselves out to yield a wage structure quite similar to the one predicted by the perfect model.

The natural market model further relaxes the assumptions of the perfect model. On the supply side, labor mobility is significantly impeded by inertia, poor information, and costs associated with loss of seniority rights, fringe benefits, and familiar friends and work environment. On the demand side the assumption that firms maximize profit is relaxed in two regards. First, workers' equity concerns over the level and distribution of profit (and thus their associated decisions about work effort, quitting, and joining a union) are included in the profit maximization calculus, and second, maximization of multiple goals by the firm's managers (promoting "the easy life," a good community image) is allowed for on the presumption that competition in most product markets is sufficiently imperfect that firms can pursue non-profit-related objectives. The result is that competitive forces arising from labor mobility on the supply side set fairly wide limits on the wage bargain, while equity concerns and the separation of corporate ownership from control cause firms on the demand side to pay distinctly different wage rates for similar types of labor.

The wage structure that emerges in the natural market is thus only loosely defined by demand and supply forces, it responds sluggishly to changes in market conditions, and it contains a number of non-competitive wage relationships (for example, wages will vary with firm and industry profitability). A corollary is that the sluggish nature of the competitive process leaves some room for monopsonistic exploitation of workers by low-profit or poorly managed firms, although inframarginal workers are more often exploited than the newly hired, and such exploitation seldom has much bearing in either structure or outcome to the textbook (Robinsonian) monopsony model. Collective bargaining and minimum wage laws in the natural labor market thus have a potentially positive role to play both in counteracting employer power over wages and in rationalizing the wage structure, while the negative impact on firms' labor costs and resource allocation in the economy is often mitigated by an increase in productivity, as management becomes motivated to operate the firm more efficiently.

The fourth type of labor market is the institutional market. The hallmark of the institutional market is that market forces are largely supplanted by organizational rules as the deciding factors in the wage and employment determination process. These rules are established by individual firms as part of their personnel policies, and by trade unions, employers' associations, and government. One function of these institutional rules is to introduce formal boundaries into labor markets by delineating who can and cannot compete for jobs, another is to set wage rates and wage differentials within firms and among firms, while another is to determine the pace and conditions of work.

A classic description of this process is contained in Kerr's article "The Balkanization of Labor Markets" (1954). He delineates two types of institutional markets: the "communal ownership" and the "private property" models. In the communal ownership model, a craft union asserts jurisdiction over all jobs in a particular occupation and geographic area (such as New York dockworkers) and through the collective bargaining process defines who can compete for jobs and the rates of pay that go with each job. Once a worker gains entrance to the market through the union hiring hall or other such device, he or she then competes for jobs on an equal basis with other union members — not through wage competition, which the union suppresses, but on the basis of skill, personal contacts, or position on the membership list.

In the private property model, by way of contrast, the competition for jobs is largely limited to those employees within a particular firm, and in some cases the range of competition is limited to only one job and one person. For entry-level jobs firms hire from the external labor market, but for most jobs above the entry level competition is restricted to people already employed within the firm. Oftentimes this competition is further restricted by the delineation of distinct job ladders in the firm along which people move vertically, but seldom laterally, and by strict policies of promotion by seniority. Since jobs in this internal labor market are largely filled from within, and because they often involve idiosyncratic skills or job tasks not found in the external labor market, the internal wage structure has to be determined administratively through a process such as job evaluation, possibly in conjunction with collective bargaining. Thus, wage determination in the institutional market, as in the natural market, has a significant element of indeterminateness and is likewise heavily influenced by equity consideration as management attempts to promote work effort, skill acquisition, employee retention, and a nonunion environment.

The fifth type of labor market identified by Kerr is the managed market. The essence of the managed market is that government actively intervenes in the wage and employment determination process to ensure that the labor market operates in a competitive fashion. Two diametrically opposite approaches are possible. One is to use government power to break up all monopolistic elements in product and labor markets, thereby creating a competitive market structure. Unions, for example, would be heavily circumscribed, and the antitrust laws would be vigorously enforced. Having accomplished these things, government could then retire to the sidelines, and market forces would bring forth the desired outcomes. The second approach improves on the undesirable performance of the natural and institutional markets by having government intervene directly on an ongoing basis in the operation of the labor market. Rather than breaking up labor unions and large firms, for example, this approach would use some form of compulsory arbitration to resolve labor disputes and a system of wage-price controls to check cost-push inflation originating from the exercise of monopoly power in labor and product markets. Government would also improve the operation of labor markets through other direct interventions, such as facilitating job searches through the provision of moving subsidies to unemployed workers, providing work for the hard-core unemployed through government jobs programs, and combating restrictive hiring practices through equal opportunity and affirmative action programs.

According to Kerr, the perfect market is unobtainable and is best thought of as a benchmark for judging the performance of the others. With regard to economic efficiency, the neoclassical and managed markets come the closest to reproducing the wage and employment outcomes of a perfect market, while the natural and institutional markets perform the least satisfactorily.

What types of labor market structures actually predominate in the American economy? Kerr states that the most common are the natural and institutional (Kerr 1950). The result, he says, is that competitive forces shape aggregate wage relationships and long-run economic trends but permit considerable indeterminacy at the local level ("The market can make the massive adjustments of reducing occupational wage differentials or raising money wages in an inflationary situation, but it can not equalize money wages in the local labor market. Local imperfections and rigidities are too powerful" [Kerr 1969, 54]). A similar point of view is voiced by the other postwar labor economists of the period. After an extensive review of empirical research on local labor markers, Lloyd Reynolds states, for example:

> Only in theory, then, does the "competitive labor market" provide an alternative to wage determination through collective

bargaining. The practical alternative is collective bargaining *versus* wage-setting by employers with rather weak competitive checks. Under nonunion conditions, the immobility of the majority of workers plus the unsystematic selection of jobs by those in search of work gives employers wide latitude in determining wage rates and other conditions of employment. An employer can offer terms considerably below those generally prevailing in an area and still secure an adequate labor force. He is subject to serious competitive pressure mainly at the peak of business cycles, when job opportunities at other plants are relatively plentiful. (Reynolds 1954, 549)

Given the (alleged) imperfect nature of real-world labor markets, it is not surprising that the postwar labor economists took a critical view of neoclassical theory, particularly with regard to the profit maximization assumption, the marginal productivity theory of labor demand, and the perfectly competitive model of markets (Lester 1946, 1952; Dunlop 1957). Their position on these matters was summarized by Frank Pierson in the introductory chapter of the book *New Concepts in Wage Determination* (Pierson 1957, 3–31). (The chapter was intended by the volume's participants to sum up the postwar view of labor markets.) With regard to competitive theory, Pierson states (pp. 18–19) that it is useful for three purposes: providing a theoretical benchmark for studying the operation of labor markets, as a guide to predicting very general or long-run tendencies in wage relationships, and as a reminder that competitive market forces place distinct limits or bounds on the administrative discretion of managers, union leaders, and government officials. As a useful tool for studying the short- to intermediate-run operation and outcome of labor markets, however, Pierson concludes (p. 18) that "competitive theory seems completely out of touch with the world of actuality. Except in a very loose or general sense, this hypothesis [the wage and employment outcomes predicted by the competitive model] affords a very poor basis for explaining wage relationships."

What type of labor market theory would better explain wage relationships? As a guiding principle, Pierson states (pp. 12–13) "If in the interest of clarity a narrow framework is used, many important elements of the subject will doubtless be excluded; if in the interest of realism a broad framework is used, anything like definite conclusions will be put completely out of reach. . . . The most fruitful approach would appear to be to formulate and test generalizations about the effects of wage changes in terms of a number of classes of cases."

Pierson is advocating, in effect, that economists formulate alternative structural models of labor markets and test their hypotheses with data from specific cases. In certain situations, such as the labor market for harvest workers, the competitive model is likely to provide valid generalizations. In most others, however (for example, Kerr's natural and institutional markets), an imperfectly competitive model will be required. The problem that arises at this point, says Pierson, is that the conventional, neoclassical theories of imperfect competition (monopsony and oligopsony) are quite unsuited to the task and need to be replaced by different models. The shortcoming of the neoclassical models lies not with one assumption or the other but, rather, with the entire approach — an approach that treats the motivational and cognitive abilities of economic agents too simplistically, that ignores dynamic feedback effects and adjustments, that assumes more competition on both sides of the market than there really is, and that neglects the important role institutions (management, unions, government) play in structuring labor markets and defining, through their rules and policies, how wages and employment are determined.

The nature of this critique suggests the direction for theory building. The postwar labor economists were, in effect, advocating a theoretical melding of the neoclassical model of markets with the theories of motivation, firm structure, and personnel management and collective bargaining practices from the closely allied field of industrial relations. The challenge, of course, is to construct this type of theory and, in particular, to ensure that it is analytically tractable and yields at least quasi-determinate results. For a variety of reasons, the postwar labor economists made relatively modest progress on this front (see Kaufman 1988; Kerr 1988). At the same time, a rival school of thought in labor economics was emerging that was to have far greater success in theory building, albeit in the opposite direction from that advocated by DKLR.

The Chicago School

A new school of thought about the competitive nature of markets emerged in the late 1940s and early 1950s that was centered at the University of Chicago. The major figures of this "Chicago school" were Milton Friedman, George Stigler, H. Gregg Lewis, and Gary Becker, with supporting contributions from persons such as Jacob Mincer, Albert Rees, Melvin Reder, and Sherwin Rosen. The point of view of the Chicago school with respect to the study and operation of labor markets would have a near-revolutionary impact on the field (and in several other areas of economics). Where the postwar labor economists had stressed the imperfectly competitive nature of labor markets, the advantages of an interdisciplinary research approach, and the potentially beneficial roles of collective bargaining and protective labor legislation, the economists of the Chicago school steered the field in the opposite direction. The result was a resurrection of competitive neoclassical theory; an approach to research that was "imperialistic" in that it sought to apply neoclassical theory to as wide a range of labor-related outcomes as possible; and a distinct skepticism, if not antipathy, toward institutional interventions in the operation of labor markets.

Clark Kerr has labeled the economists of the Chicago school the "neoclassical restorationists," a term that accurately depicts their approach to labor market theory, research, and policy issues (Kerr 1988). The neoclassical theory of wage determination advanced by Alfred Marshall, John Bates Clark, John Hicks, and other economic theorists during the early part of the twentieth century emphasized the primacy of market forces in the determination of wages and terms of employment and, while these economists admitted that competition in labor markets is less than perfect, they nevertheless maintained that in most cases the pattern of wages and employment closely corresponds in the long run to that predicted by competitive theory. A particularly explicit statement of this position is made by Hicks: "For the general tendency for the wages of labour of equal efficiency to become equalized in different occupations (allowance being made for other advantages and disadvantages of employment) has been a commonplace since the days of Adam Smith. . . . The movement of labour from one occupation to another, which brings it about, is certainly a slow one; but there is no need to question its reality" (Hicks 1932, 3).

This viewpoint was never widely accepted in labor economics proper in the pre–World War II years, dominated as it was then by the institutionalists, and it was largely discredited across the entire spectrum of the economics discipline for reasons already cited (the events of the Depression; the publication of important theoretical works by Keynes, Robinson, and Edward Chamberlain [1933] that emphasized the superiority of theories of imperfect competition). One of the few places where the neoclassical theory of competitive markets continued to find a core base of adherents was the University of Chicago. The most outspoken advocate of competitive markets at Chicago was an economic theorist named Henry Simons. It was in large part Simons, through both his teaching and writing, who provided the intellectual bedrock for what later emerged as the Chicago school in economics (Director 1948; Reder 1982). (The economic theorist

Frank Knight is also credited with having played a role in the founding of the Chicago school, albeit one that is more indirect and with less relevance to labor issues.) It is thus with Simons and his ideas that I will start.

Simons advanced several key propositions. First, he maintained that a system of competitive markets is essential for both economic efficiency and political freedom. He states, for example, that "the great enemy of democracy is monopoly, in all its forms: gigantic corporations, trade associations, and other agencies for price control, trade-unions — or, in general, organization and concentration of power within functional classes. . . . The existence of competition within such groups, on the other hand, serves to protect the community as a whole and to give an essential flexibility to the economy" (Simons 1948, 43).

Second, he argues that in most cases product and labor markets are relatively competitive and the monopoly elements that exist are generally short-lived and of not much quantitative importance (with the exception of those protected by government). He says, for example, that "monopsony in the labor market is, I think, very unsubstantial or transitory" and "enterprise monopoly [monopoly in the product market] is also a skin disease, easy to correct when and if we will, and usually moderate in its abuses" (Simons 1948, 129).

Third, given his view that most labor markets are competitive, Simons argues that the major imperfection that prevents labor markets from functioning as effectively as they might is government-sanctioned restrictions on trade. The greatest and most pernicious of these restrictions is the encouragement and protection of labor unions and collective bargaining through the National Labor Relations Act and other such laws. (Other examples include minimum wage laws and occupational licensing requirements.) With regard to unions, Simons states: "Industrial monopolies are not yet a serious evil. . . . The hard monopoly problem is labor organization. Here are monopolies, actual and imminent, with really great power, economic, political, and military" (Simons 1948, 35), and (pp. 121–122), "For my part, I simply cannot conceive of any tolerable or enduring order in which there exists widespread organization of workers along occupational, industrial, functional lines." His solution to the labor monopoly problem is twofold: deregulate labor markets (remove the legal protections given to unions) and promote greater competition among business firms (thus curbing the ability of unions to raise wages).

Simons died in 1947, but his point of view was passed on to, and in large part adopted by, a younger generation of economists who had been graduate students at Chicago in the 1930s and who were subsequently hired as professors there. The two most important of these students were Milton Friedman and George Stigler, both of whom went on to become Nobel laureates in economics. Friedman and Stigler, together with colleagues on the faculty, such as labor economist H. Gregg Lewis, and numerous doctoral students, such as Gary Becker (later to win a Nobel prize), Jacob Mincer, Albert Rees, and Melvin Reder, fashioned an approach to economic analysis and policy perspective so distinctive that it became known in labor economics (and a number of other fields) as the Chicago school.

Like Simons, Friedman and Stigler maintained that most labor markets are competitive. By "competitive," however, they do not mean that labor markets meet all the assumptions of the competitive model, such as zero costs of mobility and perfect information, for clearly no such labor market exists. Friedman and his wife, Rose, for example, openly acknowledge that labor markets contain a variety of imperfections: "Of course, competition by other employers is sometimes strong, sometimes weak. There is much friction and ignorance about opportunities. It may be costly for employers to locate desirable employees, and for employees to locate desirable employers. This is an imperfect world, so competition does not provide complete protection" (Friedman and Friedman 1979, 246). The contention of the Chicago School, however, is that these imperfections, while very real, are nevertheless relatively unimportant in the sense that the actual outcomes of labor markets, such as the pattern of wage differentials among occupations or employment levels among firms, correspond fairly closely to the levels that would be predicted by the perfectly competitive model (allowance being made for markets to reach a new equilibrium after an unexpected shift in demand, supply, or both). Friedman states as much in an earlier article on the economic effects of labor unions (also see Reder 1982). In response to critical comments by Paul Samuelson on the realism of competitive theory, Friedman states, "The question is whether it [competitive theory] gives you the right answer, and I would argue that it substantially does" (Friedman 1951, 254). He goes on to say, "The important point is that forces [noncompetitive elements] which bulk large when you look under the microscope at the individual case, but which vary from firm to firm and industry to industry, are likely to bulk small when you look at the aggregate."

Also like Simons, Friedman and Stigler were strongly opposed to most forms of institutional interventions in labor markets. As described earlier, both the institutionalists and the postwar labor economists were sympathetic to collective bargaining and minimum wage laws (at least if not used to excess), because they believed market imperfections allowed employers to pay less than competitive, full-employment wages to certain groups of workers and these devices helped rationalize the wage structure across firms and regions and removed arbitrary or inequitable wage differentials within firms, and because firms could offset a moderate increase in labor cost through increased management efficiency, sales effort, and so on, thus reducing the likelihood of a negative employment effect. Given their belief in the competitive nature of labor markets, the Chicago economists denied all these assertions and maintained, instead, that collective bargaining and minimum wage laws were harmful to both workers and the economy.

Stigler's article on the economics of the minimum wage (Stigler 1946) illustrates this point of view. Stigler states that minimum wage laws are traditionally justified as a means to achieve two objectives: reduction of employer control over wages and amelioration of poverty. With respect to the former, he concludes (p. 364) that employers' monopsony over wages is not a quantitatively important problem. Stigler justifies this assertion, in part, by arguing that scant empirical evidence exists that an increase in the minimum wage law leads to an increase in employment (a predicted outcome under certain situations according to the standard monopsony model).

Stigler then goes on to analyze the impact of a minimum wage law on a competitive labor market. He states (p. 358): "Each worker receives the value of his marginal product under competition. If a minimum wage is effective, it must therefore have one of two effects: first, workers whose services are worth less than the minimum wage are discharged ... or second, the productivity of low-efficiency workers is increased [and they keep their jobs]." The latter option (the shock effect), according to Stigler (p. 359) "is at present lacking in empirical evidence" and, he goes on to say, is not likely to be quantitatively important in the low-wage industries affected by a minimum wage (textiles, for example), because these industries have highly competitive product markets that force managers to operate the firm efficiently in the first place.

Stigler thus concludes that the likely effect of a minimum wage law is the first option (layoffs of low-productivity workers). His overall assessment is that the competitive model fits most labor markets reasonably well, and its chief prediction (that employment will decline in response to a minimum wage) is borne out by historical experience. As a poverty-fighting device, therefore, Stigler argues that a minimum wage law is substantially flawed because it causes many low-wage workers to lose their jobs.

By the mid 1960s the Chicago school had become the dominant intellectual force in labor economics, a position it was to strengthen over the next two decades. The rise to power of the Chicago school in academe, coupled with political and economic trends in the country that favored the Chicago perspective, not only substantially shifted the opinion of American labor economists toward a more free market view of labor markets but also led to major innovations in the application of competitive theory to the analysis of labor issues. The postwar labor economists had heavily criticized competitive theory because, in their view, it provided an overly narrow and simplistic view of how labor markets work, thus leading to incorrect predictions about economic relationships and misguided implications concerning social and economic policy. The economists of the Chicago school staged a major counterattack against the critics, a counterattack that proceeded along four fronts.

The first line of attack was to rebut the charge that competitive theory is inherently flawed because it is an unrealistic portrayal of real-world labor markets. In a well-known essay, Friedman (1953) argues that the correct test of a theory is not the realism of its assumptions but its predictive ability (also see Stigler 1949). Thus, from Friedman's point of view, Paul Douglas or the postwar labor economists might be right as a matter of theoretical realism that real-world labor markets often don't match the assumptions of competitive theory, but this fact is also irrelevant so long as competitive theory yields predictions consistent with observed labor market outcomes. In effect, says Friedman, so long as the outcomes under study accord with the predictions of the theory, it can be assumed that the decision making under investigation occurs *as if* it takes place in a competitive market.

Given that predictive accuracy, not the realism of assumptions, is to be the criterion for choosing among theories, it still might be thought that the imperfect market theories of the postwar labor economists would fare better than competitive theory. However, Friedman and Stigler also undermined this possibility. They claimed (for example in Friedman 1953) that a theory, if it is to be truly a *theory* rather than a descriptive or taxonomic device, must yield refutable hypotheses of an "if A then B" nature about substantive aspects of market behavior. Looked at from this point of view, the rival models of imperfect competition that occupied the middle ground between competition and monopoly (most particularly Chamberlain's model of monopolistic competition, but also the explicit and implicit labor market models of DKLR) were intellectually barren, for they yielded few testable hypotheses not already available from existing, simpler theories. The effect, then, was to narrow the choice between alternative structural models of labor markets to the competitive model versus the monopsony model. Since the number of one-company towns and the extent of overt employer collusion in labor markets were thought to be small and declining in significance (Bunting 1962), this effectively meant that the competitive model in all but rare cases had the field to itself and was the economist's main tool for studying labor markets.

An example of the power of these arguments is provided by H. Gregg Lewis in his analysis of the long-term decline in weekly hours of work. The postwar labor economists argued (see, for example, Reynolds 1955) that application of competitive market theory to this subject was inappropriate because most firms gave workers little choice over desired work hours and most of the impetus for change in work hours came from institutional sources (unions, overtime laws, public pressure on firms). Lewis dismisses the importance of these institutional factors, however, on the argument that consideration of employer preferences "would only complicate the theory . . . without substantial gain in interpreting the data" and that "the economic role of unions in the long-run decline of average hours worked . . . is surely a minor one" (Lewis 1956). He then goes on to use the neo-classical labor-leisure model to deduce in terms of income and sub-stitution effects the impact on workers' desired work hours of an increase in the wage rate. Assuming that the negative income effect dominates the positive substitution effect, the result is predicted to be a decline in work hours. Since this is exactly the pattern observed over time, Lewis argues that the data support (or at least do not contradict) the neoclassical theory.

The third line of attack pursued by the Chicago school was to admit the importance of certain market imperfections but to argue that their existence was quite consistent with neoclassical theory and a competitively determined efficient allocation of scarce resources. The critics of competitive theory alleged that market imperfections (such as limited mobility, poor information) caused wage rates and other outcomes to diverge significantly from competitive levels, with the implication that a free market system falls short of maximum attainable economic efficiency and that this situation could be improved through various institutional interventions. The Chicago economists sought to show, however, that the market imperfections cited as so damaging to the theory were actually themselves an efficient outcome generated by a rational weighing of benefits and costs by economic agents. Thus, while admitting the substantive importance of market imperfections on the one hand, they nevertheless deny on the other that these imperfections cause a serious problem either for the theory or the economy.

Two examples will illustrate the nature of this argument. First, the postwar labor economists had found that many workers have very limited knowledge of alternative job opportunities and, as a consequence, often accept the first job offered (see Reynolds 1951). This finding was taken as evidence that competitive forces on the supply side of the market are relatively weak. Stigler sought to neutralize this criticism by arguing that information is a scarce resource and thus it would be uneconomic (irrational) for workers to invest in perfect information about job opportunities. He argues (Stigler 1962) that labor market information is like any other good — efficiency is promoted if workers invest in additional job searching only so long as the marginal gain in earnings outweighs the marginal cost. If the marginal benefit of additional searching declines rapidly and the marginal cost of searching increases sharply, Stigler's model suggests that acceptance of a first job offer may actually be quite consistent with neoclassical theory (if not competitive theory, a point I will return to shortly).

A second example concerns firms' ability to pay workers less than competitive wages. Competitive theory predicts that firms pay workers the value of their marginal revenue product, for otherwise the workers will leave the firm and take a job elsewhere. The postwar labor economists (see Lester 1954) disputed the validity of this proposition on the grounds that specific job skills and other such factors impose significant mobility costs on employees and thus allow firms some margin to pay less than market wages. In his book *Human Capital* (1964), Gary Becker rigorously develops the theory of specific on-the-job training and shows that firms necessarily pay workers less than their marginal revenue product in the post-training period as a means to recoup the cost of providing the training. He thus remarks (p. 28), "Although a discrepancy between marginal product and wages is frequently taken as evidence of imperfections in the competitive system, it would occur even in a perfectly competitive system where there is investment in specific training."

The fourth line of attack pursued by the Chicago school, and one that has been implicit in several of the examples cited previously, was to redefine "competitive theory" so that it is at once broader in concept and application and less vulnerable to attack and empirical refutation. As previously described, in response to critics the Chicago economists sought to insulate competitive theory by arguing that alleged deviations from reality were themselves the product of rational, economizing behavior by economic agents. The long-run effect of this argument has been to shift the entire locus of the debate from a test of the predictions of competitive theory per se to that of a theory of rational behavior, where rational behavior means action consistent with maximization of self-interest in response to a set of known (or estimated) benefits and costs.

This line of thought has been most extensively promoted and practiced by Becker, who labels this revised paradigm "the economic approach" and describes it as follows: "The combined assumptions of maximizing behavior, market equilibrium, and stable preferences, used relentlessly and unflinchingly, form the heart of the economic approach as I see it" (Becker 1976, 5). The economic approach, as defined by Becker, thus subsumes competitive theory (the term *market equilibrium* almost always means competitively determined prices and incomes) but does not depend on competitive theory to retain its validity, and in fact can be used to rationalize departures from competitive conditions (as illustrated by Stigler's theory of labor market information). Becker has applied the economic approach to a host of subjects once thought to be outside the pale of labor economics, such as discrimination, drug addiction, marriage and divorce, fertility, criminal behavior, and the allocation time to market and nonmarket activities (see Becker 1957, 1976). Although a number of these activities do not take place in a competitive market (or in any market at all), the ability of this type of theory to yield interesting hypotheses, and the congruence of these hypotheses with at least a modicum of empirical evidence, has nevertheless convinced many economists of the power of both "competitive reasoning" in the realm of theory and "competitive forces" in the day to day operation of labor markets.

In addition to the theoretical arguments cited above, the Chicago view of labor markets also benefited greatly from the near revolution in the techniques and methodology of empirical research in labor economics that occurred in the post-1960 period. The case study, participant-observer type of investigation performed by the postwar labor economists was displaced by a research style that relies on computers, econometric statistical techniques, and large-scale secondary data sources. Thus, the short-run frictions and human complexities so evident to the postwar economists in their close-up studies of individual labor markets largely wash out in the aggregate, disembodied labor markets contained on computer data tapes. Likewise, the indeterminacy in economic relationships emphasized by the postwar labor economists is typically impounded in the error term of the regression equation and treated by Chicago economists as random variation due to unmeasurable factors, while the predicted relationships emphasized by competitive theory are frequently regarded as vindicated if the regression coefficients for the relevant independent variables are statistically significant, even if the quantitative impact of these variables is relatively small. Finally, modern research methods focus attention on those issues and relationships that can be quantified and subjected to statistical analysis, an approach that favors an "imperialistic" economic perspective over an interdisciplinary one and that focuses attention on quantitative aspects of labor market behavior (such as union wage effects) at the expense of qualitative or hard to measure aspects (for example, the impact of unions on reducing arbitrary discipline and discharge).

The Cambridge Group

The last set of economists to be considered in this chapter is the "Cambridge group." Associated with MIT and Harvard University (either as professors or former graduate students) in Cambridge, Massachusetts, these economists are the principal intellectual rivals to the Chicago school in current-day labor economics. Members of this group include the economic theorists and Nobel laureates Paul Samuelson and Robert Solow and labor economists such as Lester Thurow, Richard Freeman, Peter Doeringer, Michael Piore, Lawrence Summers, George Akerlof, and Paul Osterman.

The perspective of the Cambridge group on the competitive nature of labor markets is in many ways a direct descendant of that advanced several decades ago by the postwar labor economists, such as Dunlop and Kerr. (Many of the Cambridge group had Dunlop as a teacher at Harvard.) Although the Cambridge group is less successful than the Chicago school in articulating a well-defined theoretical and methodological approach to the study of labor markets (hence the use of the term *group* rather than *school*), their work is nevertheless distinguished by several common themes.

First and foremost is rejection of the Chicago claim that labor markets can be treated *as if* they are perfectly competitive. Solow states, for example:

> I understand perfectly well that it is not the job of theory to get the details right. A map on the scale of one inch to the mile does not show every bend in the road. But you expect the general direction to be right. . . . Yet in today's preferred style the labor market is usually modelled as just clearing or, more subtly, producing efficient contracts. Bits of realism appear here and

there in the literature but have not made much headway. You do not have to be a congenital skeptic to doubt that this sort of map gives a useful picture of the lay of the land (Solow 1990, xvi–xvii).

In a similar vein, Thurow states, "To my mind, mainstream American economists reflect more an academic need for an internal theoretical consistency and rigor than it reflects observable, measurable reality" (Thurow 1983, xvi). He goes on to say of labor markets (p. 215), "If one were ranking various economic markets along a continuum by the extent to which they reflected the postulates of the price-auction [competitive] model, financial markets would probably be placed at one end and labor markets at the other." Finally, there is the comment of Paul Samuelson that "If each morning people could be hired in an organized auction market, the world would be a very different one — not a slightly different one, but a substantially different one" (Samuelson 1951, 322).

The claim of the Cambridge group that labor market outcomes are not usefully viewed as the product of a competitive market is based on what they consider to be certain crucial "deviant observations." The most cited example is the extent and persistence of unemployment in many labor markets (Thurow 1975, 1983; Solow 1990). According to competitive theory, an excess supply of labor in the market should precipitate a downward bidding of the wage until demand equals supply and full employment is restored. During recessions, however, wage rates exhibit a marked rigidity in the downward direction, and widespread unemployment frequently lasts for a considerable time. Proponents of the Chicago school attempt to rescue competitive theory through several arguments: wage rigidity is due to man-made market imperfections, such as unions and minimum wage laws; wage rigidity stems from implicit agreements made by firms to reduce income variability for risk-averse workers; and observed unemployment represents a voluntary choice to remain out of work until wage offers improve. Cambridge economists reject these arguments on the grounds that they are neither plausible nor supported by convincing empirical evidence.

A second commonly cited deviant observation is the considerable dispersion of wage rates that exists in most labor markets for similar types of labor (Freeman 1988). According to the simplest of competitive models, a single uniform wage rate should be paid by all firms in a labor market for similar workers doing similar jobs. A more sophisticated model, based on Adam Smith's theory of compensating wage differentials, predicts that wages will vary among workers and jobs in a manner such that differences in net advantages and disadvantages due to risk of injury, amount of skill required, and so on are equalized. This supply-side approach is typically the one used by Chicago economists to explain interfirm and interindustry wage differentials, because it provides an explanation for such differentials that is consistent with a competitive market equilibrium (Rosen 1986). The Cambridge group, however, rejects this argument, citing numerous empirical studies (for example, Krueger and Summers 1987) that find that a large portion of pay differentials are related to demand-side factors (such as firm and industry profitability, race and gender of the workers) that are quite likely noncompensating in nature.

What accounts for these deviant observations? The economists of the Cambridge group say the Chicago school assumes that labor markets operate much as commodity markets when, in fact, the two types of markets are quite different. On this matter Solow says: "One important tradition within economics, perhaps the dominant tradition right now . . . holds that in nearly all respects the labor market is just like other markets. It should be analyzed in much the same way that one would analyze the market for any perishable commodity, using the conventional apparatus of supply and demand. Common sense, on the other hand, seems to take it for granted that there is something special about the labor market" (Solow 1990, 3). What is the nature of this special factor? The answer, according to the Cambridge group, is that the service being traded in the labor market diverges from all others because it is embodied in a human being.

The human essence of labor fundamentally alters the operation of labor markets in several respects, these economists argue. One is that the supply of labor, and most particularly work effort, becomes a function of the psychological process of motivation. An inanimate factor such as a machine tool or ton of coal does not have to be "motivated" to provide its services — it will yield the same productive services regardless of the price paid for it, whether it is utilized in a pleasant or dreary workplace, and whether management is considerate or autocratic. Employees, however, are far different. What firms actually buy (or, more correctly, rent) from workers is their time; the actual amount of labor services provided is a choice made by the employee. This choice, in turn, is influenced by a host of psychological and social considerations, such as the perceived fairness of the rate of pay, the characteristics of the work to be performed (interesting versus boring, for example), the race, gender, and personality of fellow workers, and the manner in which management treats employees.

A second key difference between labor and other production factors involves the cognitive process of learning. An increase in the productivity of an inanimate factor such as an industrial robot can be obtained either by purchasing an improved model on the market or by using engineers and technicians to augment its capabilities. Increasing the productivity of employees, on the other hand, frequently requires a different approach. Many job skills that determine an employee's productivity are specific to the firm and the task at hand and, thus, cannot be readily purchased on the market. Likewise, it is typically impossible to reengineer human beings to increase their speed, dexterity, or knowledge. Therefore, the acquisition of new employee skills frequently entails a process of learning on the job through formal training programs, informal instruction from workmates, and trial-and-error experience. The challenge for firms, then, is to structure the employment relationship so that it facilitates maximum learning and on-the-job training. Among other things, this means providing employment security for workers so that they have an incentive to acquire the training; paying above-market wages so that workers do not leave the firm once it has invested in their training; filling job vacancies above the entry level through a system of promotion from within to facilitate the learning of new, higher-level skills; and allocating new job opportunities to workers not on the basis of who will work for the least rate of pay but on who is the most trainable.

These considerations, the Cambridge economists claim, lead firms to adopt organizational structures and administrative rules concerning human resource policies that fundamentally alter the operation and outcomes of labor markets (Doeringer and Piore 1971). The result, in turn, is the deviant observations noted above. Why, for example, don't unemployed workers bid down wages in recessions until a new demand-and-supply full-employment equilibrium is reached? One part of the answer is that firms find wage cuts counterproductive because they undermine the morale and work effort of existing employees; another part is that firms are deterred by the costs of training from replacing existing employees with new hires who are willing to work for less. Likewise, why do wages vary so greatly among firms and industries for similar workers and jobs? Part of the answer is that the existence of internal labor markets partially insulates company wage decisions from competitive forces, thus allowing companies greater discretion in establishing pay rates and ranges; a second part is that worker mobility in response to wage differentials is impeded by the costs of leaving one firm for another (due, in part, to personnel practices such as promotion by seniority, vesting requirements in pension plans, and the like); and a third part is that wages vary directly with the level of profits in a firm or industry, because workers perceive it unfair (and therefore reduce work effort or become interested in collective bargaining) if they don't share in those profits.

These considerations have important implications for labor market theory. Competitive theory, the Cambridge economists say, is useful as a frame of reference for thinking about the operation of labor markets and for explaining certain long-run trends. Thus, Solow states: "It does not follow from any of this that the ordinary forces of supply and demand are irrelevant to the labor market, or that we can do without the textbook apparatus altogether. It only follows that they are incomplete and need completing" (Solow 1990, 22). This "completing process" moves in several directions.

One direction for theory is the elaboration of alternative structural models of labor markets. In current-day labor economics it is fashionable to distinguish between only two labor market structures, perfect competition and monopsony. Since most economists view the monopsony model as anachronistic, this leaves the competitive model. A better approach, the Cambridge group believes, is to build alternative labor market models around distinct forms of "employment systems" (Osterman 1987). An example, if not entirely successful, is the dual labor market model (Piore 1970; Bulow and Summers 1986). An alternative conceptualization is seen in Thurow's (1975) "job competition" and "wage competition" models of the labor market.

A second direction for theory is the incorporation of more realistic human behavior assumptions in models of labor markets. An example is the introduction of equity and fairness considerations into theories of wage determination. One approach along this line is the development of efficiency wage models (Akerlof and Yellen 1990). Another suggested line of attack is the broadening of the profit maximization assumption to include multiple goals and satisficing behavior on the part of firm management. Efforts in this direction have utilized the burgeoning literature on principal-agent theory. Yet another behavioral dimension that the Cambridge group emphasizes is the dynamics of interpersonal relations, particularly as it pertains to the conditions promoting cooperation versus competition in work groups. Work on this subject has utilized game theory, such as the prisoner's dilemma model.

Finally, it is not surprising that the Cambridge economists take a more sympathetic view of labor unions and protective forms of labor legislation than their Chicago counterparts. Richard Freeman and James Medoff, for example, have argued that the monopoly model of unions typically assumed by Chicago school economists provides an overly negative view of the effect of unions on economic efficiency. While it is true, they say, that union bargaining power leads to above-competitive wage rates and a resulting misallocation of resources, the "voice" function of unions leads to a number of positive economic effects typically ignored or downplayed by Chicago economists.

Echoing the position of Commons and Slichter, Freeman and Medoff claim that many types of working conditions are public goods that are, as a consequence, underproduced in a nonunion labor market (because each individual worker will act as a free rider, hoping to enjoy the benefits of better conditions but without suffering the risk of speaking up to management). Collective bargaining provides a way of overcoming this market defect and thus improving the performance of labor markets. The voice function of collective bargaining also leads to gains in efficiency by reducing quitting and promoting increased productivity through improved management practices and employee morale. Both of these union contributions are generally overlooked in competitive models of the labor market, given the assumption in such models that firms always minimize cost and mobility is relatively costless (skills are portable in the market).

Conclusion

I have attempted here to cast light on two related questions: are labor markets competitive, and is competitive theory a useful tool for understanding the operation and outcome of these markets? My purpose has not been to provide an explicit answer to these questions, as valuable as that might be, but rather to describe the evolution of thought on these matters from the time of Adam Smith to the present.

This review suggests several conclusions. It is clear, for example, that there has been a wide range of opinion on both issues over the years. The two end points in the spectrum of thought are represented by the institutionalists on the "negative" side and the Chicago school on the "positive" side. Viewed in the context of two centuries of thought, the middle position is probably best represented by Adam Smith and by the postwar labor economists. It is also clear, however, that over the past three decades the weight of opinion in American labor economics has shifted away from the historical "middle" and toward a more competitive or free market perspective.

Why has this shift occurred? The most one can do with this question is to engage in informed speculation. From my perspective the answer has several parts. The first is related to the change over time in the structural characteristics of labor markets. Although hard research evidence on this matter is largely absent, I have argued elsewhere that several factors have worked to increase the competitiveness of labor markets in the post–World War II period (Kaufman 1989, 1990). It seems highly likely, for example, that labor markets are closer to the competitive ideal because of the increased geographic mobility of labor, improved job market information, the reduction in occupational barriers to entry brought about by improved access to institutions of higher education, reduced collusive practices among employers, less unionization among workers, and (since the 1980s) increased competition in product markets. Other powerful factors that have worked in the opposite direction include restrictions on labor mobility due to the growth in importance of fringe benefits (and associated concerns with pension vesting, health insurance availability, and so on), a growth in the firm-specific nature of job skills for a significant share of the work force (which reduces mobility and creates bilateral monopoly conditions in wage determination), the creation of some type of sheltered internal labor market by an increasing proportion of firms (a trend partly reversed in the 1980s, however), and the formalization and spread of human resource management practices and the attendant growth in influence of administrative rules and regulations concerning allocative decisions such as hiring, firing, pay, and promotion.

The net impact of these factors on the competitive nature of labor markets is uncertain, but a reasonable case can be made that labor markets have moved in a more competitive direction, a trend that is consistent with, and helps explain, the rise to power of the Chicago school. The shift in thinking toward a more competitive view of labor markets cannot be attributed solely to structural changes, however, for two other developments also played an equally, if not larger, role.

One of these is the positive impact on the labor market of various types of institutional intervention. There is little doubt, for example, that the earnings of minority workers and the number of female lawyers and doctors would remain depressed below, and the incidence of workplace injuries elevated considerably above, the level that would prevail in a truly competitive, barrier-free labor market were it not for the passage of civil rights, affirmative action, and occupational safety and health legislation. An institutional intervention of a different type, but one of much greater importance, is the use of activist, Keynesian-inspired monetary and fiscal policies to reduce macroeconomic instability and involuntary unemployment.

Among economists of the pre–World War II era, the persistent, widespread presence of unemployed job seekers was seen as the single greatest factor accounting for noncompetitive outcomes in labor markets. With thousands of unemployed workers outside the plant gates, employers no longer faced competitive pressure to pay a compensating wage differential for risk of injury or to hire a black worker with equal productivity to a white worker. If there is any economic lesson of the twentieth century, it is that full employment is the surest guarantor of competitive wages and conditions for workers, for only then are employers motivated by a prospective shortage of labor to "do the right thing." A corollary lesson is that — the wishful thinking of certain macroeconomists notwithstanding — it is a vain hope to expect that money or real wage cuts in labor markets will restore the economy to a full-employment equilibrium. Thus, even though Chicago economists claim with some justification that labor markets perform *as if* they are competitive, this outcome reflects more the guiding hand of government, which they decry, than the presumed equilibrating forces of demand and supply in labor markets.

The other consideration accountable for a significant part of the pronounced shift toward a more competitive view of labor markets among economists is the divorce of theory from reality. Under the influence of the Chicago school, it has become a serious methodological weakness to check the accuracy of assumptions against the facts, to interview managers, union officials, or workers about their motives or actions, or to conduct a participant-observer case investigation of a specific labor market. Worse, theory development has become an end in itself, as the greatest professional rewards go to those economists who show the most ingenuity and technical virtuosity in either successfully applying neoclassical, competitive theory to a hitherto unexplored subject or in using it to rationalize a troublesome deviant observation. In empirical work, in turn, hypothesis testing is all too often turned on its head, so that the goal becomes affirmation of the theoretical model rather than a disinterested testing of the facts. One must conclude that the move toward a more competitive view of labor markets partly reflects the lamentable detachment most economists have from the real-life version of the subject they are studying, the near complete absence of empirical studies of individual labor markets (an exception is Leonard 1989) and of those assumptions most crucial to the validity of the competitive model (a perfectly elastic labor supply curve to the firm, a cost-minimizing wage policy by employers), and the distorting influence imparted to labor market research by the preoccupation many economists have with the development and testing of theory for its own sake.

In a number of respects great advances have been achieved in our understanding of labor markets. Unfortunately, knowledge of the operation of individual, real-world labor markets, and the degree to which their outcomes approach competitive levels, is not one of them (a conclusion also reached in Freeman 1988). I suspect part of the reason for this is a fear of what will be found and the damage this knowledge will inflict on the elaborate theoretical edifice and comfortable policy conclusions built up in labor economics over the past 30 years.

References

Akerlof, George A., and Janet L. Yellen. 1990. "The Fair Wage-Effort Hypothesis and Unemployment." *Quarterly Journal of Economics* 105 (May), 255–284.

Ashenfelter, Orley, and Richard Layard. 1986. *Handbook of Labor Economics.* Amsterdam: North Holland.

Becker, Gary S. 1957. *The Economics of Discrimination.* Chicago: University of Chicago Press.

———. 1964. *Human Capital.* New York: Columbia University Press.

———. 1976. *The Economic Approach to Human Behavior.* Chicago: University of Chicago Press.

Blum, Solomon. 1925. *Labor Economics.* New York: Henry Holt.

Bulow, Jeremy, and Lawrence Summers. 1986. "A Test of Dual Labor Markets with Application to Industrial Policy, Discrimination, and Keynesian Unemployment." *Journal of Labor Economics* 4 (July), 376–414.

Bunting, Robert L. 1962. *Employer Concentration in Local Labor Markets.* Chapel Hill: University of North Carolina Press.

Cain, Glen. 1976. "The Challenge of Segmented Labor Market Theories to Orthodox Theory." *Journal of Economic Literature* 14 (December), 1215–1257.

Chamberlain, Edward. 1933. *The Theory of Monopolistic Competition.* Cambridge, Mass.: Harvard University Press.

Commons, John R. 1921. "Industrial Relations," in John R. Commons, ed., *Trade Unionism and Labor Problems*, Second Series. New York: Augustus Kelly. pp. 1–16.

Commons, John R., and John B. Andrews. 1936. *Principles of Labor Legislation*, 4th revised ed. New York: Harper & Row.

Director, Aaron. 1948. "Prefatory Note," in Henry Simons, *Economic Policy for a Free Society.* Chicago: University of Chicago Press. pp. v–vii.

Doeringer, Peter B., and Michael J. Piore. 1971. *Internal Labor Markets and Manpower Analysis.* Lexington, Mass.: D. C. Heath, Lexington Books.

Dorfman, Joseph. 1963. "The Background of Institutional Economics," in *Institutional Economics: Veblen, Commons, and Mitchell Reconsidered.* Berkeley: University of California Press. pp. 1–44.

Douglas, Paul H. 1934. *The Theory of Wages.* New York: Macmillan.

Dunlop, John T. 1957. "The Task of Contemporary Wage Theory," in George Taylor and Frank Pierson, eds., *New Concepts in Wage Determination.* New York: McGraw-Hill. pp. 117–139.

———, ed. 1961. *Potentials of the American Economy: Selected Essays of Sumner H. Slichter.* Cambridge, Mass.: Harvard University Press.

Freeman, Richard B. 1988. "Do the Newer Generation of Labor Economists Know More than the Older Generation? in Bruce E. Kaufman, ed., *How Labor Markets Work,* Lexington, Mass.: Lexington Books. pp. 205–232.

Freeman, Richard B., and James Medoff. 1984. *What Do Unions Do?* New York: Basic Books.

Friedman, Milton, 1951. "Some Comments on the Significance of Labor Unions for Economic Policy," in David McCord Wright, ed., *The Impact of the Union.* New York: Kelley & Millman. pp. 204–234.

———. 1953. "The Methodology of Positive Economics," In Milton Friedman, *Essays in Positive Economics.* Chicago: University of Chicago Press. pp. 3–43.

Friedman, Milton, and Rose Friedman. 1979. *Free to Choose.* New York: Harcourt Brace.

Hicks, John R. 1932. *The Theory of Wages.* London: Macmillan.

Kaufman, Bruce E. 1988. "The Postwar View of Labor Markets and Wage Determination," in Bruce E. Kaufman, ed., *How Labor Markets Work.* Lexington, Mass.: Lexington Books. pp. 145–203.

———. 1989. "Labor's Inequality of Bargaining Power: Changes Over Time and Implications for Public Policy." *Journal of Labor Research* 10 (Summer), 285–298.

———. 1990. "Labor's Inequality of Bargaining Power: Myth or Reality?" *Journal of Labor Research* 11 (Spring), 151–166.

———. 1993. *The Origins and Evolution of the Field of Industrial Relations.* Ithaca, N.Y.: ILR Press.

Kerr, Clark. 1950. "Labor Markets: Their Character and Consequences." *American Economic Review* 40 (May), 278–291.

———. 1954. "The Balkanization of Labor Markets," in Social Science Research Council, *Labor Mobility and Economic Opportunity.* New York: John Wiley & Sons. pp. 92–110.

———. 1969. *Marshall, Marx and Modern Times.* London: Cambridge University Press.

———. 1988. "The Neoclassical Revisionists in Labor Economics (1940–1960) — R.I.P.," in Bruce E. Kaufman, ed., *How Labor Markets Work.* Lexington, Mass.: Lexington Books. pp. 1–46.

Keynes, John M., 1936. *The General Theory of Employment, Interest, and Money.* New York: Harcourt.

Krueger, Alan, and Lawrence Summers. 1987. Reflections on the Inter-Industry Wage Structure," in Kevin Lang and Jonathan Leonard, eds., *Unemployment and the Structure of Labor Markets.* New York: Basil Blackwell. pp. 17–47.

Leonard, Jonathan S. 1989. "Wage Structure and Dynamics in the Electronics Industry." *Industrial Relations* 28 (Spring), 251–275.

Lester, Richard A. 1946. "Shortcomings of Marginal Analysis for Wage-Employment Problems." *American Economic Review* 36 (March), 63–82.

———. 1952. "A Range Theory of Wage Differentials." *Industrial and Labor Relations Review* 5 (July), 433–450.

———. 1954. *Hiring Practices and Labor Competition.* Princeton: Industrial Relations Section, Princeton University.

Lewis, H. Gregg. 1956. "Hours of Work and Hours of Leisure," in Industrial Relations Research Association, *Proceedings of the Ninth Annual Meeting.* Madison, Wis.: IRRA. pp. 196–206.

Marshall, Alfred. 1961. *Principles of Economics,* 9th (Variorum) ed., vol. 1. London: Macmillan.

McNulty, Paul J. 1980. *The Origins and Development of Labor Economics.* Cambridge, Mass.: MIT Press.

Millis, Harry A., and Royal E. Montgomery. 1938. *The Economics of Labor* (vol. 1, *Labor's Problems and Progress,* 1938; vol. 2, *Labor's Risks and Social Insurance.* 1938; and vol. 3, *Organized Labor,* 1945). New York: McGraw-Hill.

Osterman, Paul. 1987. "Choice of Employment Systems in Internal Labor Markets." *Industrial Relations* 26 (Winter), 46–67.

Pierson, Frank C. 1957. "An Evaluation of Wage Theory," in George Taylor and Frank Pierson, eds., *New Concepts in Wage Determination.* pp. 3–31.

Piore, Michael J. 1970. "Jobs and Training: Manpower Policy," in Samuel Beer and Richard Barringer, eds., *The State and the Poor.* pp. 53–83.

Reder, Melvin W. 1982. "Chicago Economics: Permanence and Change." *Journal of Economic Literature* 20 (March), 1–38.

Reynolds, Lloyd. 1951. *The Structure of Labor Markets.* New York. Harper and Brothers.

———. 1954. *Labor Economics and Labor Relations,* 2nd ed. Englewood Cliffs, N.J.: Prentice-Hall.

———. 1955. "Research and Practice in Industrial Relations," in Industrial Relations Research Association, *Proceedings of the Eighth Annual Meeting.* Madison, Wis.: IRRA. pp. 2–13.

Robinson, Joan. 1933. *The Economics of Imperfect Competition.* London: Macmillan.

Rosen, Sherwin. 1986. "The Theory of Equalizing Differences," in Orley Ashenfelter and Richard Layard, eds., *Handbook of Labor Economics,* vol 1. Amsterdam: North Holland. pp. 641–692.

Rottenberg, Simon. 1956. "On Choice in Labor Markets." *Industrial and Labor Relations Review* 9 (January), 183–199.

Samuelson, Paul. 1951. "Economic Theory and Wages," in David McCord Wright, ed., *The Impact of the Union.* New York: Harcourt Brace. pp. 312–360.

Simons, Henry C. 1948. *Economic Policy for a Free Society.* Chicago: University of Chicago Press.

Slichter, Sumner H. 1931. *Modern Economic Society,* rev. ed. New York: Henry Holt.

———. 1947. *The Challenge of Industrial Relations.* Ithaca, N.Y.: Cornell University Press.

Smith, Adam. 1776. *An Inquiry into the Nature and Causes of the Wealth of Nations.* New York: The Modern Library.

Solow, Robert M. 1990. *The Labor Market as a Social Institution.* New York: Basil Blackwell.

Stigler, George. 1946. "The Economics of Minimum Wage Legislation." *American Economic Review* 36 (June), 358–365.

———. 1949. *Five Lectures on Economic Problems.* London: Longmans, Green.

———. 1962. "Information in the Labor Market." *Journal of Political Economy* 70, Part 2 (October), 94–105.

Thurow, Lester C. 1975. *Generating Inequality.* New York: Basic Books.

———. 1983. *Dangerous Currents: The State of Economics.* New York: Random House.

Webb, Sydney, and Beatrice Webb. 1897. *Industrial Democracy.* London: Longmans, Green.

6

Wage Differentials and Minimum-Wage Effects

■ ————————————— ■

Richard A. Lester

This chapter deals with two interrelated subjects. One is certain wage differentials — size-of-company, interindustry, and inter-establishment — in a labor market area that have proved difficult to explain by standard competitive theory. The other subject is the employment effects of increases in legal minimum wages, in a state or nationwide, that are inconsistent with expectations or predictions based on competitive labor market analysis. The chapter draws on research findings that extend over half a century. Particularly fruitful have been the decades of 1945 to 1955 and 1982 to 1992. In recent years some younger economists have made significant contributions in these subject areas.

Wage Differentials by Plant and Company Size

A prominent feature of manufacturing wage structures in this country and abroad has been the employer-size wage differential — the fact that there is a positive relationship between wages paid and size of company and plant.

Employer-size wage differentials are often calculated and presented by using the largest size category (firms or plants with 1,000 or more employees) as a base. In a paper of mine (Lester 1967) such wage indexes were presented by seven size categories for 21 representative industries or branches of industries, using 1954 U.S. Census of Manufacturing data. All except three of the industries had the distinct pattern of wage index numbers increasing as size of establishment increases. The index figures for wages in Table 6.1, taken from a table in the 1967 paper, provide a simple average for the 21 industries.

As Table 6.2 shows, a similar pattern of employer-size wage differentials has characterized the wage structures of certain European countries and Japan. Indeed, the pattern of such differentials for the United Kingdom and France resembles that for the United States in Table 6.1 except that the spread of wages between the smallest and largest categories for the United States is somewhat greater — 74 to 100 — than for Britain and France. For West Germany, the spread between the smallest and largest size categories is quite small: 91 to 100. The opposite is the case for Japan, with the spread in 1960 being from 55 to 100. By the 1970s, however, the size-of-firm wage differential seems to have been more nearly like that in this country (Oi and Raisian 1985, 2–3, Appendix Table 2).

Table 6.1. Wages by plant size for manufacturing industries, 1954

No. of plant employees	Index of wages
50– 99	74
100–249	77
250–499	81
500–999	87
1,000+	100

Source: Lester 1967, 59 (Table 2).

Table 6.2. Wage differentials by size of manufacturing establishment, 1960

No. of employees	United Kingdom*	France	Italy	West Germany	Japan
50– 99	82	78	85	91	55
100–249	83	81	87	94	72
250–499	85	81	92	99	85
500–999	90	89	92	99	88
1,000+	100	100	100	100	100

Source: Data from Koji Taira, "Wage Differentials in Developing Countries: A Survey of Findings," *International Labour Review* 93 (March 1966), 285.
Note: The ratio for each size class is the median of the ratios for eight manufacturing industries.
* Figures for the U.K. are from 1954.

A comprehensive study by Charles Brown, James Hamilton, and James Medoff (*Employers Large and Small*, 1990) adds considerably to our knowledge and understanding of the wage effects of different company and plant sizes. Their study includes material on manufacturing and on employment in communications, transportation, and retail trade. In their analysis, Brown, Hamilton, and Medoff make a serious effort to control for any differences in work force quality and in working conditions between small and large companies or establishments.

Brown, Hamilton, and Medoff's principal findings in summary form are as follows (with page references):

1. Both large firms and large workplaces pay money wages that are about one-third higher than are paid by small ones (pp. 3, 43).
2. Firm size has a similar effect on expenditures for fringe benefits (such as life insurance, health insurance, pensions, paid vacations): fringe benefit expenditures are more than 30 percent higher for large firms than for small firms (pp. 35, 43, 47).
3. Unionization tends to dampen the employer-size wage effect. Workers in large unionized firms earn only 14 percent more than their counterparts in small unionized firms (p. 32).
4. Taking into account the observable indicators of employee quality such as education, training, experience, and occupation, employees of large firms have, on balance, a size-wage differential of 10 to 13 percent (p. 33).

From their examination of the data, Brown, Hamilton, and Medoff conclude that it "is still an open research question" why large employers do pay such firm-size wage premiums to their employees (p. 42).

In a 1990 paper, Charles Brown and James Medoff thoroughly examine and test a number of explanations that have been offered for employer-size wage differentials. Their findings "strongly suggest that differences in employee quality by size of firm and size of establishment can explain about one half of the total size-wage differential" (Brown and Medoff, 1028). They find that (1) the existence of measurable differences in working conditions "seems not to explain much of the size-wage differential," (2) "the threat of unionism to large employers does not explain the size premiums," and (3) "within industries, market power does not explain the size-wage premium" (p. 1056).

The authors conclude that they do not have "the answers to the question why large employers pay their workers more than small employers do." They find that "the employer-size wage effect remains a fact in need of an empirically based theory" (p. 1057). Commenting on an early version of the Brown-Medoff study, Richard Freeman said that they had "found that there are significant differentials by size of firm that cannot be readily explained by standard competitive theory" (Freeman 1988, 209).

A recent study by Lucia Dunn (1984) examines the effect of firm size on wages, fringe benefits, working conditions, and the disutility of work, and finds that "the appropriation" by labor of some of "large firms' higher profits is the dominant influence" in the firm-size relationship. The study uses samples of employers and employees in the plastics industry from a metropolitan area in the northeast and a nonmetropolitan area in a midwestern state. All firms included in the study were organized by national unions.

The paper concludes with its findings on three explanations commonly advanced for the existence of higher wages in larger firms. These are: (1) the worker skill and discipline requirements are no greater than in small firms, so that factor cannot be the cause of the wage-size differential; (2) there is no difference in the disutility of work in the small- and medium-size firms, but that factor may play some role in explaining the size-wage differential in larger firms with over 4,000 employees. Through organized bargaining efforts, labor in large firms appropriates some of the large firms' higher profits; that is the dominant influence in the wage–firm size relationship. (Dunn 1984, 35–36).

In commenting on the Dunn paper, Orley Ashenfelter notes that the findings are derived from data for only one industry in which there are no returns to scale, and that there is a need to demonstrate that any rents in the economic system are likely to be correlated with firm size (Ashenfelter 1984, 81–82).

Interindustry Wage Differentials

A significant pattern of wage differentials among manufacturing industries was prevalent in this country well before World War I. Certain industries have had comparatively high wage scales or structures; these include airframe manufacturing, automobile assembly, chemicals, and steel. Industries that have had low wage scales include cotton textiles, fertilizer, food preparation and canning, and leather and leather products.

Studies in the post–World War I period found that high wages tend to be paid in industries where labor costs are a small percentage of total production costs, profit margins are relatively high, and the industry tends to be dominated by a few large firms, which affects product competition (Cullen 1956; Garbarino 1950; Ross 1950).

The influence that company wage policies can have on interindustry wage differences is demonstrated by experience in the automobile and oil industries. In 1914, Henry Ford boldly established a $5 minimum wage for an eight-hour workday in all Ford operations, in the South as well as the North. Ford stated that his wages before the $5 minimum averaged "about 15 percent above the usual market rate," and he thought of the resulting large increases in pay for all Ford workers as a form of profit sharing (Ford 1922, 126–128). Now it might be called rent sharing. By instituting and carrying out a companywide program of wage uniformity in the early days when the Ford Motor Company was the major automobile producer, a nationwide wage pattern was established for the industry that, with few deviations, characterized it thereafter.

The oil industry illustrates another aspect of interindustry differentials in pay. The early policy adapted by the Standard Oil Company of paying "at least the prevailing scale of wages for similar work in the community" (Hicks 1941, 56) meant that wage scales in petroleum refining were among the highest in each district or labor market area where the oil company was operating. By the time I made my study of company wage policies in 1947, an oil industry wage pattern had been established involving cooperation by the leading firms so that wage-level changes in the industry were made at the same time and to the same extent (Lester 1948, 15, 17, 18). One reason that oil companies did not wish to exceed the wage scale of high-paying employers in the locality was because that might antagonize them. Such concern, however, was not generated by a high level of company nonwage benefits (for example, employee pensions, hospital and medical care, and group life insurance), in which the petroleum industry's record has been outstanding. In 1959, companies in that industry were spending over 12 percent of gross payroll (37 cents an hour) on private benefit plans, which was almost twice as much as the next highest industry in terms of employee benefits (Lester 1964, 338). It would be interesting to try to determine the extent to which compensation in the form of benefits for production workers (and also for management) in oil companies has really involved rent sharing.

In a 1987 paper, Alan Krueger and Lawrence Summers present a thorough study of the interindustry wage structure. They conclude from their analysis and from earlier studies by others that the competitive labor market model cannot provide a plausible explanation of the pervasive pattern of interindustry differentials "without the introduction of non-competitive considerations or additional constraints" (Krueger and Summers 1987, 18, 37). They also say that "there are reasons to believe that considerations other than profit maximization influence the wage structure," and if managers were to maximize a utility function including both profits and the well-being of the production employees, the situation might resemble that in industries having a high wage differential (pp. 39, 40). The authors "conclude that industry wage differentials reflect in large part rent sharing between firms and workers" and endure because the payment of high wages is not very costly for firms for efficiency wage reasons (p. 18). In further support of their findings, they state: "We have stressed the rent sharing aspect of wage setting as an explanation for differences in the inter-industry wage structure because of the difficulty of accounting in any other way for the similarity in the wage pattern for all different types of workers" in the company (p. 41). No effort was made to explain company variation in the amount of rent sharing over time.

Interemployer Differentials in a Labor Market Area

The structure of wages in manufacturing plants in a city or an industrial area is the result of various factors and influences on both a national and a local basis over an extended period of time. Among them, of course, are the size-of-plant wage differentials and the inter-industry wage differentials already examined. My 1948 study of the wage policies and practices of 107 manufacturing companies, with 2 million employees distributed around the country, included 88 multiplant concerns (Lester 1948, 8). It showed that such large companies, following varied wage policies, could cause persistent wage differentials at the local level. Thirteen of the companies with operations in a number of states were following a policy of paying a uniform wage scale for their production employees, wherever their plants were located (pp. 18–20). Companywide uniformity in wage scales then was especially prevalent in the flat glass, automobile assembly, and aircraft assembly industries.

Especially when one is dealing with wage differentials in a local labor market, one must bear in mind that money wages are administered prices and that noncash compensation (benefits) is also administered.

The New Haven labor market study

Lloyd Reynolds's examination of the New Haven, Connecticut, labor market provides a detailed analysis of the wage differentials among 28 manufacturing companies (Reynolds 1951). His findings include the following with respect to wage differentials:

1. The larger plants "tend to be the high-wage plants" (p. 221).
2. The range of interplant differentials is indicated by the fact that, in mid-1948, "the starting rate for inexperienced workers varied from about 60 cents per hour in the lowest [paying] plants to $1.18 in the highest plant" (p. 221).
3. The "dispersion of plant wage levels changed very little between 1940 and 1948" (p. 222).
4. Nonwage terms of employment, such as employee benefits and plant conditions, served "to accentuate interplant wage differentials rather than to offset them" (p. 221).

"Quality of labor" is difficult to measure but, using a variety of evidence, Reynolds found that the "difference in average quality of workforce in different plants is considerably less than the difference in their wage levels" (p. 219). Thus, quality of labor was no more than a part of the explanation for the interplant wage differentials in New Haven during that time.

The Trenton labor market study

My two-stage study of the Trenton, New Jersey, labor market in the early 1950s, which included an examination of interplant wage differentials, lent support to the findings of the New Haven study (Lester 1954, 1955). Some selected factual material from that study may assist in understanding the wage differentials. The managers of 82 manufacturing plants were systematically interviewed in 1951 and 1952. The plants made up about 70 percent of the manufacturing employment in the area of the study. Thirty of the plants each had over 500 employees, and 34 plants were either branch plants or subdivisions of companies with headquarters elsewhere. The personnel managers of some 30 of those companies had an association that met monthly, so they were presumably informed on the wages and employment practices of their constituent companies and could thereby serve their mutual interests. The first part of my study dealt with the situation before the new Fairless Steel plant was completed (Lester 1954). The second part examined the situation that existed in mid-1954 after employment in the area had expanded by a combined total of 14,000 jobs, including those at the Fairless plant, two aircraft manufacturing plants, and a federally owned shell plant. The result was a significant labor shortage in the area (Lester 1955).

The interviews with management showed that about half of the plants tended to conform to an industry wage pattern. That was true, for instance, of steel, auto parts, and airplane assembly plants. The other half of the plants were guided in wage policy largely by local wage conditions. Some industry categories like rubber, pottery, and metal processing were using their industry pattern and the local wage distribution about equally as guides (Lester 1954, 78).

One way of trying to establish the extent of wage differentials in a locality is to have a number of plants manufacturing the same kind of product, using the same standard equipment, and requiring the same level of training or lack of training. Those conditions nearly existed for the starting or entrance wage for male workers at four plants producing hard rubber goods and four plants producing rubber hose. For the four hard-rubber plants, the starting rate of the highest paying plants was 14 percent above that for the lowest paying plant. For the four rubber-hose plants, that wage differential was 13 percent. The comparable percentages for skilled maintenance employees (first-class machinist or electrician) were 5 percent for the four hard-rubber plants and 15 percent for the four rubber-hose plants (Lester 1954, 75–77). Examples from other industries are provided in the report.

A number of factors help to explain why economic forces failed to cause significant reduction in interplant wage differentials, even in such a tight labor market. Interplant movement of workers was discouraged by policies and practices that attach workers to their companies. These include: (1) hiring new employees at the bottom level, (2) filling upper-level jobs by in-plant training and promotion opportunity based on seniority, (3) gearing pension benefits and amount of vacation to length of service, and (4) following an "anti-pirating" hiring code and cooperating with management at other plants on employee interplant movement. Such discouragements to interplant mobility explain why managers said, in interviews in 1951–52 and in mid-1953, that they did not feel that they were in competition for labor with any other companies, even companies that were located nearby and manufacturing some of the same products. In the initial interviews, managers said that employees generally were firmly attached to the company after a year of employment. In the follow-up interview in the first half of 1953, when unemployment in the area was down to 2.2 percent, many managements said that their employees were still tightly attached after a year of service, but some managers in soft-goods lines said that the period of service before attachment had become longer (Lester 1954, 59–68, 83–87; Lester 1955, 72–74, 80–81).

These two labor market studies — New Haven and Trenton —

help to illuminate the factors responsible for the existence and persistence of significant wage differentials among manufacturing establishments in two medium-size cities in the 1940s and 1950s. Several of the findings of the studies are difficult to explain by means of standard competitive theory.

Employment Effects of Minimum Wages

I had been studying wage differentials in the South and also serving as chairman of the tripartite Southern Textile Commission of the War Labor Board, when an article by George J. Stigler, "The Economics of Minimum Wage Legislation," appeared in the June 1946 issue of the *American Economic Review.* I presented some critical comments on Professor Stigler's paper (Lester 1947) and he made a rejoinder (Stigler 1947).

The basis for our differences can be briefly stated. In his analysis of the effects of a minimum wage increase, Professor Stigler makes certain assumptions about the low-wage industries most affected by minimum wage action. The cotton textiles industry is prominent on his list of the 14 low-wage industries that are said to be subject to "competitive wage determination." Stigler claims that employers in competitive industries "do not have control over the wage rates they pay for labor" (Stigler 1946, 358, 359). That deduction from competitive theory is obviously incorrect in fact. In manufacturing industries, employers generally decide and quote their wage rates for production workers, except where wages are determined by collective bargaining. There was then relatively little union organization in cotton textiles in the South, though there was much in the North. Professor Stigler also asserted: "Each worker receives the value of his marginal product under competition." Presumably with no exceptions.

My paper provided a detailed criticism of Stigler's paper, based, in part, on my studies of wage differentials in low-wage manufacturing industries and in local labor markets in the South (Lester 1947, 142–148). Those studies found wage differentials that were difficult to explain by competitive theory. This was particularly true of the wage differentials in six cotton textile communities in North and South Carolina, each with 7 to 12 mills located fairly near to one another in the community (Lester 1946a, 254–256 and 1946c, 154–157). Stigler also neglected to take account of significant race and sex wage differentials in parts of the industry (Lester 1947, 143; Hindricks 1938, 89–90, 95–105).

The impact on employment

The U.S. Department of Labor has made studies of experience under state and federal minimum wage legislation, beginning in the early years of this century. Of particular interest has been the employment effects of minimum wage increases in particular industries.

In 1957 and 1959, John M. Peterson undertook a critical "reexamination" of the Department of Labor's findings on employment effects of minimum wages in three service industries under state laws and in three different manufacturing industries under the Fair Labor Standards Act (Peterson 1957, 1959). Peterson based his analysis of the employment effects of minimum wage increases on "the competitive model of the firm," which assumes "a horizontal labor supply curve and a smoothly declining labor demand curve," so that a minimum wage increase will, by itself, "reduce employment and reduce it more, the larger the wage increase" (Peterson 1957, 413). In his reexamination, Peterson apparently adopted Stigler's assumptions.[1]

In my response to Peterson's paper interpreting experience in specific minimum wage cases, I pointed out that wage differentials of varying size and economic justification, as shown in wage studies like mine on the cotton textile industry, should be taken into account in analyzing the employment effects of minimum wages. To the extent that an increase in the minimum wage serves to reduce or eliminate insupportably low wages (including those due to race, sex, and other forms of discrimination), the increase should not force a reduction in employment.

Firms directly affected because they have wages significantly below a new minimum can use various means of adjustment that may not involve a reduction in employment. Some of those means are indicated by the firms producing the same product with the same machinery whose wages already meet or exceed the new minimum. Experience with the increase in the minimum wage from 75 cents to $1.00 under the Fair Labor Standards Act in 1956 showed that management was able to increase productivity and cut costs in a number of specific ways (Lester 1960, 254–256; Lester 1964, 516–519).

In my comment on Peterson's paper, I pointed out that analysis of the data showed considerable lack of support for his thesis that a definite inverse relationship exists between minimum wage increases and employment in the affected firms.[2] By 1959, material from *Studies of the Economic Effects of the $1.00 Minimum Wage*

(Department of Labor) had become available for an analysis of the effects of the minimum, and I used it in my comment and in the 1964 edition of my book, *Economics of Labor*.

In the book, I sought to test the proposition that the more wages of firms are raised by a new minimum, the larger will be the reduction in those firms' employment. For that purpose, I made use of the data for ten low-wage segments of manufacturing in the South that the Department of Labor had selected for a special study of the effects of the increase in the minimum hourly wage from 75 cents to $1.00, which took effect March 1, 1956. In each industry segment, employment in the high-impact establishments (those that would require for compliance an increase of between 16 and 29 percent of their preexisting total wages) is expressed as a percentage of the segment's total employment, reported four different times over a period of one and a half years. Interestingly, the percentage that represented the high-impact portion of an industry segment's total employment was practically constant or increased slightly over the period in four of the industry segments — a result opposite to what would be predicted by Peterson's model. All but one of the other five industry segments showed relatively small but definite declines in the employment percentage for high-impact establishments. Clearly, the results of this study are mixed and do not support the proposition that a increase in a minimum wage will soon lead to a reduction in the affected firm's employment in proportion to the relative size of the wage increase.[3]

Some recent studies

An elaborate study was made by David Card of the effects of the increase in California's state minimum hourly wage from $3.35 to $4.25 on January 1, 1988 — an increase made while the federal law's minimum remained at $3.35 (Card 1990). The state law applies to most workers not covered by the federal law. About half of the workers under the state law are in the retail trade industry, which includes eating and drinking establishments.

The study found that the employment effects of the increase in the minimum were, if anything, positive rather than negative. Even in the low wage retail trade, Card could find no evidence of an adverse impact on employment (Card, 1992, p. 51). He observed that groups with a higher fraction of low-wage workers do not appear to have suffered any losses in employment (p. 44). Rather than an adverse employment effect, the data point toward an increase in teenage employment in California following the rise in the minimum wage (pp. 52–53). Card concluded: "Clearly, these findings are inconsistent with a conventional competitive model of the low-wage labor market" (p. 52).

The effects of two increases in the federal minimum on the fast-food industry in Texas were studied by Lawrence Katz and Alan Krueger (1992). The increases in the federal minimum under the Fair Labor Standards Act were from $3.35 an hour to $3.80 on April 1, 1990, and from $3.80 to $4.25 in April 1991. Most of the data used in the study were obtained in two sets of phone interviews with restaurant managers or assistant managers. The first of 167 interviews was done in December 1990, and the second set of 330 interviews in August 1991; the second set included another interview with 110 of the managers and assistant managers involved in the first set. The fast-food industry in Texas was chosen because Texas is a large state and because that industry has a high proportion of low-paid workers.

Looking at 102 establishments for which they have complete data for the period extending from before to after the 1991 increase in the minimum wage, the authors find that "employment growth was positively related to the size of the wage increases mandated by the minimum wage" (Katz and Krueger 1992, 15). In summary, Katz and Krueger conclude: "Our surveys provide little evidence supporting significant adverse effects of minimum wage increases in employment. Direct measures of employment and wages at the survey dates indicate that employment increased substantially more rapidly from December 1990 to August 1991 in firms where the minimum wage increase of April 1991 had a substantial bite than in firms less constrained by the minimum wage increase" (pp. 18–19). Of interest is the study's finding "that the price of a full meal tended to decline in restaurants with large mandated wage increases relative to restaurants not much affected by the minimum wage change" (p. 21), which shows firms were not adjusting in their product pricing in a way that could adversely affect their employment.

In a 1991 paper, David Card analyzes the effect on wages and employment of an increase in the federal minimum to $3.80 on April 1, 1990. He measures the relative impact of the new federal minimum wage in a state or other unit by the percentage of workers who were earning wages between $3.35 an hour (the old minimum) and $3.80 (the new minimum) in 1989. By that method, the impact was quite large in low-wage states like West Virginia, Mississippi, and Louisiana, where over 10 percent of the workers in the state had earnings between the old and the new minimum in the year 1989. In Card's paper, he gives special attention to teenage workers, one-fourth of whom earned a wage between the old and the new minimum in that year, and to the retail trade industry, where one-half of all worker's earnings were within the same range, between the old and the new minimum.

For one type of analysis Card classifies the states into three groups based on the percentage of their workers affected by the minimum wage. These are 13 "low-wage states," each of which had more than over 40 percent of its teenage workers in the affected wage range in 1989; 12 "high-wage states," each of which had less than 20 percent of its teenage workers in that range; and 26 "median-wage states," each of which had affected teenage workers between those two percentages.

Card found that "the data suggest the rise in the federal minimum wage increased teenage wages and increased employment in the low-wage states," and "that the minimum wage increased average wages slightly in the median-wage states, with no measurable effect on employment." Card adds: "There is certainly no indication of the adverse employment effects predicted by conventional models of minimum wages (Card 1991, 10). The results of the individual state analysis are consistent with the results of the analysis by state groups. "Although the rise in the federal minimum wage apparently had a positive effect on average teenage wages in many states, there is no indication that the wage increases lead to employment losses" (p. 13).

In summarizing his findings, Card states (p. 17): "There is no evidence of a negative employment effect of higher minimum wages on teenage workers in the retail trade sector. Neither is there evidence of any decrease in hours among workers whose wages were raised by the new minimum. These conclusions are consistent with and reinforce the conclusions from my earlier analysis of the increase in the California minimum wage."

Card and Krueger have made a thorough analysis of the effects that the increase in the state minimum-wage law had on fast food stores in New Jersey compared with fast food stores in neighboring eastern Pennsylvania, where there was no increase in the minimum wage (Card and Krueger, 1994). They found that employment in the fast food industry increased in New Jersey relative to Pennsylvania, and there was no evidence that the increase in New Jersey's minimum wage reduced employment in fast food restaurants in the state. They point out that their findings are difficult to explain by the standard competitive model.

Concluding Observations

The material in this paper spans half a century, beginning with the burst of wage and labor market studies after World War II that led to a questioning of the competitive model of the labor market, and to an alternative conception of the way labor markets operate and maintain a structure of wage differentials difficult to explain by competitive theory.

My criticism of George Stigler's paper on minimum wages was part of an extended exchange I had with him and Fritz Machlup in 1946 and 1947 (Lester 1946b, 1947; Machlup 1946, 1947; Stigler 1946, 1947). In that controversy, my position rested in part on the responses of southern employers to independent increases in their wages, and on the findings in wage and employment studies that were not compatible with neoclassical theory.[4]

In their paper on the interindustry wage structure, Krueger and Summers remark that their study leads them to conclude that the observed patterns "cannot plausibly be rationalized without the introduction of noncompetitive considerations or additional constraints" (Krueger and Summers 1987, 37). What those considerations and constraints might be and how they could be integrated with competitive theory, the authors do not explain. It would be interesting if something like that could be worked out.

I am reminded of Fritz Machlup's attempt, on the twentieth anniversary of our controversy, to integrate the profit-maximum model of the firm with alternative approaches in his paper, "Theories of the Firm: Marginalist, Behavioral, Managerial" (Machlup 1967). With skillful and elaborate exposition, Machlup thinks that he has worked out a basis for "peaceful existence of allegedly antagonistic positions." However, he insists that, on the issue of the effects of an increase in minimum wages on the employment of labor, the only fruitful method of analysis under competitive conditions is the model of "simple marginalism based on unadulterated profit maximization" (Machlup 1967, 31). Unfortunately, my esteemed former colleague did not live to read the papers by David Card, Lawrence Katz, and Alan Krueger and Lawrence Summers.

Many textbooks may need to have their treatment of wage differentials and minimum-wage effects altered in view of the contents of this paper.

Author's Note

I am grateful to David Card and Alan Krueger for comments and suggestions.

Notes

1. In his two papers, Peterson refers to my writings several times but omits any reference to the exchange I had with George Stigler on minimum wages (Stigler 1947; Lester 1947).
2. My comments on Peterson's papers and his reply appear under the title "Communications: Employment Effects of Minimum Wages" in the January 1960 issue of *Industrial and Labor Relations Review*.
3. For more details on this case see Lester 1964, pp. 520–522.
4. For historical and analytical material dealing with issues raised in the Machlup-Lester-Stigler controversy, see chapters by Bruce Kaufman and Richard Freeman in Bruce E. Kaufman (ed.) *How Labor Markets Work*.

References

Ashenfelter, Orley. 1984. "Commentator's Remarks," in Betty Boch et al., eds., *The Impact of the Modern Corporation*. New York: Columbia University Press. pp. 79–82.

Brown, Charles, James Hamilton, and James Medoff. 1990a. *Employers Large and Small*. Cambridge, Mass.: Harvard University Press.

———. 1990b. "The Employer Size-Wage Effect," *Journal of Political Economy* 97 (October): 1027–1059.

Card, David. 1992a. "Do Minimum Wages Reduce Employment? A Case Study of California, 1987–89," *Industrial and Labor Relations Review* 46 (October): 38–54.

———. 1992b. "Using Regional Variation in Wages to Measure the Effects of the Federal Minimum Wage," *Industrial and Labor Relations Review* 46 (October). 22–37.

Card, David, and Alan Krueger. 1994. "Minimum Wages and Employment: A Case Study of the Fast Food Industry in New Jersey and Pennsylvania." Princeton University and NBER Working Paper. Forthcoming.

Cullen, Donald E. 1956. "The Interindustry Wage Structure, 1899–1950," *American Economic Review* 46 (June): 353–369.

Dunn, Lucia F. 1984. "The Effects of Firm Size on Wages, Fringe Benefits, and Work Disutility," in Betty Boch et al., eds., *The Impact of the Modern Corporation.* New York: Columbia University Press. pp. 5–58.

Employer Expenditures for Selected Supplementary Remuneration Practices for Production Workers in Manufacturing Industries, 1959. January 1962. Bulletin no. 1308, U.S. Bureau of Labor Statistics.

Freeman, Richard. 1988. "Does the New Generation of Labor Economists Know More Than the Old Generation?" in Bruce E. Kaufman, ed., *How Labor Markets Work.* Lexington, Mass.: D. C. Heath. pp. 209–232.

Garbarino, Joseph W. 1950. "A Theory of Interindustry Wage Structure Variation," *Quarterly Journal of Economics* 64 (May): 282–305.

Hicks, Clarence J. 1941. *My Life in Industrial Relations.* New York: Harper.

Katz, Lawrence F., and Alan B. Krueger. 1992. "The Effect of the Minimum Wage on the Fast Food Industry." Hindricks, A.F., *Wages in Cooton Goods Manufacturing,* U.S. Bureau of Labor Statistics, Bulletin No. 663, 1938, *Industrial and Labor Relations Review.* 46 (October) 6–21.

Kaufman, Bruce. 1988. "The Postwar View of Labor Markets and Wage Determination," in Kaufman, ed., *How Labor Markets Work.* Lexington, Mass.: D. C. Heath. pp. 145–203.

Krueger, Alan B., and Lawrence H. Summers. 1987. "Reflections on the Inter-Industry Wage Structure," in Kevin Lang and Jonathan Leonard, eds., *Unemployment and the Structure of Labor Markets.* Oxford: Basil Blackwell. pp. 17–46.

Kwoka, John E. 1980. "Establishment Size, Wages, and Job Satisfaction: The Tradeoffs," in John J. Siegfried, ed., *The Economics of Firm Size, Market Structure and Social Performance.* Washington, D.C.: Federal Trade Commission, pp. 359–379.

Lester, Richard A. 1946a. "Diversity in North-South Wage Differentials and in Wage Rates within the South." *Southern Economic Journal* 12 (January), 238–262.

———. 1946b. "Shortcomings of Marginal Analysis for Wage-Employment Problems." *American Economic Review* 36 (March), 63–84.

———. 1946c. "Wage Diversity and Its Theoretical Implications." *Review of Economics and Statistics* 28 (August), 152–159.

———. 1947. "Marginalism, Minimum Wages and Labor Markets." *American Economic Review* 34 (March), 135–148.

———. 1948. *Company Wage Policies: A Survey of Patterns and Experience.* Princeton: Industrial Relations Section, Princeton University.

———. 1954. *Hiring Practices and Labor Competition.* Princeton: Industrial Relations Section, Princeton University.

———. 1955. *Adjustment to Labor Shortages, Management Practices and Industrial Controls in an Area of Expanding Employment.* Princeton: Industrial Relations Section, Princeton University.

———. 1960. "Communications: Employment Effects of Minimum Wages." *Industrial and Labor Relations Review* 13 (January), 254–264.

———. 1964. *Economics of Labor,* 2nd. ed. New York: Macmillian.

———. 1967. "Pay Differentials by Size of Establishment." *Industrial Relations* 7 (October), 57–66.

———. 1973. "Manipulation of the Labor Market," in Gerald G. Somers, ed., *The Next Twenty-five Years of Industrial Relations*. Madison, Wis.: Industrial Relations Research Association. Pp. 47–56.

Machlup, Fritz. 1946. "Marginal Analysis and Empirical Research." *American Economic Review* 36 (September), 515–554.

———. 1947. "Rejoinder to an Antimarginalist." *American Economic Review* (March), 148–154.

———. 1967. "Theories of the Firm: Marginalist, Behavioral, Managerial." *American Economic Review* 57 (March), 1–33.

Oi, Walter, and John Raisian. 1985. "The Impact of Firm Size On Wages and Work." Unpublished paper.

Peterson, John M. 1957. "Employment Effects of Minimum Wages." *Journal of Political Economy* 65 (October), 412–430.

———. 1959. "Employment Effects of State Minimum Wages for Women: Three Historical Cases Reexamined." *Industrial and Labor Relations Review* 12 (April), 406–422.

———. 1960. "Reply: Employment Effects of Minimum Wages." *Industrial and Labor Relations Review* 13 (January), 264–273.

Reynolds, Lloyd G. 1951. *The Structure of Labor Markets*. New York: Harper.

Ross, Arthur M., and William Goldner. 1950. "Forces Affecting the Inter-industry Wage Structure," *Quarterly Journal of Economics* 64 (May), 254–261.

Stigler, George J. 1946. "The Economics of Minimum Wage Legislation." *American Economic Review* 36 (June), 358–365.

———. 1947. "Professor Lester and the Marginalists." *American Economic Review* (March), 154–157.

Studies of the Economic Effects of the $1.00 Minimum Wage, Effects in Selected Low Wage Industries and Localities. January 1959. Washington, D.C.: U.S. Department of Labor.

Taira, Koji. 1961. "Japanese Enterprise Unionism and Inter-firm Wage Structure." *Industrial and Labor Relations Review* 15 (October), 33–51.

Tan, Hong W. 1982. "Wage Determination in Japanese Manufacturing: A Review of Recent Literature." *Economic Record* 52 (March), 46–60.

7

Modeling Third World Labor Markets

■ —————————————— ■

Lloyd G. Reynolds

Two models of Third World labor markets appear in the literature. One is the dualistic model, which distinguishes two sectors of the economy differing in wage level and in the principles governing the determination of employment. This model was originated by W. A. Lewis, and it was further developed in the Fei-Ranis model, the Harris-Todaro model, and other writings.[1] The other is the familiar neoclassical model, in which the economy is treated as an integrated whole, with the same principles governing wage and employment determination in all activities. This model has also been elaborated and enriched over the past 40 years, through work on the returns on education and training and the many other variables which enter into individual earnings functions.

Which of these models does the actual operation of Third World labor markets most nearly resemble? In addressing this question I am very conscious of variability within the Third World, embracing as it does more than a hundred countries and the bulk of the world's population. Every oddity of labor market behavior that one can imagine appears in one country or another. No statement about labor markets can be equally true of all. One must deal with median behavior, with a range of variation about the median that is considerably wider than that in the "developed" world.

A further difficulty is that Third World labor markets have been little investigated; most of the investigation has been driven by policy concerns, such as the sources of poverty and underemployment, and the skewed distribution of personal incomes. In only a handful of studies is the structure of labor markets the central concern. In what follows I shall draw for illustrative purposes on superior studies from Kenya, Indonesia, and Mexico, but their experience is not necessarily typical on their respective continents.[2] Left out of account are China, North Korea, and Vietnam, whose government structures differ from those in the remainder of the Third World.

Dualistic Models

Arthur Lewis set out to portray how a capitalist economy expands through reinvestment of industrial profits. The purpose is "to provide a mechanism explaining the rapid growth of the proportion of domestic saving in the national income in the early stages of an economy whose growth is due to the expansion of capitalist forms of production." Thus, it is not specifically a less developed country (LDC) model. It is perhaps better regarded as a model of early capitalist development in Britain.

The focus on capitalist profits as a source of saving dictates the division of the economy into a *capitalist* sector, in which employees work for wages and generate profits, and a *noncapitalist* or subsistence sector characterized by self-employment. The subsistence sector (and the surplus labor it contains) is not coterminous with agriculture. It includes handicraft workers, petty traders, domestic servants, and others as well as farmers.

The capitalist sector is neoclassical, with employers equating the marginal productivity of labor to the market wage. Neither wage earners nor subsistence workers save; all saving comes from capitalist profits (though it is not necessary to assume that all profit is saved). The increase in capital stock raises the demand schedule for labor, which may also rise through technical progress.

The noncapitalist sector, which functions mainly as a labor reservoir, is less clearly outlined. Implicitly, agriculture is peasant- or owner-operated agriculture. Farmers earn a subsistence wage, apparently related to their average rather than their marginal productivity. And, again by implication, traders, artisans, and other noncapitalist workers earn the agricultural wage. The marginal productivity of man-hours in the noncapitalist sector is normally positive. But the marginal productivity of *workers* is assumed to be zero; that is, as workers are withdrawn for industrial employment, those remaining do enough additional work that output does not fall.

There is a "wage gap" between the subsistence wage and the market wage in the capitalist sector, a gap large enough to induce workers to transfer as rapidly as there are jobs for them. The labor supply curve to the capitalist sector is infinitely elastic at the market wage. In fairness, Lewis does not assert that the capitalist wage will in fact remain constant. Normatively, it is desirable that the wage level *should* remain constant, since this maximizes the rate of increase in capitalist employment, output, and profits. Eventually, if capitalist expansion is rapid enough to outrun population growth, the surplus labor reservoir will run dry and employers will face a normal forward-rising labor supply schedule. The Lewis model is not "tight" in a formal sense. There are many loose ends. But the system captures major features of the British case: the initial labor slack in the preindustrial economy, the agriculture-industry wage gap, the lag of real wages during the early decades of industrial growth, and the profit share of output at first rising and later stabilizing or declining. If theory is the artful simplification of reality to get at fundamentals, the Lewis model deserves the high repute it has enjoyed in the literature.

As the Lewis model captures early British growth, vintage 1750 to 1850, the Fei-Ranis model offers a stylized Japan, vintage 1864 to 1920. Here the sectoral division is between agriculture and non-agriculture, which operate on different economic principles. Agriculture is organized by landlords who employ wage earners at a constant institutional wage. Nonagricultural production is organized in capitalist firms, which pay a wage above the agricultural level, and which maximize profit by equating labor's marginal product to that wage. Because of the existence of redundant labor in agriculture (workers who can be withdrawn with no decrease in agriculture output), the supply schedule of labor to industry is infinitely elastic at a constant real wage. As in Lewis, saving out of profits is a major source of capital accumulation; but it is no longer the only source, as landlords are also assumed to save. The transfer of labor from agriculture continues until all redundant labor has been withdrawn from agriculture. Beyond this shortage point, the labor supply curve to industry turns upward.

A variation on the Lewis model was introduced by Michael Todaro, based on his observations in Kenya. There, the urban wage level is set by institutional forces at a level well above the rural wage, the gap being more than sufficient to stimulate migration from the countryside. As excess migrants accumulate in the city, the queue of those seeking urban employment increases. The inducement to migrate depends on the wage gap discounted by the probability of finding an urban job. Eventually, when this probability has fallen sufficiently, migration ceases. The stock of urban unemployed is equilibrated not by the wage gap but by the probability of finding urban employment.

It is worth noting that none of these models was drafted by a labor economist and that, with the possible exception of the Todaro model, the labor market does not occupy center stage. The unlimited supply of labor to the urban sector, along with the underlying redundant labor in agriculture, is an expository device that facilitates the expansion of output and profits in the capitalist sector, which is the centerpiece of the development process. Also, the models are "competitive" in the broad sense of relying on economic motivation in private markets. Only in the Todaro variant is the urban wage level institutionally determined. In both Lewis and Fei-Ranis, the wage gap is just sufficient to keep the migration current flowing. These pictures of the labor market are of course vastly simplified, another sign of their origins in a branch of the theory of development rather than in labor economics. There are no wage differentials in either the urban or rural sectors; hence there is no scope for individual wages to vary in respect to changing demand or supply conditions.

The "Developed Country" Model

The model of the developed country, described in great detail in texts on labor economics, is part of the larger corpus of neoclassical theory. The multitude of submarkets for labor, and the wage rates that indicate and regulate the supply-demand balance in each market, form an integrated whole. Changes in wage relations depend on changes in demand for specific types of labor. Departures from equilibrium are temporary and functional, in that they tend to call forth an adequate supply in each submarket. Employment in each submarket is determined by equating the marginal productivity of labor to its marginal cost. The system as a whole is one of moving equilibrium, tending toward full employment.

While labor markets and their interrelations are broadly competitive, this means workable competition rather than perfect competition. It leaves room for elements of monopoly and monopsony, for limited information on both sides of the market, and for a good deal of fumbling about rather than instantaneous adjustment. Some economists choose to emphasize the elements of imperfection, while others have insisted on the predominant influence of competition. Over the years, opinion seems to have moved in the latter direction. Wage differences that were at one time viewed as queer, noncompetitive, institutionally determined, have turned out to be explainable as a rational response to market conditions.

This brings me to the central issue of this paper: are the labor market phenomena observed in the less developed world susceptible to the same *kind* of explanation used for higher-income economies? Are they broadly competitive, if not perfectly competitive? Or, on the contrary, does the picture more nearly resemble that found in dualistic models of economic development? I shall look in turn at rural labor markets, rural-urban migration and the existence of surplus labor, and the characteristics of urban labor markets.

The Rural Labor Market

Mexico shows the typical Latin American division of land holdings into minifundia and latifundia. The majority of the rural population, some 77 percent, live on holdings of less than 5 hectares. At the other pole of the distribution, the 3.1 percent of farmers with 50 hectares or more account for 63 percent of the available cropland. There is thus a large and well-established rural labor market. Small farms have excess labor available for sale, while large farms need to hire large amounts of labor, particularly at seasonal peaks. In addition there are substantial numbers of landless workers.

The tradition of migration to the United States for varying periods of time is well established. But greater in volume is the amount of migrating labor within Mexico itself. For small farmers the amount of income from off-farm production typically exceeds the value of farm output. The range of opportunities for off-farm employment is wide. In addition to hired work on larger farms, it includes employment in urban industries, commerce, and services, as well as work as an independent artisan. In one poor and remote region of Oaxaca, the value of artisan production amounted to 32 percent of all household income, well above the 19 percent originating in crop production. Gregory concludes: "It is thus amply clear that, in virtually all the regions that have been studied, regions with very different quantitative and qualitative endowments of land, off-farm employment has accounted for a substantial, if not dominant, proportion of the total for both cultivators and their families."[3]

Wages are flexible, varying with the season and the part of the country in question, and the minimum wage system does not seem to have much binding effect. Wages are lowest on small farms, higher as farm size increases, and considerably higher still in urban activities. Rural people are well acquainted with this wage ladder, and take advantage of it as opportunity offers.

The trend of real wages is not easy to discover, because of difficulties in adjusting for rapid inflation by use of imperfect price indexes. Wage data and household consumption surveys, however, both suggest a large rise in per capita income, and also a narrowing of differentials between the agricultural and nonagricultural sectors. During the 1970s median agricultural earnings in 26 of the 32 states increased considerably more rapidly than those originating in the remainder of the economy. There was also a narrowing of differentials between richer and poorer states. The intersectoral and intrasectoral narrowing that appears to have occurred would be expected only as labor supply conditions generally became tighter, a finding which conflicts with the surplus labor hypothesis.

Turning from Mexico to Indonesia, and specifically to Java, one visualizes the countryside as a rich tapestry of rice fields in varying shades of green and yellow. The cultivation is carried out through a complex intermingling of family labor and hired employees, the proportions varying with size of landholdings and season of the year. On average, more than a third of the man-hours worked in rural Java are worked by employees, usually paid on a daily contract. The distribution of landholdings is quite unequal, with the top 10 percent of families typically owning one-third to one-half of the village land. Small landholders thus devote a considerable part of their time to wage labor; there is also a substantial landless population, amounting to 20 or 30 percent of all families, for whom wage labor is the only resort.

Rice cultivation — normally two crops per year — is the leading production activity, but far from the only one. Indeed, field studies show that less than half of the days worked are devoted to growing rice. Other prominent activities are trading, handicrafts, and the care of livestock and fish ponds. Those who sell their labor for wages thus have a range of alternative economic opportunities.

The preeminence of rice is confirmed by the higher earnings opportunities in that sector. One study found that rice wages were 36 rupiahs per hour for harvesting, and 24 per hour at the earlier stage of transplanting the seedlings. Other activities yielded only 6 to 10 rupiahs per hour, and are thus marginal or fill-in activities, engaged in when work in the rice fields is unavailable. One result is an infinitely elastic supply of labor for rice growing, at the markedly higher rice wage. Man-hours of labor flow into the rice sector to meet seasonal peaks and are withdrawn as activity ebbs.

Wages in the rice sector, while always well above earnings in other rural activities, are by no means uniform. They vary from village to village and by season of the year, the harvest bringing a peak in wage rates as well as in employment. They vary also by size of farm, with large estates paying substantially more than small holdings. One study found that the wage earnings for all farm workers in West Java was 200 rupiahs per day. Estate workers, however, averaged 360 rupiahs per day. Larger landowners use a higher wage level to attract workers from greater distances and to build continuing relations with those workers from year to year, and they are perhaps more selective in the qualities they require of prospective employees.

These differences in earnings, within the rice sector and outside it, are well understood by the villagers and call forth appropriate supply adjustments. Households tend to choose the available combination of activities with the highest total return. There is also a clear relation between high returns per unit of labor and the economic status of the household. Additional workers from relatively high-income households are drawn into the labor market at higher wages during the busy harvest season. Kinship relations are important: close relatives receive from one-fourth to one-half of what they harvest; shares of one-sixth to one-eighth are given to women from neighboring households. Shares of one-tenth to one-twelfth are given to distant villagers who fall outside the first two categories. There is no single wage that applies throughout a region and is paid to all harvesters.

In Kenya, there are two submarkets for agricultural labor: small-holder cultivation, and the large estates specializing in such crops as coffee, tea, and pyrethrum. In smallholder cultivation the amount of hired labor used is on the order of 10 percent. Most of this is seasonal, only about 30 percent of the hired labor force being employed throughout the year. Sales of labor are in the expected direction — from smaller units to larger units. But they are insufficient in size to come close to equalizing marginal products per hectare, which decrease as the size of the holding increases. There is a serious financial constraint on the hiring of labor. To hire one full-time agricultural worker costs about 2,000 shillings per year. For smallholders, the average annual income is only about 3,600 shillings, and they are typically not eligible for bank credit.

The estate labor market pays higher wages, typically by 20 to 30 percent. The estates practice something approaching factory like supervision of the labor force, which is engaged mainly in picking operations, and estates are consequently able to enforce a higher level of productivity. The gap in productivity between estate and smallholder labor is even larger than the wage gap, indicating a substantial use of monopsony power by the estate owners. This has apparently decreased somewhat over time, due mainly to improvement of transport facilities, but some degree of monopsony still remains.

Over the period 1963 to 1974 a combination of factors — expansion of land area, an increase in land concentration, and changes in the cropping pattern and the composition of livestock — raised the demand for labor in smallholder agriculture by about 63 percent. The smallholder labor force remained roughly constant. There was a large decline in labor input per unit of output, and this increase in the productivity of labor must have served to increase real wages. Estimates of the increase in real wages over the period range from 44 to 57 percent. Collier and Lal conclude that "the increase in real wages between 1963 and 1974 is qualitatively compatible with a competitive market framework of demand and supply." There is some geographic segmentation of the market. A labor shortage in Coast Province coexists with a labor surplus in western Kenya. But still, "the changing monopsony position of the estates aside, the framework of a competitive market appears applicable for the study of changes in agricultural wage rates."[4]

Rural-Urban Migration and "Surplus Labor"

Migration is highly selective — by age, by educational level, by kinship ties with those who have already settled in the city. Most migrants are young, and the migration rate falls off rapidly with increasing age. The more highly educated workers are much more likely to move than are those with little education. Many migrants have relatives already living in the city, relatives who provide access to jobs and temporary financial support. These observations have been confirmed many times over in studies of migration within developed as well as less developed countries.

Internal migration in Mexico is very large, the flows dwarfing the much-publicized migration to the United States. The annual growth rate of the urban population from 1940 to 1970 was 4.8 percent, compared with only 1.5 percent for the rural population. The estimated net migration from rural to urban areas in the 1960s alone was 3.75 million. Migration accounted for 40 percent of the population growth in Mexico City during this decade and for an even higher percentage in other rapidly growing cities, such as Monterrey.

This movement is often presented as involving immiserization — people forced off the land by population growth and resorting to self-employment in tertiary activities in the city. The evidence suggests, however, that the bulk of the movement is a rational response to perceived economic opportunities. The migrants conform to the characteristics already noted. They are relatively young, better educated than those who do not migrate, and they move from lower-income to higher-income regions of the country. This movement has not been sufficient to erode interregional differences of income, but it has held them in check. Interregional differentials widened from 1900 to 1940, but have declined moderately since that time.

The migrants seem to fit into the urban labor market quite rapidly. One quarter of them had assurance of employment before moving, and 60 percent found a job within two weeks of arrival. Between one-half and three-fourths found their first job with the assistance of friends or relatives, a proportion not very different from that in the United States. The majority of these jobs, to be sure, were at the unskilled manual level in manufacturing and construction, and to a lesser extent in services. Contrary to a popular view, the percentage going into services has been declining, from more than 50 percent in the 1930s to only 27 percent in the 1960s. All the sample surveys agree that, in most cases, migration involves an immediate improvement in the economic status of the individual — typically, a large increase in earnings as well as greater stability of employment. And over the years migrants move up the occupational ladder at a rate at least equal to that of those born in the city.

Gregory worked hard to discover the "surplus labor" which is supposedly characteristic of Mexico, but he failed to find much of it in either the rural or the urban sector. Open unemployment rates in major metropolitan areas during the 1970s were in the range of 6 to 8 percent, with no upward trend. Efforts to get at hidden or discouraged unemployment through surveys asking whether the respondent would like a full-time job turn out to have been seriously flawed. More than two-thirds of the males answering "yes" to this question were students, while more than three-fourths of the women were homemakers, a status that precludes work except on a part-time basis. Efforts to measure underemployment by assuming that all workers wish to work a full-time year also yield exaggerated estimates, particularly for rural areas where some seasonality of operations is unavoidable. As further evidence, Gregory notes that the acceleration of Mexico's economic growth, which got under way in 1978, led to widespread labor shortages by 1980. The large labor surplus that was thought to exist failed to materialize.

A prominent feature of the Indonesian labor market is the high incidence of temporary or "circular" migration. A sample survey of villages in West Java found that two-thirds of the migrants were temporary, that is, not meeting the criterion of being absent from the home village for six months or more. Indeed, about one-fourth of the temporary migrants were commuters, who worked in town but returned every night to their village home. In the city, temporary migrants work mainly in the informal sector. About 40 percent are engaged in small-scale distribution, and another 16 percent in transport. Permanent migrants, by contrast, are engaged mainly in formal and permanent employment. About 43 percent of them are employed as wage earners in the private sector, and an additional 22 percent have public-sector jobs.

The phenomenon of surplus labor is related to the distinction already noted between the high-wage rice sector and all other activities. Surplus labor appears to exist only in the slack seasons of rice production. The fact that additional workers from relatively high-income households are drawn into the labor force (at higher wages) during the busy season suggests that there is full employment during that season. When the harvest demand slackens, workers from high-income households drop out of the labor force, while landless and other low-income workers retreat to marginal activities to make ends meet. Surplus labor exists only in the sense of an infinitely elastic supply of labor at the high rice wage. In the slack season it does not mean idleness, but rather a reallocation of time to other activities yielding substantially lower earnings.

In the cities, open unemployment rates for men run around 5 percent. Unemployment is heavily concentrated in the lower age groups, and is linked with education. The higher a young person's educational level, the greater the likelihood that he or she will be unemployed for substantial periods of time. This can reasonably be interpreted as waiting for a job appropriate to one's educational level, depending meanwhile on family support. Unemployment rates for those with postelementary education do not drop to normal levels until the 30 years and older age group. A sizable proportion of those with secondary education or above continue to seek employment through their late twenties. This is a common phenomenon in Asian countries, but the unemployment rates in Indonesia are unusually high.

In Kenya there has been substantial migration to Nairobi, and in lesser measure to other urban centers. During the 1960s the population of Nairobi grew at an annual rate of 10.3 percent per year, of which about 8 percent was due to migration. During the 1970s the growth rate fell to 5.0 percent, of which only 2 percent was due to net migration. Interestingly enough, there are large migration flows in both directions between rural and urban areas. The estimates of gross migration are about double those of net migration. Those returning to the *shamba* fall into three categories: women for whom Nairobi serves as a marriage market, many of whom return to the *shamba* after marriage; the less successful younger male workers, many of whom return to the country after five to ten years of urban experience; and more successful and better educated older workers, for whom going back to the country is a form of retirement.

Almost all of the migrants are young people, the modal age group being 20 to 24 for both men and women, and there is a clear relation with education. During the 1970s, however, the propensity of educated young people to migrate fell off rapidly. While 80 percent of secondary school graduates were migrating in the early 1960s, this had fallen to 10 percent by the end of the 1970s. Collier and Lal conclude that "the pace of urbanization slowed sharply in the 1970s. The rapid rates of growth experienced in the 1960s should therefore be interpreted as a temporary response to the particular circumstances of the Independence era. This deceleration of urban growth coincided with an acceleration in educational output. Despite this conjunction, those with little education were not bumped out of the urban labor market. Instead, the adjustment was borne by those with secondary education revising their expectations and accordingly reducing their propensity to migrate."[5]

There was an upsurge of employment opportunities in Nairobi in the 1970s, with formal wage employment rising by more than 50 percent to 217,300 in 1979. During the same period the number of unemployed fell from 18,400 to 16,300, and it fell even more as a percentage of the labor force. In addition, some 35,000 were estimated to be self-employed or employed in the informal sector. These figures, combined with the complaints of labor shortage from estate employers in the rural sector, would appear to refute the existence of any appreciable labor surplus in the Kenyan economy. The Harris-Todaro model, which involved excessive migration from country to city and a piling up of (primarily educated) unemployed in the cities, seems to have been an overgeneralization of the peculiar circumstances of the early 1960s, which did not continue in later decades.

The Urban Labor Market

Mexico has now experienced more than 50 years of sustained economic growth, and its economic structure has shifted toward the proportions characteristic of a developed country. The agricultural labor force stabilized around 1950 and has increased little since that time. In 1980, 5.4 million people were employed in manufacturing, mining, electricity, and construction, compared with 5.6 million in agriculture. The largest increases in employment were in commerce, finance, and services, which accounted for 8.4 million workers. The rapid increase of employment in the secondary and tertiary sectors is still continuing at a rate in excess of 5 percent per year, and the agricultural labor force is steadily shrinking in relative terms.

The rapid growth of employment in service activities is sometimes interpreted as supply- rather than demand-determined. The service sector is regarded as an infinitely expandable sponge, ready to absorb a labor force that is incapable of finding satisfactory wage employment. Thus it is believed that workers are forced into marginal employment in easily entered subsectors such as trade and domestic service, often as self-employed or unpaid family workers. Gregory examines this hypothesis with some care, coming to the conclusion that it is wrong — that the service sector is demand-driven and that workers seek those jobs. Perhaps the most convincing evidence is that real wages in the service sector have risen consistently over time, at a rate comparable with that in secondary activities. This has been true particularly of domestic servants. As demand for domestics continues to rise, propelled by a high income-elasticity of demand in middle-income households, while supply shrinks with the spread of education and the slackening of rural-urban migration, wages of domestics are likely to rise faster than the general wage level.

There is a well-established wage ladder in the Mexican economy. There is, first of all, a large differential between earnings in the rural and the urban sectors, a differential sufficient to induce large city-ward migration. Within the city, earnings are lowest in the industrial sector, somewhat higher in commerce, and highest of all in the service sector, which along with low-paid domestics includes large numbers of higher-paid workers in the professions and in government. There are also large differentials according to the size of the employing establishment. In industry in 1975 the annual earnings were as follows: in firms employing 1 to 25 workers, 12,000 pesos; 26 to 100 workers, 17,185 pesos; 101 to 500 workers, 22,116 pesos; and more than 500 workers, 28,236 pesos. Similar differentials exist in the commerce and service sectors. There has been some narrowing of these differentials since 1960, to be sure, which is compatible with a general shortage of available labor.

The general level of wages has risen since 1960 at an estimated rate of 3 percent per year. This rise is supported by advances in productivity, apparently at an even higher rate, leading to a widening of profit margins. In 1975, for example, net value added per employed person in establishments of 500 or more workers was 74,546 pesos. This compares with remuneration per paid employee of only 30,425 pesos, or about 40 percent of value added. This combination of wages rising less rapidly than productivity, leading to a widening of profit margins, is a common feature of the early decades of modern industrial growth. It was seen also in nineteenth-century Britain and the United States, and in twentieth-century Japan.

Although there is a comprehensive minimum wage system in Mexico, with minima varying by region and between rural and urban workers over most of the period studied, this does not seem to have been a major influence on the movement of real wages. Gregory concludes that, "while institutional intervention in the labor market in the form of legal minimum wages and collective bargaining enjoys high visibility, it would not appear to have played a decisive role in determining the course of wages in most of the labor market."[6]

In Indonesia, as I noted earlier, there is a distinction between nonpermanent migrants and permanent migrants to the city. The supply price of nonpermanent migrants is low because their absence from the family may mean little change in family output, and because they are typically single workers with no dependents to support. Their earnings in urban activities would therefore be expected to approximate the rural wage level. The supply price of permanent migrants is higher because they do have dependents. In time they find their way into permanent jobs in the formal sector, at higher levels of wages.

Within the formal sector there is a wage ladder, outlined as follows in the World Bank Mission Report[7]:

Category of labor	Daily earnings (rupiahs)
Agriculture, men, Central Java	210
Plantation, permanent workers, Java	302
Construction, unskilled workers, Jakarta	409
Manufacturing, unskilled labor	
Domestic firms, low K/L ratio	296
Domestic firms, high K/L ratio	504
Foreign firms	760

Large firms with a high capital-labor (K/L) ratio, and in particular large foreign-owned firms, appear to constitute a distinct high-wage sector. Why do these firms pay wages well above those prevailing elsewhere in the economy? Part of the difference is explainable by differences in worker characteristics. High-wage firms can establish higher standards for access to employment — for example, employing only high school graduates. They can insist on regular attendance at work, as is evidenced by lower absenteeism rates and lower rates of labor turnover. They usually have formal training programs. Thus they gradually develop a stable group of employees with relatively high seniority and job experience, which leads to higher productivity.

These considerations, however, are not sufficient to explain the size of the differentials. The Mission Report goes on to note that, in such cases, "the durability and smoothness of employer/employee relations enter the objective functions of employers, at least as much as the desire for cost-minimization. Thus the rent or surplus, created within the firm through technical progress or on-the-job training, tends to get shared between employer and employees. . . . Clearly, this phenomenon is more likely if the share of the wage bill in total costs is small. . . . Also it will be especially important in foreign-owned or multinational firms in which there is considerable social/political pressure to share profits with the workers."

Finally, despite relatively high wage rates in the modern sector firms, labor costs were often only about 10 percent of total costs (though this would be somewhat higher if salaries were included along with wages). Employers can readily afford to be generous. The report notes incidentally that the influence of minimum wage legislation or trade unions on wages is virtually negligible.

The excellent study of Kenya by Collier and Lal devotes almost a hundred pages to analysis of the nonagricultural labor market, including an exhaustive study of firm hiring policies and an extended discussion of the relation between education and earnings. I can touch here on only a few salient points from this unusually detailed and thoughtful book.

The authors note at the outset that the well-known association between wage level and size of firm can reasonably be explained by economic considerations: the hierarchical nature of large organizations, the consequent need for greater care in initial recruitment, the association of earnings with lengthening job experience in a permanent employment relationship, and other aspects of employment familiar from the theory of human capital. They note, too, that union organization is strongly correlated with size of the employing unit, and that this can explain much of what might otherwise be interpreted as a union wage premium.

Their particular concern is to examine how the wage structure has responded to external shocks impinging on it during the 1960s and 1970s. Has the wage structure been reasonably flexible and responsive? Or have rigid wages, determined by institutional forces, been unresponsive to change? In general, they come out with a finding that market pressures have been effective in modifying wage differentials in expected directions. For example, there was a large increase in the urban minimum wage in the 1950s, which they interpret as an effort by the colonial authorities to stave off political unrest during the waning years of colonial rule. The immediate effect was a sharp reduction of differentials between skilled and unskilled labor, an urban wage explosion, and an exacerbation of urban unemployment. During the 1970s, however, minimum wage policies were reversed and differentials widened once more.

The other striking development was the great expansion of primary education in the early years of independence. A wave of primary school graduates hit the labor market in the late 1960s at rates which could not immediately be absorbed. Given time, however, the wage structure bent to accommodate this influx. Earnings of groups for which education is especially important — teachers, nurses, lower-level clerical employees — lagged behind the general pace of wage advance, but the specter of "educated unemployment" gradually receded.

Collier and Lal conclude:

> The models of the Kenyan labor market which continue to imprison thought are still implicitly based on the exceptional period of the decade from the late 1950s to the late 1960s, when policy-induced distortions led to the outcomes which various theorists attempted to rationalize in terms of institutionalist, segmented labor markets. . . . We have shown, first, that wages are not rigid in the face of imbalances in the demand or supply of particular kinds of labor. . . . Secondly, the asserted role of completed years of education as a screening device in the labor market is not valid for either manual or white-collar labor. For jobs where educational background is important, it is examination performance (which is a test of ability and hence of potential productivity) rather than years of schooling which is used as a recruitment criterion. . . . Thirdly, there are no inherent structural imbalances in the labor market which would necessitate high and rising unemployment as an accompaniment of rising urban formal sector employment. That current unemployment rates at around 6 percent are above those in rural areas is proba-

bly due to the minimum wage laws which have further exacerbated youth unemployment.[8]

A Summary Word

I should repeat the cautions I stated at the outset concerning the dangers of overgeneralization. In the Third World one is dealing with upwards of a hundred national economies, for many of which detailed labor market information is virtually absent. The three case studies on which I have relied here are not necessarily typical.

The fact remains that these studies, which were done by experienced investigators and with unusual care, show a striking consistency in their results. Dual labor market theories do not stand up well in the light of the evidence. There is no evidence of wage rigidity. Instead of a single rural and urban wage, the studies reveal a great variety of wage rates for particular kinds of labor. The whole wage structure moves generally upward, as rising productivity is translated into higher incomes. But the relation of particular wage rates to each other changes over the course of time, in ways susceptible to explanation as a response to market developments.

Neither is there much evidence of the existence of surplus labor. The seasonal lulls of the agricultural production cycle are reasonably well filled by handicrafts, trade, repair work and other "marginal" activities. The amount of idle time may also increase, but idleness does not necessarily mean involuntary unemployment. It may instead represent a rational balancing of leisure against returns from low-income activities. Rates of measured unemployment are within the range observed in the developed countries, and show no tendency toward a secular increase.

Instead of surplus labor, one should perhaps think in terms of adequate labor supply, a supply that does not restrain the increase of employment by modern-sector employers. These employers often, perhaps typically, offer more than the supply price for low-skilled labor, and the skills needed for higher-level jobs are developed mainly by training and promotion within the firm.

It should not be forgotten that surplus labor models were developed to highlight the role of capital accumulation in the process of economic development. They have served this function quite well; their plausibility is strengthened by the fact that the urban wage level, while not rigid, has generally lagged some distance behind increases in productivity. This has permitted the wide profit margins

221

characteristic of modern activities in less developed countries, and these profits can be devoted to further expansion. Labor economists should not complain that Lewis and his followers were not specialists in the detailed operation of labor markets, and that economists who do have this expertise can easily poke holes in their models.

On the positive side, these studies should be encouraging to Western labor market specialists. Labor markets in the less developed countries bear a distinct family resemblance to our own. Market pressures do operate with compelling force. The apparatus of modern labor economics, including human capital theory, which has done so much to explain and rationalize differences in earnings in the United States and elsewhere, can also be applied in the LDCs with illuminating results.

In the United States we also have a wage ladder stretching all the way from minimum wage jobs to the higher reaches of scientific and professional employment. At first glance, the ladder in most developing countries appears to have wider gaps than ours, larger differences between top and bottom. I suspect that these wide differences in earnings are largely a transitional phenomenon, and will gradually be eroded in subsequent decades by improvement of market information, continued accumulation of human capital, and the other changes that accompany economic progress. If this is true, LDC labor markets are close to our own in essential structure if not yet in demonstrated performance.

It may be that policy-induced distortions of the wage structure are more prevalent in the less developed countries. There is an almost irresistible tendency to try to increase welfare by misguided tinkering with prices. This mainly takes the form of minimum wage legislation and public-sector wage and employment policies. But here also one can learn from experience; as failure of these efforts becomes evident, public resources may be turned toward more fruitful lines of endeavor.

Notes

1. See in particular W. Arthur Lewis, "Economic Development with Unlimited Supplies of Labor," *Manchester School* 22 (May 1954), 139–191; "Unlimited Supplies of Labor: Further Notes," *Manchester School* 26 (January 1958), 1–32; and "Reflections on Unlimited Labor," in Lewis's *International Economics and Economic Development* (New York and London: Academic Press, 1972).

See also John C. H. Fei and Gustav Ranis, *Development of the Labor-Surplus Economy: Theory and Policy* (Homewood, Ill.: Richard D. Irwin, 1964); and J. R. Harris and M. Todaro, "Migration, Unemployment and Development: A Two-Sector Analysis," *American Economic Review* 60 (March 1960), 126–142.

2. Paul Collier and Deepak Lal, *Labor and Poverty in Kenya, 1900–1980* (New York: Oxford University Press, 1986); *Indonesia: Wages and Employment*, World Bank Mission Report. Washington, D.C.: International Bank for Reconstruction and Development, 1985); and Peter Gregory, *The Myth of Market Failure: Employment and the Labor Market in Mexico* (Baltimore: Johns Hopkins University Press, 1986).

3. Gregory, 113.

4. Collier and Lal, 150.

5. Collier and Lal, 245–246.

6. Gregory, 261.

7. *Indonesia*, 99.

8. Collier and Lal, 275–276.

8

Occupational Wage Differentials

■ ─────────────────── ■

Albert E. Rees

Of the many kinds of differentials that make up our complex wage structure, occupational differentials are probably the most fundamental. Wage differentials among industries can be viewed as being composed largely of differences in the occupational structure of the industries' work forces. Wage differentials by race, sex, size of establishment, and union status all are pervasive and important, but all are substantially smaller than occupational differentials.

Economists have been interested in occupational wage differentials for more than two hundred years. In *The Wealth of Nations*, first published in 1776, Adam Smith discussed the differences in pay among occupations and advanced two major theories of occupational wage differentials. The first of these we now call the theory of investment in human capital and the second the theory of compensating wage differentials.

The theory of investment in human capital holds that occupations that require a large investment in education or training must pay more than other occupations so that the workers who have made these investments will obtain a fair return. If this were not true, too few workers would be trained for the occupation and its earnings would eventually rise. As Adam Smith put it:

> When any expensive machine is erected, the extraordinary work to be performed by it before it is worn out, it must be expected, will replace the capital laid out upon it, with at least the ordinary profits. A man educated at the expense of much labor and time to any of those employments which require extraordinary dexterity and skill, may be compared to one of those expensive machines. The work which he learns to perform, it must be expected, over and above the usual wages of common labor will replace to him the whole expense of his

education, with at least the ordinary profits of an equally valuable capital. It must do this too in a reasonable time, regard being had to the very uncertain duration of human life, in the same manner as to the more certain duration of the machine.[1]

In the past 40 years, the theory of human capital has been greatly elaborated, beginning with the work of T. W. Schultz, Gary S. Becker, and Jacob Mincer.[2] Let me mention briefly a few of the salient features of this elaboration. These writers have made it clear that investment in human capital includes the earnings forgone while a student of working age is in school, as well as direct outlays such as tuition. They have shown that on-the-job training, whether formal or informal, is also investment in human capital. If the training is useful to employers other than the one who provides it (what Becker calls "general training"), the trainee will bear all or part of the cost through lower wages during the training period. Finally, these writers began the process of estimating rates of return on education and training, to which many others have since contributed.

The theory of compensating wage differentials holds that workers must be paid more to do unpleasant or hazardous work and will accept less to do work that is especially prestigious or rewarding. For example, Smith writes: "The trade of a butcher is a brutal and odious business; but it is in most places more profitable than the greater part of common trades. The most detestable of all employments, that of public executioner, is, in proportion to the quantity of work done, better paid than any common trade whatever."[3] Smith writes as though all workers find being a butcher equally odious, which is really a special case of the theory. If 2 percent of the work force do not find it odious to be a butcher and butchers comprise only 1 percent of employment, then it will not be necessary to pay a compensating differential.[4]

In the past 25 years, several estimates of compensating differentials have been made, especially of the premiums for hazardous work. It is harder to estimate risk premiums than it is to estimate returns on human capital in the sense that data from different sources produce a wider range of estimates.

In addition to the two sources of occupational wage differentials discussed by Adam Smith, two more should be mentioned. One of these is trade unions and the other is gender. It is now well established that American unions raise the wages of their members relative to the wages of similar workers who are not unionized by something in the neighborhood of 15 percent. This produces differentials between heavily unionized occupations and those with few if any union members. It is also well established that because in general women earn less than men, occupations that are heavily female will pay both men and women less than occupations that are heavily male.[5]

With at least four major forces contributing to the pattern of occupational differentials, it is hard to sort out the contributions of each. Most of the work that attempts to do so involves sophisticated econometrics. Rather than attempting to review this voluminous work here, I shall try to illustrate the principal forces at work by examining some occupational wage data for the years 1949, 1979, and 1990. Although some important changes in differentials among these years will be noted, the dominant impression is that differentials have been amazingly stable over this period.

Table 8.1 shows data on median weekly wages for selected detailed occupations for the calendar year 1990, separately for men and women. The data come from the Current Population Survey, a monthly sample survey of the labor force. Because of sampling error, estimates of median weekly wages are not shown where the estimated number of workers in the group is less than 50,000. In addition to showing the weekly wage in dollars, I have calculated each wage as a percentage of the wages for all occupations combined, including the many occupations not shown in the table.

Two general features of the table should be noted. First, occupational wage differentials are very large. For both men and women, the highest-paid occupation, lawyer, makes five times as much as the lowest. Even this understates the size of occupational differences in earnings, since many of the lawyers, physicians, and accountants with the highest earnings are partners in or sole proprietors of practices rather than wage or salary workers, and are therefore not included in the wage data in this table. It should also be noted that none of the wage data in this paper includes employer contributions for such benefits as health care and pensions. Since such contributions are larger and more frequent in the better-paid occupations, the dispersion of wages among occupations understates the dispersion of total compensation. The second noteworthy general feature of Table 8.1 is that in every occupation where data are shown for both sexes, men earn more than women.

Lawyer and physician are the two most highly paid occupations for both men and women. Both professions require large amounts of professional training. Lawyers generally attend law school for three years after college, and physicians attend medical school for four years. Physicians then serve an internship in a hospital before they are qualified to practice independently. In addition to these invest-

Table 8.1. Median weekly wages of full-time wage and salary workers, 1990 — selected detailed occupations, by sex

	Men			Women		
	No. workers (in thousands)	Median weekly wage	Percent of all occupations	No. workers (in thousands)	Median weekly wages	Percent of all occupations
All occupations	49,015	$ 485	100.0	36,068	$ 348	100.0
Accountants and auditors	550	644	132.8	636	483	138.8
Physicians	198	978	201.6	68	802	230.5
Registered nurses	76	616	127.0	1,104	608	174.7
Teachers, college and university	376	808	166.6	164	620	178.2
Teachers, elementary school	200	575	118.6	1,111	513	147.4
Clergy	246	441	90.9	22	—a	—
Lawyers	285	1,178	242.9	105	875	251.4
Airplane pilots and navigators	74	910	187.6	2	—a	—
Cashiers	231	242	49.9	850	210	60.3
Secretaries	28	—a	—	3,154	343	98.6
Private household workers	12	—a	—	298	171	49.1
Cooks, except short order	585	248	51.1	417	206	59.2
Structural metalworkers	52	569	117.3	—	—	—
Assemblers	578	370	76.3	432	287	82.5
Rail transportation occupations	104	716	147.6	3	—a	—
Farm workers	492	234	48.2	70	202	58.0

Source: Data from the Current Population Survey, Employment and Earnings, January 1991, Table 56.
a. Median wage not shown when estimated number of workers is below 50,000.

ments in human capital, there is another factor raising the median wages in these professions. According to the 1980 census, in both professions the median male worker worked more than 41 hours a week, while for men in all occupations, median weekly hours were between 35 and 40. Estimates of mean hours worked from census data show lawyers working an average of 47 hours a week, compared with 41 for all college graduates.[6]

The third profession in the table that requires substantial formal education is college and university teaching. Most college professors have a Ph.D., a degree that requires a minimum of four years of study after college, and often more. Although college teachers earn substantially more than the average for all occupations, they are well below salaried lawyers and physicians. This probably reflects a negative compensating differential. College teachers may be sacrificing earnings for the great independence their profession offers and for the job security provided by academic tenure.[7]

An even clearer example of the effect of nonpecuniary benefits on wages is found in the case of clergy. Male clergy earn only 91 percent as much as males in all occupations. However, the great majority of male clergy are college graduates, and many have graduate training in theology.[8] An estimate of the monetary return on education for the clergy shows it to be substantially negative.[9] Many clergy receive income in kind, especially housing. More important, the profession has high prestige, and presumably most clergy find their work very satisfying and in keeping with their values.[10]

The table also shows three more professions that require formal professional education at the college level or beyond. These are accounting, elementary school teaching, and nursing. The last two of these are professions in which women are far more numerous than men. Earnings in accounting are about one-third above the average for all occupations for both sexes. For nursing and elementary school teaching, the relative earnings of women are substantially higher than those of men. Indeed, male registered nurses have median weekly wages only $8 above their female colleagues, the smallest such difference in the table.

Three of the occupations in the table do not necessarily require higher education, but require substantial occupational training through trade school, apprenticeship, or on the job. These are airplane pilots, rail transportation occupations, and structural metalworkers. All are almost exclusively male and have earnings above the average for all male occupations. Indeed, the average earnings of airplane pilots are above those of college and university teachers. In addition to a return on vocational training and experience, two other factors are at work here. Many airplane pilots and structural metal-workers and virtually all railroad operating employees are members of strong unions. In addition, all three occupations may command a wage premium because they have a higher than average risk of accidental death or occupational injury.[11]

The occupations I have not yet discussed all have wages below the median for all occupations. They include two clerical occupations, secretary and cashier, a semiskilled factory occupation, assembler, two service occupations, cook and private household worker, and farm worker. Secretary is by far the most common occupation in the table, and it is almost entirely female. Secretaries' median wage lies just below the median for all women. Most have probably had some specialized training in vocational school. Skills required for the other occupations whose wage lies below the median for all occupations are largely learned on the job or in the home. Two of the entries in the table are at less than half the median wage for all occupations: male farm workers and female private household workers. Male cooks earn barely more than half the median for all occupations. If I were using the mean rather than the median as the measure of central tendency, this poor showing would have been moderated by the high wages of chefs in expensive restaurants.

Published data on median wages by detailed occupation have only been available for a few years. To examine trends in differentials, I turn to another data source, the decennial census. Table 8.2 shows median annual income for selected occupations in 1949 from the census of 1950. The occupations have been chosen so as to match as closely as possible those in Table 8.1. No 1949 income data were published for airplane pilots or for assemblers.

The concepts underlying the two tables differ in two important ways. First, the 1949 data include income from all sources, not just wages and salaries. This means that in such professions as medicine, law, and accounting the 1949 data include sole practitioners and partners, while the 1990 data do not. Second, the 1949 data include part-time workers, while the 1990 data do not. The dispersion of incomes among occupations is substantially larger in Table 8.2 than in Table 8.1, but because of the conceptual difference I just mentioned, one cannot tell how much of this, if any, represents a real narrowing of occupational wage differentials over the past 40 years.

Nevertheless, the pattern of differences among occupations is strikingly similar in the two tables. Apart from physicians, where the conceptual differences could account for the apparent change, there are three other notable changes. First, the relative position of nurses has improved markedly since 1949. This no doubt represents a

Table 8.2. Median income of the experienced civilian labor force, 1949 — selected detailed occupations, by sex

	Men			Women		
	Number with income (in thousands)	Median income	Percent of all occupations	Number with income (in thousands)	Median income	Percent of all occupations
All occupations	38,286	$2,668	100.0	13,766	$1,575	100.0
Accountants and auditors	301	4,002	150.0	52	2,632	167.1
Physicians	154	8,115	304.2	10	3,475	220.6
Nurses, professional	—a	—	—	343	2,127	135.0
University professors, n.e.c.	88	4,348	163.0	25	3,106	197.2
Teachers, n.e.c.	268	3,456	129.5	744	2,394	152.0
Clergy	144	2,412	90.4	—a	—	—
Lawyers and judges	148	6,257	234.5	5	3,616	229.6
Cashiers	—a	—	—	168	1,585	100.6
Stenographers, typists, and secretaries	1,387	2,138	135.7	—a	—	—
Private household workers	64	1,176	44.1	1,177	652	41.4
Cooks, except private households	192	2,241	84.0	215	991	62.9
Structural metalworkers	52	3,428	128.5	—a	—	—
Locomotive engineers	68	4,590	172.0	—a	—	—
Locomotive firemen	53	3,688	138.2	—a	—	—
Farm laborers and foremen, except unpaid family workers	1,257	940	35.2	110	574	36.4

Source: Data from U.S. Census of Population, 1950. Characteristics of the Population, U.S. Summary, Table 129.
a. Not shown separately.

combination of the rapid growth of the health care industry on the demand side, combined with the opening of traditionally male occupations to women, which could have restricted the supply. (Note the large difference in the number of women physicians between the two tables).

A second major change is the sharp decline in the relative position of women in the two clerical occupations shown, secretaries and cashiers. This suggests that the increase in the number of women in the labor force may have increased supply to these occupations more rapidly than demand grew, or that the skills required may have been reduced by changes in technology. The third large change is the decline in the position of male cooks, for which I do not venture an explanation.

Although occupational differentials may have narrowed since 1949, over the shorter period since 1979 these differentials appear to have widened. This is in keeping with the evidence for other kinds of wage differentials over the same period.[12]

Table 8.3 shows median earnings data for selected occupations for 1979 from the census of 1980, again matching as closely as possible the occupations in Table 8.1. No separate data are available for structural metalworkers. The data are restricted to labor earnings, excluding property income. The median earnings, though not the number of workers, are confined to full-time year-round workers. In both these respects, Table 8.3 is conceptually closer to Table 8.1 than is Table 8.2. However, Table 8.3 does include the earnings of self-employed practitioners and partners, which explains the apparent decline in the relative position of male physicians between 1979 and 1990. With this single exception, all the occupations that require extensive education or training have a better relative position in 1990 than in 1979. On the other hand, there are four occupations that require little formal training whose relative position is much worse in 1990 than in 1979: assemblers, cashiers, farm workers, and cooks.

The increased dispersion of occupational earnings in the 1980s suggests that the demand for educated labor expanded during the decade more rapidly than the supply, while the demand for less educated workers did not. One explanation for this is that changes in the pattern of international trade led to the substitution of imported goods for low-skilled domestic labor.[13] Another may be that the availability of educated labor led employers to hire people with more training than was really needed for their jobs.

It is hard to foresee any developments that will improve the demand for uneducated labor in the next few years. To avoid ending up

Table 8.3. Median earnings of full-time, year-round workers, 1979 — selected detailed occupations

	Men			Women		
	No. of workers with earnings (in thousands)	Median earnings	Percent of all occupations	No. of workers with earnings (in thousands)	Median earnings	Percent of all occupations
All occupations	57,971	$ 17,107	100.0	41,602	$ 10,134	100.0
Accountants and auditors	620	20,560	120.2	376	12,821	126.5
Physicians	370	52,916	309.3	57	22,585	222.9
Registered nurses	76	16,337	95.4	1,201	14,898	147.0
Teachers, postsecondary	398	23,725	138.7	225	16,626	164.1
Teachers, elementary	569	16,644	97.3	1,874	12,610	124.4
Religious workers	279	12,096	70.7	41	8,208	81.0
Lawyers and judges	450	32,328	189.0	72	18,503	182.6
Airplane pilots and navigators	74	28,171	164.7	1	14,721	145.3
Cashiers	294	12,370	72.3	1,438	7,852	77.5
Secretaries	47	14,480	86.7	3,801	10,261	101.3
Private household occupations	26	7,291	42.6	521	4,707	46.4
Cooks	586	9,192	53.7	737	6,810	67.2
Assemblers	827	14,405	84.2	793	9,517	93.9
Rail and water transport occupations	278	22,415	131.0	5	15,286	150.7
Farm occupations, except managerial	695	8,551	50.0	156	6,718	66.3

Source: Data from U.S. Census, 1980, Detailed Population Characteristics, U.S. Summary, Part A, Table 281.

in such poorly paid occupations as cashiers and cooks, Americans will need to be trained for better-paid occupations. The United States now does an excellent job of training people for the learned professions, as demonstrated by the large and growing number of foreign students in our colleges and universities. It does a much poorer job than many European countries of providing adequate vocational guidance and vocational training to those who do not go on to college. Improved skills training for these groups could both improve the international competitiveness of the American economy and narrow the occupational wage distribution.[14]

Notes

1. Adam Smith, *The Wealth of Nations.* (New York: Random House, 1937.) Book 1, chap. 10, p. 101.
2. See in particular T. W. Schultz, "Investment in Human Capital," *American Economic Review* 51 (1961), 1–17; Gary S. Becker, *Human Capital: A Theoretical and Empirical Analysis with Special Reference to Education* (New York: National Bureau of Economic Research, 1964); and Jacob Mincer, *Schooling, Experience and Earnings* (New York: National Bureau of Economic Research, 1974).
3. Smith, book 1, chap. 10, p. 100.
4. See Albert Rees, "Compensating Wage Differentials," in Andrew Skinner and Thomas Wilson, eds., *Essays on Adam Smith* (Oxford: Clarendon Press, 1975).
5. This "crowding" hypothesis was first advanced by Barbara R. Bergmann in the context of racial wage differentials, in "The Effect on White Incomes of Discrimination in Employment," *Journal of Political Economy* 79 (March/April 1971), 294–313. As applied to gender differences, it has been the basis for comparable-worth legislation affecting public employees in some states and cities. Such legislation raises pay in heavily female occupations to the level of more heavily male occupations that are judged to require equivalent skills.
6. Sherwin Rosen, "The Market for Lawyers," Henry Simons Lecture, University of Chicago Law School, April 1990.
7. See Albert Rees, "The Salaries of Ph.D.'s in Academe and Elsewhere," unpublished paper, Industrial Relations Section, Princeton University. Included in this paper is a discussion of the problems in comparing academic and nonacademic salaries that arise from the ten-month academic year and from academics' consulting income.
8. See *U.S. Census of Population, 1980,* Detailed Population Characteristics, U.S. Summary, Section A, Table 282, for religious workers, a somewhat broader category than clergy.

9. See David A. A. Stager, "Monetary Returns to Post-Secondary Education in Ontario," Ph.D. dissertation, Princeton University, 1968.

10. In general, the relationship between pay and occupational status is positive; see Henry Phelps Brown, *The Inequality of Pay* (New York: Oxford University Press, 1977), chapter 4. But this is true in large part because of the positive association between status and education, not because workers dislike high-status jobs.

11. A study by the Society of Actuaries in 1967 showed railroad brakemen, railroad conductors, locomotive firemen, and structural ironworkers all having substantially higher age-adjusted death rates than all males. See Richard Thaler and Sherwin Rosen, "The Value of Saving a Life: Evidence from the Labor Market," in Nestor E. Terleckyj, ed., *Household Production and Consumption* (New York: National Bureau of Economic Research, 1975), p. 288. In addition, data from the Bureau of Labor Statistics show high rates of occupational injury for structural metalworkers. See Norman Root and Deborah Sebastian, "BLS Develops Measure of Job Risk by Occupation," *Monthly Labor Review* 104 (October 1981), 26–30.

12. See, for example, Chinhui Juhn, Kevin M. Murphy, and Brooks Pierce, "Accounting for the Slowdown in Black-White Wage Convergence," in Marvin H. Kosters, ed., *Workers and Their Wages: Changing Patterns in the United States* (Washington D.C.: American Enterprise Institute Press, 1991), pp. 114–117.

13. See Kevin M. Murphy and Finis Welch, "The Role of International Trade in Wage Differentials" in Kosters, ed., *Workers and Their Wages.*

14. For a detailed exposition of this point, see *America's Choice: High Skills or Low Wages!* (Rochester, N.Y.: National Center on Education and the Economy, 1990).

III

Other Great Issues

9

On Labor's Bargaining Disadvantage

Melvin W. Reder

*. . . the common wages of labour, depends everywhere upon the con-
tracts usually made between those two parties whose interests are by
no means the same. . . . In all such disputes the masters can hold out
much longer. . . . Many workmen could not subsist a week . . . and
scarce any a year without employment. In the long-run the workman
may be as necessary to his master as his master is to him; but the
necessity is not so immediate.*
    Adam Smith, *The Wealth of Nations* (book I, chap. 8, 58–59)

*The want of reserve funds and of the power of long withholding their
labour from the market is common to nearly all grades of those whose
work is chiefly with their hands. But it is especially true of unskilled
labourers. . . .*

*Turning next to the highest grades of industry, we find that as a rule
they have the advantage in bargaining over the purchaser of their
labour. . . .*

*If further evidence were wanted that the disadvantages of bargain-
ing under which the vendor of labour commonly suffers, depend on his
own circumstances and qualities, and not on the fact that the particular thing which he has to sell is labour; such evidence could be found
by comparing the successful barrister or solicitor or physician, or
opera singer or jockey with the poorer independent producers of vend-
ible goods.*
    Alfred Marshall, *Principles of Economics*, 8th ed. (London and
    New York: Macmillan, 1920; book VI, chap. 4, 568–569)

*The relationship between workers and their capitalist employer is
formally structured by the ownership and control of the means of
production. . . . Within a given legal and economic context, the employer can do better than to simply hire workers and let them work as*

they please. The level of profits therefore depends — at least to some extent — on the power of capital over labor.
Samuel Bowles, "The Production Process in a Competitive Economy," *American Economic Review* 75, no. 1 (March 1985), 19

Though from the inception of economic thinking, the notion of bargaining has shared a conceptual domicile with the idea of market, the cohabitation of these concepts has been fraught with strain. Bargaining has always been recognized as an aspect of the process by which markets determine prices (the higgling of the market), but the primary concern of economic theory has been the interrelation of equilibrium prices (that is, prices that have been already determined in some manner) and not the possible interrelation of the manner in which prices are determined and the prices (and quantities) that result.[1]

Obviously, overt bargaining is one of the ways in which prices can be determined. But while there is an appreciable amount of literature on the theory of bargaining, this literature has not devoted much attention either to the possible effects of setting prices mainly through bargaining (rather than through, say, auction markets) or to the consequences that might follow if certain classes of economic agents were relatively disadvantaged in the bargaining process. In this chapter I shall address only the matter of bargaining disadvantage and confine the argument exclusively to the case of hired labor.

In keeping with customary usage, I shall use the terms *laborer, worker,* and *employee* interchangeably, although it is on the concept of employee that my argument will focus. It is clear that when Smith and especially Marshall spoke of labor being at a bargaining disadvantage they had in mind primarily unskilled labor. Highly skilled labor, and especially members of professions, were considered to be in a different and more favorable bargaining position and not subject to the same degree of bargaining disadvantage, or to any disadvantage whatever.[2]

Both Smith and Marshall considered unskilled laborers to have but little in the way of liquid assets and therefore to be chronically in the position of a distressed seller unable to hold out for the "fair market value" of his services. It is not clear what either of them would have replied to the assertion that competition among employers would, sooner or later, raise wages to a long-run competitive equilibrium that was independent of the vicissitudes of the adjustment process. Both of them, especially Smith, contended that employers (masters) frequently were parties to implicit oligopsonistic agreements to hold down wages; if valid, this contention could form the basis for such a reply.[3] But it is not clear that either really intended to make employer coalition in restraint of labor market competition the normal case.

Moreover, some of the remarks of both Smith and Marshall suggest that the ascription to workers of inferior power "to hold out" was meant to apply to situations of collective bargaining rather than to individual wage negotiations. Nevertheless, some of Marshall's other remarks (for example in book V on p. 335), and his comparison of the bargaining power of highly skilled and unskilled workers, make sense only if interpreted as referring to wage negotiations between individual workers and employers who compete in hiring.

Attempting to reconcile the fragmented remarks either of Smith or Marshall on the bargaining power of labor with what they said of wage determination in other contexts would constitute a difficult exegetic exercise irrelevant to my present purpose.[4] It is enough to note that both of them believed that (at least) unskilled laborers were at a bargaining disadvantage that was somehow related to a deficiency of resources, and that this disadvantage impaired their ability to "hold out" in the event of a disagreement over terms of employment, but that neither of them attempted systematically to relate this belief to an account of how wages were determined in the long run. It is clear that they believed that this disadvantage existed both under collective bargaining and in competitive labor markets. Further, it is worth noting that neither of them explicitly introduced the notion of unemployment (at the community level) into the discussion of bargaining power.

It is difficult to discuss bargaining power in the context of a competitive labor market without recognizing a critical difference between labor and inanimate inputs: labor can withhold effort. For my purpose here, it is unnecessary to recapitulate the insights and errors associated with the belated recognition of the importance of this distinction for the neoclassical theory of production. This is because, following Herbert Simon's (1950) introduction of the distinction between contracts of sale and contracts of employment,[5] there has come a gradually increasing recognition of the necessity of considering how method of compensation relates to worker productivity, with the result that it is now customary to consider employees as (utility maximizing) agents rather than as (inanimate) units of input.

One important milestone on the path from the labor demand function of the 1950s to the efficient employment contract of current literature is the famous paper by Alchian and Demsetz (1972) in which they presented the idea that an efficient employer must monitor the behavior of his employees to impede "shirking."[6] A second milestone is Shapiro and Stiglitz's article (1984) that introduced to economic theory the commonsense idea that the expected cost of losing one's job affects the performance of a rational employee and, indirectly, the behavior of his employer.[7] The major practical implication of this idea is that the wage and disciplinary policies of employers are related to the current level of unemployment.

It would be fair to say that recognition of the importance of employer monitoring and the role of unemployment in the enforcement of employee discipline, constitutes a belated acceptance by mainstream economists of Marx's distinction between labor and labor power and the related idea that capitalist production involves the extraction of surplus value from hired workers, with the threat of unemployment (the "reserve army of the unemployed") functioning as an instrument to extract effort.[8] However, as in the case of Marshall, I shall avoid textual exegesis as much as possible in order to concentrate on the issue at hand.

To summarize: some distinguished economists have claimed that, in one sense or another, labor is at a bargaining disadvantage in negotiating with employers. However, there is no consensus on what it is that causes this disadvantage. And there is a strong countertradition in economic theory that holds that labor is simply one of many economic services, none of which exhibits price behavior with noteworthy special characteristics under competitive conditions.

While the issue of labor's alleged bargaining disadvantage is longstanding, it can hardly be said to be on the front burner in the contemporary research kitchen. Despite exceptions, modern economists seem not to find the issue to be of great interest.[9] This is unfortunate because there is a widespread, though understandably confused, popular belief often vented in courts and legislatures that "ordinary" workers — at least when not unionized — are at the mercy of their employers.

This belief is reflected in labor laws that even now (in the 1990s) give special — albeit diminished — protection to labor unions and that, in many states, attempt to limit the legal right of employers to fire at will. This belief is also reflected in common modes of speech and thought in which it is suggested that it is prudent for employees to fear the wrath of the boss, and that the "giver" of employment should be considered as a public benefactor whose employees have reason to be especially grateful.

Without belaboring the matter, I feel that it is an important though neglected task of the economics profession to specify the circumstances under which employees might be at a bargaining disadvantage, and to show the implications of such a disadvantage, where it exists. Despite the remarks of Smith, Marshall, and others, conventional price theory has no place for a notion of bargaining advantage or disadvantage. As a result both students and the general public are left with a poorly defined notion of bargaining advantage and no clue as to how, in any formulation, it might be related to the corpus of economic theory. What follows is an attempt to remedy this situation.

In the ensuing discussion I shall discuss several different versions of the concept of bargaining disadvantage. Although I consider these to be among the more important versions, I do not suggest that they exhaust the possible interpretations of this concept.

Bargaining without an Employment Relationship

Except where the contrary is explicitly stated, I abstract from unions, monopsony, and combinations of employers throughout this essay. Not that I consider such phenomena to be infrequent or unimportant, but I feel that in their presence there is no presumption that labor is at a bargaining disadvantage. Unions are sometimes "stronger" than the employers (or employer associations) with whom they deal, and at other times not. In any case, I shall consider only situations where there is competition on both sides of the labor market. That is, I shall focus on situations in which many noncooperating employers negotiate contracts with many noncooperating workers. It is assumed that a worker can contract with no more than one employer, but that an employer may contract with more than one worker.

In this idealized labor market each potential employer-worker pair somehow reaches (or fails to reach) a mutually acceptable contract within some finite, short time interval. In the event of failure, both worker and employer seek out alternative contracting partners, but with no guarantee that one will be found within any specified time interval, or of the terms obtainable. At any given time, barring flukes, the contract terms that the various (successful) pairs reach are permitted to differ, and it is expected that there will usually be both unengaged workers and unfilled job vacancies.

For convenience, assume that all workers are known to be of the same productivity; to have identical levels of wealth and the same risk-averse utility function. Each utilizes the same bargaining (negotiating) tactics, with a reservation wage equal to a common expected value plus a disturbance, distributed randomly over individuals; an individual's reservation wage (that is, his personal disturbance) is unknown to prospective employers.

Employers are assumed to be profit-seeking firms (expected value maximizers) rather than possibly risk-averse individuals, and accordingly they are assumed to be risk neutral. For simplicity, assume them to adopt identical bargaining tactics and to have a maximum hiring wage rate equal to a common expected value plus a disturbance, distributed randomly over the population of employers. The maximum hiring wage of any individual employer is unknown to any of the workers with whom the employer negotiates.

The contracting process consists of workers moving through a congeries of employers, bargaining for an arbitrary fixed time interval with the one first encountered and moving on to another in the event a contract is not reached. The contract is assumed to cover exactly one period of employment, after which the contracting process is repeated with all participants acting independently of previous contracting. In the event of a failure to reach a contract, the worker loses the potential earnings of one employment period and the employer loses the potential earnings from employing that worker for one period.[10]

In setting his reservation wage, a worker balances the prospect of gain from encountering an employer willing to pay an above-average wage against the danger of loss from encountering one unwilling to pay as much as the average and, as a result, being unemployed for a period. Since the worker is assumed to be risk averse, he will choose a reservation wage below the level that would maximize his expected earnings, thereby enhancing his employment prospects and so limiting his downside risk of earnings loss on account of unemployment. This wage would be less than what he would accept if he were risk neutral.[11] As it is plausible to suppose that an individual's degree of risk aversion diminishes with his wealth, it is similarly plausible to suppose that among relatively wealthy workers, bargaining disadvantage is less than among poorer ones, possibly disappearing at some sufficiently high level of wealth.

This argument captures the essence of one of Marshall's arguments in support of the idea of labor's bargaining disadvantage — the "hungry worker" argument (book V, 335–336). That is, workers are needy sellers of a perishable service and employers are aware of this and accordingly hold out for lower wages than those at which they could hope to make hires if workers were richer. This corresponds to many popular images and literary descriptions of how nonunion labor markets function when workers are without financial reserves.

Nevertheless, the argument says nothing about the role of the employment relationship. A worker differs from an employer only in being risk averse. His bargaining disadvantage is simply that of any risk-averse seller dealing with a risk-neutral buyer. I will now consider how the employment relationship might generate bargaining disadvantage.

The Employment Relationship and Unemployment

Following Simon, one may distinguish between a contract of sale and a contract of employment. In the former, the transaction is completed upon the exchange of money (for example) for the "consideration"; that is, the transaction is completed instantaneously. Under a contract of employment, the employer makes an unconditional commitment to pay for one period of time, regardless of worker performance.[12] Obviously, the employer has the expectation of obtaining performance sufficient to justify the promised compensation. But it is up to the employer somehow to induce the necessary effort, and to monitor the result.

To rationalize the effort-inducing (labor extraction) process, assume that all workers and employers expect that the employment relation will continue for at least one more period, provided that the worker is perceived to perform satisfactorily. The worker has the option of arbitrarily limiting his effort (shirking) in the first period, for whatever reason, at the risk of not being rehired for the second period, should the employer be dissatisfied with the resulting performance. The effort that this risk induces depends on the size of the expected loss from not being rehired and the worker's effort responsiveness to the threat of income loss. For simplicity, assume initially that the amount of resources per period that an employer devotes to monitoring a given employee is technologically fixed.

If a worker could with certainty obtain equally attractive alternative employment at the end of the first period, regardless of whether he had been dismissed, there would be no way in which his employer could induce him not to shirk; he would be indifferent as to whether or not he was rehired. This state of affairs could not be satisfactory to a rational employer, who would either stop offering employment or find a way to make workers stop shirking.

For simplicity, assume for a moment that all employers are equally attractive to members of the pool of prospective workers, and therefore offer the same wage rate, in an initial situation in which workers believe that they can change employers without loss, and shirk accordingly. Each employer would then try somehow to enhance his relative attractiveness to induce his workers to stop shirking. One way of doing this would be to attempt to pay a wage above the going rate. But this would be futile, since all the other employers would be attempting to do the same, with the result that the common wage rate would increase without any change in relative wages among employers.

Without elaborating irrelevant details, assume that the common wage rate increases until there is sufficient excess supply as to make the expected interval of unemployment consequent on nonrenewal long enough to entail a painful loss of earnings. Somewhere in the vicinity of this wage rate, workers would begin to balance the marginal utility of greater shirking against the expected loss of income from not being rehired, and would adjust their effort accordingly. Thus an equilibrium would emerge, with individual workers optimizing an effort-dismissal risk trade-off in accordance with the combination of wage rate and expected unemployment duration generated by the workings of the labor market.[13]

In this way, without cooperating, employers would in effect act to set both a wage rate and an expected loss from being unemployed that were high enough to make workers fear a dismissal notice and extend effort accordingly. In such a situation, a worker would be at a bargaining disadvantage in the sense that any seller would be at a disadvantage in a market with persisting excess supply. But the precise meaning of this in the context of an employment contract needs explication.

Consider the following possibility: in a situation of excess supply an employer, about to hire a worker at the going wage, might demand a small return payment (a kickback) as a condition of completing the hiring. If the kickback demanded were small enough, it would be worth it for a rational worker to pay rather than continue job searching, which raises a question as to why such demands are not (normally) made. The answer is that it is more efficient for the employer to reserve the use of his superior bargaining power for obtaining additional effort *as needed* from the worker on pain of dismissal in the event of refusal. To fix ideas, the reader may suppose that the additional effort takes the form of unpaid overtime, which must be rendered on demand.

The essence of the matter is that an employment contract is by definition incomplete: in exchange for a specified money payment by the employer, a worker agrees to perform incompletely described acts "as directed" during some specified time interval.[14] If the employer's technology were deterministic, the required acts could (in principle) be spelled out and the incompleteness removed, but in practice this is rarely feasible. Consequently the employer finds it efficient to pay a wage higher than that at which the worker would be indifferent to dismissal, and to extract effort as required by the production process from workers bribed to be compliant.

For such an employment contract to make sense, it must be assumed that there is some conventional level of effort expected from a worker as a condition of being retained. "Additional" effort is measured with this as a base. Similarly it must be assumed that there is some upper boundary to the amount of effort that the employer can demand without either paying more or causing the worker to quit.

In a nutshell, an efficient employer offers a wage rate sufficiently high to obtain worker effort as required by the production process without danger that the worker might quit. While the minimum wage level adequate for this purpose will vary inversely with the percentage of unemployment in the labor force, my argument here does not warrant the theoretical elaboration necessary to establish the functional relation between these variables. Suffice it to say that in the situation described, the worker is led to feel "grateful" that the boss does not demand still more. Put yet another way, the employment contract is designed so that the worker will respond to unanticipated variations in the production requirements of the employer, but the employer need not respond analogously to unanticipated changes in the household situation of the worker.[15]

It is to be emphasized that for this state of affairs to persist, the employer must be offering a wage rate above that which would clear the market; that is, jobs must be perceived as being scarce and employed workers must be correspondingly anxious to retain their positions. In other words, in the situation just described, the obverse side of the worker's bargaining disadvantage is that his wage rate must be *above* the level at which he, as well as his employer, is indifferent as to whether the employment relation is ruptured.

However, this situation arises only in a very particular type of employment arrangement. Briefly, consider the more important of its special characteristics, and their relation to the possibility of employee bargaining disadvantage. First, in this type of employment arrangement, the worker's compensation is completely unrelated to performance except insofar as failure to perform at some minimum level will lead to dismissal: hence the only motivating instrument available to the employer is the threat of dismissal. But in many employment relationships, given satisfaction of some minimum performance requirement, compensation varies directly with current performance, and in others promotion is conditional on satisfactory performance over a substantial period of time.

In such arrangements, the worker's motivation to perform may be quite independent of the level of unemployment and the associated fear of job loss. Consequently, the extent of the worker's bargaining disadvantage, if any, may be dependent simply on the degree of his risk aversion. In short, fear of nonpromotion or loss of potential bonuses and the like could provide worker motivation — and reflect bargaining disadvantage — even in a world where unemployment was unknown. One need not be concerned with the percentage of hired workers who are motivated by fear of job loss relative to the percentage of those who fear unfavorable treatment despite security of employment. The only point is that fear of job loss is not a necessary condition for the existence of worker bargaining disadvantage.

Second, as noted, I assumed that the technique of monitoring worker performance was technologically determined, and therefore insensitive to changes either in other aspects of the production process or in the characteristics of worker utility functions. While facilitating exposition, this assumption is usually if not always counterfactual, though it can be abandoned without altering the substance of the argument.[16]

To summarize: where the only means of disciplining a shirking employee is dismissal, employee bargaining disadvantage is manifested as a willingness to accept employer-imposed changes in working conditions, while being unable to effect changes (in working conditions) of the employee's own design. This aspect of employee bargaining disadvantage does not depend on a difference of risk aversion between workers and employers, nor does it imply that compensation is less than it would be in the absence of this bargaining disadvantage. This is in marked contrast to the bargaining disadvantage associated with greater risk aversion in the absence of an employment relation, as discussed earlier in this chapter (see "Bargaining Without an Employment Relationship").

Exit and Voice

There is yet another potential source of employee bargaining disadvantage: unwillingness of the employer to negotiate. This possibility is hinted at in some of Marshall's remarks, but it can be most readily appreciated if approached via Albert Hirschman's distinction between "Exit" and "Voice."[17] In deciding the terms of an employment relationship — either ongoing or newly contemplated — the parties may negotiate, or one of them may make a take-it-or-leave-it offer. Negotiation involves the taking of time and trouble to preserve the possibility of further relations and exemplifies the use of Voice by both parties. A take-it-or-leave-it offer constitutes a threat to use Exit (to terminate the relationship) and effectively deprives the other party of the opportunity to use Voice.

There are two possible reasons that a bargainer would make a take-it-or-leave-it offer. The first is that he or she wishes to negotiate with a large number of parties and does not have time to negotiate separately with each (and finds it unsatisfactory to delegate the authority to negotiate). For such a bargainer the efficient procedure is to post the minimum contract terms that are sufficient to attract his desired number of contracting partners. This, of course, corresponds to the practice of large firms that post hiring terms and select workers from among the job applicants. And, more generally, it corresponds to the practice of posting (and rigidly adhering to) list prices on articles of low value that are sold frequently.[18]

Typically, it is the employer who posts hiring terms and the worker who accepts them or leaves. This is due mainly to the fact that efficiency considerations often lead one employer to hire many workers, and only rarely to a single worker accepting more than one employer.[19] As a result it is typically the employer who finds that it is more efficient to post unalterable terms of employment than to bargain separately with each of a number of potential employees, and to make the terms sufficiently attractive to recruit (or retain) the desired number. Accordingly, it is usually the worker who finds himself with no influence over the conditions of employment beyond the power of Exit.

The second reason for refusing to negotiate over contract terms with a given individual is the perceived linkage of terms in one contract with what will then be required in others: "If I do it for you, I'll have to do it for everybody." This concern can be operative even where the value of retaining an individual would warrant the time and trouble required to negotiate a mutually satisfactory contract if its terms could be kept secret.

Whatever the reason, an employer policy of refusing to negotiate contract terms with individuals creates (or reflects) an asymmetry in the employment relation between employer and employee. Because the employment relation, by its very nature, requires that the worker listen to (and follow) changing instructions, the employer is always using Voice to vary the worker's effort (and associated disutility).

The worker's position, in contrast, permits no such use of Voice; his role is to follow instructions. Changes in his personal situation that require absence from work or reduced effort are strictly limited by "company policy," which is generally unresponsive to the needs of (low-rank) individual workers.[20]

As before, the worker accepts this asymmetry because the pay is too good to warrant quitting. Existence of this pay level reflects the employer's desire for a work force that accepts company policy without question in preference to one that is paid less, but whose members are able to negotiate changes in work rules and other aspects of employment on pain of quitting. In other words, whatever the low-rank worker feels about the adequacy of his pay, he is powerless either to alter the terms of employment or to prevent the employer from altering them: his only option is to quit.[21]

The situation is very different for a high-ranking employee: varying with his rank, matters relating not only to his own working conditions but also to location of plants, development of new product lines, policy on environmental issues, and so on, may be discussed with him, with his opinions affecting the final decision. Similarly, the star performer on a sports team, in the theater, on a sales force, or even on a faculty can insist on having a say in virtually any policy decision that he or she feels is important. The power to do this obviously stems both from the credibility of the employee's threat to quit and from the organization's concern to keep him or her from developing an attitude inimical to high productivity.

The critical difference between the star and the spear-carrier lies in the perceived difference in the difficulty of replacing them. The differences in "quality" among individuals of star (or high executive) rank are considered to be of such importance as to warrant incurring large costs in search and negotiation to secure the best available candidate. To avoid such costs, great efforts are made to keep incumbents from leaving or becoming dissatisfied.

By contrast, the differences among spear-carriers are perceived as negligible: a few general characteristics suffice to determine whether an individual satisfies a given job description and should be hired to fill it. Their departures would entail only a small cost of replacement, and if their dissatisfaction resulted in shirking they could be fired with impunity. Hence, given adequate compensation, they have no bargaining power. Their complaints about company policy, even on matters vital to their individual well-being, would be ignored: the time and trouble required to alter policy would cost more than letting them quit and hiring replacements.

It is important not to exaggerate the insensitivity of employers to the concerns of low-rank workers. Varying with managerial style, especially as regards willingness to delegate authority on personnel matters to lower levels of management, company policy may give considerable latitude to low-rank employees in choosing items from a package of fringe benefits of given cost to the employer; in choosing break times and vacation times; and even in making within-shop changes in methods of production. However, the objects among which choice may be exercised and, most important, the limits to the cost entailed by such exercise, are usually set by company policy, which is tightly controlled by those at higher levels of management. Moreover, such matters as product quality, protection of the environment, location and closure of plants, corporate mergers, and the like, are almost always considered to be beyond the purview of all but a very few top-ranking employees, and not subject to negotiation with any of the others.

In short, the "bargaining power" of a worker vis-à-vis a given employer may vary with the issue.[22] In addition, the willingness to take time and trouble to negotiate with individual employees depends critically on company policy concerning the delegation of authority to lower levels of management: often it is only the worker's immediate supervisor who is aware of his particular skills and the importance of retaining and utilizing them.[23] Hence the probability that a given worker's bargaining power is conditioned on the discretion accorded his immediate supervisor.

These qualifications notwithstanding, most workers properly feel that their compensation and working conditions are governed by company policy, which they may take or leave but which they cannot negotiate on individually. Of course, workers who resent the rejection of their individual requests as "contrary to company policy" may combine to make a joint request, to which it may behoove the employer to listen and respond. That is, collective Voice may be effective where individual Voice goes unheard. The obvious institutional means for expressing collective Voice is a union, which prompts the question of whether and to what extent unionization gives bargaining power to workers who would otherwise be without it.

The answer is not so simple as proponents of unionism tend to suggest. To be sure, the presence of an effective coalition of workers — whether called a union or not — may compel an employer to negotiate where he would refuse to negotiate with any individuals. But this does not necessarily confer Voice on the individuals. To act collectively requires some method of representation, and Voice can be exercised only through those *individuals* who are selected as representatives.

For an individual worker who desires to become a union spokesperson, and who has the skills and energy to do so, unionization may indeed provide an opportunity to engage in bargaining over the terms of his own employment, as well as those of his fellow workers. But for the many workers who lack the requisite combination of tastes and aptitudes, the problem of influencing the union organization through a political process replaces that of negotiating with the employer.

Depending on legal requirements, organizational structure, and traditions, unions may be either monolithic and insensitive to the individual needs of their members, or the opposite; or they may be somewhere in between. It is not obvious that in dealing with a union organization an individual worker has more bargaining power than he or she would have in dealing with an employer. In a large union, policy may conflict with an individual's preferences on any of a variety of issues, and, like a large employer, the union organization may find it too costly in time and trouble to alter policy to meet the demands of a single individual, or even of a small group.

When dealing with an employer who refuses to negotiate, an individual has the options of Exit or of joining a union that might take up his cause. When dealing with a union that will not negotiate on an issue that might require a change of its policy, an individual may Exit[24] or use Voice in the form of an attempt to change union policy. While not useless, the efficacy of this latter channel for Voice is highly variable both with the individual involved and with the circumstances of the dispute.[25]

The notion of employee bargaining disadvantage has (at least) three variants:

1. Typically, the worker is poorer than his employer and consequently less risk averse. Hence, in the absence of an employment relation, the typical worker accepts a lower average wage than he could obtain under similar conditions if he were wealthier and (therefore) less risk averse.

2. Most employers find it efficient to set terms of compensation such that their employees would rather tolerate occasional pressure for increased exertion and occasional worsening of working conditions than quit. Bargaining disadvantage consists of being induced to tolerate a situation in which working conditions will vary in response to changes in the employer's "needs," but not in response to the worker's. Although this form of bargaining disadvantage may arise from fear of unemployment, unemployment is not a necessary condition: the combined effects of worker risk aversion and the

difference in expected compensation corresponding to superior performance (as judged by the employer) may be enough to induce compliant behavior.

3. Employee bargaining disadvantage arises from the fact that the transaction cost for the employer of negotiating terms of employment with an individual worker exceeds the cost of letting him quit or refuse an offer of employment. That is, the worker is given a take-it-or-leave-it offer even though he and the employer, jointly, could find acceptable contract terms that would cost no more (except for the cost of negotiation). Hence employment terms are set by the employer, with the worker having no opportunity to negotiate; this is perceived as a bargaining disadvantage.

The first and third types of bargaining disadvantage may be eradicated by formation of a union. A union may be able to compel an employer to bargain over the details of company policy where no one of its members acting in isolation could do so. However, a union may itself be insensitive to the demands of its individual members. The underlying reason that some employees lack bargaining power is that their goodwill (willingness to refrain both from shirking and quitting) is not important either to their employer or to their union.[26]

Counterintuitively, except for the first variant (risk aversion), it does not follow that removing an individual employee's bargaining disadvantage would lead to an increase in his compensation. On the contrary, one type of employee bargaining disadvantage exists because employers (sometimes) find it efficient to make the terms of employment so attractive that employees will acquiesce in demands for additional effort rather than quit or risk dismissal because of shirking. If employers were, for some reason, to find it less important to be able to elicit additional effort from workers, they might be able to reduce both wages and employee bargaining disadvantage.[27]

One root of employee bargaining disadvantage is the employee's unwillingness to accept the consequences of refusing to accede to employer demands. Such consequences are not tantamount to destitution: in a society where small stocks of capital are widely distributed, opportunities for self employment in handicrafts, personal services, and small-scale retailing are also widespread.[28] And in such situations, whether as boss or as one of a few employees, an individual would not encounter the frustration of being too unimportant to warrant his employer's taking the trouble to negotiate individual terms of employment.

However, in such situations the worker's productivity and therefore his wage are likely to be far below what it would be were he to accept employment in a multiemployee establishment where he might be too unimportant to bargain with. That is, for low-rank employees, bargaining disadvantage is a concomitant of the economies of scale that make high(er) wages possible, and is tolerated in order to obtain these benefits.

At the risk of belaboring the obvious, I will remark that because an employee is at a bargaining disadvantage, it does not follow that his or her level of utility would be higher if it were somehow possible to remove the disadvantage. At least in the second and third cases just noted, the employee is "bribed" to accept a bargaining disadvantage. The worker might bemoan the poverty that leads him to accept such an offer but, given his utility function, he would repeat the decision under similar circumstances. Whether it is socially desirable to permit transactions that have such consequences is another matter.

Notes

1. I recognize that this statement is somewhat overstrong. There has been some consideration of hysteresis where prices (and quantities) are path dependent. There has also been considerable discussion of price setting in a multiperiod context where the process of price setting is highly salient. However, in such discussions the distinction between the procedure by which prices are set and the resulting pattern of price-quantity behavior, and, a fortiori, the interrelation of the two, is not explicitly analyzed (as, for example, in Arthur Okun, *Prices and Quantities*, (Washington, D.C.: Brookings Institution, 1980).

2. Indeed, as is revealed in the passage quoted at the start of this chapter, Marshall contended that professional workers held a bargaining advantage over the purchasers of their services.

3. As Smith put it, "Masters are always and everywhere in a sort of tacit, but constant and uniform combination, not to raise the wages of labour above their actual rate." *Wealth of Nations*, book I, chap. 8, 59.

4. The difficulty of reconciling the various strands in Marshall's account of wage determination is magnified by his espousal of an "efficiency wage" theory (book VI, chap. IV, 569). Characteristically, Marshall was fully cognizant of the difficulty of reconciling his theory of wages with necessary "practical" qualifications: "whereas in fact the difference between the two cases [i.e., labour and commodity markets], though not fundamental from the point of view of theory, are yet clearly marked, and in practice often very important." (book V, chap. II, 336).

5. H. A. Simon, "A Formal Theory of the Employment Relationship," *Econometrica*, July 1951, 293–305.

6. A. A. Alchian and H. Demsetz, "Production, Information Costs and Eco-

nomic Organization," *American Economic Review* 52 (December 1972), 777–795.

7. C. Shapiro and J. Stiglitz, "Equilibrium Unemployment as a Worker Discipline Device," *American Economic Review* 74 (June 1984), 433–444.

8. The concept of surplus value is discussed in Marx, *Capital*, vol. 1, chap. 7–10. For a good brief discussion of the subject in the context of modern economic theory, see Samuel Bowles, "The Production Process in a Competitive Economy," *American Economic Review* 75, no. 1 (March 1985), 19. This discussion is very pertinent to the argument of this chapter.

9. The notable exceptions being economists associated with the radical political economy movement of the past 20 years. A good introduction to their work is in Bowles, "The Production Process in a Competitive Economy."

10. I assume that an employer is (somehow) capable of bargaining simultaneously with as many individual job candidates as he or she desires, while the candidates are unaware of the ongoing negotiations with others. It is contrary to the spirit of the argument to assume that an employer pays all workers at the same rate — despite their identical productivity — though it would not change any essential point if he or she did. Asymmetrically, a worker is assumed to negotiate with only one employer at a time.

11. For this discussion to make sense, it is necessary to permit employers to differ in the maximum wage they would pay — to a stubborn bargainer — to avoid failing to make a hire. To accommodate this need without attributing irrationality to some of them, assume that employers differ in the characteristics of their products, with some standing to lose more than others from a small variance of employment and output. Plausibly, the more variance-averse employers would pay higher (average) wages to avoid missing opportunities to hire.

12. This simplified notion of an employment contract is applicable only to a small sector of the labor force, at best. As will be seen, consideration of incentive payments, deferred compensation, and the like may alter the argument.

13. The details of the argument necessary to establish the existence and characteristics of this unemployment equilibrium are essentially the same as in Shapiro and Stiglitz, op. cit., and are of no particular interest in this context.

14. The idea that an employment contract involves an incompletely specified effort obligation by the employee is also conveyed by the concept of shirking and the related counterefforts of the employer, introduced by Alchian and Demsetz.

15. To speak of the employer's "production requirements" in this context is in keeping with the assumption that the employer is a pure profit maximizer and therefore uninterested in any other objective. However, the common image of employee bargaining disadvantage is strongly

associated with the picture of the boss as someone gratifying his vanity or whims at the expense of the disadvantaged employee.

16. Bowles's analysis of the production process ("The Production Process in a Competitive Economy," pp. 18–24) contains a development of the idea that, as an aspect of optimization, the employer trades off greater intensity of supervision (implying greater probability of an employee's being detected in the event of shirking) against higher wage rates (implying greater loss in the event of being caught shirking). From a formal point of view, the employer's choice between wage rate and intensity of supervision is analogous to the lawmaker's choice between more severe punishment for detected lawbreakers and greater use of resources for policing to increase the probability of detecting criminals. (See G. J. Stigler, "Optimum Enforcement of Laws," *Journal of Political Economy* 78 [May 1970], 526–536.)

Bowles (pp. 27–29) argues that the profit-maximizing trade-off between wage rate and supervisory intensity is not socially efficient, because more intensive supervision requires greater net outlay of resources while payment of higher wages does not. However, if worker utility functions are exogenous, as is usually assumed, this argument will hold only where workers are risk neutral. In the case of risk aversion, the greater expected loss from being caught shirking when there is a higher wage rate reflects a psychic cost to the worker that must be set against the resources saved from less intensive supervision.

I suspect that Bowles would insist that because worker utility functions are not exogenous, but are "produced" as a joint product along with ordinary commodities, the argument of the preceding paragraph would be relevant only to capitalist economies. Under some alternative set of institutional arrangements, workers would — might? — shirk less at a given intensity of supervision and therefore make higher wages possible without reduction of profits (or of any other income share). Appraisal of such an argument is beyond the scope of this essay.

17. A. O. Hirschman, *Exit, Voice and Loyalty* (Cambridge, Mass.: Harvard University Press, 1970). R. B. Freeman and J. L. Medoff, in *What Do Unions Do?* (New York: Basic Books, 1984), utilize the Exit-Voice dichotomy in discussing collective bargaining. However, apart from a common indebtedness to Hirschman, my arguments are quite different in style and purpose.

18. While it is not the only reason for the phenomenon of the rigid list price (*pris unic*), avoidance of the transaction costs of bargaining is an important one. And the phenomenon occurs mainly in cases where the dollar magnitude of the individual transaction relative to the net sales of the firm is small. That is, in small transactions the potential gain from skillful bargaining — and the correlative price variation across transactions — is insufficient to offset the transaction cost involved. Where the individual item is of relatively great value (for example, an automobile), or where the buyer is offering to purchase an unusually

large quantity, the list price loses its rigidity and negotiation occurs. By analogy, a large firm does not negotiate terms of employment with hourly wage employees, but does so with a few high-ranking executives.

19. It will not be seriously denied that the predominance of the one employer–many workers employment pattern is rooted in scale economies of management and the minimum efficient size of capital equipment. It is similarly obvious that the one worker–many employer pattern is very uncommon because of the waste in travel time and setup costs associated with serving a plurality of employers. However, there are examples of the latter employment pattern in professional service, such as medicine, law, and accounting. In such cases it is to be expected that in dealing with small clients the "employee" will be the party setting the terms on a take-it-or-leave-it basis.

20. The variations in worker effort that are permitted by company policy differ across firms and job levels. Typically, the worker is granted some limited "rights of choice" as part of the implicit terms of the employment contract. Further variations in required effort and attendance may be permitted at the discretion of the immediate supervisor, however there are always limits set by policy. Policy, itself, is sometimes altered on appeal to supervisors, but the resistance to such alterations is well known. In short, the assumption that the worker has no Voice is an exaggeration, but low-rank employees have very little Voice as compared with employers.

21. This assertion reflects an implicit assumption that the worker cannot bargain by a partial withdrawal of effort sufficient to lower productivity but not enough to warrant dismissal (call it "sulking"). Occasionally an employee's special skills or isolation from other workers may be such as to permit him to bargain by sulking. In most cases, however, the bad example set by a sulker, and the resulting effect on overall productivity, will make an employer unwilling to tolerate such behavior.

22. I am greatly indebted to Clark Kerr for pointing out the significance of worker participation in shop-floor management decisions for the issue of worker bargaining power.

23. It is very often the case that it requires an appreciable period of time for a worker to acquire — and to show his supervisor that he possesses — special skills or knowledge.

24. In the absence of constraint on withdrawal from the union, Exit means simply leaving the union. Where there is some element of compulsion to join (or remain in) a union, Exit may also involve quitting one's job or, in extreme cases, withdrawing from a trade or an industry.

25. Several readers have suggested that this discussion does not give sufficient credit to the achievements or the potential of union Voice. Accordingly, I wish explicitly to disclaim any judgment of the performance or the potential for utilizing union Voice. My only point is that, varying in degree with the union's organizational structure and with the characteristics of the union members and their employer, the

individual worker may find problems (costs) in obtaining access to union Voice.

26. In this context, the union analogue of "refraining from shirking or quitting" would be "refraining from making trouble within the organization."

27. I do not go so far as to claim that employee bargaining disadvantage is typically associated with wages higher than would prevail in its absence. This is because employee bargaining disadvantage is the net result of a number of factors. In particular, the effect of risk aversion may be to lower the wage rate at which workers become compliant to employer demands for "additional effort" enough to more than offset the upward push (to wages) resulting from such demands.

28. Similarly, in a society with a social safety net, unemployment need not entail destitution. It is the employee's unwillingness to accept what society offers the unemployed that provides a support for his bargaining disadvantage.

10

Two (or Three) Ways of Thinking about Unemployment

■ ─────────────── ■

Robert M. Solow

There are, of course, many ways of thinking about unemployment, and many models of the labor market. Perhaps a broader phrase would be better, like "attitudes of mind." In any case, I want to distinguish two mind-sets with which economists can approach — and have approached — the explanation of unemployment and the discussion of policy aimed at the problem of unemployment, if it is a problem.

Unemployment as Pathology

The first general attitude presumes that unemployment in excess of some small, necessary, "frictional" level is a pathology of the market system — or at least that it is something to be regretted. This weak way of putting it allows for the possibility that someone might accept this view of unemployment but still believe that an attempt at corrective policy would likely do more harm than good.

There is no *necessary* implication that unemployment is a great social evil. That depends on how the existing amount of unemployment is distributed over the working population, and on the quality of the social safety net. Still it is fair to say that most economists who think about unemployment as pathology regard it as a bad thing especially because loss of income is not the only cost of unemployment to the unemployed; there are psychological costs and damages to the social and family fabric as well. Besides, unemployment is an index of general economic slack. Even if the unemployed are tolerably well off, potential output is being wasted in an economy that is far from satiation. Most economists who take this view of unemployment favor public policy to correct the pathology. That is a correlation, not an implication. But the connection is pretty close. If one thinks that unemployment is a market failure one is likely to see public policy as a natural response. The appropriate policy choice will depend on one's preferred model of the labor market.

According to this way of thinking, there will be at any time a level of employment worth calling "full employment." It need not be knowable to any great degree of accuracy. Anything short of full employment is then at least a partial failure; how much of a failure is also hard to know, because the amount of underemployment and partial employment should be factored into any evaluation, if they can be approximated. Overfull employment is also a failure. The usual presumption is that it will manifest itself in wage and price inflation pretty quickly. Shortfalls from full employment and full capacity no doubt put some pressure on prices and wages in the other direction, but apparently not so promptly or reliably.

This way of thinking is not tied to a firm belief as to whether excessive unemployment is an equilibrium or disequilibrium phenomenon. Those two possibilities shade into one another in practice; there is not much observable difference between persistent excess unemployment and very slowly decreasing excess unemployment. Those who hold this first view have developed a variety of ideas about the mechanism of the pathology. Nominal or real wage inflexibility is one such mechanism, but not the only one; there are others. In any case, wage inflexibility can arise in several different ways, and the best choice of policy may depend on the particular way it arises. I will return to this point later.

Unemployment as an Occupation

So much for the first way of thinking. There is an alternative view that is currently more popular among professional economists, and perhaps only among them. According to this way of thinking, if the volume of employment is at rest, moved only by fairly slow-moving trends, it can legitimately be described as an equilibrium. There is no compelling reason — at least none convincingly advanced — to abandon the presumption that an equilibrium amount of unemployment is a satisfactory amount of unemployment, maybe the best feasible one. From this point of view imperfect wage flexibility, while it may have something to do with monopoly power in the labor market, is mainly an indicator that not being employed is an acceptable occupation to those who are not employed.

The general tenor of this view is expressed by the locution "natural rate of unemployment." The phrase does not explicitly make a claim of optimality, but not many people would be attracted by the idea that it ought to be a social goal to achieve an unnatural rate of unemployment. Of course, policies directed at the structure of the labor market could change the natural rate itself. So the implicit claim is a claim of "constrained" optimality, meaning the best that can exist under the circumstances. I think it promotes calm discussion to use a neutral phrase like the "equilibrium" amount of employment or nonemployment. One can then discuss whether the equilibrium has desirable or undesirable properties.

To say that a particular amount of employment is an equilibrium means that no significant number of participants in the labor market feels impelled to disturb the going situation by taking an action that is actually available. There is an old and unprofitable argument as to whether observed unemployment is or is not "involuntary." Why unprofitable? Anyone old enough to remember "The Jack Benny Show" on radio may remember an episode in which the footsteps of the legendarily stingy Jack Benny are heard walking down the street. A voice calls out, "Your money or your life." There follows an interminable silence while Benny reflects. Suppose he refuses the money and is killed. Is that voluntary? Suppose he gives up his wallet. Is that voluntary? Benny did not want to be held up. On the other hand, he was (voluntarily) walking in a part of town where there is a known probability of being held up, so he has chosen to run a certain risk. If you roll the dice and they come up snake eyes, it is too late to complain. Of course Benny could have moved to another city, or carried an AK-47.

This is clearly becoming a theological argument. It is surely better to stick to neutrally definable concepts like equilibrium. One can then say, as one would in any other market, that the labor market malfunctions if it can sustain an equilibrium in which the real wage exceeds the marginal consumption value of leisure for any significant number of people who are not employed. (The relevant real wage must be currently paid in jobs that the nonemployed are capable of doing.) There is obviously something wrong with an economy in which the obviously desirable transactions cannot or do not take place. Those who adopt this second way of thinking about unemployment seem generally to presume, as an article of faith, that no such gap is likely to persist — not at the natural or equilibrium rate anyway. For protagonists of this view, "equilibrium" tends to mean "market clearing," and that rules out any persistent difference between real wage and marginal value of leisure *by definition*. No one else has to accede to that self-limiting choice, however.

A certain dynamic story usually goes along with the theory of a natural rate of unemployment, although it is not the only possible one. According to this accelerationist story, the rate of wage (and price) inflation increases whenever the unemployment rate is lower than the natural rate, and decreases (presumably into negative values) whenever current unemployment exceeds the natural rate. One implication is that the natural rate or equilibrium rate is the only unemployment rate that is compatible with steady inflation. Indeed it is compatible with steady inflation at any historically given rate, the cumulative result of past deviations from the natural rate. (This story can obviously be refined by allowing for lags here and there, but the moral of the story is unaffected.)

There is a temptation here. One sometimes hears it said that unemployment is below the natural rate. How is that known? Because inflation is accelerating. Why is inflation accelerating? Because unemployment is below the natural rate. It is possible to use language so that the statement "unemployment is below the natural rate" *means* "inflation is accelerating." It would seem to be more straightforward just to state the observable fact that inflation is accelerating.

Rigorous application of this locution is a way of defining the natural rate of unemployment. Suppose that the natural rate thus defined should turn out to be pretty nearly constant for substantial periods of time or, if not constant, moving slowly in a predictable way. That would confirm the accelerationist model, and it would then do little harm to identify accelerating or decelerating inflation with an unemployment rate below or above the natural rate. Something like that may have been true for the United States between the 1950s and the 1980s. Even that is not entirely clear, however, and even if it were, it would not be a solid enough foundation for a very tall structure of theory. The picture is entirely different in the large European economies. There, in the 1950s and 1960s, the equilibrium unemployment rate appears to have been very low, maybe below 2 percent of the labor force. Extension of the accelerationist story to the 1970s and 1980s, however, requires that the equilibrium unemployment rate jump up fairly suddenly to 7 or 8 percent or even higher before — perhaps — turning down again in some places. This will not do at all. If the accelerationist model is to be taken seriously, the implied equilibrium unemployment rate has to be a fairly stable number.

Otherwise we are back to a convoluted and tendentious use of language for persuasive purposes.

An Alternative Possibility

The choice between these two ways of thinking is not simply a choice between equilibrium and disequilibrium views of the labor market, as I hope to have made clear. Nor is it just a matter of ideology, although ideology no doubt plays a role, and a larger role the closer one gets to policy matters. The choice rests on a judgment about the way the labor market operates. This is a judgment that ought to be based on observation, but I have also tried to emphasize that neither casual characterization nor mechanical econometrics is likely to be an adequate foundation for judgment. My goal here is to suggest a little widening of the range of possibilities, in a way that allows a point of entry for the institutional factors that have long been the stuff of labor economics.

One such possibility would be to imagine that the labor market is capable of many equilibrium configurations (employment, real wage rates, vacancies, other characteristics). An especially interesting case arises if there is a whole interval of equilibria — a range of unemployment rates, say — any one of which would persist if once achieved. To describe these as equilibrium unemployment rates is just to say that they generate no significant internal forces leading to change. To say that there are many equilibria is not necessarily to opt for any sort of fundamental indeterminacy. Which equilibrium the economy occupies — now or eventually — may be historically determined, traceable to some initial conditions that might have been otherwise and to the dynamics that intervene between a disturbance and the achievement of a new equilibrium.

An equilibrium of this kind is probably not the result of simple market clearing. I am not suggesting, for instance, that the demand curve and the supply curve in the labor market both happen to have infinitely elastic segments that overlap. That is possible but unlikely. The idea, instead, is that the institutions of the labor market are such that they tolerate a range of unemployment rates without any pattern of wage changes or other manifestations that will cause the volume of employment to change. These institutions have to be spelled out.

In my Royer lectures at Berkeley (published as *The Labor Market as a Social Institution*, 1990) I discussed one possible rationalization for this kind of outcome in terms of a rationally founded and formally or informally transmitted wish not to rock the boat, not to do anything that might return the labor market from its current institutional form to something approaching unbridled competition. (The basic idea, described in a little more detail in my lectures, was worked out by Frank Hahn and myself, and independently by the Swedish economist and game theorist Jörgen Weibull.) Similar results can probably be deduced from other settings. The important thing is that the representation of the "supply" of labor is no longer an upward-sloping curve connecting the volume of employment and the real wage, but is rather a "thick" two-dimensional area showing that labor-market supply conditions can be satisfied by a range of levels of employment corresponding to a given real wage, and therefore by a range of real wage rates corresponding to a given level of employment.

An Indecisive Test

In the Royer lectures I explored one simple — no doubt excessively simple — way of giving effect to this idea. Go back to the accelerationist model described earlier: it says that inflation accelerates or decelerates accordingly, as the current unemployment rate is below or above the equilibrium unemployment rate. Now suppose that the equilibrium unemployment rate is the average of the observed unemployment rates in the past five years, and not some more permanent quantity. Then the model says that inflation accelerates or decelerates as the current unemployment rate is below or above its (backward) five-year moving average.

This is a drastic change. The "natural rate" version of the accelerationist model says that the equilibrium unemployment rate is the unique one that allows steady inflation. Anything else, maintained for a long time, will cause an explosion of inflation or deflation. The alternative says that *any* unemployment rate can be an equilibrium in that sense. As soon as an unemployment rate has been maintained for five years, it has all the properties of an equilibrium; in particular, steady inflation is compatible with any steady unemployment rate. It would of course be a simple matter to modify the model so that not any unemployment rate could be an equilibrium, but only those that are neither too high nor too low.

I reported at the time on a very simple preliminary test of this hypothesis, without frills. I compared its ability to explain the unemployment-inflation nexus for the United States, 1955 to 1986, with that of a traditional accelerationist model possessing a constant equilibrium unemployment rate (estimated from the data to be 5.5 percent). The traditional model was superior, but by a narrow margin. It seems quite likely that a few plausible improvements — like the truncation of the range of equilibria as just suggested — could narrow the gap still further.

The postwar period for the United States is known to be a favorite testing ground for the natural-rate hypothesis, which was, after all, developed in that environment to fit those circumstances. The European history is much less congenial, because average unemployment rates were very low early in the period and very high later on, without any commensurate change in the propensity to inflate. Any attempt to account for those facts with an accelerationist model and a constant equilibrium rate of unemployment is bound to fail. I want to report briefly on some experiments with European data, not to peddle this simple version of multiple equilibria but to indicate how wide open the field is for other theories.

These experiments are confined to three large European economies — France, West Germany, and the United Kingdom — for the years 1955 to 1990. There is much to be learned from the experience of other countries with different institutional settings, but my purpose is not comparative and I do not know enough about the institutional differences to make intelligent inferences anyway.

The first step was to verify the suspicion that the accelerationist model is a total loss for this period in these countries. That turned out to be the case. The most straightforward vehicle for such a test is the one proposed by Franco Modigliani and Lucas Papademos, developed by Donald Nichols, and picked up in my Royer lectures (where references will be found): it is a regression of the acceleration of inflation on the unemployment rate. If this equation does a good job, the accelerationist–natural rate hypothesis is supported, and the constant equilibrium rate of unemployment can be calculated. In the event, this simple model has no explanatory value at all. (The squared correlation coefficients are 0.10, 0.01, and 0.03, respectively.) The alternative model with the constant equilibrium unemployment rate replaced by a five-year moving average of observed unemployment rates is slightly better on average but still not much good; the values of R^2 are 0.09, 0.08, and 0.06.

An obvious second step was to allow the equilibrium unemployment rate to have a time trend. To my mind this verges on data mining, but it is probably harmless here. With a quadratic trend, the squared correlation coefficients rise to 0.16, 0.06, and 0.08. If the moving-average model is also given the benefit of a quadratic trend, it generates R^2 of 0.15, 0.11, and 0.11. The conclusion has to be that simple accelerationism does not describe the experience of these three countries; if it did, there would be some slight evidence of the sort of floating equilibrium rate that I am using to exemplify the possibility of a range of equilibria.

Another Test

Next I turn to a different sort of dynamic story that may nowadays be replacing accelerationism in professional popularity and that certainly works better in contemporary Europe. In this story the focus is on the real wage itself rather than on the rate of change of real or nominal wages. The idea is that there is at any time an equilibrium real wage. It depends on productivity and perhaps on the unemployment rate. The presumption is that the equilibrium real wage will be lower in a softer labor market. In this error-correcting model, the real wage is not always at its equilibrium level. When it is higher it tends to decrease; when it is lower it tends to rise. In practice the interpretation is less clear-cut. The current unemployment rate can enter in two ways. As just mentioned, it can be a determinant of the equilibrium real wage. But one might suspect that the adjustment dynamics will also depend on the current unemployment rate: even if the real wage is above its equilibrium, say, its tendency to fall back toward equilibrium could be attenuated, and might even disappear, in a tight enough labor market, and it could be accentuated when the unemployment rate is high. These two roles of the unemployment rate will be hard to disentangle in practice. For my purpose it is not very important to do that.

Before reporting the results of this experiment, I would make two more comments about my empirical use of the model. First, it would be possible to measure the influence of productivity on the equilibrium real wage using the smoothed productivity trend in each country as an independent variable. Instead I have used a quadratic trend in each case, with coefficients determined by the data. This cannot make a major difference for the comparison I propose to make. Second, I have described the equilibrium real wage and the local dynamics as being determined in part by the unemployment rate. It is always open to interpret this as the difference between the unemployment rate and some neutral or equilibrium or even "natural" level, and this is what I shall do.

When the error-correction model is applied to France, it fits reasonably well with $R^2 = 0.53$, which is not bad considering that the dependent variable is the annual proportional change in the real wage. (By the way, the explanatory power is not to be compared with that of the accelerationist model, because the dependent variables are quite different.) The model makes fair sense in that all the variables appear with the right sign, but there are some weaknesses. The unemployment rate enters in the right way but fails to be of statistical significance. In the case of France, it is not absolutely clear that either the equilibrium real wage or the dynamics really depends on the rate of current unemployment, nor is it clear that they do not. A second weakness is that the speed of adjustment of the real wage toward its equilibrium is quite slow, only 10 percent of the gap being eliminated in a year.

For Germany and the United Kingdom the story is generally considerably better. In the case of Germany, all the variables enter appropriately and with clear statistical significance. The fit is good: $R^2 = 0.59$. It is estimated that the real wage moves a third of the way toward its equilibrium in the course of a year. That seems to make intuitive sense.

In most respects the case of the United Kingdom is similar. The model has the right general shape; all the independent variables appear with the correct sign and statistically significant coefficients. It looks as if the real wage responds more amply to the unemployment rate than it does in Germany and just about as much as it does in France (although the French coefficient is not well determined). According to the estimates a trifle more than one-third of a real-wage disequilibrium is eliminated in one calendar year. The only noteworthy difference is that the model explains less than in Germany or France, with $R^2 = 0.30$. This is to be expected; Britain is notorious for having generated rising real wages even during the period of greatest unemployment under the Thatcher government. That is a description, however, not an explanation. It strikes me as just the sort of fact that needs to be explained by historical-institutional analysis and not by mining the data for a better-fitting model.

The error-correcting model seems to be a reasonable description of the three large European economies (with reservations in the case of France). I am not in the business of producing wage equations, however; I am exploring the notion of equilibrium in the labor market. In this model, the level of unemployment is meant to determine an equilibrium (productivity-adjusted) real wage. That is algebraically the same thing as relating the real wage to the distance of the unemployment rate from some fixed reference point. Now I want to see what happens if this model is replaced by one in which the equilibrium real wage is determined by the deviation of the unemployment rate from its five-year retrospective moving average. In other words, I want to play around with the idea that a given real wage can become, by habituation, compatible with any unemployment rate within reason. I add that last qualifier to indicate that the range-of-equilibria story could undoubtedly be improved by making plausible — even necessary — adjustments, but that would be a never-ending game and is not now to the point. Here are the results of a simple experiment.

In every case, the moving-average-equilibrium model outperforms the fixed-equilibrium model, ever so slightly. In each of the three countries the structure of the estimated model remains sensible and the speed of adjustment changes only trivially. The squared correlation coefficient rises to 0.54 in France, 0.61 in Germany, and 0.33 in the United Kingdom. I do not think anything portentous should be read into this consistent slight improvement. The message is lower key than that. If one asks these data to discriminate between a model in which the equilibrium real wage is determined by the absolute size of the unemployment rate and a model in which the equilibrium real wage is determined by the excess of current unemployment over (or under) its recent average level, the result is that there is not much advantage to be gained either way. I take this to mean that stories with a unique equilibrium in the labor market have not earned their popularity. The field is open to plausible scenarios in which many equilibrium unemployment rates are possible.

A secondary lesson is that it will probably be hard to find unambiguous empirical evidence in favor of one sort of story or the other. Conviction may have to come from different, perhaps qualitative or anecdotal, sources of evidence.

Relevance for Policy

This theoretical issue about the nature of labor market equilibrium has important practical consequences. I do not mean to suggest that theory and econometrics move the world, only that holding a particular theory of labor market equilibrium would incline an observer to prefer certain sorts of policies to others. For instance, those who find the natural-rate concept congenial and plausible would accept that the equilibrium rate itself, and therefore eventually the observed amount of unemployment, can be changed by policies affecting the structure and institutions of the labor market. Therefore legislation or regulation affecting industrial, occupational, and regional mobility; reducing or increasing transaction costs, including hiring and firing costs; reducing or increasing unemployment insurance coverage, duration, and benefits; and changing the legal status of labor unions would all change the equilibrium unemployment rate in fairly predictable ways, and thus the course of events as well.

Many such policy moves entail difficulties because they would weaken institutions and customs to which people are bound by interest or devotion. Others are problematic because they almost certainly have major distribution implications very near the surface; when there are big winners and big losers, either within or between social classes, efficiency arguments have an air of unreality. Granted those difficulties and subtleties, debate about such measures takes a routine form.

The more controversial question is: what is the likely effect on employment and nonemployment of demand-side policies, of actions whose direct effect is to increase or decrease the nominal or real demand, or both, for produced goods and services. The intellectual history locates the natural-rate idea in the assertion that demand-side policies will have at most temporary effects on employment and nonemployment. Instead the unemployment rate will gravitate toward the equilibrium rate, or else it will eventuate in accelerating inflation or deflation. (I have often asked rhetorically whether partisans of the accelerationist model actually believe the deflation half of that implication, but I am still not sure about the appropriate reply.) The accelerationist story was intended to discredit the textbook-Keynesian model that led to the conclusion that policy-induced expansion of nominal demand would reliably increase unemployment on a sufficiently long-run basis to matter. The critique applies to the theoretical and empirical foundations of all versions of textbook-Keynesian doctrine, whether based on equilibrium or disequilibrium modeling, on nominal-wage rigidity or on some version of the Phillips curve.

The notion that the labor market may admit a whole range of equilibria is directly relevant to this sort of policy debate. In a narrow sense, somewhere within the range of labor market equilibria may be a configuration that is worth calling "full employment." A more exact version of this statement is that, when there are many equilibria, some may be unambiguously better than others, with all parties to the employment transaction coming out ahead. Then there is another possible role for demand-side policy: to shift the economy from an unsatisfactory equilibrium to a better one. Another way of putting it is to say that public policy is a way of replacing an inefficient noncooperative outcome of a "game" with a superior cooperative outcome.

That is the good news. If the institutions of the labor market allow a range of equilibria, then demand-side policies can be effective. They operate by picking out one of the available equilibrium unemployment rates. Anyone looking at recent history might easily conclude that if one were "picking out" an unemployment rate for Europe and, more recently, North America, one might be inclined to pick out a lower one. The general importance of this enlargement of possibilities is that the fatalism implied by the natural-rate version of equilibrium theory turns out to be linked to a very narrow version of equilibrium theory. The evidence supporting that model of the labor market is unconvincing, to say the least.

There is bad news, too. No body of evidence supports a multiple-equilibrium picture of the labor market, either. Even if there were such evidence, the policy implications are not necessarily optimistic. For example, the moving-average accelerationism I have used as a trial horse implies that the act of moving from one steady unemployment rate to another entails a permanent rise in the rate of inflation. This can be seen by following a stylized case. Start with steady unemployment and steady inflation; the deviation of the current unemployment rate from its past average is zero. Now do whatever is necessary to lower the unemployment rate a few tenths of a point and hold it there. Initially the current unemployment rate is below the backward-looking moving average, so inflation accelerates. The same will be true for each of the first few years, although decreasingly so, and thus inflation continues to accelerate. Eventually the moving average catches up with the new steady unemployment rate and inflation stabilizes. But it is higher than it was when the process started. (This is entirely apart from the likelihood that there is a lower limit to the range of equilibrium unemployment rates.) I had better emphasize that I hold no particular brief for moving-average accelerationism. I have used it merely as a device to show how special and how unconvincing the natural-rate hypothesis really is.

Final Note

The error-correction model is an alternative to accelerationism. It does not single out a unique — or any — equilibrium unemployment rate. It is just one equation with two unknowns, the real wage and the unemployment rate. (There could, of course, be other variables, exogenous and endogenous; I am just illustrating a principle.) To determine both variables, we need another equation involving them. The error-correction model represents the supply side of the labor market, but not in any simple Marshallian sense. It gives the wage-unemployment pairs compatible with the institutions of the labor market. The additional equation would presumably represent the demand side of the labor market, in the loose sense that it would be the vehicle by which the product-market situation of firms affects labor market outcomes. If the supply-side model allows for a range of equilibria, then even a strict demand curve for labor would determine only a range of eligible wage-unemployment pairs. Something else, which I imagine to be historical contingency, would be needed to produce determinacy.

Here, and also in the description of the supply side of the market, is the point of entry for the intimate, contextual sort of labor economics that I once learned from such guides to the field as John Dunlop, Clark Kerr, and Arthur Ross. I hope I am right in thinking that there is a revival of that approach.

Author's Note

I want to thank Ms. Aparna Rao, an undergraduate economics student at MIT, for her excellent research assistance.

References

Nichols, Donald A. 1987. "The Decline of the Natural Rate of Unemployment." Unpublished paper, University of Wisconsin–Madison.

Solow, Robert M. 1990. *The Labor Market as a Social Institution.* Cambridge, Mass., and Oxford: Basil Blackwell.

Weibull, Jörgen. 1987. "Persistent Unemployment as Subgame Perfect Equilibrium." Seminar Paper No. 381, Institute for International Economic Studies, Stockholm, Sweden.

Appendix

Following are the regression equations underlying the discussion of the error-correction model found in the body of the chapter. The data are from the Organization for Economic Cooperation and Development's *Historical Statistics*.

Let w_t be the natural logarithm of the real wage in year t. Then the basic error-correction hypothesis is that

$$w_t - w_{t-1} = -b[w_{t-1} - (c + dt + et^2 + fu_t)]$$

where b, c, d, e, and t are parameters, and the expression in round parentheses is the hypothetical equilibrium value of the (log) real wage in year $t-1$. So the regression equation is

$$w_t - w_{t-1} = a_0 + a_1 t + a_2 t + a_3 w_{t-1} + a_4 u_t$$

The estimated speed of adjustment is $-a_3$. If u^* is an equilibrium unemployment rate, then $a_y u_t$ can be interpreted as $a_4(u_t - u^*)$ and a_0 by $a_0 + a_4 u^*$.

The least-squares estimates (with t statistics) are given in Table 10.1.
The same regression, with the $u_t - u_t^*$ where $u_2^* = \frac{1}{5}(u_{t-1} + u_{t-2} + u_{t-3} + u_{t-4} + u_{t-5})$ gives the values shown in Table 10.2.

The least-squares estimates (with t statistics) are given in Table 10.1.
The same regression, with the u_t replaced by $u_t - u_t^*$ where $u_t^* = \frac{1}{5}(u_{t-1} + u_{t-2} + u_{t-3} + u_{t-4} + u_{t-5})$ gives the values shown in Table 10.2.

Table 10.1.

	a_0	a_1	a_2	a_3	a_4	R^2	DW
France	−0.23	.0010	−.00015	−.098	−.0005	0.53	2.08
	(1.80)	(3.52)	(2.10)	(1.82)	(0.93)		
Germany	−1.00	.0022	−.00021	−0.34	−.00098	0.59	1.31
	(2.84)	(2.63)	(2.05)	(3.09)	(3.42)		
U.K.	−1.41	.017	−.00022	−0.36	−.00041	.30	1.6
	(2.87)	(2.89)	(2.65)	(2.94)	(1.57)		

Table 10.2.

	a_0	a_1	a_2	a_3	a_4	R^2	DW
France	−0.23	.011	−.00022	−0.89	−.00047	0.54	1.70
	(1.15)	(2.27)	(3.48)	(1.13)	(0.98)		
Germany	−1.08	.029	−.00043	−0.34	−.013	0.61	1.56
	(3.00)	(3.11)	(3.21)	(3.15)	(4.01)		
U.K.	−1.52	.0020	−.00034	−0.37	−.0054	0.33	1.66
	(2.56)	(2.38)	(2.33)	(2.63)	(1.67)		

11

American Exceptionalism in the Labor Market: Union-Nonunion Differentials in the United States and Other Countries

■ ——————————————— ■

Richard B. Freeman

The voluminous empirical literature on the economic effects of trade unions reviewed in Freeman and Medoff (1981), Lewis (1986), and in the *Handbook of Labor Economics* (Ashenfelter and Layard 1986) is based largely on U.S. data and experience. While American economists occasionally pay attention to unions in Britain and elsewhere, and specialists in other countries have made some quantitative analyses of union effects comparable to those for the United States, researchers rarely look across country lines to try to differentiate which union-nonunion effects are "universal" and which are rooted in the distinctive features of national labor relations systems. The resultant insularity contributes to the gap between abstract theories of unions as maximizing agents of their members and the institutional reality of their operation in different countries.

How do union-nonunion wage gaps in other Organization for Economic Cooperation and Development (OECD) countries compare with those in the United States? Do unions in other countries reduce wage dispersion, raise fringe-benefit shares of compensation, lower quitting rates, and increase tenure with employers, as they do in the United States? Do the effects of unions on productivity and profits found in the United States generalize to other economies?

This study seeks to answer these questions by estimating union-nonunion wage and other outcome gaps in microdata for individuals from ten countries covered in the pooled 1987–1989 International

Social Survey Programme (ISSP) surveys and by contrasting the results of studies using other data sets with those for the United States. The 1987–1989 ISSP contains more countries than the 1985–1987 ISSP surveys analyzed by Blanchflower and Freeman (1992). In addition, the 1989 "work orientations" module includes questions about job satisfaction and labor relations not contained on earlier files.

The method of analyzing union effects across countries in this study — contrasting outcomes for union and nonunion workers within a country — differs from studies that relate macroeconomic variables to taxonomies of labor relations systems in cross-country regressions (Crouch 1985; Bruno and Sachs 1985; Grubb, Jackman, and Layard 1983; Calmfors and Driffil 1988; Freeman 1988b). Here the principal units of observation are individuals within countries, whereas the principal units of observation in those studies are country aggregates.

My primary data analysis finds that:

• Unions raise wages by widely different amounts across countries, with union-nonunion wage gaps being largest in the United States.

• Unions reduce the dispersion of earnings among members in virtually all countries — the apparent result of ubiquitous "standard rate" wage policies.

• Union workers generally report lower job satisfaction and more conflict with management at workplaces than nonunion workers.

The review of existing studies shows that:

• Unions raise fringe benefits in several countries besides the United States, but they are unlikely to do as much in countries where government mandates large fringe-benefit expenditures.

• Unions reduce voluntary quitting and turnover in other countries, as in the United States.

• Unions have disparate effects on the level and growth of productivity. Positive productivity effects in the United States appear linked to large union wage effects.

• Unions reduce profits in the United States and the United Kingdom — countries with decentralized bargaining — but are unlikely to have such effects in countries with centralized wage setting.

What explains this pattern of findings? Why does unionism have similar effects on dispersion, exit, fringes, and satisfaction across countries but different effects on wages, productivity, and profits?

Viewing what unionism does to dispersion, fringes, exit, and satisfaction as reflecting the "voice" of unions and what unionism does to wages and profits as reflecting "monopoly" wage effects, the simplest explanation of the empirical results is that voice is the universal aspect of unionism while the monopoly wage effects result from the United States' decentralized wage-setting system. Finding an exceptionally large union wage effect in the United States is, moreover, consistent with explanations of falling private-sector union density in the United States that stress the incentives that huge union-nonunion wage gaps give management to oppose unions and the institutional rules that allow management to act on that opposition.

Union Effects across Countries

A priori, should one expect unionism to produce similar or different union-nonunion wage gaps and other outcome gaps across countries? Simple union maximizing models give no reason to expect union wage effects to differ systematically across countries. Such models relate differences in wage effects to differences in worker utility functions (for earnings versus employment security) and in employer demand for labor. There is little one can say a priori about these factors; indeed, economists generally forswear relating differences in outcomes to differences in tastes and would expect roughly comparable labor demand curves across countries (absent institutional interventions). By contrast, knowledge of the institutional systems governing labor relations across countries generates clear predictions about the likely effects of unionism in different settings.

On the wage side, the key institutional difference among labor markets is the degree of centralization of wage setting. In the United States thousands of local unions bargain over detailed collective contracts that set members' wage rates, while management determines the wages for nonunion workers subject to market constraints. In Scandinavia and Austria unions often negotiate national wage agreements with employer associations and enter into agreements with the government and employer federations that link wage settlements to national economic policies. Australian unions argue wage cases before arbitration tribunals that issue orders covering the bulk of the work force. French unions and German unions negotiate industry or regional agreements whose terms the Ministry of Labor can extend to nonunion workers. In Japan enterprise unions bargain at the firm level, while union federations engage in the Shunto Offensive to determine national wage patterns.

To the extent that institutions represent more than the crowing of Cantillon's cock,[1] these differing arrangements can be expected to produce different union-nonunion wage gaps. *Centralized bargaining systems should, in particular, produce relatively small wage gaps*, since the wages of union and nonunion workers are governed largely by the same agreements. As the United States has the most decentralized bargaining system, I expect American union wage premiums to be larger than those in other countries.

On the "voice" or representation side of the union ledger, there is an institutional difference between English-speaking OECD countries and Sweden as a group and the continental European countries. In the English-speaking countries and Sweden, unions are the sole institution for worker collective voice whereas in virtually all Western European countries, mandated works councils represent workers, union or not, at local workplaces. This should produce greater union-nonunion outcome gaps for voice-related variables in the English-speaking countries and Sweden than in countries with works councils. However, councils tend to be more active where unions are strong, and in most council elections workers vote for union slates, suggesting union-nonunion differences in voice-related outcome gaps even in these settings.

Finally, there are differences across countries in the role of unions in national politics. Many countries have labor or socialist parties. The United States does not. This could lead to differences in the reliance on government versus collective bargaining in determining wages and fringe benefits. Since legislated solutions impose the same outcomes on workers regardless of union status, union movements that rely more on legislation than collective bargaining will produce smaller union-nonunion gaps. However, AFL-CIO support for occupational health and safety legislation, civil rights legislation, and the like in the United States shows that even unions in decentralized wage-setting systems without a labor party often go the legislative route.

Problems in comparing union effects across countries

Comparing the effects of unionism on microeconomic outcomes across countries by estimating outcome differences between union and nonunion workers (other factors held fixed) is tricky for conceptual and data reasons.

First, union membership measures different things outside the United States than in the United States, making it a potentially less valid measure of union activity in foreign labor markets. In the United States, exclusive union representation of 50 percent or more of workers sharply differentiates union and nonunion labor. In other countries, the demarcation between member and nonmember is not necessarily the best dividing line between workers influenced and not influenced by collective bargaining. In Sweden, where almost all workers are union members, a more appropriate contrast might be made between workers in strong unions or federations (LO) and those in weaker unions or federations (TCO, in years past). In Spain, where few workers are union members but where union-dominated works councils can strike against enterprises and where unions have conducted successful general strikes, the analogue to the union-nonunion comparison may be between active and inactive councils. Similarly, density of union membership or existence of a works council might be taken as better measures of potential union influence on enterprise decisions in Germany than simple union-nonunion worker comparisons. Even in the United Kingdom, whether a worker is in a plant where the employer recognizes the union or whether the workplace is a closed shop may offer more valid indicators of union influence on outcomes than union membership.

When union membership is a less valid measure of union influence than it is for the United States, membership (M) will differ from the true measure of union influence (UI) by an error term (u):

$$M = UI + u$$

Since union-nonunion comparisons are most appropriate for the United States, measurement error is likely to produce a greater downward bias in the estimated effect of unionism on outcomes in other countries. This raises the possibility that measurement error rather than the systemic nature of labor relations systems might produce smaller union-nonunion gaps overseas.

A second problem in comparing union effects relates to the different levels of union density across countries. Consider Sweden again, where union density is on the order of 85 percent of the work force. Since so few workers are outside unions, there is a good chance those workers or their workplaces are "odd," creating a selectivity bias in comparisons of union and nonunion workers. In addition to selectivity, moreover, density is likely to affect outcomes by influencing the "power" of unions to affect outcomes: union wage gaps in the United States tend to rise with the percentage organized (Freeman and Medoff 1981b). As Sweden is not included in the ISSP, and as most countries have union-membership densities between 30 percent and 60 percent, the problem case is actually the United States, with its extremely low level of unionization. Differences in union effects between the United States and other countries may be due in part to the American low density.

A third problem is that the same nominal outcome may have different importance in different countries. Wages are generally a larger share of labor cost in the United States than in European countries, so a given union wage effect will have a greater impact on costs in the United States than in Europe. In Japan bonuses are a significant share of pay and must be included in any study of union wage effects. In most European countries, governments mandate many fringe benefits, leaving unions little scope to raise fringes for members. To the extent that differences in union effects on fringe benefits reflect differential union reliance on legislation rather than collective agreements, union-nonunion differentials in fringes are a poor measure of union influence on the provision of fringes.

The empirical issue facing this study is that of differentiating differences in union-nonunion outcome gaps due to institutional arrangements from "spurious gaps" — differences due to the validity of measures or differing levels of density or differing importance of outcome measures. Unfortunately, the ISSP data do not allow me any simple statistical way to control for spurious differentials. The ISSP has only one question relating to unionism — "Are you a member in a trade union at present?" — which rules out using other variables to measure union influence or as instruments for membership. The outcome variables are earnings, wage policies that affect earnings, and job satisfaction. Absent econometric "proof" of causal relations, I try to assess the potential bias in results on the basis of the more refined studies from the U.S. union effect literature, and by comparing union-nonunion gaps in different outcome variables.

Empirical Analysis

In this section I present ordinary least square (OLS) cross-section regression estimates of union-nonunion differentials for the United States and nine other developed countries. I eschew more complex structural models because U.S. experience shows that those models yield unreliable estimates of union effects that add little to our stock of knowledge (Freeman and Medoff 1981; Lewis 1986) and thus are unlikely to cast much light on differences across countries.[2] Studies in the United States that compare workers before and after being a union member generally confirm the findings of cross-section regressions, though they usually yield smaller union-

277

nonunion gaps (Freeman 1984; Lewis 1986). I have argued that while cross sections overstate union gaps for selectivity reasons, longitudinal studies understate those effects, providing a boundary on the true union effect (Freeman 1984). If selectivity and measurement biases are similar across countries, such problems will not affect my comparisons.

The International Social Survey Programme data

The data used in this study are the 1987–1989 survey files of the International Social Survey Programme, a program of cross-national collaboration carried out by research institutes that conduct annual surveys of social attitudes and values. The ISSP coordinates national social science surveys to produce a common set of questions asked in identical form in the participating nations. The surveys contain information on union membership and various outcome variables for ten OECD countries: Austria, Australia, Germany, United States, Italy, Norway, Netherlands, United Kingdom, Ireland, and Switzerland. I have pooled the files for three years to increase the sample size and the number of countries: Ireland and Norway are included in the 1989 survey only; Australia is in the 1987 survey; Switzerland is in the 1987 group, although it is not a member of ISSP; and Italy's files contain union data for 1987 and 1989 but not for 1988. While the ISSP is the most readily available cross-country data set, it is still far from ideal. There are more questions on attitudes than on objective labor market circumstances; earnings relate to yearly earnings rather than hourly pay; and despite the effort for comparability, not every country asks the same questions each year.

Table 11.1 presents estimates of the rate of unionization for employed workers in the ten countries for several different groups. The first column gives densities for all employed workers: it has the lowest density figures. The remaining columns are limited to wage and salary workers, and show higher densities of the magnitudes generally found in other data sets (Freeman 1989). While there are some differences between the ISSP figures and those reported from other sources, these data confirm the key fact about unionization for this study: the extraordinary low level of union density for the United States. In these data, just 18 percent of U.S. wage and salary workers are unionized compared with a median figure for other countries of 45 percent. When I limit the sample to full-time workers or to manual workers or to the intersection of those sets, the density rates rise, but the gap between the United States and the other countries remains huge.

To see if unionization has different effects on wages across ISSP countries, I estimated earnings equations for the log of wage and salary earnings. In cases where the data were reported in categorical units, I used the midpoint of the category as the relevant earnings figure. To maintain comparability across countries, the regressions include only basic control variables: experience (age-schooling-6), experience squared, education, sex, the logarithm of hours worked the previous week, and manual status. I limited the sample to wage and salary workers. Because several countries, including the United States, obtain annual earnings, I also include a dummy for full-time workers, so as to reduce the danger of misconstruing differences in weeks worked for differences in pay.

Table 11.2 presents my estimated union-nonunion wage differential (and standard errors) for each country and contrasts the U.S. differential from the median differential. The first column gives results for all workers, while the second gives results for the manual workers who are generally the bulwark of unionism. The Table 11.2 differentials accord reasonably well with estimated union wage effects for the limited countries for which union effects have been

Table 11.1. Rates of unionization of employed workers in the ISSP survey, 1987–1989

Country (sample size for all)		All employed	Wage and salary		Full-time	
			All	Manual	All	Manual
United States	(2,179)	16	18	24	19	27
United Kingdom	(2,148)	40	45	50	47	53
Ireland	(976)	36	46	30	48	49
West Germany	(2,670)	27	21	36	34	39
Austria	(1,918)	43	49	54	52	57
Australia	(945)	64	68	67	70	69
Italy	(814)	—	31	35	33	37
Netherlands	(2,083)	30	39	43	42	47
Norway	(1,318)	54	57	63	63	63
Switzerland	(671)	37	37	35	37	37
Median density, except U.S.		37	45	43	47	49
U.S. minus median		−21	−27	−20	−28	−22

Source: Tabulated from 1987–1989 ISSP surveys. Australia and Switzerland data are available for 1987 only. Norway is available only in 1989. Ireland is available for 1988 and 1989. Italy did not have a union question in 1988. Italy did not ask self-employed workers union status, so the tabulation in column 1 includes them as nonunion workers.

estimated in other data sets. The ISSP-based estimate of 0.33 for the United States is in the high range of U.S. Current Population Survey (CPS)–based estimates of union-nonunion wage differentials for the United States (Freeman and Medoff 1984; Lewis 1986), potentially because it relates to annual earnings. The ISSP-based estimate of 0.14 for the United Kingdom is modestly above the 10 percent or so reported in extant British studies (Blanchflower; Blanchflower and Oswald). The estimates for Australia are low, however, compared with those found in more detailed studies (Mulvey 1986; Kornfeld 1990), and the estimates for Germany are smaller than those reported by Blanchflower and Freeman for earlier ISSP surveys. I attribute some of these differences to the modest sample sizes and to sampling error.

This said, there is no gainsaying the most striking finding in the table: the high union-nonunion differential in the United States. The U.S. differentials of 0.33 and 0.40 dwarf those for the other nine countries. The second highest differential is for Ireland and the third highest for the United Kingdom (and Austria, in the first column). The Austrian results differ noticeably from the negligible union effects reported by Blanchflower and Freeman. For all workers the

Table 11.2   Regression coefficients and standard errors on union dummy variables: wage and salary workers, by country, 1987–1989 ISSP

	All workers	Manual workers
United States	.33 (.05)	.40 (.07)
United Kingdom	.14 (.02)	.17 (.04)
Ireland	.21 (.03)	.15 (.04)
West Germany	.10 (.02)	.07 (.03)
Austria	.14 (.02)	.14 (.03)
Australia	.03 (.05)	−.07 (.08)
Italy	.04 (.03)	.08 (.04)
Netherlands	.09 (.03)	.08 (.03)
Norway	.03 (.02)	.12 (.04)
Switzerland	.05 (.04)	.12 (.07)
Median, except U.S.	.05	.12
U.S. minus median	.28	.28

Source: Based on multivariate regressions of log earnings on the following variables: years of schooling, experience (age-schooling-6), years of experience squared, log of hours worked, dummy variables for sex, married status, full-time work, and year, as well as union status.

Note: Log refers to the natural logarithm, standard error in parenthesis. Sample consists of wage and salary workers only.

estimated wage union effects in the other relatively centralized wage-setting systems are either moderate (West Germany, Netherlands) or small (Italy, Norway, Australia). They are moderate for manual workers in all of these countries, though insignificant (negative) in Australia, and also in Switzerland.

Evidence from other studies on union-nonunion wage differentials for countries not covered in the ISSP — Japan, Canada, and Sweden — confirms the finding that the U.S. has the largest union wage premium (see Table 11.6). In Japan union wage effects are small except for women, presumably because the Shunto Offensive sets wage patterns for the entire country, and union effects on bonuses and severance pay do not come close to producing a differential of the United States' magnitude (Nakamura, Sato, and Kaniya 1988; Osawa 1989). In Canada, which has a labor relations system similar to that in the United States, non-ISSP estimated differentials are smaller than comparable estimated differentials in the United States: 1970s and 1980s differentials on the order of 10 to 20 percent (Gunderson 1982; Simpson 1985) compared with 20 to 25 percent differentials in the U.S. CPS (Freeman and Medoff 1984; Lewis 1986). While I am uneasy about wage differentials for Sweden, due to the high degree of unionization, they appear to be small as well. In short, *U.S. unionism produces greater union-nonunion differentials than unionism in other advanced countries.*

Interpretation

Is it correct to interpret the higher union wage premium in the United States as being due to decentralized wage setting as opposed to, say, low density? Might not the observed high union-nonunion wage differential in the United States be an artifact of sample selectivity, so that if workers were ranked by the potential for a union differential, the United States would include only those with a high potential while countries with higher densities include workers with lower potential differentials?

I doubt that selectivity explains the results. First, since employers as well as workers affect union density in the United States, the direction of the selectivity effect is uncertain: employers will fight hardest against unions that have the most potential for raising wages and will accept unions where they have the least potential. Evidence that union wage differentials are greater the greater the extent of unionization in a sector (Freeman and Medoff 1981b; Lewis 1986, 147) is, at the minimum, inconsistent with the notion that reduced density produces larger differentials. Second, to the extent that density or measurement factors account for the U.S. having greater union-nonunion wage gaps than other countries, I would expect similar differences in other market outcomes. Density in a country is the same for all outcomes, and I am using the same mismeasured union-influence variable on the right side of the equation. In fact, as the remainder of this section shows, union-nonunion gaps in other outcomes are quite similar across countries. Only on wage differences is the United States an extreme outlier.

The question naturally arises as to why there is any union effect in the centralized wage-setting countries. There are two mechanisms for this: wage drift at plants, which is potentially more important for unionized workers; and the speed of adjustment of wages toward nationally determined levels, which is potentially faster where unions are stronger. Wage drift has long been important in Europe and the subject of attention in West Germany, Sweden, and the Netherlands. The small union differential in Italy may also raise some questions, for Italy is not widely recognized as having a highly centralized wage-setting system. In fact, however, with the *scala mobile* dominating changes in wages in the 1970s and early 1980s, industry agreements followed by enterprise or individual wage setting, the Italian system closely resembles those of such corporatist states as Sweden (Erickson and Ichino 1992).

Dispersion of earnings

By raising the wages of organized workers relative to otherwise comparable less-organized workers, unions increase wage dispersion. By pushing standard-rate wage policies, on the other hand, unions reduce dispersion among organized workers. And by increasing the wages of union, manual workers relative to nonunion, nonmanual workers, unions also lower inequality. Microdata sets available in the 1970s for the United States showed that the lower dispersion of pay among union workers and between white-collar and blue-collar workers in unionized settings dominates the increased dispersion due to the union differential on otherwise comparable workers, producing a net reduction in wage inequality (Freeman 1980; 1982). Is this a general feature of unionization?

To answer this question I calculated the standard deviation of log earnings of union and nonunion workers for all workers and full-time wage and salary workers in each ISSP country. The results in Table 11.3 reveal markedly lower standard deviations among unionists than among nonunionists in virtually all cases. In contrast to the Table 11.2 finding of greater union-nonunion wage differentials in the United States, moreover, the differences in standard deviations of earnings in the United States, while large, are similar in magnitude

Table 11.3. Standard deviation of log earnings between union and nonunion wage and salary and full-time wage and salary workers by country, 1987–1989 ISSP

	All workers			Full-time workers			Manual workers		
	Union	Nonunion	Difference	Union	Nonunion	Difference	Union	Nonunion	Difference
United States	.84	1.12	-.28	.68	.82	-.14	.86	1.17	-.31
United Kingdom	.67	.83	-.16	.59	.67	-.08	.67	.76	-.09
West Germany	.38	.61	-.23	.35	.53	-.18	.33	.58	-.25
Austria	.49	.67	-.18	.43	.57	-.16	.50	.65	-.15
Australia	1.01	1.08	-.07	.63	.62	.01	.86	.85	.01
Italy	.37	.52	-.15	.37	.46	.09	.31	.42	-.11
Ireland	.77	.81	-.04	.48	.63	-.15	.72	.67	.05
Netherlands	.49	.68	-.17	.41	.54	-.13	.47	.54	-.07
Norway	.43	.71	-.28	.29	.53	-.24	.40	.67	-.27

Source: Calculated from ISSP data, using same data sets as in Table 11.2.

to those in the other countries. The smallest differences in dispersion in these data are for Australia and Ireland, where among manual workers dispersion among unionists is slightly larger than among nonunion workers.

Finding that unionization is associated with lower earnings dispersion outside the United States is consistent with other work (see Table 11.6). Metcalf (1990), and Blanchflower and Oswald (1988a) report lower wage inequality among union than nonunion workers in the United Kingdom. Kupferschmidt and Swidinsky (1989) report a similar result for Canada in cross-section and longitudinal data. Lemieux (1992) finds that unions reduce the overall variance of wages for men but not for women in Canada and account for 40 percent of the greater variance in wages among men in the United States than men in Canada by the differing level of unionization. As for the small estimated effect of unionization on dispersion in Australia, Kornfeld (1990) reports only modest union-nonunion differences in variances of earnings among young Australian workers.

Finally, U.S. studies relate the lower dispersion among union versus nonunion workers to explicit pay policies — union preference for standard-rate modes of wage setting as opposed to personalized or merit pay setting. The 1989 ISSP asks, "At your workplace, in deciding on pay for two people doing the same kind of work, how important is the standard rate — giving both employees the same pay?" There are four possible answers: it is the most important element in pay (compared with how well the employee does the job, experience, tenure, sex, family responsibilities, education, and formal qualifications); it is second most important; it is third most important; or the item is not chosen (that is, it is fourth, or less important). In addition, the ISSP asks for the importance of "how well the employee does the job" in wage setting, as well as the other factors. Surprisingly, given the uniformity of results on the greater use of standard rates at union workplaces in the United States, the ISSP shows American union members reporting less use of standard rates and greater importance given to quality of work on the job than nonunionists (Table 11.4). The situation for other countries shows that unionization is associated with greater use of standard rate policies and that less weight is given to how well the worker performs on the job in determining pay in five of seven cases; unionization has practically no effect on these factors in Germany, while Ireland shows the reverse pattern. In light of the odd result for the United States, which is contrary to surveys of actual company wage-setting policies (Freeman 1982), I am loath to make much of the responses to this question. Perhaps the way in

Table 11.4. Percentage of wage and salary workers stating that standard-rate wage policies or quality of work are important in setting wages, by union status and country, 1989 ISSP

	Percentage reporting standard rate is among top three factors			Percentage reporting quality of work is most important factor		
	Union	Nonunion	Difference	Union	Nonunion	Difference
United States	15	19	−4	70	64	6
United Kingdom	43	31	12	48	60	−12
West Germany	34	34	0	29	28	1
Austria	24	17	7	33	45	−12
Italy	18	15	3	33	33	0
Ireland	32	34	−2	51	45	6
Netherlands	27	18	9	56	60	−4
Norway	34	24	10	19	34	−15

Source: Tabulated from 1989 ISSP data, from two questions: "At your workplace, in deciding on pay for two people doing the same kind of work, how important is the standard rate — giving both employees the same pay?"; and "At your workplace, in deciding on pay for two people doing the same kind of work how important is how well the employee does the job?"

285

which the ISSP worded the question — in terms of the importance rather than existence of explicit policies — affected the answers.

Satisfaction

One of the more surprising findings from analysis of unionization in the United States is that union workers tend to report themselves less satisfied with their job than similarly situated nonunion workers paid the same wages (Freeman 1978; Borjas 1979). The ISSP asked workers, "How satisfied are you in your main job?" and allowed for seven responses, ranging from completely satisfied to completely dissatisfied. The responses in Table 11.5 show that in six of the eight countries, including the United States, union workers evinced markedly less satisfaction at their job than nonunion workers. In addition, a similar pattern appears to be true for Australia, which was not covered in the 1989 ISSP (Miller).

The ISSP contains one additional question relating to potential discontent associated with union voice. It asks workers about "relations at the respondent's workplace between management and employees." Consistent with the relative job satisfaction reported, in all countries proportionately fewer union than nonunion workers report that relations are "very good" or "quite good" (Table 11.5).

My interpretation for these patterns is that union voice involves active criticism of company decisions, particularly during contract negotiation periods, when workers have to be dissatisfied to support tough negotiations for economic benefits. Absent longitudinal information, the data are also consistent with the alternative explanation that poor working conditions lead to dissatisfaction and unionization (Miller).

Other Effects of Unionization

Since the ISSP lacks information on several important economic outcomes that unionization might influence, I rely on other studies to assess country differences in how unions affect employment, provision of fringe benefits, job tenure and turnover, productivity, technical change, and profits. Because these comparisons use different data and statistical models, they are subject to considerable uncertainty, particularly with regard to estimated magnitudes. Most of the studies are for decentralized wage-setting countries such as Canada, the United Kingdom, Japan, and Australia, where one might expect effects of unionization similar to those in the United States. There is

Table 11.5. Job satisfaction and labor-management relations at the workplace, by country and union status, ISSP 1989

	Percentage of workers completely or very satisfied in their job			Percentage of workers who view management and employee relations as very good or quite good		
	Union	Nonunion	Difference	Union	Nonunion	Difference
United States	52	39	13	69	54	15
United Kingdom	40	34	6	74	59	15
West Germany	43	37	6	85	80	5
Austria	45	48	-3	75	73	2
Netherlands	42	32	10	67	54	13
Italy	30	30	0	63	56	7
Ireland	60	44	16	87	75	12
Norway	46	39	7	76	67	9

Source: Tabulated from ISSP 1989 questions: "How Satisfied are you in your (main) job?" with seven possible answers, and "In general how would you describe relations at your workplace between management and employees?" with five possible answers.

only limited evidence for countries in which wage setting is more centralized. The available studies, summarized in Table 11.6, while limited, support the generalization that *unions in other countries have similar effects on voice-related outcomes as they do in the United States*, but they show a more disparate picture for monopoly wage related outcomes.

Table 11.6. Summary of extant quantitative micro-based findings on the impact of unionization on outcomes across countries, 1970s and 1980s

Outcome	Estimated effect of unions / Sources*
Wages	
U.S.	20–25% increase / Freeman and Medoff 1984; Lewis 1986
U.K.	0–10% increase / Blanchflower 1984; Blanchflower and Oswald 1988c
Australia	9% increase / Mulvey 1986; Kornfeld 1990
Canada	10–20% increase / Gunderson 1982; Simpson 1985
Japan	No increase (men); 10% increase (women) / Nakamura et al. 1988; Osawa 1989 Negative / Brunello 1992
Germany	Unionization effect is positive but correlated works council effect is negative / FitzRoy and Kraft 1985
Dispersion and effect of characteristics on pay	
U.S.	Unions lower, reduce merit pay / Freeman and Medoff 1984
U.K.	Unions lower, reduce merit pay / Metcalf 1990; Blanchflower and Oswald 1988a
Canada	Unions lower pay / Kupferschmidt and Swidinsky 1989 Unions lower pay for men but not for women; have bigger effect on the pay of less skilled men and more skilled women / Lemieux 1992
Employment	
U.S.	Evidence that unions reduce employment / Leonard 1986; Freeman and Medoff 1984; Freeman and Kleiner 1990a Strong evidence that they increase temporary layoffs / Freeman and Medoff 1984
U.K.	Unions reduce employment / Blanchflower et al. 1989
Germany	Works councils lower employment growth / Büchtemann and Kraft 1992
Fringe benefits	
U.S.	Unions increase benefits; share of spending on benefits / Freeman and Medoff 1984
U.K.	Unions increase likelihood of health and safety committees and fringes / Millward and Stevens; Green et al. 1985
Japan	Unions raise bonuses, severance pay / Nakamura et al. 1988
Canada	Unions raise pensions / Kupferschmidt and Swidinsky 1989
Sweden	LO negotiates insurance schemes / Edebalk and Wadensjö 1989

Turnover and job tenure

U.S.	Unions lower quits; raise tenure / Freeman and Medoff 1984
Japan	Unions lower quits / Muramatsu 1984; Osawa 1989
Australia	Unions raise tenure / Kornfeld 1990; Miller and Mulvey 1991a, 1991b
	Unions lower quits / Miller and Mulvey; Drago and Wooden 1991
U.K.	Unions reduce quit rates / Wilson et al. 1990
	Unions raise tenure / Elias 1992

Productivity

U.S.	Union effect mixed depending on industry, but generally positive / Belman 1989; Freeman (five studies in addition to Belman's)
U.K.	Union effect mixed; under debate / Metcalf 1990; Callaghan 1989; Machin 1988; Noland and Marginson 1990
Japan	Positive effect / Muramatsu 1984
	Active joint consultation committees also positive / Morishima 1991
	No effect / Brunello 1992
Germany	Unions positive but works councils negative / FitzRoy and Kraft 1985
	Works councils positive / Addison et al.

Technological change / Productivity growth

U.S.	Unions have mixed effect on adoption of new technologies, depending on industry and technology / Keefe 1989; Eaton and Voos 1989
	Unionized industries and firms have slower productivity growth; do less R & D / Belman 1989
Canada	Unions have no effect on adoption of computer-based technologies / Betcherman 1988
U.K.	Unions have positive impact on adoption of microelectronic process technology / Daniel 1987
	Productivity growth higher in some years under unionization / Wadhwani 1989

R & D and Investment

U.S.	R & D lower in unionized industries or firms / Hirsch and Link 1987; Hirsch 1990
	Investment lower in unionized firms / Hirsch 1990
U.K.	R & D lower in unionized industries / Ulph and Ulph 1989
	Investment the same under unionization / Wadhwani 1989

Profits

U.S.	Unions reduce profits; share value of firm / Belman 1989
U.K.	Unions reduce profits / Blanchflower and Oswald 1988b; Machin 1988
Germany	Works councils have insignificant negative effect / Addison et al.
Japan	Unions reduce return on capital and sales / Brunello 1992

* See References for information on studies listed.

Employment

Consider first the effects of unionization on employment and the growth of employment. Consistent with the existence of a sizable union wage effect in the United States, there is evidence that U.S. unions decrease employment in the private sector.[3] Leonard (1992) and Freeman and Kleiner (1990a) report negative effects of unionization on employment; Freeman and Medoff (1984), and Allen (1988) find that firms substitute workers not covered by collective bargaining for union members, reducing employment of the union members; and Carter, Linneman, and Wachter (1990) report slower growth of unionized employment in industries with higher union wage differentials. For the United Kingdom, Blanchflower, Millward, and Oswald (1989) find a substantial negative union effect on employment growth from 1980 to 1984.[4] Büchtemann and Kraft (1992) show that the presence of a works council in Germany is associated with slower employment growth. The only other study of union employment effects in other countries of which I am aware is one of Malaysia (not reported in the table because it is a developing country), where Standing (1991) also finds smaller employment growth under unionization. I know of no studies of union effects on employment per se in other countries, though the modest wage effects shown in Table 11.2 suggest modest employment effects as well.

Quits and tenure

Turning to quits and tenure, for Japan both Muramatsu (1984) and Osawa (1989) find markedly lower quitting rates in union sectors than in nonunion ones. For the United Kingdom, Elias reports lower turnover among unionists in the United Kingdom than among otherwise comparable nonunion workers; Wilson, Cable, and Peel (1990) find that union presence is strongly negatively related to quits, with quits some 4 percent lower in strongly unionized closed shops than in nonunion enterprises. For Australia, Kornfeld (1990) reports union effects on tenure and quits among young workers that appear, if anything, to be larger than those found among young Americans. Miller and Mulvey report a 45 percent differential in tenure between union and nonunion workers in Australia, and a quit rate that is lower by 6.3 percentage points; and one difference from the U.S. unions: Australian unions are associated with lower layoffs, rather than the higher layoffs associated with unions in the United States. Using plant-level data, Drago and Wooden (1991) report that in the Australian context "more direct measures of union voice (notably presence of union delegates) . . . exhibit a strong negative relationship to quits" (p. 234). The only study with results inconsistent with the union "exit-voice" trade-off is Kraft's (1986) analysis of 60 German metal manufacturing firms, in which detailed questions on individual voice reduce turnover more than unionism.

Fringes

With respect to fringe benefits, virtually all U.S. studies show that unions raise fringes, particularly pension benefits (Freeman and Medoff 1984). Studies for other countries yield a similar finding. For Britain, Millward and Stevens, and Green, Hadjimatheou, and Small (1985) report that unionization raises provision of fringes. For Canada, Kupferschmidt and Swidinsky (1989) find that pensions are more likely under unionization. For Japan, Nakamura, Sato, and Kamiya (1988) report that the bonus share of labor cost and severance pay are higher in unionized firms. For Australia, Kornfeld (1990) finds greater probabilities of pensions for unionized than nonunion workers. There is no information on the relation between unionization and fringe benefits in the more centralized labor relations systems. Given the high mandated level of nonwage labor costs in many of these countries, I would expect relatively small union-nonunion differences, not because workers fail to use union voice to gain fringe benefits, but because unions operate largely through political pressure on the state or affect all workers through bargaining.[5] Edebalk and Wadensjö (1989) show that in Sweden the LO negotiates contractual insurance for members, gaining them greater replacement of income than for nonmembers.

Productivity and productivity change

Estimates of the effect of unions on productivity are subject to controversy. The preponderance of studies in the United States indicate a positive union productivity effect (see the summaries in Belman 1989 or Freeman 1991), but there are enough counterexamples (Hirsch 1990) to suggest that the *state of labor relations, rather than unionization and collective bargaining per se, determines productivity.* The limited studies overseas are consistent with this result. Muramatsu's (1984) analysis of value added in Japan found a positive union coefficient but may not have adequately controlled for the effects of firm size on productivity (in Japan unionization is concentrated in large firms). Consistent with a "collective voice" interpretation of the effect of unionism on productivity, Morishima (1991) reports positive productivity effects in Japanese firms with more active management-labor joint-consultation committees. On the other hand, Brunello (1992) finds no union effect on Japanese productivity in his sample of firms.[6] Whether productivity is higher or lower under unionization in the United Kingdom is the subject of debate. Metcalf (1990) interprets the evidence for the early 1980s as indicating that productivity is lower under unions but notes that productivity grew more rapidly in unionized settings thereafter, potentially erasing the early 1980s productivity gap. Callaghan (1989) and Nolan and Marginson (1990) disagree with Metcalf's assessment of the early-1980s studies. The inconclusive nature of the British evidence indicates that even in a country whose union structure has long been lambasted as inefficient, it is difficult to find compelling evidence for negative productivity effects. For Germany, studies of the effect of works councils and union density on productivity in the workplace yield a mixed picture. FitzRoy and Kraft (1985) report positive union effects but negative effects for works councils. Addison, Kraft, and Wagner (1992) report inconclusive works council effects on total factor productivity.

Studies of productivity change and technological progress for the United States have shown: (1) productivity growth is slower, to a modestly and statistically insignificant degree, in unionized settings (see Belman 1989 for a summary of studies); (2) new technologies are adopted as rapidly in union as in nonunion settings (Eaton and Voos 1989); (3) R & D and investment spending are lower under unionization (Hirsch and Link 1987; Hirsch 1990). Studies for the United Kingdom and Canada confirm some but not all of these findings. They show that unions do not adversely affect the speed of adaptation (Daniel 1987; Betcherman 1988); and find for the United Kingdom lower R & D-to-sales ratios in more heavily unionized industries (Ulph and Ulph 1989). By contrast, U.K. evidence that union firms had faster increases in productivity during the years 1980 to 1984 than nonunion firms (and had similar rates of increase in other years) runs counter to U.S. findings, as does evidence that unionization is unrelated to investment (Wadhwhani 1989). As neither the U.S. nor the British studies contain adequate controls for the age or maturity of union and nonunion plants and industries, I am leary of interpreting the different results as reflecting genuine differences in union impacts. Perhaps they reflect the fact that British unions grew rapidly in the 1970s, which placed them in new industries and plants, whereas American unions failed to organize new firms and sectors and thus were concentrated in parts of the economy facing slow productivity and limited investment. This interpretation is consistent with Hirsch's (1990) fixed-effects analysis of the lower productivity growth and investment in unionized firms in the United States: controlling for "firm effects" in various ways, he concludes that the observed correlations are due largely to the location of unions in declining sectors.

Profits

One of the most important findings from U.S. research has been that unionization is associated with markedly lower profitability (see Belman 1989 for a summary of 11 U.S. studies). Estimates of the effect of unions on profits in the United Kingdom (Blanchflower and Oswald 1988b; Machin 1988) show a similar pattern. In the United States, the profits effect results from the large effect of unions on wages, which exceeds the positive effect of unions on productivity. In the United Kingdom, the profits effect results from a moderate effect of unions on wages and little union effect on productivity. For Germany, Addison, Kraft, and Wagner (1992) report insignificant effects of works councils on profits. The only case of a positive unionization-related effect on profits is Morishima's (1991) finding that Japanese firms with active joint-consultation committees have higher profits than those with less active committees. Brunello (1992), by contrast, reports slight negative effects on profitability.[7]

While the estimated profits effects are not sufficiently precise to determine whether unions reduce profitability more in the United States than in the United Kingdom, and while estimates are lacking for the effects of unions on profits in other countries, I infer from the wage and productivity findings that the profits effect is especially large in the United States. If the standard method of estimating union-nonunion wage differentials is reasonably correct (or biased in a similar way across countries), the 20 to 25 percent higher wage (and moderate productivity offset) implies that U.S. unionized firms will be at a significant cost disadvantage compared with foreign unionized competitors, as well as with nonunion U.S. competitors.

The evidence in this paper and elsewhere on the economic effects of unionization in different countries suggests that many of the findings reported for the United States in *What Do Unions Do?* (Freeman and Medoff 1984) are not only supported by ensuing analysis for the United States (Mishel and Voos 1991) but also generalize to other countries. American exceptionalism in union-nonunion differences is found not so much in outcomes influenced by the "voice" side of the institution but rather in outcomes on the "monopoly wage" side. Union wage effects are larger in the United States than elsewhere because of the decentralized wage-setting system. This in turn seems to underlie the large positive productivity effect, and the substantial adverse profits effect in the United States.

The near uniform effect of unions on dispersion of earnings; the negative effect of unions on quits and the positive effect on tenure with the firm; and the negative relation between unions and satisfaction in different settings suggest, further, that the voice component of unionization is more universal and less dependent on the system of labor relations than are monopoly wage effects. From this I conclude that voice factors must be intrinsic in any general theory of trade unionization.

Author's Note

In preparing this chapter I have benefited from the assistance of Yan Zhang.

Notes

1. This is the cock that crows every morning before sunrise and believes *post hoc ergo procter hoc* that its crowing makes the sun rise. John Dunlop used the example in labor economics classes to make the point that participants in labor relations often overestimate their importance and effect on outcomes compared to market forces. I believe he was taught the cock story by John Hicks.
2. Such models require correct specification of the structure of a complex system, and yield wildly divergent results depending on the structure chosen. While one can criticize ordinary least squares analyses for failing to take account of such issues as simultaneity in unionization and outcomes, selectivity of union members, and so on, OLS provides a robust description of the patterns in the data.
3. The U.S. data do show higher employment in unionized settings in the public sector. See Freeman (1986b) and Freeman and Ichniowski (1988). This is attributed to the role of unions in raising demand for public services and increasing public-sector budgets for unionized activities.
4. Whether the U.S. and British union effects on employment growth reflect short-term adjustments or long-term slower growth rates in unionized workplaces is open to question (Wadhwani 1989; Pencavel 1989).
5. Addison, Kraft, and Wagner report that they detected no evidence for effects of works councils on nonwage costs, but note that their equation for such costs was sufficiently poor that they did not report the regression.
6. Brunello reports negative effects for some firms, but this is due to interaction terms that seem to obscure the basic result. His OLS productivity regression gives an insignificant positive coefficient on unionization that

I take as the basic finding. Interactions of unionization with other variables suggest the need to look separately at production functions for different groups. Leaving out interactions gives the main result.
7. Again, I ignore Brunello's interaction model and focus on the basic OLS regression.

References

Addison, J. T., K. Kraft, and J. Wagner. (1992) "German Works Councils and Firm Performance," first draft of a paper prepared for *Employee Representation: Alternatives and Future Directions*, B. Kaufman and M. Kleiner, eds. Madison, Wis.: Industrial Relations Research Association Series.

Allen, S. (1988). "Human Resource Policies and Union-Nonunion Productivity Differences." National Bureau of Economic Research Working Paper no. 2744.

Ashenfelter, O., and R. Layard, eds. (1986). *Handbook of Labor Economics.* Amsterdam: North-Holland.

Bean, R. (1989). *International Labour Statistics.* London: Routledge.

Belman, D. (1989). "Unions, the Quality of Labor Relations and Firm Performance," mimeo. Washington, D.C.: Economic Policy Institute.

Betcherman, G. (1988). "Technological Change and Its Impacts: Do Unions Make a Difference?" *Proceedings of 1987 Annual Meeting of the Canadian Industrial Relations Association.*

Blanchflower, D. G. (1984). "Union Relative Wage Effects: a Cross-Section Analysis Using Establishment Data," *British Journal of Industrial Relations* 22, 311–332.

————(1990). "Fear, Unemployment and Pay Flexibility," National Bureau of Economic Research Working Paper no. 3365.

Blanchflower, D. G., and R. Freeman. (1992). "Unionism in the United States and Other Advanced OECD Countries," *Industrial Relations* 31, no. 1 (Winter), 56–70.

Blanchflower, D. G., N. Millward, and A. J. Oswald. (1989) "Unionisation and Employment Behaviour," National Bureau of Economic Research Working Paper no. 3180.

Blanchflower, D. G., and A. J. Oswald. (1988a). "Internal and External Influences upon Pay Settlements," *British Journal of Industrial Relations*, 26, no. 3 (November) 363–370.

————(1988b). "Profit-Related Pay: Prose Discovered?" *Economic Journal*, September, 720–730.

————(1988c). "The Economic Effects of Britain's Trade Unions," Centre for Labour Economics Paper no. 324, London School of Economics.

————(1989). "International Patterns of Work" in *British Social Attitudes: the International Report*, R. Jowell, S. Witherspoon, and L. Brook. eds. New York: Gower.

Blasi, J. (1988). *Employee Ownership: Revolution or Ripoff?* Cambridge, Mass.: Ballinger.

Block, R., et al., eds. (1987). *Human Resources and the Performance of the Firm.* Madison, Wis.: Industrial Relations Research Association.

Blyth, C. (1979). "Level of National Bargaining," in *Collective Government and National Policies.* Paris: Organization for Economic Cooperation and Development.

Borjas, G. (1979). "Job Satisfaction, Wages, and Unions," *Journal of Human Resources* 14, no. 1 (Winter).

Brunello, Giorgio (1992). "The Effect of Unions on Firm Performance in Japanese Manufacturing," *Industrial and Labor Relations Review* 45, no. 3 (April), 471–487.

Bruno, M., and J. Sachs. (1985). *Economics of World Stagflation.* Cambridge, Mass.: Harvard University Press.

Büchtemann, C. F., and K. Kraft (1992). "The Effects of the Employment Promotion Act and Works Council on Employment Growth," unpublished manuscript, University of Fribourg.

Callaghan, W. (1989). "Trade Unions, Pay, Productivity and Jobs," mimeo, Trades Union Congress, London.

Calmfors, L. and J. Driffil (1988). "Bargaining Structure, Corporatism and Macroeconomic Performance," *Economic Policy* 6, 13–62.

Crouch, C. (1985). "Conditions for Trade Union Wage Restraint," in *The Politics of Inflation and Economic Stagnation,* L. Lindberg and C. S. Maier, eds. Washington, D.C.: Brookings Institution.

Daniel, W W. (1987). *Workplace Industrial Relations and Technical Change.* New York: Pinter.

Drago, R., and M. Wooden (1991). "Turnover Down Under: Trade Unions and Exit Behaviour in Australia," *The Journal of Industrial Relations,* June, 234–248.

Eaton, A E., and P. B. Voos (1989). "Unions and Contemporary Innovations in Work Organisation, Compensation, and Employee Participation," mimeo, Economic Policy Institute, Washington, D.C.

Edebalk, P. G., and E. Wadensjö (1989). "Contractually Determined Insurance Schemes for Manual Workers," in *The Political Economy of Social Security,* B. A. Gustafsson and N. A. Klevmarken, eds. Amsterdam: North-Holland, Elsevier Science.

Elias, P. (1992). "A Study of the Effects of Training, Unions and Employment Status on Labour Mobility," Institute for Employment Research, University of Warwick, unpublished manuscript.

Erickson, C., and A. Ichino (1992). "Wage Differentials in Italy: Market Forces, Institutions, and Inflation," paper presented at National Bureau of Economic Research Conference on Differences and Changes in Wage Structures, July 23–34.

FitzRoy, F. R., and K. Kraft (1985). "Unionization, Wages and Efficiency — Theories and Evidence from the U.S. and West Germany," *Kyklos* 38, 537–554.

Freeman, R. (1978). "Job Satisfaction as an Economic Variable," *American Economic Review* 68 (May), 135–141.

——— (1980). "Unionism and the Dispersion of Wages," *Industrial and Labor Relations Review* 34 (1), 3–23.

——— (1982). "Union Wage Practices and Wage Dispersion within Establishments," *Industrial and Labor Relations Review* 36 (1), 3–39.

——— (1984). "Longitudinal Analysis of the Effect of Trade Unions," *Journal of Labor Economics*, 2 (1), 1–26.

——— (1986a). "Unionism Comes to the Public Sector," *Journal of Economic Literature*, March, 24, 41–86.

——— (1986b). "The Effect of the Union Wage Differential on Management Opposition and Organising Success," *American Economic Review* 76, 92–96.

———, ed. (1988a). *Immigration, Trade, and the Labor Market*, National Bureau of Economic Research Summary Report.

——— (1988b). "Labour Market Institutions and Economic Performance," *Economic Policy* 6, 64–80.

——— (1990). "On the Divergence in Unionism Among Developed Countries," in *Labour Relations and Economic Performance*, Renato Brunetta and Carlo Dell'Aringa, eds. Hampshire, England: Macmillan.

——— (1991). "Is Declining Unionization of the U.S. Good, Bad or Irrelevant," in *Unions and Economic Competitiveness*, Lawrence Mishel and Paula B. Voos, eds. Washington, D.C.: Economic Policy Institute.

Freeman, R., and C. Ichniowski. (1988). "When Public Sector Workers Unionize," University of Chicago Press for NBER.

Freeman, R., and M. Kleiner (1990a). "The Impact of New Unionisation on Wages and Working Conditions," *Journal of Labor Economics*, January.

——— (1990b). "Employer Behavior in the Face of Union Organizing Drives" *Industrial and Labor Relations Review*, April.

Freeman, R., and J. Medoff. (1981a). "The Impact of Collective Bargaining: Illusion or Reality?" in J. Steiber, R. McKersie, and D. Mills, eds. *U.S. Industrial Relations 1950–1980: A Critical Assessment*. Madison, Wis.: Industrial Relations Research Association.

——— (1981b). "The Impact of the Percentage Organised on Union and Nonunion Wages," *Review of Economics and Statistics*, November.

——— (1984). *What Do Unions Do?* New York: Basic Books.

Freeman, R., and J. Pelletier. (1990). "The Impact of Industrial Relations Legislation on Union Density in the UK and Ireland," *British Journal of Industrial Relations*, April.

Friedman, M. (1962). *Capitalism and Freedom*. Chicago: University of Chicago Press.

Green, F., G. Hadjimatheou, and R. Smail (1985). "Fringe Benefit Distribution in Britain," *British Journal of Industrial Relations*, 261–280.

Grubb, D., R. Jackman, and R. Layard (1983). "Wage Rigidity and Unemployment in OECD Countries," *European Economic Review* 21 (1), 11–50.

Gunderson, M. (1982). "Union Impact on Wages, Fringe Benefits, and Productivity," in *Union-Management Relations in Canada,* M. Gunderson and J. Anderson, eds. Boston: Addison-Wesley.

Hirsch, B. (1990) *Labor Unions and the Economic Performance of U.S. Firms.* Kalamazoo, Mich.: Upjohn Institute.

Hirsch, B. and A. N. Link (1987). "Labor Union Effects on Innovative Activity," *Journal of Labor Research* 8, 323–332.

Johnson, G. (1981). "Changes over Time in the Union/Non-Union Differential in the United States," mimeo, University of Michigan.

R. Jowell, S Witherspoon, and L. Brook, eds. (1989). *British Social Attitudes: The International Report.* Gower.

Keefe, J. (1989). "Do Unions Hinder Technological Change?" mimeo, Economic Policy Institute, Washington, D.C.

Kerr, C., et al. (1964). *Industrialism and Industrial Man,* Oxford: Oxford University Press.

Kornfeld, Robert (1990). "Effects of Unions on Young Workers in Australia," mimeo, Harvard University.

Kraft, K. (1986). "Exit Voice in the Labor Market: An Empiricial Study of Quits," *Journal of Institutional and Theoretical Economics* 142 (December), 697–715.

Kumar, P., M. Coates, and D. Arrowsmith (1988). *The Current Industrial Relations Scene in Canada.* Kingston, Ontario: Industrial Relations Section, Queens University.

Kupferschmidt, M., and R. Swidinsky (1989). "Longitudinal Estimates of the Union Effect on Wages, Wage Dispersion, and Pension Fringe Benefits," University of Guelph, Ontario.

Lemieux, T. (1992). "Unions and the Distribution of Wages in Canada," unpublished manuscript, Princeton University.

Leonard, J. (1986). "Employment Variability and Wage Rigidity: A Comparison of Union and Non-union Plants," mimeo, University of California, Berkeley.

Lewis, H. G. (1986). *Union Relative Wage Effects: A Survey.* Chicago: University of Chicago Press.

Linneman, P., and M. Wachter (1986). "Rising Union Premiums and the Declining Boundaries among Noncompeting Groups," *American Economic Review* 76, 103–108.

Linneman, P., M. Wachter, and W. Carter (1990). "Evaluating the Evidence on Union Employment and Wages," *Industrial and Labor Relations Review.*

Machin, S. (1988). "Unions and the Capture of Economic Rents: An Investigation Using British Firm Level Data," mimeo, Department of Economics, University College, London.

Metcalf, D. (1990). "Unions and Productivity," *British Journal of Industrial Relations.*

Miller, Paul. (1991). "Trade Unions and Job Satisfaction," Australian Economic Papers.

Miller, P., and C. Mulvey (1991a). "Trade Unions and the Distribution of Paid Overtime," *Journal of Industrial Relations*, June, 220–233.

———(1991b). "Australian Evidence on the Exit/Voice Model of the Labor Market," *Industrial and Labor Relations Review* 45, no. 1 (October), 44–57.

Millward, Neil and Mark Stevens, *British Workplace Industrial Relations*, 1980–1984. London: Gower, 1986.

Mishel, L., and P. Voos, eds. (1991). Unions and Economic Competitiveness. Washington, D.C.: Economic Policy Institute.

Morishima, M. (1991). "Information Sharing and Collective Bargaining in Japan: Effects on Wage Negotiation," *Industrial and Labor Relations Review* 44, no. 3 (April), 469–485.

Mulvey, C. (1986). "Wage Levels: Do Unions Make a Difference?" in *Wage Fixation in Australia*, J. Niland, ed. Sydney: Allen and Unwin.

Muramatsu, K. (1984). Chapter in *Economic Analysis of the Japanese Firm*, M. Aoki, ed. Amsterdam: North-Holland.

Nakamura, K., H. Sato, and T. Kamiya (1988). *Do Labor Unions Really Have a Useful Role?* Tokyo: Sogo Rodo Kenkyujo (in Japanese).

Nolan, P., and P. Marginson (1990). "Skating on Thin Ice? David Metcalf on Trade Unions and Productivity," *British Journal of Industrial Relations*.

Osawa, M. (1989). "The Service Economy and Industrial Relations in Small- and Medium-Size Firms in Japan," *Japan Labor Bulletin*, July

Pencavel, J. (1989). "Employment and Trade Unions," draft manuscript (mimeo), Stanford University, 25–47.

Simpson, W. (1985). "The Impact of Unions on the Structure of Canadian Wages: An Empirical Analysis with Microdata," *Canadian Journal of Economics* 18, 164–181.

Standing, G. (1991). "Do Unions Impede or Accelerate Structural Adjustment? Industrial versus Company Unions in an Industrializing Labour Market," World Employment Program, International Labor Office Working Paper 47.

Ulph, A., and D. Ulph (1989). "Labor Markets and Innovation," *Journal of the Japanese and International Economies* 3, no. 4 (December).

Visser, J. (1989). *European Trade Unions in Figures*. Netherlands: Kluwer Deventer.

Wadhwani, S. (1989). "The Effect of Unions on Productivity Growth, Investment, and Employment: A Report on Some Recent Work," *British Journal of Industrial Relations*

Walsh, K. (1985). *Trade Union Membership: Methods and Measurement in the European Community*. Luxembourg: Eurostat.

Walsh, K., and A. King. (1986). *Handbook of International Manpower Comparisons*. New York: New York University Press.

Wilson, N., J. R. Cable, and M. J. Peel (1990). "Quit Rates and the Impact of Participation, Sharing and Unionization: Empirical Evidence from UK Engineering Firms" 28, no. 2 (July), 197–213.

Wood, W. D., and P. Kumar (1980). *The Current Industrial Relations Scene in Canada*. Kingston, Ontario: Industrial Relations Centre, Queens University.

IV

Internal Labor Markets: A New Exploration

12

Internal Labor Markets: Theory and Change

■ ─────────────── ■

Paul S. Osterman

The idea of internal labor markets — originally propounded by Clark Kerr in 1954 and John Dunlop in 1966 — has proved durable and fruitful. It is by now apparent to even the most market oriented economist that many of the rules that determine economic outcomes and social welfare originate within the firm and are in a nontrivial sense chosen by the firm. Because many workers spend long stretches of their careers within the shelter of enterprises, understanding these rules is very important.

The central idea of internal labor markets (ILMs) was set forth by Kerr in his description of "institutional labor markets." Kerr argued that these labor markets created noncompeting groups and that one of the central boundaries was between the firm and the external labor market. Kerr identified "ports of entry" as the link between the inside and outside, and described the implications for labor mobility of the boundaries and rules. Dunlop coined the term "internal labor markets" and provided a description of one group of central rules, those concerning job ladders. He applied his analysis to an important policy problem, the interpretation of job vacancy data, and by doing so showed the practical utility of the concept.

In the 1970s Doeringer and Piore (1971) provided a full description of the rules of blue-collar ILMs as well as the trade-offs among the rules (for example between hiring criteria and training procedures). Doeringer and Piore also began the process of linking analysis of ILMs back to mainstream labor economics through their discussion of how specific human capital helps cement employee attachment to firms.

These classic ILM studies set the stage for later work in several ways. First, while all of the original authors recognized that there are various alternatives for organizing work, each emphasized almost exclusively blue-collar industrial models, and within these, the traditional unionized pattern (which might then have been the central tendency even in the nonunion sector). Much of the recent work on ILMs has focused on variation, both within the blue-collar world and between blue-collar and other types of employment.

Second, none of the classics developed well-structured explanations of why ILMs arise, and the need to do so has invited a wide range of theoretical efforts. This has led to development of elaborate microeconomic models of long-term employment relationships as well as to efforts by sociologists to explain these institutions in noneconomic terms. To date these efforts have not been integrated, but this essay will attempt to provide a framework that encompasses several approaches.

Third, what drove early research on ILMs was the observation that labor mobility could not be understood as simply the result of unfettered supply and demand forces in the market. As a result these investigations focused on explaining the movement of labor and the rules governing its allocation. In undertaking this task the researchers took as given the external environment of the firm (economic and regulatory) as well as the firm's competitive strategy. Recent work has introduced these considerations more directly into an analysis of ILMs.

As I have already suggested, the study of internal labor markets attracts scholars of divergent backgrounds. For mainstream economists the challenge is to explain the rules within a framework that preserves the core ideas of maximization and efficiency. Institutional economists do not deny the impact of standard economic considerations, but they emphasize the interplay of economic, political, and social forces. This orientation has been reinforced by recent interest in international comparisons. There is also a vibrant body of sociology literature on the subject, albeit one that has not been fully incorporated into the discourse within economics. Since stable work groups lead to the formation of norms, customs, and interpersonal comparisons, ILMs provide sociologists with an opportunity to illustrate and explore the importance of these phenomena. In addition, variation across enterprises in the extent and content of rules suggests that sociological models that focus on the diffusion and adaption of institutional practices, independently of their efficiency properties (for example, the search for legitimacy via mimicry), can be fruitfully applied to ILMs.

The nature of research on ILMs has also expanded. The initial investigations were largely field-based, and the ideas rested on interviews with firms and unions. The power of this approach is demonstrated by the fact that many of the insights developed in this manner have survived. Confidence in these observations has, however, been strengthened by studies based on representative samples of firms (Baron and Bielby, 1986; Pfeffer and Cohen, 1984; Delaney, Lewin, and Ichniowski, 1989; Osterman, 1984, Osterman, forthcoming) as well as by more thorough examinations of particular practices such as firm-based wage setting (Groshen, 1991), long-term tenure (Abraham and Medoff, 1984), and part-time work (Rebitzer and Taylor, 1991). In the course of this research the original concept, while generally affirmed, has been modified in important ways. For example, sensitivity has been heightened to the fact that a firm is not a unitary employment system but rather consists of a set of ILM subsystems that may operate on quite different principles (Osterman, 1984, 1987). It also seems apparent that the correlates of ILM practices include a mixture of technical, economic, and social considerations (Bielby and Baron, 1983).

In surveying this rich line of research there appear to be two useful purposes that an essay such as this might serve. The first is to sort out the alternative theories that have been generated to explain ILMs. The second is to understand how ILMs have changed in the past twenty years.

Sorting out theory is important, but if done in isolation the exercise is likely to be both arid and inconclusive. I say arid because, unless grounded in data and specific cases, it would be difficult to keep in mind just what it is I am trying to explain, and the results would be inconclusive because of the obvious fact that no single model is likely to be completely satisfactory. Also, most models are sufficiently elastic that they can be made (to appear) to cover more than was originally intended.

A better strategy is to begin with the data, and in this case the data are the substantial shifts that seem to have transpired in work organization. These shifts render the traditional image of ILMs at least partially obsolete, and it is important to document them in their own terms. In addition they provide a handle on the various models because, after describing the shifts, one can ask which theories are best able to explain what occurred. Thus, rather than arguing in the abstract about models, and rather than applying the models to a static description, one can treat recent changes as data to be explained and search for the theory with the best "fit."

Before turning to recent shifts in the organization of work, there is one definitional issue to clear up. The Doeringer and Piore description of ILMs focused on closed job ladders and ports of entry, and this has tended to stick in peoples' minds as the central defining characteristic of ILMs (see, for example, Althauser and Kalleberg, 1981). I think that a more expansive definition — which includes wage systems, job classifications, rules regarding the deployment of labor, and rules regarding employment security — is more helpful.

These various categories of rules fit together in a logical system, and it does not make sense to isolate one rule and ignore the others. For example, narrow job classifications, wages attached to the job, few restrictions on the ability of the firm to lay off workers, and strict seniority are mutually reinforcing set of practices, while broad classifications, wages attached to individuals rather than jobs, ease of deployment, and high levels of job security constitute another logical cluster. Anyone familiar with the literature will recognize the first cluster as the traditional American model, while the second is a model associated (at least until recently) with leading-edge American firms and with the Japanese model.

It is much more helpful to think in these terms rather than focusing on any particular rule, such as the presence or absence of job ladders. The idea of a system of rules that fit logically together enables one to make sense of broader differences in ILMs. Thus, for example, both Japanese and traditionally organized American automobile firms have closed job ladders, yet there are very substantial differences along other dimensions that add up to quite distinct ILM arrangements. ILMs conceived in these broader terms come to represent the overall human resource management strategy of an enterprise, and by thinking of ILMs in this way one can ask more ambitious questions. However, this more expansive perspective introduces difficulties for theoretical models that purport to explain one rule (for example, wage premiums above market levels) but that appear ignorant of the fact that the said rule is part of a larger system.

The Evolution of Internal Labor Markets

The stylized facts concerning the evolution of internal labor markets in the United States would go as follows. Prior to the Depression and World War II, large industrial firms gyrated between several strategies of organizing work, including the foreman-centered "drive system" with few rules and arbitrary management authority, and the "American plan" with its emphasis on paternalism, welfare benefits, and more regularized employment relationships. The great unionizing drives of the Depression, combined with the diffusion of standardized union practices by the War Labor Board, led decisively to the triumph of the standard union model (with strict job classifications, seniority, grievance procedures, and so on) over its alternatives (the most complete history of these alternatives is found in Jacoby, 1985).

From the mid-1940s to the mid-1970s this model — which is essentially what Doeringer and Piore described — dominated both the union sector and the largely imitative nonunion firms. Toward the end of this era a competing model emerged, one which placed much greater emphasis on direct communication with workers and on innovations such as team production and quality circles (Kochan, Katz, and McKersie, 1986). This structure was motivated in part by its superior performance and in part by its ability to keep unions at bay. It emerged in a progressive segment of the American nonunion sector (for example, at IBM), but it also gained momentum from the spread of Japanese transplants, such as the Honda factory in Ohio, which organized work according to the Japanese model. The more traditional sector, union and nonunion, was torn between adoption of the new model (variously termed the "transformed model," the "salaried model," the "high commitment model," the "mutual gains model," or the "high performance" model) and defense of old structures. The playing out and resolving of this tension is the current ILM "story" of greatest interest and importance.

Adding to the turmoil and uncertainty are broader shifts in the economy that undermine standard assumptions. These shifts include heightened economic volatility, which threatens the job security implicit for high-tenure workers in the traditional system. In addition, the combination of technical change and the increased education levels of the labor force may alter firms' calculation of the best locus for training and undermine the traditional reliance on job ladders and closed internal markets. Both of these macroeconomic shifts make employment unstable and reduce long-term employment within an enterprise. Indeed, many commentators now assert that workers must expect to change jobs far more frequently than in the past. Implicit in this assertion is the idea that the closed, traditional ILM is of declining importance.

The foregoing represents an amalgam of various views about recent trends, but if there is such a thing as a consensus this would be it. It remains to be seen, of course, just how much evidence there is to support the various assertions.

Recent Changes in Internal Labor Markets

In this section I will address three questions concerning the evolution of ILMs: (1) are ILMs still important, or are they dissolving? (2) is the character of ILMs changing? and (3) how much international variation is there in the structure of ILMs in similar industries? Taken together these seem to be the three questions that emerge naturally from the preceding narrative and that are likely to have the most important implications for theories of ILMs.

Are ILMs still important?

Do people still spend long periods of their working life within the shelter of a single employer? The extreme alternative would be a return to a high-turnover spot market in which at least one side of the market, either employers or employees, sees little advantage in maintaining stable employment.

There are several trends commonly remarked on that suggest that ILMs are of diminishing relevance. These include growing white-collar and managerial layoffs, which erode stability in what has heretofore been the most secure segment of the labor market; the rise of contingent or temporary employment arrangements; an alleged growing reliance on educational institutions rather than firms for training; and the emergence of regional networks as the locus of careers, rather than single organizations.

Any of these developments, if important, would reduce the amount of time a person works with a single employer, and a relatively straightforward test for this would be to ask whether the distribution of worker tenure has changed over time. If ILMs are becoming less important, then this should be picked up in surveys that ask employees how long they have worked for their current employer.

The May 1979 and May 1988 Current Population Surveys asked respondents how long they had worked for their current employer. The top half of Table 12.1 shows the job tenure distribution for all employed workers in those two years, and it is apparent that there was no change in the distribution. The bottom half breaks the sample out by sex, and the conclusion of stable tenure distributions remains. However, these findings may be deceptive, since the age distribution of the labor force changed between the two periods (the labor force in 1988 was slightly older). Furthermore, one would expect that the impact of ILMs on tenure would show up most strongly in middle-aged workers, who have passed the period of high turnover and exploration that characterizes younger employees.

Table 12.2 is limited to employees in two age categories — 35 to 44 and 45 to 60 — and here there is some reduction of job tenure between 1979 and 1988 that is limited entirely to males. For men in both age groups there is a lower share of employees in the two high-tenure groups in 1988, with the drop being as large as 5.6 percentage points for the oldest group of men. By contrast, for women in the 35- to 44-year-old group there is an increased share in the high-tenure categories in 1988, and the proportions remain constant for the older group of women. These patterns remain unchanged when the data are broken down by educational group, which suggests that the findings are not limited to any single occupational subgroup.

Taken as a whole, these data show that long-term employment relationships retain their centrality for men and, indeed, are of increasing importance for women.[1] If one had to draw only one conclusion from these data, it would be that long-term relationships have an ongoing importance. The more extreme statements about the demise of ILMs and the substantial restructuring of career patterns are not true.[2] However, for men there is a deterioration, with a clear and nontrivial drop in the fraction of middle-aged workers in stable employment relationships. Furthermore, this decline occurred in the 1980s, a period of sustained growth in jobs and declining unemploy-

Table 12.1. Job tenure 1979 and 1988, all age groups

Years with current employer	1979	1988
0–2	46.6%	44.4%
3–5	18.1	19.2
6–10	15.2	15.9
11–15	8.1	8.3
16+	12.0	12.0

	Men		Women	
	1979	1988	1979	1988
0–2	41.9%	40.4%	52.4%	48.9%
3–5	17.0	19.0	19.5	19.4
6–10	15.8	15.9	14.3	15.9
11–15	9.3	8.8	6.4	7.1
16+	15.7	15.7	7.2	7.8

Source: Current Population Survey.

Table 12.2. Job tenure 1979 and 1988, ages 35 to 60

Years with current employer	Men age 35–44		Men age 45–60	
	1979	1988	1979	1988
0–2	27.7%	28.2%	17.4%	21.7%
3–5	15.9	18.0	10.9	12.7
6–10	20.4	19.4	13.9	13.3
11–15	20.5	15.1	12.9	10.3
16+	15.3	18.6	44.7	41.7

Years with current employer	Women age 35–44		Women age 45–60	
	1979	1988	1979	1988
0–2	44.8%	39.3%	26.7%	28.5%
3–5	22.1	20.6	18.2	17.4
6–10	17.2	20.1	21.0	19.9
11–15	9.6	11.2	13.2	13.3
16+	6.1	8.7	20.6	20.7

Source: Current Population Survey.

ment rates. It is apparent, then, that a portion of my discussion of ILMs must seek to explain this fraying around the edges of the standard employment pattern for men.

Contingent Employment   One commonly noted pattern, which might underlie some of these developments, is the increased use of contingent workers. This is a complicated issue to sort out, because several forces are at play. In part, growing use of contingent employees may reflect the disassembling of ILMs as firms seek to reduce job security and implied commitments to incumbent employees. On the other hand, the transformed model requires increased employment security, and one way firms may attempt to provide this is by surrounding a core labor force, which receives the security, with a buffer of peripheral employees. For example, the Saturn automobile manufacturing contract (an exemplar of the transformed model) permits General Motors to staff 20 percent of the labor positions with workers who are not covered by security pledges.

Interviews with large white-collar employers show them to be increasingly employing temporary-help staff, outside consultants, contract workers, and the like. These employees work at all skill levels; the use of such temporaries is not limited to clerical workers but includes occupations such as engineers, computer programmers, and draftspersons (Applebaum, 1989; Magnum et. al, 1985; Osterman, 1984).[3] Data on the increase in temporary-help employment is also suggestive. Figures supplied by the employer's association (the National Association of Temporary Services) show payroll increasing from $3 billion in 1980 to $6 billion in 1985 (*New York Times,* October 24, 1985). Hartman and Lapidus (1989) report that the constant dollar payroll of temporary-help firms grew by 754 percent in the 1970s and 236 percent in the 1980s.

The use of formal temporary-help agencies is, in fact, an understatement of the extent of this practice. It is common for companies to establish in-house temporary pools, internalizing the advantages and avoiding fees. The best available survey (a national probability sample of 1,200 firms in six industries: health, business service, finance and insurance, retail, transportation, and manufacturing) found that between 25 percent and 35 percent of firms with more than 250 employees had established such internal pools (Magnum et al., 1985).

It does not necessarily follow that the growing use of contingent employees shifts the job tenure distribution toward the lower end. One alternative possibility is that when firms externalize functions by shifting employment to outside contractors, workers at the same time develop stable employment relationships with those contractors. An example of this would be an increase in the amount of legal work corporations delegate to law firms where the partners and associates have long-term (or at least not shorter term) employment. One might also speculate that employees in temporary-help firms tend to be new labor market entrants who in different circumstances would have exhibited other forms of unstable work attachment.

While there is certainly some truth to these arguments, they do not seem fully convincing. First, in the example of the law firms it must also be true that the corporate lawyers who used to do legal work in-house and whose business has been externalized have therefore lost their jobs. This should show up in the data. Second, the spirit of much of the discussion of contingent employment, and the observations of temporary-help firms, suggest that these jobs are inherently less stable than the work they replace.

Another paradox lies in the associated gender patterns. Many employees of temporary-help firms are women, yet I have just shown that women's job tenure is increasing.[4] One explanation, therefore, is that women who work in temporary-help firms are substituting for men in previously long-term jobs. The other possibility is that the decline of men's tenure is due to the spread of contracts (explicit or implicit) like the Saturn contract. This agreement creates a buffer or contingent group of workers whose occupation or industry assignment remains with the original firm, not with a temporary-help employer, yet whose employment security is more tenuous than that of regular employees.

In the end, one is left with a substantial dollop of speculation. There is a slight deterioration in the extent of long-term employment relationships among middle-aged men, and there is an increase in various forms of contingent employment relationships. However, only guesswork connects these two developments. Furthermore, there is no systematic evidence on other explanations for the dip in men's tenure. Clearly more work is necessary to understand shifting tenure patterns.

Has the Character of ILMs Changed?

The foregoing evidence suggests that ILMs remain important albeit with some deterioration. There remains the important question of whether their character is changing in other respects. Is the transformed model capturing the field?

There are two kinds of evidence on this question: anecdotal and survey-based. The former is widely available and suggestive but is, of course, subject to numerous caveats. The latter is extremely uneven. In this section, I will present data of both kinds, but in the end the portrait will be fuzzy and incomplete. Data simply are not adequate to reach a definitive judgment about the distribution of ILM practices or the trend.

Three of the most widely cited examples of transformed ILMs are General Motors (the Saturn program), Corning, and Xerox.

Corning, with its headquarters in upstate New York, had closed nearly 35 plants in the 1970s and 1980s, with no end in sight.[5] In 1986, however, the firm decided to reverse its decline in manufacturing by dramatically altering work systems and ILM rules. The firm built two greenfield factories, one in West Virginia and one in New York, which were organized around "high-performance work systems." These proved successful enough that Corning began retrofitting other, existing plants.

The retrofitting process typically involves establishing a joint union-management team that visits other companies, attends workshops, and develops a common vision of what the new work systems might look like. This is followed by an "awareness program" in which all employees in the plant attend workshops. Subsequently joint design teams, working with consultants, reorganize work flows, change job descriptions, organize and attend training, and establish training programs for the work force. Typical results are a reduced number of job classifications and team production. These shifts in work rules and work flow are also usually linked to a new compensation system that puts substantial emphasis on performance pay. The performance targets are established by a joint union-management committee. Employees are promised that no layoffs will be implemented as a result of the reorganizations, but the firm retains the right to implement layoffs due to product market developments.

At Xerox Corporation, early experiments with quality of work life (QWL) programs evolved into far-reaching changes in work organization (Cutcher-Gershenfeld, 1989). This process, which began in 1980 in the company's Webster, New York manufacturing facility, had as its initial impetus the loss of low-end market share to the Japanese. The initial and halting QWL experiments eventually led to employee involvement in a wide range of previously managerial decisions (such as outsourcing), problem-solving teams aimed at specific issues, the creation of work teams for normal production, management's agreement to no-layoff pledges, much broadened job assignments with new classifications, and experiments with gain-sharing pay systems. The ILM of the manufacturing system at Xerox clearly came very close to the ideal of the transformed or salaried model.

Recent events in some U.S. automobile industry plants are by now widely known. The most far-reaching changes have taken place at the General Motors Saturn plant, in which the union and management jointly designed the production system and the product, and in which job classifications have nearly been eliminated and job security is essentially guaranteed. Similar initiatives have occurred in many other auto plants, albeit in less dramatic circumstances (Katz, 1985).

Such shifts in ILM systems are not limited to the union sector in heavy industry. Kochan, Katz, and McKersie (1986) report numerous examples of nonunion firms that have opened new plants along the lines of the transformed model or altered the ILM of existing plants. They also describe partially unionized firms whose nonunion plants are consciously intended to provide a transformed counterweight to the more traditional union work settings. Typical is the electronic cable plant of TRW that employs an all-salaried work force, a pay-for-knowledge compensation system, only nine job classifications, and team production (Kochan, Katz, McKersie, 1986, p. 96). Anil Verma, whose research provided the details on the TRW case, provides data on a multiplant firm that includes new nonunion, old nonunion, and old union plants. The new nonunion plants have an average of six job classifications, compared with an average of 65 in the old nonunion and 96 in the old union plants (Verma, 1983). In a twist on this theme,

Cappelli and Sherer (1989) describe a very interesting experiment at Cummings Engine in which ILMs were redesigned to permit employees to remain within the union bargaining unit but to work according to the ILM rules that applied to nonunion supervisors.

In these examples the ILM rules have changed substantially and in a reasonably similar direction — a direction that might be taken to represent the path along which American firms are moving as they restructure their internal labor markets. It is apparent that the underlying ideas or inspiration come from the experience of observing Japanese firms and from ideas taken from leading American nonunion firms, such as IBM. Is it correct to believe that this transformed model is winning out?

The recent experiences of two leading nonunion "transformed" firms, IBM and Digital Equipment Corporation (DEC), raise warning flags. Both IBM and DEC are companies that most observers believed to be the closest American equivalents to the Japanese model of commitment, lifetime employment, extensive training, and so forth. Yet recently both companies retreated from this model. Digital laid off, for the first time in its history, several thousand employees. IBM implemented a number of financial incentives that, when combined with increasingly strict performance standards, are designed to force employees to leave. Indeed, the firm recently enacted a strict new performance review system under which the bottom 10 percent of workers will come under pressure to resign. By all accounts the atmosphere in both companies has changed dramatically.

Observers in a wide range of other companies report that efforts to reorganize or transform ILMs — via introduction of work teams, expansion of training, or provision of job protections — are surprisingly slow. In recent contracts, Boeing included a number of provisions aimed at involving employees more fully in decisions about work organization and technology, but these have not been implemented, and the company and union have not been able to agree on how to organize a joint training fund they established. In the nonunion sector, Eastman Kodak has repeatedly swung back and forth between a strategy of building commitment and employee participation and widespread layoffs, which undermined the other efforts.

The war of the anecdotes leads to an inconclusive result, but at the minimum, anecdotal data do cast doubt on the view that the transformed model is triumphing. Unfortunately there are no survey data that shed a brighter light. An ideal data set would measure a wide range of ILM rules for a panel of firms over time. With such data one could classify the firms into types and see how the distribution of those types was changing.

The closest such data, although not longitudinal, was collected by Osterman (see Osterman, forthcoming). These data are a survey of 875 establishments, hence avoiding the risks of questions directed to corporate headquarters about the entire organization. The sample was drawn from the Dun and Bradstreet file and is representative of private sector establishments with fifty or more employees. The survey asked about a wide range of internal labor market rules including the role of seniority in hiring and promotion, compensation systems, employment security, and the use of contingent employees.

One section of the survey examined the use of self-directed work teams, quality circles, total quality management, and job rotation. In addition to asking whether the practice was in place, data was also collected on the percentage of "core" employees involved. "Core" employees were defined as the nonmanagement workers most directly involved in producing the good or service, and they could be both blue and white collar.

Among the key results was that thirty-five percent of establishments had at least two of these practices in place, involving fifty percent or more of "core" employees. Additional analysis tested explanations for which establishments did and did not adopt these practices. Among the central findings were that establishments most likely to adopt these practices were those that competed in international markets, that were part of larger organizations, that used high skill technology, that followed a market strategy based on quality and variety rather than price competition, and that espoused values that emphasized employee wellbeing. The size of an establishment, the presence or absence of unions, and the time horizons of management did not prove important.

In addition to attempting to identify what might be thought of as the exogenous determinants of the use of flexible work practices, Osterman also sought to understand what set of human resource practices supported the use of these systems. He found that high levels of training, use of contingent compensation plans, and a strong voice for the human resources department were important. Surprisingly, it did not appear that employment security commitments played an important role.

There are a number of other studies that have sought to examine the distribution of specific practices, although the survey by Delaney, Lewin, and Ichniowski is the only other effort that sought to capture the full range of ILM practices.[6] For example, a sense of how widespread new compensation systems are can be gained from a 1987 survey conducted by the American Productivity Center. The center found that 32 percent of responding firms reported having profit-sharing arrangements, 28 percent reported having individual incentives, 14 percent had small group incentives, and 13 percent had gain sharing (Mitchell, Lewin, Lawler, 1990, p. 23).

Turning to teams and quality of work life, the Work in America Institute estimates that about 25 percent of U.S. workers are covered by some type of employee involvement program, although the depth and quality of these programs vary considerably (Gershenfeld, 1987, p. 131). However, this estimate is very much on the high side compared with those in the literature. A 1982 survey of firms with over 500 employees, conducted by the New York Stock Exchange, estimated that 14 percent of all firms and 52 percent of manufacturing firms used quality circles and that 20 percent of all firms and 59 percent of manufacturing firms had implemented either teams or other forms of work redesign. However, only a relatively small fraction (perhaps one-fourth) of employees at firms that had such programs in fact participated in them (Russell, 1988, p. 380). Finally, in a survey of Fortune 1000 firm headquarters, Lawler, Mohrman, and Ledford (1992) found that 56% reported having quality circles in their organization, and 4,795 had self managed work teams. However, less than 20% of employees were involved.

An additional, and very provocative, source of data about trends in ILM systems comes from examining the practices of Japanese transplants in the United States. These transplants are important because they provide American firms with examples or illustrations of alternative practices, and I will discuss this role later in the chapter. For now I can simply ask whether we know what these firms are doing.

The best publicized of the transplants are the large automobile assembly factories — Honda, Mazda, New United Motor Manufacturing, Inc. (NUMMI), and so on — and all reports suggest that these firms are organized along the lines of the transformed model (see Brown, Reich, and Stern, 1991; Shimada and MacDuffie, 1987; Adler, 1991). However, these enterprises may not be typical of the much larger number of Japanese-owned companies that have emerged in recent years. The evidence that is available on these firms suggests considerable diversity.

One striking study, by Ruth Milkman, surveyed 50 Japanese-owned electronic assembly plants in California with more than 100 employees. She collected data on ILM rules and found that "the Japanese owned plants in California bear little resemblance to the Japanese management model. Relatively few have quality circles or the equivalent; flexible teams are even more exceptional; and most of the managers we interviewed laughed outright when asked about just-in-time delivery or the like. One 'Japanese practice' is more

316

typical of these plants, however; most are committed, in principle, to avoiding layoffs. However, even this is tempered by the fact that these plants typically have high turnover rates." (Milkman, 1991, pp. 79–80).

These findings are provocative because one surely cannot argue that the owners of these firms were not aware of, and not accustomed to, alternative models and their presumed productivity advantages. There is, however, counterevidence. Florida and Kenny (1991) surveyed Japanese transplants that supply parts to the large Japanese automobile assemblers. They found a very high rate of adoption of transformed practices: for example, 76 percent of the suppliers use work teams and 79 percent have workers maintain their own machines. They also found substantial union avoidance (Milkman also observed this) and considerable use of contingent or temporary workers. This pattern of supply firms adopting transformed practices at the behest of their customers is informally confirmed by anecdotal evidence I collected about midwestern supplier networks that implemented a range of transformed practices in response to their customers' demands for innovations such as statistical process control.

In short, just as American firms seem torn between alternative ILM systems, so do Japanese-owned firms that are located in America. There is obviously movement away from the traditional model as it was developed in the 1940s through the 1960s, but it is not clear how far this shift has gone.

International variation

The final element of "data" with implications for the evolution of ILMs is the very substantial variation across nations in how ILMs are organized to produce similar products. While some years ago this point might have been controversial, by now it is almost commonplace in the discussion of international competitiveness, although it has yet to be fully incorporated in the ILM literature. At least since Ronald Dore's *British Factory, Japanese Factory* (1973), we have known that Japanese ILMs differ in many important respects from comparable American ones on dimensions such as wage ratios (Japanese pay their managers many fewer multiples of worker wages than do Americans), job security (the core of workers at large Japanese firms are protected from layoffs), job rotation and training (there is much more of both in Japan), and career paths (movements from blue- to white-collar ranks are more common in Japan).

While the Japanese comparison is by now well known, it is often not understood that other nations also differ from U.S. patterns. In German firms, for example, job security is also stronger, employees are involved in personnel decisions via their participation in works councils, there appear to be lower ratios of supervisors to frontline employees, and there is a much greater emphasis on formal skill-based training systems as a gateway to promotions.

These international comparisons create problems for arguments that make technology and product markets the central determinants of ILM structure. It may still be the case that product markets and technology are important in the sense that they restrict the range of alternatives[7] or alter the relative costs and benefits of various ILM systems. However, the international evidence makes clear that there must be more to the story.

In summary, these are my conclusions from the review of recent developments in ILMs:

1. As judged by data on job tenure, long-term employment in ILMs remains important. In fact, it is of growing relevance for women. Among middle-aged men there is a noticeable decline in the percentage in extended employment relationships, but the dominate pattern remains lengthy spells in ILMs.

2. Although the central tendency in employment is clearly stability, the evidence on the growth of contingent employment relationships also suggests there is some slippage around the edges. Some firms are seeking to establish looser relationships with a portion of their labor force. It will take further research to reveal whether this development can explain the tenure patterns noted above.

3. Many firms are seeking to implement significant shifts in the organization of their ILMs. These shifts typically involve more flexible job boundaries, greater attention to training, more communication with the labor force, movement toward performance-based pay systems, and — at least in some cases — enhanced job security. At the same time, these transformations are not diffusing as rapidly as might have been predicted some years ago, and there appear to be important obstacles. While it is hard to know which way the balance will tilt, it does seem fair to conclude that the rules regarding ILMs are much more open to question than in the past. Both the changes and the barriers are important "facts" that can be brought to bear on theory.

4. There is considerable international variation in the organization of ILMs in firms that operate in similar product markets using similar technology.

Understanding How Internal Labor Markets Evolve

The foregoing material can be thought of as the data against which I will try to develop a credible theory of the development of ILMs. In making this effort I of course have a great deal of prior research and theorizing from which to draw, but this does not necessarily make the task easier. A nice way to illustrate the problem is to consider the following two quotations, which describe the same ILM phenomena — the determinants of the careers of senior executives in large corporations. The first passage is from Robert Jackall's ethnographic study of three large firms, and the second is from Sherwin Rosen's review of the economic literature concerning the market for executives.

> . . . more frequent is the case where those with the power to do so foist or allow blame to fall on the unwary or inexperienced underlings . . . the most feared situation is to end up inadvertently in the wrong place at the wrong time. Yet this is exactly what happens in a structure that systematically diffuses responsibility . . . big corporations implicitly encourage scapegoating by their complete lack of any tracking system to trace responsibility . . . managers see [what happens] as completely capricious but completely understandable . . . what does matter when things go wrong is agility and political connections . . . most important they can "outrun their mistakes" so that when blame time arrives the burden will fall on someone else. At the institutional level, the absence of tracking responsibility becomes crucial. (Robert Jackall, 1988, pp. 85–90)

> How a career develops depends upon the quality of the person's previous work, what talents were demonstrated at lower positions, and the talent of other people available to be selected . . . this process can be modeled as a tournament. Competitors with the highest score on some performance criteria are declared winners and get promoted to a better job . . . within firm competition can sometimes be structured to approximate socially optimum incentives by adjusting the wage structure across ranks . . . competition generated by these kinds of relative performance evaluation can lead to moral hazard problems. (Rosen, 1990, pp. 33–39)

In Jackall's world (and the generalizations are supported by numerous anecdotes in the three firms) moral hazard is everything and efficiency is an afterthought, if that. In Rosen's world (which is supported by data on wage structures derived from several firm surveys) efficiency is at the core of firm structure, and moral hazard is a troublesome side issue, but not one that undermines the basic model or that suggests that the models are on the wrong track. Both purport to be representations of the rules governing careers in large private enterprises.

It is perhaps discouraging that two scholars can have such radically different views of the same question; if the question were actually this constrained, however, it would not be too difficult to make progress. Choosing between two such views is difficult, but is perhaps easier — given their sharp differences — than answering the broader and fuzzier question of why National Steel has transformed its ILM while U.S. Steel has remained traditional. What combination of economic, political, and social factors explains these divergent outcomes? When national differences are added, the problem becomes even more difficult.

To make progress, I will first identify the core ideas of the competing models and then try to show how they can fit together to provide a coherent explanation of the patterns.

Performance One set of ideas suggests that ILM structure is determined by performance considerations. Employment rules are determined by the firm's calculation of which configuration will produce the most output given the environment (chiefly product markets, technology, and labor force characteristics). This is a view traditionally associated with economic models, although I will add additional elements to it.

The most long-standing explanation of why ILMs improve performance is that they reduce the costs for firms of training the work force and retaining skilled labor. By creating incentives for people to remain with the employer (for example, compensation schemes that are "back-loaded") and disincentives for them to move (other firms force movers to start at the bottom of a job ladder), ILMs help resolve the bargaining problems inherent in the provision of specific human capital.[8] The evidence on this general point has always been the wage returns on job tenure, and although there have been several recent papers that argue this is not as high as sometimes assumed (Abraham and Farber, 1987), the evidence is still strong that these returns are substantial (Topel, 1990).

More recently, economic theorists have emphasized new explanations of why long-term employment relationships enhance efficiency and hence performance. These explanations include the minimizing of transaction costs, the resolution of agent-principle problems, and job stability flowing from above-market-clearing efficiency wages (Wachter and Wright, 1990; Williamson, Wachter, and Harris, 1975; Akerlof, 1984). Although models based on each of these ideas have been developed independently, I think it is best to think of them as part of a more general class of explanations that emphasize the issue of *control*. The firm is seen as having to solve the problem of how best to elicit effort from its labor force while minimizing the ability of employees to act in their personal interest rather than in the firm's interest.[9] These problems are especially serious when complexity or size render direct supervision of employees difficult. ILMs help resolve the problem by providing long-term opportunities to observe employee behavior (the transaction costs argument), by creating employee investment in the firm and hence raising the costs of cheating or poor effort (the bonding and implicit contract models), and by establishing an employment framework that permits development of wage systems that harmonize agent and principal interests (agent-principal and efficiency wage explanations).

The two foregoing groups of performance-based explanations for ILMs flow largely from the economics literature. There is, however, a third class of performance-centered explanations whose origin lies more in the industrial relations, human resource management, and organizational sociology fields. Particular ILM configurations may induce greater employee commitment, not because of fear of unemployment or loss of wage premiums, as posited by the economic models, but because of increased identification with the goals of the organization. This heightened commitment may in turn lead to more effort, more attention to quality, lower turnover rates, and other behaviors that enhance productivity.

The most commonly cited example of the relationship between ILM structure and commitment is Japan. Most casual observers believe that Japanese employees are more committed to their employer and that this does in fact lead to the performance-enhancing behaviors I have listed. In a recent important study Lincoln and Kalleberg (1990) analyzed a sample of workers drawn from manufacturing firms in Japan and America. Surprisingly they did not find higher average levels of commitment in Japan than in the United States.[10] However, they did find that in both Japan and the United States some aspects of ILMs, particularly employee welfare programs and employee participation in quality circles and other forms of joint decision making, were associated with heightened commitment.[11] Assuming that this commitment improves performance — an assumption I will examine later — this line of thought suggests a different performance-based rationale for some types of ILM systems.

It is important to understand that the salience of each variant of a performance-based explanation is conditioned on external conditions or constraints. One obvious example is technology. The nature of the technology has a significant impact on the relative importance of specific skills in the production process. Technology also plays a role in determining the ease or difficulty of directly monitoring employee performance. Other external constraints include the skills that the labor force brings to the firm (and hence the nature of the education system) and the characteristics of product markets (high volatility and consequent frequent shifts in product characteristics affect optimal supervision practices).[12]

Custom, Norms, and Political Contests An alternative perspective, quite different in spirit from performance-based explanations, interprets ILMs as work rules that represent the outcome of social processes within organizations. These social processes may be the relatively invisible inertial impact of norms and custom enforced through employee pressure or they may be the result of active power struggles.

Custom and norms emerge naturally out of the fact that when groups exist for extended periods they develop a history and a sense of what is appropriate and inappropriate. These norms include rules regarding output (Roethlisberger and Dickson, 1939; Roy, 1954) and also job demarcations, promotion procedures, and the like.

More active contests among factions within an organization can also shape the ILM rules. In the course of such struggles the kinds of performance considerations discussed earlier may underlie management motives, but even this is not necessarily true. Management itself may be driven by self-interest or ideology to retain certain powers or structures that bear little direct relationship to productivity.

The literature is replete with illustrations of these points. Jacoby (1984) describes the struggles of personnel staff against foremen, with the personnel department seeking to establish a legitimate role for itself. Various ILM rules such as job posting resulted from this conflict. The phenomena continues: Baron, Davis-Blake, and Bielby (1986) show that job titles tend to proliferate in organizations that employ relatively large proportions of personnel specialists.[13] Elbaum (1984), in his discussion of wages in the steel industry, documents how the modern wage structure reflects long-ago political struggles among different factions of the steel union. Indeed, the persistence of customary wage differentials in the face of shifting market conditions has long been observed by industrial relations scholars. Middle managers and foremen have resisted shifts in ILMs that transfer power to employees, and the resulting structures represent a compromise (Klein, 1989).

The external environment: Constraints and guidance

Along some dimensions the impact of the external environment on ILM structure is so obvious as to not require much comment. Government regulations regarding wages or equal employment opportunity are clearly reflected in organizational rules regarding such matters. During World War II, for example, the War Labor Board, in an effort to maintain labor peace, implanted personnel practices within firms, and these practices remained in place long after the war ended. The government was also influential in establishing ILM rules in the railroad and airline industries.

There are, however, more subtle channels of external influence. Maurice, Sellier, and Silvestre (1986) show how the differing educational systems of France and Germany are reflected in organizational rules within firms. Because German schools impart both more skill and more respect for authority flowing from formal credentials than does France, the ratio of supervisors to workers is much lower in German workplaces, and promotion paths between high-level blue-collar jobs and low-level supervisors are more open. The extensive debate about the role of Japanese culture in supporting the supposedly distinctive characteristics of the Japanese ILM is another illustration of the impact of an external environment (Dore, 1973; Lincoln and Kalleberg, 1990). There are also international differences in norms governing appropriate pay differentials across levels within an organization, and these differences do not appear to be related to corresponding variation in labor supply or demand.

The external environment also acts on firm decisions through the coercive channels of imitation. The sociology literature on institutionalism or isomorphism (for example, DiMaggio and Powell, 1983) argues that institutions seek legitimacy by imitating powerful actors in their environment. Hence Pfeffer and Cohen (1984) find that organizations regulated by government agencies are more likely to adopt particular formalized internal employment rules than are other organizations. Baron, Jennings, and Dobbin (1986) describe how professional personnel organizations diffused particular practices after World War II in an effort to maintain and expand their status within firms. One can surely speculate that there is a substantial element of mimicry in the spread of "transformed" ILM models today.[14]

Explaining the Data

How well do the alternative perspectives I have described explain the ILM patterns in the 1980s? As a first step, consider the following analogous question: what leads to a change in relative wages across occupations? It is helpful to think of the process as a set of three rings.

Within the first ring the impetus for such a wage shift comes from supply and demand developments, for example a technological shift that might increase the demand for a particular skill. This impetus is similar to the performance considerations I have already cited and sets off a series of reactions. In a frictionless universe the outward shift in the demand curve would yield a temporarily higher wage, which over time would be gradually offset by appropriate supply responses. In the short run, at least, the wage structure would shift.[15]

If, in the inner ring, performance considerations start the process in motion, how it actually plays out is modified in the second and third rings. Internal firm customs, norms, and politics modify the thrust of market forces. Historical differentials, the problems of dramatically increasing the wages of one group within an organization, fears of compression if the wages of entry-level employees rise sharply relative to incumbents, the competing demands of managers elsewhere for resources, and fears of wage inflation as other groups seek to maintain their customary relative standing, all taken together, influence the outcome. None of this is to say that the relative wages of the affected group do not rise; the performance considerations are indeed powerful. However it is easy to imagine a vice president for human resources limiting the size and timing of the wage increase for the reasons just cited.[16] Hence the impact of performance concerns is refracted and modified to an important extent by the considerations in the second ring.

In the United States, the third ring — the external environment — is less important to understanding wage changes. At the bottom of the labor market, the minimum wage and the "social wage" (welfare and other benefits) influence the wage structure, but these are much less important further up. Wage and hours legislation — the requirement that time and a half be paid for overtime — may be important, and so may equal employment opportunity considerations. Even mimicry can be important if, for example, a portion of the wage increase takes the form of performance pay, an innovation which has been spread via the business press. All in all, however, this third ring probably would exert a much weaker effect than the other two.

It should be apparent that explaining the evolution of the wage structure is complicated and that all three rings play some role.[17] Yet wages are a single measurable variable. Understanding the evolution of work organization, with its many dimensions and trade-offs among these dimensions, must be even more difficult. This said, how can one apply the models to recent ILM shifts?

It is evident that transformations, and attempted transformations, in ILM structure were initiated by performance considerations. In some industries American firms appeared to be less productive than their foreign competitors, and the organization of work was apparently the culprit.[18] It is clear that performance concerns drove the adoption of innovations such as team production, quality circles, cross-training, and so on. These ideas had been around for a long time and received considerable academic discussion, and even press attention, as part of the movements to humanize work. The federal government's 1972 report *Work in America* exemplified these interests. However, the innovations did not penetrate until they were perceived to be tied to performance, and this came about when the workplace innovations were incorporated into the overall production system and when competitors showed there were payoffs to such efforts.

In thinking about the nature of the performance considerations behind ILM shifts, economic explanations centering on control do not, at first blush, seem adequate. It is certainly plausible that efforts to improve quality, for example, may lead employers to improve control of the labor force. However, most observers of foreign ILM models tend to emphasize employee cooperation and commitment more than control, at least as control is normally understood. That is, the control models in the economics literature, with their emphasis on monitoring, wage profiles, and optimal incentive structures, do not seem to capture what underlies the gains made in transformed ILMs.

But even if control as it is typically described is not what explains recent changes, it may nonetheless be true that commitment is simply a more subtle form of control, one that is grounded in social psychology rather than economic principles. Put differently, do these new production systems succeed simply because they are a cleverer way of controlling the work force and eliciting effort, for example by using work teams to monitor the performance of peers? Japanese firms refer to their employees as "members." Does this capture a distinctive reality, or is it a mask for control?

The best available American evidence on this question comes from the experience of automobile firms that have adopted transformed ILM systems (these provide the best evidence simply because they have been studied most closely), and my reading of this research is that while control considerations remain important — and may be accomplished more effectively in transformed systems — the dimension of commitment is in fact real and distinctive.

Paul Adler conducted a series of intensive interviews in the General Motors–Toyota NUMMI plant in California (Adler, 1991). This plant implemented the Toyota system of team work, just-in-time inventories, continuous improvement, and employee responsibility for quality along the line. Taken together, these constitute a new production system. The production changes alone do not necessarily buy commitment, as Mazda learned in Flat Rock, Michigan.[19] At NUMMI, however, the new system was combined with management behavior shifts. For example, one of Adler's interviewees says, "NUMMI's managers are generally pretty good at considering suggestions when workers make them. They respect workers' ideas. NUMMI's managers always get back with: 'Its a great idea' or 'It's a good idea but . . .' This is what we like to see. At GM, you were lucky if they wrote the idea down; as soon as you left the room you knew the idea was headed for the garbage can" (Adler, 1991).

NUMMI was also explicit about offering strong job security pledges and respecting worker power along the assembly line (in terms of workers' ability to stop the line to correct quality problems). The consequences of all of these policies is that NUMMI is judged to have made tremendous gains on productivity and quality (MacDuffie and Krafcik, 1992), but my point here is that these gains are not ones that can be easily attributed to control, at least not as it is traditionally understood.

Adler provides numerous examples of workers making small suggestions that accumulate into substantial savings (such as the color coding of circuit breakers or replacing chrome water fountains with metal), as well as improved worker behavior, such as voluntarily picking up cigarette butts off the floor in the work area. Control models focus on shirking, cheating, misreporting, absenteeism, and the like; they do not satisfactorily explain *positive* voluntary behaviors such as these. Nor do they explain what Adler's quotes reveal is the explicit *reciprocal* nature of these actions: they are in response to management demonstrations of commitment to the labor force (which take the form of job security, concern with health and safety, respect for suggestions, and the like). Shimada and MacDuffie (1987)

326

use the phrase "giving knowledge to the machine" to characterize employee contributions in transformed systems.

There are elements of control in transformed systems: as Adler points out, the absence of buffers makes errors and problems along the line much more visible to supervisors, and teams do put pressure on peers with respect to absenteeism. Most dramatically, at least at NUMMI, is the heavy use of time and motion studies to decrease cycle time and hence to reduce employee discretion over their behavior along the assembly line.

In short, however, it does appear that commitment is a genuinely distinctive dimension of performance, separate from control. At the core of the difference is the idea of reciprocity. Management in fact gives up something significant: it transfers power to gain commitment. This suggests that there is a trade-off between control and commitment. Delineating the nature of that trade-off is an important theme for future work.

At the same time, the line between control and commitment is not always clear, and transformed ILM systems may achieve higher performance via gains in both dimensions. This explains the dilemma facing unions in such settings, as they seek to protect employees from intensified control and yet avoid challenging the gains from commitment.

Traditional economic considerations can more successfully explain the development of core-periphery employment patterns. Moving to high-commitment ILMs is costly because of the heightened job security implicit in such arrangements. To reduce costs, management excludes as many employees as possible from the core. How far one can go along these lines is determined by how deeply into an organization contingent employment can penetrate before it has adverse performance impacts, and by the supply of willing contingent employees.[20] For firms that adopt contingent employment relationships without ILM transformations, cost considerations alone seem to dominate.

If performance explains the emergence of new forms of ILMs in the United States, what can explain their halting progress? In part the answer is again performance. It would appear that there are many circumstances in which the traditional mode of organizing work is superior (or at least as good) and probably cheaper. One important clue here is found in the transplanted Japanese electronic assemblers cited earlier. There is no obstacle to transformed ILMs that one can plausibly cite other than that the firms believe the traditional work organization is the most profitable, given their market and technology.[21]

The impetus given to transforming ILM systems by performance considerations has also been refracted by the customs, norms, and politics of organizations. In the union sector, for example, it has taken some time for many unions to believe, or at least grudgingly accept, that work-rule changes are the price of remaining in business. The time this has taken, and the compromises that have been reached, are reflected in ILM outcomes.

Performance pressures are also filtered through managerial politics and custom. As I have already noted, transformed work systems are often a direct threat to first-line supervisors, and these concerns can be an obstacle to change. Considerable anecdotal evidence also suggests that middle managers find the devolution of authority inherent in transformed systems to be a threat, or a violation of norms, and often resist. It is easy to understand why a traditionally trained manager would find it difficult to pay close attention to employee suggestions. There are also barriers at the more senior management level. Full implementation of the transformed system requires expenditures of resources on large commitments (employment continuity) as well as small ones (consistent responses to employee suggestions for improvements related to comfort and safety). Where a union is present, senior management may find it difficult to accept the degree of cooperation that is typically necessary. In the absence of a union, management is likely to fear that empowering the labor force is the first step toward unionization. Taken together these concerns are often enough to block adoption of the transformed ILM system.[22]

The best evidence of the importance of the third ring — the external environment — comes from international comparisons. One example is skill: the United States lacks the deep vocational training programs of Germany, and such training can ease the introduction of new work systems.[23] In addition United States managerial culture is hostile to the transformed model because of its restriction of legitimate goals to maximize stockholder interests. This stands in contrast to the broader stakeholder perspective of both Japan and Germany. In addition to the bias inherent in a stockholder versus stakeholder perspective, the problem of transforming ILMs is exacerbated by an emphasis in the United States on short-term gains. This emphasis is not a logical part of stockholder systems, but it does appear to be characteristic of the American managerial system, and it makes it more difficult to justify long-term investments in training and enhanced employment security. In both Germany and Japan legal restrictions and the national culture lead firms to be much more reluctant both to follow a hire-fire strategy and to adopt the ILM associated with such a policy.[24]

To summarize, what do recent events reveal about the merits of alternative ILM theories? In some sense I have ducked the question by arguing, via the analogy of the three rings, that no single model is adequate and that many of the contenders have a role in the story. This may not seem clean, but it fairly reflects a complex world. However, some additional progress has been made. I have argued that performance-based models are central to explaining the recent drive for change in ILMs and that the norms, customs, politics, and mimicry models shape the actual outcome, which results from the initial performance impulse. These performance models are contingent on a variety of considerations, such as technology and product markets, and also on the external environment in which the firm finds itself.

I have also argued that we need to work with a broader view of performance models than is typically permitted in the economics literature. Economics stresses control, but recent events seem equally driven, if not more, by efforts to obtain commitment. Central to commitment is reciprocity, that is, managers giving up control. When reciprocity is added, commitment becomes more than a new and sly way of obtaining control. Nonetheless the line between commitment and control is not always clear.

Finally, the reader may be troubled by the ring analogy, because it implies a series of sequential, not simultaneous, steps and because it appears to give primacy to performance. The sequential structure is simply a conceit intended to indicate which factor is most important and to permit clear exposition. In reality all factors may be in play at once. Giving primacy to performance is, I think, historically contingent but accurate for the current period. By contrast, when the War Labor Board essentially imposed ILM patterns in a variety of industries, or when personnel staff diffused them through professional associations, other rings may have claimed center stage. Furthermore, although the impetus for change comes from performance researchers may be more struck, and more interested, in why transformations occur so haltingly. In that case the other rings should occupy their attention.

There has been a great deal of useful and important research on ILMs and our understanding of these institutions has progressed a great deal. However, an obvious research task to be undertaken is the collection of nationally representative data on the distribution of ILM types and on the change in that distribution over time. As the reader no doubt noticed, much of the evidence deployed here is anecdotal and impressionistic, and there is no good reason to permit that to continue.

There are, in addition, several themes that have been insufficiently addressed in the literature. The first is white-collar or managerial ILMs, and the second concerns placing ILMs in a broader context.

Any casual reader of the ILM literature will immediately observe that most of the material is drawn from the blue-collar manufacturing world. Whether the central models and descriptions are equally valid for managerial ILMs or in the service sector more generally is an open question. On the one hand the core constructs (control or commitment) must be important in other settings. However, the contexts in which these ideas are set may be quite different.[25]

In addition there is a great deal of talk in the business press about the flattening of organizational hierarchies, white-collar job insecurity, and the impact of technical change on white-collar skills and tasks. Other work suggests that new work forms, such as ad hoc teams for product development, are increasingly important (Ancona and Caldwell, 1987). Some observers speak of the "Taylor-ization" of service work while others emphasize that quality is key in the service sector and thus high-commitment systems are important there also. All of these developments, or alleged developments, can be systematically examined in the context of ILMs.

Some of the economics literature on agent-principal issues, compensation models, and tournament mobility have managers as their focus, but the empirical evidence is slim relative to the theories. There is also a large "careers" literature that is most closely associated with human resource management as it is taught in business schools. Much of this literature is very prescriptive and managerial, and when it is more academic it tends to be grounded in the psychology or ethnography literatures. It rarely asks about explanations for variation across organizations, nor does it seek general explanatory models. Finally, there is very little work of any kind concerning employment patterns in the service sector. Clearly, expanding the ambit of ILM research beyond blue-collar employment represents a major challenge.

An additional challenge to future ILM research is to embed ILMs in a framework that is broader than the terms in which they have been typically conceived. As I noted in the introduction to this essay, the early ILM researchers took public policy and the firm's competitive strategy as givens and focused on the labor market implications of ILM institutions. However, ILMs are important because they have substantial impacts on the welfare of individuals (along the dimensions of pay, job security, skill acquisition, and so on) and on the competitiveness of firms and the economy. This suggests that it is important to place ILMs firmly in both a public policy and a business strategy perspective.

We currently have a very poor understanding of how to deploy policy levers to influence ILMs. If, for example, we wished as a matter of policy to encourage the diffusion of the transformed ILM model, we would not know where to start. As I have already indicated, the simple prescription of more training is not convincing. Some experience suggests that interventions in firms around a particular issue (for example, the introduction of statistical process control) can lead to broader changes as the firm trains its labor force and reorganizes work (Batt and Osterman, 1993). There has been very little systematic research along these lines, however, and almost none on the broader question of the how (or whether) to attempt transformations in the external environment that would in turn induce firms to shift ILM patterns.

In a similar vein, only recently has research begun to place ILMs in the context of competitive strategy. The productivity consequences of alternative ILM patterns are poorly understood. How work organization fits with market strategy (such as variety or quality) is not well developed. In these and other ways, the firm's employment system should be more systematically linked to other aspects of its strategy and structure.

These limitations aside, it is apparent that ILMs provide a fruitful research arena for a variety of disciplines and intellectual perspectives. This will doubtlessly continue to be true. Whether ILMs will also be an arena in which the disciplines and perspectives can reach a mutually rewarding accommodation remains to be seen.

Author's Note

Research support for this work was provided by the Spencer Foundation. I am grateful to Rosemary Batt, Peter Cappelli, Thomas Kochan, James Rebitzer, and Maureen Scully for their comments.

Editors' Note

This essay was originally written for this book. At the author's request, we have granted permission for portions of the chapter to be published in the Industrial Relations Research Association's volume entitled *Research*

Frontiers in Industrial Relations and Human Resources, edited by David Lewin, Olivia S. Mitchell, and Peter D. Sherer.

Notes

1. It is important to remember that many individuals in the lower tenure categories in the tables are in the early stages of a long-term employment relationship, and hence the fraction of the labor force that is ever in a long-term employment relationship is larger than the proportion in such a relationship at any cross section. See Hall (1982) for a discussion of this.
2. I have in mind the commonly heard assertions that the average worker will have to change his or her employer many more times than in the past.
3. Hartman and Lapidus (1989, p. 1567) report that 45 percent of workers employed by temporary-help services are clerical, 20 percent are in blue-collar manufacturing jobs, and 15 percent in technical/professional specialties. Mangum et al. (1985) report that their survey showed that 62 percent of respondents used temporary workers in clerical jobs, 43 percent for production jobs, 46 percent as professional workers, and 41 percent as service workers.
4. The increase in women's tenure is influenced by supply developments as well as by the demand-side factors emphasized here.
5. The material on Corning is taken from interviews I conducted in the company. Similar information has been widely reported in the business press.
6. A great deal of effort and imagination went into the collection of these data. Unfortunately, the response rate was only 6.5 percent and thus it is not entirely clear what one should make of any findings.
7. The classic example is that the dispersed character of construction, particularly home construction, discourages formation of firm-based ILMs.
8. ILMs also make it safe for senior workers to pass on skills, since they are protected, by virtue of job ladders, from competition from their "students."
9. The more power workers have, the more serious is the firm's control problem. This power can take various forms, including knowledge that workers have but managers do not, and the ability to affect production at key "choke points."
10. When they manipulated the data by estimating commitment levels via a two-stage instruments procedure Lincoln and Kalleberg did find higher levels of commitment in Japan.
11. This supports the argument developed in Cappelli and Sherer (1991), that ILMs represent an important link in the organizational behavior literature between individual behavior (in this case commitment) and context.
12. For a more extended discussion of the interaction between performance-

based objectives of the firm and external constraints in the establishment of ILM patterns, see Osterman, 1987 (this paper does not, however, discuss the theme of commitment).

13. Of course, there is a question about direction of causality. Complex organizations may require personnel specialists.

14. The mimicry models are convincing in a number of respects, and certainly in my own interviews with managers I have been struck by the frequency with which they explain their own policies by reference to practices they have heard of at other firms. However, copying may simply be a cheap form of economic search. The mimicry models also tend to leave open the question of where the initial ideas come from and, more troubling, what role is played by performance in determining which models are ultimately selected and survive.

15. In a textbook world, in the long run the former structure would reemerge as the supply responses reached completion.

16. In response to the objection that "market discipline" (such as quit rates or difficulty in recruitment) would thwart such administrative action, one can point to the substantial variation within a geographical area of wages for comparable jobs (Goshen, 1991; Dunlop, 1957). Doeringer and Piore (1971) discuss a number of adjustment mechanisms that firms can use in lieu of wage increases to adjust the size and quality of their labor force.

17. In a recent article Erica Goshen (1991) reviews various theories for why wages for comparable skills and occupations vary by firm. She rejects most standard neoclassical models and instead places greatest emphasis on efficiency wage and rent sharing explanations. However, she notes that the direct evidence on these models is very weak, and one is left with the view that even after many years of research on wages, we still cannot develop a convincing explanation for variation across enterprises.

18. In other industries, American firms seem to more than hold their own in international competition. The relationship of this success to ILM structure is less well understood, since much research has (unfortunately, in my view) been concentrated on declining industries.

19. At the Mazda plant in Flat Rock, Michigan, a production system and ILM that initially appeared to have the same characteristics as at NUMMI broke down under employee complaints about work pace and health and safety. A difficult industrial relations climate emerged, culminating in the election of a dissident union group and challenges to company policy (see Fucini and Fucini, 1990).

20. Rebitzer (1991) shows that in the petroleum refining industry, heavy use of contingent employees is associated with increased risk of accidents.

21. The contingency of the performance gains probably helps explain the mixed findings in the literature that seeks to establish a link between work organization and outcomes such as productivity. There are investigations that suggest such links (MacDuffie, 1991; Cutcher-Gershenfeld,

1991), but there is also quality research with findings much more on the neutral or negative side (for example, Wall et al., 1986). If one had to make a bet, the safer one, given the research and given the international evidence, would be that transformed systems do provide a performance boost. However, the mixed findings in the research give one pause, as do the serious methodological problems that characterize this line of work. The greatest methodological problem is that much of the research consists of studies of "best practice" — settings in which the researcher knows in advance that there was some success. It is not at all clear from this style of research what would happen were the "treatment" administered to a random firm. Given the possible costs of making the transition, it is evident why caution is a reasonable strategy.

22. The survival rate of QWL plans is low. According to Paul Goodman (1980), of the plans established in the 1970s, only 25 percent managed to last for five years. It is not clear whether programs in the 1980s had better prospects.

23. Skill alone is not the explanation, however, since Japan provides relatively little school-based vocational training; firms instead train intensively in the context of ILMs. American firms could choose to follow a similar strategy.

24. Levine and Tyson (1990) point to another external environment issue. When only a few firms implement transformed systems, their heightened commitment to employment security may have an adverse selection effect, as employees who would be fired in other environments gravitate to the transformed firms. It is hard to assess how important this is, although it may help explain some of the extensive investment in selection and hiring that characterizes some of the start-up transformed firms.

25. Rosabeth Kanter wrote of a group of managers, "People in the same position disagreed among themselves about its place in the organizational career map. Twenty distribution managers identified seven routes to their jobs . . . and they imagined that there were three likely and seven rare moves from their job." (Kanter, 1978, p. 132). A description of a traditional blue-collar job ladder would be quite different.

References

Abraham, Katherine, and Farber, Henry, 1987. "Job Duration, Seniority, and Earnings," *American Economic Review* 77 (June), 278–297.

Abraham, Katherine, and Medoff, James, 1984. "Length of Service and Layoffs in Union and Non-Union Groups," *Industrial and Labor Relations Review* 38 (October), 87–97.

Adler, Paul, 1991. "The New 'Learning Bureaucracy': New United Motor Manufacturing, Inc.," mimeo, October, University of Southern California.

Akerlof, George, 1984. "Gift Exchange and Efficiency Wages," *American Economic Review* 74 (May), 79–83.

Althauser, Robert, and Kalleberg, Arne 1981. "Firms, Occupations, and the Structure of Labor Markets," in Ivan Berg, ed., *Sociological Perspectives on Labor Markets* (New York: Academic Press), 119–145.

Altonji, Joseph, and Shakotko, Robert, 1987. "Do Wages Rise with Job Seniority?" *Review of Economic Studies* 54 (July), 437–460.

Ancona, Deborah, and Caldwell, David, 1987. "Management Issues in New Product Teams in High Technology Companies," in David Lewin, David Lipsky, and Donna Sockell, eds. *Advances in Industrial Relations,* vol. 4 (Greenwich, Conn.: JAI Press).

Applebaum, Eileen, 1989. "The Growth of the U.S. Contingent Labor Force," in Robert Drago and Richard Perlman, eds., *Microeconomic Issues in Labor Economics* (New York: Harvester Wheatsheaf).

Baron, James, and Bielby, William, 1986. "The Proliferation of Job Titles in Organizations," *Administration Science Quarterly* 31 (December), 561–586.

Baron, James, Davis-Blake, Alison, and Bielby, William, 1986. "The Structure of Opportunity: How Promotion Ladders Vary Within and Among Organizations," *Administrative Science Quarterly* 31 (June), 248–273.

Baron, James, Jennings, P. Devereaux, and Dobbin, Frank, 1988. "Mission Control? The Development of Personnel Systems in U.S. Industry," *American Sociological Review* 53, (August), 497–514.

Baron, James, and Pfeffer, Jeffrey, 1988. "Taking the Workers Back Out: Recent Trends in the Structuring of Employment," in Barry Straw and L. L. Cummings, eds., *Research in Organizational Behavior,* vol. 10 (Greenwich, Conn: JAI Press), 257–304.

Batt, Rose, and Osterman, Paul, 1993. *A National Framework for Employment and Training Policy: Lessons from Local Initiatives* (Washington, D.C.: Economic Policy Institute).

Bielby, William, and Baron, James, 1983. "Organization, Technology, and Worker Attachment to the Firm," in Donald Trieman and Robert Robertson, eds. *Research in Social Mobility* (Greenwich, Conn.: JAI Press), 77–115.

Brown, Clair, Reich, Michael, Stern, David, 1991. "Skills and Security in Evolving Employment Systems; Observations From Case Studies," mimeo, Institute of Industrial Relations, University of California, Berkeley.

Cappelli, Peter, and Sherer, Peter D. 1991. "The Missing Role of Context in OB: The Need for a Meso-Level Approach," in L. L. Cummings and Barry Straw, eds., *Research in Organizational Behavior,* vol. 13 (Greenwich, Conn.: JAI Press), 55–110.

———1989. "Spanning the Union/Nonunion Boundary," *Industrial Relations* 28, no. 2 (Spring), 188–205.

Cutcher-Gershenfeld, Joel, 1991. "The Impact on Economic Performance of a Transformation in Workplace Relations," *Industrial and Labor Relations Review* 44 (January), 241–260.

———, 1989. "The Institutionalization of Organizational Change: A Case Study of Xerox and the ACTWU," in Fred Foulkes, ed., *Human Resource*

Management: Text and Cases, second ed. (Englewood Cliffs, N.J.: Prentice Hall).

Daly, Anne, 1986. "Education and Productivity: A Comparison of Great Britain and the United States," *British Journal of Industrial Relations,* July, 251–266.

Daly, A., Hitchens, D. M., and Wagner, K., 1985. "Productivity, Machinery and Skills in a Sample of British and German Manufacturing Plants," *National Institute of Economic Review,* February, no. 111, 48–61.

Delaney, John, Lewin, David, and Ichniowski, Casey, 1989. *Human Resource Policies and Practices in American Firms,* BLMR Report no. 137 (Washington, D.C.: U.S. Department of Labor).

DiMaggio, Paul, and Powell, Walter, 1983. "The Iron Cage Revisited: Institutional Isomorphism and Collective Rationality in Organizational Fields," *American Sociological Review* 48, 147–160.

Doeringer, Peter, and Piore, Michael, 1971. *Internal Labor Markets* (Lexington, Mass.: D. C. Heath).

Dore, Ronald, 1973. *British Factory, Japanese Factory* (Berkeley: University of California Press).

Dunlop, John, 1966. "Job Vacancy Measures and Economic Analysis," in *The Measurement and Interpretation of Job Vacancies: A Conference Report,* National Bureau of Economic Research (New York: Columbia University Press), 1966.

————, 1957. "The Task of Contemporary Wage Theory," in G. Taylor and F. Pierson, eds., *New Concepts in Wage Determination.* New York: McGraw-Hill, 117–139.

Elbaum, Bernard, 1984. "The Making and Shaping of Job and Pay Structures in the Iron and Steel Industry," in Paul Osterman, ed., *Internal Labor Markets* (Cambridge, Mass.: MIT Press), 71–108.

Florida, Richard, and Kenney, Martin, 1991. "The Transfer of Japanese Industrial Organization to the U.S.," *American Sociological Review* 56 (June), 381–398.

Fucini, J., and Fucini, S., 1990. *Working for the Japanese* (New York: Free Press).

Gershenfeld, Walter, 1987. "Employee Participation in Firm Decisions," in Morris Kleiner, et al., eds., *Human Resources and the Performance of the Firm* (Madison, Wis.: Industrial Relations Research Association), 123–158.

Goodman, Paul, 1980. "Realities of Improving Quality Work Life," *Labor Law Journal* 31 (August), 487–494.

Groshen, Erica L., 1991. "Sources of Intra-Industry Wage Dispersion: How Much Do Employers Matter?" *Quarterly Journal of Economics* 106 (August), 869–885.

Hall, Robert, 1982. "The Importance of Lifetime Jobs in the U.S. Economy," *American Economic Review* 72 (September), 716–724.

Hartmann, G., et al., 1983. "Computerized Machine-Tools, Manpower Consequences and Skill Utilization: A Study of British and West German

Manufacturing Firms," *British Journal of Industrial Relations* 23, no. 2, 221–231.

Hartman, Heidi, and Lapidus, June, 1989. "Temporary Work," in Commission on Workforce Quality, *Investing in People* (Washington, D.C.: U.S. Department of Labor), 1561–1608.

Ichniowski, Casey, 1990. "Human Resource Management Systems and the Performance of U.S. Manufacturing Business," NBER Working Paper no. 3449 (September).

Jackall, Robert, 1988. *Moral Mazes: The World of Corporate Managers* (New York: Oxford University Press).

Jacoby, Sanford, 1985. *Employing Bureaucracy* (New York: Columbia University Press).

Kanter, Rosabeth Moss, 1977. *Men and Women of the Corporation* (New York: Basic Books).

Katz, Harry, 1985. *Shifting Gears: Changing Labor Relations in the U.S. Auto Industry* (Cambridge, Mass.: MIT Press).

Katz, Lawrence, 1986. "Efficiency Wage Theories: A Partial Evaluation," in Stanley Fischer, ed., *NBER Macroeconomics Annual* (Cambridge, Mass.: MIT Press).

Kerr, Clark, 1954. "The Balkinization of Labor Markets," in E. Wright Bakke, ed., *Labor Mobility and Economic Opportunity* (Cambridge, Mass.: MIT Press), 92–110.

Klein, Janice, 1989. "Why Supervisors Resist Employee Involvement," *Harvard Business Review* 62 (September–October), 87–95.

Kochan, Thomas, Katz, Harry, and McKersie, Robert, 1986. *The Transformation of American Industrial Relations* (New York: Basic Books).

Kochan, Thomas, and Osterman, Paul, 1991. "Human Resource Development: Does the United States Do Too Little?" paper prepared for the American Council on Competitiveness, 1991.

Lawler, Edward, Mohrman, Susan, and Ledford, Gerald, 1992. *Employee Involvement and Total Quality Management; Practices and Results in Fortune 1000 Companies* (San Francisco: Jossey Bass).

Levine, David, and Tyson, Laura D'Andrea, 1990. "Participation, Productivity, and the Firm's Environment," in Alan Blinder, ed., *Paying for Productivity* (Washington, D.C.: Brookings Institution), 183–244.

Lincoln, James, and Kalleberg, Arne, 1990. *Culture, Control, and Commitment: A Study of Work Organization and Work Artifacts in the United States and Japan* (Cambridge: Cambridge University Press).

MacDuffie, John Paul, 1991. *Beyond Mass Production: Flexible Production Systems and Manufacturing Performance in the World Auto Industry.* Ph.D. dissertation, MIT Sloan School of Management.

MacDuffie, John Paul, and Krafcik, John, forthcoming. "Integrating Technology and Human Resources for High Performance Manufacturing: Evidence from the International Auto Industry," in Thomas A. Kochan and Michael Useem, eds., *Transforming Organizations* (New York: Oxford University Press).

Mangum, Garth, Mayhill, Donald, and Nelson, Kristin, 1985. "The Temporary Help Market: A Response to the Dual Internal Labor Market," *Industrial and Labor Relations Review* 38, (July), 599–611.

Maurice, Marc, Sellier, François, and Silvestre, Jean-Jacques, 1986. *The Social Foundations of Industrial Power* (Cambridge, Mass.: MIT Press).

Maurice, M., Sorge, A., and Warner, M. 1980. "Societal Differences in Organizing Manufacturing Units: A Comparison of France, West Germany, and Great Britain," *Organization Studies* 1, 59–86.

Milkman, Ruth, 1991. *California's Japanese Factories: Labor Relations and Economic Globalization,* (Los Angeles: UCLA Institute of Industrial Relations).

Miller, Katherine, and Monge, Peter, 1986. "Participation, Satisfaction, and Productivity: A Meta-Analytic Review," *Academy of Management Journal,* 727–753.

Mitchell, Daniel J. B., Lewin, David, and Lawler, Edward 1990. "Alternative Pay Systems, Firm Performance, and Productivity," in Alan Blinder, ed., *Paying for Productivity* (Washington, D.C.: Brookings Institution), 15–94.

New York Stock Exchange, 1982. *People and Productivity: A Challenge to Corporate America* (New York: New York Stock Exchange).

Osterman, Paul, 1987. "Choice Among Alternative Internal Labor Market Systems," *Industrial Relations* 26 (February) 46–67.

——, 1988. *Employment Futures: Reorganization, Dislocation, and Public Policy* (New York: Oxford University Press).

——ed., 1984. *Internal Labor Markets* (Cambridge, Mass.: MIT Press).

——1991. *The Productivity Consequences of Alternative Internal Labor Market Arrangements* (Stockholm: Swedish Delegation on Productivity).

——1987. "Turnover and the Performance of the Firm," in Morris Kleiner et al., eds., *Human Resources and the Performance of the Firm* (Madison, Wis.: Industrial Relations Research Association), 275–318.

——, 1984. "White Collar Internal Labor Markets," in Paul Osterman, ed., *Internal Labor Markets* (Cambridge, Mass.: MIT Press).

——. "How Common is Workplace Transformation and How Can we Explain who Does It?" *Industrial and Labor Relations Review,* forthcoming.

Pfeffer, Jeffrey, and Cohen, Yinon, 1984. "Determinants of Internal Labor Markets in Organizations," *Administrative Science Quarterly* 29, 550–572.

Rebitzer, James, 1991. "Short-Term Employment Relations and Labor Market Outcomes: Contract Workers in the U.S. Petrochemical Industry," mimeo, MIT Sloan School of Management.

Rebitzer, James, and Taylor, Lowell, 1991. "Do Labor Markets Provide Enough Short Hour Jobs? An Analysis of Work Hours and Work Incentives," mimeo, MIT Sloan School of Management.

Roethlisberger, F. J., and Dickson, William, 1939. *Management and the Worker* (Cambridge, Mass.: Harvard University Press).

Rosen, Sherwin, 1990. "Contracts and the Markets for Executives," NBER Working Paper no. 3542, December.

Roy, Donald, 1954. "Quota Restriction and Goldbricking in a Machine Shop," *American Journal of Sociology* 60, 255–266.

Russell, Raymond, 1988. "Forms and Extent of Employee Participation in the Contemporary United States," *Work and Occupations* 15, 374–395.

Shimada, Haruo, and MacDuffie, John Paul, 1987. "Industrial Relations and Humanware: Japanese Investments in Automobile Manufacturing in the United States," working paper, MIT Sloan School of Management.

Steedman, H., and Wagner, K., 1987. "A Second Look at Productivity, Machinery and Skills in Britain and Germany," *National Institute of Economic Review*, November, no. 122, 81–86.

Stinchcombe, Arthur, 1965. "Social Structure and Organization," in James March, ed., *Handbook of Industrial Organization* (Chicago: Rand McNally), 142–193.

Topel, Robert, 1990. "Specific Capital, Mobility, and Wages: Wages Rise with Job Seniority," NBER Working Paper no. 3294 (March).

Verma, Anil, 1983. "Union and Non-Union Industrial Relations at the Plant Level," Ph.D. dissertation, MIT Sloan School of Management.

Wachter, Michael, and Wright, Richard, 1990. "The Economics of Internal Labor Markets," *Industrial Relations* 29, (Spring), 240–262.

Wall, Toby, et al., 1986. "Outcomes of Autonomous Work Groups: A Long-Term Field Experiment," *Academy of Management Journal* 29, 280–304.

Williamson, Oliver, Wacter, Michael, and Harris, Jeffrey, 1975. "Understanding the Employment Relation: The Analysis of Idiosyncratic Exchange," *Bell Journal of Economics* 6 (Spring), 250–280.

Yellen, Janet, 1984. "Efficiency Wage Models of Unemployment," *American Economics Review* 74 (May), 200–208.

13

Managing the Workplace: From Markets to Manors, and Beyond

■────────────────────────────■

Sanford M. Jacoby

Earlier than other nations, the United States developed a specialized branch of management — personnel management — for dealing with the administration of employment and industrial relations. One reason for this early specialization was the relatively large size of American firms, which, as business historian Alfred D. Chandler has shown, were the first companies in the world to adopt a system of managerial capitalism. In addition, American companies manifested a strong tendency toward self-restraint in the employment relationship, because of the relative weakness, prior to the 1930s, of both government regulation and trade unionism.

Personnel management had roots in various Progressive reform movements that placed a high value on rational administration as a social good and on the legitimation of authority through technical expertise. This gave personnel management a strong professional orientation during its early years, which, in turn, had a liberalizing effect on personnel managers and the firms employing them. Professionalism was an impetus for managerial self-restraint and for employment reform. But it brought the personnel manager into repeated conflict with line management and caused a repudiation of the professional model during the 1920s. After 1933, attempts were made to revive the professional element in personnel management. In unionized firms, this proved difficult to achieve, but elsewhere a new kind of professionalism emerged, one that was built on sophisticated, science-based personnel techniques. Ultimately this new professionalism — dubbed "human resource management" — became the dominant tendency in mainstream American corporations.

By examining the history of the personnel management profession in the United States, much can be learned about the process by which American corporations went about replacing a market-oriented employment system with one that was more bureaucratic, stable, and rule-bound. The study of personnel management thus provides a window on the process of internal labor market formation. It also permits us to gauge the impact of unionism on management and, conversely, to see the impact of management on unions, especially during periods of union decline such as the 1920s and the decades since 1970.

The method taken here, then, is to focus on professionalization and to tie that process to larger changes taking place outside the corporation. This is quite different from previous attempts to analyze the development of personnel management. One standard approach — the philosophical — conceptualizes the field's history as a succession of managerial creeds and styles, each more sophisticated and democratic than its predecessor. Starting with paternalism, personnel management is said to have progressed through scientific management, human relations, and various new forms of participative management. But this philosophical approach ignores the more mundane content of the personnel manager's tasks and creates artificial distinctions between essentially similar ideas. An alternative approach — the organizational — presents personnel management as an offshoot of firms' increased size and complexity. Entrepreneurial duties were differentiated and delegated to specialized managers and centralized managers. But the focus on bloodless organizational forms obscures the content of personnel management — how it differed over time and what made it unique in the United States. And both approaches are too linear, since they imply a continuous unfolding of managerial competence, organizational rationality, or both.[1]

This essay is divided into three parts. First, the traditional system of foreman management is described. This is followed by an examination of the early origins of the personnel management profession. Finally, the modern development of personnel management is examined, both during the heyday of unionism (1933 to 1960) and during the more recent phase of the "new" human resource management.

The Foreman and Employment

The foreman (and other first-line supervisors) enjoys relatively little status within the modern managerial hierarchy. He has been called "the forgotten man of management," a phrase that evokes an earlier period when foremen were recognized as a critical element in the administration of the factory. Indeed the foreman of the nineteenth and early twentieth centuries exercised considerable control over factory production and employment.

Production management entailed the authority to make decisions regarding the method of production and the ability to control a product's cost and quality. Where skill mattered, as it did in many nineteenth-century industries, foremen and skilled workers shared the task of managing production. Often they knew more about the technology of production than a firm's owners. They had mastered a body of arcane knowledge that Frederick W. Taylor called "the principal asset or possession of every tradesman."

The relative amount of power held by the foreman depended on the collective ability of skilled workers to preserve their autonomy in production. Union working rules and informal codes of behavior protected the skilled workers' freedom to decide how to produce an item without interference from a supervisor. The type of technology in use determined the total amount of power to be shared. Foremen and skilled workers had greater control of production under unit and small-batch techniques, where a high degree of craft skill was essential to production, than they did under newer machine-paced and continuous-flow techniques of production.[2]

Technology imposed few constraints on the foreman's authority in the employment sphere. Whether in a machine shop or on an assembly line, the foreman was given free rein to manage the acquisition, allocation, pricing, and supervision of labor. To the worker the foreman was a despot, not often benevolent, who made or interpreted employment policy as he saw fit. An observer remarked that, "The foreman and the gang bosses are the most important means by which the workmen come into contact with the management — they *are* the management to the worker."

The foreman's control over employment began at the factory gate. Hiring often was random or arbitrary. Unemployed workers would gather in front of a factory on mornings when a firm was hiring. The foremen stood at the head of the crowd and picked out those workers who had managed to get near the front. Sometimes apples were tossed to the throng; if you caught an apple, you had a job. Foremen could also be less arbitrary, hiring their friends or relatives of those already employed. Many relied on ethnic stereotypes to determine who would get a job or which job they would be offered. Perhaps the most common method of obtaining employment was to bribe the foreman with whiskey, cigars, or cash.[3]

The foreman also determined the wage rates of the individuals he hired. On either a piecework or daywork basis, foremen could and did set widely varying wage rates for individuals in the same department. It was common practice for foremen to "beat the applicant down from the wage he states he wishes to the lowest which the interviewer believes he can be induced to accept." Employment records rarely were kept before 1900. Only the foreman knew with any accuracy how many workers were employed in his department and what rates they received.

A firm's owners expected the foreman to hold labor costs down despite or because of the latitude they gave him in determining rates. This meant paying a wage no greater than the "going rate" for a particular job. But it also meant striving to keep effort levels up so as to reduce unit labor costs. The prevailing wage simply was a ceiling on unit labor costs.

To maintain or increase effort, foremen relied on a variety of methods collectively known as "the drive system" — close supervision, abuse, profanity, and threats. Workers constantly were urged to work harder, move faster, and look lively. Foremen might bribe some workers to set a faster pace for the rest of the group. Said Sumner Slichter, "The dominating note of the drive policy is to inspire the worker with awe and fear of the management, and having developed fear among them, to take advantage of it."

The fear that the drive system aroused ultimately was founded on the threat of dismissal. The foreman was free to utilize the discharge as he saw fit, and discharges were liberally meted out. The threat posed by dismissal depended on labor market conditions, with a tight market tending to undermine the drive system. But when the labor market loosened and workers were plentiful, as was often the case between 1870 and 1915, a discharge could be devastating to a worker's livelihood.[4]

Employment was volatile under the drive system, and few workers had anything resembling equity in their jobs. When layoffs came, it was the rare employer who ordered his foremen to systematically reduce the work force. Employment security was determined by the same particularistic criteria as hiring and promotions. Bribes were a common method of ensuring that one's job was secure.

There was a system of employment here, although it wasn't bureaucratic. Foremen weren't entirely unpredictable, nor did they rely solely on threats to maintain order and elicit effort. They had many favors to dispense to those whom they befriended or to those who bought their friendship. Personal ties and loyalty counted for much, although future managers were distressed by the particularism and brutality that infused the traditional system of employment. Yet where employment first achieved a semblance of rational organization, systematization, and standardization, these features were not a managerial innovation but were imposed from below.

Trade unions curbed the foreman's prerogatives in employment and gave the skilled worker considerable control over the terms of his employment relationship with the firm. Strict rules and equitable procedures governed hiring, promotion, wage determination, discipline, and employment security. When professional managers later instituted bureaucratic methods of employment, they incorporated numerous features of the employment system skilled workers had fashioned for themselves, and extended these to the less skilled.[5]

The Roots of Personnel Management

Industrial engineering

The trend after 1880 was toward larger establishments and faster throughput time in manufacturing operations. An important factor behind these developments was the increased application of science to industry, a process personified by the engineer. Aside from purely technical achievements, the engineers were responsible for introducing new methods of production management to industry. Until 1915, discussions of plant administration, cost accounting, and related topics rarely were found outside of engineering journals and magazines.

The engineers employed in the older metal-working industries were the primary source of the innovations that led to the bureaucratization of production. In these industries there already existed an entrenched system of production management. If plant size and operating speeds were to continue to increase, control of production would have to be wrested from foremen and skilled workers.

The engineers developed administrative innovations that displaced traditional methods of production management. Early production control systems told the foreman which units he was to produce, the order in which operations were to be performed, and the method by which the operations were to be carried out. Industrial engineers like Frederick W. Taylor called for transferring all "brain work" done by foremen and skilled workers to "brain workers" in a central planning department. The foreman's directive and conceptual duties in production were assumed by engineers and managers far removed from the shop floor. Routinized aspects of the foreman's duties were assigned to specialized clerical personnel. The process resulted in a steady increase in the ratio of administrative to production employees.[6]

There was more to this reorganization of production than a bloodless reworking of authority lines and cost control methods. The bureaucratization of production management entailed a zero-sum transfer of initiative away from the foreman and skilled worker to the managerial expert. Foremen did not take kindly to this shrinkage in their zone of discretion. One engineer noted that foremen "resented taking instructions from abrasive, soft-handed college men who had never themselves poured a mold or run a machine."

Despite their forays into production management, the industrial engineers left relatively untouched the other important area of the foreman's duties. The overall lack of attention to employment matters should not be construed as a lack of concern, however. Rather, it represented the engineers' somewhat naive belief that most employment and labor relations problems could be solved by a properly devised incentive wage scheme. Consequently, the development of a bureaucratic system of employment lagged behind the rationalization of other spheres of the firm.

It would, however, be incorrect to argue that the engineers contributed nothing to the development of modern personnel management. Engineering instead was an exemplar for the processes of bureaucratization and professionalization that were central to the rise of systematic personnel management.[7]

Elements of the engineers' bureaucratizing impulse came into play when the first American personnel departments were established in the decade after 1900. These early departments often were little more than payroll offices, reflecting the engineers' stress on accurate records, orderly procedures, and the departmentalization of routinized functions.

At a more general level, the path that the bureaucratization of employment followed after 1915 had parallels to the path taken in production. The foreman's employment duties were routinized and transferred to staff departments. Information formerly part of the foreman's "secret" store of knowledge, such as wage rates and job content, was appropriated by the personnel manager, much as the secrets of production were appropriated by the engineer. The rhetoric used by personnel managers to attack foremen — that they weren't specialists, that they were overly busy with other duties, that their methods weren't scientific — was similar to that used by the engineers.[8]

The issue of professionalism, which was a prominent theme in the engineering literature between 1890 and 1920, provided a more subtle link between the engineers and personnel management. The engineers became deeply concerned about the autonomy and influence they would wield in the large corporations where they increasingly found themselves employed after 1890. A related dilemma involved reconciling their allegiance to their employers with their professional pretensions and corresponding social responsibilities.

The industrial engineers involved in the reorganization of production, and Frederick W. Taylor in particular, were more concerned with the structure of the emerging corporate bureaucracy than were engineers in other specialties. Questions that plagued other engineers, such as the role of the expert in the corporate hierarchy, arose naturally in the course of the industrial engineer's work. Taylor, an independent consulting engineer, was obsessively concerned that his clients accept his recommendations in entirety and respect the expertise and autonomy of his associates.

Fundamental to Taylor's system was his appeal to science and to professional expertise as legitimators of the engineer's attempts to rationalize production management. Taylor claimed to have discovered an entirely new system of "scientific management" in which scientific laws were substituted for traditional decision making. Taylor and other industrial engineers used the authority of technical expertise to attack the "rule of thumb" methods used by foremen and skilled workers. But the science of management also involved a transfer of initiative away from the firm's owners and a restriction of their traditional powers. Some employers regarded Taylor's system as an impetuous obstruction of their prerogatives, because it questioned their natural superiority.[9]

Taylor's professional ideology shaped the outlook of other specialists employed in corporate bureaucracies. First, it provided a formula for undermining the status quo within the firm by questioning traditional methods of organization and forms of authority. By virtue of his technical expertise, the trained professional could claim a directive role that reduced the authority of those above and below him in the corporate hierarchy. Second, Taylor's scientific stance pointed the way to the professional's self-image as an arbiter of conflicts between management and workers. The professional allegedly could act in the best interests of both groups, because he had an invariant measure of social welfare — the science of production and human behavior. The belief that industrial conflict could be ameliorated by trained professionals dispassionately applying science to industry became the leitmotiv of the early personnel management movement.

Taylor's stress on expertise as opposed to customary forms of authority lent recognition to efforts then under way to professionalize management by teaching it in schools of business. By linking science to management, Taylor undercut the traditional academic disdain of commerce. His system occupied a central place in the curricula of the new business schools at such universities as Dartmouth, Harvard, and Pennsylvania. Supporters of these developments had high hopes that the professionalization of management would humanize industry by injecting liberal values into the firm. At a meeting of the Efficiency Society in 1912, Thomas N. Carver, a Harvard economist, argued that "the various schools of business are doing more for the labor problem than all the industrial reformers put together."[10]

Advocates of professional personnel management had similar hopes. Repeatedly it was emphasized that the personnel manager had to be a "big man," imbued with the liberal temperament that a university education was supposed to impart. The professionalization of employment management would pacify industry by placing the professional, a man of science and class neutrality, in charge of finding a private solution to the "labor problem." The personnel manager was viewed as the catalyst whose expertise, neutrality, and broad vision would bring "the business conscience . . . into alignment with the social conscience."[11]

Having drawn these parallels, it still is a fact that the content of personnel management had sources wider than industrial engineering and Taylorism. The typical analysis of employment in the prewar engineering literature was simply a call for more clerks and better incentive wage plans. Robert F. Hoxie's 1914 survey of employment methods in use at scientifically managed firms found "little uniformity" in selection and hiring techniques and "at best a separate labor department is established."[12]

The so-called social justice movement of the Progressive Era provided the other sources of a systematic approach to personnel management. The movement was peopled with middle-class professionals — social workers, settlement house workers, educators, and ministers — who shared the engineers' idealization of scientific expertise and rational administration. These individuals were imbued with a humanitarian ethic of uplift and social reform that made them more sympathetic than the engineers to the immigrant working class. Yet despite their humanitarianism, their writings and programs contained distinct strains of social control and elitism. The reformers in this group rationalized the stresses and strains of a rapidly industrializing society. The reforms they introduced helped to strengthen existing institutions and steer social change from more radical paths. Industrial welfare work and the crusade to reform the labor market were two branches of the social justice movement that had direct links to the emergence of professional personnel management.[13]

Welfare work

In 1914 the National Civic Federation listed over 2,500 companies that were engaged in some type of welfare or betterment work. One strand of welfare work may be traced to the period of recurring labor unrest between 1877 and 1894, when employers sought to undermine the unions, and to win the loyalty of their skilled workers away from them, through the use of quasi-pecuniary incentives such as profit sharing, pensions, and stock bonus plans. Another strand was rooted in the companies' belief that the cause of labor unrest, social tension, and a perceived decline in the work ethic was the worker — the intemperate, slothful worker or the ignorant, immigrant worker prey to radical nostrums. To uplift or better their employees, firms experimented with a variety of programs ranging from instruction in citizenship and child care, to thrift clubs and compulsory religion, to company housing, lunchrooms, outings, glee clubs, magazines, and contests. The idea was to use the firm to recast the worker in a middle-class mold, making him sedulous, sober, and loyal.

This paternalistic element in companies' welfare work reflected its origins in social work, mission work, and the settlement house movement. It was the private-sector analogue to the "search for order" that professional welfare workers then were conducting in American cities. Many of those engaged in industrial welfare work, as administrators and publicists, had backgrounds in those fields. They believed that their moralistic paternalism would improve workers' lives and change some of industry's cruder aspects. One early welfare worker said of her colleagues that they went into welfare work "with faith in its power to meliorate industrial conditions."[14]

Like the industrial engineers, welfare workers tried to scientize and professionalize their programs for industry. Conferences sponsored by the National Civic Federation and the Young Men's Christian Association brought together welfare workers from different firms to discuss the latest developments in the field. The new schools of social work and business offered courses in industrial welfare work. The claim that welfare workers had a special competence in building character and morale, in "human relations," became the justification for their authority in the firm.

Welfare workers regularly encountered resistance from line executives and foremen who resented intrusions into their domain. The welfare workers spoke a foreign language of morale, human relations, and sympathy. Line executives and foremen were interested only in cost, speed, and output. Welfare workers came to believe that conflicts with line management could be alleviated if their authority were vested in a separate department, free of interference from the line.[15]

By 1910 firms had begun to centralize their welfare programs in a single department with clearly defined responsibilities. A few of these departments were on a par with other major corporate divisions, but in most firms the welfare department remained subordinate to the manufacturing division. The welfare worker in these firms, said one observer, "has not yet been assimilated into the operating organization. . . . He deals largely with matters outside the regular routine of industry operations, he has to do primarily with the men while *off* the job rather than *on* the job. . . ." This explains the dearth of employment topics in the welfare work literature. Most welfare departments posed little real threat to the foreman's autonomy, since they lacked independent authority and a mandate to intervene in employment management. The drive system could and did coexist with paternalism.

However, welfare work created a distinctive role for the management of labor. Labor was becoming the province of the specialist, and labor-related policy was turning into a decision variable subject to rational determination. The specialization of function involved in the creation of welfare departments marked the beginning of efforts to develop employment policies that weren't subordinate to the firm's traditional short-run emphasis on production. This distinguished welfare work from forays by industrial engineers into the labor area, and these developments set a bureaucratic precedent for the personnel manager and the personnel department.[16]

Welfare work also gave future personnel managers an ideology of expertise that legitimated the scope of their corporate interventions. As specialists in human relations, personnel managers were expected to possess tact, sympathy, and "other qualities which tend to promote harmony all through the plant." The first American personnel management textbook, published in 1920, told the personnel manager of his "special need to know about people, about their physical and mental construction, about human nature." Personnel managers invoked their expertise in human relations to justify transferring authority away from the foreman. Thus, because "the foreman may not naturally be a good interviewer," hiring was supposed to be left to "a specialist known to be a good judge of men." Foremen were accused of insensitivity to workers' grievances, and the personnel manager was to be permitted to intervene in shop floor disputes because of his "diplomacy" and "broad understanding of human nature."

The human relations ideology in personnel management meshed with the contemporary ethos of uplift and expert-led reform. Henry S. Dennison, a prominent liberal employer, told a gathering of personnel managers in 1917, "You will humanize industry. You will give the corporation a soul." But personnel managers could not forget that any improvement in human relations was a means to the end of greater worker loyalty and effort. Many personnel managers saw no contradiction between their roles as workers' advocate and owners' representative. Yet some came to view their profession as an independent force for reform in industry. Events after World War I would serve to remind them that human relations and their professional identities could not be ends in themselves.[17]

Vocational guidance

American educators after the turn of the century came to believe that the primary goal of schooling was the efficient preparation of youth for the job market. Vocational schools and curricula were developed to link the schools more closely to industry and to satisfy what was presumed to be a less able group of immigrant students. Children of different class and ethnic backgrounds were said to differ greatly in their innate capacities and interests. Vocational education sought to match the "manually minded" child to his "destiny" in the labor market. The problem for vocational educators was to devise a democratic scheme to ensure that children would end up in the courses and schools that suited them. This was the task of vocational guidance: to allow children and parents to choose the education they wanted, but to make their choices consonant with the counselor's perception of need.[18]

Vocational guidance counselors turned to science to buttress the authority of their advice. In the burgeoning discipline of psychology they found scientific evidence of the heritability and variability of capacity, as well as scientific methods to classify individuals. Testing and classification were adopted as the preferred regimen for vocational counselors, being more persuasive than manipulation and cajolery. Vocational guidance became the science of allocating the manually minded to their appropriate niches and the art of scaling down their aspirations. This was a long way from the egalitarian common school ideology of the nineteenth century.[19]

There was, however, a group of educational and child labor reformers in the vocational guidance movement who believed that guidance should be more than an effort to fit children to particular curricula or jobs. Leading this group was Meyer Bloomfield, a former settlement house worker who had introduced vocational guidance to the Boston schools in 1910. Bloomfield organized the National Vocational Guidance Association in 1913 and was largely responsible for popularizing vocational counseling as a new profession.

Bloomfield had been heavily influenced by Great Britain's 1909 "Report of the Royal Commission on the Poor-Laws and Relief of Distress." He was impressed by the commission's finding that youth who entered "blind alley jobs" (casual employment) suffered high unemployment and long-term disadvantages in the labor market. Bloomfield thought that vocational guidance could be used to regulate the youth labor market by scrutinizing the jobs that employers offered those leaving school. If the schools were going to assist industry by training children in marketable skills, then they had the right to monitor employers to ensure that decent, stable jobs were provided.

Bloomfield's program for reforming the labor market via the schools included follow-ups on those leaving school, surveys of employment conditions in local industries, selective placement of graduates in exemplary jobs, and closer contacts with local employers. Vocational counselors were to encourage employers to rationalize their hiring procedures, educate and train their young workers, and promote from within.[20]

In 1914 Bloomfield began to have doubts that the schools were "the most suitable agency to attempt the organization of the labor market for the young." One educator observed in 1915 that few of his colleagues wanted "the responsibility of influencing the conditions of industry in favor of human welfare." The vocational guidance movement soon lost its reforming zeal as it became integrated into the educational bureaucracy. Bloomfield, still believing that vocational guidance would lead to "a more intelligent and generous treatment of employees by business leaders," redirected his energies from the schools to industry.[21]

While still active in the vocational guidance movement, Bloomfield founded the Employment Managers' Association of Boston (EMAB), the first organization of its kind in the United States. The EMAB was intended to be a professional association of local employment and personnel managers, but few firms in the Boston area had personnel departments when the group was formed in 1912 — and the same was true of the rest of the nation. Many of the early supporters of Bloomfield's efforts to promote professional personnel management were, like Bloomfield, proselytizers and reformers drawn from the ranks of the vocational guidance, industrial education, and labor market reform movements. Personnel management was not well known outside of those movements and a few progressive firms. It was an idea whose time had not quite yet come, although the efforts of Bloomfield and others to spread its concepts and techniques laid the foundation for its phenomenal growth after 1915.

Bloomfield and his supporters thought that the establishment of personnel departments would bring to industry "some idea of what fitness and future means in the career of the worker." Professional personnel managers would introduce vocational methods to industry and thus ensure that school graduates continued to receive guidance and training. Bloomfield advocated, and personnel departments later adopted, such vocational techniques as written job specifications, internal promotion plans, and rational selection procedures. Bloomfield stressed the importance of scientific hiring methods and carefully following up on new workers. These techniques were supposed to rationalize the labor market, make employment less casual, and provide something akin to a career for manual workers.[22]

Bloomfield also thought that the establishment of personnel departments would "help unravel the tangled web" of youth and adult unemployment. Other labor market reformers in groups like the American Association for Labor Legislation (AALL) were attracted to the idea of organizing the labor market through voluntary, private measures as an alternative to national labor exchanges and unemployment insurance. The AALL claimed that personnel departments could permanently reduce unemployment levels by making hiring and firing more efficient, by administering transfers in lieu of layoffs, and by taking other steps to stabilize employment.

Liberal followers of Frederick W. Taylor and his Taylor Society became ardent advocates of the new approach to unemployment, because it held the promise that a major social problem could be solved by the same efficient managerial techniques then being applied to production. This brought the industrial engineers into the ranks of what was to become a national personnel management movement. During the depression of 1914 and 1915, groups sprang up in major cities to discuss unemployment problems and promote personnel management by local employers. The groups were organized by Bloomfield, as well as by members of the Taylor Society and the AALL. The first national conference of personnel managers was held in 1916, and when a national association was founded in 1918, these groups were chartered as local chapters.[23]

Thus the disparate strands that would compose the personnel

management movement were being twisted together in the years before America's entry into World War I. Efficiency, the engineers' watchword, with its connotations of scientific method and bureaucratic order, infused the welfare work and vocational guidance movements at the same time that employment reform began to be taken seriously by the engineers.

Common to all three groups and the personnel management movement they gave rise to was the ascendance of the expert, the professional reformer and problem solver. The roots of personnel management are to be found not only in the technical imperatives imposed by the increased size and complexity of firms — which created the empty slots in the managerial hierarcy — but also in the professional ideology of those who filled these slots. As it was adapted to an industrial setting, this ideology implied that personnel managers were to be a third force in the firm; their professional ethics and neutral stance would mitigate industrial conflict. Bloomfield thought that personnel managers should serve "in a unique mediating capacity." Others stressed the importance of maintaining an independent personnel department as "the only place in the plant where the outside point of view gets in."

Those in the personnel management movement who were most concerned with the issue of professionalism tended to be the persons most sympathetic to the unions. An emphasis on professional standards and ideals linked the movement to an agenda of priorities beyond the employer's short-term interests. Men like Bloomfield, Morris L. Cooke, and Boyd Fisher, as well as former socialists like Algie Simons and Ordway Tead, believed that professional personnel management could introduce enlightened ideas about collective bargaining to industry. The precise relation of the personnel manager to the union rarely was specified, but these liberals envisioned some sort of joint control exercised by judicious managers and responsible, accommodative trade unions. Professionalism protected the movement's progressive character at the same time that it made its ends more acceptable to workers. Bloomfield had what he admitted was a "fanciful" idea that someday workers would pay part of the personnel manager's salary.[24]

World War I

The personnel management movement grew rapidly after 1915 with the onset of war-induced labor shortages and a massive increase in strikes. By 1920 personnel departments had been created in one out of every four manufacturing establishments employing more than 250 workers. The federal government helped to speed the adoption of personnel departments by training hundreds of personnel managers in wartime emergency courses. Various wartime labor agencies promoted personnel management, believing it would standardize conditions in war industries and thus reduce the likelihood of disputes. Popular and academic publications carried numerous articles on "the new profession of handling men." The 1920 convention of the Industrial Relations Association of America, a national organization of personnel managers, attracted more than two thousand participants.[25]

Personnel managers made deep raids into the foreman's territory during and after the war. Recruiting and selecting employees was the most common function taken over by the new personnel departments. In other areas, such as wage determination, promotions, and transfers, personnel departments introduced uniform rules and procedures that curbed the foreman's discretion. Personnel managers also appropriated the foreman's disciplinary and discharge prerogatives. Foremen were more resentful of this aspect of personnel management than any other. They considered their drive system of harsh discipline and quick dismissals to be essential to maintaining order on the shop floor. That a worker could appeal a discharge to the personnel department was said to be "demoralizing to the discipline of the factory." The personnel manager's ideal of an independent, professional department brought him into head-on conflicts with foremen and other line managers.[26]

Foremen had powerful allies in their fight with personnel managers. Plant superintendents and works managers often took the foreman's side in disputes with the personnel department. This was a problem that the industrial engineers had never encountered. Production officials were skeptical of the new employment methods, because they led to few immediate, easily measured improvements in output or cost. The restraints that personnel managers imposed on foremen were viewed as a hindrance to the goal of high-speed production. Personnel managers complained that they had a harder time "selling" personnel management to production executives than to foremen. They invoked their professional independence to alleviate these conflicts, and they called for strong personnel departments with a status equal to that of the firm's other functional divisions.

Employers tolerated these conflicts in the face of unprecedented labor scarcity and militance. The traditional system for maintaining effort and discipline no longer was effective with unemployment at rock-bottom levels. Labor productivity sank while quit rates rose. Personnel management promised to alleviate these problems by improving worker morale and the firm's capacity to retain labor. It also weakened the potential appeal of trade unions by preempting the reforms that skilled workers had been pushing for, themselves. For less skilled workers, personnel management brought many of the benefits that the trade union had given to the more skilled, including allocation by rule, enhanced employment security, and rudimentary grievance mechanisms. Sumner Slichter wondered if personnel management wasn't "a backfire against unionism, an attempt to forestall changes in industrial government by changes in managerial methods."

Yet others saw the mitigation of the drive system by bureaucratic controls as a notable instance of managerial self-restraint. Sidney Hillman, president of the Amalgamated Clothing Workers Union, addressed a conference of personnel managers in 1920 and noted that personnel departments had begun to curb the influence of production elements in management. He expressed the hope that this shift of power would continue in the future. Professional personnel management was a force for the reform of traditional employment methods, although it was held back by the persistence of old attitudes and beliefs.[27]

The ideology of the drive system continued to exert a strong hold on line managers and employers despite the efforts of personnel managers to convince them of the virtues of an alternative approach. In 1919, Joseph Willits, a prominent economist, pointed to the prevalence of "the Bourbon employer" who felt that "the events of the war have justified his previous beliefs as to the essential depravity of American workmen." Willits thought that the war had hardened, rather than softened, the employer's belief that restraint led to a reduction in effort and discipline. The persistence of this ideology — that liberality undermined discipline, that foremen had to be upheld in disputes with workers, that labor was a commodity — made it difficult for personnel managers to expand their influence either within or beyond the minority of firms that had initiated personnel departments by 1920.

The 1920s

By mid-1920 it was evident that the beliefs that had stymied the progress of personnel management were growing in intensity. An open-shop movement spread from state to state, while the Red Scare hysteria gripped the nation. Postwar hopes for social reconstruction and cooperation were replaced by calls for a "return for normalcy." Hostility to Progressive reform movements became widespread. A prominent personnel manager warned that if labor markets softened, employers would "seize with avidity what they consider a long-deferred opportunity to put the screws down."[28]

A split appeared in the personnel management movement several months before the onset of the depression of 1921 and 1922. A conservative faction in the movement launched a broad attack on their more liberal colleagues. It is not clear whether they were motivated by a genuine disagreement with the liberals or by fears about their own futures. Yet they were able to articulate a program for the movement that was more in tune with the new mood of the times, a mood that was to prevail throughout the 1920s.

The most common charge leveled by the conservatives was that personnel managers had gone too far in blaming the foreman for industry's problems and stripping him of his authority. They argued that foremen should be given greater discretion to allocate, discipline, and discharge workers. The personnel department was to be a staff auxiliary to the production division rather than an independent department. In this new view, the personnel manager no longer would be an impartial force for change within the firm; he would have to give up his professional pretensions. The new model of personnel management promised to restore allocational flexibility and preserve authority relations on the shop floor at a time when calls for "a return to business principles" and a reassertion of discipline were on the increase. Those personnel managers who adopted this model presumably would stand the greatest chance of weathering the oncoming depression.[29]

The depression revealed that a personnel department was not essential to the maintenance of either morale, effort, or stability. Unemployment rates in manufacturing reached over 20 percent in 1921. With this came a decline in strikes and turnover, as well as a sharp increase in labor productivity. Many firms cut back or completely eliminated their personnel departments during the depression. One employer noted, "People are now willing to work hard and do it more cheerfully than heretofore. Therefore, personnel departments as such are not so great." Personnel departments that survived the depression lost their status as independent units and were integrated into manufacturing or production divisions. Ordway Tead estimated in 1923 that there was only a handful of establishments where the personnel manager still held a major administrative post. A 1923 survey of personnel departments that were still in existence found a marked tendency toward decentralization of what was termed the "control" of personnel activities.[30]

Although these moves were touted as cost-cutting necessities, the decline of personnel management had more to do with the desire to restore discipline. In 1928, after the dust had long settled, the director of the American Management Association said that "more personnel men lost their jobs because they were given and used too much authority, because they usurped the prerogatives of the line organizations and consequently interfered with normal disciplinary procedure, than because of business depression." After the depression, personnel departments conformed to the new model of personnel management. Foremen assumed many of their old prerogatives, and personnel managers were restricted from interfering in the allocation, payment, and disciplining of workers. Personnel management faded from public attention during the quiescent labor atmosphere of the 1920s. The proportion of large establishments with personnel departments grew much more slowly than before, rising from 25 percent in 1920 to 34 percent in 1929.[31]

Throughout the 1920s the American Management Association (AMA) was the leading exponent of the decentralized, conservative model of personnel management. The AMA called for giving the foreman, who was termed "a teacher and a diplomat," complete autonomy in the daily management of employees. The personnel manager merely would "supply the tools" that others would use to manage employment. An AMA executive said that the time was past for "building castles in the air about independent industrial relations departments owing allegiance to nobody." The idea of professionalism in personnel management now was viewed as archaic or worse. Arthur H. Young, one of the founders of the AMA, predicted that "Those employment managers who have looked upon their jobs as more or less professional will probably find that they have no more jobs left."[32]

Liberals in the personnel management movement were bitter about the shift away from professionalism and reform. Mary B. Gilson castigated the AMA for "turning the clock back a considerable distance in regard to the development of centralization in the selection and training of workers as well as in safeguarding discharges, because of their blind zeal in defending what they called the foremen's 'rights.' " Morris L. Cooke, a champion of professional ethics in engineering and president of the Taylor Society in the 1920s, criticized the AMA for being "essentially a mutual-aid organization and not a professional society."

The decentralized model of personnel management left the foreman with considerable power, yet firms with personnel departments still were relatively more attractive places to work during the 1920s. Many other firms did not initiate personnel departments during the 1920s or failed to replace the departments they had discontinued during the depression. At these firms, said economist Leo Wolman, "there was a reversion to older methods."[33]

Modern Personnel Management

The heyday of unionism, 1933–1960

Personnel management experienced a renaissance in the wake of the New Deal and a surge in labor organization. The spread of collective bargaining elevated the status and authority of the personnel department. A personnel manager at a large nonunion firm noted that the new wave of unionism had given the personnel department "a function of great importance in management's eyes." Newly created or beefed-up personnel departments began to implement definite employment and grievance procedures to ward off unionization. At other firms, personnel departments were not established until after a union had organized their employees. The proportion of large establishments with personnel departments rose dramatically from 34 percent in 1929 to 64 percent in 1935.

Most personnel managers and trade unionists had no great love for each other. But their mutual interest in restraining foremen, improving morale, and developing rules to guide employment decisions led to a partial coalescence of the goals of the two movements. As before, personnel managers assimilated union goals by creating a bureaucratic structure of restraint, equity, and security. The new unions assimilated management's goals by making reasonable demands that in effect furthered the project initiated by personnel managers during World War I. The result was a rapid expansion in the use of centralized, bureaucratic employment procedures after 1933.[34]

Foremen now were subjected to sharp pressures from above and below. They complained that the personnel department took away their responsibilities, did not solicit their advice, and failed to back them up in disputes with employees — complaints that were similar to those heard between 1916 and 1920. But extensive unionization created new difficulties for the foreman. Union grievance mechanisms, allocational rules, and bargaining processes took away much of his power and authority. One industrial relations expert noted in 1940 that foremen "no longer controlled the employment of the men who worked under them; even if they did recommend the discharge of an incompetent worker, the union usually could get him reinstated; they no longer had a say in the setting of production standards. . . . In general, they were pretty well kicked around by both sides." The foreman was becoming the forgotten man of management.

In contrast to the foreman, the personnel manager now enjoyed unprecedented authority. Personnel departments expanded in size and were placed on an equal footing with other management divisions. Liberal conceptions of personnel management as a third force crept back into prominence in this atmosphere of resurgence.

Personnel managers again imagined themselves to be the men in the middle who would bring workers and managers to a better understanding of each other. Harold F. North, personnel manager at Swift, wrote in 1940 that "the good personnel man must be absolutely sincere in his determination to be fair to both management and employees. . . . He carries no brief for either. It will be impossible for him to be impartial in his judgment if he has any axes to grind." Yet in unionized firms it now was more difficult for personnel managers to project themselves as being an impartial, third force. The unions had become deeply and widely entrenched. Adversarial industrial relations precluded independent personnel management.[35]

Personnel departments in nonunion firms had relatively more leeway to function as a third force. In these settings personnel managers emphasized their neutrality and their independent role as guarantors of the employee's "rights." James C. Worthy of Sears, Roebuck argued that the personnel manager should help to build democratic ideals within the firm, including "fundamental notions of participation, human dignity [and] freedom to speak one's piece." But Worthy, like some of his predecessors during the 1920s, was skeptical of the claim that personnel managers could function as independent professionals. "To be effective," said Worthy, "the basis of personnel administration must be the individual business organization. The object of the personnel manager should be closer and more effective integration within his own organization." Worthy argued that personnel management could never achieve, nor should it strive for, the independence of other professions. In a nonunion establishment, it was more important that the personnel manager appear as an independent professional, but less desirable that he act like one.[36]

Although it was difficult to recreate the earlier model of personnel professionalism, new elements entered into personnel management after 1933 that bolstered its professional image. One of these was a set of sophisticated, science-based personnel techniques initially developed by university researchers. Starting in the 1920s, academics from several disciplines had begun to study the determinants of employee attitudes, particularly employee "morale," which was variously interpreted as esprit de corps or employee loyalty. As in other kinds of attitude research, psychologists relied on data derived from standardized questionnaires, while sociologists and anthropologists tended to favor more quantitative information, such as that obtained in the studies at Western Electric's Hawthorne plant. In trying to shed light on the link between supervision and morale, the Hawthorne researchers developed the method of nondirective interviewing, which encouraged workers to discuss freely with an interviewer whatever was on their mind.[37]

Elton Mayo, a Harvard Business School professor, wrote several influential books that summarized the Hawthorne research for a lay audience. Mayo is credited with sensitizing managers to the importance of psychological motives and the role of informal social groups in the workplace. During the 1940s, a group of university-based researchers who sought to extend Mayo's insights and apply them to industry came to be known as the "human relations" movement. In contrast to earlier strands in personnel management, human relations was less concerned with using the workplace as a stepping stone to social reform. Also, it had little to say about bureaucratic employment methods, and what it *did* say was often critical. Rather than focus on employment structures, the human relations researchers turned their attention to the worker's psyche and to his personal relationships at work, particularly the relationship between employee and supervisor. During the Second World War, the government's Training within Industry (TWI) program — developed by Mayo's colleague Fritz Roethlisberger — used public funds to teach foremen how to "work with people" and to "treat people as individuals." Through the use of sophisticated behavioral techniques like sociodrama, sociometry, and role playing, foremen were trained to be gentle persuaders. TWI boasted that the course, which was given to half a million foremen in private industry, raised war production by reducing conflict and dissatisfaction at work.[38]

In light of these claims, union leaders and their supporters became suspicious of the behavioral scientists who were promoting human relations. A slew of prominent social scientists — including Daniel Bell, Reinhard Bendix, and Clark Kerr — attacked the human relations school for its unitary premises and disregard of unions. As consultants to industry, the human relations researchers were castigated as "servants of power" and "cow sociologists" because they purportedly helped employers to manipulate their employees and to suppress unions. But the critics missed some important points. First, few of them directed their fire at the new techniques for managing small groups developed by Kurt Lewin and his followers, techniques that would later become critical to the "team approach" developed in the 1970s. Second, while the ideas of prominent researchers like Mayo and Roethlisberger were heavily criticized, the critics spent less time considering how human relations ideas were translated into industrial practice.[39]

Along with foreman training, a widely used human relations technique was the employee attitude survey. Attitude surveys helped managers to pinpoint employee problems and rectify them before they became a festering issue that might attract union organizers to a nonunion firm or cause a strike in a unionized setting. In unionized firms, surveys allowed managers to bypass the union as a source of information on worker attitudes and thus stay one step ahead in the competition for employee loyalty. A surge in the use of attitude surveys occurred after the Second World War: each year after 1944 saw a steady increase in the number of firms using surveys and by 1954, about two in five large firms had conducted at least one survey. What accounts for this surge? Obviously a primary factor was management's attempt to reduce the tensions associated with the rise of mass unionism and governmental regulation of the labor market. But another factor was the creation of stronger linkages between personnel managers and consultants based or trained in the universities. Because of their numerous contributions to the war effort, behavioral and social scientists enjoyed great prestige outside the university after the war. Managers were more eager than ever before to hire them as technical consultants to design employee relations programs. One psychologist said in 1948 that managers had become "psychologically-minded," ready to embrace the notion that "the whole question of efficiency boils down to one thing: understanding the MOTIVATIONS of your employees and taking steps to SATISFY them." By 1948, 30 percent of large corporations had a psychologist on staff, while others employed sociologists, psychiatrists, and anthropologists.[40]

As attitude testing and leadership training were catching on in the corporate world, research on these subjects was burgeoning in the universities. Three times as many studies relating job factors to employee attitudes were published between 1950 and 1954 as had appeared between 1940 and 1944. The military — through agencies such as the Office of Naval Research — heavily supported research in these areas, including the Ohio State University studies of leadership and the employee morale studies done at the University of Michigan's Institute for Social Research. Private companies also funded many of these studies by hiring university researchers to survey their employees and by contributing funds for the development of survey instruments. For example, in 1950 the personnel department at

Sears, Roebuck commissioned the University of Chicago's Industrial Relations Center to develop an attitude survey that Sears and other companies could use. These ties among government, universities, and corporate personnel departments were not unprecedented; similar nexuses had existed during the First World War. What *was* new was the large volume of subsidized research and the extent to which behavioral scientists and personnel managers became dependent on each other.[41]

The relationship between personnel managers and behavioral scientists was symbiotic; both sides profited from it. For behavioral scientists, industry provided research issues, research sites, consulting fees, and support for the new industrial relations institutes established after the war. To take advantage of these opportunities, academics had to learn a whole new etiquette for establishing cooperative relationships with business clients. For personnel managers, linking up with university-trained researchers had several advantages. First, it provided technical assistance in solving various personnel "problems." Second, it conferred legitimacy on personnel managers and on the new science-based personnel techniques, casting both of them in the light of neutral, scientific reason. For example, when Pitney Bowes hired researchers from Dartmouth's Tuck School to conduct an attitude survey, the employees were given a brochure containing photographs of Dartmouth, of sealed cartons being loaded into a car headed there, and of the Tuck researchers tabulating the survey data.[42]

Conscious of their status as semiprofessionals and seeking to bolster it, personnel managers in the late 1940s and 1950s experienced a burst of professional consciousness. New professional associations were formed, along with professional journals and codes of ethics. In addition to behavioral science, the personnel manager's domain of professional knowledge included familiarity with government labor regulations — everything from the Fair Labor Standards Act to the National Labor Relations Act to wage controls — and with the arcana of collective bargaining. Inside the universities, business schools and the new industrial relations institutes offered specialized degrees certifying knowledge in these areas. Enrollments boomed in the postwar years, when personnel was seen as a "hot" field for returning GIs to enter.[43]

During these years, however, the gap widened between "labor relations" and "employee relations." Labor relations departments, found in unionized firms, increasingly concerned themselves with collective bargaining and contract administration. Few labor relations managers had time to delve deeply into behavioral science issues, and they often were skeptical of them. However, some unionized firms created separate employee relations departments to manage day-to-day employee matters exclusive of the collective bargaining relationship; this was where the new behavioral science approach took hold. Exceptionally effective in this regard was General Motors, the first of the big three automobile manufacturers to develop a coherent industrial relations strategy after the war. The GM approach was Janus-like; the unions were faced with a tough adversary in bargaining and contract administration, while the employees saw a more human visage as the company sought to establish direct personal ties with them. The company created an employee relations department in 1945, whose director, Harry B. Coen, was an ardent opponent of unionism. Said Coen, "I do not believe in making the union contact the only one between our employees and ourselves. . . . I am hopeful that we as a staff can deal with it in such a manner that the union aspect will be only one little segment, or whatever segment it cares to be." Among other duties, Coen's department was in charge of conducting attitude surveys at GM plants around the country.[44]

Things did not always go smoothly at General Motors. The problem for Coen (and for employee relations managers at other unionized firms) was that unions were quick to condemn attitude surveys and other such projects as efforts to bypass, undermine, and weaken the union. Also, union leaders boldly disparaged claims to neutrality made by employee relations managers and their consultants. One union official told a conference of managers: "Whereas you gentlemen present yourselves to the workers as specialists and as technicians and as detached professionals, they sort of chew at the end of their cigars, or spit after they have swallowed a little tobacco from the end of their cigarettes, and say, "Yes, but who is paying you?" To make matters more complex, employee and labor relations managers occasionally found themselves in conflict with each other. The labor relations department wanted smooth relations with the union and judged its performance by strike and grievance-rate levels. The employee relations department, however, looked at measures of employee morale, which were weakly related to (or even negatively correlated with) the presence of a union.

In partially unionized companies like TRW, employee relations departments worked at keeping new plants union-free, while labor relations departments sought to establish "mature" relations with unions in already organized plants. Of course, such problems did not exist in nonunion firms. As a result, large nonunion firms (and the employee relations departments of some unionized companies, such as AT&T) formed the seedbed for a new approach to personnel management, one that first appeared in the 1960s.[45]

Developments since 1960: Human resource management

The so-called new human resource management (which has made "personnel management" archaic) is based on techniques whose origins lie in psychological and social scientific research on the workplace. Starting in the late 1960s American corporations began to speed up their adoption of these techniques, both recent innovations and more traditional approaches. For example, the proportion of manufacturing firms conducting attitude surveys rose from 21 percent in 1963 to 45 percent in 1981. Newer techniques also appeared, including those associated with the quality of work life (QWL) and a variety of organization development methods such as participative problem solving, task forces, team building, and employee involvement programs. While the precise mix of techniques varied from company to company, once a firm used some of them, it was more likely to adopt others. Nonunion companies, with their early start in this area, were the first to implement the new human resource management en bloc.[46]

There were other reasons for the association of "new" and "nonunion." Nonunion firms (and nonunion divisions of partially unionized companies) typically were the fastest growing companies of the day, hence they had sufficient resources (what economists term "organizational slack") to experiment and innovate. Also, nonunion companies employed relatively large numbers of white-collar technical and professional workers, a highly educated group with special needs. Managing these employees required personnel policies that promoted communication and small group decision making, precisely the outcomes that could be achieved with attitude surveys and organizational development (OD) techniques. Finally, human resource managers in these nonunion firms were more "psychologically minded" than their colleagues in older, unionized companies. While human resource managers in nonunion firms came from a variety of backgrounds, those in charge of labor relations in unionized firms increasingly had backgrounds in a single discipline — the law — which reflected the growing regulatory complexity of labor-management relations. They were therefore less comfortable dealing with behavioral scientists and slower to appreciate the advantages that could be derived from new techniques like OD.[47]

But even heavily unionized firms eventually jumped on the human resource management bandwagon. This was partly a response to the economic problems confronting them. Many were old-line industrial firms that hoped the new human resource management would allow them to compete more successfully in an increasingly competitive world market (as was the case with the Saturn project at General Motors). Another impetus was a managerial sense that unions had become vulnerable. Union organization in the private sector was in decline throughout most of the 1960s and 1970s. Inside unionized firms, power shifted from the labor relations function to employee relations managers, as companies adopted a more aggressive posture. Priorities shifted from maintaining stability in union-management relations to confronting weak unions and, where possible, undermining or even eliminating them. As a result of such internal power shifts, human resource managers in unionized firms today are less likely to accept the inevitability of unions. And they are less skeptical of behavioral science techniques than were their predecessors of the 1950s. Thus, the human resource functions in unionized and nonunion firms have more in common with each other now than they did 40 or 50 years ago.[48]

Today there still is a professional strain in human resource management, although it is unclear precisely how deeply it runs. A survey of American human resource executives found slightly more than one-half exhibiting a strong to moderate professional orientation based on their attachment to their occupation and their interest in the field as a whole. Professional organizations and journals exist in abundance, as do specialized degree programs in the universities. Within nonunion companies, human resource departments administer employee complaint systems, and they try — not always with success — to serve as a neutral mediator between employees and line management. These developments would have pleased early advocates of a professional approach to personnel management.[49]

But professionalism today has a more restricted meaning than it did 80 years ago. Few modern human resource managers conceive of themselves as agents of social change within their organizations. Instead, professionalism — including the reliance on behavioral science jargon — often is little more than a technocratic gambit to secure greater prestige and pay within the corporate hierarchy. The strategy has not been without success. A survey of Fortune 500 companies found that, at an increasing rate, companies are elevating their top human resource managers to higher levels within the organization, often to positions that report directly to the company's chief executive officer. Thus, the modern human resource manager is more often a part of management, and management is not the independent force for reform that men like Brandeis, Taylor, and Bloomfield hoped it might prove to be. Also, it is difficult for human resource managers to maintain a thoroughly professional orientation, since, as James Worthy warned, "sooner or later loyalty to the profession is likely to come into conflict with loyalty to the organization." The human resource manager has to steer a tricky course between a professional and a managerial orientation, between advocacy and adjustment, and between equity and costs. Like their counterparts of an earlier period, today's human resource managers still risk ostracism by their fellow managers if they veer too much toward advocacy of the employees' rights.[50]

Yet we are entering new and uncharted waters. The great upsurge of unionization that lasted from 1933 to 1960 is over. So is the period of union shrinkage that lasted roughly from the 1960s into the 1990s. By the year 2000, private-sector unionization is likely to be so low (it is predicted to reach less than 5 percent of the labor force) that little further shrinkage will be likely to occur. The upsurge of unionism marked a period when stable job structures and bureaucratic personnel management took hold; its current decline is occurring as firms adopt more individualized and behaviorally sophisticated forms of employment.

What is the future likely to hold? In part this question turns on the ability of the new human resource management to provide a satisfying substitute for unionism. The experience of the 1920s — when a weakened labor movement led some companies to shrink or close their personnel departments — suggests that retrogression of this kind is not unlikely. Indeed, in some companies the new human resource management has brought a weakening of bureaucratic job structures for so-called contingent (part-time or temporary) employees. Whether unions will be able to capitalize on any future discontent, as they did in the 1930s, in turn will depend on their ability to again develop new forms of workplace representation appropriate to a more educated and individualistic work force.

There is reason to believe that human resource managers may once again become linked to larger movements for societal change. During the 1980s, human resource managers often found themselves to be the chief advocates for affirmative action policies inside their organization. And with the new national search for economic competitiveness, it is possible that human resource managers will become more involved with public education and urban public policy, just like their predecessors in the Progressive Era.

Notes

1. Charles R. Milton, *Ethics and Expediency in Personnel Management: A Critical History of Personnel Philosophy* (Columbia: University of South Carolina Press, 1970); Cyril C. Ling, *The Management of Personnel Relations: History and Origins* (Homewood, Ill.: R. D. Irwin, 1965); Leonard R. Sayles and George Strauss, *Managing Human Resources* (Englewood Cliffs, N.J.: Prentice-Hall, 1977): 3–68; Raymond Villers, *Dynamic Management in Industry* (Englewood Cliffs, N.J.: Prentice Hall, 1960): 75–114.
2. Thomas H. Patten, Jr., *The Foreman: Forgotten Man of Management* (New York: American Management Association, 1969); Frederick W. Taylor, *The Principles of Scientific Management* (New York: Harper, 1911): 31–32; Daniel Nelson, *Managers and Workers: Origins of the New Factory System in the U.S., 1880–1920* (Madison: University of Wisconsin Press, 1975): 34–42; Dan Clawson, *Bureaucracy and the Labor Process: The Transformation of U.S. Industry, 1860–1920* (New York: Monthly Review Press, 1980): 71–166; David Montgomery, "Workers' Control of Machine Production in the Nineteenth Century, *Labor History* 17 (Fall 1976): 486–492; Benson Soffer, "A Theory of Trade Union Development: The Role of the 'Autonomous' Workman," *Labor History* 1 (Spring 1960): 141–163; "The Characteristics of a Foreman," *Engineering Magazine* 36 (February 1909): 847.
3. Sumner H. Slichter, *The Turnover of Factory Labor* (New York: Appleton, 1919): 372; Joseph H. Willits, "Steadying Employment," *The Annals* 65 (May 1916): 72; H. Keith Trask, "The Problem of the Minor Executive," *Engineering Magazine* 38 (January 1910): 501; Fred H. Rindge, Jr., "From Boss to Foreman," *Industrial Management* 53 (July 1917): 508–509; C. J. Morrison, "Short-Sighted Methods in Dealing with Labor," *Engineering Magazine* 46 (January 1914): 568; David Brody, *Steelworkers in America: The Nonunion Era* (Cambridge, Mass.: Harvard University Press, 1960): 120.
4. Slichter, *Turnover*: 319, 202; John P. Frey and John R. Commons, "Conciliation in the Stove Industry," U.S. Bureau of Labor Statistics *Bulletin* no. 62 (Washington, D.C.: U.S. Government Printing Office, 1906): 128; Ernest M. Hopkins, "A Functionalized Employment Department as a Factor in Industrial Efficiency," *The Annals* 61 (September 1915): 117; John R. Commons, "Labor Conditions in Meat Packing and the Recent Strike," *Quarterly Journal of Economics* 19 (November 1904): 8. Driving occurred under daywork systems, where the effort wage was indeterminate, as well as in the new incentive wage systems, which were calculated to reduce unit costs as output rose. But it also was prevalent in piecework, partly in response to workers' restriction of output. Lloyd Ulman, *The Rise of the*

National Trade Union (Cambridge, Mass.: Harvard University Press, 1955): 549–551.

5. Alexander Keyssar, *Out of Work: The First Century of Unemployment in Massachusetts* (Cambridge: Cambridge University Press, 1986); Dwight T. Farnham, "Adjusting the Employment Department to the Rest of the Plant," *Industrial Management* 58 (September 1919): 202; Jacob H. Hollander and George E. Barnett, *Studies in American Trade Unionism* (New York: Holt, 1906); David A. McCabe, *The Standard Rate in American Trade Unions* (Baltimore: Johns Hopkins University Press, 1912); Sumner H. Slichter, *Union Policies and Industrial Management* (Washington, D.C.: Brookings Institution, 1941); Harry A. Millis and Royal E. Montgomery, *Organized Labor* (New York: McGraw-Hill, 1945): 389–485; Ulman, *The Rise of the National Trade Union*: 305–333, 536–566.

6. Frederick W. Taylor, *Shop Management* (New York: Harper, 1919): 110, 122; Joseph A. Litterer, "Systematic Management: The Search for Order and Integration," *Business History Review* 35 (Winter 1961); Alfred D. Chandler, Jr., *The Visible Hand: The Managerial Revolution in American Business* (Cambridge, Mass.: Harvard University Press, 1977): 280–281; Joseph A. Litterer, "Systematic Management: Design for Organizational Recoupling in American Manufacturing Firms," *Business History Review* 37 (Winter 1963); Henry Towne, "The Engineer as Economist," *Transactions of the ASME* 7 (1886); Harrington Emerson, *Efficiency as a Basis for Operation and Wages* (New York: Efficiency Press, 1912); Reinhard Bendix, *Work and Authority in Industry: Ideologies of Management in the Course of Industrialization* (New York: Wiley, 1956): 214–218.

7. Miner Chipman, *Efficiency, Scientific Management and Labor* (New York: Harper, 1916): 65; Frederick W. Taylor, "A Piece Rate System: A Step Toward Partial Solution of the Labor Problem," *Transactions of the ASME*, 16 (1895); C. Bertrand Thompson, "Wages and Wage Systems as Incentives," in Thompson (ed.), *Scientific Management: A Collection of the More Significant Articles Describing the Taylor System of Management* (Cambridge, Mass.: Harvard University Press, 1914). Among those who argue that engineering made few contributions to personnel management are Leland H. Jenks, "Early Phases of the Management Movement," *Administrative Science Quarterly* 5 (December 1960): 430; and Daniel Nelson, *Managers and Workers*: 78. Braverman impressively documents the effect of scientific management on the skilled worker, although he downplays the very similar effect on the foreman. Harry Braverman, *Labor and Monopoly Capital* (New York: Monthly Review Press, 1974).

8. Henry Eilbirt, "The Development of Personnel Management in the United States," *Business History Review* 33 (Autumn 1959): 346; Fred W. Climer, "Cutting Labor Cost in Seasonal Business," *Manufacturing Industries* 13 (May 1927).

9. Monte Calvert, *The Mechanical Engineer in America, 1830–1910: Professional Cultures in Conflict* (Baltimore: Johns Hopkins University Press, 1967): 63–85, 189–195; Edwin T. Layton, *The Revolt of the Engineers*

(Cleveland: Case Western Reserve Press, 1971): 57–69, 140; Samuel Haber, *Efficiency and Uplift: Scientific Management in the Progressive Era, 1890–1910* (Chicago: University of Chicago Press, 1964): 55; Daniel Nelson, *Frederick W. Taylor and the Rise of Scientific Management* (Madison: University of Wisconsin Press, 1980): 181–180; Henry Towne, "The General Principles of Organization Applied to an Individual Manufacturing Establishment," *Transactions of the Efficiency Society* 1 (1912).

10. Meyer Bloomfield, "What Is an Employment Manager?" *Industrial Management* 52 (March 1917): 879; Melvin T. Copeland, *And Mark an Era: The Story of the Harvard Business School* (Boston: Little, Brown, 1958): 26, 159; Elliot Goodwin, "Is There a Profession of Business and Can We Really Train for It?" *Transactions of the Efficiency Society* 5 (June 1916); Louis D. Brandeis, *Business: A Profession* (Boston: Small Maynard, 1914); Thomas N. Carver, "The Redistribution of Human Talent," *Transactions of the Efficiency Society* 1 (1912): 363.

11. Slichter, *Turnover:* 409–410.

12. Robert F. Hoxie, *Scientific Management and Labor* (New York: Appleton, 1915): 31–32; Walter M. McFarland, "The Basic Cause of Increased Efficiency," *Engineering Magazine* 36 (December 1908).

13. Samuel P. Hays, *The Response to Industrialism, 1885–1914* (Chicago: University of Chicago Press, 1957): 71–115; Robert H. Wiebe, *The Search for Order: 1877–1920* (New York: Hill & Wang, 1967); Roy Lubove, *The Professional Altruist: The Emergence of Social Work as a Career* (Cambridge, Mass.: Harvard University Press, 1965); Allen F. Davis, *Spearheads for Reform: The Social Settlements and the Progressive Movement, 1890–1914* (New York: Oxford University Press, 1967).

14. Edward Berkowitz and Kim McQuaid, "Businessman and Bureaucrat: The Evolution of the American Social Welfare System, 1900–1940," *Journal of Economic History* 38 (March 1978): 124; Stuart Brandes, *American Welfare Capitalism, 1880–1940* (Chicago: University of Chicago Press, 1976); Robert Ozanne, *A Century of Labor-Management Relations at McCormick and International Harvester* (Madison: University of Wisconsin Press, 1967): 32–40; Arthur Mann, *Yankee Reformers in the Urban Age* (Cambridge, Mass.: Harvard University Press, 1954): 84–85; Mary Barnett Gilson, *What's Past Is Prologue: Reflections on My Industrial Experience* (New York: Harper, 1940): ix.

15. Stephen J. Scheinberg, "The Development of Corporation Labor Policy, 1900–1940" (Ph.D. diss., University of Wisconsin, Madison, 1966): 21–75; Mary B. Gilson, "The Relation of Home Conditions to Industrial Efficiency," *The Annals* 65 (May 1916): 278–279; Mary Van Kleeck, "The Professionalization of Social Work," *The Annals* 101 (May 1922).

16. Charles U. Carpenter, "The Working of a Labor Department in Industrial Establishments," *Engineering Magazine* 25 (April 1903); L. A. Boettiger, *Employee Welfare Work: A Critical and Historical Study* (New York: Ronald Press, 1923): 128; Slichter, *Turnover:* 431–434.

17. Fred H. Colvin, *Labor Turnover, Loyalty and Output* (New York:

McGraw-Hill, 1919), 108; Ordway Tead and Henry C. Metcalf, *Personnel Administration: Its Principles and Practice* (New York: McGraw-Hill, 1920): 5; Slichter, *Turnover:* 231, 385; Henry S. Dennison, "What the Employment Department Should Be in Industry," *Proceedings of the Employment Managers' Conference,* U.S. Bureau of Labor Statistics *Bulletin* no. 227 (Washington, D.C.: U.S. Government Printing Office, 1917): 80.

18. Marvin Lazerson, *Origins of the Urban School: Public Education in Massachusetts, 1870–1915* (Cambridge, Mass.: Harvard University Press, 1971); Charles A. Bennett, *History of Manual and Industrial Education* (Peoria, Ill.: Manual Arts Press, 1937); Charles Eliot, "Industrial Education as an Essential Factor in Our National Prosperity," National Society for the Promotion of Industrial Education *Bulletin* 5 (1908): 13; Sol Cohen, "The Industrial Education Movement, 1907–1917," *American Quarterly* 20 (Spring 1968): 98.

19. Frank Parsons, *Choosing a Vocation* (Boston: Houghton Mifflin, 1909); John M. Brewer, *History of Vocational Guidance: Origins and Early Development* (New York: Harper, 1942): 57; Harry D. Kitson, *The Psychology of Vocational Adjustment* (Philadelphia: J. B. Lippincott, 1925): 186–225.

20. Meyer Bloomfield, *The Vocational Guidance of Youth* (Boston: Houghton Mifflin, 1911): 3–8, 13–16, 23; Meyer Bloomfield, "The School and the Start of Life," in Bloomfield (ed.), *Readings in Vocational Guidance* (Boston: Ginn, 1915): 679–720; Owen Lovejoy, "Vocational Guidance and Child Labor," U.S. Bureau of Education *Bulletin* no. 14 (Washington, D.C.: U.S. Government Printing Office, 1914): 13–15, 62–63, 80. A blind alley job was defined as one lacking in stability and advancement, one "which offers little opportunity for growth in skill or knowledge . . . and which does not usually lead to a better occupation." John M. Brewer, *The Vocational Guidance Movement* (New York: Macmillan, 1918): 289.

21. Frank E. Spaulding, "Problems of Vocational Guidance," in Bloomfield (ed.), *Readings:* 324.

22. Meyer Bloomfield, *Youth, School and Vocation* (Boston: Houghton Mifflin, 1915): 48, 68–86; Meyer Bloomfield in U.S. Senate, Commission on Industrial Relations, *Final Report and Testimony,* vol. 1 (Washington, D.C.: U.S. Government Printing Office, 1916): 393; Ralph G. Wells, "The Work Program of the Employment Managers' Association of Boston," *The Annals* 65 (May 1916): 111; Meyer Bloomfield, "Introduction," in Roy W. Kelly, *Hiring the Worker* (Boston: Engineering Magazine, 1919): 2. A 1923 survey of employment departments found that only 15 percent had been established prior to 1915. Robert F. Lovett, "Present Tendencies in Personnel Practice," *Industrial Management* 65 (June 1923): 329.

23. Meyer Bloomfield, "General Discussion," *American Labor Legislation Review* 4 (May 1914): 350–352; John B. Andrews, "A Practical Program for the Prevention of Unemployment in America," *American Labor*

Legislation Review 5 (November 1915): 585–587; Richard A. Feiss, "Scientific Management Applied to the Steadying of Employment and Its Effect in an Industrial Establishment," *The Annals* 61 (September 1915): 103–111; Herman Feldman, "The New Emphasis in the Problem of Reducing Unemployment," *Bulletin of the Taylor Society* 7 (October 1922): 176–177; Malcolm C. Rorty, "Broader Aspects of the Employment Problem," *Industrial Management* 52 (February 1917): 723.

24. Meyer Bloomfield, "Problems of Industrial Management," *Proceedings of the Employment Managers' Conference,* U.S. Bureau of Labor Statistics, *Bulletin* no. 247 (Washington, D.C.: U.S. Government Printing Office, 1919): 157; Meyer Bloomfield, "A New Profession in American Industry," *London Daily News* (January 16, 1919), reprinted in Daniel Bloomfield (ed.), *Selected Articles on Employment Management* (New York: H. W. Wilson, 1919): 117–118; Joseph H. Willits, "Development of Employment Managers' Associations," *Monthly Labor Review* 5 (September 1917): 85.

25. Sanford M. Jacoby, *Employing Bureaucracy: Managers, Unions, and the Transformation of Work in American Industry, 1900–1945* (New York: Columbia University Press, 1985); Paul H. Douglas, "War Time Courses in Employment Management, *School and Society* 9 (June 7, 1919): 962; Meyer Jacobstein, "Government Courses for Training Employment Managers," U.S. Bureau of Labor Statistics, *Bulletin* no. 247 (Washington, D.C.: U.S. Government Printing Office, 1919): 19.

26. K. Huey, "Problems Arising and Methods Used in Interviewing and Selecting Employees," *The Annals* 65 (May 1916); Herbert Feis, "The Requirements of a Policy of Wage Settlement," *The Annals* 100 (March 1922); Feis, "Transfer and Promotion of Employees," *Iron Age* 103 (June 5, 1919): 1519; Feis, "Hiring, Discharge and Transfer: A Symposium," *Industrial Management* 58 (August 1919): 159; Meyer Bloomfield, "Employment Management Department," *Industrial Management* 52 (January 1917): 557.

27. Sumner H. Slichter, "Review of Personnel Relations in Industry," *Administration* 2 (August, 1921): 261–263; Sidney Hillman, "Organized Labor in Industry," in *Proceedings of the Industrial Relations Association of America,* part 2, Chicago 1920: 98–102.

28. Allen M. Wakstein, "The Origins of the Open-Shop Movement, 1919–1920," *Journal of American History* 51 (December 1964): 460–475; Robert K. Murray, *Red Scare: A Study in National Hysteria, 1919–1920* (Minneapolis: University of Minnesota Press, 1955); Dudley R. Kennedy, "The Future of Industrial Relations," *Industrial Management* 59 (March 1920): 558.

29. Charles Piez, "Trends in Management: What Is the Business Outlook Today?" *Factory* 26 (January 1, 1921): 32; E. S. Cowdrick, "What Are We Going to Do with the Boss?" *Industrial Management* 60 (August 1920): 195.

30. Paul H. Douglas, "Personnel Problems and the Business Cycle," *Admin-*

istration 4 (July 1922): 18–23; William L. Chenery, "Personnel Relations Tested," *The Survey* (May 21, 1921): 236–237; Ordway Tead, "The Field of Personnel Administration," *Bulletin of the Taylor Society* 8 (December 1923): 240; Robert F. Lovett, "Tendencies in Personnel Practice," *The Service Bulletin*, Carnegie Institute of Technology, Bureau of Personnel Research (February 1923).

31. W. J. Donald, "The Newer Conception of Personnel Functions," *Factory and Industrial Management* 75 (March 1928): 514–515; Jacoby, *Employing Bureaucracy:* 167–206.

32. "The Personnel Content of Management," *American Management Review* 12 (April 1923): 3–6; Sam A. Lewisohn, "Management's Part in Personnel Administration," *Personnel Administration* 9 (August 1922): 3–4; T. G. Portmore, "Selecting Employees to Meet the Needs of the Foreman," *American Management Review* 13 (April 1924): 3–5; Chenery, "Personnel Relations Tested": 237.

33. Gilson, *What's Past Is Prologue:* 101; Morris L. Cooke to E. O. Griffenhagen, December 22, 1926, Cooke Papers, Franklin D. Roosevelt Presidential Library, file 38, box 61; Leo Wolman and Gustave Peck, *Recent Social Trends in the U.S.* (New York: McGraw-Hill, 1933): 830.

34. James C. Worthy, "A Working Philosophy of Personnel Management," unpublished paper delivered to a meeting of the Industrial Relations Association of Chicago, June 11, 1951: 9; Jacoby, *Employing Bureaucracy:* 233.

35. Lawrence A. Appley, "The Foreman's Place in an Employee Educational Program," *Personnel Series* no. 33 (New York: American Management Association, 1938): 27–28; Ira B. Cross, Jr., "When Foremen Joined the CIO," *Personnel Journal* 18 (February 1940): 277; Harold F. North, "The Personnel Man's Functional Relationships," *Personnel Series* no. 45 (New York: American Management Association, 1940): 17–18; Ordway Tead, "Industrial Relations, 1939 Model," *Personnel Journal* 17 (November 1938): 166–167.

36. James C. Worthy, "Changing Aspects of the Personnel Function," *Personnel* 25 (November 1948): 166–175.

37. Jeanne L. Wilensky and Harold L. Wilensky, "Personnel Counseling: The Hawthorne Case," *American Journal of Sociology* 57 (November 1951): 265–280.

38. War Manpower Commission, *The Training within Industry Report, 1941–1945* (Washington, D.C.: U.S. Government Printing Office, 1945): 128, 204–222; Jacoby, *Employing Bureaucracy:* 269.

39. Daniel Bell, "Adjusting Men to Machines," *Commentary* 3 (June 1947): 79–88; "Deep Therapy on the Assembly Line," *Ammunition* 7 (April 1949): 47–51; Loren Baritz, *The Servants of Power* (Middletown, Conn.: Wesleyan University Press, 1960); Henry Landsberger, *Hawthorne Revisited: Management and the Worker, Its Critics, and Developments in Human Relations in Industry* (Ithaca, N.Y.: Cornell University Press, 1958): 85; James C. Worthy, "Management's Approach to Human Rela-

tions," in Conrad Arensberg (ed.), *Research in Industrial Relations* (New York: Harper, 1957): 14–24; Clark Kerr and Lloyd H. Fisher, "Plant Sociology: The Elite and the Aborigines," in Mirra Komarovsky (ed.), *Common Frontiers of the Social Sciences* (Glencoe, Ill.: Free Press, 1957): 281–309. Kerr and Fisher were dubious of the human relations claim that society's great problem was social disorganization, and they similarly doubted that the solution to this supposed problem was to provide workers with an "enveloping and satisfying plant life." Yet Kerr, for one, realized that there were elements within human relations that might constitute the basis for a new "democratic or participative management." See the discussion of management in Clark Kerr, et al., *Industrialism and Industrial Man: The Problems of Labor and Management in Economic Growth* (Cambridge, Mass.: Harvard University Press, 1960).

40. George K. Bennett, "A New Era in Business and Industrial Psychology," *Personnel Psychology* 1 (Winter 1948): 473–477; Gerald Gordon, "Industrial Psychiatry: Five Year Plant Experience," *Industrial Medicine and Surgery* 21 (December 1952): 585–588; Joseph Tiffin, "How Psychologists Serve Industry," *Personnel Psychology* 36 (March 1958): 372–376. On employer attitudes to unions after the war, see Clark Kerr, "Employer Policies in Industrial Relations, 1945–1947," in Colston Warne (ed.), *Labor in Postwar America* (Brooklyn: Remsen Press, 1949): 43–76.

41. Frederick Herzberg, *Job Attitudes: Review of Research and Opinion* (Pittsburgh: Psychological Service, 1957); Sanford M. Jacoby, "Employee Attitude Testing at Sears, Roebuck and Company, 1938–1960," *Business History Review* 60 (Winter 1986): 602–632; David Noble, *America by Design: Science, Technology, and the Rise of Corporate Capitalism* (New York: Knopf, 1977); Sanford M. Jacoby, "Employee Attitude Surveys in American Industry: An Historical Perspective," *Industrial Relations* 27 (Winter 1988): 74–93.

42. Rensis Likert and Ronald Lippitt, "The Utilization of Social Science," in Leon Festinger and Daniel Katz (eds.), *Research Methods in the Behavioral Sciences* (New York: Dryden Press, 1953); S. Avery Raube, "Experience with Employee Attitude Surveys," *Studies in Personnel Policy* no. 115 (New York: Conference Board, 1951).

43. "Should Industrial Relations Men Be Given Professional Status?" *Industrial Relations* 4 (December 1946): 27–28; Charles A. Drake, "Developing Professional Standards for Personnel Executives," *Personnel* 19 (March 1943): 646–655; Dale Yoder, "Professional Associations in Manpower Management," *Personnel Journal* 27 (June 1948): 43–46.

44. Coen is quoted in Reinhard Bendix, *Work and Authority in Industry: Ideologies of Management in the Course of Industrialization* (New York: Wiley, 1956): 329; Chester E. Evans and LaVerne N. Laseau, *My Job Contest* (Washington, D.C.: Personnel Psychology, 1950).

45. "The Workers' Poll That Kicked Up a Fuss," *Business Week*, February 19, 1955: 31; "Principles and Applications of Job Evaluation," in *Studies*

in Personnel Policy no. 62 (New York: Conference Board, 1944): 7; Sanford M. Jacoby, "Reckoning with Company Unions: The Case of Thompson Products," *Industrial and Labor Relations Review* 43 (October 1989): 19–40.

46. Harold M. F. Rush, *Behavioral Science: Concepts and Applications* (New York: Conference Board, 1969); Rush, *Organization Development* (New York: Conference Board, 1973); Charles C. Heckscher, *The New Unionism: Employee Involvement in the Changing Corporation* (New York: Basic Books, 1988).

47. Anil Verma and Thomas A. Kochan, "The Growth and Nature of the Nonunion Sector within a Firm," in Kochan (ed.), *Challenges and Choices Facing American Labor* (Cambridge, Mass.: MIT Press, 1985); Fred K. Foulkes, *Personnel Policies in Large Nonunion Companies* (Englewood Cliffs, N.J.: Prentice Hall, 1980).

48. D. Quinn Mills, "Management Performance," in Jack Stieber (ed.), *U.S. Industrial Relations, 1950–1980: A Critical Assessment* (Madison, Wis.: Industrial Relations Research Association, 1981): 99–128; Sanford M. Jacoby, "The Future of Industrial Relations in the United States," *California Management Review* 26 (Summer 1984): 90–94; Thomas A. Kochan and Peter Cappelli, "The Transformation of the Industrial Relations and Personnel Function," in Paul Osterman (ed.), *Internal Labor Markets* (Cambridge, Mass.: MIT Press, 1984): 133–162.

49. Dalton E. McFarland, *Cooperation and Conflict in Personnel Administration* (New York: Foundation for Management Research, 1962): 134; Harrison M. Trice, *An Occupation in Conflict: A Study of the Personnel Manager* (Ithaca, N.Y.: ILR Press, 1969): 23–35; Foulkes, *Personnel Policies*, 299–322.

50. Worthy, "Working Philosophy": 4.

14

Organizations and Human Resources: Internal and External Markets

■ ─────────────────── ■

John T. Dunlop

Resources are said to be allocated among enterprises by the market medium and directed within firms by administrative fiat. D. H. Robertson used the phrase "islands of conscious power in this ocean of unconscious cooperation, like lumps of butter coagulating in a pail of buttermilk."[1] But organizations other than business enterprises — households, nonprofit institutions, and governmental units — command the disposition of resources. The relative area of "milk surface" or "butter" varies accordingly, not merely with the extent of enterprise integration but also with the importance of these other directive "lumps."[2]

Instead of the analogy of a milk pail, Herbert A. Simon prefers the more modern figure of a visitor approaching from Mars viewing the areas of organizations and the market transactions connecting them.[3] His space visitor asks whether "organizational economy" would not be a more appropriate characterization of our world than "market economy." Simon reminds us that, since most producers are employees of firms, not owners, "profit-making firms, nonprofit organizations, and bureaucratic organizations all have exactly the same problem of inducing their employees to work toward the organizational goals."[4] He concludes, "The attempts of the new institutional economics to explain organizational behavior solely in terms of agency, asymmetric information, transaction costs, opportunism and other concepts drawn from neo-classical economics ignore key organizational mechanisms like authority, identification, and coordination, and hence are seriously incomplete."[5] Likewise, the assertion that "labor economics became applied or empirical microeconomics"[6] cannot be sustained.

Simon proposes that the behavior of organizations is to be understood with "empirically valid postulates about what motivates real people in real organizations" (not abstract profit maximization). He says that "such postulates can be derived from four organizational phenomena whose roles are amply documented in the literature on organizations: authority, rewards, identification [loyalty], and coordination."[7] Peter Doeringer put it well when he stated that "Effort control and labor efficiency in a wide variety of workplace settings seem to hinge far more on the choice of organizational technologies than on technological imperatives and economic incentives. The history of innovation and diffusion of social technologies at the workplace suggests a progression away from traditional economic conceptions of labor efficiency. . . ."[8] The literature of industrial relations and the experience of business executives, union officials, human resources specialists, government administrators, and mediator-arbitrators treat these questions daily, and they also reflect on these issues in the development of human resources structures and policies.

Neither D. H. Robertson's pail of buttermilk nor Herbert Simon's Martian perspective of earth as a patchwork of green masses (organizations) interconnected by red lines (markets) makes any explicit reference to labor markets as distinct from such markets as those for raw or finished goods, services, or finance.[9] But they both call attention to the issues that involve the exterior "wall" of the organization and the structure of internal activities and relations within that wall.

This chapter presents both a general overview of internal policy formulation and decision making in organizations as they relate to human resources, and a discussion of the organization's interrelations with its external complex of markets. "Internal organization and market organization coexist in active juxtaposition with one another."[10]

Industrial Relations Systems

At any given time every large-scale organization may be said to be a part of or associated with an industrial relations system.[11] In this country, the Department of Agriculture is a part of the federal government system, Union Pacific is part of the railroad system, and an

assembly plant of the Ford Motor Company is a part of the automobile system; an organization may also be associated with a system, as a large hospital may resemble many others of comparable
size in its human resources rules and patterns; or a very large organization may be so distinctive as to be regarded as a free-standing
system in itself, as might be said of IBM.[12]

The environment in which an industrial relations system operates, I divide into three broad contexts — market or budgetary, technological, and the power context, or the status of the actors and their
relations as defined by the polity. There is a continuing dynamic
interaction between changes in the environment of an organization,
its internal structure and policies, and the output of human resources rules and policies.

For the present purposes of calling attention to the interactions
between the environment of an industrial relations system, the
boundary of that organization, and its internal structures applicable
to human resources, the environment or context for a given industrial relations system may be subdivided into the following categories:

1. The cluster of surrounding product and supply markets, often
   the channel of markets from materials suppliers through retailers to consumers,[13] or the budgetary constraints facing a
   nonprofit or governmental organization;
2. The technologies;
3. The labor markets for certain key jobs;
4. The community or locale of the activity of workers;
5. The size of the organization;
6. The age of the organization;
7. The related educational and training facilities internal and
   external; and
8. The appropriate legal rules affecting human resources.

In my experience, specifying these elements of the environment of
an organization tends to define and constrain rather narrowly — but
not totally — the human resources options and decisions facing its
managers and employees at any one period of time.

For instance, the community and the age of the organization are
likely to go far in specifying the age and many other demographic
characteristics of the enterprise's work force. The cluster or channel
of surrounding markets, particularly product markets, tends to influence the character of competition the organization faces, and these
markets and technologies have significant influence on the size of
the organization. For nonprofit and governmental organizations, the

budget serves as an analogous determinant. Legal rules in this country shape whether employees or other workers have government protection in seeking union representation; whether particular employees are within or outside the appropriate unit; and whether certain overtime, health and safety, or other regulations apply. The technologies and the markets influence, in turn, the likely job classifications or occupations of employees. All these factors influence compensation and benefits for specified job classifications in an organization.

Beyond these eight features of the environment of an industrial relations system, there are two additional major elements, internal to an organization, that may be significant for its human resource policies and its boundary definitions: (1) the existence of some form of labor organization with explicit policies on a variety of issues that affect the choices of the management of the organization; and (2) a distinctive managerial philosophy toward employees, or employees in certain categories, that shapes a wide range of the organization's human resource decisions, such as hiring, layoffs, training, supervision, or management style. (Management may also have a policy or philosophy with respect to its relations with labor organizations that shapes its behavior in a given environment or context).

All together, these ten features of the environment of an organization and its internal human resource situation tend to predispose, in my experience, the boundaries and the specifics of an organization's human resource decisions and policies.

The Evolution of Internal Labor Markets

A brief sketch of the development of employment in the United States during the twentieth century and the major means of structuring internal work forces provides background for the current diversified forms of internal labor markets, which will be outlined later in this chapter. The sectoral distribution of employment is described in Table 14.1.

It would also be helpful to know the employment size of establishments in each sector and the extent of changes over the century.[14] Table 14.2 provides some information for one year. In 1986 it was reported there were 3.8 million enterprises in the U.S. and a total of 5 million establishments, with aggregate employment of 91.2 million employees.

Table 14.1. Employment by sectors

Sector	Number employed (in thousands)				
	1899 or 1900	1929	1946	1960	1990
Total population	76,000	121,767	141,389	180,671	251,523
Civilian labor force	27,172	49,180	57,520	69,628	121,787
Agricultural employment	10,912	10,450	8,320	5,458	3,186
Mining	659	1,057	862	712	711
Construction	1,315	2,392	1,683	2,926	5,136
Manufacturing	5,365	10,570	14,703	16,796	19,111
Transportation	1,908	3,051	4,061	4,004	5,826
Trade	2,892	8,028	8,375	11,391	25,888
Finance	325	1,592	1,675	2,628	6,739
Services	3,204	6,628	4,697	7,378	28,240
Government	994	2,923	5,595	8,353	18,322

Sources: John W. Kendrick, *Productivity Trends in the United States,* 1961, p. 308; *Economic Report of the President,* 1992, p. 344–345; cf. Stanley Lebergott, *Manpower in Economic Growth: The American Record Since 1800,* 1964, p. 514.

Table 14.2. Establishments and enterprises by sector and firm size, 1986

Sector	Total establishments	Total enterprises	500 or more employees	
			Establishments	Enterprises
Agriculture, forestry, fishing	115,700	104,764	2,587	89
Mining	51,666	33,841	7,961	159
Construction	566,810	527,058	10,099	405
Manufacturing	491,740	359,039	72,943	4,373
Transportation, communication, public utilities	222,734	137,112	47,753	797
Wholesale trade	576,491	419,441	52,685	510
Retail trade	1,402,906	1,046,302	151,799	1,769
Finance, insurance, real estate	448,604	271,863	94,647	1,331
Services	1,143,869	906,562	100,518	5,205

Source: The State of Small Business: A Report of the President, 1988, pp. 62–63, 90–91. Data are available for various size intervals, from 1 to 4 employees to more than 10,000 employees in the enterprise.

Outside of agriculture, there has been a growth over the years in the extent of self-employment: 3.8 million people were self-employed in 1900, 5.1 million in 1929, 6.4 million in 1960, and 8.8 million in 1990.[15]

The transformation of the economy and society over the century has been associated with declines in agricultural employment and expansion in enterprises in industry and services and in government employment. Such changes are reflected directly in exterior labor markets, in the growth of nonagricultural self-employment and in casual markets, and in the structuring of larger internal labor markets for civil service in governments, in formal personnel policies, and in collective bargaining agreements.

The intellectual means and techniques for the development of formal internal labor markets in larger establishments were developed over the past century by a series of concerns reflected in scientific management, civil service reform, job evaluation, worker compensation, and training policies, as well as by programs enhanced by the shutdown of mass immigration, wartime shortages, the growth of union organization, and government regulation of the labor market, particularly with the New Deal.[16]

The objective changes in the economy — within sectors, in the emergence of large enterprises and workplaces, and in the ideas and arrangements developed to govern and manage these workplaces, made it quite obvious to a new generation of economists in the 1940s, who were exposed in practical terms to labor markets and labor-management-government issues, that conventional (external) labor market theory was grossly inadequate. It neglected a vast range of activities within the walls of organizations as well as their forms of interaction with exterior markets.

Substantive Human Resource Policies

In considering the consequences for human relations policies of environmental influences and internal choices among philosophies of managements and policies of unions, a brief list of the major substantive areas for human resource decisions may be helpful. Policy in some of these areas may be relatively stable over long periods of time, and other policies may be subject to more frequent change:

- Breadth or span of jobs and occupations[17];
- Length of hierarchy or job ladders;

- Training processes and requirements, including safety;
- Discharge and discipline;
- Layoff and promotion processes;
- Methods of wage and salary payments;
- Wage and salary levels, relative to various external markets;
- Wage and salary structure, internal differentials;
- Benefit components of compensation such as health care and pensions, including retirement policies;
- Racial and gender composition of work force, affirmative action;
- Process for resolving controversies between employees and management;
- Executive compensation.

Major Patterns of Human Resource Management

Virtually all organizations in the United States, as distinct from those in other countries, have had their human resource policies and administrative procedures shaped by one or two pieces of legislation that were enacted in the 1930s. The Fair Labor Standards Act, originally passed in 1938, excludes from overtime provisions millions of employees classified as executive, administrative, and professional, as well as many others defined by industry or other complex exceptions. Running through most enterprises and organizations today is the distinction between "exempt" and "nonexempt" employees. Internal labor markets — ladders of promotion, points of entry, methods of wage or salary payment, some benefits — are significantly shaped by this boundary.

The other important statute enacted in the 1930s was the Labor-Management Relations Act, along with comparable legislation for the public sector, that in general terms defined bargaining units and provided for administrative certification by an administrative agency. These bargaining units typically exclude confidential, professional, managerial, supervisory, casual, part-time and temporary employees, and guards are required to be in a separate unit. Thus an organization is segmented for human resources purposes in still other ways under collective bargaining. There are additional pieces of legislation that shape internal human resource policies, such as the law eliminating age as a basis for compulsory retirement, except in the case of managers with pensions above a specified amount. The

Railway Labor Act establishes distinctive units and rules for railroad and airline employees.

Internal labor market boundaries are alone shaped by "the appropriate legal rules affecting human resources," and the drawing of these lines is often complex and contentious. In the United States, therefore, unlike in other countries, internal labor markets are at the outset typically divided into three separate areas: production and maintenance employees, including large-scale white-collar operations; white-collar and guard units related to production and maintenance; and exempt supervisory, managerial, and executive classifications of employees.

The discussion that follows is concerned with identifying eight categories of internal labor markets — outside of those involving supervisory, managerial, and executive personnel — that are particular to an establishment. The discussion does not apply to a multiestablishment enterprise as a whole, since the flow of workers between enterprises, for example, is not often centrally determined in a multiunit organization, except as common collective bargaining agreements may govern personnel policies and provide for centralized hiring and other policies for a number of enterprises.[18]

Each of these eight types of labor markets has its internal coherence among substantive human resource management policies, and each is contrasted with other major patterns of management and examined in relation to exterior markets. The brief descriptions that follow necessarily take the form of caricatures, but they illustrate the principal patterns of contemporary human resource management. Far too often academic discussion in this field has proceeded on the presumption of a single category: large-scale, capital-intensive manufacturing, as in automobiles or steel.

Small enterprises

In very small enterprises — except when they are incorporated into a sectorwide industrial relations system, as with a small ladies' garment contract shop, a small hotel, or a construction contractor that is part of an association under a collective agreement — decisions as to human resources are often made on a personal basis rather than as a matter of any general policy. Wages and benefits, training, and promotions, for instance, tend to be looked at in terms of individual employees, rather than on a formal job-classification basis.

In 1986, 3.6 million of the 3.8 million business enterprises in the United States employed fewer than 50 employees. In aggregate these small enterprises employed 25.4 million people, approximately 28 percent of all employees. (The firms that employed more than 500 employees — 14,698 enterprises — accounted for 46 million employees, more than half of all employees.[19])

National human resources analysis and policies need to recognize the large role of small enterprises. Such enterprises often do not offer health insurance (probably fewer than half the employees are covered in some form) and pensions are less frequently available. On average these enterprises tend to have lower wage rates and their workplaces are less safe. They go out of business more frequently, therefore providing less stable employment.[20] There are some small enterprises, of course, that do not fit this description, such as small firms of doctors, lawyers, and other professionals. But there are literally a few million small enterprises that do accord with this characterization, and they represent one major type of human resource environment and personalized management style.

The external market operates relatively directly in these small enterprises. There is comparatively little internal market.

Participants in worker pools
There are numerous managements that have few if any human resource policies of their own other than the policy of participating in temporary employee pools for some or many categories of labor they require. These enterprises draw labor to the enterprise as needed and then return it to the pool. The pool recruits workers with the necessary skills, is responsible for the skills of the workers in various occupations or classifications, determines wages and benefits, and administers a range of human resources policies — all, of course, for a fee.

The pool, or temporary agency, may be specialized to an occupation or may cover a wide range of activities. Many construction and maintenance activities, and maritime services including longshoring, fit this model. So do some pools of specialized workers, such as banquet waiters or types of professional nurses. It is well known that specialized temporary employee services have expanded rapidly in recent years in clerical, administrative, and accounting occupations. An enterprise following this pattern decides under what circumstances and to what degree it uses these "temps," but most of the human resources policies listed above are also subcontracted.[21]

Some agencies may get involved in the recruitment of part-time, contingent, and free-lance workers for an employer, and some have "head-hunting" roles and specialize in finding managerial and professional personnel sought for regular employment. Worker participants from an outside pool narrowly reflect the outside market, and their rates, benefits, and work rules may bear little relationship to the internal market. The arrangements between these pools and individual enterprises vary a great deal. As a rough estimate, as many as 7 million workers may be involved in this human resource management model.

Owner-Operators

This arrangement typically requires the worker to share with management some of the costs of capital equipment, operations, or travel, or some of the risks of operations, such as workplace-related accidents. In return the worker may receive a share of the value of the product, as fishermen receive part of the value of the catch in the New Bedford fishing industry and as farmer workers receive a share of the value of the crop in the harvesting of cucumbers in northwest Ohio. In the over-the-road trucking industry, the drivers are often owner-operators rather than employees, and they set mileage or trip rates for different pieces of equipment traveling between specific points.[22] The responsibility of owner-operators and owner-managers for such matters as workers' compensation, Social Security tax, and other human resource policies often depends on complex legal arrangements, contracts, and agreements. Some professional partnerships and enterprises resemble these owner-operator relationships.

As a type of human resource management, the owner-operator relationship involves recruitment by the owner-manager, a definition of the costs and risks, and some definition of the gross rewards of the owner-operator that are quite different from those of the ordinary employee. Typically there is no worker pool (apart from collective bargaining) to administer compensation or other personnel policies beyond the owner-operator contract; within some general legislative or regulatory constraints as to maximum hours or age for child labor, the worker develops work arrangements within the owner-operator contract. Several million workers may be involved in this human resource pattern.

Civil service

In this country, human resource policies and management in civil service are ordinarily minutely prescribed by centralized regulation, which is administered in turn by special procedures. Collective bargaining agreements may also govern the workplace. Any single agency or unit is rather narrowly constrained as to description of jobs and operations, ladders of promotion, processes of discipline, layoffs that are temporary or permanent, wages and salaries, benefits, affirmative action, and so on. Indeed almost all the substantive policies are prescribed by legislation, including such items as salary, pensions, and health care in the federal government, and pensions and many features of health care in municipal governments in Massachusetts, for example. In government there may be specialized job families, as for firefighters, police, and teacher classifications in local communities, and the foreign service and the military jobs in the federal government. Appeals procedures regarding actions by a single agency or management typically provide for review by a civil service commission or other specialized body.

While there are wide differences among governmental jurisdictions and among occupations — among, say, federal executive branch professionals, postal workers, and local police — the 18 million government employees in the United States constitute a differentiated arena of human resource management. The scope and style of management is specialized in the face of exterior determination of human resource policy.

Multitier internal labor markets

This type of human resource management characterizes many large-scale establishments in manufacturing, utilities, and some services.[23] Management necessarily arranges (in the absence of collective bargaining) the specified points of hiring or "ports of entry";[24] the rules of internal movement and exit from the internal market by reason of retirement, layoff, or discipline; the structure of wages and salaries and often job evaluation; methods of wage payment; pensions, health, and other benefits; formal education and training, and informal learning that arises from promotion paths; coverage of vacations and time off; the definition and breadth of jobs; affirmative action programs, and so on. Substantial and specialized capital equipment in the production process tends to provide more tiers of specialized job classifications. Basic steel production and rolling operations provided a well-known example of this, with 35 layered labor grades among production and maintenance job classifications.[25] In some cases entry into these tiers may be only at the bottom classification, while in others entry may be made at several points.

The multitiered internal market provides the largest opportunity for management to develop the most comprehensive human resource policies. There are more decisions to be made over a wider range within the purview of the enterprise. The impact of the exterior labor market is indirect and restricted, while product markets constrain aggregate costs in a general way, arising as a consequence of new entrants to the industry and imports from outside the country.

Far too much of the discussion of private-sector human resource policy has presumed this multitiered internal market. Only a small minority of all enterprises and organizations are characterized by such environments and opportunities. It may provide perspective to note that in 1986 there were 4,373 enterprises — with 72,943 establishments — that had more than 500 employees; they employed 14.8 million out of a total establishment employment of approximately 100 million that year. Discourse on one in seven jobs is scarcely a basis for a national human resource policy or even a private-sector one, or for a general analytical discipline.

Short-tier internal labor markets

This type of human resource management characterizes many retail stores, as in food chains, and service industries generally. In these short-tier organizations, which have four or five levels of employment, the industrial relations system and its environment dictates specialization of functions, but there are few long lines of occupational promotion and few compensation grades. In a supermarket, typically there are levels of baggers, shelvers, check-out clerks, managers of departments, and store managers. In general, there is less room for options in human resource policies than there is in multitiered, capital-intensive manufacturing, and the influence of the exterior market is likely to be more direct, particularly on entering job classifications.

Clerical-oriented organizations

A number of enterprises are significantly comprised of white-collar occupations as in banking, insurance, commercial businesses, and some public agencies and nonprofit organizations.[26] At the same time, several job families in these enterprises may be joined with other occupations in one of the previously noted types of industrial relations systems, such as worker pools and large-scale enterprises. Organizations that generate these types of clerical occupation patterns as the dominant or influential jobs often tend to develop distinctive policies that reflect the demography of the workplace. The predominance of women workers historically has tended to affect wage levels adversely and to generate some specified types of fringe benefits.[27] The sources of supply in the exterior markets may also represent specialized training, as in secretarial schools. Turnover rates may be distinctive, and specialized governmental regulations may apply. These occupations and job families constitute a significant number of employees in the private sector, perhaps as many as 12 million.

Technical and professional amalgams

This type of a model characterizes a number of high-technology enterprises, professional and research groups, consulting firms, and in some respects institutions of higher education. Acute-care hospitals are also to be placed in this category, as reflected by the National Labor Relations Board rule, supported by the Supreme Court, that established eight employment units in such hospitals: registered nurses, physicians, other professionals, technical employees, skilled maintenance employees, business office clerical employees, guards, and others.[28]

Employee loyalty may be to the profession or to the problem or process dealt with, rather than to the institution or enterprise.[29] Key personnel may be tempted to leave one organization and join another or to start a new one. The organization and its management, as such, may have little cohesion or control. Employees are highly trained outside the enterprise; internal hierarchial relationships are of limited relevance, and equity forms of compensation or private consulting may be significant instruments of human resource strategy. Internal relations are more entrepreneurial than bureaucratic. Academic institutions have the internal policy of tenure that formalizes this distinctive pattern for human resources in the professorate and in apprentice positions.

These eight distinctive groupings of human resource policies are derived from the structural and environmental industrial relations

Table 14.3. Estimated number of workers or employees by type of internal organization, 1990*

1. Small enterprises	31 million
2. Participants in worker pools	7 million
3. Owner-operators	2 million
4. Civil service	18 million
5. Multitier internal labor markets	15 million
6. Short-tier internal labor markets	15 million
7. Clerical-oriented organizations	12 million
8. Technical and professional amalgams	10 million
Total	110 million

Note: Large-scale enterprises are significant in mining, manufacturing, transportation, communication and public utilities, finance and insurance, some services, and government.
* Excludes agriculture (3 million), private households (1 million), and the self-employed (9 million) — a total of 13 million workers.

systems that surround and encompass the enterprise. Rough estimates of the prevalence of each type, as reflected by the numbers of the workers involved, are summarized in Table 14.3.

These categories of internal arrangements are related to exterior markets in varied and distinctive ways as has been noted in passing in the preceding discussion. A more formal classification of their dynamic interactions follows:

1. The exterior market may operate largely directly within the enterprise (as in many small enterprises or in many manpower pools).

2. Each key job may be a port of entry, existing with little promotion or transfer. In such cases the exterior market operates relatively directly within the internal market[30] (as in some types of craft-tiered internal markets and technical and professional amalgams).

3. The exterior labor markets may constrain, only very generally, the extent to which an internal job classification or group may be out of line with rates in the external markets. The experiences with skilled-trade differentials or new biotechnology positions in an internal market are illustrative of this.

4. The internal labor markets may be influenced by product markets, by their constraint on the competitiveness of the enterprise, or by budgets.

The real world is not confined to pure types but contains enterprises with a variety of units, departments, or parts of enterprises with different types of human resource policies that are linked together or combined. The combination typically creates a variety of internal human relations problems. Which category is to dominate? Which pattern of wage or salary differentials is to prevail? Which fringe benefits? What are to be the connections between the segments for movement of personnel across internal boundaries? The congruence of human resource policies among units may also influence the boundaries of the enterprise.

It may be helpful to identify some of the major internal wage and salary issues that arise in these mixed types of organizations. Wage, salary, and benefit determination always involves a delicate balancing of internal and external considerations for the job classification schedule as a whole.[31]

• Any internal job ranking plan is certain to provide different wage and salary relationships than exist for similar jobs in the outside labor markets. These differences may be large or small. The organization has greater discretion the higher its level of wage or salary rates is relative to the outside markets and the fewer the ports of entry.

• The broader the scope of the organization, measured by its range of job classifications, the greater the potential for disparities between internal and external wages and salaries.[32]

• The broader the scope of the organization subsumed under a single job ranking plan, as in the case of a plan for public employees in all operations of a state government, the greater its vulnerability to pay equity claims based on the charge that some employees (women) are underpaid relative to values ascribed to predominantly male occupations found in local labor markets. In general, the narrower the scope of the organization the less vulnerable it is.

• Any internal job ranking plan is concerned with the tilt of the wage or salary line between the lowest- and highest-paid classifications. What are the previously existing differentials for skill, responsibility, and the like? What should they be?

• A multitier internal market provides greater opportunities for promotion, with a given turnover rate, than more limited hierarchies.

• A major internal compensation policy choice relates to the roles of automatic progression within and among job classifications, merit evaluation, and length of service, and the role of general wage or salary increases.

• The method of wage payment, apart from time-related rates, such as individual piece rates or group incentives or bonus plans, is a separate decision; so is the package of fringe benefits. Some environments and internal human resource policies are congruent with some methods of wage payment and not with others.

The human resources setting and structural predispositions of an enterprise are determined by the types of environments or industrial relations systems involved. These structural policies typically persist for long periods, and they do not depend primarily on the philosophy adopted by management toward the human resources of the organization or on the collective bargaining policies developed with a labor organization, although they do make some differences in some cases. Nor can these policies, including the structural wage decisions, be related simply to microeconomic concepts of the maximizing behavior of parties engaged in contracting. The persistent wage dispersion for identical job classifications in any geographically local labor market in part reflects the major types of human resource management noted earlier and the way in which enterprises, with different mixes of units, respond to the wage and salary issues just noted, which involve a balancing of internal and external considerations.

The Role of Management Philosophy and Collective Bargaining

It is fundamental, in my view, to an understanding of human resource policies to keep the influence and predispositions of the environment conceptually separate from the independent effects of the philosophy and policies of management toward human resources and the policies of any collective bargaining relationship in the specified environment. There are at least two reasons for this separation in analysis. First, in my experience with many cases, the modifications introduced by policies of management toward human resources, or through collective bargaining, are often relatively minor over the long term compared with the large structures of human resource arrangements, although attitudes, a degree of performance, and even productivity may be influenced.[33] Second, there are serious dangers in the presumption of academics that all is variable in the human resources policy of an organization. For example, it may be wrongly thought that employment security and stability can readily be introduced into construction (without major changes in the environmental context), or that participatory relationships can be introduced into civil service without systemic change, or that extensive training and career development can be introduced into short-tier internal labor markets.

A great deal of the recent discussion about the transformation of human resource policies fails to distinguish between the influence of internal management philosophy and the constraints of the larger environment. By the philosophy of management, what is meant is management's attitudes toward the human resource components of the organization, the attitudes of principals toward agents, within a given environmental setting. In a sense these policies are the organizational behavior phenomena Herbert Simon refers to as authority, rewards, identification, and coordination.

From an industrial relations and managerial perspective it may be useful to contrast two different approaches or prototypes of management.[34] The first handles employees (workers) in a semimilitary fashion under the classic guidelines: organize, deputize, and supervise. The second approach defines a mission for employees (workers), empowers them broadly, and then measures and rewards their performance. These contrasting philosophies may result in somewhat different human resource policies in a given setting, and in somewhat different performance.

A collective bargaining relationship, involving some likely compromise between the philosophies of management and the aspirations of the labor organization, likewise may result in somewhat different human resource policies in a given setting, and somewhat different performance.[35]

In my view most of the changes in human resource policies that have taken place in recent years, particularly in large manufacturing, are very much the direct consequences of changes in the environmental or external setting — greater global competition, layoffs and the quest for job security, new technology, changes to accommodate inventory controls, and the influence of regulatory developments relating to such matters as affirmative action, pensions, and health and safety.[36] With some exceptions, the basic structural features of the industrial relations systems and human resource policies have not fundamentally changed. In a relatively few cases, changes in management philosophy and collective bargaining policies have affected outputs and internal processes, but the main dimensions of the respective systems are relatively unchanged. There appears to be no widespread transformation in substantive human resource policies in process broadly, across various environments, in the United States.

Balkanization of Labor Markets

Clark Kerr's justly celebrated chapter with the above title is in part derived from his own earliest research in agricultural labor and in migration into the Seattle area during the early World War II era.[37] The highly organized San Francisco labor markets provided contrasting illustrations of the "guild" model for craft workers and the "manorial" model for industrial-type workers tied to the enterprise. "Institutional rules put added structure into labor markets. . . . Institutional markets create truly non-competing groups. . . . Not all jobs are open at all times to all bidders except in the structureless market."[38]

A major intellectual influence in developing this general analysis of labor markets was no doubt Lloyd Fisher, Kerr's friend and mine, who had been research director of the Longshoremen's and Warehousemen's Union.[39] Fisher came to Harvard for two years and completed his doctorate with Professor J. D. Black and myself in 1949 before returning to Berkeley. Fisher's analytical formulation of the "structureless market" for harvest labor in California and related discussions were to have a significant influence on Clark Kerr's ideas on the structure of labor markets.[40] So was Kerr's experience with the War Labor Board in dealing with the internal wage structure and forms of job evaluation in many industries, including the West Coast Airframe Industry and the National Meat Packing Commission, which Clark Kerr chaired.

I found Fisher's structureless market a point of departure for describing various "structured" labor markets.[41] Fisher's work was assigned in my courses, and it helped to suggest a group of six other doctoral dissertations on various types of labor markets: Jack Stieber's on the basic steel wage structure[42]; Richard Freeman's on college-trained manpower[43]; D. Q. Mills's on construction markets[44]; Peter Doeringer and Michael Piore's on "internal" labor markets[45]; and James Scoville's on the job content of the economy.[46,47]

The emphasis on the diversity of internal labor markets and their structuring, whether imposed by management, labor organizations, collective bargaining, or by government — including the interconnections with exterior markets — was enriched for me by these detailed dissertations and by an expanding industrial relations practice.

The eightfold typology of industrial relations systems and associated internal and external labor markets is a logical outgrowth of these earlier formulations. The major structural features are relatively independent of labor organizations or collective bargaining, although the rules of the structure may be more formalized and reinforced by both.

Questions for Workers and Managers

Any operational perspective on the human resource decisions of an establishment or enterprise raises the following sorts of questions for human resource policies in each type of industrial relations system:

• How does a worker get inside the "skin" of the enterprise, through what portals? Or is the employment arrangement one of participating in temporary employment pools or as an owner-operator?[48] What are the mechanisms and the terms for exit? What are the relations between external and internal markets, and how significant are these connections for the particular organization?

- What jobs do workers actually perform? What is the job content packaged in each job classification? What is the range of activities workers are required to be able to perform?
- How are jobs related to one another in patterns of movement, promotions, transfers, or downgrading? What are the relevant job families or job clusters?[49] What are the particular paths to each position?[50]
- How are positions compensated: wages, salaries, bonuses, and benefits? What are the relative pay positions?
- What are the formal and informal training arrangements? What measures are concerned with health and safety?
- How are various categories of employees managed?
- How are productivity and quality of performance assured?
- What internal adjustments are made in the way these questions are answered with significant reduction or expansion, in the need for labor services (temporary or long-term)?
- How are differences between managers and workers resolved?
- What arrangements come to be made in the exterior labor markets to accommodate to the operation of the internal markets of various types? (Public unemployment insurance or private supplementary unemployment benefits affect the interaction of internal and external markets; social security may affect exit by retirement.) What procedures are developed for further training?

These sorts of questions have constituted the focus of industrial relations research over the years, in which Clark Kerr and his colleagues on the Labor Market Research Committee Social Science Research Council played an initiating role. These questions also incorporate many of the concerns of organizational behavior, certainly as summarized by Herbert Simon.[51] It is an unacceptable position, in my view, to define an internal labor market simply as a "set of explicit or implicit, more or less long-term agreements between a firm and its workers,"[52] for this ignores the richness and complexity of the questions just enumerated and the diversity of the eight human resource management models and their relations to exterior markets.

The questions have little or no resonance with the concerns of microeconomics and the explanatory value of the "new institutional economics," with its emphasis on agency, risk aversion, asymmetrical information, transaction costs, and so on, taken singly or in integrated treatment. No microeconomics studies examine the structure of internal markets, the differences among job classifications and categories of employees, and their connections to exterior markets, except in the most abstract fashion. It is strange indeed, that the so-called new institutional economists appear to know so little of the institutions of the internal and external labor markets in the various organization types I have described.

Internal and External Markets: A Summary

1. The black box of organizations — business enterprises as well as nonprofit and governmental organizations — is an appropriate focus of study for an understanding of human resource policies. The commonality of internal patterns and behavior in treating human resources among these profit and nonprofit organizations raises questions as to the primacy of current microeconomics analysis to such behavior.

2. The environment or the context of the organization significantly shapes its internal human resource structure and substantive policies, as well as its interactions with exterior labor markets.

3. The industrial relations systems that encompass organizations help to identify at least eight major types of human resource management: small enterprises, participants in employment pools, owner-operators, civil service, multitier internal labor markets, short-tier internal labor markets, clerical-oriented organizations, and technical and professional amalgams. In these different settings human resource policies and structures are significantly predisposed.

The large-scale capital-intensive type of enterprise, in which there is typically the greatest room for internal human resource policy development and which has received most attention, characterizes no more than one in seven jobs and covers fewer employees than are in small enterprises or in civil service–type organizations. Analytical tools need to be able to encompass and interpret all eight management types and hybrids.

No one model of internal labor markets is appropriate to all establishments; no pattern of insider-outsider relations is general;[53] and no relationship between internal and external labor markets is standard.

4. Within limits, if the organization recognizes a labor union, management philosophy or collective bargaining may alter the human resource structures and policies predisposed by an enterprise's environment or by dramatic or gradual changes in that environment. The consequences of managerial philosophy and bargaining relate to the full range of substantive policies. The complexities of such poli-

cies are not simply understood or shaped by the tools of micro-economics, or by persuasive evidence related to the maximizing behavior of parties engaged in contracting. As Robert M. Solow has stated: "Wage rates and jobs are not exactly like other prices and quantities. They are much more deeply involved in the way people see themselves, think about their social status, and evaluate whether they are getting a fair share out of society."[54]

5. External and internal labor markets are both relevant, in different settings and degrees, for managers and workers (and their organizations) and for public policy issues. Conventional economics can contribute modestly to understanding external labor markets, but microeconomics (the new institutional labor economics) has little to contribute, in my view, to an understanding of internal labor markets, for the discussions of participants or for public policy. Internal labor markets are congenial and responsive to the tools of industrial relations, including organizational behavior.

Notes

1. D. H. Robertson, *The Control of Industry* (New York: Harcourt, Brace, 1923), p. 84.
2. John T. Dunlop, *Wage Determination under Trade Unions* (New York: Macmillan, 1944), p. 8.
3. Herbert A. Simon, "Organizations and Markets," *Journal of Economic Perspectives* 5, no. 2 (Spring 1991), p. 26.
4. Ibid., p. 28. On some parts of the globe, Simon states, the Martian visitor would see "little black dots" for families and villages.
5. Ibid., p. 42; also see, John T. Dunlop, "Industrial Relations and Economics: The Common Frontier of Wage Determination," *Proceedings of the Thirty-Seventh Annual Meeting*, December 28–30, 1984, Industrial Relations Research Association, pp. 9–23; Sanford M. Jacoby, "The New Institutionalism: What Can It Learn from the Old?" in *The Economics of Human Resource Management*, Daniel J. B. Mitchell and Mahmood A. Zaidi, eds. (Cambridge, Mass.: Basil Blackwell, 1990), pp. 162–186.
6. William Darity, Jr., ed., *Labor Economics: Modern Views* (Boston: Kluwer-Nijhoff, 1984), p. 5.
7. Simon, "Organizations and Markets," p. 30.
8. Peter B. Doeringer, "The Socio-Economics of Labor Productivity," in *Morality, Rationality, and Efficiency*, Richard J. Coughlin, ed. (Armonk, N.Y.: M. E. Sharp, 1991), p. 114. Also see Richard C. Edwards on internal labor markets in *Labor Market Segmentation*, Richard C. Edwards, Michael Reich, and David M. Gordon, eds. (Lexington, Mass.: D. C. Heath, 1975), pp. 3–26.

9. Edmund S. Phelps "found it instructive to picture the economy as a group of islands between which information flows are costly: To learn the wage paid on an adjacent island, the worker must spend the day traveling to that island to sample its wage instead of spending the day at work." *Microeconomic Foundations of Employment and Inflation Theory* (New York: W. W. Norton, 1970), p. 6.

10. Oliver E. Williamson, "Emergence of the Visible Hand: Implications for Industrial Organization," in *Managerial Hierarchies, Comparative Perspectives on the Rise of the Modern Industrial Enterprise*, Alfred D. Chandler, Jr., and Herman Daems, eds. (Cambridge, Mass.: Harvard University Press, 1980), p. 194. Also see George H. Hildebrand, "External Influences and the Determination of the Internal Wage Structure," in *Internal Wage-Structure*, J. L. Meij, ed. (Amsterdam: North-Holland, 1963), pp. 260–299; John T. Dunlop, "The Task of Contemporary Wage Theory," in *The Theory of Wage Determination*, John T. Dunlop, ed. (London: Macmillan, 1957), pp. 3–27.

11. John T. Dunlop, *Industrial Relations Systems* (New York: Henry Holt, 1958), pp. 1–128. Revised Ed. (Boston: Harvard Business School Press, 1993), pp. 43–130.

12. D. Quinn Mills, *The IBM Lesson: The Profitable Act of Full Employment* (New York: Times Books, 1988).

13. See Janice H. Hammond, "Coordination in Textile and Apparel Channels: A Case for 'Virtual' Integration," Working Paper no. 92-007, Graduate School of Business Administration, Harvard University, 1991.

14. "Plants have been declining in average size measured by employment, but with output per hour rising more rapidly than the fall in hours per plant, average output per plant has grown by roughly 2 percent per year." F. M. Scherer and David Ross, *Industrial Market Structure and Economic Performance* (Boston: Houghton Mifflin, 1990), p. 119. See John T. Dunlop, "The American Industrial Relations System in 1975," in *U.S. Industrial Relations: The Next Twenty Years*, Jack Stieber, ed. (East Lansing: Michigan State University Press, 1958), pp. 33–34. For a discussion of nineteenth-century developments, see Alfred D. Chandler, Jr., *The Visible Hand: The Managerial Revolution in American Business* (Cambridge, Mass.: Harvard University Press, 1977), p. 372.

15. For recent data, see Current Population Survey, "Major Industry and Class of Worker." Also, Edward F. Denison, *Trends in American Economic Growth, 1929–1982* (Washington, D.C.: Brookings Institution, 1985), pp. 33–39, 82; Stanley Lebergott, *Manpower in Economic Growth: The American Record Since 1800* (New York: McGraw-Hill, 1964), pp. 364–383, 513.

16. See Frederick Winslow Taylor, *Scientific Management, Comprising Shop Management: The Principles of Scientific Management, Testimony before the Special House Committee* (New York: Harper and Brothers Publishers, 1947); Robert F. Hoxie, *Scientific Management and Labor* (New York: Appleton, 1921); Alfred D. Chandler, Jr., *The Visible*

Hand: The Managerial Revolution in American Business (Cambridge, Mass.: Harvard University Press, 1977); Elton Mayo, *The Social Problems of an Industrial Civilization* (Boston: Division of Research, Graduate School of Business Administration, Harvard University, 1945); Sumner H. Slichter, *The Turnover of Factory Labor* (New York: Appleton, 1919); and Slichter, *Union Policies and Industrial Management* (Washington, D.C.: Brookings Institution, 1941).

17. James G. Scoville, *The Job Content of the U.S. Economy, 1940–1970* (New York: McGraw-Hill, 1969).

18. Sanford M. Jacoby, "The Development of Internal Labor Markets in American Manufacturing Firms," in *Internal Labor Markets*, Paul Osterman, ed. (Cambridge, Mass.: MIT Press, 1984), pp. 23–69.

19. *The State of Small Business: A Report of the President* (Washington, D.C.: U.S. Government Printing Office, 1988), pp. 62, 90.

20. John T. Dunlop, "Is Small Beautiful at the Workplace?" *Villanova Law Review* 33, no. 6, (1988), pp. 1059–1071; Charles Brown, James Hamilton, and James Medoff, *Employers Large and Small* (Cambridge, Mass.: Harvard University Press, 1990).

21. See Richard S. Belous, *The Contingent Economy: The Growth of the Temporary and Part-time and Subcontracted Workforce* (Washington, D.C.: National Planning Association, 1989); Peter B. Doeringer, *Turbulence in the American Workplace* (New York: Oxford University Press, 1991), pp. 140–155.

22. See D. Daryl Wyckoff and David H. Maister, *The Owner-Operator: Independent Trucker* (Lexington, Mass.: Lexington Books, 1975); D. Daryl Wyckoff, *Truck Drivers in America* (Lexington, Mass.: Lexington Books, 1979), pp. 85–107.

23. See John T. Dunlop, "Job Vacancy Measures and Economic Analysis," in *The Measurement and Interpretation of Job Vacancies*, A Conference Report of the National Bureau of Economic Research, (New York: National Bureau of Economic Research, 1966), pp. 32–38; Peter Doeringer and Michael J. Piore, *Internal Labor Markets and Manpower Analysis* (Lexington, Mass.: Heath Lexington Books, 1971); also see Paul Osterman, ed., *Internal Labor Markets* (Cambridge, Mass.: MIT Press, 1984); Michael L. Wachter and Randall D. Wright, "The Economics of Internal Labor Markets," in Daniel J. B. Mitchell and Mahmood A. Zaidi, eds., *The Economics of Human Resource Management* (Cambridge, Mass.: Basil Blackwell, 1990), pp. 86–108.

24. See Clark Kerr, "The Balkanization of Labor Markets," reprinted in *Labor Markets and Wage Determination: The Balkanization of Labor Markets and Other Essays* (Berkeley: University of California Press, 1977), pp. 21–37.

25. *Job Description and Classification Manual: For Hourly Rated Production, Maintenance and Non-Confidential Clerical Jobs*, United Steelworkers of America, AFL-CIO and Coordinating Committee Steel Companies, 1971.

26. See George P. Shultz, "A Nonunion Market for White Collar Labor," in *Aspects of Labor Economics: A Conference of the Universities — National Bureau Committee for Economic Research* (Princeton, N.J.: Princeton University Press, 1962), pp. 107–155.

27. John T. Dunlop, ed., *Potentials of the American Economy: Selected Essays of Sumner H. Slichter* (Cambridge, Mass.: Harvard University Press, 1961), pp. 368–370.

28. *American Hospital Association* v. *National Labor Relations Board, et. al.*, pp. 90–97, decided April 23, 1991.

29. Clark Kerr, *The Uses of the University* (Cambridge, Mass.: Harvard University Press, 1963), pp. 42–44; also see Clark Kerr and Marian L. Gade, *The Many Lives of Academic Presidents: Time, Place and Character* (Washington, D.C.: Association of Governing Boards of Universities and Colleges, 1986).

30. See Dunlop, "Job Vacancy Measures and Economic Analysis," p. 34, Figure 1a.

31. John T. Dunlop, "Labor Markets and Wage Determination: Then and Now," in Bruce E. Kaufman, ed., *How Labor Markets Work* (Lexington, Mass.: Lexington Books, 1988), p. 53; John T. Dunlop and David W. Johnson, *Job Evaluation in Non-Teaching (Non-Administrative) Jobs in Education* (Washington, D.C.: National Education Association, 1991), pp. 11–15.

32. See E. Robert Livernash, ed., *Comparable Worth: Issues and Alternatives* (Washington, D.C.: Equal Employment Advisory Council, 1980), pp. 3–21, 79–106.

33. John T. Dunlop, "A Decade of National Experience," in Jerome M. Rosow, ed., *Teamwork: Joint Labor-Management Programs in America* (New York: Pergamon Press, 1986), pp. 12–25.

34. See Daniel Q. Mills, *Rebirth of the Corporation* (New York: John Wiley and Sons, 1991). Also see the remarks of John F. Welch, Jr., CEO of General Electric Company, *Wall Street Journal*, March 3, 1992, p. B-1.

35. See the significant history of collective bargaining in the copper industry by George H. Hildebrand and Garth Mangum, *Capital and Labor in American Copper, 1845–1990: A Study of the Linkages between Product and Labor Markets* (Cambridge, Mass.: Harvard University Press, 1992).

36. See Dunlop, "A Decade of National Experience," pp. 12–25; "Have the 1980's Changed Industrial Relations?" *Monthly Labor Review*, May 1988, pp. 29–34.

37. Clark Kerr, "The Balkanization of Labor Markets," in E. Wight Bakke, ed., *Labor Mobility and Economic Opportunity* (Cambridge, Mass.: MIT Press, 1954), pp. 92–110; reprinted in Clark Kerr, *Labor Markets and Wage Determination* (Berkeley: University of California Press, 1977), pp. 21–37.

38. Ibid., pp. 24, 29.

39. Kerr and Fisher wrote a number of pieces together and discussed others relating to the workplace: "Effect of Environment and Administration

on Job Evaluation," *Harvard Business Review*, May 1950; "Multiple Employer Bargaining: The San Francisco Experience," in R. A. Lester and J. Shister, eds., *Insights into Labor Issues* (New York: Macmillan, 1948), pp. 25–61. Two articles, "Labor Markets: Their Character and Consequences" *American Economic Review*, May 1950; and "Plant Sociology: The Elite and the Aborigines" in *Common Frontiers of the Social Sciences*, Mirra Komarovsky, ed., (New York: The Free Press, 1957), explicitly credit Lloyd Fisher.

40. Lloyd H. Fisher, "The Harvest Labor Market in California," *Quarterly Journal of Economics*, November 1951; Fisher, *The Harvest Labor Market in California* (Cambridge, Mass.: Harvard University Press, 1953). Clark Kerr and I wrote a joint foreword to this volume; Lloyd Fisher's untimely death occurred shortly before the book was published. The "structureless" labor market has five characteristics, according to Fisher: (1) there are no unions with seniority or other rules allocating workers; (2) the relation between the employer and workers is transitory and impersonal; (3) the workers are unskilled; (4) payment is by unit or product; (5) little capital or machinery is utilized.

41. John T. Dunlop, "Job Vacancy and Economic Analysis," in *The Measurement and Interpretation of Job Vacancies: A Conference Report*, National Bureau of Economic Research (New York: Columbia University Press, 1966), pp. 27–47.

42. Jack Stieber, *The Steel Industry Wage Structure: A Study of the Joint Union-Management Job Evaluation Program in the Basic Steel Industry* (Cambridge, Mass.: Harvard University Press, 1959).

43. Richard B. Freeman, *The Market for College-Trained Manpower: A Study in Career Choice* (Cambridge, Mass.: Harvard University Press, 1971).

44. Daniel Quinn Mills, *Industrial Relations and Manpower in Construction* (Cambridge, Mass.: MIT Press, 1972); John T. Dunlop and D. Quinn Mills, "Manpower and Construction: A Profile of the Industry and Projections to 1975," *The Report of the President's Committee on Housing*, vol. 2 (Washington, D.C.: U.S. Government Printing Office, 1968), pp. 239–286.

45. Peter B. Doeringer and Michael J. Piore, *Internal Labor Markets and Manpower Analysis* (Lexington, Mass.: D. C. Heath, 1971).

46. James G. Scoville, *The Job Content of the U.S. Economy, 1940–1970* (New York: McGraw-Hill, 1969).

47. Mention should also be made of various volumes in the Wertheim Series in Industrial Relations, particularly Vernon H. Jensen, *Hiring of Dock Workers, and Employment Practices in the Ports of New York, Liverpool, London, Rotterdam and Marseilles* (Cambridge, Mass.: Harvard University Press, 1964).

48. "A large part of the behavior of the system now takes place inside the skins of firms, and does not consist just of market exchanges. . . . Why are not all the actors independent contractors?" Herbert A. Simon, "Organizations and Markets" ibid., p. 25.

49. John T. Dunlop, "The Task of Contemporary Wage Theory," in *New Concepts in Wage Determination*, George W. Taylor and Frank L. Pierson, eds. (New York: McGraw-Hill, 1957), pp. 117–140; also see E. Robert Livernash, "The Internal Wage Structure," ibid., pp. 140–172.

50. The analyses of "general" and "specific" training by Gary S. Becker (*Human Capital* [New York: National Bureau of Economic Research, distributed by Columbia University Press, 1964], pp. 8–29) need to recognize the different configurations of internal labor markets and training. My experience suggests that, with some exceptions, the distinction between general and specific training is often neither operational nor useful.

51. Herbert Simon, "Organizations and Markets," ibid., pp. 30–42.

52. Michael L. Wachter and Randall D. Wright, "The Economics of Internal Labor Markets," in Daniel J. B. Mitchell and Mahmood A. Zaidi, eds., *The Economics of Human Resource Management*, (Cambridge, Mass.: Basil Blackwell, 1990), p. 86.

53. See Assar Lindbeck and Dennis J. Snower, *The Insider-Outsider Theory of Employment and Unemployment* (Cambridge, Mass.: MIT Press, 1988).

54. Robert M. Solow, *The Labor Market as a Social Institution* (Cambridge, Mass.: Basil Blackwell, 1990), p. 22.

15

Explicit Individual Contracting in the Labor Market

David Lewin

The best known form of explicit contracting in the labor market is the collective bargaining agreement struck between organized workers and management. Despite the continuing decline of unionism and, consequently, collective bargaining in the United States, some 150,000 collective bargaining agreements covering roughly 11 million private-sector workers are presently in effect (Bureau of National Affairs 1991; Wafilewski 1992). Furthermore, data on collective bargaining contracts continue to be collected on a systematic basis, and thus it is possible to gauge the extent of such bargaining at a particular point in time and to observe changes over time.

In contrast, there are no recurring systematic data presently available concerning explicit individual contracting in the labor market. Anecdotal, popular, and case accounts of individual employment contracts (usually about conflicts over such contracts) surface from time to time, but these do not effectively substitute for systematic data by which one can determine the extent or changing incidence of explicit individual employment contracts.

Despite this data gap, and in part because of it, in this chapter I will analyze current and potential future uses of explicit individual employment contracting in the labor market. The first section of the chapter draws on the implicit contracting and psychological contracting literatures to derive a conceptual foundation for the analysis of explicit individual employment contracting. The second section broadens this foundation to incorporate concepts drawn from the human resource management and industrial relations literature, and presents new evidence and empirical analyses of explicit individual contracting in the labor market. In the third section I describe and analyze selected case examples of explicit individual employment contracting in three U.S. firms, emphasizing the diversity of such contracting arrangements. The fourth section draws on this study's main conclusions to derive a forecast for the future of explicit individual contracting in the labor market.

Conceptual Foundations

The notion of implicit contracting in the labor market and in the employment relationship has been emphasized by economists and psychologists. Recent work by economists uses implicit contracting models to explain such phenomena as long-term employer-employee attachments, turnover, work effort, fringe benefits, variable compensation schemes, and employee voice mechanisms (Lazear 1992; Mitchell 1988; Ichniowski 1992; Kleiner 1992; Lewin and Mitchell 1992). In brief, this work begins with the stylized fact that it is often difficult for the employer to observe and monitor employee job performance. Therefore, employers are motivated to structure compensation schemes that pay workers less than the value of their marginal product early in their careers, and more than the value of their marginal product later in their careers. This in turn leads to upward-sloping age-earnings profiles for workers and long-term employer-employee attachments. Put differently, the upward-sloping age-earnings profile reflects the payment of efficiency wages by employers at individual points along the profile.

Under this arrangement workers are encouraged to monitor their own job performance, and workers whose performance is below target are encouraged to leave the firm — that is, to quit. But the central tendency under this implicit contracting arrangement is for workers to perform to targeted requirements (rather than shirk) and to remain in their jobs because later in their careers they will in effect receive pay premiums. Quitting early in their career means that workers will lose such premiums.

Employers also have a generalized incentive to keep turnover low due to the costs of recruitment, screening, hiring, and training, and because of the benefits they receive from paying wages below marginal product early in employees' careers. (Employers who attempt to discharge workers at the point at which pay just equals marginal product presumably will be dissuaded from doing so by the fact that information about such a practice will be efficiently traded in the labor market; the firm, having acquired a reputation for engaging in this practice, will eventually be unable to attract workers.) However, employers also have a generalized incentive to encourage workers to leave the firm later in their career, when their pay premiums are the greatest. For this purpose, employers adopt fringe benefit plans that are typically backloaded (Mitchell 1992) — they provide the largest payouts for the last few years of service — and that are sometimes sweetened to encourage "early" retirement (Lazear 1979).

The concept of implicit contracting in the labor market can also be applied to the use of team or group incentives. Such incentives, especially in the form of profit-sharing and employee stock ownership plans for workers, have become widespread in the United States (Delaney, Lewin, and Ichniowski 1989). Basically, these plans reward employees based on team or group performance and do so after the fact — a form of payment for output as distinct from payment for input, which is in the form of salaries or wages. The possibility of such after-the-fact payments being made forms part of the implicit contract between the firm and the worker.

A major analytical issue in the area of team incentives involves motivation and the free rider problem. Why should an individual worker put forth the effort to perform to target when the efforts of others on the team will result in meeting the performance target? In other words, what is the motivation for the individual worker not to shirk under a team-based incentive plan? One answer is that the individual may know his or her coworkers well (perhaps even be related to them) or may feel a sense of altruism toward or identification with them. Programs of team-based employee involvement and participation in decision making are intended to strengthen such mutual identification. Another answer is that the team may engage in reciprocal monitoring to prevent shirking or to raise the cost to a worker of his or her failure to achieve the performance target. The Hawthorne experiments long ago showed that work groups can develop powerful norms supporting the achievement of organizational performance standards (Roethlisberger and Dickson 1939), and a more recent study of a U.S. paper mill showed how work groups strongly enforced production objectives under a newly introduced team concept of work organization (Ichniowski 1992). Such reciprocal monitoring within a work team appears to require some type of groupwide monetary incentive, such as a profit-sharing plan. Again, the use of reciprocal monitoring together with team incentives can be viewed as constituting some of the terms of the implicit contract between the employer and the employee.

The notion of a psychological contract between the employer and the employee has long been used by industrial and organizational psychologists to refer to the set of expectations, beliefs, and attitudes that each party has with regard to the other (Schein 1980). Psychologists generally emphasize the importance of a proper match or fit between the parties' expectations, beliefs, and attitudes, and contend that mismatches along these dimensions of the employment relationship will result in dysfunctional consequences for the employee and the employer.

For example, following the Hawthorne experiments a stream of research explored the phenomenon of individual and work group restriction of output (Mathewson 1931; Roy 1952; Stagner 1956). Such behavior typically occurs in response to certain management actions, including unilateral changes in the organization of work, speedup of production processes, discharge of workers for cause, reductions in pay rates, and alterations of other terms and conditions of employment. Whatever their specific form, these and related management actions are sometimes judged by workers to violate the norms of their implicit psychological contracts with employers, hence the consequent restriction of output. In unionized settings, workers have sometimes responded to certain management actions by engaging in work slowdowns and strikes (that is, in particular forms of restriction of output); in these instances, workers judge management to have violated the terms of both explicit collective bargaining contracts and implicit psychological contracts (Kornhauser, Dubin, and Ross 1954; Karsh 1958).

More recently, studies of organizational entry have found that employee job performance and tenure are positively associated with "realistic" job previews, which provide job applicants with a balance of positive and negative organizational attributes and characteristics, in contrast to traditional job previews, which heavily emphasize positive organizational attributes and characteristics (Wanous 1992). The main conclusion of this research is that employees who enter an organization with a realistic picture of it are more likely than others to find the terms of their psychological contract with the organization actually met, leading to positive individual and organizational outcomes.

A plethora of research on employee absenteeism from and lateness to work finds that these behaviors are significantly associated with perceived violations of the norms of the psychological contract (Mobley 1982; Clegg 1983). Such violations, which may take many forms, apparently set off a sequential process of reduced employee commitment to the organization, heightened employee dissatisfaction with the organization, and increased employee withdrawal from the organization (Mowday, Porter, and Steers 1982; O'Reilly and

Chatman 1986). Moreover, employee withdrawal may proceed past the absenteeism and lateness stages to "voluntary" departure — that is, quitting — and several studies report significant negative associations between employee commitment and turnover, and between employee job satisfaction and turnover (Porter et al. 1974; Mobley 1982).

Even more recently, concepts of procedural justice, organization culture, and employee voice have been used to analyze employee attachment to and withdrawal from work organizations. The procedural justice literature focuses on the extent to which various organizational processes, especially the allocation of rewards, are judged by workers to meet expected standards of fairness. Perceived violations of such standards are associated with decreased employee commitment to and increased employee withdrawal from the firm (Sheppard, Lewicki, and Minton 1992). Similarly, organizations with strong cultures — that is, organizations whose members share common values and beliefs that are typically expressed in various rites, rituals, and symbols and that are systematically passed on to new members — are characterized by high employee commitment and low employee withdrawal (O'Reilly 1989; O'Reilly, Chatman, and Caldwell 1990). A strong organizational culture is widely regarded by researchers as a social control mechanism (O'Reilly 1989) and is often claimed to be a prerequisite for the successful introduction and implementation of team-building initiatives and broadened employee involvement and participation in decision making (Lawler 1986; Siehl and Martin 1990; Levine and Tyson 1990).

As to the concept of employee voice, most research in this area proceeds from Albert Hirschman's exit-voice-loyalty model, which posits that the exercise of voice will be negatively associated with exit (that is, withdrawal) behavior (Hirschman 1970). In the employment context, voice can be exercised through labor unions, grievance procedures, or both. While large-scale cross-sectional research shows that unionism is significantly negatively associated with employee quits, or exit (Freeman and Medoff 1984), longitudinal research on individual unionized and nonunion firms shows that the exercise of voice through grievance and grievance-like procedures is positively associated with voluntary and involuntary employee exit from the firm (Lewin and Peterson 1988; Lewin 1987a, 1992). Further, employee loyalty (a proxy for commitment) is significantly negatively associated with grievance filing (the exercise of voice) in the firm (Boroff and Lewin 1991; Lewin 1994). Indeed, evidence from this research also supports the conclusion that employees who exercise voice via grievance filing are likely to suffer reprisals for doing so —

which appears to constitute a violation of explicit contracts in unionized settings and implicit contracts in nonunion settings.

All of this research is consistent with, in fact embedded in, the older notion of a psychological contract between the employee and the employer. Concepts of procedural justice, organizational culture, and employee voice offer new insights into the dynamics and consequences of mismatches between employee and employer expectations, attitudes, and beliefs. In most settings, which is to say nonunion settings, these expectations, attitudes, and beliefs are part of implicit individual contracts between employers and employees. Given the large amount of attention that economists and psychologists have paid (from markedly different perspectives) to implicit individual contracting in the labor market, and perhaps especially given the evidence that the terms of such contracts can be and are transgressed, it is important to consider whether or not such implicit contracting will be supplanted by explicit contracting in the labor market.[1] Prior to doing so, however, I will examine the extent to which individual explicit labor market contracting is presently practiced in the United States.

Measuring and Modeling Explicit Contracts

As I have noted, systematic data on explicit individual labor market contracting in the United States are generally not available. However, a special survey of individual labor market contracting conducted in 1990 under the auspices of the University of California at Los Angeles (UCLA) Institute of Industrial Relations provides some relevant data in this regard. The survey was conducted among a sample of business units of publicly held U.S. firms listed in Standard and Poor's Compustat financial reporting file.[2]

As is shown in Table 15.1, among the 1,274 businesses that responded to the UCLA survey, about 31 percent use explicit individual contracts, which are typically referred to as employment contracts. The incidence of such contracts is greatest among professional employees, followed by managerial personnel, while manufacturing and financial service businesses practice individual employment contracting considerably more than do businesses in other industry categories. Explicit individual employment contracts are also more prevalent among unionized than nonunion businesses, younger than older businesses, smaller than larger businesses, and multinational than domestic businesses.[3] A logit-type regression analysis of these data, which treated the aforementioned variables as structural characteristics of firms, showed that the incidence of explicit individual contracting differs significantly by occupation, industry, unionization, age of business, and geographical scope of business, but not by size of business.

Based on economic theorizing about implicit contracting in the labor market and behavioral science theorizing about the psychological contract in the employment relationship, a variety of factors other than the structural characteristics of firms may influence decisions by business organizations to adopt (or not adopt) explicit individual employment contracts. For example, businesses that use work teams may attempt to curb potential shirking and free-rider

Table 15.1. Incidence of explicit individual contracting, by firms' structural characteristics

	Explicit contracting	
Characteristics of firm	Yes (%)	No (%)
Total sample ($N = 1,274$)	31	69
Occupation		
Managerial	36	64
Professional	42	58
Clerical	14	86
Production	23	77
Unionization		
High unionization	37	63
Low unionization	28	72
Industry/sector		
Agriculture, mining, construction	13	87
Manufacturing	43	57
Transportation, communications, public utilities	27	73
Wholesale and retail trade	21	79
Finance, insurance, real estate	39	61
Services	28	72
Firm size		
Large	30	70
Small	33	67
Firm age		
Old	27	73
Young	37	63
Geographic scope		
Multinational firm	39	61
Domestic firm	27	73

Source: UCLA Institute of Industrial Relations Explicit Contracting Survey, 1990.

problems, and to strengthen the motivational basis of teamwork, by practicing explicit individual contracting. Similarly, businesses that use variable pay arrangements for employees — for example, gain sharing, profit sharing, bonus, stock option, or stock ownership plans — may be especially likely to practice explicit individual contracting to formalize and underscore the potential financial gains to employees from achieving specified performance goals.

The rapidly growing literature on human resource management suggests still other factors that may affect the incidence of explicit individual employment contracting. Various subsets of this literature provide theoretical or empirical support for the positive influences of employee information-sharing programs, flexible job design programs, employee training programs, and targeted, validated selection practices on firm performance (Kleiner and Bouillon 1988; Morishima 1991; Katz and Keffe 1990; Osterman 1988; Mangum, Mangum and Hansen 1990; Fossum 1990; Hunter and Schmidt 1982; Arvey and Faley 1988). Businesses that have adopted such practices may also be likely to practice explicit individual contracting as a way of "binding" employees to the firm and raising the probability of realizing "returns" on these new initiatives.

Another subset of the human resource management literature emphasizes the linkages between a business's human resource policies and practices and its overall strategy — so-called strategic human resource management. Ostensibly, the stronger this linkage, the more likely that human resource policies and practices will contribute to the performance of the business (Kochan, Katz, and McKersie 1986; Kleiner et al. 1987; Lewin 1987b). One empirical measure of this linkage is the extent to which a business's senior human resource official is involved in the strategic planning process (Delaney, Lewin, and Ichniowski 1989; Lewin and Mitchell 1992). For purposes of this chapter, it is suggested that businesses with a "strong" link between human resource management strategy and business strategy are especially likely to practice explicit individual employment contracting, in part as a way of strengthening this linkage and in part to reflect the concept embedded in this linkage, that human resources are assets in which current investments yield future returns (Strober 1990; Flamholtz 1985).

From the aforementioned literature in procedural justice, organizational culture, and employee voice, it is possible to derive the proposition that businesses with formal systems of dispute resolution — grievance and grievance-like procedures — will be more likely than businesses without such systems to practice explicit individual employment contracting. The presence of a formal dispute resolution system in a business indicates that certain expectations and beliefs about the employment relationship have gone beyond the informal shared-values stage to the explicit codification stage. Thus, a logical next step may be to codify certain other dimensions of the employment relationship in explicit individual contracts. Additionally, however, businesses that have been charged with race, sex, or age discrimination by current or former employees, or with wrongful termination by former employees, are more likely to engage in explicit individual contracting than businesses that have not been so charged.

The UCLA survey elicited data on financial and nonfinancial participation programs, information sharing, flexible job design, training programs, selection practices, grievance systems, and discrimination and wrongful termination activity in the responding businesses, thereby making it possible to test for the effects of these variables on the use of explicit individual employment contracting. Table 15.2 presents descriptive statistics for this set of variables, and Table 15.3 presents the results of regression analyses in which the incidence of explicit individual employment contracting among the firms that responded to the UCLA survey served as the dependent variable.

The data in Table 15.2 suggest that the incidence of explicit individual employment contracting varies markedly by the human resource management characteristics of firms. Specifically, the incidence of explicit individual contracting varies positively with firms' use of financial participation, information sharing, and employee training programs as well as with selection test validation, senior human resource executive involvement in business planning, formal grievance procedures, and experience with employment discrimination and wrongful discharge litigation. By contrast, the incidence of explicit individual contracting varies negatively with firms' use of employee nonfinancial participation programs and flexible job design programs.

The regression results presented in Table 15.3 refine and extend these findings.[4] Firms with employee financial participation (FP), information sharing (IS), and formal training (TRAIN) programs, and those that have experienced employment discrimination or wrongful termination litigation (DISC), are significantly more likely to practice explicit individual employment contracting than are firms without such characteristics (column 2). The validation of selection tests (VALID), use of grievance procedures (GP), and involvement of senior human resource officials in business planning (HRI) are positively but not significantly related to the incidence of explicit employment contracting, while programs of employee nonfinancial participation

(NFP) and flexible job design (FJD) are negatively but not significantly related to the incidence of explicit contracting. Moreover, these findings generally hold when selected firm structural characteristics are included in the regression analysis (column 3).[5]

The dichotomous (yes-no) dependent variable used to this point does not capture the scope of explicit individual employment contracting in two respects: the proportion of a firm's work force that is covered by such contracts, and the terms and conditions of employ-

Table 15.2. Relationships between incidence of explicit individual contracting and firms' human resource management characteristics

Human resource management characteristics	Incidence of explicit individual contracting (%)
Employee financial participation program (FP)	
Yes	36
No	26
Employee nonfinancial participation program (NFP)	
Yes	29
No	33
Information sharing program (IS)	
Yes	35
No	27
Flexible job design program (FJD)	
Yes	29
No	32
Employee training program (TRAIN)	
Yes	35
No	27
Employee selection test validation (VALID)	
Yes	34
No	28
Human resource executive involved in business planning (HRI)	
Yes	35
No	28
Formal grievance procedure (GP)	
Yes	33
No	30
Employment discrimination/wrongful termination litigation (DISC)	
Yes	37
No	27

Source: UCLA Institute of Industrial Relations Explicit Contracting Survey, 1990. Total number of cases: 1,068.

Table 15.3. Regression estimates of the incidence of explicit individual contracting (t-values in parentheses)

1	2	3
Independent variable	Dependent variable	
	Explicit contracting	Explicit contracting
Constant	3.03	2.87
	(2.04)	(1.95)
FP	2.64*	2.45*
	(1.23)	(1.12)
NFP	−0.63	−0.59
	(−0.42)	(−0.38)
IS	1.92*	1.77*
	(0.91)	(0.84)
FJD	−0.44	−0.40
	(−0.30)	(−0.28)
TRAIN	1.83*	1.69*
	(0.87)	(0.81)
VALID	1.23	1.17
	(0.88)	(0.79)
HRI	1.42	1.31
	(1.02)	(0.94)
GP	1.27	1.19
	(0.78)	(0.71)
DISC	2.23**	2.11**
	(0.92)	(0.85)
Proportion of managerial and professional employees (MGR-PROF)	—	1.58*
		(0.73)
Firm in manufacturing or financial services sector (MFG-FIRE)	—	1.83*
		(0.87)
Firm operates outside U.S. (MNC)	—	1.54*
		(0.71)
Percent of workers unionized (UNION)	—	1.02
		(0.69)
R^2	.28	.33
Number of cases	1,042	1,016

* Significant at $p = < .05$.
** Significant at $p = < .01$.

ment that are covered by such contracts.[6] The UCLA survey provided direct data on (estimates of) respondent firms' employee coverage by explicit contracts, and these were used to test scope-of-
coverage regression equations, the results of which are reported in
Table 15.4. Several individual questions included in the UCLA sur-

Table 15.4 Regression estimates of percent of employees covered by
explicit individual contracts (t-values in parentheses)

1	2	3
Independent variable	Dependent variable	
	% of Employees covered	% of Employees covered
Constant	2.67	2.45
	(2.13)	(1.93)
FP	2.56*	2.32*
	(1.23)	(1.13)
NFP	−2.36*	−2.15*
	(−1.09)	(−1.04)
IS	2.04*	1.92*
	(0.93)	(0.86)
FJD	−2.01*	−1.87*
	(−0.91)	(−0.90)
TRAIN	1.96*	1.79*
	(0.92)	(0.85)
VALID	0.82	0.76
	(0.59)	(0.55)
HRI	1.30	1.21
	(0.82)	(0.79)
GP	0.99	0.97
	(0.65)	(0.64)
DISC	2.39**	2.16**
	(0.98)	(0.89)
MGR-PROF	—	1.64*
		(0.73)
MFG-FIRE	—	1.82*
		(0.81)
MNC	—	1.73*
		(0.84)
UNION	—	1.18
		(0.76)
R²	.34	.39
Number of cases	327	323

Note: Based on data for firms with explicit individual contracts.
* Significant at $p = < .05$.
** Significant at $p = < .01$.

vey were used to construct a terms-and-conditions scope-of-coverage variable (index), and responses to these questions served as the data for testing the relevant regressions equations, the results of which are reported in Table 15.5.[7]

From Table 15.4 it can be observed that, as with the incidence of explicit individual contracting, the proportion of a firm's employees covered by explicit individual contracts is significantly positively associated with several human resource management characteristics of firms: the use of financial participation, information sharing, and formal training programs, and experience with discrimination or wrongful termination litigation (column 2). Several structural characteristics of firms are also positively associated with the proportion of employees covered by explicit contracts, namely, the proportion of managerial and professional employees in the firm (MGR-PROF), presence of the firm in the manufacturing or financial services sector (MFG-FIRE) and the extent to which a firm operates outside of the United States (MNC) (column 3).[8] The use of nonfinancial participation and flexible job design programs are significantly negatively associated with the proportion of a firm's employees covered by explicit individual contracts. On balance, then, the incidence of explicit individual contracts and the percentage of a firm's employees covered by such contracts are for the most part influenced by common human resource management and structural variables.

The findings reported in Tables 15.3 and 15.4 for the financial participation (FP), nonfinancial participation (NFP), and flexible job design (FJD) variables are especially notable, not only because the signs on the coefficients of NFP and FJD are opposite of those that were predicted (that is, they are negative rather than positive), but also because of the recent emphasis in U.S. business on rethinking the ways in which work is organized and employees are utilized and rewarded. Initiatives to enhance the flexibility of work arrangements, to involve employees more fully in workplace and organizational decision making, and to increase the relative proportion of variable pay (or pay at risk) in the compensation package have become widespread in recent years (Delaney, Lewin, and Ichniowski 1989; Kochan, Katz, and McKersie 1986). Yet apparently only the last of these initiatives is positively associated with the use of explicit individual contracting in the labor market. When it comes to designing more flexible jobs and involving employees more fully in decision making via programs of nonfinancial participation, employers seemingly prefer to treat these arrangements as part of implicit contracts with employees.

Somewhat different dynamics, however, are at work with respect to the scope of terms and conditions included in explicit individual contracts, as is evident from the regression results presented in Table 15.5. They show that the scope of coverage is significantly negatively associated with the use of financial *and* nonfinancial participation programs, information sharing programs, and the presence of griev-

Table 15.5. Regression estimates of scope of terms and conditions covered by explicit individual contracts (t-values in parentheses)

	1	2	3
		Dependent variable	
	Independent variable	Scope of terms and conditions	Scope of terms and conditions
Constant		2.38	2.19
		(1.94)	(1.82)
FP		−2.17*	−2.06*
		(−0.96)	(−0.92)
NFP		−2.31*	−2.16*
		(−1.04)	(−0.95)
IS		−1.98*	−1.89*
		(−0.91)	(−0.87)
FSD		−1.15	−1.09
		(0.79)	(−0.76)
TRAIN		−0.81	−0.76
		(−0.59)	(−0.57)
VALID		0.50	0.46
		(0.36)	(0.34)
HRI		1.73*	1.61*
		(0.83)	(0.72)
GP		−1.87*	−1.76*
		(−0.89)	(−0.82)
DISC		1.04	0.96
		(0.71)	(0.69)
MGR-PROF		0.87	0.81
		(0.60)	(0.58)
MFG-FIRE		1.77*	1.68*
		(0.82)	(0.77)
MNC		0.73	0.67
		(0.48)	(0.45)
UNION		1.62*	1.54*
		(0.73)	(0.70)
R^2		.31	.35
Number of cases		324	311

Note: Based on data for firms with explicit individual contracts.
* Significant at $p = < .05$.

ance procedures, and significantly positively associated with senior human resource executive involvement in business planning, presence of the firm in the manufacturing or financial services sector (MFG-FIRE), and the percentage of the firm's work force that is unionized (UNION) (columns 2 and 3). Recall that financial participation and information sharing programs were previously found to be significantly positively related to the incidence of explicit individual contracts and to the proportion of a firm's employees covered by such contracts. Further, the firm's use of formal training programs and its experience with discrimination or wrongful termination litigation, which were also significantly related (in opposite directions) to the incidence of explicit individual contracts and to the proportion of a firm's employees covered by such contracts, are not significantly related to the scope of terms and conditions included in explicit individual contracts. Hence, the scope of terms and conditions included in explicit individual contracts in U.S. firms is apparently subject to a somewhat different set of determinants from those that influence the incidence of and proportion of employees covered by explicit contracts.

Case Examples of Explicit Individual Contracting

Among the specific terms and conditions covered by explicit individual contracts in the firms that responded to the UCLA survey, the most prevalent were those pertaining to employee access to so-called trade secrets.[9] The typical contract provision requires the employee to agree not to reveal trade secrets of the firm to competitors during and (for a specified period) following the employee's tenure with the firm. In return, the employee is given access to these trade secrets that are sometimes associated with an upgrading or promotion of the employee and, more broadly, with continuity of employment.

The most common trade secrets in this regard take the form of components of the production process in manufacturing firms and lists of customers or clients in service firms. Other trade secrets pertain to customer credit ratings, supplier-vendor financial information, inventory valuation, computer programs, and security procedures. Provisions for and restrictions on employee use of trade secrets are most often found in explicit individual contracts with professional personnel — notably scientists and engineers — and appear to be most prevalent among firms that serve as defense contractors and subcontractors. Nevertheless, clerical and production employees are also sometimes parties to explicit individual contracts that contain trade secret provisions.

Explicit individual employment contracts for executive and managerial personnel sometimes contain provisions barring such personnel from revealing the firm's strategic planning process and written business plans to competitors during and following the executive or manager's tenure with the firm. Such contracts also often contain language restricting the executive or manager for a specified time period from opening or joining a business that is a direct competitor of the firm in question. Provisions pertaining to personal nonwork behavior are also more prevalent in explicit individual contracts with managerial than with nonmanagerial personnel, according to the UCLA data.[10]

To better illustrate the uses to which explicit individual contracts are presently being put by U.S. firms, I will briefly consider three examples of such contracts, one in an aerospace firm, another in a financial services firm, and the last in a hotel and restaurant firm. To preserve confidentiality, the firms are referred to below as Firm A, Firm F, and Firm H, respectively. The data for this comparison were obtained from site visits, field interviews, and archival analysis in three firms that were among those that responded to the 1990 UCLA survey and that subsequently agreed to participate in this phase of the study.[11]

Firm A

This large aerospace firm produces aircraft, aircraft components, and a wide variety of other aviation products, largely for the U.S. Air Force. As of 1990, some 80 percent of its business was done under contract with the Department of Defense. About 75 percent of the firm's 36,000-member work force has signed explicit individual employment contracts, and this proportion rises to almost 100 percent for the firm's managerial and professional employees.

Virtually all of these explicit individual contracts contain a trade secrets provision, which reads in part as follows:

> As a condition of continued employment with [Firm A], the employee agrees not to reveal to competitors, suppliers, or employees of other units of [Firm A] information about [Firm A's] products, production processes and components, subcontractors, inventories, accounting methods, and financial reports. Violation of this provision will result in disciplinary action by [Firm A], including possible termination of employment.

The written contract containing this and other provisions is proferred to the job applicant in the late stages of the employment-selection process, that is, just prior to hiring. Failure of the job applicant to sign the contract will result in the applicant's not being hired by Firm A. According to the personnel data supplied by this firm for the period from 1986 to 1990, about 2 percent of job applicants who make it through the employment-selection process to this stage refuse to sign explicit individual employment contracts. Also during this period, four cases of individuals who violated the trade secrets provision of their explicit contracts with Firm A were discovered, and all four cases resulted in termination from the firm.

For senior executive and managerial personnel of Firm A, explicit individual contracts contain the following provision:

> As a condition of continued employment with [Firm A], the employee agrees not to reveal to competitors, suppliers, government officials, or employees of other units of [Firm A] information about [Firm A's] business plans, business strategy, or customers. Violation of this provision will result in disciplinary action by [Firm A], including possible termination of employment. Further, upon separation from [Firm A], the employee agrees not to seek employment with or become employed with a competitor company for a period of three years following such separation. Violation of this provision will result in legal action by [Firm A] against the former employee.

Employee agreement to these provisions is required for the employee to be placed in a senior executive or managerial position with Firm A. According to personnel data supplied by this firm for the period from 1986 to 1990, during which time Firm A made 34 appointments to senior executive and managerial positions, three individuals refused to sign explicit individual contracts containing the provisions shown above. Further, during this same period two senior executives who left the firm went to work for competitors of Firm A, which subsequently brought legal action against them. One of these executives then left his new employer, and the other was dismissed by his new employer upon receipt of notice of Firm A's legal action.

Firm F
This financial services firm provides investment banking, personal banking, brokerage, and related services to a mix of corporate, business, and individual clients. Approximately 80 percent of its 2,400-member work force has signed explicit individual employment contracts, and this proportion rises to 100 percent for professional

personnel (for example, investment bankers and stock brokers) and senior executives. The explicit contracts used by this firm are lengthy and cover such matters as trade secrets, fiduciary responsibilities, and treatment of customers. In addition, however, these contracts specify the compensation arrangement between individual employees and firm and are "renegotiated" annually. An example of the compensation provision of one such explicit contract reads as follows:

> During 1989, [the employee] will be paid a salary of $112,000.00 by [Firm F]. [The employee] will be eligible to participate in the 1989 bonus pool provided that he remains continuously employed with [Firm F] during 1989. The bonus pool will provide [the employee] with no less than four percent of his base salary, and may reach up [sic] to 20 percent depending upon the certified 1989 financial results for [Firm F]. The determination of the size of the bonus pool and its allocation among members of [Firm F] will be at the discretion of the Management Committee."

Beginning in 1986, Firm F expanded the provisions of its explicit contracts with individual employees to encompass certain aspects of personal behavior, especially in the area of substance abuse. Selected provisions of this new "standard contract" read as follows:

> As a condition of employment with [Firm F], the employee agrees not to use illegal substances, including drugs. Upon discovery by [Firm F] of the use of such substances by an employee, the employee will be dismissed and referral may be made to proper authorities for subsequent legal action.

> As a condition of employment with [Firm F], the employee agrees to submit to tests for substance and chemical dependency. The results of such tests, including the bodily fluids extracted from the employee, will remain the property of [Firm F].

> [Firm F] retains the right to make known to proper authorities and inquiring commercial enterprises the results of tests for chemical and substance dependency performed on the employee. The employee agrees to waive his right to bring legal action against [Firm F] in the event that such test results are made known to government authorities, commercial enterprises, or other inquiring organizations and parties.

As with Firm A, Firm F presents explicit individual contracts containing these and other provisions to job applicants late in the employment-selection process, just prior to hiring. According to personnel data provided by Firm F for the period from 1986 to 1990, approximately 24 percent of job applicants to managerial and professional positions who made it through the early stages of the employment-selection process refused to sign explicit contracts proferred to them by the firm. Also during this period, some 3.5 percent of Firm F's employees were dismissed for violating one or another provision of their explicit contracts with the firm.

Firm H

This firm is in the hotel and restaurant business and operates more than 1,000 such establishments in the United States and abroad. It has about 160,000 employees worldwide, of whom approximately 80 percent work in the United States. Historically, Firm H has had high employee turnover rates, averaging 100 percent annually across various occupational specialties, and approaching 400 percent annually for jobs such as desk clerk, reservations agent, and bell captain. Historically as well, Firm H has maintained explicit individual employment contracts only for a few senior executives and certain security personnel.

Beginning in 1988, however, Firm H decided to adopt explicit individual contracting for a variety of hotel and restaurant personnel at selected locations. The rationale for this decision was that such contracting would help reduce employee turnover, lengthen employee job tenure, and enable Firm H to secure a larger (and more certain) return on its investment in employee training. Such training was deemed necessary to bring new employees up to "threshold" levels of reading, writing, computing, and customer relations skills, but the problem for the firm was that it had little or no way to ensure that new employees would remain with the firm long enough to permit the training to, in effect, pay off. Explicit contracting was judged by Firm H's senior management, especially its senior human resources executives, to be a partial solution to this problem. In addition, achievement of these human resource objectives was considered critical to achieving a key business objective, namely, increased customer satisfaction.

The explicit contract offered by Firm H to prospective employees (in selected locations) contains the following provision:

> As a condition of employment with [Firm H], [the employee] agrees to participate in company-provided training which will begin immediately upon [the employee's] hiring by [Firm H] and which will last for three weeks. Following successful

completion of the training program, [the employee] will receive a six percent base pay increase and a full-time work
assignment. Following six months of satisfactory performance
in this work assignment, [the employee] will receive a five
percent increase in base pay. [The employee] agrees to remain
employed with [Firm H] for 15 months from today, at which
time [Firm H] and [the employee] will jointly decide if the
employment relationship shall be continued.

Other provisions of this explicit contract and other policies of Firm
H allow the employment relationship to be ended by either party
earlier than specified in the contract.[12] Data provided by Firm H for
the period from 1989 to 1990 indicate that approximately 4 percent
of job applicants to whom offers of employment were made rejected
the offers because of unwillingness to sign explicit employment
contracts. Further, some 6 percent of employees hired during this
period left their employment prior to the ending dates specified in
their explicit contracts with Firm H. But these data also showed that
Firm H's hotel and restaurant establishments that used explicit individual employment contracts had lower average employee turnover
rates, longer average employee job tenure, and higher (measured)
levels of customer satisfaction than establishments that did not use
such contracting arrangements. Largely on the basis of these findings, Firm H decided in 1991 to extend the use of explicit employment contracting, from about 20 percent to 40 percent of its hotels
and restaurants in the United States.

As the examples provided by Firms A, F, and H indicate, there is no
uniform or perhaps even standard type of explicit individual employment contract presently prevailing in the U.S. labor market. This is
in contrast to the uniformity of contracts that develop under collective bargaining between unions and employers, and apparently as
well to the uniformity of employment agreements that develop between individual workers and firms in countries (primarily in Western Europe) with antidischarge legislation (Bain 1992).

However, this diversity of explicit individual employment contracts appears quite consistent with economists' notions of implicit
contracting in the labor market and with psychologists' concepts of
psychological contracting in the employment relationship. Absent
active institutions, such as labor unions, works councils, or employee rights legislation, in the structuring of explicit individual
employment contracts, the provisions of such contracts can be expected to vary according to the characteristics of firms, the preferences of management, and the characteristics and preferences of
employees. Indeed, this is consistent with the previously observed

variation in the scope of terms and conditions included in explicit individual contracts, with the variation in the proportion of firms' employees covered by such contracts, and, most basically, with the fact that such contracts exist in some but not other firms.

Nevertheless, perhaps the most interesting question about explicit individual contracting in the labor market is whether or not it will become more dominant or fade from the scene in the years ahead. This question is taken up next, using the evidence presented here as a point of departure.

The Future of Explicit Contracting

Assuming that the data obtained from the sample of firms included in the UCLA survey can be generalized to the business sector as a whole, it appears that a larger proportion of the U.S. work force is presently covered by explicit individual employment contracts than by collective bargaining contracts — roughly 24 percent versus 13 percent. Thus, to a substantial extent, explicit individual contracting has supplanted explicit collective contracting in the U.S. labor market, and the differential incidence of these two contractual forms may widen if predictions of further decline in the unionization of the U.S. work force are taken seriously (Freeman and Medoff 1984; Lewin, Mitchell, and Sherer 1992).

The major "unknown" in all of this concerns the potential conversion of implicit or psychological contracts into explicit contracts. What factors may drive such conversion? The empirical findings and case examples presented in this chapter suggest that increased employer use of financial participation programs, information sharing programs, and employee training programs will contribute to a rising incidence of explicit individual employment contracting and to enlarged proportional coverage of employees by such contracts; so too will a rising incidence of employment discrimination and wrongful termination litigation, relative growth of employment in managerial and professional occupations and in the financial services sector, and enhanced multinational operations of U.S. firms.

Conversely, increased employer use of nonfinancial participation and flexible job design programs is likely to be associated with a decline in the incidence of explicit individual employment contracting and in the proportion of employees covered by such contracts. This is because these human resource management initiatives, more than most others, are typically grounded in the concept of organizational culture, which places strong emphasis on organizational members' "voluntary" (rather than contractual) adherence to a set of core or shared values (O'Reilly 1989). The dominant core value in so-called strong organizational cultures is commitment to the organization (Lawler 1986), and employee nonfinancial participation programs — for example, quality circles, quality-of-working-life improvement schemes, and autonomous work teams — and flexible job and work design programs are intended to enhance such commitment on the part of employees (Cooke 1990). Further, the idea of organizational commitment is closely akin to earlier ideas about attitudes, expectations, and beliefs that stem from the concept of psychological contracting in the employment relationship. And, as in the case of psychological contracting, the members (managers and employees) of "high-commitment" firms characterized by programs of employee nonfinancial participation and flexible job design appear to prefer implicit contracts or shared understandings to explicit individual employment contracts.

However, it is far from certain that the incidence of or employee coverage by nonfinancial participation and flexible job design programs will increase over the next several years. Various threats and challenges to such programs have been identified elsewhere (Lewin 1989b, 1991; Aaron 1992), and perhaps chief among them are the differential "risk preferences" of senior executives and employees with respect to highly participative, flexible work organizations. Employees, or a substantial subset of them, may prefer less participation and flexibility (risk) in work than senior executives who are imbued with enhancing their firms' competitiveness via the development of strong-culture, high-commitment work organizations. Put differently, organizational culture is a mechanism of social control, and as with other such mechanisms employees may prefer less control or to have a formal say in the control process. But just as employees have increasingly been rejecting unionism as a form of workplace participation, they are also likely to reject too much workplace and organizational participation in other forms.[13] Therefore, the apparent dampening effects of employee nonfinancial participation and flexible job design programs on explicit individual contracting in the labor market are unlikely to grow and may well shrink in the next several years.

A more positive case for the growth of explicit individual contracting can be made on the basis of aforementioned initiatives in the areas of employee financial participation, information sharing, and employee training. Firms are increasingly likely to seek more formal arrangements for securing returns on investments in variable pay, information sharing, training programs, and worker self-monitoring, and employees are increasingly likely to expect that these terms and conditions of employment will be put in writing. Enhanced product market competition and use of human resources to achieve strategic business objectives underly this prediction about firm behavior, while the passing of the era of having a "career with the company," and increased use of formal contracting in other spheres of social and economic life (such as for appliance repair and maintenance, various insurance coverages, and credit card usage) are among the factors underlying this prediction about employee expectations and behavior. These forces, in turn, will produce a higher incidence of explicit individual labor market contracting and a higher proportion of employees covered by such contracting arrangements than presently exist, though changes in the scope of terms and conditions under explicit individual employment contracts are far more problematic and difficult to forecast.

Finally, it is also likely that explicit individual labor market contracting will exhibit a certain dualism, segmentation, or, in Kerr's terminology, "balkanization." The incidence of such contracting is greater — and likely to be greater still — in managerial and professional labor markets than in others; in manufacturing and financial service firms than in others; in firms with highly structured internal labor markets rather than in firms with unstructured or nonexistent internal markets; and in firms with variable pay, information sharing, and training programs than in firms without such programs. Thus, while it would stretch credulity to predict that every firm and every employee will soon be party to explicit individual employment contracts, it is plausible to expect that explicit individual contracting will become the new dominant institutional arrangement in U.S. labor markets during the 1990s.

Notes

1. This is hardly the first time that a common industrial relations idea, issue, or problem has been studied by scholars from different disciplines with little or no cross-fertilization. For a more generalized treatment of this phenomenon, see Kaufman 1989, Lewin 1989a, and Cummings 1989.
2. A 40 percent sample of the roughly 5,500 "business lines" listed in the 1990 Compustat II file was selected for the purpose of administering the explicit contracting survey. The initial mail survey was followed by one written and one telephone follow-up survey, yielding an overall 53 percent response rate.

3. For the unionization, firm size, and firm age variables, the distribution of respondents was split at the mean to create high-low, large-small, and old-young categories, respectively. Geographical scope was measured by the proportion of the firm's work force employed outside the United States. As before, the distribution of respondents was split at the mean to create two categories, in this case, multinational and domestic.

4. Examination of the zero-order correlation matrix for the independent variables used in the regression analysis showed no significant multicollinearity. Because this is an "early stage" study of explicit contracting in the labor market, an argument can be made for retaining all of the theoretically motivated independent variables even in the presence of multicollinearity. It is also because this is an early stage study that formal modeling and hypothesis specification have been deemphasized.

5. In effect, these structural characteristics are treated as control variables in the regression analysis.

6. This multiplicity of measures of explicit individual labor market contracting is closely similar to the multiplicity of measures of strike activity — for example, the number of strikes, the number of workers on strike, and work hours and days lost due to strikes (see Kaufman 1992). As with strikes, an argument can be made that the incidence of labor market contracting is less meaningful than the number or proportion of employees covered by such contracts or the scope of terms and conditions included in such contracts.

7. Six items comprise this scope-of-coverage variable, with a five-point scale used for each item. Hence the explicit contract scope-of-coverage index ranges between 6 and 30. The mean score on this index among respondent firms was 16.5, with a standard deviation of 2.4.

8. The variables MNG-PROF and MFG-FIRE are constructed dichotomous variables, with yes = 1, no = 0.

9. The term *trade secrets* is in fact rarely used in the explicit individual employment contracts that were examined during the course of this study. Instead, these contracts often refer to "proprietary" processes, data, and knowledge.

10. Among the responding firms with explicit individual employment contracts, about 17 percent made reference to personal, nonwork behavior in the case of contracts with managerial personnel, compared with 11 percent in the case of contracts with nonmanagerial personnel. Among the personal, nonwork behaviors mentioned in these contracts were alcohol, drug, and gambling dependency, and physical and mental well-being.

11. The site visits, field interviews, and archival analysis were conducted between August 1990 and October 1991. Three other firms have since agreed to participate in a companion study, which is part of the UCLA Project on Explicit Labor Market Contracting.

12. These provisions include general or industry-specific business conditions necessitating layoffs; the sale or relocation of establishments; and

the employee's personal health, financial considerations, and family circumstances. Basically, Firm H does not press unwilling employees to remain in its employ, and chooses not to attempt legally to enforce its explicit contracts with non-managerial personnel. Still, Firm H believes that the main contribution of explicit contracting is to codify the relationship between company-provided training and the employee's subsequent pay and career progression within the firm.

13. Indeed, employees (or a substantial proportion of them) may regard the concept of a strong organizational culture as an ideology of management that, as with prior ideologies, primarily seeks to retain the authoritative control of management over employees (see, for example, Bendix 1956).

References

Aaron, Benjamin. 1992. "A Legal Perspective on Employee Voice," *California Management Review* 34 (Spring), pp. 124–138.

Arvey, Richard D., and Robert H. Faley. 1988. *Fairness in Selecting Employees*, 2nd. ed. Reading, Mass.: Addison-Wesley.

Bain, Trevor. 1992. "Employee Voice: A Comparative International Perspective," paper presented to the 44th Annual Meeting of the Industrial Relations Research Association, New Orleans, January.

Bendix, Reinhard. 1956. *Work and Authority in Industry.* New York: Harper.

Boroff, Karen, and David Lewin. 1991. "Loyalty, Voice, and Intent to Exit a Nonunion Firm: A Conceptual and Empirical Analysis." Los Angeles: UCLA Institute of Industrial Relations, Working Paper no. 211.

Bureau of National Affairs. 1991. *Basic Patterns in Union Contract.* Washington, D.C.: Bureau of National Affairs.

Clegg, W H. 1983. "The Psychology of Employee Lateness, Absence, and Turnover," *Journal of Applied Psychology* 68 (December), pp. 88–101.

Cooke, William. 1990. *Labor-Management Cooperation.* Kalamazoo, Mich.: Upjohn.

Cummings, Larry L. 1989. "Comments on Models of Man in Industrial Relations," *Industrial and Labor Relations Review* 43 (October), pp. 93–96.

Delaney, John Thomas, David Lewin, and Casey Ichniowski. 1989. *Human Resource Policies and Practices in American Firms.* Washington, D.C.: U.S. Department of Labor, Bureau of Labor-Management Relations and Cooperative Affairs, Bulletin no. 139.

Flamholtz, Eric G. 1985. *Human Resource Accounting.* San Francisco: Jossey-Bass.

Fossum, John A. 1990. "New Dimensions in the Design and Delivery of Corporate Training Programs," in Louis A. Ferman et al. eds., *New Development in Worker Training: A Legacy for the 1990s.* Madison, Wis.: Industrial Relations Research Association, pp. 129–156.

Freeman, Richard B., and James L. Medoff. 1984. *What Do Unions Do?* New York: Basic Books.

Hunter, John E., and Frank L. Schmidt. 1982. "Ability Tests: Economic Benefits versus the Issue of Fairness," *Industrial Relations* 21 (Fall), pp. 293–308.

Hirschman, Albert O. 1970. *Exit, Voice, and Loyalty.* Cambridge, Mass.: Harvard University Press.

Ichniowski, Casey. 1992. "Human Resource Practices and Productive Labor-Management Relations," in David Lewin, Olivia S. Mitchell, and Peter D. Sherer, eds., *Research Frontiers in Industrial Relations and Human Resources.* Madison, Wis.: Industrial Relations Research Association, pp. 239–271.

Karsh, Bernard. 1958. *Diary of a Strike.* Urbana: University of Illinois Press.

Katz, Harry C., and Jeffrey H. Keefe. 1992. "Collective Bargaining and Industrial Relations Outcomes: The Causes and Consequences of Diversity," in David Lewin, Olivia S. Mitchell, and Peter D. Sherer, eds., *Research Frontiers in Industrial Relations and Human Resources.* Madison, Wis.: Industrial Relations Research Association, pp. 43–75.

Kaufman, Bruce E. 1989. "Models of Man in Industrial Relations Research," *Industrial and Labor Relations Review* 43 (October) pp. 72–88.

———. 1992. "Research on Strike Models and Outcomes in the 1980s: Accomplishments and Shortcomings," in David Lewin, Olivia S. Mitchell, and Peter D. Sherer, eds., *Research Frontiers in Industrial Relations and Human Resources.* Madison, Wis.: Industrial Relations Research Association, pp. 77–129.

Kerr, Clark. 1954. "The Balkanization of Labor Markets," in E. Wight Bakke, ed., *Labor Mobility and Economic Opportunity.* Cambridge, Mass.: MIT Press, pp. 92–110.

Kleiner, Morris M. 1992. "Employee Voice: An Economic Perspective," paper presented to the 44th Annual Meeting of the Industrial Relations Research Association, New Orleans, January.

Kleiner, Morris M., and Marvin L. Bouillon. 1988. "Providing Business Information to Production Workers: Correlates of Compensation and Profitability," *Industrial and Labor Relations Review* 41 (July), pp. 605–617.

Kleiner, Morris M., et al., eds. 1987. *Human Resources and the Performance of the Firm.* Madison, Wis.: Industrial Relations Research Association.

Kochan, Thomas A., Harry C. Katz, and Robert B. McKersie. 1986. *The Transformation of American Industrial Relations.* New York: Basic Books.

Kornhauser, Arthur, Robert Dubin, and Arthur M. Ross, eds. 1954. *Industrial Conflict.* New York: McGraw-Hill.

Lawler, Edward E., III. 1986. *High-Involvement Management.* San Francisco: Jossey-Bass.

Lazear, Edward P. 1979. "Why Is There Mandatory Retirement?" *Journal of Political Economy* 87 (December), pp. 1261–1284.

———. 1992. "Compensation, Productivity, and the New Economics of Personnel," in David Lewin, Olivia S. Mitchell, and Peter D. Sherer, eds., *Research Frontiers in Industrial Relations and Human Resources.* Madison, WI: Industrial Relations Research Association, pp. 341–380.

Levine, David I., and Laura D'Andrea Tyson. 1990. "Participation, Productivity, and the Firm's Environment," in Alan S. Blinder, ed., *Paying for Productivity.* Washington, D.C.: Brookings Institution, pp. 183–237.

Lewin, David. 1987a. "Dispute Resolution in the Nonunion Firm: A Theoretical and Empirical Analysis," *Journal of Conflict Resolution* 31 (September), pp. 465–502.

———. 1987b. "Industrial Relations as a Strategic Variable," in Morris M. Kleiner et al., eds., *Human Resources and the Performance of the Firm.* Madison, Wis.: Industrial Relations Research Association, pp. 1–41.

———. 1989a. "Models of Man in Industrial Relations Research: Why Psychology Is Not the Sine Qua Non," *Industrial and Labor Relations Review* 43 (October), pp. 89–92.

———. 1989b. "The Future of Employee Involvement/Participation in the United States," *Labor Law Journal* 40 (August), pp. 470–475.

———. 1991. "Internal Challenges to Human Resource Management in U.S. Business," paper presented to the National University of Singapore–UCLA Conference on the Future of HRM: International Perspectives and Challenges, Singapore, February.

———. 1992. "Grievance Procedures in Nonunion Workplaces: An Empirical Analysis of Usage, Dynamics, and Outcomes," *Chicago-Kent Law Review* 66(3), pp. 823–844.

———. 1994. "Conflict Resolution and Management in Contemporary Work Organizations: Theoretical Perspectives and Empirical Evidence," in Samuel A. Bacharach, Ronald L. Seeber, and David J. Walsh, eds., *Research in the Sociology of Organizations*, 12, forthcoming.

Lewin, David, and Daniel J. B. Mitchell. 1992. "Systems of Employee Voice: Theoretical and Empirical Perspectives," *California Management Review* 34 (Spring), pp. 95–111.

Lewin, David, Olivia S. Mitchell, and Peter D. Sherer. 1992. *Research Frontiers in Industrial Relations and Human Resources.* Madison, Wis.: Industrial Relations Research Association.

Lewin, David, and Richard B. Peterson. 1988. *The Modern Grievance Procedure in the United States.* Westport, Conn.: Quorum.

Mangum, Stephen, Garth Mangum, and Gary Hansen. 1990. "Assessing the Returns to Training," in Louis A. Ferman et al., eds., *New Developments in Worker Training: A Legacy for the 1990s.* Madison, Wis.: Industrial Relations Research Association, pp. 55–89.

Mathewson, Stanley B. 1931. *Restriction of Output among Unorganized Workers.* New York: Viking.

Mitchell, Daniel J. B. 1992. "Social Insurance and Benefits," in David Lewin, Olivia S. Mitchell, and Peter D. Sherer, eds., *Research Frontiers in*

Industrial Relations and Human Resources. Madison, Wis.: Industrial Relations Research Association.

Mitchell, Olivia S. 1988. "Worker Knowledge of Pension Provisions," *Journal of Labor Economics* 17 (Spring), pp. 21–39.

Mobley, William N. 1982. *Employee Turnover: Causes, Consequences, and Control.* Reading, Mass.: Addison-Wesley.

Morishima, Motohiro. 1991. "Information Sharing and Collective Bargaining in Japan: Effects on Wage Negotiation," *Industrial and Labor Relations Review* 44 (April), pp. 469–485.

Mowday, Rick T., Lyman W. Porter, and Richard W. Steers. 1982. *Employee-Organizations Linkages: The Psychology of Commitment, Absenteeism, and Turnover.* New York: Academic Press.

O'Reilly, Charles A. 1989. "Corporations, Culture, and Commitment: Motivation and Social Control in Organizations," *California Management Review* 31 (Winter), pp. 9–25.

O'Reilly, Charles A., and Jerry A. Chatman. 1986. "Organizational Commitment and Psychological Attachment: The Effects of Compliance, Identification, and Internalization on Prosocial Behavior," *Journal of Applied Psychology* 71 (September), pp. 492–499.

O'Reilly, Charles A., Jerry A. Chatman, and David F. Caldwell. 1990. "People, Jobs, and Organizational Culture: A Q-Sort Approach to Assessing Fit," paper presented to the Annual Meeting of the Academy of Management, San Francisco, August.

Osterman, Paul. 1988. *Employment Futures.* New York: Oxford University Press.

Porter, Lyman, et al. 1974. "Organizational Commitment, Job Satisfaction, and Turnover Among Psychiatric Technicians," *Journal of Applied Psychology* 59 (June), pp. 603–609.

Roethlisberger, F. J., and William J. Dickson. 1939. *Management and the Worker.* Cambridge, Mass.: Harvard University Press.

Roy, Donald. 1952. "Quota Restriction and Goldbricking in a Machine Shop," *American Journal of Sociology* 57 (April), pp. 427–442.

Schein, Edgar H. 1980. *Organizational Psychology,* 3rd ed. Englewood Cliffs, N.J.: Prentice Hall.

Sheppard, Blair H., Roy J. Lewicki, and Jeffrey Minton. 1992. *Organizational Justice.* Lexington, Mass.: Lexington Books.

Siehl, Carol, and Joanne Martin. 1990. "Organizational Culture: A Key to Financial Performance?" in Bruce Schneider, ed., *Organizational Climate and Culture.* San Francisco: Jossey-Bass, pp. 234–265.

Stagner, Ross. 1956. *Psychology of Industrial Conflict.* New York: Wiley.

Strober, Myra H. 1990. "Human Capital Theory: Implications for HR Managers," *Industrial Relations* 29 (Spring), pp. 214–239.

Wafilewski, Edward J., Jr. 1992. "Collective Bargaining in 1992: Contract Talks and Other Activity," *Monthly Labor Review* 114 (January), pp. 3–20.

Wanous, John P. 1992. *Organizational Entry,* 2nd ed. Reading, Mass.: Addison-Wesley.

V

The New Industrial State II: What Form Is It Taking?

16

Countervailing Power: Memoir and Modern Reality

■━━━━━━━━━━━━━━■

John Kenneth Galbraith

In 1952, just over 40 years ago, I published a small volume entitled *American Capitalism: The Concept of Countervailing Power*. I am not sure why it was denoted *American* capitalism; perhaps in the stern mood of the time, I was concerned to stress my association both with capitalism and with country. On reflection, however, only Senator Joe McCarthy would have thought that important.

The essential idea of the book can be stated briefly. It held that economic power, both monopolistic and monopsonistic, is not held in check by competition, as classical orthodoxy strongly held, and certainly not alone by competition. Any exercise of power induces a countervailing development: against the power of the producer of goods and services is arrayed the power of the buyer, that of the chain store or other mass distributor or, more improbably, that of the consumer or farm cooperative. The first begets the second. And in the most visible and socially contentious manifestation of counter-vailing power, the employer of labor brings into being the trade union as a countering force. In an unduly long step, I outlined a new and effective social equilibrium in which the original power of sellers or buyers is competently neutralized in this way.

The implications of this argument for established theory were not slight: instead of competition, there was bilateral and socially self-neutralizing monopoly. There were similar implications for public policy. For half a century and more, the defining economic need had been adequately enforced antitrust legislation. Now I proposed that adverse exercise of economic power induced its own solution. I did not fail to mention that over the years since its enactment the Sherman Act had been most effectively an instrument against labor unions.

I was aware of the strength of my assault on accepted ideas and ideology. The comprehensively benign role of competition was basic in the established economic faith and so also were the means for ensuring it. I legitimatized fully the trade union, which had always enjoyed in the aforementioned orthodoxy a slightly insecure position as an impairment of the otherwise pure current of competition.

My argument did not go unnoticed. The American Economic Association scheduled a session at its next annual meeting in Washington to denounce the break with established orthodoxy. This was normal. And, as a footnote, my dissent from the general rule and benignity of competition made its way into the literature and even into the textbooks.

I have not pursued these particular ideas with any great energy myself, although I am far from averse to doing this when it seems appropriate. I am led to return to the subject here, for it bears on some of the modern developments as regards labor and labor unions. And I am encouraged to do so because Gus Tyler, an old friend, a noted trade union official, and a sometime opponent in sharp debate over foreign policy, has recently written an admirably lucid and learned paper on the subject.[1] The questions to be addressed are: What is the present state of the trade union position, and what has happened to the countervailing power that seemed so evident and so promising four decades back in the years immediately following the Second World War?

None of this is to say that the trade union is disappearing. As Tyler wrote, "The AFL-CIO can still boast that, at present, it represents more workers than at any time in its history, in absolute if not in relative numbers."[2] What has happened is that unions — or to be more specific, the solid body of the movement — are no longer in the industries where they exercised countervailing power in opposition to strong employers. Instead they have shifted to the service industries, and notably to government as well as education, where union membership is extensive.

In the service industries, however, the role of the unions is very different. There they enforce minimum standards of pay and treatment against what are frequently weak, even fragile operators or, as in the case of the public employers, where the resources are set by firm legislative limits on the available funds.

Strong unions — a vigorous exercise of countervailing power — require strong employers, something I did not stress sufficiently in my earlier writing. At that time, this strength was in manufacturing, but since 1970, employment in the manufacturing sector, which once accounted for more than a quarter of the labor force, has fallen to around 17 percent. The production of manufactured goods has moved away from American unions to Japan, Korea, Taiwan, and elsewhere. There has also been movement within the United States away from the centers of traditional union strength, a point that Tyler emphasizes.

Yet more important, I would urge, is the fact that unions have now found that they have less to fear from employer power than from employer incompetence and bureaucratic sclerosis. And they have been especially damaged by the financial insanity of the past decade — the mergers and acquisitions mania and the leveraged buyouts, leading to a stifling debt burden and to plant sales and closings, all with a widely adverse effect on workers and unions as well as on the firms themselves.

There has been a further serious attack on union strength in the English-speaking countries, one that comes from macroeconomic policy.

In recent times Republican administrations have been thought, not surprisingly, to be antilabor. Much has been made of President Ronald Reagan's historic stand against the air traffic controllers; this, it was held, put labor in its place for the duration. Far more damaging to unions has been the reliance on monetary policy as an anti-inflation measure and, more than incidentally, as a way of rewarding those with money to lend. There is no error in our time so comprehensively accepted as the notion that monetary policy is socially and politically neutral.

A strong monetary policy works against inflation by curtailing investment and consumer borrowing and expenditure, and, finally, by forcing resistance to wage claims, notably by creating unemployment. The ultimate effect is on union claims. In Western Europe and Japan this effect is mitigated by much more comprehensive collective bargaining, which holds wage claims more or less to what can be afforded from existing prices. The wage bargain is part of the anti-inflation process. In the English-speaking countries the wage bargain is left, instead, to macroeconomic policy. The strong employer is forced into battle with the union; the weak service-industry employer must appeal to the union for help, or at least moderation, so that he may survive.

I have long maintained that successful trade unionism in the United States should require as a supplement to macroeconomic policy a collaborative anti-inflation policy between employers and the state, based on the European model. In few matters could one claim less success.

There was another effect of modern macroeconomic policy on the unions. In the late Carter administration and during the Reagan years, high interest rates, the counterpart of a strong monetary policy, brought an inflow of investment funds, thus bidding up the dollar. Imports were subsidized, exports penalized, and American industrial strength was deeply impaired. The movement of industry to other countries was abetted, in fact subsidized. It is perhaps no comfort to unions that the situation was no less disastrous for employers.

It is Tyler's view that for unions the worst may be past. A revival of American industrial strength, and therewith the strength of American industrial workers, may be the next great change. The Schlesinger cycles of public concern and self-concern will make their immutable way. That is certainly to be hoped, but I confess that I am less than optimistic. Not all economic writing can have a happy ending. The diminished power and the lack of effectiveness of American industrial corporations, now more evident than in the past, stands as a major and, one supposes, continuing adverse influence. So does the fully accepted commitment to a macroeconomic policy destructive to unions and much more. The future of the trade union I cannot believe to be very bright.

Notes

1. Gus Tyler, "Laboring to Counter Balance Concentrated Capital," *Challenge*, September/October 1991, pp. 4–11.
2. Ibid., p. 8.

17

A Decade of Concession Bargaining

■───────────────■

Daniel J. B. Mitchell

That there were dramatic events in union wage determination during the 1980s is not a controversial assertion. Nor is the premise open to much debate that events in the 1980s generally were adverse to the interests of unions and their members. It is easy enough to point to unscheduled contract reopenings (General Motors and Ford, 1982), wage cuts (USX, 1983 and 1987), contracts annulled under bankruptcy proceedings (Continental Airlines, 1983), the introduction of unusual contract features such as two-tier plans (American Airlines, 1983), and strikes that led to replacement of union workers (Phelps-Dodge, 1983). Controversy sets in, however, once further interpretation of these developments is attempted.

Often the big-picture question that is posed is whether the developments of the 1980s were normal and expected reactions to changes in the economic climate. Unfortunately that question is vague, since it fails to specify what "normal" characteristics should be expected. Different observers have different perspectives on just which characteristics of union wage behavior are important. Some observers, for example, emphasize copycat pattern bargaining as the key feature of union behavior. Others, including myself, see long-term contracts with relative insensitivity of wages to short-term business cycle pressures as being much more important (Ready 1990; Mitchell 1990; Freedman 1982).

Another approach is to focus on trying to explain the diversity of reactions in the myriad wage negotiations during the 1980s. For example, one can ask whether the economic condition of particular employers or industries determined their bargaining outcomes (Bell 1989). However, such microeconomic perspectives may allow the big picture to escape. It would hardly be surprising if it were found, for example, that unions made concessions to assist floundering enterprises in some instances. They clearly did, as with the wage cuts at the money-losing United Press International news service.

In this chapter, therefore, an intermediate course is charted. I argue that there was indeed a structural break during the 1980s. The break is defined by wage settlements that were lower than might have been expected based on historical relationships. However, the break was not entirely without precedent nor was it without explanation. As I have elsewhere discussed, the early 1960s was a period with some parallels to the 1980s (Mitchell 1982).

The buildup of wage pressure and the later release of that pressure ought not be viewed as a regular, pendulum-type oscillation. The process of rising pressure in the 1970s and the release in the 1980s set in motion forces that changed the environment of bargaining and made a simple return to past conditions unlikely. In short, the 1990s are unlikely to feature a simple return to union bargaining as it existed in the 1970s. Nonetheless, two aspects of union bargaining remain largely as they were in the 1970s (and before). These are the features of union bargaining already identified as most important in my opinion: long-term contracts and a relative insensitivity of union wages to short-term business-cycle influences.

Past Approaches to Modeling Union Bargaining

Union bargaining has long proved puzzling to economists. Early approaches took unions to be monopolists who set an optimum price (wage) while operating along the employer's demand curve for labor. The difficulty with this simple approach was fourfold. First, while monopolists maximize profits in the basic model of price theory, it was hard to specify exactly what unions would maximize. The demand-curve-as-menu idea imposed a wage-employment trade-off on the union, and there was no obvious optimum point in that trade-off. In the internal political context in which unions operate, which could be said to be better, increments of wages or employment? How is that judgment made? A neat answer was not possible.

Second, even if an optimum trade-off point could be specified, it was not clear from the model how downward wage rigidity could be explained. Monopolistic prices (wages) may be higher than competitive prices. But in the simple economic model they are not downwardly inflexible. While ad hoc utility functions for unions could always be rigged to explain wage rigidity, such explanations were often strained (Cartter and Marshall 1972). Even modern explanations exhibit strained assumptions. A recent model, for example, assumes that unions can organize nonunion firms at will and, hence, make up for any membership losses due to demand declines by freely adding more workers from nonunion firms (MacDonald and Robinson 1992).

Third, as more recent theorists have noted, it was unclear why unions would want to operate inefficiently by simply taking the demand curve as given, setting a wage, and then letting the employer set the employment level. Efficient bargains should involve both wage and employment combinations. Yet, aside from reactive work-rule responses to automation, it appears that unions do leave employment decisions mainly to the determination of employers.

Fourth, and probably the most critical difficulty, the historical emphasis on union bargaining objectives often led to a neglect of the employer side of the bargaining relationship. The interaction of union and employer in the context of an adversarial negotiation — one in which each side can potentially inflict great harm on the other — was therefore given insufficient attention. Paradoxically, institutional industrial relations scholars tended to reinforce the de-emphasis on the combat aspect of negotiations. These scholars emphasized the infrequency of strikes and their small impact on the overall economy. Their motive in doing so was largely to suggest a laissez-faire public policy toward "emergency disputes." However, the potential costs of a dispute that may be of little concern macroeconomically could well be of great moment to the parties immediately concerned.

I do not attempt here a complete solution to all of these problems in the modeling of union wage setting. However, a general approach to interpreting the developments of the 1980s will be sketched, one that avoids the fourth problem — neglect of the employer-union interaction. It will be seen that taking due account of that interaction and marrying it to other views of the union wage process that developed in the 1970s and 1980s provides an adequate explanation of the wave of concession bargaining that characterized the 1980s. At the same time, the experience of the 1980s, because it did put the collective bargaining process under stress, helps illuminate fundamental aspects of that process.

Incidence of Concession Bargaining

Defining a concession bargain poses a conceptual problem, since all bargains in principle involve a give-and-take element. For empirical purposes, however, it has been useful to define concession bargains as a nominal wage freeze or cut. By such a definition, these bargains have the advantage of being relatively easy to identify from available data. Moreover, if one accepts the notion that a nominal zero in wage change determination is something of a "magic number" — a floor below which movement is difficult — then using zero as a basis for defining concessions makes sense. Some theorists will object to a nominal definition of concessions and insist that any approach should be defined in real terms. However, there is sufficient evidence of nominalism in wage setting to justify the proposed definition (Mitchell, 1993).

Table 17.1 applies the nominal definition, and alternatives, to two data sets. The first is the U.S. Bureau of Labor Statistics (BLS) series on major union settlements in the private sector (those involving 1,000 or more workers). The second is based on the Bureau of National Affairs, Inc. (BNA) series on business-sector settlements involving 50 or more employees. While the former is presented in terms of the proportion of *workers* affected, the latter is measured in terms of the proportion of *settlements.* Use of workers gives a sense of the general economic importance of the concession movement; use of settlements gives insight into the decisions of individual bargainers.

The broad definition of concessions in the BLS series (defining concessions as first-year freezes or cuts in the basic wage) suggests that concession bargaining peaked in the period 1982 to 1985 and then began to fall off. Thus, there is a suggestion of a cyclical element in the concession movement. Economic expansion in the second half of the decade reduced concession frequency. If it is assumed that a union contract lasts an average of two to three years, then in the early years of concession bargaining, a very conservative estimate would be that at least one-third of workers under major contracts directly experienced a concession under the broad definition.[1] Although some repeat concessions occurred in later years, enough new contracts involved concessions to suggest that the true proportion by the end of the 1980s was much higher.

At the peak of the business cycle in 1990, in contrast, relatively

Table 17.1. Concession bargaining trends

Year	Major private settlements: workers covered by concessions — BLS		All business sector settlements involving concessions — BNA		
	Broad[a]	Narrow[b]	Broad[a]	Intermediate[c]	Narrow[b]
1981	8%	5%	3%	2%	1%
1982	44	2	12	7	1
1983	37	15	29	21	6
1984	23	5	27	21	7
1985	37	3	25	14	4
1986	30	9	37	15	5
1987	27	4	34	16	4
1988	22	2	27	12	2
1989	8	1	18	5	*
1990	4	*	10	3	*
1991	11	*	10	5	1

Source: Bureau of Labor Statistics (BLS) data from *Current Wage Developments.* Bureau of National Affairs (BNA) data drawn from *Daily Labor Report.*

Note: Major private settlements refers to those covering 1,000 or more workers. All business-sector settlements refers to those covering 50 or more workers and covers certain quasi-commercial public enterprises such as transit systems.

a. First-year settlements involving basic wage freeze or decrease.

b. First-year settlements involving basic wage decrease. For all-business-sector sample, figures for 1981–82 based on estimates from author's concession data file.

c. Broad definition excluding settlements involving lump-sum bonuses and cost-of-living-adjustment payments. Estimates based on author's concession data file.

* Less than 0.5%.

few workers were subject to newly negotiated concessions. Defining concessions narrowly as only first-year wage cuts produces a much lower incidence rate throughout the decade, but also suggests that by the 1990 business cycle peak, concession bargains had largely disappeared. The low frequency of wage cuts compared with the high frequency of wage freezes reinforces the notion that nominal zero is indeed a magic number, a point of strong resistance, in union wage settlements.

BNA data using the broad and narrow definitions produce much the same impression, although they suggest more lingering of concessions in the late 1980s and early 1990s under the broad definition. However, it is possible — using information from the BNA biweekly tabulations — to adjust the broad definition to exclude two potential sources of de facto first-year wage increases, cost of living adjustment (COLA) clauses and lump-sum bonuses. Making such an exclusion produces the intermediate definition shown on Table 17.1.[2]

The intermediate series suggests a greater concentration of concession bargaining in the years 1983 and 1984 and, therefore, a lessened significance of concessions in the late 1980s. Unions may have officially agreed to basic wage freezes, but often they obtained pay increases through indirect means in later years. Using the intermediate definition for the second half of the 1980s, the more rapid decline of concessions reinforces the idea that economic expansion reduced concession bargaining.

Accompanying Background Features of the Concession Movement

One of the most notable developments during the 1980s was the decline in union representation of the private work force. Although relative unionization in the private sector had been eroding gradually since the 1950s, the 1980s featured a large absolute loss. Overall, union representation (private and public) fell absolutely from 22.5 million to 19.1 million workers during 1980 through 1990.[3] The drop in absolute unionization was more than fully accounted for by losses in the private sector, that is, union representation in public employment rose absolutely (but not proportionately) while private representation dropped substantially in relative and absolute terms. More than 80 percent of the drop in private representation came from the large (major) contracts covering 1,000 or more workers. That is, the large-contract sector suffered disproportionate losses.[4]

Sectoral explanations

Because the 1980s is widely perceived as a period of American deindustrialization, it is often assumed that the decline in unionization mainly reflected changes in the industrial composition of the work force. Union representation was concentrated in heavy industry traditionally, and it might have been supposed that shifts away from manufacturing would explain the representation drop. In fact, however, changing industrial composition — while a negative for unions — explains only one-sixth to one-fourth of the drop in the number of workers represented. The remaining decline, therefore, must be attributed to other influences, including heightened management resistance, changes in worker attitudes, and reduced union organizing efforts.

Management resistance

Management resistance can take several forms. In the case of new union organizing, management might take a hard line by firing union sympathizers and threatening other workers. Such tactics are illegal under existing labor law, but as many observers have noted, the penalties are comparatively low and slow in coming. The degree to which such tactics intensified in the 1980s and the effect this might have had on union representation rates has been the subject of some controversy (Weiler 1983; LaLonde and Meltzer 1991). Nonetheless, it would be difficult to point to a host of significant changes on the legal side that made union organizing any *easier* during this period.[5] The search by union representatives, ranging from top officials to dissident activists, for alternatives to traditional National Labor Relations Board (NLRB) organizing suggests that the road was harder (AFL-CIO Committee on the Evolution of Work 1985; Bureau of National Affairs 1991a; La Botz 1991).

Management might also resist new unionization by the soft approach of providing desirable working conditions that nonunion workers would feel were preferable to what a union could provide. There is in fact a long history of such managerial approaches, including the provision of unionesque personnel practices such as grievance arbitration (Foulkes 1980). Such approaches appeared to become more prominent in the 1980s, although there is no handy time series available. It is important to stress that what nonunion workers might expect from unionization is not a constant; the perception by such workers of events in the union sector could alter their views. And, indeed, there is some evidence suggesting that adverse developments affecting union workers led to skepticism of potential nonunion recruits about what unionization could achieve (Farber 1990).

Finally, as a managerial strategy, previously unionized firms might seek to expand their nonunion operations and to shrink their older, unionized plants. Such tendencies were documented by researchers in the 1980s and reported in the popular press (Verma 1985). For example, General Electric's internal rate of unionization declined from 50 percent in 1981 to 35 percent in 1988, and it was typically the newer plants that were nonunion (Bernstein 1988). In some cases in the 1980s, there were dramatic conversions of unionized companies to de facto nonunion status through replacement of union workers during labor disputes. The histories of Continental Airlines and Eastern Airlines fall squarely into this category.

It is important to note, however, that there was a sharp division of results between the public and private sectors during the 1980s. In the government sector, unions just about held their own in terms of representation and, in fact, represented over 40 percent of employees throughout the period. Almost none of the unexplained loss of union representation was located in the government sector. Also noteworthy is the fact that concession bargaining in the public sector was relatively minor until the recession of 1990–91. Thus, there seems to be some correlation between representation characteristics and bargaining strength.

In contrast to circumstances in public employment is the *pervasiveness* of the loss in private employment. Pervasiveness in the private sector is a more important aspect of the concession story than the details of its precise industrial location. The pervasiveness is closely related to the notion of a structural shift in both representation and wage determination rather than a limited phenomenon concentrated in a few depressed industries.

Union organizing

Although evidence on managerial resistance and nonunion employee attitudes must be based on casual and spotty evidence, there are some direct data on union organizing efforts. For instance, the frequency of NLRB representation election (which is largely a reflection of union organizing) was cut roughly in half from fiscal year 1980 to fiscal year 1983, and it remained low thereafter. The result of such elections was 73,106 potentially new unionized workers in fiscal year 1990. This number represents a relatively trivial sum, given the declines in unionization that occurred in the 1980s and the ongoing losses of union-represented workers from plant closings and other turnover in the labor force.[6] Even those workers "won" under NLRB elections did not necessarily remain in the union sector unless a first contract was successfully negotiated, and such first contracts were not always achieved (Cooke 1985).

Union "win rates" in NLRB elections showed a modest cyclical influence (falling in the recession trough of 1982) but remained below 50 percent throughout the period. If unions only pushed for elections when the perceived odds were close to fifty-fifty, then the drop in election frequency could be a sign of increased worker resistance to organization. Alternatively, the drop could be due to declining organizing effort on the union side (Flanagan 1984).[7] It seems likely that both occurred during the 1980s. In any case, these trends led to projections during the 1980s of unionization rates at the 5 percent level by the turn of the century (Bronars and Deere 1989).

Work stoppage data

Union aggressiveness seemed to fall in existing bargaining situations. There was a general decline in the yearly number of major strikes between 1980 and 1991.[8] In theory, strikes are the mutual outcome of the bargaining process, that is, they can be attributed to management as much as to the union. However, it has appeared to be both useful and realistic to assume asymmetric information — less information — on the workers' side than on management's, and therefore to view strike incidence as more of a reflection of union policy than of management (Ashenfelter and Johnson 1969). Seen in this way, the decline in strike frequency fits well with the decline in union-initiated representation elections.

For those workers who did strike during this period, however, the strikes in which they participated had a significant duration, that is, they remained costly. With the exception of low figures in 1982 and 1991 (recession years), a typical striker experienced a stoppage lasting roughly three weeks, until the late 1980s when the strike duration rose to more than four weeks.[9] Strikes were infrequent, but when they were initiated, the result was often a dispute of considerable intensity. Confrontations increased in intensity in the late 1980s as business conditions improved.

Great disputes, lesser disputes, and worker attitudes

Sometimes conflicts in industrial relations become sufficiently dramatic that they receive widespread public attention. Disputes of this type do not necessarily involve large numbers of workers nor need they be in "economically important" situations. Rather, they need only have sufficient human interest features to capture media coverage.[10] Although the effect of the outcomes of such "great disputes" on attitudes of both union and nonunion workers was intangible, they certainly had an influence on perceptions of what a union could accomplish. If nonunion workers perceive that unions lead to "trouble" (especially job loss), they are less likely to be organizable. And if union workers develop similar perceptions, they are more likely to be willing to make concessions.

Probably the most significant dispute of the concession era was that of the federal air traffic controllers. This dispute is often cited in popular discussions as the cause of concession bargaining, presumably because of the president's involvement and the early timing of the event (1981).[11] However, the reality was more complicated. The controllers were federal employees who were forbidden by law from striking. Past history — including endorsement of Ronald Reagan in the 1980 presidential election — distanced the controllers' union from the rest of organized labor, especially potential allies among airline unions (Northrup 1984).

If the controllers' strike had been the falling domino that began concession bargaining, one might have expected the initial spillover to be in the government sector. State and local governments suffered revenue losses during the recession of the early 1980s and could have used labor-cost reductions. But in fact, as already noted, concession bargaining was relatively rare thereafter in the public sector (Mitchell 1986, 1988)

It is more likely that the combination of later great disputes, particularly those in private employment, helped foster the spread of concession bargaining. The lesson that could be drawn by workers (union and nonunion) was that bitter disputes could lead to job loss, even — as in the Hormel case — if the union itself were not replaced.[12] Companies and individuals, notably Frank Lorenzo, mastermind of the Continental Airlines bankruptcy, developed reputations for successfully taking on unions.[13] For senior union workers — those most likely to influence union decision making (Freeman and Medoff 1984) — strike losses of the Continental variety could produce a devastating cut in income.

Still more intangible in its effect, but hardly helpful to unions, was the spread of concessions and confrontations to labor relations in the news media. Although, for example, the saga of United Press International's restructurings under bankruptcy and its accompanying wage cuts were not at the level of a great dispute, journalists were certainly aware of it. They might also have been aware of concessions at the *Boston Herald-American*, the *Oakland Tribune*, the *New York Post*, the *St. Louis Globe-Democrat*, and others. Even *Consumer Reports*, the product-testing magazine with origins in the left-wing politics of the 1930s, was on the AFL-CIO boycott list in 1984. It ultimately reached agreement on a contract with no first-year wage increase and unlimited rights to contract out work from the bargaining unit.

Among the great disputes of the period, only one is directly tied to journalism. That one — the *New York Daily News* case — seemed at first to have a happy ending. But the mysterious death of financier and white knight Robert Maxwell, and the dissolution of his worldwide holdings, left the newspaper's outlook clouded.

Of course, not all of the disputes in the 1980s resulted in union disasters. One might cite, for example, the successful organizing campaign of Harvard University clerical employees after a long campaign for union avoidance by the university, or the recognition of farm workers as contractors supplying Campbell Soup. The Service

Employees' "Justice for Janitors" campaign — based heavily on external publicity — scored some notable successes. After a bitter struggle, the United Mine Workers achieved gains at Pittston Coal.

Obviously, dispute outcomes varied during the 1980s. Lesser disputes in which labor lost can also be cited are, for example, the Catholic Archdiocese of Los Angeles — a traditional ally of organized labor — successfully avoided unionization of its cemetery workers after a lengthy and acrimonious conflict. An attempt by unions to influence corporate policy at the conglomerate Pacific Enterprises by mobilizing employee shareholder votes in a corporate employee stock ownership plan ultimately failed.[14] In both of these cases, union officials probably thought they had a good chance of succeeding initially.

And even some happy endings had mixed connotations. A long dispute at Colt Industries in which strikers were replaced was ultimately settled when the strikers and their union bought the company and discharged the replacements. But the strikers were out of work for more than four years (Paltrow 1991). After a lengthy strike in 1986–87, workers at USX (formerly US Steel) accepted wage decreases (as had workers at other steel companies) but won some limits on subcontracting.[15] Still, the most noteworthy element of the USX dispute was that it was clouded in media obscurity. In the 1980s, a major strike at USX went largely unnoticed while in the 1950s, say, such a strike would have invited presidential attention. A union that once could use the economic importance of its industry to leverage public intervention now found itself on its own.

Generally, employers felt free in the 1980s and early 1990s to test limits and previous understandings. In Las Vegas, some hotel owners sought to deviate from the trade association patterns; even multi-employer hotel settlements were sometimes achieved after bitter impasses.[16] Steel companies dropped out of their multiemployer bargaining association, as did many intercity trucking companies. Westinghouse pushed for variations in its settlements from those of parent company General Electric. The 1986 East Coast longshore negotiations produced port-by-port deviations in response to competition from nonunion ports. Railroads sought to create subsidiaries to avoid existing union agreements and to "contract out" for electricity generation within their diesel locomotives (which were to be owned by third parties).[17]

Union pressure for legislation amending federal labor law to prohibit the use of permanent replacements during strikes is an indication of a change in employers' self-imposed constraints in labor disputes. The argument that union lobbyists had to face was that the court decision permitting such replacements dated back to the late 1930s. Why, critics asked, overrule it now? From the union perspective, although there had always been an undercurrent of the use of such replacements, employers generally behaved as if they thought such tactics would not be wise. Employers, they argued, had once been more self-restrained.[18]

One factor explaining the shift away from self-restraint in management bargaining tactics was the increased uncertainty of product markets.[19] Factors such as deregulation, exchange-rate changes and trade competition, pressures from financial markets and the product market for corporate control, and seeming changes in the optimum scale of the enterprise all seemed to push the labor market in an atomistic direction (Mitchell 1989). The notion that product-market stability and insulation contributes to industrial peace is an old one (Kerr 1964). Insecurity in the 1980s contributed to a break in managerial habits. The result was a more confrontational approach that sometimes led to bitter strikes (even as the frequency of strike activity fell).

Public sympathy for strikers seemed to wane in the 1980s. Polls suggested that the average person agreed with President Reagan's termination of the striking air traffic controllers.[20] While it might not have been surprising that business travelers continued to fly on Continental and Eastern Airlines, it was more surprising that the blue-collar clientele of Greyhound Bus continued its patronage during strikes. Public support of a grape boycott was instrumental in organizing California farm workers in the 1960s and 1970s, but resumption of the boycott in the 1980s produced no such effect.[21]

Toward the end of the decade, public opinion polls began to show some elevation in status for unions and union officials (Bureau of National Affairs 1991b). It is possible that, if they continue, these shifts could be translated by unions into bargaining and organizing gains. But the shifts could simply be the result of a growing sense that unions are the underdog — a perception of union weakness. At any rate, slippage in union membership means that fewer people are in regular contact with unions and, therefore, that mobilization through boycotts or political action is more difficult.

In short, the atmosphere surrounding industrial relations in the 1980s was influenced by ongoing events and evident trends. Given the difficulties experienced by unions in earlier years, it is not surprising that an undercurrent of concession bargaining continued even in the late 1980s, as unemployment rates fell and the economy reached a business-cycle peak. These contract characteristics are discussed in the next section.

Changing Contractual Features

Apart from the direct wage settlements, important changes occurred in the way pay was delivered under union contracts during the 1980s. On the other hand, not all aspects of union contracts were heavily modified. Those features most widely discussed have been contract duration, use of COLA clauses, use of bonus payments under lump-sum provisions and profit sharing, and two-tier wage plans.

Contract duration

While other contractual features were modified in the 1980s, the principle of using a long-term contract to embody the union-management relationship continued intact. It might have been thought that uncertainty would produce shorter contracts during a period of transition. But Table 17.2 shows no evidence of such a trend. It is important to recall that the use of long-term contracts was historically a *management* demand. Such contracts were designed to stabilize industrial relations and avoid frequent strikes and negotiations (Jacoby and Mitchell 1984). Thus, if the 1980s represented a period in which bargaining strength shifted to the management side, the tendency would be for contracts to lengthen. As an example, the petroleum industry, which had long featured two-year contracts (with no COLA), switched to a three-year contract in early 1990, when oil prices were low.

Apart from nominal contract duration, de facto duration can be shortened through the inclusion of reopener clauses in union agreements. These may simply allow the reopening of negotiations on some provision, such as wages, at a defined date within the agreement's duration, as in the 1988 bituminous coal contract.[22] Or such reopenings may be triggered by some event, such as the reaching of a certain level of inflation. There was some increase in the proportion of reopeners in union agreements in the early 1980s. However, the proportion with reopeners was never high, and therefore the scope for shortening de facto duration was small. Overall contract duration was not shortened during the concession era, either explicitly or through reopeners.

COLA coverage

Cost of living adjustment coverage had become widespread during the 1970s, especially within the major contract sector. A combination of high inflation and (as theoretical purists would prefer) inflation

Table 17.2. Characteristics of concession settlements

Year	Average contract duration (months)		COLA elimination as % of COLA contracts (NC)	COLA limits as % of COLA settlements (NC)	Lump-sum bonuses (NC)	Profit sharing (NC)	Two-tier wages (NC)
	All	NC					
1981	24	24	14%	25%	0%	10%	0%
1982	30	31	25	57	0	8	5
1983	29	33	13	62	4	8	13
1984	29	32	13	63	14	5	15
1985	31	34	14	52	49	8	17
1986	33	34	41	68	58	8	13
1987	33	35	33	62	62	6	16
1988	35	37	20	38	69	10	7
1989	39	39	18	39	74	2	2
1990	39	40	20	38	66	1	3
1991	36	39	23	27	49	6	0
Total (1980–91)	32	34	22%	56%	44%	7%	11%

Source: Data file maintained by author, based on biweekly surveys published in the *Daily Labor Report*.
Note: NC = nonconstruction.

uncertainty led to increased COLA coverage. Still another influence was the wage controls program under the Nixon administration, whose rules favored COLA increases over regular wage increases.

COLA clauses, or escalator clauses, posed particular problems for management in the late 1970s and early 1980s, leading to a strong managerial desire to "do something" about COLA payments. Especially in a nominalist world, a commitment to adjust wages according to movements in the Consumer Price Index (CPI) entails a risk. Employer "ability to pay" need not move with the CPI. This problem will be particularly acute if there are elements in the CPI — such as food and energy prices — that are volatile and subject to influences outside the core economy.[23] Also, apart from volatile prices, the CPI contained a misleading mortgage interest component until it was modified in the early 1980s. This component exaggerated the measured inflation rate (and boosted COLA-linked wages artificially) (Mitchell 1982b).

Management resistance to COLAs first took the form of reducing the "quality" of COLA payouts rather than the quantity of COLA coverage. COLAs were increasingly qualified with caps, "corridors," and other limits as the era of concession bargaining began. These features effectively reduced COLA risk for employers by reducing the amount of wage increase associated with a 1 percent increase in the CPI. In some cases, the COLA was rendered virtually meaningless by contract limitations. For example, the 1984 contract between the Newspaper Guild and the Consumers Union provided for COLA increases if inflation exceeded 9 percent. Yet actual CPI inflation in 1984 was only 4 percent. A 9 percent inflation rate seemed very unlikely at the time, and the provision might best be seen as a face-saving retention of the COLA principle rather than as a genuine COLA clause.

Later in the concession era COLA clauses were actually dropped. While COLA coverage of workers in the major union sector averaged 56 to 60 percent during the first half of the 1980s, it fell to about one-third by 1991. BNA data (which include smaller agreements) reflect the same trend: COLAs were found in only 26 percent of agreements in 1989, down from 48 percent in 1983. Reduced inflation rates in the middle of the decade undoubtedly helped foster this declining trend.

Within concession bargains (Table 17.2), COLA eliminations continued throughout the years 1981 to 1991. However, eliminations were more common in the later years of the period than the earlier. COLA limits (such as caps) were more prevalent in the earlier years. Thus, in concession bargaining, employers sought to limit COLAs if they could not remove them outright. Removals became easier in the later years, when inflation was low (and seemed unlikely to burst out) and when memory of past inflation of the 1970s and early 1980s had dimmed.

The evolution of the Teamsters' Master Freight Agreement illustrates the shifting ground under COLAs. In 1982, the contract was reopened early. The new agreement had no basic wage increase (a concession), and the COLA — while continued — carried a provision diverting most of the money generated to supporting benefits. During 1985 to 1988, the contract featured a "guaranteed" COLA, really just a deferred set of specified wage increases unrelated to the CPI. A genuine CPI-linked COLA was restored in the 1988 agreement, as the economy recovered and inflation acceleration seemed more likely. However, the 1991 contract — negotiated during a recession — went back to the so-called guaranteed COLA, that is, to no genuine COLA.

Generally, concession contracts that retain active COLA clauses can be viewed as less severe from the union perspective than those without COLAs. Table 17.3 shows that COLA concessions were less likely to involve wage decreases than others. COLA concessions were also less likely to contain lump sums, a feature suggesting that lump sums were viewed as substitutes for COLA (and other) wage increases.

Lump-sum bonuses and profit sharing

The use of bonus payments became prominent during the late 1980s. By 1988, 44 percent of workers under major contracts received lump sums, a peak value. Thereafter, lump-sum coverage declined. Within the concession settlement sample, it is apparent that lump sums were a 1980s innovation (although minor bonus payments existed before). Three-fourths of new concession settlements contained lump sums by 1989, a proportion that fell off thereafter.

There are two competing explanations for management's efforts to push lump sums. One is that it was simply a way to reduce labor costs by substituting, for example, annual 3 percent bonuses for 3 percent wage increases in the context of a three-year contract. The former leaves the basic wage unchanged at the end of the contract; the latter raises the base wage by 9 percent. This was the view generally found in press accounts (Uchitelle 1986).

An alternative explanation is that the lump sums were intended to be a variable component of pay, a kind of ersatz profit sharing, as is often said of bonus payments in Japan (Freeman and Weitzman 1987).[24] Under this interpretation, lump sums were designed to shift product-market risks to workers and to create greater flexibility in labor costs. One study suggests a linkage between use of lump sums and economic uncertainty in the industry (Erickson and Ichino

Table 17.3. Associated features of nonconstruction concession settlements

All Nonconstruction settlements

Characteristic	COLA	No COLA	Lump sum	No lump sum	Profit sharing	No profit sharing	Two-tier wages	No Two-tier wages	Wage decrease	No Wage decrease
COLA	—	—	13%	27%	15%	21%	21%	21%	14%	22%
Lump sum	29%	49%	—	—	28	46	43	45	10	50
Profit sharing	5	7	4	9	—	—	7	7	17	12
Two-tier wages	11	11	11	12	12	11	—	—	14	11
Wage decrease	9	15	3	22	34	12	17	13	—	—
Proportion with characteristic	21	79	44	56	7	93	11	89	14	86

Nonconstruction settlements without wage decreases

Characteristic	Lump sum	No lump sum	Profit sharing	No profit sharing
COLA	14%	30%	17%	22%
Lump sum	—	—	38	51
Profit sharing	4	6	—	—
Two-tier wages	10	11	14	11
Proportion with characteristic	50	50	5	95

Source: Data file maintained by author based on biweekly surveys published in the *Daily Labor Report.*

1990). But another finds no evidence of added wage flexibility due to lump sums (Bell and Neumark 1991).

It is possible to find anecdotal evidence of employer usage of lump sums that fits both interpretations. Lump sums in the automobile industry seem to have been used as substitutes for basic wage increases. Since the auto industry also has used profit sharing since the 1982 concessions, it may be that management did not see a need for yet another form of flexible pay.[25] But in the aerospace industry, and at Boeing in particular during the 1989 negotiations, a case can be made for the flexibility argument.

Boeing's management took a prolonged strike to preserve the lump sum principle in the face of a "dump the lump" campaign by the Machinists' union. Large profits at Boeing were reflected in large lump sum payments in the final settlement, a strategy that seemed aimed at reinforcing the notion of lump sums as flexible pay. Still, reports of pressure from the U.S. Department of Defense behind the scenes in aerospace bargaining suggest that holding down labor costs — rather than just making them variable — was part of the motive for lump sums in the industry as a whole, even if not at Boeing.[26]

The recession period of 1990 to 1992 provides mixed evidence on employer intentions for lump sums. Thirteen of 20 major contracts negotiated between July 1990 and June 1991 simply eliminated the lump sum. Such elimination could be in keeping with using lump sums as flexible pay (and reducing them during recessions). However, total elimination of the lump sum clause seems extreme if the intent was to use them in the future. Only 7 new contracts retained the lump sum; 5 with a reduced amount.

Lump sum concessions were less likely than others to include profit sharing (and profit sharing concessions were less likely to contain lump sums). This negative correlation might be interpreted as a substitution of one for the other, from the managerial perspective. But the association is partly confounded by the tendency for wage decreases to be negatively linked to lump sums and positively linked to profit sharing.

It would seem to make little sense to cut wages and then give back the cut in the form of a lump sum bonus. On the other hand, tying a wage decrease to profit sharing *does* make sense if the idea is to trade a present concession for the possibility of a future recoupment, dependent on eventual profitability. Still, when wage decrease concessions are removed, the negative association of profit sharing and lump sums is weakened but not removed. On balance, however, the case for viewing lump sums in aggregate as de facto profit sharing (a pay flexibility interpretation) remains weak.

As for profit sharing itself, there was a notable sixfold increase in the number of union workers covered under profit sharing from 1980 to 1988. Yet of the 462,000 workers reported as covered by profit sharing in 1988, more than 70 percent were in transportation equipment jobs and may be assumed to be largely concentrated among the major automobile companies. About 7 percent of all contracts surveyed in 1988 had profit sharing, a figure comparable in magnitude to the proportion of concession contracts containing them throughout the period 1981 to 1991.

During the mid-1980s, a flurry of academic and public policy interest in profit sharing developed, in part due to the Weitzman proposal to stimulate such plans for reasons of macroeconomic stabilization (Weitzman 1984). However, it appears that profit sharing made only a limited foray into union contracts outside automobile manufacturing. There was some penetration, however, in the deregulated airline industry.

Two-tier wage plans

Union contracts have always had features whereby new entrants earn less for some period than longer-service incumbents. In addition, pay progression by seniority is not unusual in union agreements. Even though they existed in small numbers before, however, the advent of concession bargaining in the 1980s saw a notable surge in negotiation of two-tier wage plans (Martin 1990; Belous 1985). Under the two-tier plans of the 1980s, new entrants hired after the contract's inception were paid according to a lower wage schedule. In some cases, the more common "temporary" variety of plan was used, under which the lower-tier scale merged with the upper tier after sufficient seniority was attained, generally a period of several years. Less frequently the two-tier plan was "permanent," that is, the scales never merged.

Two-tier plans were sometimes "sold" by management to a reluctant union as an alternative to a general wage cut (that would include incumbents). Given unions' political process, in which the yet-to-be-hired do not vote, it is not surprising that the two-tier plan was often the preferred alternative. However, as Table 17.3 shows, general wage cuts were slightly more likely to accompany two-tier plans in concession contracts. In some cases, two-tier arrangements were sold to union members not as devices to fend off wage cuts but rather as a way to permit employment expansion (and increased union membership) by lowering incremental labor costs to competitive levels.

Two-tier plans could offer labor-cost savings only in situations in which there was rapid turnover of the work force (so that new hires were frequently added to the payroll) or when the firm expected to expand its employment level. Supermarkets fit the former case. Airlines, which saw new market opportunities in deregulation, fit the latter. Not surprisingly, therefore, two-tier wage systems were especially common in these two industries. Indeed in the airline industry, having two tiers came to be de rigueur so far as Wall Street analysts were concerned; even airlines that were not expanding came under pressure to negotiate them.[27] As Table 17.2 shows, two-tier wage plans in new concession settlements peaked in the mid 1980s and then declined. Two-tier features were found in 28 percent of all contracts (concession and nonconcession) in 1989.[28]

Because of their wage-lowering component, two-tier wage plans tend to reduce average labor costs as the proportion of workers in the lower tier increases. Apparently, there have been sufficient savings due to lower-tier hires to improve shareholder wealth perceptibly in firms adopting two-tier plans (Thomas 1990). While it might be thought that workers in the lower tier would resent their lower pay status, research on employee attitudes has not always found this result (Cappelli and Sherer 1990). In some cases, employees in the lower tier may feel that the existence of that tier allowed them to find work.

Nonetheless, complicated political forces are unleashed within the union between the tiers. And not all research suggests contentment with two-tier pay systems on the part of bottom-tier workers (McFarlin and Frone 1990). Moreover, two-tier proposals have been known to lead to contract rejections (as in the case of Teamster car haulers in 1985) and strikes (as in the United Airlines-pilot negotiations of 1985).

It appears that management in the 1980s often did not believe that two-tier systems would be stable in the long term (Jacoby and Mitchell 1986). And indeed there began to be a steady flow of narrowings and eliminations of two-tier plans, especially as labor markets tightened in the late 1980s. However, in some cases — even those viewed by unions as victories — the solution was to hold back wage increases in the upper tier to allow the lower tier to catch up.[29]

The Sectoral Pattern of Concession Bargaining

Apart from the general recession of the early 1980s, deregulation and foreign trade competition are often cited as factors contributing to concession bargaining (Lipsky and Donn 1987). As Table 17.4 illustrates, these influences certainly played a role. Industries falling in the deregulated sector showed a peak in concession activity in 1984 and 1985.[30] Moreover, when account is taken of the contractual features of the concessions, those in the deregulated sector seem most severe. For example, the proportion of first-year basic wage decreases is highest in this group. Deregulated firms — particularly airlines — were also especially prone to adopting two-tier wage plans as part of their concession packages.

Table 17.4. Rates of concession bargaining

	1 All industries	2 Deregulated industries	3 Trade sector	4 Other	5 Construction industry
1981	3%	13%	1%	2%	0%
1982	12	19	10	11	13
1983	29	17	24	36	62
1984	27	46	20	37	65
1985	25	47	32	20	27
1986	37	21	50	24	30
1987	34	20	51	22	30
1988	27	23	29	22	40
1989	18	0	26	9	15
1990	10	3	10	5	6
1991	10	0	9	8	11
Severity index[a]	+.22	−.33	+.42	−.24 (−.06)	−.43
Percent wage decreases	16%	32%	10%	21% (20%)	22%
Percent two- tier wages	9	20	7	10 (19)	2
Percent lump sums	33	17	52	14 (31)	*
Percent profit sharing	5	20	6	3 (20)	*

Source: Data file maintained by author based on biweekly surveys published in the *Daily Labor Report.*

Note: Column 1 based on published BNA tabulations. Columns 2–4 based on estimates of the author. Column 5 based on published BNA tabulations, 1981–1986, and estimates of the author thereafter. Data in parentheses refer to nonconstruction component of "other" sector.

a. Severity index is defined as a weighted average of contracts with unlimited COLAs (+2), limited COLAs (+1), lump sums (+1), profit sharing (+1), two-tier plans (−1), and decreases (−2), where the weights are the proportion of contracts with each characteristic.

* Less than 0.5%.

Industries subject to foreign trade competition showed a peak in concession activity in 1986 and 1987 — in the aftermath of the substantial appreciation of the U.S. dollar (1980 to 1985).[31] However, concession activity in the trade sector exhibited the least severe contractual features relative to other sectors. Indeed, the most severely impacted sector in Table 17.4 is construction, a component of the "other" sector. Construction settlements were influenced by the significant expansion of nonunion competition. Union wage pressures in construction in earlier periods seem, in turn, to be important factors in this expansion (Mitchell 1981). There were some relaxations of the Davis-Bacon Act protection of union contractors on federally funded projects; however, these were delayed by litigation and do not seem to be central explanations of the concession trend.[32]

It is more important to stress the sectoral diversity and (as previously noted) the pervasiveness of union wage concessions than to determine precise sectoral determinants of concession intensity.[33] Table 17.5 lists industries by the year in which they first appeared in the concession data base I have maintained. Almost all industries are represented, and most appear in the 1981 to 1984 period. This pervasiveness suggests a shift in wage norms during the concession era (Mitchell 1985; Perry 1986; Wachter and Carter 1989).[34]

It has already been suggested that the high level of publicity given to labor disputes that had unhappy outcomes for unions was part of the mechanism by which such a norm shift could spread. Cross-industry linkages through unions themselves is another explanation. While some unions — such as the Laborers Union and the Communications Workers Union — were involved in concessions in only one or two industries, other unions made concessions in many industries. That is, industries in which concessions were made are linked to other industries through one or more union connection. For example, the Teamsters negotiated concessions for truck drivers in construction and in retail foodstores. The Teamsters also represent many non–truck driver occupations in other industries.

Causes of the Structural Shift

As I noted at the outset, there are difficulties in defining a structural shift in union bargaining and, therefore, there has been controversy surrounding the concept. It has already been shown that if "structural shift" means, say, an end to long-term contracts, then no such shift has occurred. Nor is there a strong case to be made for viewing

Table 17.5. Industry composition of concession settlements by year of first appearance

1981
Metals
Motor vehicles
Retail foodstores
Machinery
Meatpacking
Airlines
Printing and publishing
Health care
Lumber and paper
1982
Construction
Public transit and intercity buses
Rubber and plastics
Trucking
Aerospace
Textiles
Food manufacturing (except meatpacking)
Instruments
Chemicals
Railroads
Hotels and restaurants
Shipping
Other transport equipment (n.e.c.)
Brick, clay, stone
Finance, insurance, real estate
Communications
Apparel
1983
Business services
Furniture
Unions (as employers)
Cement
Entertainment
Mining
Warehousing
Glass
Education
1984
Retail (except foodstores)
Leather
Petroleum
Tobacco
Utilities
1985–1991
Agriculture, forestry, fishing
Miscellaneous services (n.e.c.)

Source: Data file maintained by author, based on biweekly surveys published in the *Daily Labor Report.*

union wage bargaining as having developed a substantial sensitivity to real economic conditions. But there does seem to have been a shift to settlements that were lower than could have been expected based on past historical relationships, particularly with regard to aggregate data. Various researchers have previously identified that type of shift in the 1980s (Erickson 1990; Bell 1989, 1991; Neumark and Leonard 1991; Mitchell 1987). Finding such a shift, of course, does not mean that wage determination must be viewed as an intractable mystery. It simply means that explanations need to be sought, and that these may not be found through simple econometric modeling.

Union/nonunion wage differentials

One candidate for a cause of the shift is the change in union/nonunion wage differentials. In the private sector, this differential peaked at about one-third in the early 1980s on a wage-only basis, according to data from the Employment Cost Index (ECI).[35] Including benefits and payroll taxes, the differential peaked at almost one-half and then fell steadily until it bottomed out in the 1990–91 recession. Such bottoming out, it might be noted, is in keeping with the long-standing finding that nonunion wage setting is more sensitive than union wage setting to short-term business cycle pressures, in part due to the absence of long-term contracts in nonunion jobs.

Unfortunately, the ECI series does not go back beyond the mid-1970s. A longer series can be developed from somewhat less satisfactory data. The BLS has maintained data on effective median wage changes under major private union contracts since the late 1950s. These data can be converted into an absolute index and compared with general private wage data (union plus nonunion combined) for that period. Figure 17.1 shows the results.[36]

The resulting series suggests that the union/nonunion wage differential declined in the early 1960s as part of an earlier concession period. There was subsequent erosion as inflation accelerated during the early Great Society and Vietnam era. A catch-up phase began in the late 1960s, interrupted briefly by wage controls. Thereafter, a dramatic widening of the differential occurred, in part linked to the use of COLAs (Mitchell 1980). By this measure, a peak was reached at the end of 1981 and concession bargaining eroded the differential through 1990.

In analyzing Figure 17.1, however, it is important to keep this caveat in mind: as the proportion of payroll going to the (major) union sector has declined over the period shown, the weight of (major)

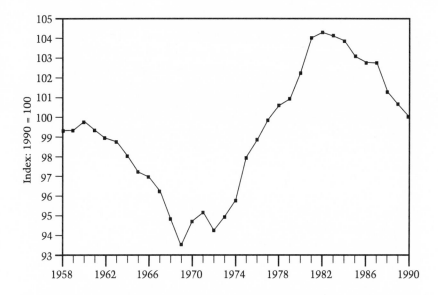

Figure 17.1. The ratio of major union pay to general pay. See text for method of calculation (1990 = 100). Source of data: U.S. Bureau of Labor Statistics.

union wages has decreased in aggregate wage measures. Hence, ratios such as that in Figure 17.1 will tend to show higher values toward the end of the period due to the smaller (major) union weight in the denominator. In short, if the ratio in Figure 17.1 is used as a proxy for the major-union/nonunion wage ratio, or the general union/nonunion ratio, it must be corrected in the early years for its downward bias.

There is no precise way to estimate this correction; if complete data were available, the union/nonunion wage ratio could be estimated directly and no proxy would be needed. However, reasonable correction values would push up the starting values on the order of 3 to 5 percent. That is, the peak values for the ratio in the early years would be close to the values attained at the peak in the early 1980s.[37] Similarly, the low values at the end of the 1980s would not be far above the lows of the late 1960s.[38]

Certainly, the notion of union/nonunion wage differentials cycling around a "normal" level is an appealing explanation for the wave of concessions in the 1980s. However, the notion by itself provides no clear indication of what "normal" is. Nor does it explain why there should be a cycle in the first place. Why should not the differential just stay at its normal level?

459

Evidence from selected major contracts

Table 17.6 presents regressions explaining annualized life-of-contract wage change for 47 bargaining pairs over the period 1970 to 1991. The data are taken from seven employer-union situations as reported by BNA's *Collective Bargaining Contracts and Negotiations* service.[39] Explanatory variables are the inverse of the monthly unemployment rate (1/U) at the inception of each contract,[40] the change in the Consumer Price Index for urban wage earners and clerical workers in the year before the contract began (CPI-1), and the annualized CPI over the life of the contract for those contracts with COLA clauses — or zero for those without them (COLA-L).[41]

Also included is the ratio of the bargaining unit's base wage (including COLA) just prior to the contract's effective date, divided by nonfarm average hourly earnings in that month (REL). To account for differences in occupation mix, and other factors that might affect the long-term wage level, the REL variable is standardized to be equal to 1 for the first contract of each bargaining pair.[42] The REL variable can be viewed as a proxy for the union/nonunion wage differential for each unit. Finally, a dummy variable equal to 1 for all settlements adopted in 1982 or later is included to represent the concession era (DUMCON).

Some general characteristics stand out. First, the inverse unemployment rate enters with the wrong sign. This aberration is due to

Table 17.6. Wage-change regressions regarding selected major settlements

	All settlements	Pre-1982 settlements	Concession-period settlements	Non-COLA settlements	COLA settlements
Constant	16.03***	17.13**	3.59	22.16***	13.78***
1/U	−21.76**	−37.15***	16.76	−32.87**	−24.59*
CPI-1	.38***	.29**	.81**	.54***	.13
COLA-L	.33***	.38***	.01	—	.67***
REL	−6.56***	−4.77	−4.97**	−11.40***	−5.10**
DUMCON	−3.56***	—	—	−1.59*	−3.61***
Adjusted R²	.82	.58	.63	.91	.85
Standard error	1.75	1.78	1.27	1.07	1.70
Observations	47	26	21	17	30

Source: Data for regressions are from Bureau of National Affairs, Inc., and U.S. Bureau of Labor Statistics, various publications.
* Significant at 10% level.
** Significant at 5% level.
*** Significant at 1% level.

the history of the 1974–75 recession in which very high unemployment rates and high wage inflation existed simultaneously. If the regressions are confined to the concession era (1982 and after), the sign reverses. This reversal is not surprising, since in the concession era, when the unemployment rate was high, wage changes were low (or negative) in the sample. However, the concession-era coefficient is not significant. In summary, a simple, real-business-conditions explanation of union wage behavior does not suffice. Union wage setting does not seem particularly responsive to real economic activity in the short term.

Second, price inflation seems to be calling the tune in combination with the relative wage variable. Non-COLA contracts are sensitive to precontract CPI inflation, perhaps using the past as a forecast of inflation during the contract's life. COLA contracts have less need of a forecast, so it is life-of-contract CPI inflation that drives them.

Third, the REL variable has the "correct" negative sign, that is, it indicates that as the unit's wage rate drifts above the general wage level, a regression-to-the-mean phenomenon enters, reducing the unit's relative wage inflation rate. However, in the preconcession period, the coefficient is not significant, indicating that the widening union differential was not a major force in retarding wage growth.

Finally, the dummy for the concession era is negative even in the presence of the REL variable. The dummy, therefore, is suggesting that "something" in that period was retarding wage change, beyond the wage differential effect. There was, in other words, a (downward) structural shift during the concession era. What caused it?

The bargaining process as a cause of the shift

As I noted earlier, economic modeling of the union wage determination process has often neglected the management side. Unions are often modeled as if they set wages unilaterally. Neglecting management means neglecting the fundamental fact that setting union wages involves adversarial bargaining. The neglect cannot be remedied with offhand references to Nash bargaining solutions; there is a genuine clash of interests and an uncertain range of outcomes.

Adversarial wage bargaining is much like international confrontation. The parties have an imperfectly known potential to do great harm to one another. They normally, therefore, have an incentive to reduce the risk of unlimited conflict to tolerable levels, to play by known rules, to communicate through understood rituals, and to avoid pushing each other "too far." As during the Cold War in the international setting, under adversarial wage bargaining there is periodic probing, testing, and even controlled conflict. That is, every once in awhile, limits are breached as an experiment by one of the parties.

As various writers have stressed (Ross 1948; Kerr 1977; Mitchell 1980), the union side's behavior can be viewed as the outcome of an internal political process reflecting member preferences and perceptions. And the union members who participate in that process have less information than the direct bargainers about the implications of their demands. Union members saw the erosion of the union/nonunion wage differential reversed in the late 1960s, accompanied by a burst of strike activity. No adverse consequences seemed to ensue in the short-term horizon they observed and so the process repeated.

CPI inflation often had foreign rather than domestic causes in the 1970s. But keeping up with the cost of living was a traditional goal not easily abandoned by union members. Similarly, although productivity growth slowed markedly in the 1970s, abandoning the post–World War II principle of steady real wage improvements — the famous annual improvement factor — was not something readily accepted.

Industrial relations scholars have characterized the union-management "deal" struck after World War II as one in which the union's role was to push for improvements and management's role was to run the business and resist union demands (Kochan, Katz, and McKersie 1986). Such a system, by its nature, does not encourage long-term thinking. Union officials and certainly their members are not supposed to be involved in the economics of operating the business. It is not surprising that to outside observers union wage behavior in the 1970s seemed to be a matter of taking the money and running (Lawrence and Lawrence 1985). But the behavior was not a matter of carefully trading off short-run gains against long-run losses. It was rather that the long-run consequences could not be clearly seen. And since the emphasis in bargaining is on the short-run damage to both sides that could result from a strike, management was also shortsighted.

Although a widening union/nonunion wage differential creates a growing incentive for nonunion management to avoid unionization, it does not immediately lead already-unionized managements to try to reverse the trend. Hence, unions did not receive early warning signals from management that devastating results would eventually follow. Already-unionized managements sought to expand nonunion operations or to contract out; to confront the union adversary directly would have meant pushing into an unknown territory of conflict for which a heavy price might be paid. Only with evidence that the cost of conflict would not be large would there be an incentive to experiment. That evidence came along in the 1980s.

The best evidence of union vulnerability would be confrontations by *other* managements in which the management side did succeed, at acceptable cost, in reversing the widening wage differential. From the management perspective, information on union vulnerability is something of a public good. A firm obtaining the information — through conflict with a union — pays the cost but does not capture most of the benefit. But severe recession, growing trade competition, deregulation, and a change in the legal and political climate induced some distressed managements to take a chance and push for concessions based on their own internal situations.

Once the initial management probes succeeded, union vulnerability was exposed and the concession movement spread. The cost of conflict was seen to be tolerable from the management viewpoint, even for nondistressed companies. Concessions turned out to be good business, noticeably improving shareholder value (Becker 1987). It is for that reason that, while one can relate specific concessions to particular causes such as deregulation, the concession movement became so pervasive and spread throughout the unionized sector.

An adversarial wage bargaining system, in short, is likely to be characterized by explosions and implosions rather than smooth and quick adjustments. Norms will appear to shift, and will be reflected as significant dummy coefficients for periods after such shifts. Just as with wars, earthquakes, and other phenomena, in which pressures build up for long periods, while we can understand the causes, it is difficult to model the precise timing of the event or even to predict what the precise results will be, once the pressure is suddenly released.

Where does this overview of the union wage concession movement leave collective bargaining? The model and interpretation sketched here suggest it is dangerous to assume that there are clockwork regularities underlying any social phenomenon, including union wage explosions and implosions. In the collective bargaining case, the wage concession era was also a period in which substantial union membership losses occurred. With a substantially increased nonunion sector as competition, a prolonged period of widening of the union wage differential now seems unlikely, although short-term cyclical movements are quite possible.

Union officials, especially at the higher levels of the union hierarchy, have learned something about the consequences of adversarial bargaining. As a consequence moves were made in some cases in the 1980s to adopt a more cooperationist stance. In the automobile industry, for example, various employee involvement initiatives were developed. Probably the most well-known example in the industry occurred at New United Motors, a General Motors–Toyota joint venture. But there were experiments in other industries, too. The U.S. Department of Labor began to publicize these developments in the 1980s through bulletins of its Bureau of Labor-Management Relations and Cooperative Programs. Along with such actions in firms with widely recognized names, such as Xerox and Harley-Davidson, the bulletins reported on smaller firms in such industries as wood products, printing, trucking, machinery manufacturing, and others.

How deeply the engagement in cooperative programs has penetrated in union circles is still an open question; certainly examples of anticooperationist dissident movements within unions are not hard to find. And not all of the situations described in the Labor Department's bulletins had happy endings. Eastern Airlines, for example, was one of the cases reported as an example of labor-management cooperation — before its takeover and its to-the-death struggle with its unions (U.S. Bureau of Labor-Management Relations and Cooperative Programs 1988). Cooperationist programs can pose difficult dilemmas for union officials, since there is an inherently adversarial aspect to employment, just as there is in any buyer-seller relationship. Union officials who advocate nonadversarial approaches are open to charges that they are the tools of management.

On the employer side, union-management cooperation is valued, but only when unionization is a fait accompli and the alternative to cooperation is continued conflict. Management's general preference is still to be nonunion if possible. Thus, in the automobile industry, the new Japanese "transplant" operations set up in the United States that were not joint ventures have remained nonunion and have resisted union organizing efforts.

Although understanding union wage determination in the 1980s does not produce clear-cut predictions about the 1990s or beyond, there are two primary lessons to be drawn. First, macroeconomic determinants of real wage trends, such as productivity growth, trade competition from abroad, and immigration, cannot be resisted indefinitely through microeconomic-level collective bargaining. They can be resisted only for a time; eventually pressure will build and force a painful "acceptance" of the external trends.

Second, since collective bargaining has an inherently adversarial element, it would be best to provide safety valves that prevent excessive wage pressure from building (as it did in the 1970s). The move toward profit sharing in the union sector, which seemed to have stalled by the late 1980s, could have provided such a safety valve.

With a significant profit-sharing element of pay, the economic conditions of the employer and (reflected through the employer) of the economy as a whole are built into payment automatically, rather than through a difficult adversarial bargaining process.

In short, there is a need to think creatively in the area of wage determination under collective bargaining. Most of the creativity in the 1980s went into such workplace practices as quality circles, autonomous work teams, and other related arrangements. It is sometimes noted that in a typical union contract, wages take up only a few pages and the bulk of the contract involves work rules and policies. But this is misleading. It may take only a few pages to describe wages, but determining them is central to collective bargaining. It was within those few pages that the pressures developed behind concession bargaining in the 1980s.

Notes

1. On a three-year cycle, the period 1982 through 1984 featured annual concession rates averaging about one-third ([44+37+23]/3 = 35). On a two-year cycle, the average for 1982 and 1983 is 41 percent. There will, of course, be some double counting of concessions under either approach if there are shorter-than-average contracts with repeated concessions.
2. Some contracts containing lump sums and bonuses may not have actuated these features in the first year. Hence, there is a slight overexclusion under the intermediate definition.
3. Consideration is given to union representation rather than membership. Some workers are represented by unions that they do not choose to join. A case can be made for viewing unionization from both perspectives. However, major union data are available only on a representation basis. It might be noted that the number of contracts reported in the BNA's biweekly survey steadily declined over the concession era. A three-year average of these numbers is appropriate, due to the typical length of union contracts. During 1980 through 1982 to 1988 through 1990, the average annual number of union settlements reported fell by 29 percent. The number of contracts in the BLS major private contract file fell by 38 percent from 1980 to 1990.
4. If the average union-represented unit falls in size, some contracts will fall below the 1,000-worker defining line for inclusion as "major," and their workers will disappear from the series. The BLS does not immediately drop such contracts from its series, however, and the overall effect of such slippage out of the series is probably quite small. Average major bargaining unit size in 1990 (slightly under 4,800 workers) was a bit larger than in 1980 (slightly over 4,700 workers).

5. There were, of course, some favorable developments from the union viewpoint. For example, the National Labor Relations Board's decision to exercise rule-making authority and to predesignate bargaining units by occupation in health care might help unions in that industry in some cases.

6. Some union representation is lost each year due to decertification elections. In fiscal year 1990, the decertification loss was 16,341 workers, bringing the potential net gain for unions down to 56,765.

7. By the early 1990s, there were calls within organized labor for devoting more resources to organizing drives (see Bureau of National Affairs 1991).

8. Budget cuts at the BLS led to the discontinuance of strike data collection after 1981 for units with fewer than 1,000 workers. However, major strikes generally involve negotiations disputes, whereas small strikes often entail minor grievances under existing contracts. The word *strike* in the text refers to any work stoppage including a lockout.

9. Because some strikes run across calendar years, reported figures underestimate strike days per striking worker.

10. As union membership fell, newspapers ceased to maintain labor reporters on their staffs. Thus, a human interest angle, rather than mere importance to the labor relations scene, was needed to attract media attention.

11. Example: "Since the controllers' strike, employers have been emboldened to take more and more militant stands." Statement of Theodore W. Kheel, noted labor attorney, quoted in Barron 1990.

12. The Hormel case arose out of a larger reconfiguration of collective bargaining in the meatpacking industry. For background, see Perry and Kegley 1989.

13. Lorenzo's reputation following the Continental dispute indirectly led to the later Eastern Airlines dispute. Organized labor thought that if a strike were won at Eastern, it would signal to the management community that the days of labor weakness were ended. On Lorenzo and the Eastern dispute, see Bernstein 1990.

14. The union did not obtain the necessary majority of votes. Subsequently, voting rules were changed to prevent a repeat union campaign.

15. Details concerning the 1986–87 dispute and its outcome can be found in Hoerr 1988, chapter 20.

16. A major strike occurred in 1984. Attempts to deviate from industry contracts were made at Binion's Horseshoe Casino in 1990 and at the Frontier Hotel in 1991–92.

17. Guilford Industries (operator of two major railroads in New England) transferred some operations to a subsidiary, Springfield Terminal Co., after a 1986 strike. It eventually signed a contract with the United Transportation Union (UTU), having effectively displaced other craft unions. Various work-rule relaxations and pay cuts resulted. The UTU had dropped out of the AFL-CIO during this period and was not bound by

no-raid rules. A similar dispute occurred when Burlington Northern switched some operations to a subsidiary, Winona Bridge. A subsequent court decision found that unless Winona Bridge was sold to an outside interest, the parent railroad's obligation to existing unions continued. The plan to contract out electricity generation surfaced during the 1986 shop-craft negotiations.

18. See Perry, Kramer, and Schneider 1982 on the law regarding the use of replacements.

19. There is only limited evidence available on the frequency with which employers have used the replacement tactic over time. A survey of employers and union officials suggests the use of replacements during strikes had increased in the 1980s relative to the 1970s (U.S. General Accounting Office 1991). A BNA survey found that employers became more willing to "consider" using replacements between 1986 and 1990 (Bureau of National Affairs 1991c).

20. See *New York Times* 1981a, 1981b. Not surprisingly, the replacement controllers many years later remained opposed to rehiring any of the strikers. See U.S. General Accounting Office (1986).

21. The United Farm Workers (UFW) particularly targeted Vons, a supermarket chain in southern California that was attempting to penetrate the Hispanic market with specialty stores. At one point, Vons agreed not to advertise grapes, although it continued to sell them. However, litigation from grape growers induced Vons to reverse the decision. The UFW also attempted to develop an environmental and health issue: the use of pesticides on grapes. While this approach did draw some public attention, the grape boycott never penetrated deeply into national public awareness.

22. In 1991, the United Mine Workers waived its option to reopen on wages under this contract, although it did negotiate a pension improvement.

23. Indeed, energy prices are production costs for most firms. Except for energy producers, energy price increases reduce ability to pay for most employers.

24. Japanese bonus payments are typically a much larger fraction of total compensation than are lump sums in the United States.

25. Profit sharing was more traditionally viewed as an incentive system, as opposed to a labor-cost flexibility system. Although the automobile industry probably viewed the decision to adopt profit sharing mainly from the latter perspective, there was interest in boosting labor productivity (witness the various experiments with quality of working life practices). At the time of the 1982 concessions, Japan was said to have as much as a $1,500 per vehicle cost advantage compared with the United States, due not only to wages but also to the labor productivity margin (see Crandall et al. 1986, pp. 22–26).

26. Having negotiated lump sums, aerospace contractors found themselves embroiled in a dispute with the BLS concerning the treatment of the bonuses in its average hourly earnings series. Bonus payments were

traditionally excluded from the calculation. However, the industry had some product contracts indexed to average hourly earnings and wanted the full labor cost reflected. Eventually the industry agreed to fund a supplemental report including the bonuses.

27. Wayne Horvitz, who was involved in concession negotiations with Western Airlines, described this pressure from the financial sector at a seminar held at the UCLA Institute of Industrial Relations on March 8, 1985. Western adopted a two-tier plan, although it was not expanding and was, indeed, struggling to stay alive. Eventually Western was swallowed by Delta Airlines.

28. In the airline industry, two factors might lead to a drop in two-tier plan usage (or a narrowing of the gap between the tiers). First, as Cappelli (1988) points out, a move toward greater oligopoly in the industry could strengthen union bargaining power. Deregulation at first produced upstart, low-cost carriers, such as People Express, that undercut the prices of established carriers. But by the early 1990s, the fallout of the deregulation movement saw the removal of such upstarts and the end of some established carriers as well, such as Eastern and Pan Am. Second, in some cases the lower-tier rate, especially for pilots, was so low that a labor shortage eventually developed by the mid-1980s. In such cases, it is in the interest of management to raise the lower tier wage or eliminate the two-tier plan. On the market for pilots in the mid-1980s, see Belous and Fischer (1986). Of course, cuts in the defense budget in the 1990s could put more former military pilots into the commercial job market.

29. At the Kenosha Leatherette and Display Company, employees in the upper tier were explicitly "red circled" (their base wages were frozen, although they received lump sums) so that lower-tier workers could catch up. Even in cases where the two-tier plan was not completely eliminated, narrowing the tier gap by freezing workers at the upper level seems to have been commonplace (International Association of Machinists 1992).

30. Deregulated industries were defined as airlines, trucking and warehousing, railroads, and communications.

31. Trade-affected industries were defined as metals, motor vehicles, rubber, machinery, aerospace, miscellaneous manufacturing, paper and lumber, textiles, food manufacturing (except meatpacking), instruments, chemicals, furniture, shipping (maritime), mining, other transportation equipment (apart from motor vehicles and aerospace), brick-clay-stone, glass, leather, petroleum, ordnance, tobacco, apparel, agriculture-forestry-fishing.

32. Although the Reagan administration tried from the beginning to make administrative changes to relax Davis-Bacon, litigation delayed implementation of significant changes until 1985. The heaviest wave of construction concession bargaining came before that.

33. Vroman and Abowd (1988) confirm that union wage moderation in the

1980s was spread across sectors and was not well explained by foreign trade and deregulation.

34. The inability to capture changes as a smoothly continuous function of measurable variables carries into nonwage aspects of industrial relations. For example, Abowd and Farber (1990) find that the upswing in management resistance and downswing in union organizing in the 1980s cannot be explained by a model relating such activities to worker quasirents.

35. The Employment Cost Index is normally presented as an index rather than as an absolute dollar value. To calculate a percentage union/nonunion differential, I benchmarked the union and nonunion indexes to the dollar figures reported for March 1991 from the same survey. However, data shown in Figure 17.1 are as of December of each year.

36. The December ECI for wages and salaries is used from 1975 onward as the measure of general pay. It is spliced to December average hourly earnings for earlier years. Before 1964, December earnings data are not available. To approximate December earnings, the average for the two years surrounding each December is used.

37. The major union sector accounts for about 60 percent of union representation and probably a larger percent of the union payroll. A plausible estimate of the weight of the union sector in total private payrolls in the late 1950s is on the order of 40 percent, so the major-sector weight was probably about 25 percent. By the early 1980s, the union weight was about 25 percent, so the major union weight would have been perhaps 15 percent. If the major union sector had a constant wage premium relative to all other private workers of, say, 30 percent at both peaks, the shifting weights would reduce the ratio bias by about 3 percent at the earlier peak relative to the later peak. If it is assumed that major union wages were equal to minor union wages and that the union/nonunion wage premium was, for example, 40 percent at the later peak, then the earlier peak would need to be boosted by about 5 percent to make the two peaks comparable.

38. An actual correction is not attempted because of the rough nature of the estimates. Among other problems, the Employment Cost Index that is used as the denominator beginning in the mid-1970s roughly fixes the union share of employment over subperiods, since a constant sample of establishments is used. The average hourly earnings index, used in the early part of the period (and spliced to the ECI) is confined to production and nonsupervisory workers and gives the union sector a still larger (but unknown) weight. For more on the weight of the union sector, see Jacoby and Mitchell 1988.

39. The pairs are General Motors and the Autoworkers; Trucking Management (a multiemployer group) and the Teamsters; USX and the Steelworkers; Atlantic Richfield and the Oil, Chemical, and Atomic Workers; General Electric and the Electronic Workers; and B. F. Goodrich and the Rubber Workers. (In some cases, the parties changed their names during

the period of regression.) Wage data for each unit was drawn from information in the looseleaf service and the *Daily Labor Report*. If a wage rate in a particular bargaining period could not be determined, it was extrapolated based on wage change data from other periods in which the wage was reported. Data on private nonagricultural hourly earnings and the CPI are from BLS sources.

40. Regressions were also run using the change in unemployment over the life of the contract. In no case did the change variable appear significant.

41. The index for urban wage and clerical workers is utilized because unions use it — rather than the more general index for urban consumers — in their COLA clauses.

42. The first contract in the sample for each pair occurs either in 1970 or (for Atlantic Richfield and USX) 1971.

References

Abowd, John M., and Henry S. Farber. 1990. "Product Market Competition, Union Organizing Activity, and Employer Resistance." Working paper no. 3353, National Bureau of Economic Research (May).

AFL-CIO Committee on the Evolution of Work. 1985. *The Changing Situation of Workers and Their Unions.* Washington, D.C.: American Federation of Labor — Congress of Industrial Organizations.

Ashenfelter, Orley, and George Johnson. 1969. "Bargaining Theory, Trade Unions, and Industrial Strike Activity." *American Economic Review* 59 (March): 35–49.

Barron, James. 1990. "The News Strike Shows Shifting Labor Relations." *New York Times*, October 28: A33.

Becker, Brian E. 1987. "Concession Bargaining: The Impact on Shareholders' Equity." *Industrial and Labor Relations Review* 40 (January): 268–279.

Bell, Linda A. 1989. "Union Concessions in the 1980s." *Federal Reserve Bank of New York Quarterly Review* (Summer): 44–58.

———. 1991. "Union Wage Concessions in the 1980s: Aggregate, Ability-to-Pay, and Institutional Explanations." Unpublished working paper, John F. Kennedy School of Government, Harvard University (September).

Bell, Linda A., and David Neumark. 1991. "Lump-Sums, Profit Sharing, and Labor Costs in the Union Sector." Working paper no. 3630, National Bureau of Economic Research (February).

Belous, Richard S. 1985. "Two-Tier Wage Systems in the U.S. Economy." Report no. 85-165 E. Congressional Research Service (August 12).

Belous, Richard S., and John W. Fischer. 1986. "Civilian and Military Pilots: The Labor Market Relationship." Report no. 86-28 E. Congressional Research Service.

Bernstein, Aaron. 1990. *Grounded: The Inside Account of How Frank Lorenzo Took Over and Destroyed Eastern Airlines.* New York: Touchstone.

Bernstein, Harry. 1988. "2 Faces of GE's 'Welchism': One Dr. Jekyll, One Mr. Hyde." *Los Angeles Times,* Part 4, January 12: 1, 22; and "For the Record." *Los Angeles Times,* Part 4, January 19: 2.

Bronars, Stephen G., and Donald R. Deere. 1989. "Union Organizing Activity and Union Coverage: 1973-1988." Unpublished working paper (November).

Bureau of National Affairs, Inc. 1991a. "AFL-CIO Leaders Seek Ways to Boost Union Membership in U.S." *Daily Labor Report,* November 15: A2.

———. 1991b. "Public Approval of Labor Leaders on Rise According to National Survey." *Daily Labor Report,* August 20: A1–A2.

———. 1991c. *Replacement Workers: Evidence From the Popular and Labor Press, 1989 and 1990.* BNA Plus Special Report. Washington, D.C.: Bureau of National Affairs, Inc.

Cappelli, Peter. 1988. "An Economist's Perspective," in Jean T. McKelvey, ed., *Cleared for Takeoff: Airline Labor Relations since Deregulation.* Ithaca, N.Y.: ILR Press. pp. 49–64.

Cappelli, Peter, and Peter D. Sherer. 1990. "Assessing Worker Attitudes Under a Two-Tier Wage Plan." *Industrial and Labor Relations Review* 43 (January): 225–244.

Cartter, Allan M., and F. Ray Marshall. 1972. *Labor Economics: Wages, Employment, and Trade Unionism,* rev. ed. Homewood, Ill.: Irwin.

Cooke, William N. 1985. *Union Organizing and Public Policy: Failure to Secure First Contracts.* Kalamazoo, Mich.: Upjohn Institute.

Crandall, Robert W., et al. 1986. *Regulating the Automobile.* Washington, D.C.: Brookings Institution.

Erickson, Christopher L. 1990. "Union Wage Growth in the 1980s: Has There Been a Structural Shift?" Unpublished working paper, New York State School of Industrial and Labor Relations, Cornell University (January).

Erickson, Christopher L., and Andrea C. Ichino. 1990. "Lump Sum Bonuses in Union Contracts: Semantic Change or Step toward a New Wage Determination System?" Unpublished working paper, New York State School of Industrial and Labor Relations, Cornell University (September).

Farber, Henry S. 1990. "The Decline of Unionization in the United States: What Can Be Learned from Recent Experience?" *Journal of Labor Economics* 8 (January, Part 2): S75–S105.

Flanagan, Robert J. 1984. "Wage Concessions and Long-Term Union Wage Flexibility." *Brookings Papers on Economic Activity* 1: 183–216.

Foulkes, Fred K. 1980. *Personnel Policies in Large Nonunion Companies.* Englewood Cliffs, N.J.: Prentice Hall.

Freedman, Audrey. 1982. "A Fundamental Change in Wage Bargaining." *Challenge* 25 (July/August): 14–17.

Freeman, Richard B., and James L. Medoff. 1984. *What Do Unions Do?* New York: Basic Books.

Freeman, Richard B., and Martin L. Weitzman. 1987. "Bonuses and Employment in Japan." *Journal of the Japanese and International Economies* 1: 168–194.

Hoerr, John P. 1988. *And the Wolf Finally Came: The Decline of the American Steel Industry.* Pittsburgh: University of Pittsburgh Press.

International Association of Machinists. 1992. "Two-Tier Rates Out at Kenosha Display." *Machinist* (January): 3.

Jacoby, Sanford M., and Daniel J. B. Mitchell. 1984. "Employer Preferences for Long-Term Contracts." *Journal of Labor Research* 5 (Summer): 215–228.

———. 1986. "Management Attitudes toward Two-Tier Pay Plans." *Journal of Labor Research* 7 (Summer): 221–237.

———. 1988. "Measurement of Compensation: Union and Nonunion." *Industrial Relations* 27 (Spring): 215–231.

Kerr, Clark. 1964. "Industrial Peace and the Collective Bargaining Environment," reprinted in Clark Kerr, *Labor and Management in Industrial Society.* Garden City, N.Y.: Anchor Books. Pp. 148–166.

———. 1977. "Economic Analysis and the Study of Industrial Relations" reprinted in Clark Kerr, *Labor Markets and Wage Determination: The Balkanization of the Labor Market and Other Essays.* Berkeley: University of California Press.

Kochan, Thomas A., Harry C. Katz, and Robert B. McKersie. 1986. *The Great Transformation of American Industrial Relations.* New York: Basic Books.

La Botz, Dan. 1991. *A Troublemaker's Handbook: How to Fight Back Where You Work — And Win.* Detroit: Labor Notes.

LaLonde, Robert J., and Bernard D. Meltzer. 1991. "Hard Times for Unions: Another Look at the Significance of Employer Illegalities." *University of Chicago Law Review* 58: 953–1014.

Lawrence, Colin, and Robert Z. Lawrence. 1985. "Manufacturing Wage Dispersion: An End Game Interpretation." *Brookings Papers on Economic Activity* 1: 47–106.

Lipsky, David B., and Clifford B. Donn. 1987. "Collective Bargaining in American Industry: A Synthesis," in David B. Lipsky and Clifford B. Donn, eds., *Collective Bargaining in American Industry: Contemporary Perspectives and Future Directions.* Lexington, Mass.: D. C. Heath. pp. 307–332.

MacDonald, Glenn M., and Chris Robinson. 1992. "Unionism in a Competitive Industry." *Journal of Labor Economics* 10 (January): 33–54.

Martin, James E. (with Thomas D. Heetderks). 1990. *Two-Tier Compensation Structures: Their Impact on Unions, Employers, and Employees.* Kalamazoo, Mich.: Upjohn Institute.

McFarlin, Dean B., and Michael R. Frone. 1990. "A Two-Tier Wage Structure in a Nonunion Firm." *Industrial Relations* 29 (Winter): 145–154.

Mitchell, Daniel J. B. 1980. *Unions, Wages, and Inflation.* Washington, D.C.: Brookings Institution.

———. 1981. "Wage Spillover: The Impact of Landrum-Griffin." *Industrial Relations* 20 (Fall): 342–346.

———. 1982a. "Recent Union Contract Concessions." *Brookings Papers on Economic Activity* 1: 165–201.

———. 1982b. "Should the Consumer Price Index Determine Wages?" *California Management Review* 25 (Fall): 5–21.

———. 1985. "Shifting Norms in Wage Determination." *Brookings Papers on Economic Activity* 2: 575–599.

———. 1986. "Concession Bargaining in the Public Sector: A Lesser Force." *Public Personnel Management* 15 (Spring): 23–40.

———. 1987. "Wage Trends and Wage Concessions: Implications for Medium-Term Economic Expansion," in *The Economic Outlook for 1987, Proceedings of November 20–21, 1986, Meetings of RSQE.* Ann Arbor: Department of Economics, University of Michigan. pp. 266–335.

———. 1988. "Collective Bargaining and Compensation in the Public Sector," in Benjamin Aaron, Joyce M. Najita, and James L. Stern, eds., *Public-Sector Bargaining*, 2nd ed. Washington, D.C.: Bureau of National Affairs.

———. 1989. "Wage Pressures and Labor Shortages: The 1960s and 1980s." *Brookings Papers on Economic Activity* 2: 191–231.

———. 1990. "Is Pattern Bargaining Dead? — Comment." *Industrial and Labor Relations Review* 44 (October): 156–159.

———. 1993. "Keynesian, Old Keynesian, and New Keynesian Wage Nominalism." *Industrial Relations* 32 (Winter): 1–29.

Neumark, David, and Jonathan S. Leonard. 1991. "Inflation Expectations and the Structural Shift in Aggregate Labor-Cost Determination in the 1980s." Unpublished working paper (November).

New York Times. 1981a. "Most in Poll Oppose Public Worker Strikes," August 16: A39.

New York Times. 1981b. "Harris Poll Finds Most Oppose the Air Strike," August 21: A18.

Northrup, Herbert R. 1984. "The Rise and Demise of PATCO." *Industrial and Labor Relations Review* 37 (January): 167–184.

Paltrow, Scott J. 1991. "Buyout Hits the Bull's-Eye at Colt's: Co-Ownership Triggers New Era for Gun Maker." *Los Angeles Times*, April 14: D1, D7, D9.

Perry, Charles R., and Delwyn H. Kegley. 1989. *Disintegration and Change: Labor Relations in the Meat Packing Industry.* Philadelphia: Industrial Relations Unit, Wharton School, University of Pennsylvania.

Perry, Charles R., Andrew M. Kramer, and Thomas J. Schneider. 1982. *Operating during Strikes.* Philadelphia: Industrial Relations Unit, Wharton School, University of Pennsylvania.

Perry, George L. 1989. "Shifting Wage Norms and Their Implications." *American Economic Review* 76 (May): 245–248.

Ready, Kathryn J. 1990. "Is Pattern Bargaining Dead?" *Industrial and Labor Relations Review* 43 (January): 272–279.

Ross, Arthur M. 1948. *Trade Union Wage Policy.* Berkeley: University of California Press.

Thomas, Steven L. 1990. "Two-Tier Collective Bargaining Agreements and

Firm Performance," in John F. Burton, Jr., ed. *Proceedings of the Forty-Second Annual Meeting,* Industrial Relations Research Association, December 28–30. 1989. Madison, Wis.: IRRA. pp. 150–154.

Uchitelle, Louis. 1986. "Bonuses Replace Wage Rises and Workers Are the Losers." *New York Times,* Section 1, June 26: 1, 31.

U.S. Bureau of Labor-Management Relations and Cooperative Programs. 1988. *Labor-Management Cooperation and Eastern Air Lines.* Bulletin 118. Washington, D.C.: U.S. Department of Labor, Bureau of Labor-Management Relations and Cooperation.

U.S. General Accounting Office. 1986. *FAA Staffing: The Air Traffic Control Work Force Opposes Rehiring Fired Controllers.* Report GAO/ RCED-87-32BR. Washington, D.C.: General Accounting Office.

Verma, Anil. 1985. "Relative Flow of Capital to Union and Nonunion Plants within a Firm." *Industrial Relations* 24 (Fall): 395–405.

Vroman, Wayne, and John M. Abowd. 1988. "Disaggregated Wage Developments." *Brookings Papers on Economic Activity* 1: 313–346.

Wachter, Michael L., and William H. Carter. 1989. "Norm Shifts in Union Wages: Will 1989 Be a Replay of 1969?" *Brookings Papers on Economic Activity* 2: 233–264.

Weiler, Paul C. 1983. "Promises to Keep: Securing Workers' Rights to Self-Organization under the NLRA." *Harvard Law Review* 96 (June): 1769–1827.

Weitzman, Martin L. 1984. *The Share Economy: Conquering Stagflation.* Cambridge, Mass.: Harvard University Press.

18

Changing Patterns in Dispute Resolution

■ ——————————————————— ■

Peter Feuille

It's 1946. The war is over, the private sector's muscle-flexing unions represent more than a third of an expanded labor force, consumers are spending their wartime savings as fast as they can and companies are furiously producing to meet the demand, the wartime controls on prices and wages have been lifted, and one of the results is a breathtaking surge in prices (14 percent by year's end). Another result is that 1946 is the most strike-prone year in American history, a record that still stands. Some of these strikes, such as those by coal miners and railroad engineers, prompt repeated calls for tough government intervention in "emergency disputes." One of the rallying cries of congressional candidates in the November elections is the need to put the clamps on the unions, and those election results produce the union restrictions of the Taft-Hartley Act several months later (passed overwhelmingly in the face of fierce union lobbying against the "Slave Labor Act" and over Harry Truman's veto). Indeed, even though union contracts are increasingly likely to contain grievance procedures that culminate in arbitration to resolve contract interpretation disputes, often the rank and file walk out the door over grievances.

Move the calendar forward. In the 1990s, the labor-management warriors of 1946 would have trouble recognizing the landscape. The union-represented share of private employment is down to 13 percent, and the unions' only stable sector is government (where they represent more than 40 percent of the work force). Strikes have fallen to their lowest levels since the early 1930s. Indeed, many unions are afraid to strike for fear that their members will be permanently replaced, and strikes over grievance disputes have all but disappeared. Instead, grievance arbitration is routinely used to resolve contract interpretation disputes (and the current version of arbitration is more formalized than it was in 1946). In public-sector negotiations in many states, interest arbitration also is used to resolve contract negotiation disputes. Worries about emergency strikes have almost completely vanished; this topic seems to have passed into the hands of the labor historians. Indeed, a succession of federal administrations have paid scant attention to union-management relations and instead have passed numerous laws designed to improve labor market conditions for all workers, along with the administrative agencies to enforce these statues. As part of this multidecade trend to provide direct protections to individual workers, disgruntled employees (mostly nonunion) have become increasingly likely to charge or sue their former employers, often on the grounds that they were discriminatorily or unfairly discharged.

In the pages that follow I will analyze some of the changes in workplace dispute processing that have occurred during the postwar period. After examining disputes over the public policy rules governing employment relationships, I will focus on how new employment terms are established, and how existing terms are interpreted. This analysis will show that strikes have come to play a significantly less visible role, and that at the same time third-party decision makers have come to play a much more prominent role. It also will show that disputes in nonunion workplaces have become a much larger concern for public policy makers than was the case during the period of union ascendancy up through the early 1960s.

Disputes over National Labor Policy

Until the early 1960s the primary objective in public policy regulation of employment relationships was to establish rules governing union-management interactions. During the subsequent years the primary objective of public policy has been to provide more direct regulation of employment terms for all employees. This shift in public policy has contributed to a similar shift in the form of workplace disputes.

During the postwar period unions and employers regularly jousted in Washington over what the union-management rules should be. There were three major legislative battles: (1) the 1947 battle over Taft-Hartley and its restrictions on union activities, (2) the 1958–59 fight over the Landrum-Griffin Act and its regulation of internal union affairs, and (3) the 1977–78 struggle over the proposed Labor Law Reform Act to modify the organizing and bargaining provisions of Taft-Hartley in a union-favorable direction. There also has been a continuing series of legislative skirmishes, including the 1951 effort to repeal Taft-Hartley's union shop election requirement; the 1965–66 efforts to repeal Taft-Hartley Section 14(b), which allows states to outlaw union shops; the 1970 proposal to more closely regulate negotiating disputes in the transportation industries; the 1974 extension of Taft-Hartley to nonprofit health care institutions; the 1975–76 attempts to allow common situs picketing; and the 1991–93 effort to prohibit employers from permanently replacing strikers. The unions lost the three major battles and won some of the skirmishes, a track record that is generally consistent with the postwar decline in union political influence at the national level.

However, the unions have scored an impressive string of victories in state legislatures during the past 30 years as they have sought and obtained the legislatively protected right to organize and bargain for millions of state and local government employees. By the late 1980s, 34 states had statutorily granted some or all of the public employees within their boundaries the right to organize and bargain, though the extent of these rights varies considerably from state to state (Schneider 1988). The degree to which these statutes favor unions is a function of the state-level political influence the labor movement can muster, and some of these laws have provided very substantial bargaining, union security, and impasse resolution rights (including either the right to strike or to use interest arbitration). Indeed, the primary postwar union political success story is told in the capitols of these states, not in the halls of Congress.

In contrast to the intermittent lobbying battles over new statutory rules, unions and employers routinely tilt at each other over how the existing rules should be interpreted. For instance, National Labor Relations Board (NLRB) figures show that in fiscal 1949 unions and employers filed a total of 5,304 unfair labor practice (ULP) charges against each other, by fiscal 1979 this ULP figure had increased to 41,259, and by fiscal 1989 ULP charges had declined somewhat to 32,401 (U.S. NLRB 1951, 1991). Because about two-thirds of these charges are dismissed or withdrawn, it is not likely that there was an eightfold increase in actual union-management rules conflicts between the late 1940s and the late 1970s. Rather, it is more likely that the parties simply became more adept at using the rules to harass each other. Similarly, the 1980s' decline in ULP charges filed does not indicate a diminution of union-management conflict, but instead is a reflection of a smaller unionized labor force and of the union assessment that during the 1980s the NLRB became more likely to favor employers in its rulings. Similarly, unions and employers in the public sector have used NLRB-type state government agencies to process and decide their rules disputes.

There is no question that the 1980s and 1990s have seen the continuation of the high "hostility quotient" in the private-sector labor relations rhetoric offered for public consumption that emerged during the 1970s (Feuille and Wheeler 1981). Most of this rhetoric has been union-inspired, for the unions have seen themselves as being on the short end of a continuing bargaining and political power imbalance that developed during the 1960s and 1970s and worsened during the 1980s. The unions believe this power imbalance to be caused by unfavorable labor relations rules that allow private employers far too much freedom to resist union organizing and bargaining efforts; they see employers engaging in serious and continuing unfair labor practices and then receiving only slap-on-the-wrist penalties.

There is considerable evidence that most private employers in the United States have not philosophically accepted unions and collective bargaining, more than 50 years after the passage of the Wagner Act (Jacoby 1990, 1991; Kochan and Katz 1988). Operationally, this has meant that nonunion and partly unionized firms have placed strong emphasis on union avoidance, and highly unionized firms have tried whenever possible to expand the nonunion component of their operations. Given this employer unwillingness to grant unions a legitimate workplace role, the relatively high level of hostility over union-management rules disputes is likely to continue. It is unlikely, though, that any significant changes in the statutory union-management rules will emerge in the foreseeable future. Employers have no incentive to seek changes in rules that operate in a primarily employer-favorable direction, and unions do not have sufficient political influence to obtain new union-favorable rules.

However, since the early 1960s the focus of national labor policy has shifted away from an emphasis on collective bargaining and toward the direct regulation of workplace conditions. Indeed, the national labor policy that has emerged during the past 30 years appears to be based on the implicit premise that collective bargaining is a decidedly inadequate vehicle through which to establish employee-favorable labor market conditions. The 1964 and 1991 Civil Rights Acts, the 1965 Executive Order 11246 requiring government contractors to practice affirmative action, the 1967 Age Discrimination in Employment Act, the 1970 Occupational Safety and

Health Act, the 1974 Employee Retirement Income Security Act, the 1988 Worker Adjustment and Retraining Notification Act regulating plant closings, the 1988 Employee Polygraph Protection Act, the 1990 Americans with Disabilities Act, and the periodic increases in the minimum wage provisions of the Fair Labor Standards Act all represent federal attempts to directly regulate employment conditions for union and nonunion employees. There have been hundreds of thousands of administrative charges and lawsuits filed under these statutes by disgruntled employees against their employers, and for the vast majority of employees these laws, rather than unions, are their main protection against unfair employer action. Additionally, the 1980s witnessed the emergence of a body of wrongful discharge common law, which to date has been regulated primarily by state courts. Most of the disputes pursued under these statutory or common law developments involve nonunion employees and employers. Accordingly, these kinds of workplace disagreements are just as much "labor disputes" as the strikes and arbitration cases that arise in unionized settings.

Disputes over the Establishment of Employment Terms

In the private unionized arena the traditional method of resolving disputes over employment terms for the next contract period is the strike threat, which is followed by an actual strike in a small fraction of cases. Strikes are less well entrenched in the more recently unionized public sector, though they are hardly unknown, and as a result there has been a comparatively greater reliance on third-party dispute resolution.

The private sector

Strike Rates There are three key lessons to be learned from decades of strike data. The first is that the vast majority of strikes occur at contract negotiation time. Contract interpretation strikes have become rare. This type of walkout may be planned (as in strikes over production standards in the auto industry) or not ("wildcat" strikes), but in any case they have greatly diminished in the wake of negotiated grievance arbitration procedures and employer unwillingness to tolerate wildcats.

The second lesson is that the proportion of negotiations that result in a strike is, on average, rather low. For instance, Gramm (1987),

McConnell (1990), and Vroman (1989), relying primarily on 1970s data for several thousand large bargaining units (those with 1,000 workers or more) found that strikes occurred, on average, about 12 to 14 percent of the time. Further, there is agreement that strike propensities generally are much lower in small bargaining units (Kochan and Katz 1988), so the overall rate at which strikes have occurred historically is probably below 5 percent of negotiations. For instance, Kochan and Katz (1988) calculated that between 1968 and 1975 strikes occurred in 2 to 3 percent of the negotiations for which contract expiration notices were filed with the Federal Mediation and Conciliation Service.

However, the third lesson is that all of this research has found huge variations in strike rates across industries, across firms and unions, and from year to year. The interindustry variation has been apparent for decades, and it is an international phenomenon (Kerr and Siegel 1954). As a result, specific strike predictions based on aggregate analyses remain hazardous. As will be discussed shortly, strike propensities have declined significantly during the 1980s and 1990s compared with earlier decades. What also has declined is the percent of work time lost due to strikes, though this type of voluntary idleness has been well under 1 percent of total work time in every postwar year except 1946.

Strike Cycles There appears to be no dispute over the finding that strikes historically have varied directly with the business cycle (McConnell 1990). There has been considerable debate over the relative importance of "economic" versus "organizational-political" causes of strikes, with evidence suggesting that the political and public policy stability of the postwar period placed greater importance on the economic variables (unemployment, wage changes, inflation, and so on) than in the prewar years (Kaufman 1982). Strikes also have been viewed as the result of mistakes (Hicks 1963), and as a consequence of incomplete information (Ashenfelter and Johnson 1969). Strikes are costly events on both sides of the table, but there is no all-encompassing theory that explains the circumstances in which some unions and employers are willing to accept such costs and others are not.

During the 1980s strike activity plummeted, even after the economy recovered from the recession of 1981 to 1983. Aggregate work stoppage figures show that the 1970s was perhaps the decade with more strikes (including lockouts) than any other in our history (U.S. Bureau of Labor Statistics 1983) and that the 1980s and 1990s may be just the reverse (U.S. BLS, 1991; U.S. General Accounting Office 1991; Bureau of National Affairs 1992). For instance, in 1977 the

Bureau of Labor Statistics (BLS) counted 5,506 strikes, and the Bureau of National Affairs (BNA) reported that there were only 706 strikes in 1991. In 1977 there were 298 large strikes (in bargaining units with 1,000 or more workers), and by 1991 this number had declined to 40.

Assuming that the BLS and the BNA used the same strike counting methods, these recent strike figures strongly suggest that strike propensities may have declined to levels not seen since the 1930s. As a result, strike research conclusions based on pre-1981 data may be of limited value in explaining why unions and employers use strikes to resolve negotiating disputes during the final two decades of this century. Anecdotal data suggest that in the 1980s the strike paradigm in this country shifted from a view of strikes as union-favorable weapons to strikes as employer-favorable weapons. One symbol of this changed perspective is the increased employer willingness to replace strikers permanently with new hires (U.S. GAO, 1991). Even though this action has been legal since 1938, it was not until the 1980s that employers began exercising this right frequently enough to make the permanent replacement phenomenon a contentious public policy issue. The Reagan administration's willingness to discharge and permanently replace 11,300 striking air traffic controllers in 1981 is often viewed as a major contributor to the increased willingness of employers to replace their own striking employees, but the impact of this federal employee strike on private-sector employers remains problematic.

National Emergency Strikes   Probably the single most visible labor relations issue during the late 1940s and 1950s was the national emergency strike. During the 1950s there was an outpouring of scholarly research on this topic (see, for example, Bernstein, Enarson, and Fleming 1955), accompanied by a great deal of handwringing over the need for government to protect the operation of "free" collective bargaining while simultaneously protecting bystanders from being harmed by such strikes. Most of this concern was directed at strikes in the transportation industries and in "national security" situations (Cullen 1968).

In a remarkable turnaround, during the past 20 years this subject has almost completely vanished from public and scholarly concern (Rehmus 1990). For instance, the Taft-Hartley Act's Title II emergency dispute procedures have been invoked only once since 1971, and in that instance (the 1977–78 coal strike) a federal district court judge rebuffed President Carter's effort to "look presidential" and refused to grant an injunction halting the strike. Similarly, the use of negotiating dispute fact-finding boards pursuant to the 1974 health care amendments to Taft-Hartley never became the norm in hospital bargaining and declined significantly after 1982. In the airline industry, only one emergency board has been appointed under the Railway Labor Act's Section 10 emergency dispute procedure since 1966, and that was a special case designed to ensure congressional passage of the 1978 Airline Deregulation Act. Only in railroad-industry negotiating disputes does the federal government still appoint emergency boards under the Railway Labor Act, and it did so in the 1980s much less frequently than in earlier decades (Rehmus 1990).

The main purpose of all of these emergency dispute intervention procedures is to provide a "cooling off" period so the parties can continue their negotiations, rather than to impose a settlement. In other words, these are strike-postponement rather than arbitration procedures, and it is apparent that federal policymakers believe that very few strikes need to be postponed. The ultimate cause of the disappearance of emergency strikes from the labor relations agenda seems to be the unions' seriously diminished ability to deprive large segments of the population of "essential" or immediately needed goods and services.

The Future of the Strike More than three decades ago Ross and Hartman predicted that the union reliance on strikes as instruments of bargaining power would decline and perhaps even "wither away" in the United States and Europe (Ross and Hartman 1960). At the time they made this prediction, strikes were indeed less frequent than in the late 1940s and early 1950s. However, in this country their prediction suffered the ignominious fate of being superseded by increased numbers of strikes in the late 1960s and throughout the 1970s, and as a result few observers took it seriously during those years.

It appears, though, that Ross and Hartman may merely have been premature rather than wrong in their forecast. The strike experiences of the 1980s and 1990s indicate that strikes are now far less likely to occur than the historical record ever would have predicted. However, this change appears to be the result of a substantial shift in bargaining power away from unions and toward employers rather than any mutual preference for the use of more "diplomatic" procedures to resolve negotiating disputes. Specifically, unions have been much less willing to call strikes during the past 10 to 12 years than previously, due to a worsened strike cost-benefit calculus (the causes of which are explored elsewhere in this volume). Strikes will not disappear, but there is no doubt that we are in the midst of a period in which strikes are a less central part of the contract negotiation process.

Further, there is nothing on the horizon that suggests a change in the diminished role of the strike. The heightened product market competition and concomitant employer resistance to union demands that were witnessed during the 1980s continues into the 1990s; the union share of the labor force continues to slide; federal labor relations policy continues to allow employers considerable freedom to resist union organizing efforts, negotiating demands, and strikes; and most private employers openly continue to pursue union avoidance strategies. In turn, these developments indicate that we have exited from a forty-year period (roughly 1935 to 1975) that represented a union-favorable aberration in the traditional pattern of U.S. corporate and government hostility toward unions (Jacoby 1990). During that period unions were able to use collective bargaining, with its strike threat method of increasing employer costs of disagreement, to obtain significant gains for workers who had little or no individual bargaining power. During much of the period, public labor relations policy, particularly the regulation of the negotiating process, was seen by scholars as a source of union power (Ross 1965). However, by the middle or end of the 1970s there was a 180-degree shift in the prevailing conventional wisdom regarding the influence of public policy (Feuille and Wheeler 1981). The continuation of this public policy, plus the continuation of widespread employer attempts to resist unions as allowed by this policy, suggest that the current distribution of relative bargaining power between unions and employers is more similar to the union-management situation in the 1920s and early 1930s than to the 1950s and 1960s. As a result, we may expect the annual number of strikes to continue at their record postwar lows.

Corporate Campaigns As strikes became less effective bargaining and organizing tools for unions, the "corporate campaign" became a selective but prominent union pressure tactic during the late 1970s and 1980s. Corporate campaigns involve union efforts to use nontraditional tactics, such as financial pressure from investors, union-initiated regulatory investigations, and adverse publicity, to make it unacceptably costly for employers to resist union organizing and bargaining efforts. The ability of these campaigns to achieve union successes is mixed, and they often are very expensive undertakings for depleted union treasuries (Jarley and Maranto 1990). Accordingly, it is very unlikely that corporate campaigns will become a regular union-management dispute resolution mechanism.

The public sector
In the government sector the strike has played a less central role in the resolution of negotiating disputes than it has in the private sector, and third-party procedures have been much more important.

The statutory right to strike is limited to certain employee groups in about ten states, though in a few other states the appellate courts have given either de jure or de facto approval to the use of strikes (Schneider 1988). Also, the strike is not the same sacrosanct event among government unions that it is in the private sector.

Nevertheless, the strike is hardly unknown in public-sector labor relations. Strikes became fairly widespread in the late 1960s by historical standards, and continued at fairly high levels throughout the 1970s (U.S. BLS, 1981). During this period strike propensities varied substantially across public employee groups, with teachers being the most strike-prone (Stern and Olson 1982). But strike rates in government have been lower than in the private sector, and government employee strikes also have been much shorter. Some research suggests that, as in private industry (Kochan and Block 1977), public employee strikes occurred because they tended to succeed (Delaney 1983, 1986). Public employee strikes tend to be more frequent in states that have legalized the strike option, and less frequent in jurisdictions that have consistently enforced strike penalties or compulsory interest arbitration (Olson 1986). During the 1980s, however, there appears to have been a significant reduction in the willingness of public employees to strike, though post-1981 government strike data are too limited to offer a precise estimate of this change.

Third-party procedures

The private and public sectors have been the scenes of very divergent experiences with the use of procedural alternatives to the strike. These mediation, fact-finding, and arbitration procedures allow varying degrees of *process control* (control over how the negotiations will be handled) and *decision control* (control over the substance of the disputed employment terms). With exceptions and allowing for oversimplification, it can be said that during the postwar period the federal government offered a variety of mediation and fact-finding services but never embraced any sort of compulsory interest arbitration (Northrup 1966; Phelps 1964). As a result of the postwar strike frenzy and the concomitant concern with emergency disputes, several states passed compulsory arbitration laws, but these became largely inactive in the early 1950s (Northrup 1966). Unions and employers occasionally have been willing to use interest arbitration to resolve particular disputes, but only by mutual agreement (Stieber 1970). In contrast, the public sector has been the scene of considerable experimentation with third-party dispute intervention, mostly in the form of compulsory procedures. This includes the adoption of interest arbitration in more than 20 states.

Mediation Ever since 1947 the federal government has provided mediation services to private-sector negotiators via the Federal Mediation and Conciliation Service (FMCS), which was created by the Taft-Hartley Act. (Prior to that, the government had — and continues to have — the authority to impose a more forceful form of mediation in railroad and airline negotiating disputes under the Railway Labor Act, and the War Labor Board possessed arbitral authority during the war years.) This intervention authority is limited, however, to situations in which a union and an employer mutually agree to participate in the mediation process, and the mediator's focus is on finding specific ways that the parties can resolve their disagreements on the issues in the dispute at hand. Larger questions about the role of labor and management in industrial society, or the impact of the dispute on the public, are invariably ignored. In Kerr's (1954) terminology, this is "tactical" rather than "strategical" mediation. There is no question that this kind of mediation has contributed to some speedier resolutions than might otherwise have been reached (Simkin and Fidandis 1986). But the fact that strike rates remained high for 30 years after the FMCS's creation in 1947 suggests that tactical mediation's contribution to industrial peace in the private sector has been modest, as was predicted four decades ago (Kerr 1954).

Mediation has played a larger role in public-sector dispute resolution. State bargaining laws frequently mandate that mediation be used whenever an impasse is reached, often as a requirement for access to more forceful third-party procedures or as a condition for engaging in a legal strike. As a result, mediation usage rates from several states suggest that a large portion of public-sector negotiations are mediated (Hoh 1984; Kochan and Katz 1988). In addition, most of the research on mediator effectiveness seems to have focused on the public sector (Carnevale and Pegnetter 1985; Gerhart and Drotning 1980; Kochan and Jick 1978; Kolb 1983). As in private industry, public-sector mediation is tactical in that the mediator helps the parties find a resolution to the dispute at hand rather than dealing with larger questions involving management, labor, and the public.

Fact-finding Easily the most misnamed dispute intervention process in history, fact-finding has suffered the ignominious fate of being scorned by unions and employers and ignored by the public. Fact-finding is a compromise between mediation and arbitration, for it allows the parties to maintain control over the outcome of the dispute while simultaneously imposing the structure and formality of interest arbitration. Fact-finders hold hearings and then issue reports with analyses and (usually) recommendations for how the dispute should be resolved, which the parties are free to accept, reject, or modify (it might be thought of as "mediation in writing"). In other words, the fact-finder has lots of process control but very little decision control.

Several states passed their own laws, many in the immediate postwar years, to provide for fact-finding in various private-sector negotiating impasses. Many of these laws were little used, and since the early 1950s their legality has been in doubt (Northrup 1966). During the postwar period most private-sector fact-finding occurred pursuant to the federal government's Taft-Hartley and Railway Labor Act intervention procedures, which were designed to handle "emergency" disputes. The historical record indicates that these kinds of procedures usually do little to assist the negotiation process and often do not result in the resolution of the dispute (Rehmus 1990), which has led to a rather jaundiced view of them.

In the public sector, fact-finding has a more widespread but similarly checkered history. It was adopted in many states during the 1960s and 1970s as a legislative compromise between union demands for the either the right to strike or compulsory interest arbitration and management's insistence that unions should have neither. It is still on the books as the terminal impasse step in 21 states (Schneider 1988), so it has not withered away. Sometimes fact-finders engage in unofficial mediation to supplement their formal and semi-adjudicatory role. As in private industry, fact-finding's public-sector history suggests that unions and employers favor it primarily when fact-finders adopt their preferred outcomes, and when this does not occur rejections of the fact-finders' efforts are routine. In spite of its limitations, it will continue to be an important part of impasse resolution in government.

In general, fact-finding appears to have suffered from a mismatch between the practitioners' high expectations about the dispute resolution services it would deliver and its actual ability to resolve negotiating disputes. In both the public and private sectors it is not always (or even usually) clear what will happen when one or both parties reject a fact-finder's recommendations. This lack of guaranteed finality means that the procedure often appears rather incomplete to practitioners and observers alike, and there is no apparent consensus about its role in the dispute resolution process. Fact-finding will continue to play a prominent role in public-sector dispute resolution in those states where neither unions nor employers are able to persuade the legislatures to adopt their more preferred dispute resolution procedures (such as the right to strike or compulsory arbitration). In the private sector, though, the continued disuse of emergency dispute procedures means that fact-finding will continue to fade from view.

Interest Arbitration in the Private Sector   It is important to differentiate between compulsory interest arbitration, the kind imposed by government that is triggered automatically or by one of the parties when an impasse occurs, and voluntary interest arbitration, the kind that requires both parties to agree that arbitration will be used to resolve their negotiating dispute. In the private sector, there is none of the former and very little of the latter. More specifically, the federal government has never had any standing authority in peacetime to impose arbitration to resolve a negotiating impasse. A series of ad hoc laws have been passed by Congress to resolve particularly intractable railroad negotiating disputes (Rehmus 1990), but each of these has been limited to the particular dispute at hand. The postwar strike wave caused eight states to pass compulsory arbitration statutes designed to prevent strikes in industries thought to have the potential for creating emergency disputes (usually public utilities; see Northrup 1966). However, these laws fell into disuse after a 1951 U.S. Supreme Court decision struck down Wisconsin's law on federal supremacy grounds (the federal government already regulated this area via the National Labor Relations Act), thereby effectively ending the experiment with state-level compulsory arbitration in the private sector.

The fact that the federal government has never given itself the standing authority to require private-sector unions and employers to arbitrate their negotiating disputes is not surprising, considering that it has been a sacred article of faith on both sides of the negotiating table that unions and employers should be free to determine their own employment terms (Phelps 1964). The only serious proposal to legislate compulsory arbitration in the past 30 years was made in 1970, when the Nixon administration sent to Congress the Emergency Public Interest Protection Act. This bill sought to cover all the transportation industries, and it proposed final-offer arbitration as one of the options the president could impose in a negotiating impasse. This bill was not supported by unions or employers, it was not reported out of committee, and the idea has not been seriously revived since (Rehmus 1990).

In contrast, selected unions and private employers have been willing to use voluntary interest arbitration when it has suited their mutual interest to do so (Stieber 1970). For instance, unions and employers in the urban transit industry had a long history of using arbitration back in the era when transit services were provided by private companies. Arbitration has also been used by some of the major airlines and their unions. By far the most visible use of interest arbitration in the private sector is major league baseball's salary arbitration arrangement for resolving salary negotiating disputes between players and clubs. This final-offer procedure is loved by the players and hated by the owners, for it has played an integral role in the dizzying escalation of baseball players' salaries (Staudohar 1989), and it occupies a prominent place in the nation's sports pages and telecasts each February.

The steel industry was the scene of the private sector's most ambitious attempt to use voluntary arbitration in lieu of strikes. By the early 1970s the strike history in that industry caused steel customers to hedge their steel-buying bets each time a contract expiration loomed. Customers would stockpile steel in anticipation of a long strike (the 1959–60 steel strike lasted 116 days), and then if a strike did not occur they would cut back their orders while they used up their inventories. This caused a boom-and-bust production cycle that the companies and the union wanted to avoid. So, in 1972 they formulated the Experimental Negotiating Agreement (ENA), which provided that their negotiations would be resolved by an arbitration panel if the parties could not reach agreement themselves (note that the word *arbitration* appears nowhere in this label). This procedure was in place and available for use during the 1974, 1977, and 1980 negotiations, though each time the parties negotiated their own agreement. The ENA procedure was quite successful in eliminating the boom-and-bust production cycle. However, it contributed to some very expensive settlements, and by 1981 the steel companies decided that they could no longer afford the procedure. As a result, they cancelled the arrangement, and there have been no noticeable efforts to revive it since then.

At the time the ENA was adopted, it was widely hailed as a progressive example of "labor statesmanship," and hopes were expressed that other unions and employers would similarly abjure the use of the strike. The rest of the private sector was unwilling to do so, however, so the ENA stands as the paramount example of how interest arbitration never became the dispute resolution method of choice in the private sector. For instance, fewer than 2 percent of the 1,717 contracts in effect during 1961–62 that were examined by the BLS provided for interest arbitration over the terms of the successor contract (U.S. BLS, 1966), and this percentage may have declined since then. This conclusion is reinforced by the fact that interest arbitration is viewed by the National Labor Relations Board as being merely a permissive subject of bargaining (Gorman 1976), so neither party can force the subject into the contract over the objections of the other party.

In sum, interest arbitration in the private sector, with few exceptions, has become a nonevent. There has been very little use of interest arbitration over time as a proportion of all negotiations, and there is not a scrap of evidence to indicate that unions, employers, or the government have any desire to expand its use.

It is rather ironic, then, that one of academia's most successful dispute resolution ideas was put forward to improve the compatibility of compulsory interest arbitration and the negotiating process, primarily in the private sector. Historically one of the arguments against compulsory arbitration was that its availability would reduce the parties' incentives to negotiate seriously, and that instead they would simply use the negotiation process to position themselves for the anticipated arbitral intervention. Accordingly, during the 1960s final-offer arbitration (FOA) was proposed as a "strikelike" dispute resolution method designed to give the parties negotiating under the umbrella of arbitration the maximum incentive to negotiate instead of merely staking out positions for the arbitration process (Stevens 1966). The Nixon administration proposed FOA in its 1970 transportation disputes legislation, it was incorporated in the baseball salary arbitration procedure and in many public-sector arbitration statutes, but it was never adopted in any private-sector labor relations legislation.

Interest Arbitration in Government   In contrast to the private sector, during the past 25 years the public sector has become the scene of a great deal of experimentation with interest arbitration, almost all of it compulsory. The federal government and several states have interest arbitration statutes covering various groups of public employees, and by now thousands of interest arbitration awards have been issued and tens of thousands of contracts have been negotiated in the shadow of arbitration.

Labor relations for most federal government employees are regulated by the 1978 Civil Service Reform Act, and one of this law's administrative agencies is the Federal Service Impasses Panel (FSIP). The FSIP has broad authority to facilitate the resolution of negotiation impasses between federal government unions and agencies. Part of its authority is the ability to impose a "final and binding" decision on the parties, or arbitration. By now such decisions have been imposed several hundred times by the FSIP, though these FSIP awards constitute a small slice of all federal government negotiations.

The U.S. Postal Service is covered by a separate interest arbitration procedure. The 1970 Postal Reorganization Act (adopted in the wake of a national postal strike) prohibits strikes by postal employees and mandates the use of arbitration to resolve negotiating disputes. During the 1970s the postal unions often relied on strike threats as their primary means of obtaining favorable settlements, and contracts often were achieved without arbitration awards. However, in the 1984 negotiations the parties could not reach agreement, and what was then the single largest interest arbitration award in this country was issued by Clark Kerr for the primary Postal Service bargaining unit. Its terms ultimately were extended to about 700,000 postal employees, and the award was notable for its deliberate attempt to slow the growth of postal wages, which by then had become substantially higher than those earned by comparable private-sector workers (Perloff and Wachter 1984).

Most of the interest arbitration action in government has occurred at the state and local levels. About 22 states have compulsory and binding interest arbitration laws for various groups of employees, most often police and firefighters (Schneider 1988). The usual public rationale for the adoption of these laws is that they prevent strikes, especially by vital public safety employees, and the fact that such strikes are usually illegal is conveniently overlooked. The real motivating force behind these laws is adroit lobbying and electoral politicking by the public-sector unions in those states to change the impasse resolution rules in a way that will give them more power at the bargaining table than they would have otherwise. Public employers agree that these laws increase union bargaining power, and they routinely lobby against the passage of these statutes (Feuille 1979).

The available evidence suggests that arbitration is indeed associated with fewer strikes than otherwise would occur (Ichniowski 1982; Olson 1986), so the ostensible public policy goal is fulfilled. However, the price paid for this objective may be high. Research shows that arbitration laws for police and firefighters lead to higher wage rates and more employee-favorable contract terms than exist in states without such laws (Feuille, Delaney, and Hendricks 1985; Feuille and Delaney 1986; Kochan and Wheeler 1975; Olson 1980). In addition, there is no question that arbitration is used more frequently than strikes (where they are legal) to resolve negotiating disputes (Olson 1988), which has led to concern that some unions and employers can become too heavily dependent on arbitrators to resolve impasses. However, most unions and employers have learned how to incorporate the availability of arbitration into their negotiating repertoires, and they have learned how to respond to procedural varia-

490

tions such as conventional and final-offer arbitration. Most negotiations end in a negotiated agreement rather than an award, and the arbitration awards that are issued almost always receive full compliance.

Compulsory interest arbitration continues to be an acceptable though controversial form of public labor relations policy in most of the states that have adopted it. It is difficult for unions to lobby such a law onto the books over employer opposition, but once the law is in place it tends to stay there. Legislatures have been unwilling to repeal arbitration laws once they have passed them, and most state appellate courts have upheld these laws in the face of constitutional challenges (which are usually brought by unhappy municipal employers covered by the law; see Grodin and Najita 1988). Because unions need a strong voice in the state legislature to obtain such laws, and because most states where unions enjoy such political influence already have passed such laws (states in the Northeast, Midwest, and Far West), it is unlikely that arbitration laws will spread to other states where unions are less influential. As a result, interest arbitration will continue to exist on an intermittent basis across the country.

One reason for the longevity of public-sector interest arbitration is that the presence of an arbitration law creates a constituency of union and employer advocates, arbitrators, public agency administrators, and academic researchers, all of whom have a stake in the continued availability and use of the procedure. This is hardly surprising given the money and prestige these individuals receive from the arbitration system. However, these are often the same people who perform research and offer normative commentary on the arbitration system. Accordingly, one should view the conventional wisdom about public-sector interest arbitration — that it works well — as first and foremost the expression of professional self-interest.

Disputes over Existing Employment Terms

In the union sector, disputes over existing employment terms, or "rights" disputes, customarily refer to grievances alleging that an employee's contractual rights have been infringed by the employer. In the nonunion sector these kinds of disputes have more flexible boundaries, for there rarely is a written employer-employee contract, and ultimately the disputes are based on competing employee and employer versions of appropriate workplace rules, procedures, and expectations. In addition, during the past 25 years employees have demonstrated an increased willingness to use government agencies and the courts in pursuit of what they believe are their statutory rights to nondiscriminatory treatment or their equitable "right" to fair treatment in the workplace, especially in discharge situations.

Unionized workplaces

Grievance Procedures   American unions and employers have negotiated a formal grievance procedure into almost every private-sector contract during the past 50 years or so, and the same process is taking place in the public sector. These procedures give unionized employees a much louder voice in personnel decisions than their nonunion peers have. Grievance procedures became the workplace norm in the 1940s and 1950s as unions bargained away their right to strike over claims of contract violations in return for employers' promising to allow grievances to be processed through the grievance procedure and taken to final and binding arbitration if the parties cannot reach their own resolution (which meant that some management decisions could be overturned by arbitrators). This union-management quid pro quo has lasted for more than 50 years, and it shows no signs of unraveling, even in the face of unions' substantially diminished ability to conduct successful strikes during the past dozen years. Further, this quid pro quo is likely to remain largely unchanged as a mutually preferred alternative to litigating grievance disputes in federal court.

There has been considerable research conducted on the grievance process. The common questions in such investigations have been: who files grievances? over what issues? how often? and what are the consequences? There has been a great deal of research into the demographic characteristics of grievance filers compared to nonfilers, and in their review of this research Gordon and Miller (1984) concluded that these studies have not yielded consistent results. In contrast, there seems to be general agreement that discipline is the single most common issue in the grievances filed (Gordon and Miller 1984; Lewin and Peterson 1988).

The yardstick most frequently used to measure grievance filing rates is the number of grievances per 100 employees per year. There is strong agreement in the research evidence that grievance filing rates vary substantially across unionized organizations (Gordon and Miller 1984; Knight 1986; Lewin and Peterson 1988). For instance, in an early 1980s study of 57 organizations Lewin and Peterson found a 15-fold variation in filing rates (from 1.6 to 24.9 grievances per 100 employees per year). If these filing rates are an accurate measure of the variation in the level of employee-employer conflict over what constitutes fair treatment at work, they diminish the usefulness of generalizations about the average number of workplace disputes.

The available data indicate that most grievances are resolved within the first two steps of the grievance procedure, most of the resolutions occur within two months of the grievance filing date, and only a small fraction of grievances are appealed to the highest step in the procedure, which is almost always arbitration (Delaney, Lewin and Ichniowski 1989; Gideon and Peterson 1979; Gordon and Miller 1984; Knight 1986; Lewin and Peterson 1988; Ng and Dastmalchian 1989). The evidence also indicates that a large proportion of all grievances are resolved in the employee's favor (defined as a resolution which fully or partly sustains the grievance), and that the type of grievance issue may have an important influence on the outcome. For instance, the proportion of employee-favorable grievance outcomes ranged from 24 percent to 58 percent across a variety of private and public workplaces in different studies (Gideon and Peterson 1979; Lewin and Peterson 1988; Ng and Dastmalchian 1989). In addition, a study of a West Coast union found that the employer won about 80 percent of the grievances over sick benefits and that employees won about 85 percent of the grievances concerning performance evaluation (Dalton and Todor 1981).

What impact do grievance procedures and grievance processing have on employers? Freeman and Medoff (1984) argue that grievance procedures, by providing an employee-voice alternative to exit behaviors (such as shirking or quitting), result in lower rates of quitting and concomitantly lower turnover and retraining costs. However, other research unambiguously indicates that in unionized manufacturing plants grievance filing rates are negatively correlated with workplace productivity (Ichniowski 1986; Ichniowski and Lewin 1987; Katz, Kochan, and Gobeille 1983; Kleiner, Nickelsburg, and Pilarski 1989; Norsworthy and Zabala 1985). It is not clear to what extent this diminished productivity is the result of the "displacement effect" — employee work time diverted from work production tasks to grievance processing — or the "worker reaction effect" — reduced effort as a reaction to perceived unfair administration of the contract (Ichniowski 1986). Whatever the cause, this research suggests that there is a substantial productivity price to be paid when grievance procedures become "distressed" (Ross 1963).

Grievance Arbitration It is not often in an industrial society that employers and unions locked in adversarial (and sometimes hostile) relationships can agree on a procedure to resolve their most difficult day-to-day disputes, live with this procedure in largely unchanged form for as long as 50 years, and obtain the repeated blessing of the highest court in the land for having done so. This is the case with grievance arbitration in unionized workplaces.

There was very substantial growth between the late 1940s and the late 1970s in the number of arbitrated grievances, and this growth testifies to union and employer willingness to rely on this administrative procedure rather than workplace disruptions to resolve contract interpretation disputes. Similarly, during the postwar period there has been a massive outpouring of writing about grievance arbitration, and with few exceptions (Hays 1966) the vast majority of this writing indicates that arbitration is a wonderful procedure. These positive characterizations are hardly surprising given, again, the large stake that most of the writers (advocates, arbitrators, interested academicians) have in the continued existence and use of the process.

Evidence shows that unions and employers each win about half of the arbitration awards issued (American Arbitration Association 1991). This result also is not surprising, given that arbitrators are selected and compensated jointly by both sides and hence must maintain their acceptability to both. What may be more surprising is that some arbitrators apparently "tilt" toward unions or employers and continue to be widely used (Block and Stieber 1987), and that there is a relatively modest level of consistency in how different arbitrators respond to the same set of facts (Thornton and Zirkel 1990). These findings suggest that union and employer expenditures on arbitrator search costs, which may be substantial, are rational investments.

By the late 1950s the contest between advocates of arbitration as an informal problem-solving process and those who viewed it as a more formal process of contractual adjudication had been decisively resolved in favor of the latter (Nolan and Abrams 1983), a description that remains accurate today. One of the notable results of the adjudicatory form of arbitration has been that courtroom trappings have become an integral part of the process (lawyers as advocates and arbitrators, court reporters and transcripts, written briefs, subpoenas, time delays, large dollar costs, and so on). Another of the notable results of this formalization of the process has been 40 years or so of continuing union and employer complaints about the cost, delay, and rigamarole associated with arbitration. But the most notable aspect of these complaints is that, with few exceptions, very little has been done to change the way arbitration operates.

Grievance Mediation   An alternative procedure is grievance mediation. In its current form, this process operates as the penultimate step in the grievance procedure, and it is followed by arbitration if mediation is unsuccessful. It usually involves having a mediator, who is also an experienced arbitrator, hold an informal conference (not a formal hearing) with the union and the employer to discuss the grievance. If this discussion does not produce a settlement, the mediator issues an advisory opinion — on the spot — which predicts how the grievance would be decided by an arbitrator. In other words, this type of mediation is a form of "peekaboo arbitration," in that the parties get an early and low-cost evaluation of their chances of prevailing in arbitration. Research shows that grievance mediation has been successful, resolving 80 percent or more of the grievances presented, and doing so much more quickly and cheaply than arbitration (Feuille 1992).

However, arbitration is not in any danger of being replaced by mediation (or anything else) as the terminal step of choice in grievance procedures. Grievance mediation has been adopted here and there, and it has produced some notable success stories (such as in the coal industry), but it is still the unusual contract that contains a mediation step in the grievance procedure, and it has not captured the hearts or the minds of most union and employer advocates. It remains to be seen how important a role mediation eventually will play in workplace dispute resolution.

Grievance Procedures and Public Policy   The Congress and especially the federal courts have heaped praise on negotiated grievance procedures, particularly arbitration. For instance, the U.S. Supreme Court has repeatedly said that, where unions and employers have promised to resolve grievances via arbitration and to accept the resulting awards as final and binding, they must live up to these promises even if the results are not to their liking (the 1960 *Steelworkers Trilogy* and its progeny). The vast majority of the time, unions and employers do so, though during the past 15 years or so disgruntled employers have become more likely to appeal adverse arbitration awards to federal court seeking judicial rulings that these awards are null and void (Feuille and LeRoy 1990). The courts reject most of these appeals, so arbitration is in no danger of becoming merely a way station on the path to an ultimate judicial resolution of grievances. In contrast, in public-sector cases the courts are somewhat less likely to defer to arbitral judgments that have been appealed by disgruntled losers (usually employers), but most arbitration awards appear to be upheld (Grodin and Najita

1988). In both sectors the arbitrator's decision usually is final and binding.

There have been periodic predictions that the increasing direct government regulation of the employment relationship will result in the courts' usurpation of grievance arbitration as a dispute resolution mechanism. This concern erupted with a vengeance among arbitrators in the wake of the U.S. Supreme Court's 1974 decision in *Alexander v. Gardner-Denver* (415 U.S. 36) that the arbitration of an African-American employee's discharge grievance did not preclude that same employee from pursuing a discharge-based discrimination lawsuit under Title VII of the 1964 Civil Rights Act in federal court (Feller 1977).

There is no question that all employees, union and nonunion, have received more and more statutory workplace rights during the postwar period. Further, the pertinent administrative agencies and the courts are the logical forum to resolve disputes about the precise extent of those rights. However, there is no persuasive evidence that the increased number of laws regulating the workplace has had any inimical impact on the demand for and supply of grievance arbitration services in unionized workplaces. In fact, during the past 25 years there has emerged a strong demand for grievance arbitration services in the public sector, and public sector employment is more regulated by statute than is private industry. In addition, there is some evidence that arbitration is gaining a foothold in nonunion workplaces, partly as a way to avoid litigation over employment disputes. The demand for grievance arbitration in the private sector may decline commensurately with the decline of union coverage in that sector, but any such reduction is not the result of employment regulation statutes.

Duty of Fair Representation   The postwar growth in grievance and arbitration procedures, the inclusion of Section 301 in the Taft-Hartley Act (which allows unions and employers to be sued in federal court for violating contracts), and a continuing stream of federal appellate court decisions requiring unions to be both diligent and fair in their representation of employee rights and interests have resulted in the widespread postwar phenomenon of the duty of fair representation (DFR) lawsuit. Among the thousands of such DFR lawsuits, the vast majority are filed against unions by employees who are disenchanted with the manner in which their union processed (or did not process) their grievance. The courts decide these lawsuits in favor of employees only about 5 percent of the time (Goldberg 1985), though the possibility of such lawsuits may make unions more careful in how they handle their members' complaints.

The nonunion sector

By now private sector employment is 87 percent nonunion (U.S. BLS, 1992), and this percentage continues to increase. During the 1970s and 1980s there was an increasing willingness on the part of nonunion employers to adopt formal grievance procedures, and in recent years there has been a concomitant increase in research on how grievances are handled in nonunion firms (including the nonunion divisions of partly unionized firms).

Grievance Procedure Growth One noteworthy aspect of this phenomenon is the fact that nonunion firms rarely attach the label "grievance" to these procedures, apparently perceiving the term as being too intertwined with unions for their taste. Instead, such labels as "complaints," "appeals," "problem solving," "fair treatment," "speak up [or out]" are used. Whatever label they use, it is apparent that significant numbers of nonunion employers have established these procedures. For instance, in three surveys of primarily large corporations about half of the respondents reported that they had a formal complaint procedure for their nonunion employees (Berenbeim 1980; Chachere and Feuille 1993; Delaney, Lewin, and Ichniowski 1989). Firms with such procedures tend to be larger than those without, and it appears that the majority of these procedures were implemented in the past 20 years (see also Scott 1965). Considering that there is no government compulsion or union pressure to provide these formal "voice" procedures, this voluntary growth is remarkable.

Why have nonunion firms been doing this? Perhaps the most frequently advanced reason is that such procedures contribute to union avoidance, a response freely given by many nonunion firms (Berenbeim 1980; Ewing 1989; Freeman and Medoff 1984; McCabe 1988). However, employers were much less willing to install these procedures for their nonunion employees during the years of union ascendancy (1935 to 1960), when the probability of being organized was much higher than during the era of union stagnation and decline (since 1960). Instead, it was during the latter period that most such procedures were established. In addition, two studies found no correlation between the presence of a nonunion grievance procedure and unionization likelihood proxies (Chachere and Feuille 1993; Delaney and Feuille 1992). The union avoidance rationale for these procedures is intuitively plausible and consistent with the long-established conventional wisdom, but it is not supported by rigorous research analyses.

A more persuasive explanation can be found in the increasing employee insistence on individualized fair treatment at work. One of

the most notable trends of the past 25 years is the increased willingness of employees to pursue fair treatment by seeking redress
through external channels. For instance, since the passage of the
1964 Civil Rights Act employees have filed hundreds of thousands of
discrimination charges with the Equal Employment Opportunity
Commission (EEOC) and related state agencies, and the number of
these charges filed each year has skyrocketed over time (from 6,133
in fiscal 1966 to 142,572 in fiscal 1988), with most being directed at
employers (U.S. EEOC 1971, 1990). Initially, employees were about
equally likely to file discriminatory hiring and discriminatory firing
charges, and in 1970 discharge claims comprised about 17 percent of
all charges filed against employers (U.S. EEOC 1971). However, by
1988 disgruntled employees were almost six times more likely to file
charges alleging discriminatory firing than discriminatory hiring
(there were about 56,000 firing charges, compared with almost
10,000 hiring charges that year, and discharge-based claims constituted half of all discrimination charges (U.S. EEOC 1990). Similarly,
the number of employment discrimination lawsuits filed in federal
court increased more than twentyfold during the period 1970 to
1989, with most of these lawsuits resulting from terminations (Donohue and Siegelman 1991).

In a parallel development, during the past 20 years or so thousands
of fired and disgruntled nonunion employees have made wrongful
discharge litigation a growth industry, and employees often prevail
in these lawsuits (Dertouzos, Holland, and Ebener 1988; Westin and
Feliu 1988). Employers have learned that the resolution of these
discrimination complaints and wrongful discharge lawsuits can be
very expensive when they lose, with six- and seven-figure damage
awards to fired employees being commonplace. Even when employers prevail the transaction costs can be formidable; one study
found that employers spent an average of $80,000 defending them-
selves in wrongful discharge litigation in California (Dertouzos, Holland, and Ebener 1988).

In other words, as the employers' probability of becoming unionized has receded markedly during the past 25 years, the probability
of an employer being charged or sued by disgruntled employees,
particularly those who are fired, appears to have increased substantially. It seems likely, then, that the demonstrated employer willingness to install grievance procedures for their nonunion employees
may be a response to this threat of charges and litigation. To the extent that a formal grievance procedure allows employee complaints
to be resolved internally, such a procedure serves the employer's
interests.

Workplace Due Process   Another noteworthy aspect of nonunion grievance procedures is that they vary substantially in the degree of due process protections that they provide to employees. In contrast to the procedural similarity that exists across grievance procedures in the union sector, nonunion grievance mechanisms exhibit a bewildering array of features that resist easy categorization. For instance, some procedures require that grievances and managerial responses be expressed in writing and others do not; some procedures specify filing and response time limits and others do not; some procedures provide for face-to-face meetings between grievants and managers and others do not; some procedures allow for employees to have representation assistance and others do not; and most nonunion procedures reserve the final decision for management (Chachere and Feuille 1993; Ewing 1989; McCabe 1988). For all the attention given to the growth of such final-step decision mechanisms as peer review panels and nonunion arbitration, these kinds of quasi-independent terminal steps are present in only a small minority of these procedures. As a result, the degree of workplace due process and grievance processing assistance provided to employees in nonunion grievance channels is significantly less than exists in unionized workplaces.

This conclusion may explain why studies of nonunion grievance processing show that grievances are filed at a substantially lower rate in nonunion establishments than in unionized firms (Lewin 1987, 1990; Lewin and Peterson 1988). However, research also shows that nonunion employees prevail in a significant proportion of the grievances they file (Lewin 1987; Ewing 1989), so the presence of a union may not be necessary for an employee to obtain redress.

One of the more disturbing findings to emerge from recent grievance research is that nonunion employees who file grievances, compared with their peers who do not file, are more likely to suffer such adverse consequences as lower performance ratings, lower promotion rates, and higher turnover (voluntary and involuntary) in the period after they filed their grievances (Lewin 1987, 1990). In addition, the supervisors of the filers suffer similar adverse consequences, compared with supervisors who do not have grievances filed against them.

Before any conclusions are offered that tie these negative consequences to the absence of unions in the eight organizations examined in these two studies (Lewin 1987, 1990), it is important to note that research using the same methodology in four unionized organizations found very similar invidious results for grievance filers (and their supervisors) compared with nonfilers (Lewin and Peterson

1988). Klass and DeNisi (1989) found comparable results when they examined performance appraisals for filers and nonfilers working for a unionized public employer.

Taken together, this research calls into question the usefulness of the prevailing exit-voice conventional wisdom about grievance procedures. This received wisdom says that voice (filing a grievance) is preferable to exit (shirking, quitting) for both employees and employers because it results in such positive outcomes as reduced quit rates, enhanced job tenure and training, increased productivity, and perhaps increased employee commitment (Freeman and Medoff 1984). However, the recent research on post–grievance resolution consequences suggests that an organizational reprisal perspective may be a more accurate framework through which to view grievance activity (Lewin 1987). Employers appear to react to grievances as if they contribute to such negative outcomes as increased transaction costs and reduced productivity, rather than such positive outcomes as reduced quitting, enhanced employee commitment, and the like.

It is very likely that nonunion grievance procedures will continue their growth. There is some evidence, for instance, that the availability and the use of these internal procedures contribute to employer-favorable judgments in wrongful discharge litigation (Feuille and Delaney 1992; Guidry and Huffman 1990). In addition, in 1991 the U.S. Supreme Court ruled that an arbitration provision covering a fired nonunion stockbroker had to be used to resolve his age discrimination claim, rather than a lawsuit filed under the Age Discrimination in Employment Act (*Gilmer v. Johnson/Interstate Lane Corp.*, 111 S. Ct. 1647). This ruling has resulted in subsequent rulings by the lower federal courts that similarly situated employees — those covered by arbitration provisions — must take their employment disputes to arbitration rather than to federal court. It is not clear how far this precedent will be pushed, but there is no question that it may help many nonunion employers look more kindly upon arbitration as a dispute mechanism.

Wrongful Discharge and Employment at Will Claims by fired nonunion employees may serve as the meeting ground between nonunion arbitration procedures and public policy. As noted, during the past 20 years there has been an explosion in the number of lawsuits filed by disgruntled fired employees claiming that they were unfairly discharged (Westin and Feliu 1988). These suits have been prompted by an increased willingness of the appellate courts in most states to grant fired employees various common law causes of action to challenge their terminations. As a result, this body of case law has eroded, though certainly not eliminated, the extent to which private nonunion employees who are not covered by a fixed-term employment contract can be terminated at will (Dertouzos and Karoly 1992). At the same time, proposals have been advanced that all American workers should be covered by legislation that guarantees that they can be discharged only for "just cause," and that fired employees be allowed to challenge their discharges via some sort of statutorily mandated arbitration procedure (Stieber 1984; Summers 1976).

Several responses to these developments have emerged. First, a small percentage of nonunion employers already have adopted arbitration procedures (BNA 1989b; Ichniowski and Lewin 1988), and the American Arbitration Association has assisted this trend by developing model arbitration procedures for nonunion settings (BNA 1989a). This trend also will be helped along by those employers who agree to explicit individual contracts of employment with their employees (a growing phenomenon examined by David Lewin in chapter 15 of this volume). Second, wrongful discharge bills were introduced into state legislatures in ten states, and in Montana such a bill became law in 1987 (Krueger 1991). This law requires that discharges must be for "good cause," it requires employees to use any internal grievance procedures, it encourages (but does not require) the use of arbitration to resolve any termination disputes, and it establishes a limit on the monetary damages that can be awarded to an employee who was improperly fired. Third, the National Conference of Commissioners on Uniform State Laws drafted and recommended that states adopt its Model Employment Termination Act (BNA 1991). This model law requires "good cause" for discharge, provides for arbitration in place of litigation for resolving termination disputes, and limits the monetary liability of employers compared with their open-ended common law exposure in a wrongful discharge lawsuit.

It remains to be seen if other states will follow Montana's lead and the National Conference's recommendation and statutorily eliminate the employment-at-will principle. There is no organized political constituency to seek the passage of such laws, for by definition the nonunion employees who would benefit most from their passage do not have an organization through which to press their views on elected officials. One reason the Montana law passed was that some employers supported it in the wake of expensive court verdicts won by fired employees (Krueger 1991). However, it is not clear if these same lawsuit pressures are sufficiently strong to give employers in other states an incentive to support wrongful discharge legislation as an alternative to the expensive verdicts and large transaction costs associated with wrongful discharge lawsuits.

It seems unlikely that the erosion of the employment-at-will principle that has occurred during the past 20 years will come to a halt now. One element apparent in just about every proposal for the statutory regulation of wrongful discharge disputes is the requirement that they be processed through some sort of arbitration procedure rather than continue to be litigated in court. If this proposal prevails, the gap between union and nonunion voice procedures will diminish substantially, at least so far as termination disputes are concerned.

The manner in which workplace disputes emerge has undergone some notable changes during the postwar period. Looking first at the unionized private sector, disputes have become much less likely to occur as disruptions to the normal workflow, whether as strikes, slowdowns, lockouts, boycotts, and so on. Contract interpretation strikes have become unusual, and have been almost completely replaced by grievance disputes processed through grievance and arbitration procedures. Contract negotiation strikes were a usually reliable instrument of union negotiating policy until about 1980, and since then they have fallen into considerable disuse in the face of heightened employer resistance supported by an employer-favorable public labor relations policy. Perhaps the most remarkable labor dispute development during the postwar era is the disappearance of the "emergency strike" as a subject of public or scholarly concern, which ultimately is a reflection of the very diminished ability of private sector unions to inflict harm on bystanders via strikes.

In the unionized public sector since the mid-1960s, strikes have become more "normal" bargaining events (whether they are legal or illegal), and public employers have realized that the sky does not fall when such strikes occur. Indeed, some states have legalized the right to strike for many public employees. At the same time, compulsory interest arbitration has become a prominent dispute resolution method, at least for those employee groups whose services are deemed essential and, more important, who also have the political skill to lobby such statutes onto the books. We have come a long way from the days when compulsory interest arbitration was only a theoretical possibility and all unions routinely condemned it. Compulsory arbitration in the private sector historically has been viewed as a mechanism to restrain union strike power. In a noteworthy turnaround, compulsory arbitration in the public sector has come to be viewed as a mechanism to restrain management bargaining power.

In 1966 Bakke lamented that U.S. union-management relations had hardened into "antagonistic cooperation," with more antagonism than cooperation. The labor relations events of the succeeding years have been consistent with this view, as unions and employers have relied on legislative battles, litigation in administrative agencies and the courts, grievance and arbitration procedures, and work stoppages, all accompanied by an overlay of adversarial and even hostile rhetoric, to press for their desired versions of union-management rules and employment terms. Further, the recently diminished level of work stoppages and the decline in the volume of unfair labor practice charges do not signify any softening of the antagonistic attitudes that unions and employers historically have displayed toward each other. So long as unions see themselves as the agents of worker resistance to management's domination of the workplace, and so long as employers resist unions as unnecessary and unproductive hindrances to effective employer-employee relationships (Jacoby 1990), union-management disputes of various kinds will be the normal order of things. The form these disagreements take will vary over time, but we are in no immediate danger of having an epidemic of genuine union-management cooperation break out and displace decades of union-management antagonism. Further, this conclusion is not altered by the fact that unions have become more politically and economically conservative than they were during the heady days of the 1940s.

As workplace disputes in the union sector have become a less compelling cause for societal concern, disputes in the nonunion sector have become steadily more important. These disputes usually emerge as individual claims, and as they emerge in publicly visible forums they appear disproportionately to involve claims generated by terminations. Whether these claims are based on antidiscrimination or other statutes or on common law exceptions to the employment-at-will principle, their unifying thread is a quest for fair treatment. The number of these kinds of unfair treatment claims seems destined to rise, especially in light of the continuing stream of civil rights and other workplace laws passed during the postwar period, the continued willingness of the courts to allow at-will employees a forum to challenge their terminations, and the increased insistence among employees that they be treated fairly at work. In short, an increasing proportion of the annual flow of workplace disputes has been uncoupled from unions, and the growth of individual contracting in the workplace, both explicit and implicit, means that this trend will continue. Indeed, although union-management collective disputes will continue to capture a disproportionate share of the headlines, it appears that the typical employer-employee dispute now is handled on an individual and nonunion basis.

One result of this trend is the continuing debate surrounding proposed wrongful discharge statutes that would require that all discharges be for good cause, and that would establish arbitration as the preferred method of discharge dispute resolution. A more pervasive result of this trend is the continuing emergence of formal grievance procedures in more and more nonunion firms (primarily large corporations), for the costs of resolving these kinds of employee claims internally is a small fraction of doing so externally. Indeed, a small number of farsighted firms have provided arbitration for their nonunion employees, particularly to handle discharge disputes. Organizational behavior researchers have viewed the spread of nonunion grievance procedures as part of the increased emphasis on organizational justice in the workplace (Sheppard, Lewicki, and Minton 1992). Further, the willingness to establish nonunion grievance and arbitration procedures is not some sort of aberration. Instead, it is merely one example of the increased willingness of employers generally to establish a sophisticated array of human resource management policies designed to enhance employee productivity and satisfaction (and which, if successful, will lessen employee interest in unionization).

In keeping with the tradition of industrial relations research, this chapter has been almost exclusively concerned with collective workplace disputes that become publicly visible and with collective or individual disputes that are processed with the assistance of third parties (via government agencies, courts, mediators, arbitrators). As a result, this analysis has emphasized those workplace disputes and dispute resolution procedures that are visible, formal, and rational. Operationally, the disputes examined here emerge as official employer-employee conflicts and are processed through institutionalized channels for handling conflicts. This focus ignores the private, informal, and sometimes nonrational nature of many workplace disputes and the equally private and informal manner in which most of these disputes are dealt with (Bartunek, Kolb, and Lewicki 1992; Kolb 1992). Such informal disputes (which are often handled under other names) are difficult to research, in large part because they leave little or no paper trail and hence are very difficult to measure. However, there should be no illusions that the emphasis in this analysis on visible and formal disputes and dispute procedures exhausts the arena of workplace conflict and its resolution.

Finally, during the postwar period formal workplace disputes have become increasingly likely to emerge via litigation and alternative dispute resolution procedures and concomitantly less likely to emerge as collective disruptions of the normal workflow. One result of this increased reliance on judicial and administrative procedures is the growth of a substantial cadre of employer and employee-union advocates, government agency administrators, mediators, arbitrators, and interested academics (these roles often overlap) who make a comfortable living handling, deciding, and studying workplace disputes. These are the same people who produce most of the research and commentary on workplace dispute systems, and in that capacity they have a strong influence on the conventional wisdom about these systems. This received wisdom emphasizes that alternative dispute resolution arrangements work well in the workplace and that there should be more rather than fewer of them, particularly as alternatives to work stoppages, unilateral employer domination of the workplace, and litigation. Accordingly, as we approach the end of a century of tumultuous change in employer-employee relations, we may be assured that the American workplace dispute resolution community remains vigilant in the pursuit of its professional self-interest.

References

American Arbitration Association. 1991. "Case Statistics Provided by Labor Arbitrators." *Study Time* (newsletter), no. 4: 1ff.

Ashenfelter, Orley, and George E. Johnson. 1969. "Bargaining Theory, Trade Unions and Industrial Strike Activity." *American Economic Review* 59: 35–49.

Bakke, E. Wight. 1966. *Mutual Survival: The Goal of Unions and Management.* 2d ed. Hamden, Conn.: Archon Books.

Bartunek, Jean M., Deborah M. Kolb, and Roy J. Lewicki. 1992. "Bringing Conflict Out from Behind the Scenes: Private, Informal, and Nonrational Dimensions of Conflict in Organizations." In Deborah M. Kolb and Jean M. Bartunek, eds., *Hidden Conflict in Organizations.* Newbury Park, Calif.: Sage Publications. pp. 209–228.

Berenbeim, Ronald. 1980. *Nonunion Complaint Systems: A Corporate Appraisal.* Research Report no. 770. New York: Conference Board.

Bernstein, Irving, Harold L. Enarson, and R. W. Fleming, eds. 1955. *Emergency Disputes and National Labor Policy.* Industrial Relations Research Association series. New York: Harper.

Block, Richard, and Jack Stieber. 1987. "The Impact of Attorneys and Arbitrators on Arbitration Awards." *Industrial and Labor Relations Review* 40: 543–555.

Bureau of National Affairs (BNA). 1989a. "AAA Issues Model Arbitration Procedures for Non-Union Settings." *Daily Labor Report* 46 (March 10): A3.

———. 1989b. "Lawyers Examine Growing Phenomenon of Arbitration in a Non-Union Setting." *Daily Labor Report* 163 (August 24): A4–A8.

———. 1991. "Draft Employment Termination Act Is Approved as Model Law by Conference of Commissioners." *Daily Labor Report* 154 (August 9): A16.

———. 1992. "BNA Data Show Most Work Stoppages Occurred in Units of Fewer Than 200 Workers." *Daily Labor Report* 75 (April 17): A1–A2, E1–E3.

Carnevale, Peter J. D., and Richard Pegnetter. 1985. "The Selection of Mediator Tactics in Public-Sector Disputes: A Contingency Analysis." *Journal of Social Issues* 41: 65–82.

Chachere, Denise R., and Peter Feuille. 1993. "Grievance Procedures and Due Process in Nonunion Workplaces." In John F. Burton, Jr., ed., *Proceedings of the Forty-Fifth Annual Meeting*. Madison, Wis.: Industrial Relations Research Association. pp. 446–455.

Cullen, Donald E. 1968. *National Emergency Strikes*. ILR Paperback no. 7. Ithaca, N.Y.: Cornell University.

Dalton, Dan R., and Todor, W. D. 1981. "Win, Lose, Draw: The Grievance Process in Practice." *Personnel Administrator* 26 (May-June): 25–29.

Delaney, John T. 1983. "Strikes, Arbitration, and Teacher Salaries: A Behavioral Analysis." *Industrial and Labor Relations Review* 36: 431–446.

———. 1986. "Impasses and Teacher Contract Outcomes." *Industrial Relations* 25: 45–55.

Delaney, John T., and Peter Feuille. 1992. "Grievance and Arbitration Procedures among Nonunion Employers." In John F. Burton, Jr., ed. *Proceedings of the Forty-Fourth Annual Meeting of the Industrial Relations Research Association*. Madison, Wis.: Industrial Relations Research Association. pp. 529–538.

Delaney, John T., David Lewin, and Casey Ichniowski. 1989. *Human Resource Policies and Practices in American Firms*. BLMR 137. Washington, D.C.: U.S. Department of Labor, Bureau of Labor-Management Relations and Cooperative Programs.

Dertouzos, James N., Elaine Holland, and Patricia Ebener. 1988. *The Legal and Economic Consequences of Wrongful Termination*. R-3602-ICJ. Santa Monica, Calif.: Rand Corporation.

Dertouzos, James N., and Lynn A. Karoly. 1992. *Labor-Market Responses to Employer Liability*. R-3989-ICJ. Santa Monica, Calif.: Rand Corporation.

Donohue, John J., and Peter Siegelman. 1991. "The Changing Nature of Employment Discrimination Litigation." *Stanford Law Review* 43: 983–1033.

Ewing, David W. 1989. *Justice on the Job: Resolving Grievances in the Nonunion Workplace*. Boston: Harvard Business School Press.

Feller, David E. 1977. "Arbitration: The Days of Its Glory Are Numbered." *Industrial Relations Law Journal* 2: 97–130.

Feuille, Peter. 1979. "Selected Benefits and Costs of Compulsory Arbitration." *Industrial and Labor Relations Review* 33: 64–76.

———. 1992. "Why Does Grievance Mediation Resolve Grievances?" *Negotiation Journal* 8: 131–145.

Feuille, Peter, and John T. Delaney. 1986. "Collective Bargaining, Interest

Arbitration, and Police Salaries." *Industrial and Labor Relations Review* 39: 228–240.

———. 1992. "The Individual Pursuit of Organizational Justice: Grievance Procedures in Nonunion Workplaces." In Gerald R. Ferris and Kendrith M. Rowland, eds., *Research in Personnel and Human Resources Management,* vol. 10. Greenwich, Conn.: JAI Press. Pp. 187–232.

Feuille, Peter, John T. Delaney, and Wallace Hendricks. 1985. "Interest Arbitration and Police Contracts." *Industrial Relations* 24: 161–181.

Feuille, Peter, and Michael LeRoy. 1990. "Grievance Arbitration Appeals in the Federal Courts: Facts and Figures." *Arbitration Journal* 45 (March): 35–47.

Feuille, Peter, and Hoyt N. Wheeler. 1981. "Will the Real Industrial Conflict Please Stand Up?" In Jack Stieber, Robert McKersie, and D. Quinn Mills, eds., *U.S. Industrial Relations 1950–1980: A Critical Assessment.* Madison Wis.: Industrial Relations Research Association. pp. 255–295.

Freeman, Richard B., and James L. Medoff. 1984. *What Do Unions Do?* New York: Basic Books.

Gerhart, Paul, and John Drotning. 1980. "Dispute Settlement and the Intensity of Mediation." *Industrial Relations* 19: 352–359.

Gideon, Thomas F., and Richard B. Peterson. 1979. "A Comparison of Alternative Grievance Procedures." *Employee Relations Law Journal* 5: 222–233.

Goldberg, Michael J. 1985. "The Duty of Fair Representation: What the Courts Do in Fact." *Buffalo Law Review* 34: 89–171.

Gordon, Michael E., and Sandra J. Miller. 1984. "Grievances: A Review of Research and Practice." *Personnel Psychology* 37: 117–146.

Gorman, Robert A. 1976. *Basic Text on Labor Law: Unionization and Collective Bargaining.* St. Paul, Minn.: West Publishing.

Gramm, Cynthia L. 1987. "New Measures of the Propensity to Strike during Contract Negotiations, 1971–1980." *Industrial and Labor Relations Review* 40: 406–417.

Grodin, Joseph R., and Joyce M. Najita. 1988. "Judicial Response to Public-Sector Arbitration." In Benjamin Aaron, Joyce M. Najita, and James L. Stern, eds., *Public-Sector Bargaining,* 2d ed. Industrial Relations Research Association series. Washington, D.C.: Bureau of National Affairs. pp. 229–265.

Guidry, Greg, and Gerald J. Huffman, Jr. 1990. "Legal and Practical Aspects of Alternative Dispute Resolution in Non-Union Companies." *The Labor Lawyer* 6: 1–48.

Hays, Paul R. 1966. *Labor Arbitration: A Dissenting View.* New Haven, Conn.: Yale University Press.

Hicks, John R. 1963. *The Theory of Wages,* 2d ed. New York: Macmillan.

Hoh, Ronald. 1984. "The Effectiveness of Mediation in Public Sector Arbitration Systems: The Iowa Experience." *Arbitration Journal* 39 (June): 30–40.

Ichniowski, Casey. 1982. "Arbitration and Police Bargaining: Prescription for the Blue Flu." *Industrial Relations* 21: 149–166.

———. 1986. "The Effects of Grievance Activity on Productivity." *Industrial and Labor Relations Review* 40: 75–89.

Ichniowski, Casey, and David Lewin. 1987. "Grievance Procedures and Firm Performance." In Morris M. Kleiner, Myron Roomkin, and Sidney W. Salsburg, eds., *Human Resources and the Performance of the Firm.* Madison, Wis.: Industrial Relations Research Association. pp. 159–193.

———. 1988. "Characteristics of Grievance Procedures: Evidence from Nonunion, Union, and Double-Breasted Businesses." In Barbara D. Dennis, ed., *Proceedings of the Forty-First Annual Meeting.* Madison, Wis.: Industrial Relations Research Association. pp. 415–424.

Jacoby, Sanford M. 1990. "Norms and Cycles: The Dynamics of Nonunion Industrial Relations in the United States." In Katherine G. Abraham and Robert McKersie, eds., *New Developments in the Labor Market: Toward a New Institutional Paradigm.* Cambridge, Mass.: MIT Press. pp. 19–57.

———. 1991. "American Exceptionalism Revisited: The Importance of Management." In Sanford M. Jacoby, ed., *Masters to Managers: Historical and Comparative Perspectives on American Employers.* New York: Columbia University Press. pp. 173–200, 235–241.

Jarley, Paul, and Cheryl Maranto. 1990. "Union Corporate Campaigns: An Assessment." *Industrial and Labor Relations Review* 43: 505–524.

Katz, Harry, Thomas A. Kochan, and Kenneth Gobeille. 1983. "Industrial Relations Performance, Economic Performance, and the Effects of Quality of Working Life Efforts: An Interplant Analysis." *Industrial and Labor Relations Review* 37: 3–17.

Kaufman, Bruce. 1982. "The Determinants of Strikes in the United States, 1900–1977." *Industrial and Labor Relations Review* 35: 473–490.

Kerr, Clark. 1954. "Industrial Conflict and Its Mediation." *American Journal of Sociology* 3: 230–245.

Kerr, Clark, and Abraham J. Siegel. 1954. "The Interindustry Propensity to Strike — An International Comparison." In Arthur Kornhauser, Robert Dubin, and Arthur Ross, eds., *Industrial Conflict.* New York: McGraw-Hill. pp. 189–212.

Klass, Brian, and Angelo S. DeNisi. 1989. "Managerial Reactions to Employee Dissent: The Impact of Grievance Activity on Performance Ratings." *Academy of Management Journal.* 32: 705–717.

Kleiner, Morris M., Gerald Nicklesburg, and Adam M. Pilarski. 1989. "Grievances and Plant Performance: Is Zero Optimal?" In Barbara B. Dennis, ed., *Proceedings of the Forty-First Annual Meeting,* Madison, Wis.: Industrial Relations Research Association. pp. 172–180.

Knight, Thomas R. 1986. "Feedback and Grievance Resolution." *Industrial and Labor Relations Review* 39: 585–598.

Kochan, Thomas A., and Richard N. Block. 1977. "An Interindustry Analysis of Bargaining Outcomes: Preliminary Evidence from Two-Digit Industries." *Quarterly Journal of Economics* 91: 431–452.

Kochan, Thomas A., and Todd Jick. 1978. "The Public Sector Mediation

Process: A Theory and Empirical Examination." *Journal of Conflict Resolution* 22: 209–240.

Kochan, Thomas A., and Harry C. Katz. 1988. *Collective Bargaining and Industrial Relations*, 2d ed. Homewood, Ill.: Irwin.

Kochan, Thomas A., and Hoyt N. Wheeler. 1975. "Municipal Collective Bargaining: A Model and Analysis of Bargaining Outcomes." *Industrial and Labor Relations Review* 29: 46–66.

Kolb, Deborah M. 1983. *The Mediators.* Cambridge, Mass.: MIT Press.

———. 1992. "Women's Work: Peacemaking in Organizations." In Deborah M. Kolb and Jean M. Bartunek, eds., *Hidden Conflict in Organizations.* Newbury Park, Calif.: Sage Publications. pp. 63–91.

Krueger, Alan B. 1991. "The Evolution of Unjust-Dismissal Legislation in the United States." *Industrial and Labor Relations Review* 44: 644–660.

Lewin, David. 1987. "Dispute Resolution in the Nonunion Firm: A Theoretical and Empirical Analysis." *Journal of Conflict Resolution* 31: 465–502.

———. 1990. "Grievance Procedures in Nonunion Workplaces: An Empirical Analysis of Usage, Dynamics, and Outcomes." *Chicago-Kent Law Review* 66: 823–844.

Lewin, David, and Richard B. Peterson. 1988. *The Modern Grievance Procedure in the United States.* New York: Quorum Books.

McCabe, Douglas M. 1988. *Corporate Nonunion Complaint Procedures and Systems.* New York: Praeger.

McConnell, Sheena. 1990. "Cyclical Fluctuations in Strike Activity." *Industrial and Labor Relations Review* 44: 130–143.

Ng, Ignace, and Ali Dastmalchian. 1989. "Determinants of Grievance Outcomes: A Case Study." *Industrial and Labor Relations Review* 42: 393–403.

Nolan, Dennis R., and Roger I. Abrams. 1983. "American Labor Arbitration: The Maturing Years." *University of Florida Law Review* 35: 557–632.

Norsworthy, J. R., and Craig A. Zabala. 1985. "Worker Attitudes, Worker Behavior, and Productivity in the U.S. Automobile Industry, 1959–76." *Industrial and Labor Relations Review* 38: 544–557.

Northrup, Herbert R. 1966. *Compulsory Arbitration and Government Intervention in Labor Disputes.* Washington, D.C.: Labor Policy Association.

Olson, Craig A. 1980. "The Impact of Arbitration on the Wages of Firefighters." *Industrial Relations* 19: 325–339.

———. 1986. "Strikes, Strike Penalties, and Arbitration in Six States." *Industrial and Labor Relations Review* 39: 539–551.

———. 1988. "Dispute Resolution in the Public Sector." In Benjamin Aaron, Joyce M. Najita, and James L. Stern, eds., *Public-Sector Bargaining,* 2d ed. Industrial Relations Research Association series. Washington, D.C.: Bureau of National Affairs. pp. 160–188.

Perloff, Jeffrey M., and Michael L. Wachter. 1984. "Wage Comparability in the U.S. Postal Service." *Industrial and Labor Relations Review* 38: 26–35.

Phelps, Orme W. 1964. "Compulsory Arbitration: Some Perspectives." *Industrial and Labor Relations Review* 18: 82–91.

Rehmus, Charles M. 1990. "Emergency Strikes Revisited." *Industrial and Labor Relations Review* 43: 175–190.

Ross, Arthur M. 1963. "Distressed Grievance Procedures and Their Rehabilitation." In Mark Kahn, ed., *Labor Arbitration and Industrial Change*, Proceedings of the Sixteenth Annual Meeting of the National Academy of Arbitrators. Washington, D.C.: Bureau of National Affairs. pp. 104–132.

Ross, Arthur M., and Paul T. Hartman. 1960. *Changing Patterns of Industrial Conflict.* New York: Wiley.

Ross, Philip. 1965. *The Government as a Source of Union Power: The Role of Public Policy in Collective Bargaining.* Providence, R.I.: Brown University Press.

Schneider, B. V. H. 1988. "Public-Sector Labor Legislation — An Evolutionary Analysis." In Benjamin Aaron, Joyce M. Najita, and James L. Stern, eds., *Public-Sector Bargaining*, 2d ed. Industrial Relations Research Association series. Washington, D.C.: Bureau of National Affairs. pp. 189–228.

Scott, William G. 1965. *The Management of Conflict: Appeal Systems in Organizations.* Homewood, Ill.: Irwin.

Sheppard, Blair H., Roy J. Lewicki, and John W. Minton. 1992. *Organizational Justice: The Search for Fairness in the Workplace.* New York: Lexington Books.

Simkin, William E., and Nicholas E. Fidandis. 1986. *Mediation and the Dynamics of Collective Bargaining*, 2d ed. Washington, D.C.: Bureau of National Affairs.

Staudohar, Paul D. 1989. *The Sports Industry and Collective Bargaining*, 2d. ed. Ithaca, N.Y.: ILR Press.

Stern, James L., and Craig Olson. 1982. "The Propensity to Strike of Local Government Employees." *Journal of Collective Negotiations in the Public Sector* 11: 201–214.

Stevens, Carl M. 1966. "Is Compulsory Arbitration Compatible with Bargaining?" *Industrial Relations* 5 (February): 38–52.

Stieber, Jack. 1970. "Voluntary Arbitration of Contract Terms." In Gerald G. Somers and Barbara D. Dennis, eds., *Arbitration and the Expanding Role of Neutrals*, Proceedings of the Twenty-Third Annual Meeting of the National Academy of Arbitrators. Washington, D.C.: Bureau of National Affairs. pp. 71–124.

———. 1984. "Employment-at-Will: An Issue for the 1980's." In Barbara D. Dennis, ed., *Proceedings of the Thirty-Sixth Annual Meeting.* Madison, Wis.: Industrial Relations Research Association. pp. 1–13.

Summers, Clyde W. 1976. "Arbitration of Unjust Dismissal: A Preliminary Proposal." In Benjamin Aaron et al., *The Future of Labor Arbitration in America.* New York: American Arbitration Association. pp. 159–195.

Thornton, Robert J., and Perry A. Zirkel. 1990. "The Consistency and Predictability of Grievance Arbitration Awards." *Industrial and Labor Relations Review* 43: 294–307.

U.S. Bureau of Labor Statistics (BLS). 1966. *Arbitration Procedures.* Bulletin 1425–6. Washington, D.C.: U.S. Government Printing Office.

————. 1981. *Work Stoppages in Government, 1980.* Bulletin 2110. Washington, D.C.: U.S. Government Printing Office.

————. 1983. *Handbook of Labor Statistics.* Bulletin 2175. Washington, D.C.: U.S. Government Printing Office.

————. 1991. *Compensation and Working Conditions* 43 (September). Washington, D.C.: U.S. Government Printing Office.

————. 1992. *Employment and Earnings* 39 (January). Washington, D.C.: U.S. Government Printing Office.

U.S. Equal Employment Opportunity Commission (EEOC). 1971. *Fifth Annual Report.* Washington, D.C.: U.S. Government Printing Office.

————. 1990. *Combined Annual Report Fiscal Years 1986, 1987, 1988.* Washington, D.C.: U.S. Government Printing Office.

U.S. General Accounting Office. 1991. *Strikes and the Use of Permanent Strike Replacements in the 1970s and 1980s.* GAO/HRD-91-2 (January).

U.S. National Labor Relations Board (NLRB). 1951. *Fifteenth Annual Report of the National Labor Relations Board, 1950.* Washington, D.C.: U.S. Government Printing Office.

————. 1991. *Fifty-Fourth Annual Report of the National Labor Relations Board, 1989.* Washington, D.C.: U.S. Government Printing Office.

Vroman, Susan. 1989. "A Longitudinal Analysis of Strike Activity in U.S. Manufacturing: 1957–1984." *American Economic Review* 79: 816–826.

Westin, Alan F., and Alfred G. Feliu. 1988. *Resolving Employment Disputes without Litigation.* Washington, D.C.: Bureau of National Affairs.

19

Unions: A Reorientation to Survive

■ ──────────────────────── ■

Michael J. Piore

In the course of the past decade, the American economy has undergone a radical institutional transformation. A salient feature of that
transformation has been the precipitous decline of organized labor.
Its dues-paying base has shrunk dramatically, both absolutely and as
a percentage of the labor force. Its political power, its bargaining
power, and its ability to command the respect and protection of the
courts and the legislature, while all more difficult to measure, have
clearly declined as well. Labor scholars' explanations for these trends
have tended to focus on changes in the environment in which labor
operates: competitive pressures emanating from globalization and
deregulation; shifts in the industrial and professional distribution of
jobs and in the age, sex, race, and geographic distribution of the labor
force. But among labor leaders trying to cope with their fate, the real
issue is not the environment itself but the organizational and institutional response to it: could they have better responded — might they
better respond now — to the hostile challenge that environmental
pressures have posed? This is a question to which labor scholars have
devoted very little attention.[1] This study constitutes the beginnings
of an effort to address these issues.[2]

The study is exploratory, an attempt to formulate a set of hypotheses rather than to provide definitive answers. It grew out of
informal conversations with a number of national AFL-CIO officials in the spring of 1987. Those conversations revealed a sense of
frustration and disappointment about their inability to reverse the
decline of the labor movement. They left the impression that, contrary to the assertions of many of their critics, unions had undertaken a variety of new initiatives in organization, bargaining, and
worker representation, and that it was despite these initiatives, not

for a lack of them, that labor's position in American society continued to deteriorate.

The feelings on the part of these labor leaders are particularly noteworthy because they contrast sharply with those expressed by American business executives interviewed for a companion study in a larger project of which the work reported here is also a part. The business leaders had made comparable changes in organizational practice, but generally expressed considerable optimism about the impact those changes would have on the competitive position of their organization, even in aspects of practice that had virtually nothing to do with labor-management relations (Piore 1991).

This study of trade union organization evolved in four stages. The initial interviews with national AFL-CIO officials constituted the first stage. In the second, a list was drawn up of union activities and activists in the Boston area generally viewed as innovative, and interviews were conducted to explore those innovations. The basic finding of this second stage was that the fundamental problems of unions in the Boston area could be traced to poor internal managerial practices, and that the innovations either failed to address these practices or were, in terms of the practices they did address, ill-conceived. In the course of exploring these issues one national union was identified that had introduced a series of internal managerial reforms in recent years: these managerial reforms seemed to have addressed virtually all of the major organizational problems that had undermined the renovative process elsewhere in the labor movement. That union, the Service Employees International Union (SEIU), coincidentally turned out to be the fastest growing international within the AFL-CIO.

The third stage of the study focused on the SEIU, and attempted, again through interviews, to identify why this particular union had introduced the organizational reforms and where the ideas for these reforms had come from. In the fourth and final stage of the study — and this chapter — I attempt to apply the SEIU's experience for American trade unions in general. The SEIU experience suggests that the underlying problem for American trade unions may not be administrative failures after all. The union is unusual not only for its internal administrative structure, but also for its unusual sense of itself as an organization, of where it fits into American society and into the ongoing debates about American social and economic policy. It is as if the SEIU defines itself in terms of these debates in the same way that other unions have historically defined themselves by the industry or the craft that they organize. This definition — odd as it may seem in terms of traditional categories of thought — is viable at a time when industry and craft have really lost their meaning, at least as a fulcrum around which to build an organizational identity. To translate this insight into a prescription for other unions, one must abandon the old debates about business and political unionism and invent an altogether new definition of what a trade union is: an institution that mediates between the economic and the social structure. And then the existing organizations must be allowed to evolve in a way that permits that mediating role to emerge.

Organizational Failings

The working hypothesis of the study at its outset was that labor's most basic problem was an excess of business unionism and a consequent loss of the ideological justification for the protective political and legal shell within which unions had operated for the first three decades of the postwar period — that unionism had lost its ideological justification (Piore 1982). The problems that emerged in the initial interviews in Boston were better described as *managerial* than as ideological or political, more indicative of inadequate appreciation of the business side of the organization, not an excess of attention to it. Three particular problems are emblematic: (1) a failure to enforce and service existing contracts, (2) an excessive diversification of organizational efforts and representational responsibilities, and (3) excessive use of outside consultants, to the detriment of internal staff training and organizational development. A number of people interviewed had other criticisms, including insufficient attention to organizing new members, autocratic leadership, excessive ideological zeal on the part of some new young organizers, undemocratic structures, and a divorce between the leadership and the rank and file. These criticisms were more difficult to evaluate, since they involved philosophies of unionization as well as managerial practice, but they are important issues in thinking about alternative organization models. They combine with the other organizational problems to suggest a general failing of union leadership to think in strategic terms.[3] But it is easiest to see this in terms of a detailed discussion of the three specific organizational issues.

Contract enforcement
Allegations that existing contracts were not effectively serviced or enforced were widespread. There were insinuations of outright corruption, sweetheart agreements, and extortion. However, in one case

in which these charges could actually be pinned down, the problem was not corruption at all, but the result of poor administration; an old, tired, or, at worst, lazy union official; and a changing business environment that rendered the old contract and collective bargaining structure obsolete. The concrete case was a laundry workers' local in which the longtime president and business agent had been displaced by a dynamic young leader and a charismatic new-left organizer whom the new president brought with him to join the local staff. The story as we pieced it together from interviews with the new leadership and background provided in other interviews was as follows.

The old president presided over an organization that represented a number of small shops. These shops had been organized and the basic contract negotiated years before, in the early postwar years or, in some cases, in the 1930s. Meanwhile the composition of the labor force had changed substantially and the competitive environment and the technology had also shifted. These changes had occurred gradually over the years, but they accelerated in the late 1970s and early 1980s. Over time, as well, the old president had grown comfortable in office and developed work habits in which he was not in regular contact with individual shops or with the rank and file. In many cases, he was probably unaware of contract violations. In other cases, he was afraid that if the contract was actually enforced, the shop would be driven out of business or the employer would file for a decertification election.

It is easy to imagine how this situation had developed not only in this local but in many old-line locals throughout New England. Collective bargaining agreements in the United States tend to be extremely detailed and complex. They govern a number of production practices and shop routines, and they tend to impose complex compensation structures involving detailed job descriptions, elaborate piecework systems, and multiple health and retirement supplements. In industries with large productive units, like steel mills and automobile plants, the local union tends to coincide with a single business unit, and the written contract is adapted to that unit's peculiarities. Even in large units, the actual agreement is modified in practice through informal ad hoc negotiations between steward and foreman on the plant floor, and there is a continual struggle by higher level officers in both the union and management to limit and control this process. When the local represents a variety of small shops, however, the contract cannot be tailored to each shop: the pressures to modify the agreement are much stronger and the task of policing the process — so that competitive pressures that undermine the industry collective bargaining structure are not unleashed — is much greater. Union officers have to travel constantly and maintain a network of stewards. Where there is high turnover and the shops are very small, the network of stewards might be better termed one of informants; aside from the business agent, there are few knowledge-able, trained union officers. If the union officers become lazy, do not travel, reduce the frequency of their visits, or lose contact with the constantly shifting membership, the network of informants deterio-rates, and contract enforcement gets out of hand, even in a firmly stable environment.

When there are new pressures, generated by technological changes and a shifting competitive structure, the tendency is even greater for changes in practice to outrun adjustments in the formal contract. In the case of the laundry workers' local — and probably a number of other small locals as well — companies under competitive pressure also stop paying into health and retirement schemes or even compro-mise stipulated wage rates. Sometimes delays of contractual pay-ments are a normal practice, due to seasonal cash flow problems or to the kinds of temporary emergencies that are endemic in poorly man-aged small businesses. Then, what appears to an outsider to be a contract violation is in effect a short-term loan from the union or, put another way, from the company's employees. When the business agent is active and his or her network of informants is extensive, it is relatively easy to catch an employer who begins abusing this process to enhance the profits of a successful business or to milk a company that is destined for bankruptcy. When the business agent loses touch with the industry, however, it takes much longer to spot these abuses. And when the agent does find out about them, he or she is in a poor position to think about how to control them. The business agent may not know enough about the competitive structure of the industry to evaluate the effect of the abuse on the viability of the contract in other shops. He or she may not be close enough to the membership to judge whether they will support efforts to enforce the agreement through a strike or a slowdown. The new laundry workers' president found, in fact, that once the situation was ex-plained to the rank and file, they were actually supportive of taking a hard line, even when they risked losing their jobs.

The effect of unenforced agreements has an impact on organized labor out of all proportion to the relatively benign process through which it appears to arise. It undermines the reputation of trade unions among the pool of unorganized workers, particularly low-income workers, who constitute the largest potential sources for union revival. These effects taint all unions, even those where this is not a major problem, although some organizers suggested that workers did recognize distinctions among different unions in this regard. Since the organizational dynamic that leads to poor contract administration is subtle and almost impossible to understand from the outside, workers generally attribute the worst motives to the officials responsible for the problem.

Consultants

The second major management problem that emerged in the interviews concerned the use of consultants. There appeared to be an excessive reliance on outsiders to perform tasks that should have been performed by permanent union staff. In a sense, this is an old problem in union management: historically, it has taken the form of hiring lawyers to negotiate contracts and manage grievance arbitrations — tasks that union business agents or even rank-and-file members could have been trained to do. This tendency to use consultants is associated with the growth of legalistic approaches to contract administration and with the rapid rise in the number of unfair labor practices associated with organizing and first-contract negotiations (Dunlop and Bok, 1970). But one might ask whether the rising importance of lawyers in union affairs is the cause or the effect of these developments. One might also ask why, even if the growing legalism is the product of autonomous factors, it is handled by outside lawyers rather than lawyers added directly to the union staff. One must suspect that resorting to outside lawyers increases the tendency for these developments to be driven by "the culture of the law" rather than by the "culture" of trade unions or of collective bargaining or of the specific industries and crafts that the union represents.

What was striking in the interviews for this study, however, was not the reliance on external lawyers but the reliance on external consultants for innovations in practice outside the traditional range of organizing and collective bargaining. One young organizer was interviewed who had been hired as a short-term consultant by the International Ladies' Garment Workers (ILGW) to *organize* electronic component manufacturers north of Boston. And a variety of other important innovations were handled by outsiders who operated independently of internal staff. Corporate campaigns, in which indirect pressure is exerted on a company (through, for example, the stockholding of union pension funds, consumer boycotts, and, although of dubious legality, subcontracting relationships), relied on outsiders not only for the research that identified the financial pressure points but also for the execution of the campaign. Thus, consultants were hired to recruit other unions with a major financial stake in the targeted company to join the campaign or to support the elaborate public relations campaigns associated with mass boycotts. The financial analysis associated with contract concessions and worker buyouts was also subcontracted, as were, to take still other examples, the legislative lobbying and electoral campaigns associated with public policy initiatives and regulatory provisions.

The use of consultants in this way may make sense in a one-shot tactical operation, and the innovations under study here tended to be viewed as such. Several respondents in interviews made it clear that corporate campaigns, in particular, were a last-resort tactic, used only after more conventional tactics had failed and a more conventional strike or organizing campaign was on the verge of collapse. (The ILGW's electronics campaign seemed to be a special project of the union president's, initiated on the spur of the moment without consulting the other officers or the staff and with no particular thought to long-term organizational development.) The result, however, is that the innovations are not incorporated into the permanent repertoire of organizing and bargaining instruments.

Even more important, a large number of the innovations involve the development of one particular capability: a detailed understanding of the economic and financial structure of an industry. The organizer hired by the ILGW to organize the electronics industry was known for his charismatic personality and his creative use of home visits, and that was apparently why he was hired. But when interviewed, he placed particular emphasis on his prior investment in research on the structure of subcontracting and the competitive relationship among firms. This information was the key to understanding what part of the industry had to be organized in order to make it possible to win meaningful contracts. This substantive knowledge, as well as the research skill through which it is acquired, is the same as that required to represent the units in collective bargaining. Therefore, if one is serious about organizing workers, this knowledge should be built into the organization that will represent them. More tellingly, however, this kind of analysis involves the same skills as are required for a worker buyout, for a corporate campaign, for an evaluation of a company's demand for bargaining concessions to stave off bankruptcy, or for the new "cooperative" labor-management relations modeled on Germany and Japan (Perry 1987). If the unions would use the consultants working on a one-shot basis in any one of these areas to develop internal staff capabilities instead, it would open up not one new tactic, but a whole range of new approaches.

A host of factors appear to reinforce the use of consultants: the financial crisis brought on by unions' declining dues-paying base makes it difficult to add permanent staff; many of the innovators have a radical political and ideological orientation that clashes with that of the established union leadership; top-notch financial and economic analysts do not fit into the traditional union pay structure. The way in which unions customarily use lawyers has set a precedent for this approach. But a fundamental reason that unions have failed to see this is that they seem to think of consultants' innovations as individual tactics, or even gimmicks, rather than thinking in terms of strategies for adapting to a new socioeconomic environment.

One particularly tragic example of this difference between seeing things as tactics and as strategy was found in a community economic development project in one of the depressed regions of Massachusetts. The director of the project saw the development as an instrument for community revival through the renaissance of the traditional industry of the city, all built on the model of Italian industrial districts or the old New York City garment industry. He thus saw a network of community services (daycare, training facilities, design and technology institutes) and physical infrastructure (industrial parks, road and bridge repairs, warehousing and shipping facilities) undergirding a structure of intercontracting small enterprises, growing out of the nucleus of firms still operating in the city. The board of his development agency was heavily weighted with union representatives and industrialists mostly sympathetic to the union. The director's grand vision was constantly being undermined, however, by the local union business agent. The business agent also saw himself as staving off the decline of the industry, but his approach consisted of making an elaborate patchwork of special deals with marginal firms, designed to keep the union in business from season to season, job to job. For him, the components of the director's economic development program were just so many more pieces in the ad hoc deals he was constructing, distributed so as to reward, punish, or balance the relationship between the unions and the different constituencies he was constantly manipulating to maintain his membership base.

The business agent was, in contrast to the old president of the laundry workers' local, a "good" manager: on top of his contacts; in touch with his members, with the economic conditions of the enterprise with which he dealt, with the politics of the city. The union made concessions to keep its members, but by design, not by default. On some very abstract level, the business agent shared the goals of the director of the economic development agency. Their differences really revolved around the breadth and depth of their vision. The director's vision grew out of an economic analysis of the industry and was linked to a complete industrial strategy. The business agent was operating from a practical understanding — built out of his experience in the city, heavily dependent on the history of particular firms with which he had dealt over the years, and conceived in terms of a limited repertoire of instruments for coping with the competitive environment. The gap between the business agent's perspective and the development agency director's could have been bridged by a staff built out of the organizing campaign in the local electronic industry, worker buyouts, and corporate campaigns, had all these things not been subcontracted to outside consultants.

Conglomeration

The third example of poor management was that national and even local unions seemed to be organizing in too many industries and occupations at once. The problem was most apparent in the remarks of the president of a clothing workers' local. Asked whether the decline of the industry in the region did not pose a threat to the union, he replied that that was nonsense; the union had a very good reputation, excellent organizers, and was organizing in all sorts of other fields — plastics, electronics, metal working, and so on. The clothing workers were hardly alone: the natural response of the labor movement appears to be to organize wherever it can, and most unions have sought members far outside their initial jurisdictions: the auto workers tried to organize Harvard University employees in Cambridge, Massachusetts; the steelworkers, parole officers in Quebec City. One can see how a union, faced with the substantial overhead of an ongoing organization and a shrinking dues structure, might be led to pick up new members wherever possible, but it seems doubtful that it can effectively organize, let alone represent, members in industries so far from the organization's initial expertise and that it is reasonable to try to acquire new expertise in so many different areas at once.[4]

The use of consultants and the tendency toward conglomeration, however, appear to represent something more than a reflexive and ill-conceived response to a new (and highly threatening) set of environmental pressures. They reflect a particular conception of a union as an organization: an organization whose core competency consists of *representing* employees, as if representation is a skill wholly divorced from the particular work in which the employees are engaged and the particular industry in which that work is performed. This leads, in turn, to the concept that union organizing consists of finding employees who need representation and selling them on the capacity of the union to provide it. In this view, the organizational activities of the union may be seen as separate from the representational activities, in the same sense that, in a business organization, the sales function is distinct from production. This concept of unions leads to organizational development and structure along these two dimensions. It does not lead the union to think of industry and occupation as being critical organizational dimensions. At best they are seen as secondary areas, requiring expertise that could be easily acquired on a case-by-case basis, as needed, through outside consultants. This view has similar implications for the use of in-house staff: it leads people to see the concentration of union membership in, for example, steel or clothing as simply a by-product of history. Such a concentration may make it economical to have a good deal of in-house industry-specific expertise, but that expertise will be viewed, like the consultants, as playing a secondary role. This conception, it may be noted, acts to limit union participation in new cooperative forms of labor relations, for such efforts require very detailed knowledge of the specific business environment.

At the national level, "reform" seems to have been dominated by a similar conception. The labor movement's major response to calls for reform has been to expand its repertoire, first by offering new services such as credit cards and insurance benefits, and second by creating new forms of associate membership (Jarley and Fiorito 1990). The new services increase the organization's "representational" capabilities; the new forms of membership facilitate its organizational capabilities by reducing the hurdle created by the National Labor Relations Board (NLRB) certification process, which basically requires a majority vote within a specified bargaining unit before a union can obtain new dues-paying members.

This approach totally fails to deal with the conflicts between representation and organization, as organizational goals are not inherently complementary goals. Within a single industry or occupation, they are complementary: organizational activities can relieve the competitive pressure from nonunion workers and, hence, increase the capacity of existing members to make claims on the resources of their employers. As the union moves outside of these economically defined jurisdictions, however, the relationship between new organizations and the interests of the existing membership becomes tenuous. There is then a conflict between organizational survival and the union's representational responsibilities. Conglomeration has enormously increased this conflict.

Such conflict is one of the major factors distinguishing unions from business organizations. The primary constituency of the business leadership is a set of stockholders, motivated almost exclusively by profit as their single, overriding goal. And profit is the predominant determinant of organizational survival and gauge of organizational health. A potential for conflict — analogous to that between union organization and worker representation — exists in the debates about hostile takeovers, short-term profit orientation, and business responsibilities to nonshareholder constituencies (customers, suppliers, employees, the surrounding community). But in the United States in the past decade, none of these conflicts has moved enough beyond debate to seriously influence the process of business organizational renewal. One result of this is that business organizations have been free to be much more draconian than trade unions in their pursuit of organizational reforms. However, this is not a distinguishing feature of the two reform processes. Even the more benign approaches used by business have not been used by labor. For example, many businesses have offered large financial settlements to their senior staff in order to vacate positions that could then be filled by employees better equipped to handle the pressures of the new environment. But it would have been difficult for labor unions to justify the use of their members' dues to replace old staff, since it was not clear that the kind of new staff that would have insured organizational survival would be in the interest of the existing members. Why should clothing workers in New Bedford care about organizing plastics firms in Lawrence? Similarly, business opened very wide debates about organizational direction: this kind of debate would seem to be much more natural in a democratic organization, like a union, than in a hierarchical one like the U.S. corporations in which it has occurred, but again, it is not at all clear that the interests of the dues-paying rank and file that would have emerged in such a debate would have coincided with those of the union organization as a continuing entity, or with those of the union leaders whose careers were tied to it.

A New Organizational Model

The SEIU: Its innovations

In the course of the initial set of interviews for this study, one union was repeatedly identified as being especially innovative and dynamic, the Service Employees International Union. It had hired as staff many people who were particularly respected by the "innovators" who were interviewed. And information in the interviews suggested that the SEIU had introduced internal managerial reforms that addressed many of the problems identified in other organizations. The focus of the later part of the study turned increasingly to those managerial reforms.

It is not necessarily correct to think of the structure of the SEIU in terms of a list of particular organizational innovations. It is not clear that this is the way in which that structure was conceived, and the innovations undoubtedly interact, so that their effects on the way the organization operates can probably not be distributed individually. Nonetheless, when an examination of these innovations was undertaken, it was as if the SEIU had devised a particular remedy to each of the items on the list of problems identified in previous interviews.

Conglomerate Union   On the surface, the SEIU is a conglomerate union. It was formed initially in the 1930s as an alliance of local unions of building service workers (essentially janitors) in several major cities (notably New York, Chicago, San Francisco, and Boston). It expanded rapidly in the postwar period, most especially in the past three decades, into health care and state and local government. The SEIU now represents a range of workers, in a variety of different industries: in enterprises distributed across the private for-profit sector, the private nonprofit sector, and all levels of government; and in occupations ranging from nurses and medical technicians, to parole officers, clerical workers, janitors, and maids. Whether this diversity is actually the hodgepodge conglomerate it appears to be is a question to which I will return later. But the union does face in spades the problem that most other unions seem to be developing as they try to compensate for declining membership by organizing outside their core jurisdiction: how to represent effectively such a diverse set of members.

The SEIU's solution to this problem is a set of internal conferences — the union has been divided internally into groups of health care workers, clerical workers, building services, and so on. The conferences serve two major purposes: they provide a way for people with common interests to come together to develop strategy, and they are a focal point for the organization of staff resources. But the conferences are also cross-connected by industry, by occupation, and by geographic area. Most members fall under at least two conference jurisdictions. This prevents the conferences from degenerating into a series of semi-autonomous organizations and the union from losing its organizational identity. A tendency to fragment along conference lines is further contained by local union structures, which are often orthogonal to the conference structure, and by a unified national staff that serves all the conferences at the same time.

Staff Management   The second organizational problem for which the SEIU has devised a solution is the supervision of local officers and business agents, to enforce work standards in membership service, contract enforcement, organizing goals, and the like. The solution is an internal planning process in which local unions work with the national and regional staff to develop performance goals and targets; these are then used as the bases for performance evaluations and are periodically updated and reviewed. The performance targets are debated and approved by the rank and file, which has a triple effect: (1) strengthening rank-and-file involvement; (2) enlisting the rank and file in the oversight process; and (3) legitimizing the oversight function exercised by the national union and whatever disciplinary measures need to be invoked.

The planning process also serves to highlight the tactical and strategic issues involved in organizing new members and in concession bargaining. In the process of setting goals, the leadership is forced to consider whether contract provisions are driving organized bargaining units out of business and what kind of organizing efforts would be required to alleviate competitive (or political) pressures that threaten the viability of those provisions. It was a lack of strategic considerations of this kind, as much as laziness or corruption, it will be recalled, that seemed to lie behind contract enforcement problems elsewhere in the Boston area. Organizing in the SEIU has been made the responsibility of local unions. It is not, as in many other organizations, a separate staff function. As a result, local unions are naturally led to consider the relationship between resources devoted to organizing and the problems of contract enforcement.

The planning process the SEIU has instituted involves considerable staff and leadership training. And another distinguishing characteristic of the SEIU had been its willingness to invest in this training. Ironically, and most notably, the union has contracted with the American Management Association to provide it.[5]

Consultants   The third organizational issue the SEIU has addressed is the excessive use of consultants. It makes much less use of consultants than other unions: over the past eight years, it has expanded its own national staff fivefold. And it has been willing to hire onto its own payroll the kinds of people — sometimes the very individuals — with whom other organizations have maintained an arms-length, contractual relationship. When outside consultants are used, they work *with* union staff and leadership in a way that serves as a training process, transferring the consultants' skills and expertise to the organization itself. This has been true of the SEIU in a whole range of activities, from corporate campaigns in organizing and bargaining to leadership training and education to legal services.[6]

Finally, the organization seems to be infused with a broad strategic perspective, which involves a sense of the interrelatedness of the different organizational components, of the union's different tactics, of the various functions its staff performs, and of various activities in which it is involved. Emblematic of the SEIU's difference in thinking is the fact, already noted, that organizing has been placed under the jurisdiction of local unions, thus ending the dichotomy between representatives and organizers.

The SEIU: why and how

Why did the SEIU develop an effective organizational response to problems that the rest of the labor movement seemed to ignore? Where did the ideas for these innovations come from? How were they introduced? Interviews within the SEIU that were designed to answer these questions constituted the third stage of the study.

The SEIU is an old AFL craft union. It was chartered in 1921 as a federation of building service worker locals in about 50 cities, and for many years it consisted basically of a series of powerful local baronies in New York, Chicago, and San Francisco, and several somewhat less powerful fiefdoms, including Boston and western Massachusetts. It has historically had a very small, weak national staff. As late as 1980, the international union's resources were largely directed at organizing, and there were fewer than 20 professionals on the international staff in Washington. The SEIU also has a tradition of considerable — in fact for much of its history, virtually complete — local autonomy. In many ways, it was a typical AFL craft union, with two exceptions. First, it did not represent the labor aristocracy; it represented what its old-timers characterized in interviews as the dregs of the labor force. That these workers were organized at all was due to the fact that they worked in an industry in which other AFL craft unions were strong and, in the beginning at least, in which workers were, like those in the more traditional crafts, ethnic Catholics. Second, the SEIU was more decentralized than most AFL unions. The AFL craft unions have historically been more decentralized than industrial unions: the pressures for coordination of policy came largely from the labor market rather than, as in industrial unions, the product market. In building services, these labor market pressures seem to have been even weaker than in the crafts, or possibly, in a basically unskilled labor market, the pressures simply could not be controlled through national policies. At any rate, if one were to calibrate the strength of the national union in the tradition of Perlman and Ulman, building service falls into a distinct class at one extreme of the spectrum along with other local industries and basically unskilled trades, such as hotel and restaurant work and laundry work. This class gives rise to substantial allegations of union corruption and mafia control, but it has also tolerated radical labor leaders and innovative organizational experiments that other unions would have stifled or expelled (Ulman 1955; Perlman 1928).

In the postwar period, the SEIU began to grow by expanding outside of building services. That expansion has been fairly steady and, in percentage terms, remarkably large throughout the postwar period, but it was particularly remarkable in the 1970s and 1980s, when the absolute numbers were also very large and the rest of the labor movement was in decline. The expansion involved movement into new industries: health care, state and local government, and clerical workers. It is unclear exactly why the union has been so successful in expanding in this way. The list of contributing factors is clear, but the relative weights of the items on that list are not. Nor is it obvious why the SEIU has been more successful than other national unions with similar resources and structural characteristics and, in the Boston area, comparable dynamism, such as the hotel and restaurant workers' union or even the laundry workers' union. The early expansion probably depended on the decisions of the national president and various local barons, and hence on their own personalities and particular histories: the local focus of the union paradoxically also gave the national president enormous power and autonomy in organizing and in national politics, so long as he did not interfere in local affairs. The union moved into the health care industry very early through the organization of building service workers at San Francisco General Hospital in 1935 and the city's private hospitals in 1941. The organization of hospital workers also put the union in the public sector. In the 1960s and 1970s, the public sector and health care turned out to be "growth" industries for unions. Public-sector organization was facilitated by new federal regulations and state and local laws giving public employees the right to organize and to bargain collectively. Nonprofit hospital workers were granted National Labor Relations Act protection in 1974, in no small measure as a result of SEIU's own lobbying efforts. Health care and state and local governments have been expanding industries since, employing a growing fraction of the labor force in most parts of the country.

The bulk of the SEIU's state and local membership came through

526

"affiliation," that is, through persuading autonomous workers' organizations to become union locals (Ichniowski and Zav 1990). This is an elaborate process, making claims on union resources comparable to those of organizing new workers, in terms of financial investments and skills. The competition is especially fierce with the AFSCME. But it was obviously facilitated by the trends in the 1970s toward collective bargaining rights for public employees and the pressure on associations to affiliate with *somebody*, to forestall raids by outsiders and (although this was probably a secondary motivation) to gain bargaining expertise. The SEIU was particularly attractive to these previously independent associations because of the autonomy it gave its locals. The SEIU also gained considerable advantage in its effort to attract associations of government workers through its prominent role in campaigns opposing cutbacks in government expenditures. This was especially important in California, where the union played a critical role in organizing opposition to the Briggs initiative in 1976. Eight years later, it affiliated the 80,000-member California State Employees Association. The SEIU role in the Briggs campaign had apparently been the personal decision of George Hardy, then the national president. The decision had been easy to rationalize in terms of the impact of the public expenditures on the welfare of the union's constituency. But the union had been in no sense compelled to expend its resources in this way, and it is hard to believe that anyone anticipated the impact this drive would have on an affiliation decision so far down the road.

Whatever initiated the process, the growth of membership had a cumulative effect, giving the SEIU additional resources to invest in any number of activities, at the very time, moreover, when other unions were forced by their declining dues base to cut back staff and expenditures. It was relatively easy, therefore, for a national president to decide to spend on both organizing and political activity, or on anything else. His funds were expanding and the local barons did not pay much attention to what he did with them: in fact, most local funds were expanding as well.

In 1980, on the eve of Ronald Reagan's Republican victory, John Sweeney became president of the SEIU. And it was Sweeney who transformed the organization, especially after 1984. He doubled the per capita tax, historically the lowest in the AFL-CIO, from $4 to $8 a month, and from 1984 to 1988 he increased the national staff from about 20 to more than 200. The new staff members were largely drawn from the ranks of the "new left" radicals who had gravitated toward the labor movement since the late 1960s. The SEIU had its pick of these "new" labor militants: few other unions were actually hiring in the 1980s, and in any case, most were afraid of the political orientation of the staff people that Sweeney hired. By common consensus within this political milieu, the SEIU picked the "best and brightest." The new SEIU staff joined a much smaller core, which Sweeney had hired between 1980 and 1984 or had inherited from his predecessor. This core group also included some new left radicals, as well as several key staffers who — although they might equally have characterized themselves as new left — had been raised as Roman Catholics and educated in parochial schools, and who therefore had a style and orientation much closer to that of the original core union leadership than did the bulk of the more recent hires, who had a secular orientation and many of whom were Jewish.

How much is this staff responsible for the organizational structure that distinguishes the union? The structure clearly has roots in the union's early history. The distrust of outside consultants, for example, might be traced to the president of the old-line Boston building service local who always hired his own staff lawyers because his was the poorest and weakest union in the area, and outside lawyers always sacrificed the union's interests for those of other clients. In 1940, the national SEIU president was jailed for embezzlement, and his successor instituted a series of reforms designed to prevent corruption; these reforms could be taken as the distant roots of the present internal management structure. Regional joint councils were established in 1942; industry conferences were created in 1974. But the organization now in place is not simply a product of the natural evolution of these earlier efforts. It is an integrated structure, self-consciously devised and instituted by Sweeney and his staff. The ideas that underlie it were drawn from the business management literature. The staff read widely in the business press and the more scholarly literature as well. Their single most important source was probably the *Harvard Business Review*. As noted, the union hired the American Management Association to do staff training.

Why did this particular staff have access to the business press, whereas staff members in other unions did not? The answer, at least in part, lies paradoxically in their left-wing ideological commitments. The career histories of the SEIU staff, and much of the secondary leadership as well, were varied. Some were essentially political activists, community organizers, or union staffers all along. Others, however, had gone into blue-collar manufacturing jobs, as school dropouts or after college graduation, often for political reasons, and had held lower-level leadership positions in other unions. Still others had wandered aimlessly into jobs organized by the SEIU: the health care and other helping professions probably attracted a disproportionate number of radically disposed people, but not all were initially politicized. A great many of these people come from middle-class backgrounds and from the upwardly mobile working class. Their brothers and sisters and college contemporaries went into the businesses toward which the business literature was actually directed — and from which the organizational innovations derived.

But the other factor that predisposed the left toward this literature was that it advocated in business exactly the kind of decentralization of power and responsibility to which the radicals were already committed ideologically. It did so, of course, for reasons of efficiency rather than democratic ideology. (The true democratic commitments of the union reforms can also be questioned, however. One of my colleagues, studying these reforms for a different purpose, was struck by how readily they lent themselves to control by an adroit leader).[7] But it nonetheless fit well with the ideology of the new left. It was also, incidently, the same literature that addressed the precise problem the SEIU faced at this juncture in its history: how to combine the advantages of the decentralized organizational structure it had inherited with the requirements of a permanent organization for strategic direction and control.

An organic organization, a moral alliance

The most notable feature of the SEIU is that despite its appearance as a conglomerate union par excellence, it is actually an organic organization; the interviews made it quite clear that the diverse membership and staff share a sense of common identity. The source of that identity is not their industry or occupation, but rather a moral vision. That vision comes out of the fact that the union, for all of its diversity, is really composed of two kinds of workers: workers in low-wage jobs (to use again the phrase of the president of an oldline janitors' local, "the dregs") and workers in the helping professions. The professionals in the latter positions have a commitment to the people they serve that goes beyond mere income or career, and the low-income workers, both actual and potential members, are an important part of the group to whom that commitment extends. For the low-income workers, the alliance with the helping professions not only legitimizes the claims that they make in their own behalf in the eyes of the public at large — who must foot the bill for the social services on which low-income communities are so dependent — but it also relieves much of the shame often associated with their positions.

Once one identifies this moral vision as being critical to the SEIU, then the process through which it emerged and is sustained within the organization becomes an additional characteristic of the organizational structure, quite possibly the key structural characteristic in the union's success. The process is not easy to identify, but it is illustrated by a debate over U.S. policy in Nicaragua, which occurred at the SEIU quadrennial convention in Toronto in 1988. The debate seemed initially to be irrelevant to the organizational focus of this study and, hence, to the line of questioning that was being pursued, but it nonetheless came up repeatedly in the interviews, and a good deal of unsolicited information about it was acquired. It was a traumatic event in the life of the organization, because it pitted the radical, new left segments of the staff and newer portions of the membership, who favored Nicaragua's Sandanista regime, against the old-line building service locals, the Catholic leadership, and the AFL-CIO, all of whom favored the U.S.-backed Contras.

The most moving, and in certain respects most telling, story was that of a business agent in one of the health care locals, who had just joined the union staff. He had come from a community organizing background and, as he himself reported, the SEIU job was particularly important to him because it had doubled his income, enabling him to continue working as an organizer and also support his new baby, resolving a conflict that had threatened his marriage. He told how he had sat listening to the convention debate about a resolution supporting the AFL-CIO position, growing increasingly agitated, until all of a sudden he found himself standing on his chair yelling, "No! No! No!" And as delegates around him began to jump on their chairs too, all he could think was, "Oh my God, there goes my job, my marriage . . .," and he began to cry. As it turns out, however, he still has his job. The issue was resolved — through floor debate, prolonged corridor discussions, and backroom negotiations — with a compromise solution that respected the moral integrity of the radically different positions represented within the union. What came through in the business agent's story, and in stories told by the other SEIU respondents as well, was that the Nicaraguan debate was a critical part of the process through which the union reaffirmed its identity as a moral organization and came to command members' allegiance to it as morally committed men and women.

The SEIU is rare, possibly unique, among AFL-CIO unions in that it allowed enough of the new left to emerge in leadership positions to have a real, divisive debate of this kind, in that it allowed the debate to actually take place, and in that the protagonists kept their jobs. Open political debate is an organizational innovation for American labor. It is very hard to find a place for such debate on the list of organizational reforms that foster union survival, particularly if one is trying to develop that list in parallel with reforms in U.S. business enterprises. And yet, in some sense, this debate is the most important organizational reform of all, because in the debate, and more precisely in the compromise through which it was resolved, the morality of the union was defined. It is that morality that gives the union its cohesion as an organization, the cohesion American unions once got first through their craft and then through their industrial structure, but have increasingly lost as their traditional jurisdictional lines have broken down. It is this organizational cohesion that American business gets through the common commitment of its dominant components to profit, and that seems to explain why U.S. business reforms generate a sense of direction and confidence while the reforms within the labor movement do not.

The Lessons of the SEIU

This study was conceived and executed in the context of two specific questions that are of pressing practical interest to the labor movement and, more broadly, to everyone concerned with the character of American life: What is responsible for the decline of the U.S. labor movement? and What structures and strategies on the part of unions as institutions could reverse, halt, or at least contain that decline? This study was avowedly exploratory and, not surprisingly, it does not yield general answers to these specific questions. It does, however, suggest two general conclusions.

The first phase of the study suggests that, whatever was initially responsible for the decline of union membership, that decline was probably exacerbated by the unions' own institutional response. National unions responded to the decline of membership (or potential members) in their original jurisdiction by picking up new bargaining units on an ad hoc basis in a range of industries and occupations outside their traditional area of expertise and so widely dispersed that they could not represent them effectively. They responded in an ad hoc and piecemeal fashion to economic pressures in the shops they represented, and the results were a series of uncentered, uncontrollable contract provisions that damaged their reputation among the rank and file, both actual and potential. The declining dues-paying base forced the cutback of staff, separating the organization from younger, more open and innovative people, and leaving a core of senior staff members, most of whom were wedded to old practices and not open to new approaches that might have been better adapted to the changed environment. They tried to compensate for internal staff weaknesses through consultants, but they frequently turned to consultants only in emergencies, seeking last-minute tactical support rather than long-term strategic advantage, and they dealt with the consultants at arm's length, in a way that had no lasting impact on the organization.

The second phase of the study, which focused on the SEIU, suggests that there were institutional remedies to these organizational failings. The conglomerate membership that emerged through ad hoc organizing responses could be effectively integrated into a single institutional structure through a matrix, or conference, structure. The improvised nature of the responses in organizing, and also in concession bargaining, contract enforcement, and more broadly in internal strategic thinking, could be overcome through internal planning and evaluation systems. Consultants could be deployed in ways that strengthen internal organizational structures, build new tactical capabilities, and contribute to strategic planning.

Neither of these conclusions really answers the fundamental questions. They do not answer these questions because, first, they do not indicate the degree to which the institutional failings of unions contributed to their decline, and second, they do not indicate whether the remedies for these failings, which were developed by the SEIU, are generalizable to other unions, or are specific to the unique circumstances of that particular organization. In a sense, this last question is the most central: if the SEIU is unique, then the other issues become an analytical morass, for it is the existence of the SEIU as an institutional alternative that makes it possible to identify the responses of other unions as *organizational failings* and to separate them from the environment in which they occurred. In other words, without the analytical purchase that the SEIU provides, we would never be able to distinguish between environmental pressures and organizational response as separate factors in labor's current difficulties.

What, then, is the lesson of the SEIU? The most direct reading of this case is that the SEIU provides a series of specific managerial remedies to the particular problems identified in the study, remedies by which other unions — or the AFL-CIO — could also overcome organizational weaknesses. This, however, would seem to be the wrong lesson to draw from this study, because the most basic problem of unions as organizations is that they have lost — or are in the process of losing — their cohesiveness as organizations. They are degenerating into a set of separate constituencies that at best have no organic relationship to each other and, in the very worst cases of plant-level labor-management cooperation, are directly competitive for work in the same company. The SEIU's managerial reforms speak to this problem, but the SEIU also has an organic identity, one that preceded the reforms and was reinforced in the period in which the reforms were instituted. That identity is probably a more important factor in the union's success than the reforms themselves and may, in fact, be a critical prerequisite for the reform process.

If this is true, then the nature of the organization's identity and the process through which it was created, not the managerial reforms, are the source of the general lessons to which labor ought to look. The identity of the SEIU, as noted earlier, grew out of linking together a group of low-income, low-status workers with workers in the helping professions, who view the low-income workers as part of the larger underprivileged and disadvantaged class that constitutes their clientele. The staff of the union has a professional identity that essentially coincides with the helping professions and thus, although the staff does not come directly out of the rank and file, it is so much like them that it reinforces the organic nature of the organization.[8]

The principle that gives the SEIU unity and cohesiveness is very difficult to define or name. Within the union, it seems to be closely connected to a kind of moral and political vision and to have grown out of debates and discussions about that vision, such as the debate about U.S. policy in Nicaragua, which otherwise seems very remote from the union's real concerns. But the underlying principles that give the organization a core identity are also closely connected to the principle of the welfare state.

The SEIU is not connected to the welfare state as an institution, but to the welfare state as an ideology that locates the ultimate responsibility for human welfare in the nation-state, as opposed to other ideologies that locate that responsibility in the family, the tribe, the ethnic or religious community, the workings of the marketplace, or in the individual him- or herself. In an ideology of human welfare, the state is not held directly responsible for the provision of any particular service or for the maintenance of a defined standard. Rather, the state is the focal point of a process through which the standards of welfare are debated and defined, and it orchestrates the ensemble of institutions through which the services, once defined, are maintained. Virtually all of the political controversy that seems to call into question the welfare state is really about the standards and "delivery systems" (public, private, charity, and the like), and it presupposes an acceptance of the idea that there are *some* standards and *some* institutions, staffed by professionals, appropriate for meeting them. In this sense, the vision or ideology that gives the SEIU its coherence corresponds to something that is generally recognized by the public at large, as well. This ideology of the welfare state can, thus, be said to define the SEIU's jurisdiction in much the same way that industries and crafts defined the jurisdictions of and gave coherence to other national unions earlier in the postwar period. It might also be noted that the welfare state as an institution is even more amorphous than the SEIU, but everyone recognizes its existence nonetheless. And the debates about standards and delivery systems in the politics of the welfare state are in some ways like the Nicaraguan debate.

This interpretation of the SEIU's success yields one general lesson: it highlights the limitations of the categories through which American labor has traditionally understood itself and through which it has been understood and evaluated by sympathetic outsiders in the academy. Two categories in particular are called into question. One is the dichotomy between craft and industrial unions, as it is used to define union jurisdictions and to understand organizational identity. The second is the dichotomy between business and ideological unionism (Piore 1991). The SEIU is a union whose ability to function effectively as a business union depends on a prior set of ideological commitments, and these commitments define a jurisdiction and identity that respects virtually no industrial or craft lines.

The SEIU's particular ideology, however, or even the notion of an "ideological jurisdiction," would seem to have little general relevance for American trade unions. A few other national unions may be able to compete with the SEIU for the *same* jurisdiction, or to carve out a piece of the adjacent territory in the ideological space of the welfare state. As noted, the AFSCME is already a competitor in certain areas, and other unions of low-income workers would seem to have — or at least to have had — that potential (Wial 1991). But the SEIU ideology would not seem to have much relevance for the United Auto Workers, for example, or the steel workers.

What may be more relevant for the rest of the labor movement is the process through which the union's organic identity emerged. That process was one that seemed to depend heavily on the decentralized structure of the union, the enormous autonomy of both local and, paradoxically, national initiatives, and the openness of internal discussion and debate. Insofar as the SEIU has lessons for organizational reform in other unions, these are the lessons that seem most salient.

But the directions in which such debate and experimentation are likely to take the rest of the labor movement will probably be very different from that which the SEIU has taken. The reasons for thinking so emerge not from this particular study, but from other parts of the larger project on the institutional transformation of the American economy, of which this study is a part. And I turn to that issue in the final section of this chapter.

Unions as Socioeconomic Mediators

To think constructively about trade union strategy, one needs to begin by reexamining the nature of trade unions, as institutions in contemporary society. The postwar literature on this subject is dominated by a debate about whether trade unions are economic institutions or political ones (Dunlop 1950; Ross 1948). But unions may also be viewed in a third and very different way, as mediating between the economic and the social structures. They are, to be sure, not the only institution that does this, and they are, on the whole, distinguished from other institutions by the fact that they are organized in the workplace and derive much of their power from the *economic* leverage they can exert there. But, this view implies, they cannot be reduced to an economic institution and, indeed, their existence is predicated on some kind of disjuncture, actual or potential, between the economy and the society in which it resides. The transformative visions, which seem so central to labor history, are understood in this view as arising from the attempt of unions to define a vision of the social structure that they would like the economy to respect and sustain. Often, this vision is simply a reflection of some previous structures that are breaking down as the economy evolves and that become a norm or ideal people would like to restore (Piore 1989).

The position of labor in the earlier postwar period was based on the then prevailing — and, in retrospect, rather particular — relationship between the economic and social realms. That relationship was one in which the household was represented in the labor market by a single dominant (generally male) wage earner, from whom it derived the bulk of its support. Moreover, the dominant earner, during that period in his life when he performed that role, was attached to a particular industry or craft, and very often to a single employer as well. (Other household members worked, to be sure, but their income was viewed as supplementary, and tended to be targeted for specific purposes.) Unions representing these single wage earners were able to focus their concerns on the social structure of the workplace itself and on increasing worker income. They had no direct interest in social structures outside of work, because on the whole the most effective thing they could do to promote any vision of that dimension of social life was to raise the income of the workers who supported it. In point of fact, unions had a rather limited vision of what they could do to affect the social structure of the workplace without compromising their ability to generate the income to sustain the household structures outside it. But that vision was sufficiently different from management's to make unions an important autonomous force in shaping the productive, workplace structures.

Most knowledgeable observers seem to agree on the recent fundamental changes in work and work experience, and these changes are fairly destructive of the socioeconomic structure by which American unions defined themselves in the earlier postwar period. There are three critical items on the list of changes. First, a part of the traditionally unionized work force is being drawn into close collaboration with management in the production process, in a way that abridges the traditional distinctions between labor and management and is inconsistent with the adversarial and legalistic structures through which unions exerted control over the social structure of the workplace in the past. Second, managers assert and most observers seem to accept that workers will typically have to move more frequently among jobs and among enterprises in the future than they have in the past, and that identifying one's work life with a single employer or even with a single industry or occupation will no longer be possible. Third, household income is no longer dominated by the earnings of a single individual but is increasingly composed of a series of components contributed by several earners. A fourth change, which is occurring in the social structure and is not generally recognized in labor market discussions, but which seems important for unions as just defined, is the emergence of social groups who make claims on income through the political process but who have no role as a group in the productive structure. The largest of groups is the aged, but there are also groups of those who have disabilities, and so-called lifestyle groups, such as gays and lesbians (Piore 1991; Piore 1989).

In earlier work, Charles Sabel and I traced the postwar union structure to a historic commitment to mass production as a vehicle for achieving technological progress and economic growth, and associated the breakdown of that structure with the emergence of flexible specialization as an alternative technological trajectory (Piore and Sable 1984). We likened flexible specialization to traditional craft production, and it is clear that many employers think of the reorganization of work in these terms. To some employers, labor-management collaboration and the demise of industry-, occupation-, or employer-specific careers are two distinct trends. The former is an outgrowth of those developments making for more and more craftlike production processes, and will actually lead to a greater commitment on the part of the firm to its work force. But the remainder of the work force — those without the core, craftlike skills — will have a very different relation to the firm; they will supplement the core workers, providing peripheral skills and easing business operations and the burden of the fixed cost of long-term commitments in an unstable, uncertain business environment.

It would seem that such developments would almost inevitably produce a bifurcated labor force with two totally different relationships to work, requiring at least two distinct kinds of union representation. The core skilled workers might be able to command incomes high enough to make them the sole support of a household unit, and in that sense they would allow the union to deal with the social structure outside the workplace in the traditional way. But the nature of social control within the workplace would definitely have to change to permit the kind of labor-management collaboration that management envisions. Indeed, it is unclear just how much space such a structure would leave for an independent unionlike institution. In any case, the identification of workers with management will be so strong as to create seemingly insurmountable barriers to cohesiveness in a union linking workers in competing profit centers within a single company, let alone across companies within an industry.

The peripheral workers will, of course, not be bound to management in the same way and will have ample need for the kind of protection a union could provide. But their major concern will be for structures that facilitate movement across enterprises and traditional industry and occupational lines, and they are likely to be attached to multiple-earner households with specific problems that realistic increases in the income of any one member are unlikely to solve. There will be plenty of space for an institution to mediate between the economic and social structure, but at least defined in this way, simply in opposition to craftlike workers, it is very hard to see how such an organization could ever achieve a cohesive identity or an organic program.

In reality, however, the clear dichotomy in this scenario is not emerging, and the prevailing trends involve enormous tensions and contradictions, which management has yet to recognize, let alone attempt to resolve. One basic problem is that many of the peripheral workers that the new "flexible" companies need to complement their core workers are also skilled, and the operative distinction between them has less to do with skill than with what the companies call their "core competency."

But there is also a second, possibly more fundamental problem: the attempt to strip the committed labor force back to a core competency group is proving in many ways to be like peeling an onion. Companies find themselves producing a range of products whose evolution involves a mix of skills and professional disciplines that is in perpetual and unpredictable flux. Companies are becoming more and more like general contractors: the environmental pressures are pushing them toward externalizing everything. Thus, long-term commitment on the part of the company is proving much more difficult to achieve than the core-periphery model envisages, although the need for labor-management collaboration, which that commitment was supposed to secure, is no less pressing.

The growth in the number of multiple-earner households creates still a third source of tension. Although undoubtedly hastened by the declining relative income of some segments of the labor force, it is a general phenomenon and is affecting even families in which one member is capable of supporting the unit. The multiplication of household earners increasingly constrains the geographic mobility of any one of its members, at the very moment when waning employer commitment requires much greater worker mobility. Thus, while unions may be frozen out of any particular workplace by increasing labor-management collaboration, there appear to be increasing ten- ϽΩ1ΩΩ, in both social and economic structures, associated with move- .nent among employers — and here there is ample room for trade unions to play a role. Moreover, the fact that even workers who collaborate with managers are likely to move in their work life across competing firms provides an opening for an institution that will structure the competition so as to facilitate this movement. (see Piore 1981; Osterman 1988; Kochan, Katz, and McKersie 1986).

This diagnosis does not speak directly to the question of organizational identity and cohesiveness that the SEIU experience has pushed to the fore. But here, too, existing trends suggest where the answers are likely to lie. First, although the concept that a well-defined set of skills underlies the terminology of core competency, crafts, or professions is proving elusive in reality, and although the technology that produces those skills is evolving in ways that seem completely random, the evolution is not in fact so drastic, and it is possible, at least in retrospect, to identify patterns. Firms, like construction contractors, do seem to draw on a definable and delimited range of skills and to do so repeatedly over time, although they cannot say precisely when a given skill will be needed. Thus, one could define groups of people who share a common "territory" within the labor market and in the productive process, especially if one were prepared to accept the kind of unorthodox approach that defines the jurisdiction of the SEIU.[9]

Second, the process of organizing the economy to address the twin problems of enabling producers to get the human resources they need and solving workers' need for reasonable employment continuity would be facilitated by geographic concentration. Since geographic concentration would also solve the problems created by the multiple-earner household, one must suspect that geography will also prove an increasingly important source of organizational identity and cohesion. Indeed, a geographic identity would be capable of merging the issues of multiemployer careers and multiple-earner households into a single cohesive organization. And one might expect such an organizational identity to emerge if one opened debate and decentralized organizational initiatives in a way that encouraged existing members to talk about the tensions they were experiencing in their work and family lives.

Author's Note

This chapter draws heavily on discussions and debates with James Shoch, who was the research assistant for the project, as well as with other faculty members and students at MIT. It was supported by the Ford Foundation and by the International Labor Organization. Without the cooperation of the trade union respondents it would not have been possible. In focusing on the current problems of trade unions, the chapter fails to convey the dedication and moral integrity of these people, which is in no sense limited to the more effective administrators among them and which distinguishes them fundamentally from the other actors in the American economy whom I have interviewed as part of the larger research project of which this is a part.

Notes

1. Nonetheless, a general bias seems to infuse the literature, carried more by the tone than the substance, that the environment cannot alone explain labor's decline; that weaknesses of leadership, organizational strategy, and structure must bear at least some of the blame. (See, for example, Farber 1990; Strauss, Gallagher, and Fiorito 1991.)
2. There is a relatively limited body of literature on union management that is germane here. See, for example, Dunlop 1990; Clark and Gray 1991; Fiorito, Gramm, and Hendricks 1991.

3. But see Stratton and Brown 1989.
4. The historical exception has been the Teamsters, but their organizational and bargaining power comes from their capacity to boycott recalcitrant establishments, and no other union can do this as effectively.
5. For a broader and somewhat different view of leadership development in the SEIU, see Easton 1992.
6. The SEIU does use an outside consultant for public relations and publicity, but apparently because that individual, for personal reasons, refuses to join the staff.
7. Personal communication from Ray Freedman, Harvard Business School.
8. For parallel arguments, see Easton 1992 and Wial 1992.
9. Similar proposals for geographic unions can be found in Heckscher 1988 and in Wial 1992. Interestingly, Wial seems to be generalizing the SEIU experience.

References

Clark, Paul F., and Lois S. Gray. 1991. "Union Administration," in George Strauss, Daniel Gallagher, and Jack Fiorito (eds.), *The State of the Unions.* Madison, Wis.: Industrial Relations Research Association. pp. 175–200.

Dunlop, John T. 1990. *The Management of Labor Unions: Decision Making with Historical Constraints.* Lexington, Mass.: D. C. Heath.

———. 1950. *Wage Determination under Trade Unions,* New York: A. M. Kelley.

Dunlop, John T., and Derek C. Bok. 1970. *Labor and the American Community.* New York: Simon and Schuster.

Easton, Susan C. 1992. *Union Leadership Development in the 1990's and Beyond: A Report with Recommendations.* Paper prepared for the Seminar on Industrial Relations, MIT Sloan School of Management, May 11.

Estey, Marten. 1981. *The Unions: Structure, Development, Management.* New York: Harcourt Brace Jovanovich.

Farber, Henry. 1990. "The Decline of Unionization in the United States: What Can be Learned from Recent Experience?" *Journal of Labor Economics* 8, no. 1 (January).

Fiorito, Jack, Cynthia L. Gramm, and Wallace E. Hendricks. 1991. "Union Structural Choices," in Strauss et al., *The State of the Unions,* 103–138.

Heckscher, Charles C. 1988. *The New Unionism: Employee Involvement in the Changing Corporation.* New York: Basic Books.

Ichniowski, Casey, and Jeffrey Zax. 1990. "Today's Associations, Tomorrow's Unions," *Industrial and Labor Relations Review* 43, no. 2 (January): 191–208.

Jarley, Paul, and Jack Fiorito. 1990. "Associate Membership: Unions or Consumerism," *Industrial and Labor Relations Review* 43, no. 2 (January): 209–224.

Kochan, Thomas, Harry Katz, and Robert McKersie. 1986. *The Transformation of American Industrial Relations*. New York: Basic Books.

Osterman, Paul. 1988. *Employment Futures*. New York: Oxford University Press.

Perlman, Selig. 1928. *A Theory of the Labor Movement*. New York: Macmillan.

Perry, Charles. 1987. *Union Corporate Campaigns*. Philadelphia: Industrial Research Unit, Wharton School, University of Pennsylvania.

Piore, Michael J. 1982. "Can the American Labor Movement Survive Re-Gomperization?" in Industrial Relations Research Association, *Proceedings of the Thirty-Fifth Annual Meeting*. Madison, Wis.: Industrial Relations Research Association.

――――. 1986. "The Decline of Mass Production and Union Survival in the USA," *Industrial Relations Journal* 17, no. 3.

――――. 1989. *Post-Reaganomics: The Resurgence of the Social Sphere in Economic and Political Life?* (Part I), Center for International Studies Working Paper, MIT, January.

――――. 1991a. "Corporate Reform in American Manufacturing and the Challenge to Economic Theory," in *Collected Essays on Management of the 1990's*. New York: Oxford University Press.

――――. 1991b. "The Future of Unions," in Strauss et al., *The State of the Unions*, 387–410.

Piore, Michael J., and Charles Sabel. 1984. *The Second Industrial Divide: Possibilities for Prosperity*. New York: Basic Books.

Ross, Arthur M. 1948. *Trade Union Wage Policy*. Berkeley, Calif.: University of California Press.

Stratton, Kay, and Robert Brown. 1989. "Strategic Planning in U.S. Labor Unions," in Industrial Relations Research Association, *Proceedings of the Forty-First Annual Meeting*. Madison, Wis.: Industrial Relations Research Association.

Strauss, George, Daniel Gallagher, and Jack Fiorito (eds.). 1991. *The State of the Unions*. Madison, Wis.: Industrial Relations Research Association.

Ulman, Lloyd. 1955. *The Rise of the National Union*. Cambridge, Mass.: Harvard University Press.

Wial, Howard. 1992. *The Emerging Organizational Structure of Unions in Low Wage Services*. Unpublished paper, Yale University Law School, March.

VI

Labor Economics in a Changing World

20

Productivity: Data and Determinants

■——————————————■
Edward F. Denison

Rising productivity has been a main cause of the enormous rise in the total national income of modern nations since the industrial revolution and the principal cause of dramatically higher real wages and living standards. From World War II to 1973 an exceptionally rapid increase in productivity made possible a parallel acceleration of the rise in real wages. After 1973 a sudden slowdown in the rate of productivity increase was matched, inevitably, by a cessation of large increases in real wages.

Information about productivity is valuable not only in the study of economic growth, living standards, and real wages but also of inflation, international competition, and many other topics. Projections of future productivity change are central to the budgetary planning of governments.

The Concepts, the Data, and the Record

Productivity is the ratio of output to one or more of the inputs used in producing that output. The most frequently used measure of productivity change in the United States is the series for output per hour in business that the U.S. Labor Department's Bureau of Labor Statistics (BLS) publishes annually and quarterly.

BLS also publishes output-per-hour series that are limited, respectively, to nonfarm business, nonfinancial corporations, and manufacturing. In addition, BLS publishes annual series for output per hour, output per unit of capital (including land), and multifactor productivity in private business, nonfarm business, and manufacturing. Multifactor productivity is obtained by dividing an index of output by a weighted average of indexes of the man-hours, capital, and land used in producing that output; the weights are the earnings of these factors of production. Private business differs from business in that it excludes government enterprises such as the U.S. Postal Service.

In all of these BLS series the numerator in the productivity calculation, output, is measured by the gross domestic product (GDP) valued in constant prices (presently, prices prevailing in 1987) that originates in the sector analyzed. GDP originating in a sector is a value-added series that measures the value of the sector's gross output minus the value of its current-account purchases of goods and services from other sectors.[1] The GDP series are prepared by the U.S. Department of Commerce's Bureau of Economic Analysis (BEA), the man-hours series by the BLS, and the series for capital input by the BLS, which uses, mainly, BEA data.

Table 20.1 shows annual growth rates of these series during two time periods: 1948 to 1973 and 1973 to 1990.[2] The former is a period in which productivity grew much faster than it had in earlier periods of comparable length. Growth after 1973 was slow — much slower, even, than before 1948. Various privately estimated series for earlier periods are available. One linked series, charted by the President's Council of Economic Advisors (*Economic Report of the President, February 1992*, p. 91), shows growth rates of private business sector GDP per hour that approximated 2 percent in 1889 to 1948, 3 percent in 1948 to 1973, and 1 percent in 1973 to 1990.

Even the most comprehensive of the productivity series described does not cover the whole economy. As defined by the BLS, the business sector excludes the services provided by employees of government (except government enterprises), nonprofit organizations (except nonprofit organizations serving business), and household workers, all of which are included in the GDP. These groups are omitted because it is impractical to measure their productivity in the same way productivity is measured in business; instead their GDP is measured as if labor productivity doesn't change (except as a result of changes in employment composition). The BLS also excludes from business the rental value of owner-occupied homes, because it has no employment counterpart. For some analyses, nevertheless, it is appropriate to compute the productivity changes that the estimates imply for the whole domestic economy. This yields growth rates for 1948 to 1973 that are lower by 0.2 or 0.3 percentage points than those

Table 20.1. Growth rates of various measures of productivity in the
United States, 1948–1973 and 1973–1990 (percent per year)

Concept and scope	1948–1973	1973–1990
Output per hour		
Business[a]	3.0	0.8
Nonfarm business[a]	2.5	0.6
Manufacturing	2.9	2.0
Nonfinancial corporations	2.4[b]	0.9
Output per unit of capital		
Private business	−0.2	−1.0
Private nonfarm business	−0.3	−1.3
Manufacturing	−0.1	−0.8
Multifactor productivity		
Private business	2.0	0.3
Private nonfarm business	1.6	0.1
Manufacturing	2.1	1.3

Source: U.S. Bureau of Labor Statistics, "Multifactor Productivity Measures, 1990,"
August 29, 1991; "Productivity and Costs," March 10, 1992, and other BLS releases
and printouts, except that 1973–1990 rates have been reduced where necessary to
allow for revision and rebasing of U.S. Bureau of Economic Analysis estimates for
output.
a. Estimates for private business and private nonfarm business are the same as these.
b. Rate for 1958–1973.

for business; in other periods differences are smaller. Series that
measure output per person employed, which has usually grown less
than output per hour because average hours have declined, are also
often used and are available from the BLS.

Table 20.2 compares U.S. rates of growth of GDP per person employed in the whole domestic economy with rates in other advanced
countries during the 1950 to 1973 and 1973 to 1990 periods, based on
unofficial BLS compilations of series provided by national statistical
agencies.[3] Two points stand out. First, both before and after 1973 this
growth rate was lower in the United States than in any other country
shown. Most of these countries grew *much* faster than the United
States. Second, in every country shown, the growth rate dropped
sharply between 1950 to 1973 and 1973 to 1990. (Pre-1973 data are
not shown for South Korea because they are available only since
1963, but South Korea is clearly an exception to the usual pattern.)
The fall to a lower growth rate typically was abrupt, starting with the
yearly change from 1973 to 1974. At about the same time growth
rates also fell sharply in many countries not shown in the table,
including the Soviet Union and the socialist countries of Eastern

Europe. Measured in percentage points the decline was smaller in the United States than in most other countries; only the United Kingdom, Canada, and Norway were exceptions. Japan and Italy, with the highest 1950 to 1973 rates, experienced the biggest declines. The average decline (unweighted) of 2.4 percentage points compares with 1.5 points in the United States. However, the average percentage decline, 58 percent, and the percentage declines in all other countries except the Netherlands were smaller than the 75 percent decline in the United States.

A growth rate lower than other industrial countries enjoyed since 1950 has not dislodged the United States from its position as the industrial nation with the highest GDP per person employed. (Only certain oil-rich Mideast countries rank higher.) The second column of figures in Table 20.3 compares 1990 levels of GDP per person employed in the countries covered by Table 20.2. GDP per person employed was highest in the United States, with Canada second,

Table 20.2. Real gross domestic product per employed person: growth rates in 14 countries, 1950–1973, and 1973–1990 and decline

| Country | Growth rate (percent per year) | | Decline | |
	1950–1973	1973–1990	In percentage points	In percent
United States	2.0	0.5	1.5	75
Canada	2.5	1.1	1.4	56
Japan	7.5	2.9	4.6	61
South Korea	NA	5.5	NA	NA
Austria	4.8	2.1	2.7	56
Belgium	3.7	2.1	1.6	43
Denmark	3.5[a]	1.3	2.2	63
France	4.6	2.3	2.3	50
Germany (West)	4.8	1.8	3.0	62
Italy	5.7	2.2	3.5	61
Netherlands	3.8	0.8	3.0	79
Norway	3.5	2.2	1.3	37
Sweden	3.4[b]	1.0	2.4	71
United Kingdom	2.6	1.4	1.2	46

Source: U.S. Bureau of Labor Statistics, "Comparative Real Gross Domestic Product, Real GDP per Capita, and Real GDP per Employed Person, Fourteen Countries, 1950–1990," July 1991 and January 1992.

Note: NA = not available.

a. 1955–1973.

b. 1960–1973.

France third at 89 percent of the U.S. level, and other West European countries ranging downward from there. GDP per person employed in Japan, despite that country's high postwar growth rate, was still only 76 percent of the U.S. level and also below many other Western countries. With its exceptionally long working hours, Japan lies still lower in a comparison of output per hour. All the countries were closer to the United States in 1990 than in 1960.

The third and fourth columns of Table 20.3 compare GDP per capita in the same countries. Percentages of the population that are of working age, labor force participation rates, and unemployment rates all vary widely among countries, so there is only a very loose correspondence between rankings by output per person employed and output per capita. The former measure provides the better starting point for productivity analysis, the latter for welfare comparisons, though neither is adequate by itself. It is notable that in 1990

Table 20.3. Real gross domestic product per employed person and per capita in 14 countries: comparative levels based on purchasing-power-parity exchange rates (United States = 100)

Country	Real GDP per employed person		Real GDP per capita		Increase in position in percentage points	
	1960	1990	1960	1990	Per employed person	Per capita
United States	100.0	100.0	100.0	100.0	—	—
Canada	77.8	92.3	71.0	93.2	14.5	23.2
Japan	23.8	76.3	29.4	80.1	52.5	50.7
South Korea	NA	43.0	9.6	37.9	—	28.3
Austria	38.7	73.9	46.4	67.1	35.2	20.7
Belgium	49.9	88.1	50.1	69.8	38.2	19.7
Denmark	52.3	68.1	61.3	71.8	15.8	10.5
France	47.0	89.1	53.7	73.2	42.1	19.5
Germany (West)	48.7	78.6	60.7	74.0	29.9	13.3
Italy	41.5	87.8	44.7	68.6	46.3	23.9
Netherlands	56.7	77.1	60.1	68.3	20.4	8.2
Norway	49.8	79.8	56.0	80.7	30.0	24.7
Sweden	51.7	67.2	66.1	74.8	15.5	8.7
United Kingdom	53.9	70.7	65.7	69.3	16.8	3.6
U.S. GDP in 1990 dollars	$31,842	$45,165	$12,030	$21,571	—	—

Source: U.S. Bureau of Labor Statistics, "Comparative Real Gross Domestic Product, Real GDP per Capita, and Real GDP per Employed Person, Fourteen Countries, 1960–1990," January 1992.

Note: NA = Not available.

Japan ranked above all European countries except Norway in GDP per capita, and that West Germany, which was well below France in GDP per person employed in 1990, was slightly higher in GDP per capita.

Comparison of the 1960 and 1990 columns in Table 20.3 shows that the lower growth rate of the United States has greatly narrowed the U.S. advantage over all the other countries in both GDP per person employed and GDP per capita, that the relative positions of other countries among themselves have changed greatly, and that positions of countries and changes in position with respect to GDP per person employed differ substantially from those with respect to GDP per capita. In the United States itself the ratio of employment to population rose sharply, and this is why all the other countries except Canada improved more, relative to the United States, in GDP per person employed than in GDP per capita. But ratios of employment to population were also changing substantially, and differently, in other countries.

International comparisons of GDP are based on the ratio of the quantity of goods and services of every type that are produced in one country to the quantity produced in another country, which has the effect of converting GDP estimates valued in national currencies to a common basis by use of purchasing power parities.[4] The results are sensitive to the structure of price weights applied to combine the various goods and services, so no one set of estimates can be considered unambiguously accurate.[5]

Nevertheless, equating GDP estimates valued in national currencies by purchasing power parities is far more satisfactory than conversion by exchange rates. The weighting problem in international comparisons is analogous to that encountered in constructing time series for a single country: the growth rates obtained depend on the year — and that year's prices — in which constant-dollar GDP is evaluated. Both geographic and temporal comparisons are affected by measurement errors as well as by the weights selected, so they are, of course, imprecise.

Time series measuring changes in output per hour in industry divisions and in industries within business should be mentioned. The BLS has available for all industry divisions, but does not publish, time series that are conceptually comparable to that for manufacturing, for which growth rates are shown in Table 20.1. Data by industry division are less reliable than those for business as a whole, partly because price series for intermediate products, required to allocate GDP among industry divisions, are incomplete and often unreliable.

For many detailed industries the BLS publishes series for output per hour in which output is measured not by the GDP, the value added in an industry, but by the gross output of an industry, which includes the value of purchases from other industries. The two procedures yield the same productivity index only if the ratio of value-added to gross output, both valued in constant prices, does not change.

Numerous productivity series have been prepared by domestic and foreign government agencies besides the BLS, by international agencies, and by private scholars. Those for the United States include series for time periods before BLS estimates begin, series for special segments of the economy, and series using different definitions of productivity.

My own analyses of the sources of changes in output and productivity use as an output measure real national income (NI), a measure of net product, in preference to real GDP. There are three differences. First, NI is measured after deduction of capital consumption. It is more desirable to maximize net product, the value of private and public consumption and net additions to the capital stock, than gross product, which includes the value of gross instead of net additions to the capital stock and, consequently, contains duplication. Second, national income measures the output attributable to labor and property resources provided by U.S. residents, whereas GDP measures the output of resources geographically located in the United States. The difference equals the net inflow of income from abroad, which consists mainly of property income. This difference does not affect output or productivity in the domestic sectors. Third, to obtain total real NI, components of consumption and investment are weighted by their base-year factor costs rather than their base-year market prices. Factor-cost weighting is conceptually preferable for productivity measurement, but the choice usually makes little difference in practice.

The Sources of Productivity Change

It is easy to enumerate the determinants of output per person employed that were responsible for its past increases, that will determine its future course, and that would need to be altered if a nation undertook to change that course. They include the quality of labor and the hours worked; the capital and land available; the state of knowledge concerning methods of producing at low cost; the efficiency with which resources are allocated among uses; the size of markets; the quality of management; and so on. But a discussion must be quantitative if it is not to be restricted to platitudes. Studies providing quantitative estimates are known as sources-of-growth analyses, or growth accounting. Research in this area has been conducted by individual scholars and has not been institutionalized, so estimates of the sources of growth are available only irregularly. The discussion of U.S. growth that follows relies on my own estimates for the period from 1929 to 1982. The "nonresidential business" sector analyzed differs from "business" in the BLS estimates in that the services of tenant-occupied as well as owner-occupied homes are omitted. Growth experience in other countries during various slices of time has been analyzed by similar methods.

It is essential to distinguish between changes in actual and potential national income. Potential NI, valued in 1972 prices in any year, is defined here as the value that NI in 1972 prices would have taken if (1) unemployment had equaled 4 percent of the civilian labor force 16 years of age and older; (2) the intensity of utilization of resources had been at the same rate every year, namely the rate which, on the average, would be associated with a 4 percent unemployment rate; and (3) other conditions had been those that actually prevailed in that year. Potential employment is the number of workers who would have been employed under the same conditions. Growth rates of potential NI and employment would be little different if 3, 5, or 6 percent, instead of 4 percent, were specified as the unemployment rate. In 1973 to 1982 (and subsequently) the gaps between actual and potential output and productivity were affected by more than the business cycle. Unemployment was above 4 percent even at business cycle peaks. Unemployment over the whole business cycle averaged higher rates than in earlier postwar cycles.

For perspective, Table 20.4 shows — for both the whole economy and nonresidential business — growth rates of NI, NI per person potentially employed, NI per hour, and NI per unit of factor input on potential and actual bases. The growth rates for 1948 to 1973 cover the period of fast productivity growth. The 1929 to 1948 rates cover the last two decades of the earlier long period of medium growth, decades that were unusual because they were dominated by the Great Depression and World War II. The 1973 to 1982 rates cover the first decade of the still-continuing period of very slow productivity growth. The terminal year was one of deep recession. All 24 of the series for potential and actual productivity, as well as the 2 for total actual NI, grew most rapidly in 1948 to 1973, much less rapidly in

1929 to 1948, and very slowly (if at all) in 1973 to 1982. Because the potential labor force increased by an extraordinary amount in the 1973 to 1982 period, total potential NI in the whole economy and in business grew at a slightly higher rate in 1973 to 1982 than in 1929 to 1948. Labor force growth has subsequently slackened.

A brief explanation of NI per unit of factor input is appropriate here. Input in the nonresidential business sector is a weighted average of labor, capital, and land used in production, or available for use in production in the case of the series calculated on a potential basis. Inputs are weighted by their estimated marginal products. Labor input reflects changes in characteristics of labor (such as education or experience) that affect productivity. It is measured by weighting groups of workers with different characteristics by their earnings, on the reasonable presumption that, for broad groups of employed persons, earnings are proportional to marginal products. Similarly, to measure capital input different types of capital goods and inventories are weighted by their values, on the presumption that their marginal products (net of depreciation) are proportional to values. In principle

Table 20.4. Growth rates of potential and actual national income and productivity measures, selected periods (percent per year)

Item	1929–1982	1929–1948	1948–1973	1973–1982
Whole economy				
Total potential national income	3.20	2.57	3.89	2.61
Per person potentially employed	1.55	1.24	2.26	0.23
Per potential hour	2.19	2.09	2.79	0.79
Per unit of potential input	1.17	1.01	1.65	0.08
Total actual national income	2.92	2.54	3.70	1.55
Per person employed	1.48	1.26	2.16	0.06
Per hour	2.16	2.11	2.70	0.75
Per unit of input	1.02	1.01	1.53	−0.27
Nonresidential business				
Total potential national income	3.14	2.48	3.82	2.66
Per person potentially employed	1.68	1.31	2.59	0.00
Per potential hour	2.30	2.09	3.08	0.63
Per unit of potential input	1.47	1.23	2.14	0.09
Total actual national income	2.77	2.44	3.58	1.26
Per person employed	1.58	1.33	2.45	−0.26
Per hour	2.24	2.11	2.96	0.51
Per unit of input	1.31	1.25	1.98	−0.37

Source: Edward F. Denison, *Trends in American Economic Growth, 1929–1982* (Washington, D.C.: Brookings Institution, 1985), pp. 84, 107, 108, 110, 111, 112, 114.

the procedure for land is the same, but given land's small weight, land has not changed enough to make weighting of plots necessary. Finally, to obtain indexes of total factor input in nonresidential business, the indexes for labor, nonresidential structures and equipment, inventories, and land are weighted by their total earnings to secure an index of total factor input. These weights are appropriate because the total earnings of each type of input are the product of the number of units and their average earnings, which will be proportional to their marginal products if factors are combined in proportions that minimize costs. To obtain total factor input in the whole economy, labor input is expanded to include persons employed by general government, households, nonprofit institutions, and the "rest-of-the-world" sector, while capital and land input are expanded to include dwellings and net claims on the rest of the world.

Sources of growth of national income per person employed (NIPPE) will be examined next. Data calculated on a potential basis will be used, to concentrate on the growth of this country's ability to produce as well as to minimize the sensitivity of results to the points at which years are divided and grouped.

Table 20.5 shows estimates of the sources of growth of potential NIPPE in nonresidential business and in the economy as a whole. Changes in employment, a major source of growth of total NI, does not appear in a table referring to NIPPE, of course. The estimates for nonresidential business will be described first, starting with factor input.

To analyze each relevant characteristic of labor, an index is constructed of the effect of changes in that characteristic on the average quality (ability to contribute to production) of a year's work. The lower panel of Table 20.6 shows growth rates of these indexes. To obtain the contribution of changes in each characteristic to the growth rate of potential NIPPE in nonresidential business, shown on the left in Table 20.5, these growth rates are multiplied by the weight of labor in total input, shown in the upper panel of Table 20.6. For example, the contribution of education to the growth rate in 1929 to 1948, 0.47 percentage point, is the product of the growth rate of the index for education, 0.60, and the labor share of earnings, 0.790. (There often is a negligible discrepancy because of rounding and an interaction term.) The input weights add up to 1, so the procedure is consistent with an assumption that if all inputs increased by 1 percent, NI would increase by 1 percent. My belief is that the economy actually operates under increasing returns to scale, but gains from economies of scale are classified as a contribution of increased output per unit of input.

Table 20.5. Sources of growth of potential national income per person potentially employed: nonresidential business and whole economy, 1929–1982 (contributions to growth rates in percentage points)

Item	Non residential business			Whole economy		
	1929–1948	1948–1973	1973–1982	1929–1948	1948–1973	1973–1982
National income per person potentially employed	1.31	2.59	0.00	1.24	2.26	0.23
Total factor input	0.08	0.45	-0.09	0.23	0.61	0.15
Labor	0.22	0.11	-0.10	0.40	0.18	-0.04
Hours	-0.25	-0.22	-0.36	-0.21	-0.24	-0.33
Average hours	-0.62	-0.39	-0.52	-0.68	-0.37	-0.46
Efficiency offset	0.27	0.05	0.12	0.39	0.04	0.10
Intergroup shift offset	0.10	0.12	0.04	0.08	0.09	0.03
Age-sex composition	0.00	-0.19	-0.31	0.00	-0.15	-0.24
Education	0.47	0.52	0.57	0.38	0.40	0.44
Unallocated	—	—	—	0.23	0.17	0.09
Capital	-0.09	0.39	0.10	-0.12	0.48	0.26
Inventories	0.02	0.10	-0.02	0.00	0.07	-0.01
Nonresidential structures and equipment	-0.11	0.29	0.12	-0.12	0.19	0.11
Dwellings	—	—	—	0.01	0.17	0.12
International assets	—	—	—	-0.01	0.05	0.04
Land	-0.05	-0.05	-0.09	-0.05	-0.05	-0.07
Output per unit of input	1.23	2.14	0.09	1.01	1.65	0.08
Advances in knowledge and n.e.c.	0.61	1.40	-0.07	0.49	1.08	-0.05
Improved resource allocation	0.36	0.38	0.09	0.29	0.30	0.07
Farm	0.33	0.26	0.08	0.27	0.21	0.06
Nonfarm self-employment	0.03	0.12	0.01	0.02	0.09	0.01
Legal and human environment	0.00	-0.05	-0.22	0.00	-0.04	-0.17
Pollution abatement	0.00	-0.02	-0.12	0.00	-0.02	-0.09
Worker safety and health	0.00	-0.01	-0.03	0.00	-0.01	-0.03
Dishonesty and crime	0.00	-0.02	-0.07	0.00	-0.01	-0.05
Dwellings occupancy ratio	—	—	—	0.22	0.32	0.21
Economies of scale	0.27	0.42	0.27	0.02	-0.01	0.01
Irregular factors	-0.01	-0.01	0.02	-0.01	0.00	0.01
Weather in farming	-0.01	-0.01	0.02	-0.01	0.00	0.01
Labor disputes	0.00	0.00	0.00	0.00	0.00	0.00

Source: Edward F. Denison, *Trends in American Economic Growth, 1929–1982* (Washington, D.C.: Brookings Institution, 1985, pp. 110, 114.)

Hours of work declined rather rapidly in all three periods, though least in 1948 to 1973, as is shown by the "average hours" line in Table 20.6. This line is approximately equal to the difference between growth rates of output per hour and output per person employed on a potential basis, as shown in Table 20.4, but it does not measure the effect of shorter hours on labor input. Before the reasons for this are discussed, another aspect of labor will be examined.

Labor is not a homogeneous mass. Skills and effort vary from person to person. It is permissible to assume that natural ability at birth has not changed in recent generations, but changes in other characteristics cannot be ignored.

The distribution of total hours worked in nonresidential business among ten groups classified by sex and age has changed greatly (Table 20.7). Changes reflect fluctuations in the age distribution of the population together with differential changes in labor force participation rates, proportions employed outside the business sector, and

Table 20.6. Potential national income per person potentially employed in nonresidential business: weights and growth rates of factor input components, 1929–1982

Input components	1929–1948	1948–1973	1973–1982
Weights			
Total	1.000	1.000	1.000
Labor	.790	.805	.829
Inventories	.051	.043	.033
Nonresidential structures and equipment	.111	.114	.100
Land	.048	.038	.038
Growth rates			
Total factor input	0.08	0.45	−0.09
Labor	0.28	0.14	−0.12
Hours	−0.31	−0.27	−0.43
Average hours	−0.76	−0.47	−0.63
Efficiency offset	0.33	0.06	0.14
Intergroup shift offset	0.12	0.15	0.05
Age-sex composition	0.01	−0.24	−0.38
Education	0.60	0.64	0.69
Capital			
Inventories	0.23	2.34	−0.60
Nonresidential structures and equipment	−1.10	2.57	1.21
Land	−1.14	−1.19	−2.59

Source: Edward F. Denison, *Trends in American Economic Growth, 1929–1982* (Washington, D.C.: Brookings Institution, 1985), pp. 87, 93, 122, and underlying work sheets.

average hours of work. The proportion of hours worked by women increased persistently as their labor force participation rates rose. The shares of hours worked by both men and women under 20 dropped as schooling was lengthened, though with an interruption associated with the postwar baby boom. After 1948, earlier retirements, stimulated by the availability of social insurance and private pensions, sharply reduced the shares of older men — the older portion of the 35- to 64-year-old age group as well as the group over 65.

The last column in Table 20.7 shows the average hourly earnings of each age-sex group expressed as a percentage of the earnings of males 35 to 64, the group with the highest earnings. An index to allow for the effect on labor input of changes in age-sex composition was calculated by weighting the hours worked by each age-sex group by its average earnings.[6] This calculation rests on the assumption that average earnings in age-sex groups are proportional to the marginal products of labor, per hour worked, of these groups. The assumption is valid insofar as earnings differentials reflect differences in the value of the work that age-sex groups actually perform. In this context it does not matter whether they reflect differences in the value of the work the groups are able and willing to perform or failure

Table 20.7. Nonresidential business: percentage distribution of total hours worked, by sex and age, and relative hourly earnings, 1929–1982.

Sex and age	Percentage distribution of hours worked				Hourly earnings[a]
	1929	1948	1973	1982	
Male	83.5	77.7	69.3	63.3	—
14–19	6.2	4.0	4.6	2.9	31
20–24	10.9	8.0	8.5	8.3	56
25–34	20.6	19.1	17.2	19.0	82
35–64	42.4	43.0	37.1	31.6	100
65 and older	3.4	3.6	1.8	1.5	75
Female	16.5	22.3	30.7	36.7	—
14–19	2.6	2.0	2.8	2.2	28
20–24	3.7	3.7	5.2	6.2	44
25–34	4.0	5.3	6.4	10.8	54
35–64	5.9	10.7	15.5	16.8	54
65 and older	0.3	0.6	0.8	0.7	45

Source: Edward F. Denison, *Trends in American Economic Growth, 1929–1982* (Washington, D.C.: Brookings Institution, 1985), p. 88.
a. Percent of earnings of males 35–64 in 1975–1979.

(because abilities are not recognized or because of discrimination in employment practices) to use abilities that are present. Discrimination introduces an error into the calculation only insofar as there are differences in pay for the same work.

Changes in the distribution of hours worked among age-sex groups had a negligible effect on output per hour in 1929 to 1948, because changes in the age distribution offset the rise in the female proportion of workers. Changes were decidedly adverse to output per hour in 1948 to 1973 and more so in 1973 to 1981, when they subtracted .31 percentage point from the growth rate. This exceeded the deduction in 1948 to 1973 by 0.12 percentage point, and the difference contributed to the slowdown in productivity growth.[7] The increase in women working has, of course, added to total and per capita NI even though it has tended to lower NI per hour and especially (because women's hours are short) NIPPE.

The effect of declining average hours on labor input will now be examined. To estimate this effect employed persons are divided among nonfarm wage and salary workers, nonfarm self-employed and unpaid family workers, and farm workers. Each of these three groups is divided between men and women, and each of these between full-time workers and part-time workers, resulting in 12 groups in all.

The general shape of a curve relating hours to output for any category of full-time workers can be described. If working hours are very long, the adverse effects of fatigue on productivity are so great that output per worker increases if hours are shortened (and output per hour increases more). The effects of fatigue are reinforced by a tendency for absenteeism, which is costly, to be excessive when hours are long, and by important institutional factors. If hours are shortened further, a point is reached below which output per worker declines while output per hour increases. At this stage, increases in output per hour only partially offset the reduction in hours worked. Finally, if hours become very short, the proportion of time spent in starting and stopping work may become so great that even output per hour declines as hours are shortened. Evidence as to the location of the critical points is inadequate, but it is impossible to measure labor input at all, or to analyze sources of growth, without introducing judgments about such curves.

Full-time nonfarm wage and salary workers accounted for more than three-fourths of the total hours worked in nonresidential business in 1982. Separately for men and women, particular curves were assumed. They implied that a small change in average weekly hours had a 30 percent offset in output per man-hour when average weekly hours per person employed were at their 1960 levels. These levels were 42.7 hours for men and 38.2 for women, figures that are reduced for vacations, holidays, sickness, and other absences and that correspond to about 46.0 and 42.2, respectively, for persons at work. It was further assumed that output per worker is at a maximum when weekly hours are ten longer and that output per hour reaches a maximum when hours are about four shorter. Full-time farm workers as well as nonfarm proprietors and unpaid family workers work very long weekly hours that have not changed much, except for a reduction in hours of the nonfarm group, since the 1960s. The assumption was made, separately for men and women in each group, that fluctuations in hours were fully offset by opposite fluctuations in output per hour. Finally, it was assumed that there is no efficiency offset to changes in average hours of part-time workers, which have persistently averaged about 17 to 19 hours a week in all groups.

Based on these assumptions, the amount of the reduction in average hours within specified groups that is offset by greater output per hour is shown in Tables 20.5 and 20.6 in the line labeled "efficiency offset." In 1929 to 1948, when full-time hours were sharply reduced from a high level, the index measuring the efficiency offset increased 0.33 percent a year, and its contribution to growth was 0.27 point. The contribution was only 0.05 point in 1948 to 1973, but it increased to 0.12 point in 1973 to 1986, when potential hours dropped more rapidly.

A second offset, labeled "intergroup shift offset," also appears in the tables. The percentages of full-time male and female workers who are nonfarm wage and salary workers have increased, while the percentages who are farm workers and nonfarm self-employed have declined; farm workers comprised 24 percent of all full-time workers in 1929, 15 percent in 1948, and 3 percent in 1982. Because average weekly hours worked by full-time nonfarm wage and salary workers are much shorter than those worked by the other groups, these shifts reduced the average hours worked by all full-time workers of each sex combined. If not offset, the movements into nonfarm wage-salary employment would reduce labor input. A full-time farm or nonfarm self-employed worker would count as far more labor input than a nonfarm wage and salary worker because of the much longer hours.

This result would not be convenient or desirable. Shifts among categories are therefore prevented from reducing labor input by the inclusion of an index, whose growth rate is shown in Table 20.6, that introduces the convention that a year rather than an hour of full-time employment (when performed by the same individual, or individuals with similar characteristics) represents the same amount of labor input in any of these three groups. If full-time workers shift from one group to another, and if they work the average hours of their old group before moving and of their new group after moving, the index of labor input is unchanged.

The estimated effect of changes in potential working hours on the growth rates of potential labor input per person employed (Table 20.6) and NIPPE (Table 20.5) is the sum of its three components and is labeled "hours" in these tables. Although average hours fell much less per year in 1948 to 1973 than in 1929 to 1948, the adverse effect on NIPPE was only slightly smaller. A rapid decline in average hours resumed after 1973. With the combined productivity offsets being little changed from 1948 to 1973, this contributed 0.14 percentage point to the decline in growth rate of potential NIPPE.

Educational background decisively conditions both the types of work a person is able to perform and his or her proficiency in any particular occupation. A continuous upward shift in the educational background of the American labor force has upgraded the skills and versatility of labor and contributed much to the rise in NI. It has enhanced the skills of individuals within what is conventionally termed an occupation, often with considerable changes in the work actually performed; it has also permitted a shift in occupational composition from occupations in which workers typically have little education and low earnings toward those in which education and earnings are higher. Education also heightens a person's awareness of job opportunities and thereby the chances that the worker is employed where his or her marginal product is greatest. A better-educated work force also is better able to learn about and use the most efficient production practices.

Increasing education has been a major source of growth in the United States since at least 1910, and especially since 1929. Table 20.8 shows percentage distributions among nine educational levels of persons employed in the business sector in three years bounding the postwar periods under consideration. Data are on a full-time equivalent basis, which is necessary because the less educated workers are the most likely not only to be underemployed but also to hold only part-time jobs. The table reveals a pervasive and massive upgrading of educational background in the U.S. labor force. Changes in the education of employed persons reflect changes in education of young people over a very long period. Members of the 1929 labor force who were 68 years old started their schooling in about 1867, while members of the 1982 labor force who were 16 years old were still in school in 1982. The educational distribution of the labor force

Table 20.8. Percentage distribution of persons employed in the business sector, by sex and years of school completed, full-time equivalent basis, selected dates (1948–1982), and 1969 weights

| Sex, and school years completed | Percent of persons employed[a] | | | Standardized earnings, 1969 (value at 8 years = 100) | 1969 weight[b] |
	1948 (Oct.)	1973 (Mar.)	1982 (Mar.)		
Male, total	100.0	100.0	100.0	—	—
No school years completed	1.5	0.4	0.2	75	87
Elementary, 1–4	7.3	2.1	1.1	89	93
Elementary, 5–7	14.6	5.7	3.4	97	97
Elementary, 8	21.0	8.2	4.0	100	100
High school, 1–3	20.2	17.5	12.8	111	111
High school, 4	23.1	38.2	39.7	124	122
College, 1–3	6.6	14.0	17.6	147	142
College, 4	3.5	8.2	12.0	189	184
College, 5 or more	2.2	5.7	9.2	219	207
Average days of school per year, persons with no college	124	149	156	—	—
Female, total	100.0	100.0	100.0	—	—
No school years completed	0.9	0.1	0.2	—	87
Elementary, 1–4	3.5	1.0	0.5	—	93
Elementary, 5–7	9.9	3.6	1.9	—	97
Elementary, 8	18.1	6.2	2.8	—	100
High school, 1–3	18.8	17.4	12.3	—	111
High school, 4	37.3	51.0	49.5	—	122
College, 1–3	7.5	14.0	19.7	—	142
College, 4	3.0	4.5	8.7	—	184
College, 5 or more	1.0	2.1	4.4	—	207
Average days of school per year, persons with no college	128	150	157	—	—

Sources: Edward F. Denison, *Accounting for United States Economic Growth, 1929–1969* (Washington, D.C.: Brookings Institution, 1974), pp. 44, 244; *Accounting for Slower Economic Growth: The United States in the 1970s* (Washington, D.C.: Brookings Institution, 1979), pp. 43, 44; *Trends in American Economic Growth, 1929–1982* (Washington, D.C.: Brookings Institution, 1985), p. 91.

a. 1948 data cover persons 18 years of age and older, 1973 and 1982 data cover persons 16 years of age and older.

b. Weights for males were also used for females.

rises because those leaving the labor force are older and, consequently, have less education, on average, than those entering it.

Attention to the relationship between education and growth sometimes focuses on college graduates, and indeed there has been a notable increase in their number. From 6 percent in 1948, the percentage of men employed in business who had completed four or more years of college increased to 14 percent in 1973 and 21 percent in 1982. However, changes at the bottom of the distribution are equally remarkable. The percentage with seven years of schooling or less fell from 23 percent as recently as 1948 to 8 percent in 1973 and 5 percent in 1982, while the number with eight years (formerly a completed elementary education) fell from 21 percent to 8 percent to 4 percent. The total percentage who had not completed high school fell from 65 percent in 1948 to 34 percent in 1973 and 20 percent in 1982. Women in the business sector are more highly concentrated at the high school graduate and incomplete college levels than are men, but the upswing in education is similar.[8]

In addition to the increase in years of schooling, the average number of days that had been spent in elementary and secondary schools per year of such schooling rose from an estimated 124 for men employed in 1948, to 149 in 1973 and 156 in 1982, and they rose nearly as much for females. The increase reflected much earlier developments in schools that had occurred in the following way. There was no increase, but actually a decrease, from the late nineteenth century to the twentieth in the length of the school year in big cities. But in towns and rural areas, school years that were initially very short rose toward big-city levels. Meanwhile, absenteeism declined greatly in all geographic areas.

Separately for men and women, indexes of the effect of changes in education on labor quality were constructed, initially based only on highest school grade completed. This required weights for each educational level. Those computed for 1969 are shown in the last column in Table 20.8. They were computed for men 25 to 64 years of age but were also used for women and for other age groups, for whom necessary data are much less ample.

Because education is correlated with many other characteristics of workers that also affect earnings, the derivation of the weights is complex. First, for persons employed in business the average earnings of full-time year-round male workers at each education level were calculated and expressed as percentages of the earnings of those with eight years of education. This was done separately for 32 groups, resulting from cross-classification by four age groups within the 25 to 64 age range, farm or nonfarm work attachment, two races, and two regions. The percentages in the next-to-last column in Table 20.8 ("standardized earnings, 1969") are weighted averages of the percentages for the 32 groups. This procedure eliminated from earnings differentials the effects of correlation among education, the four characteristics just listed, and sex (because only data for men were used). The standardized differentials so obtained were reduced to eliminate the effect of correlation among education, earnings, and academic aptitude and socioeconomic status of parents. The adjusted differentials shown in the last column of Table 20.8 (or similar ones for another year) are the proper weights to use in constructing an index that measures the effect of changes in highest school grade completed on labor input.

Such indexes were constructed by applying these weights (or for earlier years, similar weights for a previous date) to annual distributions of employed persons similar to those in Table 20.8. An allowance was then added to take account of changes in the number of school days per year. This allowance was made only for persons who did not continue beyond high school, because those entering college are presumed to have made up deficiencies in earlier education before admission. The indexes for the two sexes were adjusted from an actual to a potential basis, and then combined by using as weights the total earnings of men and women in the business sector. Growth rates of this final education index are shown in Table 20.6, and the contribution of additional education to the growth of potential NIPPE in nonresidential business is shown in Table 20.5.

Increased education was a major and even an increasing source of growth. Over the whole 1929 to 1982 period it contributed 0.51 percentage point, or 30 percent, of the 1.68 percent growth rate of potential NIPPE. The contribution, as measured, increased from 0.52 percentage point in 1948 to 1973 to 0.57 point in 1973 to 1982 and thus moderated the post-1973 productivity slowdown. The moderation was confined to the early part of the period as the contribution peaked at 0.59 point in 1973 to 1979, then receded to 0.52 point by 1979 to 1982.

The index does not reflect changes in the quality of education, apart from the allowance for school days per year. Quality of education is widely thought to have deteriorated recently, the main quantitative evidence for this being Scholastic Aptitude Test scores, which declined for two decades until they began a weak recovery about 1982. Until well into the productivity slowdown period, at least, omission of test scores from the procedures was unimportant because over decades scores have moved in cycles, rather than following a steady trend. This pattern assures that changes in a series for the average test scores received by employed persons when they were students would be small and gradual, very muted in comparison with movements in student scores. Nevertheless, it is obvious that lowering the quality of education — whether it stems from the schools themselves, changes in the family, attitudes of parents and students toward schools, television, or other causes — can affect productivity adversely, and indications that it has done so are persuasive.

The negative impacts of changes in hours of work and the age-sex composition of hours worked offset the positive effect of education, so that the net change in the quantity and quality of work per person employed, on a potential basis, was moderate. It was, however, declining: its contribution to the growth of potential NIPPE fell from 0.22 percentage point in 1929 to 1948 to 0.11 in 1948 to 1973 and −0.10 in 1973 to 1982. The drop of 0.21 percentage point in the period after 1973 contributed appreciably to the productivity slowdown.

Capital is the next determinant of NIPPE to be examined. Capital used in nonresidential business consists of fixed capital (nonresidential structures and equipment) and inventories. Over the 1929 to 1982 period as a whole, input of fixed capital per person potentially employed grew 0.9 percent a year and contributed 0.11 percentage point to the growth rate of potential NIPPE. Inventories, with a slightly higher growth rate but much smaller weight, contributed 0.05 percentage point.

The growth rate of capital input per person potentially employed has been volatile, as shown in Table 20.6, even though the rate of employment growth is among the important determinants of capital requirements. From 1929 to 1948 fixed capital per person potentially employed actually declined as a result of the intervening depression, when demand was weak, and the war, when resources available to produce capital goods were severely restricted. Meanwhile, inventories increased only a little. During the period of fast growth between 1948 and 1973 both fixed capital and inventories increased rapidly. The capital shortage present in 1948 contributed to this fast growth, especially at the beginning of the period, so it is uncertain whether the capital stock was permanently reduced by the depression and war. After 1973 the growth rate of fixed capital per person employed dropped sharply and that of inventories turned negative. Thus capital contributed more to *changes* in the growth rate of potential NIPPE, even between periods as long as those shown in Table 20.5, than it did to the long-term rate itself: 0.48 point or 38 percent to the increase between 1929 to 1948 and 1948 to 1973, and 0.29 point or 11 percent to the subsequent drop between 1948 to 1973 and 1973 to 1982.

Discussion of the complex changes in saving and investment behavior that affected the 1973 to 1982 change in capital input per person potentially employed is prohibited here by space limitations, but three points must be noted.[9] First, growth of *total* capital input dropped only a little between 1948 to 1973 and 1973 to 1982, whereas the growth rate of potential employment jumped from 1.2 percent to 2.7 percent. Second, actual output and employment were persistently below potential, reducing capital requirements and the rate of return and, consequently, the demand for capital. Third, the growth rate of the gross stock of fixed capital (the value of the stock without deduction of accumulated depreciation) per person potentially employed fell more than that of the net stock. To measure input (net services) of fixed capital, I weight indexes of gross stock three-fourths and net stock one-fourth. Introduction of net stock into the capital input measure is only a convenient way to allow for deterioration in the contribution of capital goods to production as they age.

The reader is cautioned that the concept of capital appropriate for productivity analysis when the design of capital goods changes is much debated. The chief conceptual issue is: should an improvement that increases a type of capital good's contribution to production but does not require more saving (that is, forgoing more consumption to pay for it) be counted as a contribution to growth made by capital or as a contribution made by advances in knowledge of how to produce at low cost? In my opinion, a useful classification of growth sources must identify cause with effect. The contribution made to output growth by advances in knowledge of all types, including design of capital goods, should be classified as such (appearing as a component of changes in output per unit of input), whereas the contribution of capital must be identified with the concept of consumption forgone. Some analysts advocate classifying as contributions of capital any gains in output that result from improvements in the design of capital goods. To measure capital this way requires equating types of capital goods produced at different times by their marginal products at a common date. Not only would this concept yield an undesirable classification, but in my opinion it also is impossible to implement.

The present estimates rely on capital stock series compiled in accordance with the common convention that capital goods having the same production cost at a common date are the same amount of capital. This results in a classification of growth sources much closer to the "consumption forgone" procedure than to the alternative I have described, but unsatisfactory in one respect: advances in knowledge that lower the production cost of unchanged capital goods are incorrectly classified as contributions of capital rather than as advances in knowledge.

The ratio of land, whose quantity is considered constant, to employment fell more than twice as fast in 1973 to 1982 as it had in earlier periods, because potential employment growth accelerated. Despite a decline in the weight of land in total input, its contribution to the growth rate of potential NIPPE in nonresidential business was −0.09 percentage point in 1973 to 1982 as against −0.05 point in both earlier periods, so it contributed to the decline in the growth rate of potential NIPPE after 1973.

Total factor input per person employed combines the offsetting positive and negative contributions of labor, capital, and land. On a net basis it contributed importantly to growth of potential NIPPE in nonresidential business only in 1948 to 1973. It accounts for 0.54 point of the 2.59 percentage point decline in this growth rate between 1948 to 1973 and 1973 to 1982.

Changes in output per unit of input contributed much more to the growth of NIPPE and to changes in its rate of growth. Output per unit of input is affected by a host of determinants, of which a few main types are separately estimated.

The more nearly resources are allocated to the uses in which they can contribute the most to the value of output, the larger is the output per unit of input. Mainly because shifting patterns of demand for labor have long been reducing the requirements for farm labor, while the actual transfer of labor has lagged, overallocation of labor to farming has been a chronic condition. As farm employment has shrunk, the fraction of total business employment thus misallocated has declined. The reduction contributed an almost constant amount, around 0.35 percentage point, to the growth rate of potential NIPPE in nonresidential business in 1929 to 1941, 1941 to 1948, 1948 to 1953, and 1953 to 1958 despite the fact that the pool of farm employment dropped from 24 percent of the sector total to 10 percent. The shift was responsible for 18 percent of the growth rate of potential NIPPE in the sector from 1929 to 1958. After 1958 the farm share of potential employment in nonresidential business continued down, reaching 3 percent in 1982, but there was not enough surplus labor left to contribute as much to growth as before. By 1973 to 1982 the contribution was down to 0.08 percentage point (Table 20.5).

Persons who are underemployed or whose labor is very wastefully utilized are also present among the nonfarm self-employed and unpaid members of their families. The reduction in the proportion of labor so employed contributed an estimated 0.12 percentage point to the sector growth rate in 1948 to 1953 but very little in 1929 to 1948 or 1973 to 1982.

These two types of reduction in misallocation of labor contributed

0.38 percentage point to the growth of NIPPE in the sector in 1948 to 1973 but only 0.09 point in 1973 to 1982. Thus they contributed substantially to the drop in the growth rate of productivity.

Government regulations intended to combat pollution began to impose significant costs on business in 1968, and new legislation to protect worker safety and health began to do so in 1969. Although some of the benefits are counted in measured output, most are not — so the costs incurred reduce output per unit of input as measured. A third change, dated as beginning about 1958, has been a rise in criminal acts committed against business and a lessened ability to rely on the honesty of other people. These problems reduce measured output per unit of input in two ways. Businesses may divert resources from the production of measured output to protection against criminal and dishonest acts in an effort to limit their losses, and (a much larger cost) criminal acts that nevertheless occur (such as shoplifting or damaging property) reduce measured output. Together, these changes in the legal and human environment subtracted 0.05 percentage point from the growth rate of potential NIPPE in 1948 to 1973 as a whole and 0.22 point in 1973 to 1982. Thus they contributed appreciably to the productivity slowdown.

Economies of scale are estimated to have enhanced the growth that would have occurred in their absence. Growth of an economy automatically means growth in the average size of the local, regional, and national markets that business serves. Growth of markets brings opportunities for greater specialization — both among and within industries, firms, and establishments — and opportunities for establishments and firms within the economy to become larger without impairing the competition that stimulates efficiency. The opportunities for greater specialization, bigger units, longer production runs, and larger transactions provide a clear reason to expect increasing returns in the production and distribution of many products, and examples of increasing returns are plentiful.

The estimates presented here assume that an increase in any other determinant of output that would have sufficed to raise nonresidential business national income by 1.0 percent under constant returns to scale actually increased it by 1.125 percent, or by an extra one-eighth. This assumption meant that the cost reductions resulting from economies of scale associated with the growth of the national market were credited with being the source of one-ninth of the growth rate of sector output and (with employment growing) a larger fraction of the growth rate of sector NIPPE: nearly one-sixth in 1948 to 1973. Reduction of gains from scale economies contributed 0.15 point to the productivity slowdown.

Irregular factors may influence growth rates in any particular time period, but the effect of the most important, fluctuations in the intensity of aggregate demand, disappears when these estimates are on a potential basis. The effects of weather on farm output and the effects of labor disputes contributed little to growth rates in the time periods shown in Table 20.5.

Advancing knowledge of ways to produce at low cost is the biggest and most basic reason for the long-term growth of output per unit of input. The term "advances in knowledge" covers both technological knowledge and managerial and organizational knowledge. It includes knowledge originating in this country and abroad, and knowledge obtained in any way: by organized research, by individual research workers, and by simple observation and experience.

The term must, however, be limited to those advances in knowledge that allow the same amount of *measured* output to be obtained with less input. The introduction of new and improved products for final sale from the business sector to consumers and government provides buyers with greater choice or enables them to meet their needs better with the same use of resources, but it does not, in general, contribute to growth as measured; rather, it results in unmeasured quality change.

The combined contributions of changes in all determinants of output that were not directly measured on an annual basis, including advances in knowledge and a group of miscellaneous determinants, is obtained as a residual and shown in Table 20.6. The miscellaneous determinants fall into seven groups:

1. Changes in personal characteristics of workers that are not measured in labor input, such as effort expended.
2. Changes in misallocation of resources, except overallocation of labor to farming and nonfarm self-employment.
3. Changes in the shortfall of actual output below what output would be if the best techniques were used.
4. Changes in the costs of business services to government, such as collecting taxes or filing statistical reports.
5. Changes in the adequacy of government services to business, such as police protection, law courts, and roads for business use.
6. Changes in the legal and human environment other than requirements for pollution abatement and worker safety and health, and dishonesty and crime.
7. Changes in productive efficiency that occur independently of changes in the other determinants identified.

One explanation for such changes is that the efficiency actually achieved is affected by the strength of competitive pressures. Another stresses the quality of management.

Interpreting the residual series obviously involves judgment. My judgment is that from 1948 to 1973 the series provides an acceptable approximation of the contribution made to growth by the incorporation of new knowledge into the process of production. If so, advances in knowledge contributed 1.40 percentage points to the 2.59 percent growth rate of NIPPE. The 0.61 percentage point residual in 1929 to 1948 probably was reduced a little by restrictive practices introduced during the Depression in the thirties, but advances in knowledge appear to have contributed much less to growth than in 1948 to 1973. From 1973 to 1982 the residual fell slightly below zero. Comparable estimates for later years are not available, but it is evident that the residual has remained very small.

What happened? Domestic expenditures for relevant R & D have not fallen, and the rate of return on such expenditures appears to have been maintained. Importing of foreign technology has increased. While direct evidence concerning advances in knowledge other than from R & D is scant, it seems unlikely that they can be responsible for most of the drop in the residual. Moreover, the decline in the growth rate of the residual after 1973 was abrupt; there was no hint of slackening through 1973, and there was a sudden decline thereafter. It is not plausible that the contribution of advances in knowledge could have changed so abruptly. Many suggestions blaming other output determinants have been made. The Mideast oil situation may have contributed 0.1 percentage point to the productivity slowdown. Nearly all the other suggestions can be rejected as either wrong or quantitatively unimportant. Among those that cannot be readily dismissed is a deterioration of management, whether as a result of the spread of false management doctrines, lower quality and inappropriate training of managers, or a shift in incentives for managers toward emphasis on short-term profits at the expense of longer-term considerations. That management is the source of the slowdown in American productivity growth is plausible but unproven, and the idea faces the objection that the productivity slowdown is worldwide. Thus the causes of the slowdown in the growth of residual productivity remain a mystery.

Turning now from discussing the sources of growth of potential NIPPE in nonresidential business to sources of growth in the economy as a whole, the right side of Table 20.5 provides similar estimates for the whole economy. Since nonresidential business covers only about four-fifths of the economy on average, changes in this sector have less effect on the growth rate of NI in the whole economy than in the sector. Contributions to the growth rate of NIPPE also differ, because the growth rates of potential employment are not the same in nonresidential business and the whole economy. In an examination of the whole economy, the contributions of capital must be broadened to include the contributions of dwellings and of net property income from abroad, both shown as separate entries in Table 20.5. The contribution of American labor employed by general government, nonprofit organizations, and households must be added. The contributions of changes in age-sex composition and education are not separated outside the business sector; they are combined with another small component as the "unallocated" contribution of labor. A small additional entry is the "dwellings occupancy ratio," which measures changes in the services provided by dwellings as a result of changes in the percentage occupied. This percentage does not move with the business cycle and, unlike changes in the intensity of use of nonresidential capital, does not disappear when NI is figured on a potential basis.

Except for the dwelling occupancy ratio, changes in measured NI outside nonresidential business occur only because of changes in inputs. Consequently, potential NIPPE grew more slowly in the economy as a whole than in nonresidential business except after 1973, when output per unit of input in business scarcely increased. Total factor input consistently contributed more to growth of potential NIPPE in the whole economy than in nonresidential business.

Growth accounting can help answer a variety of questions about American productivity, only some of which could be discussed or even mentioned here. How much has American productivity grown, and what have been the sources of its growth? What changes have occurred in the rate of productivity growth, and what were the reasons for such changes? How much of the difference between productivity levels observed at two dates is due to differences with respect to position in the business cycle — or, more exactly, to the intensity with which employed resources are used? How do levels of productivity in other countries differ from the level in the United States, and what is responsible for the differences? How do growth rates of productivity in other countries differ from the rate in the United States, and what is responsible for the differences? What is the relationship between international differences in productivity levels and growth rates? What will be the future growth rate of productivity? How much would any action, or change in policy, that may be proposed alter the future growth rate? Or, alternatively, how could the future growth rate of productivity be changed by any given amount? A recent review of the literature gives examples of all these uses of growth accounting in the analysis of productivity.[10]

Stimulation of Growth

The rate of growth of national product depends on myriad decisions by the individuals, firms, and other organizations that comprise the nation. Almost any action that promotes growth of potential output per hour requires a perceived, and usually an actual, sacrifice by some participants in the society. It may be working harder; studying more to prepare for future employment; devotion of time and effort to raising one's children in the way they should go; consuming less either to save more and thus permit more rapid accumulation of the country's physical assets or to finance research and development; loss of a monopolistic position; abandonment of special privileges in tax codes, subsidies, and government services, or of a special favor in other aspects of the law; changing jobs or line of business to accommodate shifts in demand or technological change, sometimes with a lasting loss of income and frequently with an intervening period of idleness; or some other shift from present to future consumption or exertion of greater effort.

Governments, including the monetary authorities, have the major responsibility for economic stabilization at a high level of activity. Though subordinate to individuals and firms, their ability to influence the growth of potential output is also crucial. It centers on the provision of an environment of law and justice; a stable currency; education; roads, streets, and other transportation facilities; disposal of sewage and pollutants; emergency services; and filling gaps left by the private sector in such growth-promoting activities as research and the provision of information.

What stands out in any reasonable analysis of growth stimulation is that steps to raise the growth of potential output are neither easy nor cheap.[11] Past periods of relatively satisfactory productivity growth, and even the modest recent 1 percent annual growth of output per hour, required devoting huge amounts of resources to growth-creating activities. To raise the growth rate by any stipulated amount requires commensurate increases in these resources unless, improbably, some strategic roadblock to growth not yet identified can be uncovered and removed.

The sources of the slowdown in productivity growth up to 1982 have been examined. As one now surveys the situation in 1992, three points stand out. First, many growth sources each contributed small amounts to the productivity slowdown. Some of these are irreversible, at least by any government policy, while others seem impermeable. Elimination of excess labor in farming can no longer be a major growth source because few farmers remain. There has been ample and justified complaint about American education but no demonstrable improvement — which, I believe, would require changes in the attitudes of parents and students quite as much as in the schools themselves. Additional steps toward tax neutrality among types of income and products would help a little, but in 1992 even preservation of the achievements of the 1986 tax law were imperiled.

Second, a dramatic decline in the rate of net national saving occurred early in the 1980s and the new rate, very low in comparison not only with past American experience but also with other advanced countries, has continued in the early 1990s. Both private and government saving fell drastically. The latter drop was largely at the federal level. A huge and persistent federal deficit, which represents dissaving, followed the tax reductions of 1982. The drop in the net national saving rate was matched in part by a drop in domestic investment and in part by a drop, to substantial negative amounts, in net foreign investment. The 1992 election campaign shows no popular nor party support for raising taxes or for other realistic steps to reduce the deficit. Meanwhile, the existence of the federal deficit and the resistance to taxes at all levels of government inhibit government spending to promote growth. Measures that can be expected, with confidence, to raise private saving without lowering government saving are simply not known.

Third, the cause of much of the post-1973 decline in productivity advance is an enigma. It probably originated in the private sector and may well be founded in short-sighted or otherwise inadequate management, as is widely believed. But in the absence of firm conclusions as to the source of the problem, one can recommend only further study, the use of a longer time frame by major investors, and promotion of vigorous competition to eliminate inefficiency.

Notes

1. To maximize statistical consistency between input and output measures, GDP is calculated as the sum of charges against gross product.
2. Data available at the time of writing (May 1992) are in a state of flux,

mainly as a result of only partly completed rebasing and revision of the Commerce Department's estimates of national product. Data in Table 20.1 for 1948 to 1973 are unrevised BLS data in 1982 prices, while those for 1973 to 1990 have been revised to incorporate changes in the BEA's estimates of real national product that resulted from changing the base year from 1982 to 1987 and from statistical revisions. Data in Tables 20.2 to 20.5 are BLS estimates that incorporate available BEA revisions. They do not incorporate data from the 1990 purchasing-power parity study, which appear to be inconsistent with data from the 1985 study.

3. U.S. growth rates are below rates shown in Table 20.1 for business output per hour in similar periods, both because average hours were falling and because Table 20.2 includes additional sectors.

4. The GDP is estimated as the sum of private and public consumption, gross domestic investment, and the excess of exports over imports.

5. The estimates for 1990 shown in Tables 20.2 and 20.3, except for Korea, are extrapolations from basic data that refer to 1985. The 1985 comparisons among the United States, Japan, Canada, Sweden, and 12 members of the European Economic Community (EEC) as a group were based on average prices for these areas; comparisons among the EEC members are based on average prices in these countries. Estimates for Korea are extrapolations from a 1980 level, based on a comparison of Korean and Japanese prices. The BLS provides a fuller description in the source cited in the tables.

6. During recent periods, weights have been changed periodically, but changes were small.

7. However, the index for age-sex composition changed course within the periods shown. Its movement was most adverse in 1964 to 1973, slightly less so in 1973 to 1979, and much less so thereafter.

8. Persons employed outside the business sector tend to have larger percentages at both ends of the distribution than those employed in business; this applies particularly to women, who have large numbers in teaching and in household employment.

9. Changes were even greater after 1982, when the federal government deficit was huge, private saving dropped, and investment by foreigners helped replace public and private domestic saving.

10. Edward F. Denison, "The Growth Accounting Tradition and Proximate Sources of Growth." Paper presented at the Conference on Explaining Economic Growth, Groningen, Netherlands, April 8–10, 1992.

11. For an evaluation of the quantitative effect of a wide range of alternatives on the growth rate, as of 1960, see Edward F. Denison, *The Sources of Economic Growth and the Alternatives before Us,* (New York: Committee for Economic Development, 1962), especially chapter 24.

21

The Specter of Affirmative Action

Jonathan S. Leonard

In the space of one week in 1991, President Bush changed his description of the Civil Rights Act of 1991 from a quota bill to a nonquota bill, and changed his threatened veto to a signature enacting the bill into law. This political about-face is emblematic of the quandary that civil rights legislation creates for political leaders. It is a fine example of mercurial decisions based on evanescent judgments. Some small changes in language provided the thinnest smokescreen for the president's change of mind, but these hardly changed the substance of the proposed law. Certainly the president did not change his mind because of some new research demonstrating the absence of quotas under the civil rights law. To the contrary, the hallmark of much of the debate over civil rights is its disjunction from empirical evidence and its reliance on specters. What had changed, along with the president's new depiction of the old quota bill, was the rise of one such specter embodying racial fear and hatred. During the long debate over the quota bill, a former leader of the Ku Klux Klan, David Duke, nearly rode the wave of racial resentment into statewide office in Louisiana. Putting a stop to Duke's image as a representative of the Republicans required the president's signature on the bill. In effect, David Duke became the chief lobbyist for passage of the Civil Rights Act of 1991.

Affirmative action has become one of the totems of domestic policy in our times — it is a lightning rod and a dividing line for political discussions. It is held up as a symbol of liberal excess, ethnic pork barrel writ large, and the decay of meritocratic values. It is also held up as a symbol of fairness, cohesiveness, and equality. This chapter examines the construction and manipulation of the symbols surrounding affirmative action, a policy that serves as a case study in the political uses of ambiguity and the control of information. The demonic or angelic specters of affirmative action will be compared with the mundane effects of the policy in the United States. As the United States has sought to balance employees' and employers' rights, its affirmative action policies have affected patterns of employment, promotion, wages, productivity, and profitability in ways that are important for understanding the nature of the policy and the ends it serves.

The United States has had an active federal policy requiring affirmative action among federal contractors since 1965 (Executive Order 11246), and a contract compliance policy barring discrimination among federal contractors since 1941 (Executive Order 8802). Despite this long history, one of the most notable characteristics of affirmative action under the contract compliance program is that few people in the United States could state the goals of the policy, and little consensus would emerge among those who could state them. Perhaps more striking, attempts to elicit this information from government officials charged with implementing policy would not greatly clarify matters. An easy way to test the ambiguity of the issue is to ask under what conditions an affirmative action policy might be declared successful and so brought to an end. Proponents of affirmative action have rarely contemplated what success might look like. A second defining characteristic of affirmative action policy is the passion with which both proponents and critics approach the idea. This has helped to inflate its symbolic importance far out of proportion to its modest accomplishments. I argue here that the first characteristic — ambiguity — is no accident but rather serves a useful political function in light of the second characteristic — sharply divided political opinions.

The distance the United States has come since 1941 in terms of the growing importance of affirmative action, expanding intervention by the federal government, and changing attitudes toward discrimination can best be judged by considering the words of Mark Ethridge, first chairman of the Fair Employment Practice Committee, which was established to supervise compliance with the 1941 executive order. In the following quotation from Ruchames (p. 28), Ethridge is shown to have sharply limited the scope of antidiscrimination policy, in a manner startling to modern readers:

> Although he defended the granting of civil rights and equal opportunity to Negroes, he also affirmed his personal support of segregation in the South. Stressing that "the committee has taken no position on the question of segregation of industrial workers," he emphasized that "Executive Order 8802 is a war

order, and not a social document," that it did not require the elimination of segregation, and that had it done so, he would have considered it "against the general peace and welfare . . . in the Nazi dictatorial pattern rather than in the slower, more painful, but sounder pattern of the democratic process."

Of course, the delicate question of how to remedy swiftly the harm done by discrimination without distorting the democratic process is still with us, as is the question of how well the democratic process can function outside an integrated society. Democratic society requires a consensus for change, but it depends on the full participation of its members. The past fifty years have witnessed a slow and at times painful process of confrontation and accommodation in the development of a consensus that provides the foundation for a lasting change in attitudes toward discrimination.

Executive orders establishing affirmative action have shifted in emphasis and in legal foundation. The Roosevelt and Truman orders had the stated goal of increasing the labor supply for defense production, and referred specifically to national defense acts. Under the Federal Procurement Act, the president could move to ensure the government's access to cheaper goods and services through the full and efficient use of human resources. In the framework of the Civil Rights Act of 1964, the president could act to combat employment discrimination. In light of this country's troubled history of group relations, perhaps the most noble goal of affirmative action is to help integrate society and ensure that all have a stake in its success.

In 1968, the Office of Federal Contract Compliance Programs (OFCCP) within the Department of Labor issued regulations requiring written affirmative action section plans (AASP), containing goals and timetables, to correct deficiencies in equal employment opportunity. These regulations have been expanded from time to time. In 1970, Order Number 4, applicable to federal contractors with 50 or more employees and a contract of $50,000 or more, required (1) a utilization study of minorities by job category, (2) goals and timetables to correct deficiencies, and (3) data collection and reporting systems to report progress toward goals. Under the executive order, federal contractors agree that they will "not discriminate against any employee or applicant for employment because of race, color, religion, sex or national origin, and to take affirmative action to ensure that applicants are employed, and that employees are treated during employment without regard to their race, color, religion, sex or national origin. Such action shall include, but not be limited to the following: employment, upgrading, demotion, or transfer; recruitment or recruitment advertising; layoff or terminations; rates of pay or other forms of compensation; and selection for training including apprenticeship" (3 C.F.R. 169 202 [1] [1974]).

Affirmative Action Politics

The language of the executive order imposes two obligations: first, not to discriminate; second, whether or not there is any evidence of discrimination, to take affirmative action not to discriminate. To say that this second obligation, as it has been developed in the regulations, has provoked a good deal of debate would be a considerable understatement. In practice, the order has not been enforced so as to ensure that employees are treated "without regard to their race, color, sex," and so on. In the words of one legal expert, Arthur Smith (p. 1028): "The affirmative action obligations imposed by the Contract Compliance Program are separate and distinct from non-discrimination obligations and are not based on proof of individual acts of discrimination. At the logical extreme, affirmative action and non-discrimination obligations can be viewed as mutually exclusive and inconsistent . . . in practice, the non-discrimination and affirmative action obligations may be incompatible when, for example, a less qualified, less senior female or black is granted a job preference that disadvantages a male or white solely on the basis of sex or race to achieve an affirmative action commitment."

The same dissonance and ambiguity is analyzed by another legal expert, Owen Fiss (pp. 235–313), in the following extracts. "The affirmative-action duty does not purport to supplant the duty not to discriminate, nor could it be understood independently of the duty not to discriminate. . . . In the typical scenario, the enforcement agency tells the employer that he not only must refrain from discrimination but must also undertake 'affirmative action.' The employer asks what 'affirmative action' is: 'What is it I have to do?' The response of the enforcement agency is essentially one of silence." After dismissing a number of possible explanations of this silence, Professor Fiss hints at one that seems plausible to him:

A third explanation of this silence is embarrassment . . . the agency is embarrassed to say what it means. This embarrassment is . . . attributable to fear of the political consequences of informing the employer precisely what is expected of him or to the uncertainty on the part of the agency as to the legality of the action it wants the employer to take. The agency wants the employer to do anything that is necessary to increase the number of black workers or to improve the relative economic position of Negroes. Of course one means of doing that is to give blacks a preference because of their color. In this instance the phrase 'affirmative action' is a technique for avoiding the political and legal consequences of the agency's directive.

Professor Fiss goes on to argue that the only affirmative action programs with a legal basis are those ordered by the courts as remedies for discrimination found under Title VII of the Civil Rights Act of 1964. He concludes, "To the extent that it is not redundant, the affirmative-action concept is either meaningless or inconsistent with the prohibition against discrimination. Most often it is used simply as a bluff."

Was the affirmative action obligation really so vague and open-ended? In 1967, the director of the OFCC, Edward Sylvester, stated: "There is no fixed and firm definition of affirmative action. I would say that in a general way, affirmative action is anything you have to do to get results. . . . Affirmative action is really designed to get employers to apply the same kind of imagination and ingenuity that they apply to other phases of their operation" (*Report of the 1967 Plans for Progress Fifth National Conference*, pp. 73–74). To be vague concerning methods is the ideal decentralized approach, but this is also vague about the critical issue of ends. What is the goal against which results are judged, nondiscrimination or increased minority and female employment? The distinct, practical question of whether the two can be distinguished in an operational sense will be explored later.

In the words of Lawrence Silberman, undersecretary of labor from 1970 to 1973: "One of the interesting things about the affirmative action concept, it is not antidiscrimination. It goes beyond that. . . . We and the compliance agencies put pressure on contractors to come up with commitments even though these contracts are not guilty of any discrimination, but because we think they are required under the Executive order to go beyond, to provide affirmative action" (*Hearings of the Senate Subcommittee on Labor, 92nd Congress, 1st Session*, p. 88 [1971]).

Speculate a moment on the sources of political support for affirmative action. Why should a politician support affirmative action? Who will support him or her for doing so? Obviously blacks and women are the largest direct beneficiaries of affirmative action, absent civil disorder, and among these groups there may be greater sensitivity to the wishes of those most likely to support their goals with votes and money. This suggests a very different conception of how OFCCP regulatory pressure may be targeted.

How does an individual employee — minority or female — gain from affirmative action? If affirmative action is viewed as a policy of antidiscrimination, he or she gains from having a broader set of choices, a feeling of justice and equal protection under the law, and, indirectly, from increased earnings — for a broader choice of employment only makes the individual better off if he or she ends up in a better job. Increasing the choice set does not by itself necessarily increase utility, and while feelings of justice may promote the authority of the state, they do not put bread on the table. The premise of this section is that political support for affirmative action depends on individual gain in the form of increased earnings.

Relating this in more formal economic terms, political support is proportional to workers' surplus: the area above the supply curve and beneath the wage. Executive Order 11246 imposes employment goals, not wage goals. For a given induced shift in employment, workers' surplus will be greater the more inelastic the supply, and will depend not at all on the elasticity of demand.

If political support is proportional to rents, then the OFCCP will elicit more support from minorities and women by targeting enforcement pressure where supply is inelastic. So affirmative action pressure should be stronger in occupations requiring high skills and high education, areas in which people are also more likely to be politically active, and which are after all, in my opinion, the true battlefield of affirmative action. It is a battlefield because it is these same cases of inelastic supply that provoke the most political backlash. Employers in these areas are more sensitive to quality differentials, have more difficulty meeting employment goals, and are under pressure to raise wages to do so. Meanwhile, as their relative wage declines, white men are seized by concern with inequity.

Affirmative action policies that are perceived as reducing discrimination gain far more support than those perceived as inducing "reverse discrimination," mandating a system of preferences, or making reparations. In opinion polls, a majority is typically against discrimination and in favor of antidiscrimination policies. A yet stronger majority is typically opposed to affirmative action. These public opinions direct clear framing strategies for political proponents and adversaries of affirmative action: to gain support, sell the program's effect in fighting discrimination; to kill the program, portray it as an institutionalized system of unfair preferences calcified into quotas.

The dilemma that affirmative action raises for politicians in the

United States can perhaps best be appreciated in noting that the U.S. Congress has not found it necessary to legislate affirmative action in employment. Its strongest support has taken the form of its failure to overthrow the policy undertaken by executive order.

This leaves the president with considerable leeway for drafting and implementing regulation. To enforce policy without benefit of potentially rancorous and divisive public debate, the executive branch has been able either to strengthen affirmative action by instituting goals and timetables, monitoring, and sanctions, or to weaken affirmative action by limiting funding and administrative support, and reducing monitoring and sanctions. Tucked away beyond the harsh glare of congressional debate, what has developed is an ambiguous affirmative action policy that attempts to placate the opposed groups without provoking a rupture; a policy promoted just enough to yield a sense of enfranchisement among minorities and women, but not so far as to incite the majority to repudiate it.

With a myopic electorate, affirmative action offers other political opportunities. A system of institutionalized preferences could be eviscerated while charging ahead under the banner of antidiscrimination. Affirmative action grew from its initial focus on racial minorities to encompass women. Over time, other policies have been added to protect veterans, older workers, and the disabled. As a policy to reduce discrimination, this is wonderful. Discrimination is bad, and there are likely economies of scope in extending the protection of antidiscrimination policy. As a system of preferences, the politics are more subtle. Each group is pleased with the promise of a relative preference. If the groups are myopic enough, none notices that preferences for all are equivalent to preferences for none. But this defines a politician's dream: a promise of more for everyone that need change nothing beyond his political popularity.

Political divisiveness over affirmative action seems to depend in part on a little-remarked aspect of these policies — the extent to which the risk of discrimination is exclusive or inclusive. Historically, the battles over legislation against racial discrimination were more prolonged and hard fought than those against disability or age discrimination; the risk is exclusive in the former case, inclusive in the latter. Racial antidiscrimination policy is seen as clearly dividing beneficiaries from contributors. The lines are less starkly drawn for sex discrimination — which can be viewed in part as redistribution within the family. Disability discrimination is an even more inclusive risk: everybody faces some risk of becoming disabled, and so of being a victim of discrimination against the disabled. At the extreme, everybody grows old — the risk of age discrimination is all-inclusive. While age discrimination can be viewed as redistribution over a lifetime, policies against age discrimination gain wide support in part because all can see themselves as eventually directly benefiting.

Proponents and critics of affirmative action are united in viewing the program in mythical proportions. To proponents, it has been a key to expanding employment opportunities for minorities and women, opening the way for their economic advance. Critics see it as a pervasive and substantial system of unfair preferences. This roaring mouse in fact had modest effects in the 1970s, and they dwindled to insignificance in the 1980s. Reviewing the development of affirmative action into "quotas," former Undersecretary Lawrence Silberman wrote: "We wished to create a generalized firm, but gentle pressure to balance the residue of discrimination. . . . Our use of numerical standards in pursuit of equal opportunity has led ineluctably to the very quotas, guaranteeing equal results, that we initially wished to avoid. . . . Thus was introduced a group rights concept antithetical to traditional American notions of individual merit and responsibility."

Silberman raises two key issues. The first is that an affirmative action program without measurable results invites sham efforts. According to the U.S. comptroller general (48 Comp. Gen. 326 [1968]), such vague requirements may also fail to conform with the requirement of federal procurement law that prospective bidders be informed of the minimum standard for a contract. On the other hand, numerical standards in the quest for equal opportunity open the door to an emphasis on equal results. The second issue raised is whether discrimination and its remedy should be addressed in terms of groups or individuals. Most of our law turns on individual rights. The surfacing of group rights under Title VII is the source of persistent tension. It raises issues of group guilt, group retribution, and group preferences. It challenges the atomistic notion of a color-, race-, and gender-blind society. And it follows directly from the standard economic definition of employment discrimination adopted by the courts — systematically treating members of a particular group differently on account of real or perceived group characteristics that are irrelevant to productivity.

In the heated political arguments over whether and what affirmative action should be, mythic visions have come to overwhelm any clear conception of what affirmative action actually is. To discern what the affirmative action obligation means, I believe it is more useful to examine the actions rather than the words of employers and regulators.

The Development of Affirmative Action in the Early 1970s

Over time the OFCCP became slightly more voluble on the subject of the details of the affirmative action obligation. Detailed regulations, including numerical goals, were introduced in 1969, after the comptroller general ruled that the affirmative action obligation was too vague to fulfill the requirement that minimum contract standards be made clear to prospective bidders (48 Comp. Gen. 326 [1968]). Numerical goals were first introduced in the manning tables embodied in the Cleveland and Philadelphia plans for construction contractors. These measurable standards to monitor compliance were extended to nonconstruction contractors in 1970, and the regulations won the tacit approval of Congress and the courts. The regulations require an affirmative action program consisting in part of a utilization analysis of the work force indicating areas in which the employer is deficient — areas of underutilization — and goals and timetables for good-faith efforts to correct deficiencies (41 C.F.R. 60-2.10 [1977]). For each job title by line of progression, the work force analysis lists the wage rate, the total number of incumbents by sex, and the number of incumbents who are black, Spanish-surnamed, Native American, and Asian.

What is underutilization? That is a question that has kept many lawyers, economists, and statisticians employed, and given birth to a whole new breed: affirmative action professionals. Underutilization is defined in the regulation as "having fewer minorities or women in a particular job group than would reasonably be expected by their availability. In making the utilization analysis the contractor shall conduct such analysis separately for minorities and women." The eight-factor test for underutilization first issued in the OFCCP's Revised Order Number 4 of 1974 reads as follows:

> (1) In determining whether minorities are being under-utilized in any job group, the contractor will consider at least all of the following factors:
> (i)   The minority population of the labor area surrounding the facility;
> (ii)   The size of the minority unemployment force in the labor area surrounding the facility;
> (iii) The percentage of the minority work force as compared with the total work force in the immediate labor area;

(iv) The general availability of minorities having requisite skills in the immediate labor area;

(v) The availability of minorities having requisite skills in an area in which the contractor can reasonably recruit;

(vi) The availability of promotable and transferable minorities within the contractor's organization;

(vii) The existence of training institutions capable of training persons in the requisite skills; and

(viii) The degree of training which the contractor is reasonably able to undertake as a means of making all job classes available to minorities."

The same eight factors are also to be used for assessing the employment of women. The ambiguity and inconsistency inherent in these standards imposes a vague and potentially overwhelming burden on the contractor. The first factor suggests that a determination of employment underutilization be based on a comparison with the local population, regardless of skills. Note also that defining the local labor area is itself a fitting subject for litigation, as in the debarment contesting case of *Timken Co. v. Vaughan* (413 F. Supp. 1183 [N.D. Ohio 1976]) in which the court slogged through the details of travel time and distance and traditional commuting practice. The second factor suggests the availability of unemployed people is what counts — the excess supply of workers. The third factor changes the emphasis from absolute to relative population. Population is exchanged for availability and skills are brought into the picture in factors four and five, and five muddies the already gray waters of "immediate labor area" by adding "area in which the contractor can reasonably recruit." Setting aside the external market, factor six suggests internal promotions and transfers must also be considered. Factor seven suggests taking into account external training institutions, and factor eight suggests internal training to make jobs available to minorities and females. This last factor shows how, in the process of translating law into regulation, the obligation of affirmative action has grown.

Affirmative action has grown from the germ of combating employment discrimination to the intimation that firms pay for training that either remedies premarket discrimination or calls for equality of result rather than equality of opportunity. It is not enough to bring all up to the starting line if some still wear the shackles of past discrimination, but the distinction between the starting line, the finish line, and the race itself has become blurred, along with the employer's burden.

While not affirmed by Congress and the courts, these detailed and growing regulations have won tacit approval by not being negated. As the Ninth Circuit Court said in the case of *Legal Aid Society of Alameda County v. Brennan*: "there can be no doubt that the essential feature of the Affirmative Action Program reflected in the regulations promulgated in Revised Order No. 4 were effectively ratified by Congress in adopting the Equal Employment Opportunity Act of 1972" (608 f.2d. 1319, 1329-39 n. 14 [1979], cert. denied, 445 v.s. 946 [1980]). It is worthy of note that the furthest Congress has been willing to stick its neck out on this issue is to refuse to negate it.

If the utilization analysis required by the regulations reveals that women or minorities are underrepresented in an establishment, then the contractor is required to submit numerical goals for the prompt and full utilization of members of protected groups, and timetables for the achievement of those goals. According to the regulations, "these goals may not be rigid and inflexible quotas which must be met, but must be targets reasonably attainable by means of applying every good faith effort to make all aspects of the entire affirmative action program work" (41 C.F.R. 60-2.13[f] & [i] [1978]).

Over and above these efforts to ensure full utilization, Revised Order Number 4 also required contractors to provide "relief, including back pay when appropriate, for members of an affected class who by virtue of past discrimination continue to suffer the present effects of that discrimination" (41 C.F.R. 60-2.1b [1978]). This relief is to be formalized in a conciliation agreement, but guidelines for affected class identification and remedies have not been issued.

Contractors are also required to "validate worker specifications . . . by job title using job performance criteria. Special attention should be given to academic experience, and skill requirements to insure that the requirements themselves do not constitute inadvertent discrimination" (41 C.F.R. 60-2.24b [1978]).

The regulation that employee selection and promotion tests be validated to ensure that they are related to job performance and are not merely a pretext for discrimination stems directly from the celebrated 1971 Supreme Court decision in *Griggs v. Duke Power Company*. Since discriminators are unlikely to confess intent, a prima facie case of discrimination can be made by showing the disparate impact across race or sex lines of personnel procedures. However, one consequence is that the baby of promoting nondiscriminatory employment for the full, fair, and efficient use of human resources may be in danger of being thrown out with the bathwater of superfluous or biased tests used as a pretense for discrimination. If all employee selection were made objectively, there could, by definition, be no discrimination. Tests appear at first sight to be more objective than interviews or other means of employee selection, so one might suppose that federal antidiscrimination policy would promote a meritocracy based on tests. Just the opposite is true. Since tests are imperfect and validation is costly, employers have dropped tests and standards that they previously found useful. Even if the contractor successfully validates a test, under Equal Employment Opportunity Commission (EEOC) guidelines [29 C.F.R. 1607.3[b] [1974]) he or she must also show that there are no other less discriminatory tests available that also predict job performance. In the words of the *Harvard Law Review*, "The validation and alternative showing requirement embodied in EEOC requirements and enforced by the OFCCP, if stringently applied, would raise the cost of testing for many employers beyond tolerable limits, forcing the abandonment of testing programs, which, although they may be valid, cannot be validated at any cost. . . . The guidelines if applied as strictly as their language allows, would encourage many employers to use a quota system of hiring."

The view is echoed by Supreme Court Justice Blackmun in a 1975 dissent: "I fear that too rigid application of the EEOC Guidelines will leave the employer too little choice, save an impossibly expensive and complex validation study, but to engage in a subjective quota system of employment selection. This, of course, is far from the intent of Title VII." The implications for productivity are drawn by a representative of a prominent, though partisan, labor law firm: "The incentive and ability of managers and supervisors to manage is threatened when random or quota selection replaces their right to evaluate and select employees based upon merit. . . the statistical parity theory invariably results in the abandonment of the 'most qualified' standard for the 'basically qualified' or 'lowest common denominator' standard or, in some cases, no selection standard at all. When projected across our entire economy, this pressure to substitute numbers and the 'lowest common denominator' standard for merit selection results in immense costs in lost efficiency, productivity, and quality" (*Albermarle Paper Co. v. Moody* [1975]).

Surveys of personnel executives by the Bureau of National Affairs show that the use of tests in employee selection had in fact declined. In 1976, 60 percent of the 160 companies surveyed reported that they had changed their selection procedures for equal employment opportunity reasons. Thirty-nine percent changed testing procedures and 31 percent revised job qualifications. Of 196 companies also surveyed in 1976, only 42 percent used ability, intelligence, or personality tests in preemployment screening. This was a drastic drop from the 90 percent of firms that used such psychological tests in a comparable 1963 survey. Most companies in 1976 considered interviews the most important aspect of the selection procedure. The concrete, measurable qualities that are the essence of tests also made them a relatively easy target for law suits. Under the pressure of Title VII law, employee selection now largely takes place through interviews rather than tests, although there is some evidence of a recent resurgence of testing. Title VII has prompted a more formally documented selection process, but not necessarily a more objective or more efficient process.

How does the government see to it that firms meet their affirmative action obligations? Field officers stated in interviews that in targeting compliance reviews they typically do not refer to an establishment's demographic record contained in official Equal Employment Opportunity forms or to its past affirmative action records. In part, affirmative action enforcement today is a game played with backward-looking mirrors. An internal affirmative action bureaucracy has become entrenched in the largest corporations, and this internal bureaucracy has goals of its own that internalize within the corporations the external government goals even when external pressure declines. Since these corporate affirmative action professionals influence the flow of information to the corporation concerning affirmative action regulation, and are usually individually committed to affirmative action, they can keep the threat of external pressure alive. Of course, one expects firms to learn over time the true extent of enforcement.

Efficient regulation may entail intense sanctions rather than extensive surveillance. Debarment, however, does not seem to be appropriate, because it is politically and economically costly to the government and need not be costly to the debarred firm. Fines or back-pay awards impose direct costs on the firms and constitute a more credible threat, since they impose lower costs on the government. Short of that, the less hard-edged pressure of adverse publicity can influence firms at little cost to the government. Publicity is a more subtle sanction, but it may be among the most powerful tool available to the OFCCP. Corporate management does not like to be publicly labeled racist and sexist, even in industries that do not sell directly to the public, perhaps because such labels encourage Title VII law suits.

"Show trials" are an efficient means of magnifying the perceived threat of government intervention. During the Carter administration the OFCCP pursued a few well-publicized debarments. Many were promptly enjoined by the courts, but not before businesses were made aware that the OFCCP was willing to use its ultimate sanction.

The literature on the early years of affirmative action can be divided into studies of process that find it mortally flawed and studies of impact that find it modestly successful. In the light of studies finding that regulatory pressure in the affirmative action program has been close to nonexistent, it is surprising that the few econometric studies of the impact of affirmative action in its first years have generally found significant evidence that it has been effective for black men (Burman 1973; Ashenfelter and Heckman 1976; Goldstein and Smith 1976; Heckman and Wolpin 1976). These few studies of the initial years of affirmative action (1966 to 1973) are not directly comparable because of the different specifications, samples, and periods they employ. Nevertheless they do find that despite weak enforcement in its early years, and despite the ineffectiveness of compliance reviews, affirmative action has been effective in increasing the employment share of black men in the contractor sector; Brown (1982) provides a review. The effects are not large, generally in the order of an increase of less than 1 percent in the black male share of employment per year. However, they do imply that even with seemingly weak enforcement, affirmative action under the contract compliance program did increase the proportion of black men in federal contractor firms in the early 1970s.

The Maturation of Affirmative Action in the Late 1970s

Enforcement of affirmative action did become more aggressive after 1973, whether measured by the increased incidence of debarment or by back-pay awards. In addition, the contract compliance agencies were consolidated into the Office of Federal Contract Compliance Programs in 1978.

Since affirmative action regulations under Executive Order 11246 apply only to federal contractors, one method of judging its effect is to compare the growth of minority and female employment at federal contractor establishments with figures at similar establishments that have no affirmative action obligation. I performed such a comparison using data on employment demographics reported to the government by 68,690 establishments in 1974 and 1980. This sample includes more than 16 million employees. (The results summarized here are reported at length in Leonard 1983 and 1984a.)

I compared the mean employment share of demographic groups in 1974 and 1980 across contractor and noncontractor establishments.

Between 1974 and 1980 black male and female employment shares increased significantly faster in contractor establishments than in noncontractor establishments. I have estimated the impact of affirmative action after controlling for establishment size, growth, region, industry, and occupational and corporate structure (Leonard 1984a). Affirmative action has similar effects even with these additional controls. I found that the employment of members of protected groups grew significantly faster in contractor than in noncontractor establishments.

Expressed as an annual growth rate, black male employment grew 0.62 percent faster in the contractor sector. For white men, the annual growth rate was 0.2 percent slower among contractors, so contractor status appears to shift the demand for black men relative to white men by 0.82 percent per year. These effects are significant at the 99 percent confidence level or better, and are robust across a number of specifications. These effects are similar in magnitude to those previously estimated by Ashenfelter and Heckman (1976) and by Heckman and Wolpin (1976).

Compliance reviews have played a significant role over and above that of contractor status. Compliance reviews — an audit of an employer's demographics and personnel procedures, with negotiations over suggested changes — are the main enforcement mechanism. For the employment of black men, the impact of a company's undergoing a compliance review is roughly twice that of its being a federal contractor. Conversely, compliance reviews have retarded the employment growth of whites. Direct pressure does make a difference. Simultaneity is unlikely to bias these estimates because, as I shall show, the probability of being reviewed hardly depends on demographics.

The total impact of affirmative action on the growth rate of employment for black men among federal contractors is, then, the weighted average of the annual 0.62 percent shift among non-reviewed contractors and the 1.91 percent shift among reviewed contractors, or 0.84 percent per year. The corresponding demand shift for black women is 2.13 percent. Regression estimates also indicate that minorities and women experienced significantly greater increases in representation in establishments that were growing and so had many job openings, irrespective of affirmative action. The elasticity of white male employment growth with respect to total employment growth is .976, significantly less than 1. The respective elasticities for black men and black women (1.22 and 1.19) are significantly greater than 1. This indicates that members of protected groups dominate the net incoming flows in both contractor and noncontractor establishments. The supply of blacks has not greatly increased, so this suggests the importance of expanding employment opportunities with broader forces, such as Title VII, that apply to all sample establishments. The efficacy of affirmative action also depends heavily on employment growth. Affirmative action has been far more successful at establishments that are growing and have more job openings to accommodate federal pressure.

Although affirmative action has lacked public consensus and vigorous enforcement and has frequently been criticized as an exercise in paper pushing, it has actually been of material importance in prompting companies to increase their employment of black men and women.

Occupational Advance

One of the major affirmative action battlefields lies in the white-collar and craft occupations. In these skilled positions, employers are most sensitive to productivity differences and have complained the most about the burden of goals for minority and female employment. It is also in this region of relatively inelastic supply that the potential wage gains for members of protected groups are the greatest.

The four econometric studies mentioned earlier, which found employment gains for blacks despite little enforcement of affirmative action in its early years, also found that while affirmative action increases total black male employment among federal contractors, it does not increase the employment share of black men in the skilled occupations (Burman 1973; Ashenfelter and Heckman 1976; Goldstein and Smith 1976; Heckman and Wolpin 1976). These studies suggest that contractors have been able to fulfill their obligations by hiring into relatively unskilled positions. Before 1974, affirmative action appears to have been more effective in increasing employment than in promoting occupational advancement.

Some might argue that such a result is only to be expected, given a short supply of skilled minorities or women. However, even in the case of a small fixed supply, affirmative action should induce a reshuffling of skilled blacks and women from noncontractor to contractor firms without any increase in overall supply being necessary. The long-run presumption behind affirmative action is that trainable members of protected groups will be considered for promotion to skilled employment. By the late 1970s, however, affirmative action was no longer as ineffective as it may have been in its early years at increasing minority employment in skilled occupations (Leonard 1984b). This difference may reflect the increasing supply of highly educated blacks, as well as the more aggressive enforcement program that developed in the middle to late 1970s.

Goals or Quotas?

The goals and timetables for the employment of minorities and women drawn from the affirmative action plans of federal contractors stand accused of two mutually inconsistent charges. The first is that "goal" is really just an expedient and polite word for inflexible quotas for minority and female employment. The second is that these goals are worth less than the paper they are written on, and that affirmative action has never been enforced stringently enough to produce significant results. What are affirmative action promises actually worth? The employment goals that firms agree to under affirmative action are not adhered to strictly as quotas, nor are they vacuous (Leonard 1985b).

Goals and timetables generally predict growth in minority and female employment shares far in excess of their own past history, and far in excess of what they will actually fulfill. In fact, they also overpromise white male employment, which reveals something of their strategy in formulating promises. They do not promise direct substitution of minority and female workers for white men; instead, they promise more for all.

But while the projections for future employment of members of protected groups are inflated, establishments that promise to employ more actually do employ more. It turns out that the affirmative action goal is the single best predictor of subsequent employment demographics, far better than the establishment's own past history, even controlling for the direct impact of detailed regulatory pressure (Leonard 1985b).

Goals set during costly compliance negotiations do have a measurable and significant correlation with improvements in the employment of minorities and women at reviewed establishments (Leonard 1985b). At the same time, these goals are not being fulfilled with the rigidity one would expect of quotas. This indicates that while establishments promise more than they deliver, the ones that promise more do deliver more. We have a policy that appears to be effective in its whole and ineffective in its parts.

The Targeting of Compliance Reviews

Affirmative action can be broadly conceived of either as a tool to fight discrimination or as a tool to redistribute jobs and earnings. That is to say, it can either pursue equality of opportunity or equality of result. Given the historical record, progress toward one goal will often entail progress toward the other. Some see discrimination as a broad enough target that it can be hit even with imperfect aim. The approach taken here is to infer the ends of affirmative action policy from an analysis of the historical record of actual enforcement.

Assertions concerning the ends of affirmative action are surprisingly common, especially when one realizes that only twice in the past has the actual pattern of enforcement been analyzed. The pathbreaking study of Heckman and Wolpin (1976) examined the incidence of compliance reviews at a sample of 1,185 Chicago-area establishments during 1972. These compliance reviews are the first, the most common, and usually the last step in the enforcement process. Heckman and Wolpin found that the probability of review was not affected by establishment size, minority employment, or change in minority employment. They discovered "no evidence of a systematic government policy for reviewing contractor firms." This first analysis of targeting studied a relatively small sample in one city during the early 1970s, before the contract compliance program reached its full stride. Additional research is needed to discover if these early findings continue to hold true. And just as important, how are such results to be interpreted?

If one were to think of the OFCCP's primary concern as fighting the most blatant forms of employment discrimination directly in the workplace, one might then expect reviews to be concentrated at establishments employing a relatively small proportion of women and black men, controlling for size, industry, and region. Indeed, the OFCCP has used formal systems for targeting reviews, such as the Revised McKersie System or the late EISEN system. These systems generally select for review those establishments with a low proportion of minorities or women relative to other establishments in the same area and industry.

But interviews with OFCCP officials in Washington and in the field suggest that these formal targeting systems were never really used. Instead, compliance officers claim they simply reviewed the firms with the most employees and the growing firms. Given an even distribution of discriminators, and the large fixed costs of review, this may not be unreasonable. I gathered additional evidence by examining the types of establishments that were actually reviewed between 1974 and 1980 (Leonard 1985a). Firms with low proportions of women or black men were not any more likely to be reviewed than those with much higher proportions.

How can this lack of a consistent targeting pattern by race or sex be explained? One explanation is that affirmative action is primarily concerned not with attacking the grossest forms of current employment discrimination, but rather with redistributing jobs and earnings to minorities and women. The model of affirmative action as an earnings redistribution program has two testable implications. The first is that no particular pressure should be applied to firms with relatively few minorities or women, since discrimination is not at issue. The second implication is that greater pressure should be brought to bear to shift demand curves where the supply of labor is relatively inelastic. In particular, this implies a higher incidence of compliance reviews at establishments with non-clerical-intensive workforces. As I have already noted, enforcement is not concentrated on establishments with few women or blacks. As to the second implication, I find evidence that reviews are significantly more likely to take place, other factors held constant, in non-clerical, white-collar establishments. Reviews are also more likely to occur at both large and growing establishments, where any costs to white men are likely to be more diffused.

Charades for the 1980s

The economic advance of blacks faltered along a number of dimensions during the 1980s. I do not know how much of this was due to weakened affirmative action, but I do know that affirmative action under the contract compliance program virtually ceased to exist in all but name after 1980 (Leonard 1987a). From a public relations perspective, the gutting of the program had a certain artfulness. With no greater staffing or budget, the OFCCP doubled the number of compliance reviews. A wondrously invigorated bureaucracy doubling its efficiency? It is easy to go twice as fast when you are just going through the motions, with more desk reviews and fewer in-depth audits. After 1980, fewer administrative complaints were filed, back-pay awards were phased out, and the already rare penalty of debarment became an endangered species. Over the same period, OFCCP staffing and real budget were reduced. This type of surface enforcement resulted not just in stagnation, but in a reversal of the advances blacks had made under affirmative action. Between 1980 and 1984, both male and female black employment grew more slowly among contractors than noncontractors (Leonard 1987a). Affirmative action, such as it was, no longer aided blacks. Consider the different response, by contractor status, of black male employment growth to the total establishment employment growth of 10 percent. Before 1980, this could be expected to result in a black male employment growth rate of 12 percent among noncontractors and 17 percent among contractors. After 1980, the comparable rates were 11 percent among noncontractors and 10 percent among contractors. The reversal of growth for black women was even more marked.

It is as though contractors were returning to a growth path they had been forced off of by previous affirmative action efforts. This is discouraging news. Affirmative action seeks to give those discriminated against a chance to demonstrate their skills, and thus to break the preconceptions on which prejudicial barriers are based. Under this model, affirmative action should serve as long-term inoculation against discrimination, and previous victims of discrimination should continue to progress even after active treatment has ceased.

The evidence supports far less optimistic views of what is at stake. The decline of black employment advances under the "affirmative inaction" program of the 1980s suggests either that affirmative action during the 1970s resulted in discrimination against whites, or that ongoing treatment is required to counteract the aftereffects of generations of discrimination, or that there is a persistence and resiliency to the taste for discrimination against blacks.

Of another form of affirmative action that developed during the 1970s we are more ignorant. Set-aside programs were enacted that set numerical goals for the share of government construction, goods, and services to be purchased from minority- or women-owned businesses. These were usually justified as a remedy for past discrimination. The impact these set-aside policies may have had is unknown — either before or after being challenged by the Supreme Court's *Croson v. City of Richmond* decision. In part this is because we have little in the way of a government contracting baseline for comparison. The incubator effect on business growth, the indirect effect on minority or female employment, the ease with which shell companies can be used to sidestep the law, or the political trade-off of throwing some small bones to minority- or women-owned firms while maintaining competitive bidding on large contracts — all are unknown.

The Impact of Title VII of the Civil Rights Act of 1964

Title VII of the Civil Rights Act of 1964, which made employment discrimination illegal, stands at the center of the federal anti-discrimination effort. While the focus of this analysis has been on affirmative action under the executive order, it should be understood that the executive order has functioned within the backdrop of Title VII's congressional mandate and substantial legal sanctions. This section will sketch some of the findings in the literature about the impact of Title VII. (For a more complete discussion, see Brown 1982; Freeman 1981; Butler and Heckman 1977; and Smith 1978.) Title VII allows individuals to bring suit with only pro forma bureaucratic oversight. More important, Title VII litigation has resulted in multi-million dollar remedies. The threat of costly Title VII litigation, largely private, has been of great importance to employers.

The major contribution of the Equal Employment Opportunity Commission, which oversees Title VII enforcement, has probably been in helping to establish far-reaching principles of Title VII law in the courts that can then be used by private litigants, rather than in directly providing relief from systematic discrimination through its own enforcement activity.

Government policies to improve the position of blacks have been multifaceted. That makes it difficult to disentangle their effects against a shifting economic background. These policies include the 1962 and 1965 Voting Rights Acts that expanded black political power, measures such as the Supreme Court's 1954 decision in *Brown v. Board of Education* that outlawed separate but equal school systems, the Civil Rights Act of 1964 and Executive Order 11246 barring discrimination in employment, and the antipoverty programs of the Great Society.

While there is broad agreement that the earnings of employed blacks increased relative to those of whites through much of the postwar period, there is continuing debate about the causes of this convergence. The logarithmic wage differential between black and white men improved from −0.48 in 1960 to −0.39 in 1970 to −0.29 in 1980. Average wages of blacks relative to whites rose from 62 percent in 1960 to 67 percent in 1970 to 75 percent in 1980 (Card and Krueger 1992, Table 1). Smith and Welch (1989) argue that migration from the rural South and improvements in black education relative to white education account for much of the convergence. Indeed, while the rate of racial convergence was particularly rapid during the 1940s, few would recommend re-creating the same circumstances today: a Great Depression to further marginalize blacks followed by the extraordinarily tight labor markets of World War II. While it is true that blacks have gained during periods of economic growth and high demand in the past, the period since 1973 charts a far more fragmented path. Part of the relative economic stagnation of blacks after 1973 is a result of the broader decline in the earnings of un-skilled workers — a decline that hit blacks harder, given their greater concentration in low-skill industries and occupations (Bound and Freeman 1992).

Migration out of the low-wage rural South clearly raised blacks' earnings, but this effect had run its course by the mid-1960s. Farley and Allen (1987) show that 14.6 percent of the black population left the South during the 1940s, and an additional 13.7 percent left during the 1950s. However, as Farley and Allen show, of the total net migration of southern blacks during the 1960s, only 15.7 percent left after 1965 — when the overall pace of economic convergence accelerated sharply.

The acceleration of black economic progress after 1965 — even among cohorts that had completed their education years or decades previously — also does not fit well with explanations in terms of more or better education. While education certainly contributes to economic advance, Card and Krueger (1992) estimate that improve-ments in school quality can explain only 15 to 25 percent of the closing of racial differentials in wages among southern-born workers between 1960 and 1980. This leaves a large potential role for some factor that increases black earnings relative to white starting in 1965 and affecting all cohorts.

The work of Richard Freeman is of critical importance in demon-strating the central role of federal antidiscrimination policy in im-proving the earnings of employed blacks (Freeman 1973, 1981). Freeman found that the upward trend in the ratio of black to white earnings distinctly accelerated after 1965, as the Civil Rights Act of 1964 went into effect. I have used cross-section data to corroborate the effectiveness of Title VII litigation: black employment share increased significantly faster during the late 1960s and 1970s in industries and states with a greater incidence of class-action Title VII decisions per firm (Leonard 1984c). While perhaps 10 to 20 percent of the observed convergence in earnings over time may be attributed to low-wage blacks dropping out of the labor force (Leonard, 1987, Butler and Heckman 1977, Brown 1982), the timing and magnitude of the changes is consistent with effective pressure under Title VII. The conclusion that federal civil rights policy, including the Civil Rights Act of 1964 and affirmative action under the contract compliance program, was "the major contributor to the sustained improvement in black economic status that began in 1965" is shared by Donohue and Heckman (1991, p. 1641) and by Heckman and Payner (1989).

One criticism of Title VII is that it has led to numerical balancing rather than to a reduction in discrimination, as firms have sought safety behind the right numbers. A facile employer response to Title VII is to ensure that all employment flow rates (hires, promotions, discharges, and so on) are the same across demographic groups, irrespective of discrimination. In time, black representation in the firm mirrors that in the relevant labor pool. However, cases such as *Connecticut v. Teal* (457 U.S. 440 [1982]) indicate that employers cannot be assured immunity from challenge under Title VII by having the "right" numbers of minority or female employees on their bottom line. Moreover, evidence of a decline in the variance of demographic employment shares is more complex and mixed than the numerical balancing theory predicts (Leonard 1987b). For example, the variance of black female and nonblack minority employment shares have increased.

Previous research suggests that Title VII litigation has played a significant role over and above that of affirmative action. Title VII has affected a larger group of employers and implemented more severe sanctions. The Supreme Court decisions of 1989 raised the burden and limited the prospects for plaintiffs contemplating adverse impact claims under Title VII. *Wards Cove Packing Company, Inc. v. Atonio* (109 S.Ct. 2115 [1989]) did this by requiring that plaintiffs demonstrate that a particular policy having an adverse impact is not a business necessity. Overturning this decision was a key element of the Civil Rights Act of 1991. In contrast to the 1960s and 1970s, the courts are now more reluctant than Congress to extend the reach of Title VII.

Despite poor targeting, affirmative action has helped promote the employment of minorities and women, and Title VII has likely played an even greater role. But has this pressure led to reduced discrimination, or has it gone beyond and induced reverse discrimination against white men? The evidence is least conclusive on this question. Direct tests of the impact of affirmative action on productivity find no significant evidence of a productivity decline, which implies a lack of substantial reverse discrimination (Leonard 1984c). However, since the productivity estimates are not measured with great precision, strong policy conclusions based on this particular result should be resisted. The available evidence is not yet strong enough to be compelling on either side of this issue.

While government antidiscrimination policies achieved some important successes between 1965 and 1980, their future contributions to improving minority economic position seem more problematic, both because the temperament of the judiciary has changed and because broader economic forces are undercutting the position of minorities. In the courts, most of the easy pickings are gone and employers have become more sophisticated. Cases that do reach the courts face a more conservative judiciary among whom the historical events of the Civil Rights movement resonate weakly. As I have already noted, affirmative action under the Executive Order virtually ceased as an effective instrument of policy after 1980. The economic environment, which had previously supported black progress, became more of an obstacle after the mid-1970s. With an increasingly open economy and technological change, the real earnings of low-skill workers plummeted in the United States. Sectors of the economy that had been gateways for black progress were hard hit. Manufacturing's share of jobs fell, as did the unions'. Overall economic growth fell below that experienced in the 1950s and 1960s. Socially, the inner cities faced mounting problems of crime, drugs, and the breakdown of the family. The result of all these adverse forces was a decline in the economic position of young black men. Controlling for years of education and experience, the logarithmic earnings differentials between blacks and whites increased from $-.136$ in 1980 to $-.179$ in 1989, with a significant negative trend (toward greater inequality) over the period between 1973 and 1989 (Bound and Freeman 1992). While the precise factors at work vary across different black subgroups, the immediate past does not bode well for the future economic well-being of blacks.

One of the rare and noble virtues of democracies is their protection of the rights of individuals and minority groups. History, after all, continues to accumulate dismal stories of the fate of minority groups under less politically open systems.

While a strong consensus in this country supports policies against discrimination, affirmative action continues to provoke sharply divided opinions. In consequence, affirmative action remains cloaked in ambiguity. The political lightning it attracts has far more to do with its symbolic importance as a totem of group rights and privileges, than with its modest practical accomplishments to date. Of course none of this precludes enacting affirmative action law (although it does help considerably if it is called something else). At the same time that the proposed Civil Rights Act of 1990 was stalled in Congress and was facing a presidential veto — quota bill that would unfairly burden employers — the nation's most explicit affirmative action law was enacted with only the slightest opposition. An employment law sold as an antidiscrimination measure, recognizing group differences and requiring employers to spend resources to overcome those differences was greeted by warm consensus. The Americans with Disabilities Act of 1990 requires that employers make reasonable accommodations for the disabled. In contrast to other civil rights laws, this act starts from the presumption that the disabled may be less productive given the current situation, and it requires employers to spend more to employ them. This is the most explicit form of affirmative action taken to date in employment, so we should not be surprised to find that it has never been described in such terms.

References

Ashenfelter, Orley, and James Heckman. 1976. "Measuring the Effect of an Antidiscrimination Program." In Orley Ashenfelter and James Blum, eds., *Evaluating the Labor Market Effects of Social Programs.* Princeton, N.J.: Princeton University, Industrial Relations Series.

Bound, John, and Richard B. Freeman. 1992. "What Went Wrong? The Erosion of Relative Earnings and Employment among Young Black Men in the 1980s," *Quarterly Journal of Economics* 107, no. 1 (February), 201–232.

Brown, Charles. 1982. "The Federal Attack on Labor Market Discrimination: The Mouse that Roared?" In R. Ehrenberg, ed., *Research in Labor Economics*, vol. 5. New York: JAI Press. pp. 33–68.

Burman, George. 1973. "The Economics of Discrimination: The Impact of Public Policy," Ph.D. dissertation, University of Chicago.

Butler, Richard, and James Heckman. 1977. "The Government's Impact on the Labor Market Status of Black Americans: A Critical Review." In Farrell E. Bloch et al., eds., *Equal Rights and Industrial Relations.* Madison, Wis.: Industrial Relations Research Association. pp. 235–281.

Card, David, and Alan Krueger. 1992. "School Quality and Black-White Relative Earnings: A Direct Assessment," *Quarterly Journal of Economics* 107, no. 1 (February), 151–200.

Donohue, John III, and James Heckman. 1991. "Continuous versus Episodic Change: The Impact of Civil Rights Policy on the Economic Status of Blacks," *Journal of Economic Literature* 29 (December), 1603–1643.

Farley, Reynolds, and Walter Allen. 1987. *The Color Line and the Quality of Life in America.* New York: Russell Sage Foundation.

Fiss, Owen M. 1977. "A Theory of Fair Employment Laws," *University of Chicago Law Review* 39, 235–313.

Freeman, Richard B. 1973. "Changes in the Labor Market for Black Americans, 1948–1972," *Brookings Papers on Economic Activity* 1, 67–120.

———. 1981. "Black Economic Progress after 1964: Who Has Gained and Why?" In Sherwin Rosen, ed., *Studies in Labor Markets.* Chicago: University of Chicago Press/National Bureau of Economic Research. pp. 247–294.

Glazer, Nathan. 1975. *Affirmative Discrimination: Ethnic Inequality and Public Policy.* New York: Basic Books.

Goldstein, Morris, and Robert S. Smith. 1976. "The Estimated Impact of the Anti-discrimination Program Aimed at Federal Contractors," *Industrial and Labor Relations Review* 29 (July), 524–543.

Heckman, James J., and Brook Payner. 1989. "Determining the Impact of Federal Anti-discrimination Policy on the Economic Status of Blacks: A Study of South Carolina," *American Economic Review* 79, no. 1 (March), 138–177.

Heckman, James J., and Kenneth I. Wolpin. 1976. "Does the Contract Compliance Program Work? An Analysis of Chicago Data," *Industrial and Labor Relations Review* 29 (July), 544–564.

Leonard, Jonathan S., 1976. "On the Decline in the Labor Force Participation Rates of Older Black Males," Thesis, Harvard College.

———. 1983. "The Impact of Affirmative Action," Department of Labor Report, July 1983.

———. 1984a. "The Impact of Affirmative Action on Employment," *Journal of Labor Economics* 2 (October), 439–463.

———. 1984b. "Employment and Occupational Advance under Affirmative Action," *Review of Economics and Statistics* 66 (August), 377–385.

———. 1984c. "Anti-Discrimination or Reverse Discrimination: The Impact of Changing Demographics, Title VII and Affirmative Action on Productivity," *Journal of Human Resources* 19 (Spring), 145–174.

———. 1985a. "Affirmative Action as Earnings Redistribution: The Targeting of Compliance Reviews," *Journal of Labor Economics* 3 (July), 363–384.

———. 1985b. "What Promises Are Worth: The Impact of Affirmative Action Goals," *Journal of Human Resources* 20 (Winter), 3–20.

———. 1986. "Splitting Blacks? Affirmative Action and Earnings Inequality within and between Races," *Proceedings of the Industrial Relations Research Association Annual Meeting* 39 (Winter), 51–57.

———. 1987a. "Affirmative Action in the 1980s: With a Whimper, Not a Bang." Unpublished paper, University of California, Berkeley.

———. 1987b. "Anti-Discrimination or Numerical Balancing: The Impact of Title VII, 1978–1984." Unpublished paper, University of California, Berkeley.

Ruchames, L. 1953. *Race, Jobs and Politics — The Story of FEPC.* New York: Columbia University Press.

Silberman, Lawrence H. 1977. "The Road to Racial Quotas," *Wall Street Journal,* August 11, p. 14.

Smith, Arthur B., Jr. 1978. *Employment Discrimination Law.* Indianapolis: Bobbs-Merrill.

Smith, James P., and Finis Welch. 1984. "Affirmative Action and Labor Markets," *Journal of Labor Economics* 2 (April), 269–301.

———. 1989. "Black Economic Progress After Myrdal," *Journal of Economic Literature* 27, no. 2 (June), 519–564.

22

Organizations and Learning Systems for a High-Wage Economy

■ ─────────────────── ■

Ray Marshall

Ideas, skills, and knowledge, embodied in people, tools, machines, and organizational structures — that is, in human and physical capital and organizational structures — have been responsible for most human progress. Human capital has been the main source of improvements in productivity throughout history. Technological progress comes about mainly through improvements in productivity by substituting ideas, skills, and knowledge for physical resources. However, the greatest improvements in productivity come from the effective organization of people and technology. The mass production system that contributed significantly to the economic preeminence of the United States during the first half of this century organized work to achieve economies of scale. The system required educated managers, professionals, and technicians, but most workers did not have to do much learning or thinking. Schools, organized according to mass production principles, mass produced students who, although literate, performed only routine work and therefore were not expected to think or learn very much. Special tracks within these schools, and elite private schools, produced the managerial, professional, and technical workers who had to think.

The basic theme of this chapter is that economic and technological changes have made learning and thinking by a whole organization, especially by frontline workers, a much more important determinant of personal, enterprise, and national economic success. Partly because mass-production learning and working systems were so deeply entrenched in the United States, we are having more trouble than many other countries adjusting to the high-performance learning and working systems required for economic success in a more competitive, knowledge-intensive, global economy. In other words, most of our learning systems are obsolete, and enterprises must now become *learning* as well as *production* systems.

I use the term *learning systems* to include families, work, community institutions, media, and political processes, not just formal schools. As I shall demonstrate later, moreover, there are symbiotic relationships between all of these learning systems.

One of the anomalies of American education is that learning, clearly an important function in schools — and indeed in life — receives very little systematic attention in most American educational institutions. Perhaps this anomaly is due to the assumption that everybody knows what learning is about and how it is done. And perhaps this assumption holds true for the kinds of learning by observation and doing that people have needed throughout most of human history. It was always clear, of course, that some people were better learners than others, but this was not a subject of much analysis, because it was assumed that intellectual ability, like physical attributes, was due mainly to genetics or innate ability — an idea that persists more in the United States than in most industrial nations, despite considerable empirical evidence to the contrary. We now know, in other words, that learning is due mainly to opportunities, supportive learning systems, and hard work, not inherited abilities.

Some of the confusion about learning also is due to the growth of formal education, which created distinctions between schooling, education, and learning. Most learning has taken place outside of formal schools — in families, workplaces, and community institutions. One of the economic realities of the 1990s and beyond is the growing dependence of high-performance economic activity on abstract and formal learning, which was much less important for most workers earlier in this century. A basic hypothesis of this chapter is that economic success requires that all learning systems be restructured to meet the requirements of a very different and more knowledge-intensive economy, and that learning must be a more explicit factor or process in economic as well as school activities.

To clarify this basic hypothesis, I will outline the nature of the economic and learning systems that helped the United States become the world's preeminent industrial economy during the first half of this century, discuss the forces that eroded the American economy's basic advantages, analyze the characteristics of high-performance organizations under modern economic and technological conditions, contrast the requirements for a high-performance economy with existing U.S. learning systems, and conclude with recommendations for public and private practices required to improve American learning systems and economic performance.

The Mass Production System

Before it started losing its relative position in the global economy during the 1960s, the American mass production system had attained unchallenged international status. While there were always many other forces at work, the success of this system caused it to dominate economic and social institutions.

Between 1900 and 1926, the United States developed the world's strongest economy. In 1913, this country accounted for 36 percent of the world's industrial output, three times that of the closest competitor, the United Kingdom. We were the world's largest producer of electricity, autos, and oil. And by 1926 we produced 45 percent of the world's industrial output, about the same percentage we attained in the 1940s (Kuznets 1946; U.S. Department of the Census 1948; Kendrick 1961).

This rapid growth in productivity and total output dramatically increased the American standard of living. Wages of American workers in 1920 were five times higher than in 1900, the output of goods and services was six times as high, and the number of wage earners almost doubled. There were, in addition, rapid increases in per capita GNP: $462 in 1897, $502 in 1900, $611 in 1910, and $711 in 1918 (Hession and Sardy 1969: 518).

While no one factor caused the American system's preeminence, there was an unprecedented confluence of mutually reinforcing factors during the first quarter of the twentieth century. Perhaps the most significant of these was the size and importance of the U.S. market, which American companies had largely to themselves. This market was nationalized by the growth of water and rail transportation systems during the eighteenth and nineteenth centuries, and by automobiles, buses, and trucks during the first half of the twentieth century. And the American market was enlarged by rapid population growth and enriched by relatively high and rising incomes.

One of the most important contributions to the development of the American economic system was technology, which is best defined as ways of doing things. Technology therefore includes ideas, knowledge, and skills, some of which immigrants brought with them and some of which were developed to meet American conditions. In the eighteenth century, economic growth depended heavily on the availability of natural resources, especially land. In the first half of the twentieth century, natural resources became much less important and technology increasingly more important — though major factors in the success of the American system were the adaptation of the world's most advanced technology to abundant natural resources and a very supportive policy and institutional environment. The high returns on investments in this environment attracted capital, technology, and people from other countries. After the 1930s, natural resources made almost no contribution to net productivity improvements — which mainly were due to advances in human capital and technology. Less than 20 percent of the improvement in productivity between the 1930s and the 1980s came from physical capital (Carnevale 1983; Schultz 1981; Baumol, Blackman, and Wolff 1989).

One of the most important American contributions to economic organizations was the mass production system, developed in the eighteenth century and made possible by the large, wealthy, and growing internal American market. The mass production system emphasized economies of scale and greatly reduced the cost of such consumer durables as the Singer sewing machine, which revolutionized home and commercial sewing, and food and tobacco products. Indeed, even Andrew Carnegie used an assembly line technique in the production of steel. He used the Monongahela River as the transmission belt for assembling the materials for producing steel. With this system, Carnegie reduced the price of steel from $36.52 a ton in 1878 to $12 a ton in 1898 (Hoerr 1988).

But the most important mass production innovation in the first half of the century undoubtedly was Henry Ford's assembly line, introduced in 1913. Ford made his first car in 1896, but he introduced the Model T, one of the greatest commercial and technological successes of all time, in 1908 (Nevins and Hill 1954). The inexpensive, technologically advanced, and dependable Model T, together with the assembly line, made the Ford Motor Company. Ford's sales skyrocketed from 10,607 cars in 1908–1909 to 730,041 in 1916–17; at the same time the price for a touring car fell from $850 to $360 and Ford's share of the auto market rose from 9.4 percent in 1908 to 48 percent in 1914. The ready availability of low-cost cars, trucks, and tractors radically transformed America's cities, factories, and farms. Productivity in the auto industry more than quadrupled between 1889 and 1919 (Kendrick 1961).

For my purposes, however, the automobile industry was important because it popularized the use of the assembly line and the "scientific management" ideas developed by Frederick Winslow Taylor between 1882 and 1911. Taylor's basic concepts built on much earlier work, especially that of Eli Whitney, who introduced an assembly line at the end of the eighteenth century to produce muskets for the federal government. A major problem for Whitney had been to produce muskets of uniform quality in sufficient quantity to meet the government's standards. He solved this problem with the assembly line and with component specialization to produce parts with fine tolerances so they could be assembled by relatively unskilled labor. This process thus helped to overcome the problem created by a shortage of skilled workers. With the assembly line, total output depended on the production system, not the skills of individual workers.

Taylor's model, developed almost 100 years after Whitney's, involved the following main elements:

1. Fragmented tasks and a minute division of labor among workers;
2. Many layers of management and technical staffs;
3. The belief that there is "one best way" to organize and perform work and that it is management's responsibility to develop this "best way" and impose it on workers;
4. The development of rigid work rules to protect the interests of both managers and workers; and
5. The belief that efficiency requires an authoritarian system in which management has unchallenged control of: (a) the design and introduction of technology; (b) investment, plant closing, and location decisions; and (c) job functions and qualifications. In short, workers were to be integral components of the production process, thoroughly integrated with the machines (Layton 1971).

Under Taylor's approach to what he called scientific management, "The worker's equal division of work was to do what he was told to do by management and his share of the responsibility was that responsibility to do what he was told. In his system the judgment of the individual workman was replaced by the laws, rules, principles, etc. of the science of the job which was developed by management. . . . The whole attitude of Taylor in this respect was described by a mechanic who worked with him. . . . Taylor would tell him that he was 'not supposed to think, there are other people paid to think around here' (Callahan 1962). Taylor's basic approach was thus to reduce the amount of skill required to produce products, not just to overcome shortages but also to reduce the skilled workers' control of the work, to transfer skills to machines and to management, who would thus gain greater control of the work (Haber 1944).

The Mass Production Schools

The accomplishments of the mass production system in industry caused its leaders to be greatly admired and its values, procedures, and structures to be widely emulated in other sectors, especially in government and the public schools. School administrators and educators, under intense attack from business and the press for being "impractical" and "inefficient," quickly adopted business and scientific management practices as defensive mechanisms (Callahan 1962; Tyack 1974: 28).

The challenge to educators was enormous. As industrial wages rose, employment in America's cities became very attractive to people on the farms and in poverty stricken areas overseas. The schools had to cope with a vast influx of uneducated people and make them fit for life in the factories, mills, and growing numbers of office and retail establishments.

Whether the schools in fact became more efficient is open to question, just as it is at least arguable that mass production and economies of scale, not scientific management, improved industrial efficiency. But there can be little doubt that large bureaucracies were created to control the schools, just as they controlled Tayloristic factories. The United States Office of Education reported that in 1889 there were, on average, 4 school administrators in each of the 484 cities for which it collected such data. Between 1890 and 1920, however, the numbers grew from 9 to 144 in Baltimore, 7 to 159 in Boston, 10 to 159 in Cleveland, and 235 to 1,310 in New York (Tyack 1974: 185).

The dictates of scientific management produced not only this bureaucracy, but also the professors of education who created, taught, and popularized a body of literature that made this system become more pervasive and institutionalized in American schools. Franklin Bobbitt, instructor in educational administration at the University of Chicago, translated Frederick Taylor's principles of scientific management into a form that could be used by school people. Bobbitt

> believed with Taylor that efficiency depended on "centralization of authority and definite direction by the supervisors of all processes performed. ... The worker [that is, the teacher] ... must be kept supplied with detailed instructions as to the work to be done, the standards to be reached, the methods to be employed, and the appliances to be used ... the results of the work of the planning department had to be transmitted to the

teachers so that there can never be any misunderstanding as to what is expected of a teacher in the way of results or in the matter of method. This means that instruction must be given as to everything that is to be done" (Callahan 1962: 89, 90).

Because school administrators could discriminate against women, teaching — almost alone among the occupations requiring a college degree — became more like a blue-collar occupation than a profession. Just as industrial managers employed workers they could control, so school managers, who were overwhelmingly men, hired as teachers women, who would follow orders and who would work for wages well below those their education might otherwise have commanded. Before the formation of factory schools, teachers were more likely to be educated young men who would teach temporarily before going on to some more rewarding occupation; men to whom no other occupation was available, including men who had handicaps; or men, such as ministers, who combined teaching with some other vocation.

All of this changed when the steady rise in student populations greatly increased the demand for teachers. School administrators turned to women because they fit better into Tayloristic schools and could be paid less than men. In 1870, women had come to account for 60 percent of the teaching force. By 1900, the figure had risen to 70 percent, and by 1925, it was 83 percent (Hofstadter, 1963: 317). But these young women were not very well educated and did not stay around very long; convention, law, or regulation required women to quit teaching when they got married or had children. As late as the 1919–20 school year, "half of America's school teachers were under twenty-five, half served in the schools for not more than four or five years, and half had no more than four years of education beyond the eighth grade" (Hofstadter 1963: 318).

The same reformers who imposed scientific management on the schools were also bitter critics of the prevailing classical curriculum, which they denounced as "academic" and irrelevant to the needs of the students (Hofstadter 1963: 331–335). Pressed by the business community to turn out students who had practical skills, and perceiving the traditional intellectual goals to be undemocratic, school leaders made the mastery of basic skills the de facto standard of American schools.

The American system in the 1920s
On the eve of the Great Depression, the American economy had reached its zenith relative to other countries. During the late nineteenth and early twentieth centuries, it enjoyed a favorable combination of mutually reinforcing markets, technologies, resources,

policies, management systems, and institutions that promoted rapid economic growth in key industries. The earliest of the country's advantages were its abundant resources and relative shortages of people, which necessitated the development of productivity-improving technology. U.S. companies at first borrowed technology from Europe and adapted it to American conditions. Later the United States became the world's leading technological innovator, and its market was particularly conducive to the development of the mass production system, whose economies of scale produced important cost advantages. Public policies permitted American businesses more freedom than their counterparts in any other industrial economy. Before the Great Depression, the federal government also supported business interests and used its power to prevent workers from organizing.

The mass production system's values influenced other institutions, especially public schools. The American education system developed into a two-tier system to reflect the mass production company. Elite schools turned out people who were prepared for managerial, professional, and technical jobs, and the public schools mass produced students for routine, mass production jobs. The elites generally thought, planned, and gave orders while the blue-collar workers were not supposed to think — they were supposed to perform routine, repetitive work and follow orders. Mass production schools, like mass production factories, contained enormous inefficiencies, but these were more than offset by economies of scale. Neither teachers nor factory workers were given high status by the system. The teachers, increasingly women, had limited power to change the system. And they were ruled by men who had very little power relative to the "successful men" who dominated the American system and who therefore imposed their values and interests on other institutions. Industrial workers revolted from time to time, but they were generally held in check by the combined power of governments and the corporations, and by labor supplies swollen by unemployment and migrants from rural areas and other countries.

The system collapses

The mass production system nevertheless faced some very serious problems. One of the most important of these, the lack of balance between aggregate demand and aggregate supply, was revealed dramatically by the Great Depression of the 1930s. Other weaknesses became more apparent in the competitive, knowledge-intensive economy of the 1970s and beyond.

The Great Depression is popularly thought to have started with the 1929 stock market crash, which sent the value of the stock traded on the New York Stock Exchange plummeting from $67.5 billion in 1929 to $22.8 billion in 1935; average stock prices fell dramatically from $89.11 to $17.35 (Berle and Means 1933). Although the stock market crash was an important event, the Great Depression had much deeper origins. In fact, the decline in automobile production from 5.6 million cars in 1929 to 1.4 million in 1932 was a much better barometer of economic conditions than the stock prices. In a very real sense the fundamental problems were the mass production system's rigidities and its inability to match demand with the system's greatly increased productive capacity. Wage increases were much smaller during the 1920s than the increase in productivity, causing workers to have inadequate purchasing power to keep the system running.[1]

Because of agriculture's importance in the economy, the farm recession that started in the 1920s was a particularly important cause of inadequate aggregate demand. American agriculture had prospered greatly from economic development, urbanization, increased foreign demand, and improvements in technology and productivity during the "golden era" between 1899 and 1919. But the agricultural boom collapsed during the 1920s. To meet mounting worldwide demand, farmers had incurred substantial debt to add 77 million acres of cropland between 1910 and 1920. The subsequent decline in demand, as productivity increased and production resumed in other countries after World War I, meant that American farmers faced serious overproduction problems (Galbraith 1961). Farmers also suffered from a cost-price squeeze, because they sold on highly competitive markets with flexible prices and bought supplies from the manufacturing sector, which had administered prices.

In the 1920s and 1930s, international markets were disrupted by policies that made it very difficult for the system to work. U.S. financial institutions and companies extended credit to foreigners to buy exports from America, but restrictive trade practices like the 1931 Smoot-Hawley Trade Act made it difficult for foreigners to earn the dollars needed to repay those loans. As the depression deepened, each country attempted to shift its unemployment to others by restricting imports and increasing exports. This led to successive retaliations, contracted trade, and a deepening depression. U.S. exports shrank from over $5 billion in 1929 to $1.6 billion in 1932, while imports fell from $4.4 billion to $1.3 billion.

The expansion of financial markets added to the economic problems. Interlocking relationships between financial institutions were such that disruptions spread quickly throughout the system, as happened after Austria's largest bank, the Kreditanstalt, was forced to close in 1931, followed shortly by the German banks. Soon thereafter Britain abandoned the gold standard, which many economists, who had little understanding of the forces that caused the Great Depression, thought would be the mechanism to maintain international stability.

Similarly, many U.S. economists thought the Federal Reserve System, organized in 1914, had stabilized the country's financial markets, but the Federal Reserve had neither the understanding nor the power to deal with the deepening depression. Indeed, the Federal Reserve had very limited power to prevent the kind of rampant speculation in stocks and other markets during the 1920s that resulted in many individuals being highly leveraged. The vulnerability of those investors almost guaranteed that any major downturn in asset values would cause financial markets to be converted into degenerating systems (Kemmerer 1950).

The New Deal and the mass production system

After the mass production system collapsed during the 1930s, the Roosevelt administration's New Deal sought to resurrect it by overcoming some of its main flaws. Agricultural price supports and other programs attempted to restore parity for farmers in order to enhance their welfare and purchasing power. Financial institutions were bolstered by deposit insurance to prevent runs on banks, as well as by regulations to prevent the speculative excesses of the 1920s, both of which had contributed significantly to the depression. Workers' purchasing power was strengthened by unemployment compensation, social security, and the encouragement of collective bargaining. Despite business leaders' resistance to New Deal policies — of which they were major beneficiaries — the Roosevelt administration left the mass production system and its economies of scale largely intact. The collective bargaining system associated with New Deal policies made only marginal changes in management's hierarchical authority, and the system of fragmented production jobs continued. The main difference, and an important one, was the fact that collective bargaining contracts gave workers more control over jobs and a larger share of the gains from the economies of scale. The system still treated workers as appendages to machines and was still adversarial, but it was relieved somewhat by the workers' ability to organize and bargain collectively and to participate in the benefits of economies of scale. The federal government also perfected supportive monetary and fiscal policies to stabilize the mass production system, increasing government spending and the money supply to stimulate growth and reduce massive unemployment.

The New Deal's policies and the mass production system were justified by the economy's amazing performance during World War II. Despite the enormous drain of the war, mass production and strong aggregate demand allowed the American economy to emerge from the war stronger than when the conflict started. Indeed when the war ended, the United States, with about 6 percent of the world's population, probably accounted for three-fourths of the world's gross product. And the average American was better off in terms of material consumption in 1945 than in 1939 (Galbraith 1987: 299–300). That strength, together with collective bargaining and progressive government policies, ushered in 20 years of the most sustained and equitably shared prosperity in history. Income distribution was more equal than in either the 1920s or the 1980s.

Global Competition and High-Performance Work Organizations

As noted in the previous section, during the first half of this century the United States developed economic policies and work organizations that produced the world's strongest economy and highest standard of living. That system required higher order thinking skills for professional, managerial, and technical elites and only basic academic skills for most workers. Work was organized so that most frontline employees did very little learning or thinking on the job. Additionally, schools and other learning systems reflected the economy's bifurcated skill requirements. This section traces the emergence of a very different economy requiring very different skills. While the United States had huge advantages in the mass production economy, it has enormous disadvantages in the more competitive, global, knowledge-intensive economy of the 1990s.

The system erodes

Toward the end of the 1960s there were growing signs that America's traditional economic system was in trouble. The main forces for change were technology and increased international competition, which combined to render anachronistic much of the traditional mass production system and its supporting institutions. These changes also dramatically altered the conditions for economic viability. In this more competitive world dominated by knowledge-intensive technology, the keys to economic success became human resources and a more effective organization of production systems, not natural resources and traditional economies of scale. Indeed, as the work of Theodore Schultz and other economists has demonstrated, the process of substituting knowledge and skills for physical resources has been the main source of improved productivity since at least the 1920s (Baumol, Blackman, and Wolff 1989; Carnevale 1983; Denison 1985; Schultz 1981). Drucker provides another illustration of this process. He points out that the strategic product of the 1920s, the automobile, was 60 percent energy and raw materials and 40 percent ideas, skills, and knowledge. The strategic product of the 1990s is the computer chip, which is 2 percent energy and materials and 98 percent ideas, skills, and knowledge (Drucker 1992).

Technology not only contributed to the globalization of markets but it also made the mass production system and traditional economies of scale less viable in high-wage countries. Although the assembly line can be automated, that is not the most efficient use of the new technology (Zuboff 1988). Computerized technology provides many of the advantages of economies of scale and scope through flexible systems, which have enormous advantages in a more dynamic and competitive global economy.

Technology makes new organizations of production possible, but competition makes them necessary for those who wish to maintain and improve incomes. This is so because a more competitive internationalized information economy has very different requirements for national, enterprise, organizational, and personal success than was true of largely national goods-producing systems. One of the most important changes for public policy purposes is that national governments now have less control of their economy. A country can no longer maintain high wages and full employment through traditional combinations of monetary-fiscal and international trade policies, administered wages and prices, and fixed exchange rates. In the 1970s and 1980s, internationalization weakened the links between domestic consumption, investment, and output that formed the basic structure of the traditional Keynesian demand-management system. The weakening of these Keynesian linkages became very clear when U.S. tax cuts in the early 1980s increased consumption but also greatly stimulated imports and therefore produced much smaller increases in domestic investment than had resulted from earlier tax cuts in less globalized markets. Indeed, imports accounted for almost all of the increased demand for capital goods following the 1981 tax cuts (Lower 1985).

The basic choice: lower wages or higher quality and productivity

These altered economic conditions do not just change the magnitude of the requirements for economic success — they fundamentally alter the necessary structures and policies. In a more competitive global economy, firms, countries, or individuals can compete in only two basic ways: they can reduce their incomes or they can improve productivity and quality (Klein 1988: 309). In the more competitive global information economy, success therefore requires greater emphasis on factors that were much less important in traditional mass production systems. These new factors are quality, productivity, and flexibility.

Quality, best defined as meeting customers' needs, becomes more important for two reasons.[2] First, as the mass production system matured and personal incomes rose, consumers became less satisfied with standardized products. Second, the more competitive environment of the 1990s is largely consumer driven; the mass production system was more producer driven, especially after governments and oligopolies "stabilized" prices. In the more competitive environments of the 1970s and 1980s, oligopolistic pricing became anachronistic; flexible prices become more important. Furthermore, the mass production system depended heavily on the ability of a few companies to control national markets; with internationalization, companies — like national governments — have much less market control. It took some time for American oligopolies, who adjusted to declining demand by reducing employment and holding prices, to understand how vulnerable they were to foreign competitors who adjusted by reducing prices and maintaining employment and capacity utilization.

Productivity and flexibility are closely related to quality. The difference in productivity today is that now productivity improvements are achieved by using all factors of production more efficiently, not, as in the mass production system, mainly through economies of scale and compatible and reinforcing interindustry shifts. Indeed, in the 1970s and 1980s interindustry shifts lowered productivity growth slightly because they were shifts, on balance, from more productive manufacturing activities to less productive services. The mass production system created enormous waste in its utilization of capital (especially inventory) and people, but this was more than offset by economies of scale. Once technology reduced traditional scale advantages, mass production companies were left with the labor and capital inefficiencies, but with much smaller scale offsets.

Flexibility enhances productivity by facilitating the shift of resources from less to more productive outputs, and improves quality by making it possible to respond quickly to diverse and changing customer needs. Moreover, flexibility in the use of workers and technology improves productivity by reducing the waste of labor and machine time. It is probably the case that flexibility, which makes it possible to deliver a variety of automated goods in a timely manner, often has at least as much to do with competitiveness (in the sense of competing on terms that make it possible to maintain and improve incomes) as lower factor costs.

Worker participation, lean management systems, and higher-order thinking skills

The fundamental issue, of course, is how to arrange production to achieve quality, productivity, and flexibility. The answer appears to be to develop high-performance production systems that develop and use leading-edge technologies. Productivity is improved by work organizations that reduce waste of materials through better inventory control, promote the efficient use of labor, and develop more effective quality controls to *prevent* defects rather detect them, as was often the case in mass production systems. High-performance systems have a high degree of employee involvement in what would have been considered "management" functions in mass production systems. Indeed, in more productive and flexible systems, the distinctions between frontline "managers" and "workers" become blurred. In short, high-performance organizations cannot be achieved through marginal changes in mass production systems — they require radical reorganization of those systems or the creation of radically different organizations.

A number of features of high-performance production systems encourage worker participation and lean management structures. First, in these systems workers must have more knowledge and skill. And skilled, educated workers are less tolerant of monotonous, routine work and authoritarian managerial controls. Second, quality, productivity, and flexibility are all enhanced when production decisions are made as close to the point of production as possible. Mass production bureaucracies were designed to achieve quantity, managerial control, and stability — not flexibility, quality, or productivity in the use of all factors of production. Mass production systems are based on managerial information monopolies and worker controls; in high-performance systems workers must be free to make decisions. To accomplish this, information must be shared, not monopolized, because machines do more of the routine, direct work and frontline workers do more of the indirect work formerly done mainly by administrative staffs.

Several features of a high-performance system reduce the efficacy of hierarchical management systems. Since machines take over more of the direct work and frontline workers take over more of the indirect work, there is less need for inspectors, schedulers, and other indirect workers. Since workers manage more of their own work, individually or in teams, there is less need for managers. Thus, the control of the flow of information, a major function of Tayloristic managers, can be performed more effectively by computers and other information technology, which can provide everybody a common data base or "score," to use an orchestral analogy. The role of managers therefore shifts from "bossing" or supervising to teaching, building consensus, and enabling and supporting frontline workers, who assume more responsibility for quality, productivity, and flexibility.

One of the most important differences between high-performance and Tayloristic systems is in the attitudes of managers and workers. As noted, the Tayloristic manager's attitude is that workers are naturally lazy and must be forced to work out of fear that they will lose their jobs or be reprimanded. Taylor's system assumed, in addition, that most frontline workers did not have to think and, indeed, were incapable of the higher-order thinking done by supervisors educated in scientific management. This attitude naturally created resentment and distrust of management by workers and their unions. Labor's distrust was exacerbated by the decline in upward mobility of skilled, non-college-educated workers, who had fewer opportunities to move into upper managerial ranks. High-performance management, by contrast, establishes trust and respect between workers and managers by assuming that most workers instinctively want to do a good job that enhances their self-worth and gains them the respect of management and their fellow workers. These managers assume, in addition, that workers and effective work organization are the keys to high performance. They assume, further, that workers understand their jobs, are capable of higher-order thinking, and are motivated by positive reward systems, which include managers who understand and value their work.

High-performance systems therefore require that frontline workers have different kinds of thinking skills than was the case in Tayloristic systems. One of the most important skills required for indirect work is the ability to analyze the flood of data produced by information technology. This means that workers must understand

and be able to use models, metrics, and other quantitative techniques. Workers who can impose order on chaotic data can use information to add value to products, improve productivity and quality, solve problems, and improve technology.

Indirect work also is more likely to be group work, requiring more communication, interpersonal skills, and teamwork. These skills are necessary because productivity, quality, and flexibility require close coordination between what were formerly more discrete components of the production process (research and development, design, production, inspection, distribution, sales, and services). These functions were more linear in the mass production system, but are more interactive in dynamic, consumer-oriented production systems.

Another very important high-performance skill is the ability to learn. Learning is not only more important than in mass production systems but it also is very different. The simplification of tasks and the standardization of technology and productivity in Tayloristic systems limits the amount of learning needed or achieved. More learning is required in a dynamic, technology-intensive workplace, and more of that learning must be achieved through the manipulation of abstract symbols, simulations, and models. For line workers, mass production systems stress learning almost entirely by observation and doing.

Learning in more productive workplaces also is likely to be more communal and cooperative. Taylor's system and cost competition encouraged adversarial relationships that impede the sharing of information between workers, managers, and suppliers. A high-performance system, by contrast, encourages the sharing of information and cooperative efforts to achieve common objectives. High-performance organizations must, in addition, find ways to measure learning and to make individual and group learning part of the organization's collective memory. These quality-driven processes create communities of interest among all of those involved in the system — managers, frontline workers and suppliers, and other participants in high-performance networks. Tayloristic organizations emphasize short-run profit maximization, which tends to create conflicts; high-performance systems emphasize quality, which tends to unify workers and managers. The mass production system also created adversarial relations designed to keep costs down through competition between suppliers. There clearly is much more learning in a community-of-interest network than in an adversarial system. Communal learning, in addition, becomes more important as a means of building the consensus needed to improve the performance of more highly integrated production processes. High-performance workers not only need to be self-managers but they also must perform a greater array of tasks and adapt more readily to change. This requires a reduction of Taylor's detailed job classifications and work rules. Well-educated, well-trained, highly motivated workers are likely to be much more flexible and productive, especially in supportive systems that stress equity and internal cohesion. Indeed, humans are likely to be the most flexible components in a high-performance system.

Other features of high-performance workplaces require greater employee involvement and higher-order thinking skills. One is the need for constant improvements in technology — or what the Japanese call "giving wisdom to the machine." Technology, as noted earlier, is best defined as how things are done. The most important factor in technology is not the physical capital itself but, as I have noted, the ideas, skills, and knowledge embodied in machines and structures. Technology becomes standardized when the rates at which ideas, skills, and knowledge can be transferred to machines or structures become very small. Standardized technology therefore requires workers to have fewer ideas and less skill and knowledge than leading-edge technology. High-performance organizations emphasize developing and using leading-edge technologies, because highly mobile standardized technologies are likely to gravitate to low-paid workers. Some American companies have responded to competitive pressures by attempting to combine high technology and low skills through automation (Keller 1989). This combination has proved to be little more productive, if at all, than standardized technology and low-skilled workers. The most productive systems therefore have highly skilled workers who can adapt, develop, and use leading-edge technology in particular production systems. And the shorter life cycle of products and technologies in a more dynamic and competitive global economy means these are important advantages to continuous innovation and creativity.

The need to pay more attention to quality and productivity is another reason for increased worker involvement. In cases where direct contact with customers is required, flexible, highly skilled employees can provide better customer service than is true of highly specialized mass production workers, who can provide only their narrow, specialized service. In manufacturing systems, moreover, even the most sophisticated machines are idiosyncratic and therefore require the close attention of skilled workers to adapt them to particular situations. With the smaller production runs permitted by information technology and required by more competitive and dynamic markets, workers must control production and be able to override machines; the mass production system usually made it very difficult for frontline workers to override machines. The mass production system's long production runs, by contrast, made it possible to amortize start-up defects over those long runs. Systems with short production runs cannot afford many start-up defects; they must therefore have workers who can override the machines if the latter malfunction or start producing defects. Quality-driven systems also must provide for more self-inspection by workers, and this must often be on the basis of visible observation to prevent defects rather than by inspections to detect them at the end of the production process. Quality improvement is facilitated by just-in-time inventory methods and other mechanisms that make defects more visible or detectable early in production processes. Productivity and quality are enhanced by early detection; otherwise, those defective components become invisible when they enter the product, and are discovered only as the products malfunction when used by customers.

Incentive systems

Since organizations ordinarily get the outcomes they reward, the explicit or implicit incentives in any system are basic determinants of its outcomes. High-performance organizations stress positive incentive systems. Mass production incentives, by contrast, tend to be negative — fear of discharge or punishment; they also are more individualistic and implicit. Mass production incentives are sometimes even perverse in that they actually impede improvements in productivity. Process- and time-based mass production compensation systems, for example, are often unrelated to productivity or quality and may even be counterproductive, as when workers fear they will lose their jobs if productivity improves.

Positive incentives enhance flexibility as well as productivity and quality. Group incentives and job security encourage flexibility by simultaneously overcoming the resistance to the development and use of broader skills and providing employers greater incentives to invest in education and training to develop those skills. Similarly, bonus compensation systems can simultaneously provide greater incentives for workers to improve productivity and quality and create more flexible compensation systems. Participative systems therefore, in themselves, create positive incentives. In essence, the high-performance system substitutes clearly defined goals and objectives and positive incentives for the mass production system's rules, regulations, supervisors, and administrators.

It would be hard to overemphasize the importance of equity, internal unity, and positive incentives for high-performance, knowledge-intensive workplaces, in part because all parties must be willing to go "all out" to achieve common objectives. In traditional mass production systems workers are justifiably afraid to go all out to improve productivity for fear they will lose their jobs. This is the reason employment security is one of the most important incentives a high-performance company can have. Similarly, the fragmentation of work within mass production systems gives workers little incentive to control quality — quality is somebody else's responsibility. A high-performance system, by contrast, makes quality control everybody's responsibility. Positive incentives are required, in addition, because the effective use of information technology gives workers greater discretion. It is difficult to compel workers to think, or even to tell whether or not they are doing it. It also is very hard to compel workers to go all out to improve quality and productivity.

One of the most important requirements for high-performance incentive systems is a high level of consensus and trust. Traditional American managers have so much trouble understanding this concept that they actually are surprised when workers refuse to accept unilaterally imposed "incentives" that will improve the workers' earnings and the firm's economic viability. It is, moreover, difficult to transform adversarial relations into cooperative ones. The most successful transformations in the United States ordinarily have required demonstrable threats to jobs and company survival.

The role of labor organizations
One of the most controversial aspects of high-performance production systems is the role of labor organizations. My own view is that the right of workers to organize and bargain collectively is an important requirement for a high-performance system. It is not coincidental that companies in industrialized countries that are taking high-value-added market share from American companies usually have much stronger worker organizations — through works councils, other workplace organizations, and trade unions — than are present in the United States.

Independent worker organizations also are required because of the fundamental nature of the employment relationship. It is difficult to have cooperative relationships between parties of unequal power. Cooperation is weakened when the stronger party makes unilateral decisions, forcing the other party to seek countervailing power. Moreover, the relationships between workers and managers are inherently adversarial as well as cooperative. Indeed, adversarial relations are functional insofar as they provide processes to resolve differences. Workers therefore need an independent source of power to protect and promote their interests in these adversarial relationships. The challenge, of course, is to maximize common interests and prevent conflicts from becoming "functionless" by worsening conditions for all parties. Additionally, it is unlikely that workers will be willing to improve productivity and quality unless they have an independent source of power to protect their interests in the process.

Workers and managers are likely to clash over the conflicts inherent in the components of a high-performance system. Management typically wants to restrain wages, for example, while workers want to increase them. Management stresses "flexibility" while workers emphasize employment security. How such clashes are worked out determines the extent to which incentives remain positive. Since incentives are critical components of a high-performance system, the nature of the relationship between unions and managers is an important determinant of whether unionized firms can be high-performance organizations. A good orienting hypothesis, therefore, is: with mutual acceptance and respect between unions and managers, unionized firms probably can achieve higher performance than nonunion firms.

Evidence

Worker Participation   I have argued that greater worker participation will improve productivity, quality, and flexibility. Unfortunately, the evidence for this proposition is difficult to establish, because many worker participation processes in the United States are relatively new, have different meanings, are qualitatively different from place to place, and never occur in isolation from other factors.

There is, however, growing evidence that worker participation and work reorganization are important factors in improving productivity and economic competitiveness (Dertouzes, Lester, and Solow 1989). This should not be surprising, of course, since labor accounts for at least 70 percent of total value added. Small improvements in labor productivity therefore can have much greater impact on total productivity than larger increases in physical capital. A 1990 Brookings study edited by Alan Blinder acknowledged the positive contribution of worker participation, though Blinder considers such productivity improvements to be "transitory," albeit potentially "impressive" (Blinder 1990, 1989/90). Blinder, like most orthodox economists, believes that "the best way to raise productivity growth, and perhaps the only way to do so permanently, is to speed up the pace of technological innovation" (Blinder 1989/90:33). The trouble with this view, of course, is the implied assumption that technological innovation is external to the production process and not an integral part of it. This view also fails to recognize that high-performance production systems with positive incentives, skilled workers, continuous learning processes, and a high degree of worker involvement have the capacity for continuous improvements in productivity and technology. The Brookings study nevertheless shows that incentive compensation systems raise wages about 11 percent an hour more than for other workers, and they do this without reducing fringe benefits or hourly wages (Blinder 1989/90:37). Blinder concludes that "worker participation apparently does help make alternative compensation plans . . . work better — and also has beneficial effects of its own. This theme was totally unexpected when I organized the conference [that led to these studies]" (Blinder 1989/90: 38).

I should note, however, that the mere existence of a formal worker participation system will not necessarily improve productivity and quality — the degree of participation and whether or not workers have independent sources of power seem to be the keys to higher productivity. For example, David Lewin and others at Columbia University studied the relationships between the financial performance of 500 publicly traded companies and their degree of employee involvement. Analysis of the data for 1987 concluded that "the mere presence of an employee involvement process was not significantly related to positive improvements in any of the financial indicators. However, the further a firm moved up the employee involvement index [measuring degrees of employee involvement] and the more employees were involved in decision-making, the greater the magnitude of financial performance. What appears to be critical is the scope or comprehensiveness of employee involvement and participation programs. High employee involvement is associated with better financial performance, particularly on the return on investment and return on asset measures" (Economic Policy Council 1990:16).

There is, in addition, abundant case study evidence of the relationship between worker participation and improved quality and productivity. Perhaps the most clear-cut and compelling evidence is from the New United Motor Manufacturing Co., Inc. (NUMMI), a joint venture between Toyota and General Motors (GM) in Fremont, California. This was a plant that GM closed in 1982 because its managers could not make it competitive. Toyota reopened it as a NUMMI plant in 1984, with a new management system but with mostly the same United Automobile Workers (UAW) members and essentially the same equipment, which was much less automated than in GM's most modern plants. One of the most important changes NUMMI

621

made was to guarantee the workers a high level of job security. Other changes include a reduction in job classes from about 100 to 4; the elimination of such management perks as private dining rooms, parking lots, private offices, and separate dress codes; and the establishment of work teams of five to ten people who set their own work standards, laid out the work area, determined the work load distribution, and assigned workers to specific tasks.

From a production standpoint there can be little doubt that NUMMI, which makes Toyota Corollas and the Geo Prism (Chevrolet Novas were discontinued in 1989, and the plant started producing light trucks in 1991), has been a success. Productivity at the plant is 50 percent higher than at the former GM plant, and in 1989 NUMMI ranked first among all GM plants in the United States. A 1988 MIT study reported that its productivity was about 40 percent higher than at traditional GM plants and was about equal that of Toyota's Japanese plants (Krafcik 1988). *Consumer Reports* judged NUMMI's Chevrolet Nova to have the highest quality of any American-built car. As a result of these successes, there has been strong interest in NUMMI among American managers.

It also should be noted that while the NUMMI experience is an improvement over the Tayloristic GM model, worker participation actually is restricted to production processes, and the work itself is still highly standardized, though the work by each employee is less standardized. GM's experience with its Saturn project (the autonomous high-performance company in Tennessee) has gone beyond NUMMI, especially in the important worker participation factor; at Saturn, as in most German or Swedish companies, workers have much more control of the production process at every level than is true at NUMMI or in most Japanese companies. Worker autonomy and control are key ingredients to steep learning curves and high performance. To some degree, NUMMI involves a Tayloristic fragmentation of work and a much faster pace than in the traditional GM plants. This system is nevertheless popular with NUMMI employees; indeed, "even the critics are enthusiastic about the system. . . . The criticisms are, with few exceptions, directed at what workers see as flaws in the implementation of the standardized work system, not the system itself" (Adler 1991:72). The NUMMI workers are supportive of the system, despite its standardization and pace, because "they set the standards themselves" and because of the personal satisfaction workers derive from superior performance (or "the instinct of craftsmanship," a motivation "accorded too little attention by managers and researchers") and "the understanding that either the plant constantly improves its performance or, independent of whether the managers are mean or nice, competitors will take its market" (Adler 1991:72).

Skills and Productivity Econometricians have consistently found that only 40 percent of competitive improvements come from direct investments, while 60 percent are due to "advances in knowledge" or "innovation" (Baumol, Blackman, and Wolff 1989). In other words, some technologies, representing the distilled ideas, skills, and knowledge of others, can be acquired externally, but most (60 percent) are developed through individual and organizational learning, most often in the production process. There is additional econometric evidence of high returns to companies from investments in the education and training of their workers (Lillard and Tan 1986). Similarly, Denison (1985) attributes 26 percent of the productivity growth between 1929 and 1982 to education and 55 percent to on-the-job learning.

Econometric studies likewise tend to confirm the conceptual view of the changing structure of U.S. industry outlined in this chapter. There is clear evidence of a large increase in the relative wages of educated workers during the 1980s. These relative changes cannot be explained by quantitative changes in the demand and supply for labor. For example, a study by John Bound and George Johnson tested the impact of various traditional demand and supply factors on wage differentials for the 1980s and concluded: "Our analysis points strongly to the conclusion that the principal reason for the increases in wage differentials by educational attainment . . . is a combination of skill-based technical changes and changes in unmeasured labor quality" (Bound and Johnson 1992: 389).

There is also a growing body of case study evidence that confirms the positive correlation between work force skills and productivity. Studies of matched plants making similar products in Britain and the Netherlands by the National Institute of Economic and Social Research in London found Dutch manufacturing companies to be 25 to 30 percent more productive than their British counterparts, despite rapid upgrading and productivity growth in Britain during the 1980s (Mason and van Ark 1992). This study found that Dutch workers were more highly skilled and were therefore capable of more self-management, experienced fewer breakdowns of equipment, and were more capable of continuous maintenance to prevent problems. The Anglo-Dutch study concluded that companies in Britain and Europe were being forced by international competition to move away from the Tayloristic mass production model, but that British plants were having more trouble than their Dutch rivals, because of "slower investment in new capital equipment" and because of "lower average levels of workforce skills and knowledge" (Mason and van Ark 1992:16). The Dutch skills advantage was due not only to more extensive skills training and education, but also to higher standards for students in Dutch junior and intermediate technical schools, which "give Dutch employers a considerable 'head start' over their British counterparts in terms of the trainability of their workforce, both as new entrants to the labour market and subsequently as adult workers who may need retraining and updating. In this context, Dutch employers are able to carry out training to given standards more quickly and cost effectively than is possible in Britain, and in many cases are able to set their training standards much higher than is possible for their British counterparts" (Mason and van Ark 1992: 17).

A comparison of productivity and foreman training in Britain and Germany reached similar conclusions. Because almost all German students who are not in full-time education at ages 16 through 18 receive apprentice training, "two-thirds of the German workforce attain examined specialised vocational qualifications (at 'craft level' or higher) — which is probably at least double the proportion attaining comparable levels in Britain" (Prais and Wagner 1988: 34). Training also is facilitated by the fact that "the level of mathematical competence of the average school leaver (at age 15–16) in Germany is substantially higher than in Britain" and the German youths' mathematics skills are developed further as an integral component of the German apprenticeship system (Prais and Wagner 1988: 34).

In large part, the German skill training system contributed to an estimated production advantage for German manufacturing establishments of 52 percent in 1977 and 40 percent in 1987 (Prais and Wagner 1988: 37). Germany had better-trained workers and foremen, contributing to German companies' superior ability to organize work for high performance. In industrial occupations "the German training system produced about seven times as many formally qualified foremen as the British system" (Prais and Wagner p. 36). As a consequence of their higher skills, studies in matched manufacturing plants showed that relative to the British, German plants had higher levels of coordination, smaller ratios of supervisors to workers, smaller rates of machinery breakdown, a higher level of automation and machine technology, and more timely product deliveries. Moreover, because their workers were not as well trained, British companies were forced to rely much more heavily than their German counterparts on wage competition. There was, of course, much more to the British competitiveness problem than workers' skills. The British labor movement had less influence on national policies than the German; Britain therefore adopted a low-wage development strategy that included weakening the unions.

Although similar detailed comparative studies have not yet been made, the experiences of most U.S. companies probably resemble those of British companies more than those of Dutch or German companies.

Unions and Productivity The diversity of union experiences makes it difficult to generalize about the impact of unions on productivity. There is, however, abundant case study evidence that in general unionized firms are more productive than nonunion firms. A very thorough review of the econometric evidence on this subject by Harvard University economists Richard Freeman and James Medoff concluded: "Modern quantitative analysis of productivity in organized and unorganized establishments and sectors offers striking new evidence on what unions do to productivity. The new work suggests that in general, productivity is higher in the presence of unionism than in its absence" (Freeman and Medoff 1984: 162–163).

Adrienne Eaton and Paula Voos (1992), among others, show that unions are more likely than their nonunion counterparts to be involved in workplace innovation, especially those cooperative arrangements, like teamwork and production gain sharing, that yield higher productivity. Nonunion firms are more likely to concentrate on profit-sharing plans that have little direct impact on productivity.

A study by Maryellen Kelley and Bennett Harrison (1992) of 1,015 U.S. metal and machinery companies found that union shops were as much as 31 percent more productive than nonunion shops. In fact, even unionized branches of large companies were more productive than the nonunion branches of those companies, using the same technology, paying similar wages, and making the same products. Kelley and Harrison found, in addition, that sites with various employee-management problem-solving teams, which sprang up in many U.S. firms during the 1970s and 1980s as an alternative to unions, were less productive than those without them.

A study of unions and competitiveness (Mishel and Voos 1992) sponsored by the Economic Policy Institute offered the following conclusions. First, at the general economywide level, collective bargaining and unionization have had "few if any" adverse effects on competitiveness. Second, although it is commonly argued that unions reduce competitiveness by raising prices above competitive levels, there is strong empirical evidence that while unions do increase wages and benefits, they do not necessarily reduce competitiveness, because competition is over quality, not just price. Quality is more likely to be maintained and improved by highly participative systems where workers are unionized. Third, since most studies show unionized firms to be more productive than nonunion firms, higher union wages are offset in part by higher productivity and in part by reducing oligopolistic profits. And fourth, while both union and nonunion sectors are trying to become more competitive through the introduction of various workplace innovations, "by the end of the 1980s, the large union employers either equaled or surpassed the large nonunion employers with regard to virtually all flexibility and productivity-enhancing workplace innovations, with the sole exception of profit-sharing" (Mishel and Voos 1992: 9).

Many studies have shown, moreover, that profit sharing has much less effect on productivity than team production and gain sharing. Eaton and Voos (1992) show that gain sharing and team productivity not only have greater potential for increasing firm performance than profit sharing, but also are a continuation of a long tradition of productivity bargaining by U.S. unions, which permits them to maintain union employment despite higher union wages.

Levine and Tyson (1990), in another survey, contend that formal worker participation systems are more likely to increase productivity where workers share the benefits, wage differentials between firms are relatively narrow, there are long-term employment guarantees, and workers are protected from unjust dismissal. These findings are compatible with my conclusions, presented earlier, on positive incentive systems.

The foregoing is not to argue, however, that industrial relations systems never have negative effects on productivity and economic performance. In Japan during the 1950s and in Germany and other countries during the 1960s, there is evidence that poor labor-management relations contributed to poor economic performance (Marshall 1987). Studies have shown national economic performance to be directly related to the availability of consensus-building processes (Bruno and Sachs 1985; Sachs 1989; Marshall 1987; Metcalf 1986; Bean, Layard, and Nickell 1986; Newell and Symon 1986). Consensus processes focus attention on the parties' common interests, while adversarial processes tend to magnify differences, however trivial. Consensus processes also provide all parties better information, which, in turn, improves collective bargaining, management, and public policy decisions.

There is considerable empirical evidence that the industrial relations climate can influence economic performance. For example, Belman notes, on the basis of an extensive review of the evidence, that

The structure of bargaining, the history of labor management relations, the environment in which firms and employees operate, and the consequent attitudes of labor and management affect firm performance. In plants and firms in which there is little trust between employers and employees, in which production workers are largely excluded from decisions affecting them, and in which there is ongoing conflict over the boundary between subjects of bargaining and those under unilateral managerial control, there will be little incentive for workers and managers to share information, workers will only produce under compulsion, and the rules of the work site — originating from conflict — will be used to assert or limit control rather than improve output. In contrast, in environments in which there is high trust, where employees and their unions are integrated into the decision process, and in which the parties accept the legitimacy of one another's goals, productivity gains and cost reductions can be realized through creative bargaining, cooperation in development of better production techniques, and a reduction in the use of restrictive work practices and monitoring. (Belman 1992: 45–46)

The Competitive Position of the United States

The previous section outlining the requirements for high-performance work organizations is based on a synthesis of my studies in the United States and elsewhere (Marshall 1987), especially as cochair of the Commission on the Skills of the American Workforce (CSAW), which examined the strategies and skill requirements of companies in the United States and six other countries — Japan, Singapore, Germany, Sweden, Denmark, and Ireland (CSAW 1990).

The commission found that firms in the United States were much less likely than their counterparts in other countries to have restructured for high performance. Indeed, fewer than 5 percent of American companies were high-performance organizations as they are defined in this chapter.

How does one explain this difference? I believe the answer is to be found in the history of the mass production system in the United States and the absence of a national economic strategy to provide incentives for American companies to pursue a high-wage strategy. Indeed, with this strategy absent, "market forces" dictate economic outcomes, and in the American context, where Taylorism and the mass production system are so deeply entrenched in learning systems and work relationships, laissez-faire policies have produced a low-wage strategy by default.

Market forces will naturally polarize incomes. The other industrialized countries in the CSAW study rejected the laissez-faire, low-wage strategy because they understood that it implied lower and more unequal incomes. Low-wage strategies, in addition, greatly restrict the ability to upgrade individuals, enterprises, or national performance. With low-wage strategies, incomes can only be maintained or improved by working harder — which clearly is self-limiting. High-productivity strategies, by contrast, emphasize substituting ideas, skills, and knowledge for physical resources — a process with enormous potential for continuous growth. Other industrialized countries have therefore adopted a variety of policies to provide incentives for companies to restructure for high performance. These include adjustment policies to shift resources from low- to high-productivity sectors, measures to strengthen collective bargaining and worker participation, active trade policies to support high-productivity industries and discourage those that can only compete through low wages, high minimum wage and income support systems, full employment policies, and active labor market and human resource development strategies.

In marked contrast to policy in most other industrial countries, American policies have encouraged companies to pursue low-wage strategies. These policies include weak collective bargaining and minimum wage protections; trade and tax policies that actually subsidize companies that shift jobs to other countries; uncoordinated macroeconomic policies that create economic instability and uncertainty as well as high real interest rates; weak immigration controls, which encourage a flow of unskilled labor from developing countries; and, most important, the absence of universal world-class learning systems for workers who are not college educated. Leaders in other countries understand that low-wage strategies subsidize inefficiency.

The greatest differences the CSAW found between the United States and other countries were in overall economic and human resource development policies and structures. While all of the other countries surveyed differed in their economies and cultures, they had developed very similar economic goals and human resource development strategies:

• They insist that virtually all of their secondary school students reach a high educational standard. We do not.

- They provide "professional" education to non-college-bound students to prepare them for their trades and to ease their school-to-work transition. We do not.
- They operate comprehensive labor market systems that combine training, labor market information, job search, and income maintenance for the unemployed. We do not.
- They support company-based training through general or payroll-tax-based financing schemes. We do not.
- They have national consensus on the importance of moving to high-productivity work organizations and building high-wage economies. We do not.

The consequences of our failure to adjust to a high-performance economy are fairly clear in the United States. Real wages were about 12 percent lower in 1990 than they were in 1969, productivity growth has stagnated, and incomes have become much more unequal. Only the top 30 percent of wage earners, generally the college educated, had higher incomes in 1990 than in 1969.

As noted, most high-income industrial countries have rejected the low-wage option because it creates lower and more unequal wages — which is exactly what we have experienced in the United States in the past 20 years. Wages in most other major industrialized economies are now higher than they are in the United States. According to the most recent U.S. census data, developed by the Economic Policy Institute, the median hourly wage of men was 14 percent lower in 1989 than it was in 1979. The only workers whose incomes had increased since 1979 were the college educated. Young male high school graduates' earnings were 26.5 percent lower in 1991 than in 1979. Among all male college graduates, earnings increased only for those with advanced degrees; young male college graduates actually earned 5.1 percent less in 1991 than they did in 1979, with most of the drop coming after 1987. Men's gains in earnings were significantly lower than those of women; between 1979 and 1991 real wages for high school dropouts declined 23.2 percent for men and 11.0 percent for women. For those with four years of college, earnings dropped 2.3 percent for men but rose 13.6 percent for women; for those with college plus two years, the gains were 10.2 percent for men and 13.2 for women. These improvements for women are relative, however, because women still earn considerably less than men, regardless of education. In 1991, for example, a woman at the eightieth earnings percentile was paid $13 an hour, only slightly more than the median $12.59 paid to a man in 1979, 12 years earlier. With declining productivity growth, we have maintained national and family incomes mainly by adding more workers. It takes about three times as much labor to achieve the same increase in national output as was achieved during the 1950s and 1960s. However, this is a less accessible option, because work force growth will slow down during the 1990s and families only have a limited amount of labor to put into the work force.

Also of concern are the political, social, and economic effects of growing inequalities in wealth and income. The United States already has the most unequal distribution of income, however it is measured, among the major industrial countries (Mishel and Frankel 1991: 260). While American manufacturing wages were the highest in the world in 1985 when measured at market exchange rates, they were thirteenth among the industrialized countries in 1990 (Neef and Kask 1991: 27).

Learning systems

As noted, the slowdown in productivity growth is a major economic problem for the United States. While economists have been unable to agree on the reasons for the slowdown, I am convinced that many of the reasons are likely to be found in the obsolescence and inefficiencies of our learning systems, broadly defined. There is growing evidence, in addition, that the decline of *public* investment accounts for much of the slowdown (Aschauer 1990, 1989a, 1989b, 1988). These failures are therefore related to inefficient public decision and learning processes relative to those of our principal competitors'.

The stress in orthodox economics on the efficiency of competitive markets is very simplistic. Competitive markets produce efficiency in the sense of reducing prices, but they do not encourage much joint learning and information sharing among sellers and between buyers and sellers. This is one of the reasons that the Japanese and Europeans have developed, and made good use of, processes that simultaneously promote cooperation and competition; they realize the importance of combining price competition with joint learning systems for productivity, quality, and the development and use of leading-edge technologies. In a highly competitive internationalized information world, the most competitive enterprises are likely to be those that are the most efficient production and learning systems.

The need to restructure schools

It became clear during the 1980s that America's public schools, our most pivotal learning systems, were in considerable trouble. It was equally clear that the same principles applied to restructuring mass production schools as to mass production companies. Early studies by Coleman and colleagues (1966, 1982), Jencks (1972), and others concluded that schools had very little to do with student achievement — which was due mainly to family income. Businesses complained that graduates lacked basic skills. Scholastic Aptitude Test (SAT) scores declined during the 1970s and early 1980s, and international comparisons of student achievement consistently ranked American students near the bottom. One should note, however, that the main point is not that the schools have deteriorated, which cannot be demonstrated very convincingly, but that the mass production school, like the mass production factory, is not likely to meet the needs of a high-performance economy.

Restructuring means making fundamental changes in the rules, roles, and relationships in schools. The principles of high-performance organizations, discussed earlier, apply to schools as well as to businesses and other organizations. According to the National Center on Education and the Economy (NCEE): "Education, like private industry, can improve by restructuring operations following some very simple principles. First, go for quality and build it in the first time whenever possible. Second, reward success in producing quality. Third, when a system for real accountability is in place, let the people on the firing line figure out how to get the job done, and get rid of as much of the bureaucracy and as many of the intervening rules and regulations as possible" (NCEE 1989:6).

A high-performance school would make student achievement the main criterion by which teachers, principals, and administrators are judged and rewarded. A restructured system would decentralize decisions about how to improve learning to teachers and schools. Policymakers would establish basic outcome objectives but would leave decisions about how to achieve those objectives to teachers, principals, child development professionals, parents, and other interested parties at the school level. In addition to using positive incentives to achieve outcomes prescribed by elected officials and policymakers, high-performance schools would be guided by professional standards based on knowledge and skills developed through research and experience.

School-to-work learning systems

One of the most serious learning problems for the United States is that, unlike our principal competitors, we have no system to facilitate the transition from school to work. As might be expected in a Tayloristic system, we do a lot for students who go to college, but almost nothing for the great majority who do not. The proportions of both students who fail to finish high school and those who receive no formal education and training for work are very high relative to other industrialized countries. There are very few incentives for schools to prevent students from dropping out and limited incentives for non-college-bound students to acquire higher-order thinking skills.

The problem is not the complete absence of work-related education and training institutions. The United States has numerous excellent technical institutes, community colleges, and apprenticeship programs, and many companies and industry associations in such cities as Boston, New York, Rochester, Chicago, and elsewhere have formed organizations to bridge the gap between school and work. These business associations provide part-time employment for students who stay in school and meet certain standards, as well as jobs for those who graduate. There are, in addition, some excellent "second chance" systems funded by federal and state governments. One successful program is the Job Corps, a mainly residential program for seriously disadvantaged young people. The very efficient computer-based learning system developed by the Job Corps and perfected by private nonprofit organizations makes it possible, on average, to improve educational attainment by 1.4 grade levels in math and 1 grade level in reading with 28 hours of instruction. The Job Corps is cost-effective, though the per-enrollee costs are relatively high — $14,776 in the Conservation Corps and $10,454 in non–Conservation Corps centers in 1986 dollars (GAO 1986) — but the Job Corps provided public benefits of 1.46 1977 dollars for each dollar spent in 1986 (Mathematica Policy Research 1982: 242, 248, 251, 253; 1983).

Second chance programs can simultaneously help students with learning problems and jobs. One of the most serious learning problems for disadvantaged young people, for example, is the loss of knowledge that occurs during summer vacations, which are much longer in the United States than in other major industrial countries. According to studies by Barbara Heynes, 80 percent of the year-to-year differences in educational achievement between advantaged and disadvantaged students is due to summer loss (Berlin and Sum 1988: 37).

Despite scattered success stories, however, American school-to-work transition processes have a number of very serious weaknesses (Glover and Marshall 1993):

1. There is no overall system to monitor, evaluate, and provide comprehensive services to seriously disadvantaged young people.

2. Funds for labor market programs are very low relative to those of

other countries and were only about one-third as high in real terms in 1990 as they were in 1978 (Levitan and Gallo 1991). Funding uncertainties made it very difficult for service providers to build solid job delivery systems.

3. Many of the federal programs are means- or income-tested and therefore carry a stigma that deters participation by employers and job seekers.

4. Unlike other countries, the United States provides no comprehensive labor exchange or labor market information system. Employers are not required to list job openings with the U.S. Employment Service, which is mainly responsible for certifying work tests for unemployment compensation and placing low-skilled workers. Because it has very few skilled job openings, few employers seek skilled workers from the Employment Service and few skilled workers register with it.

5. Although U.S. companies spend between $30 billion and $40 billion on formal education and training activities, very few companies actually provide education and training, and very little is spent on frontline workers. Company training has been found to yield high returns to companies and workers, but most training goes to relatively well-educated management and technical workers and white men (Lillard and Tan 1986). As noted earlier, very little learning takes place in Tayloristic firms, and interfirm relationships based on price competition alone provide very poor learning systems.

Families as learning systems

The quality of human resources depends significantly on what happens to families. The family as an institution is a major force behind the preservation of physical and cultural linkages between the past, present, and future. Mounting empirical evidence suggests, for example, that the nature of the relationship between parents or other caregivers and infants and young children can have lasting effects on the children's cognitive, social, and emotional development (Hamburg 1987). A large body of international research also demonstrates close relationships between health and cognitive development. The mother's health, especially, will influence the baby's health, and the parents' thinking skills and emotional stability or instability will be transferred to their children. Children are particularly likely to acquire the important values that guide their personal conduct from parents, reinforced by learning from their extended family, peers, and community institutions. Child development therefore depends on the extent to which families make conscious efforts to structure learning. Moreover, a major determinant of family welfare is likely to be the parents' education, which has become increasingly correlated with levels of family income (Marshall 1991).

The family, like the surrounding economy and society, is much less stable than it was earlier in this century. Children no longer learn about their parents' work by firsthand observation and experience, and they no longer gain a sense of personal satisfaction from contributing to the family's material welfare. Parents also spend less time with fewer children, and a greater number of fathers than ever before abandon or never care for their children. At the same time, however, the increased earnings of women have made it possible for them to improve the material welfare of their families and for parents to give higher priority to the educational development of their children if they wish to do so.

The main family problems are due to the following facts: too many households have members who work full-time for wages below the poverty level, too many children are born into poor households, too many women receive inadequate prenatal care, too many fathers do not support their children at all, and too many children are born to unwed mothers who are unable to care for them and to mothers whose drug addictions are transmitted to their children. On all of these indicators, the American experience is much worse than that in any other major industrial country.

The problem of child poverty in America is getting worse. Children as a group are becoming poorer, but the problem is particularly acute for minorities, who will constitute most of the growth of the U.S. work force for the rest of this century and into the next. Nearly half of all black children and a third of all Hispanic children are poor. By 2000, a third of all children will be black or Hispanic; their number will increase by 25 percent during the last ten years of the century, compared with a 0.2 percent increase for whites. By 2000, 16 million American children — one in four — will be poor if present trends continue. More than one-fifth (20.6 percent) of all children were poor in 1987.

Though the problem of poverty among children is worse for minority groups than for whites, no one should assume that only minorities are poor. In fact, the poverty rate among white children is higher than the overall rate in any other major industrial country (Children's Defense Fund 1989).

Summary, Conclusions, and Recommendations

The main theme of this chapter is that traditional learning systems are inadequate if the United States is to remain a high-income, world-class, democratic country. My recommendations for restructuring our learning systems are as follows.

Establish an economic policy council to build consensus on national economic goals, and develop strategies to achieve those goals. The council's first order of business should be to build support for a high-wage economic development strategy and for greater equity in economic opportunity.

Public policy should also aim to strengthen families, to make them more effective learning systems. Major components of such a policy should include guaranteed income support for families with children, regardless of their ability to collect child support from absent parents; programs to involve parents actively in their children's education; national health insurance modeled on the Canadian system; child care; parental leave; and full funding for the very successful Head Start and Women, Infants and Children (WIC) food, education and nutritional programs.

Adopt the following measures, as recommended by the Commission on the Skills of the American Workforce (CSAW 1990), to promote a high-quality work force in the United States and to give employers incentives to develop high-performance work organizations.

1. Performance standards should be established that all students should be expected to meet by age 16. Standards would be established nationally and benchmarked according to the highest standards in the world. Students who meet these standards would be prepared for work, higher education, or technical training for work. Student performance assessment should be based on examinations for which students should be able to prepare, and assessment should provide multiple opportunities for success rather than one high-stakes chance for failure. Under present arrangements the constant standard for graduation is time in school, and the variable is student achievement; with world-class standards in place, the variable would be time in school and the constant would be minimum learning requirements. The objective should be tough standards that almost

all students would be expected to meet, but not all in the same amount of time.

2. The states should take responsibility for assuring that virtually all students meet the standards stipulated in the previous recommendation. They should therefore fund alternative learning environments for those who, for whatever reason, cannot meet these standards in regular schools. More than 20 percent of students currently in school drop out before graduation. These inadequately prepared young people will constitute more than one-third of the frontline workers during the 1990s. Under present arrangements, regular schools have limited incentive to prevent students from dropping out, and very few of these students receive additional education and training in the Job Corps or other "second chance" systems. The creation of local youth centers in each labor market would help reclaim dropouts and provide alternatives for those who do not perform well in regular schools. These youth centers would provide alternative learning environments, perhaps building on the computer-based learning system developed by the Job Corps.

A number of incentives and disincentives for schools, young workers, and employers should accompany the creation of youth centers. First, if by the age of 16 students are not making satisfactory progress toward the required minimum standards, they should be allowed to leave school and take all of the money allocated for their education with them to the youth center. This would create an incentive for schools to do more to prevent students from dropping out. Second, once the youth centers are in place, young people under 18 should not be allowed to work unless they meet the minimum standards or are in a program to meet them. While this may seem draconian, it is nowhere near as debilitating as permitting dropouts to get trapped in deadend jobs.

3. A comprehensive system of technical certificates and associate degrees should be created for the majority of students and adult workers who do not pursue baccalaureate degrees. The absence of skill-training programs for the great majority of workers who do not receive baccalaurate degrees puts Americans at a tremendous competitive disadvantage. Other industrial countries have multiyear programs to teach technical skills to those workers who do not attend college. The United States, as I have noted, does a lot for those who go to college, but almost nothing for those who do not. As might be expected in an economy where Tayloristic practices are deeply entrenched, we have one of the most elitist education systems of any major democratic industrial economy. This system served us well in

the past but puts us at a serious disadvantage in today's competitive, knowledge-based world.

We should therefore provide a series of advanced technical certificates across a broad range of service and manufacturing occupations. As with our most effective apprentice programs, the standards for these certificates should be set by employers and workers in the private sector, with assistance from academic and government experts. The achievement of technical certificates would provide incentives for workers, knowledge to employers about workers' qualifications, a means of evaluating technical and professional learning systems, and greater labor market flexibility. Students would pursue these certificates through a wide range of institutions — community colleges, technical institutes, proprietary schools, and joint labor-management programs.

4. Four years of postsecondary education or training should be provided for all students who meet the minimum standards for graduation from high school. Defraying the rising cost of education and training is a major problem for middle- and low-income families in the United States, and it is contributing to the growing polarization of income. The provision of ready access to postsecondary education would therefore be in the national interest. This entitlement could be financed in a number of ways. One way would be to provide loans that could be repaid as a surtax on earnings after training is completed. Loans could be made from surpluses in Social Security funds, making it possible for those funds to be repaid, with higher yields, when they will be needed for retirement purposes in the twenty-first century. There is abundant evidence that investments in postsecondary education could yield high personal and social dividends, as was seen with the GI Bill after World War II. Loans also might be repaid, or entitlements earned, through national service. Indeed, a national service program also could provide resources to meet many needs in the areas of human service, public infrastructure, and environmental protection.

5. All employers should be given incentives and assistance to invest in the further education and training of their workers and to pursue high-productivity forms of work organization. As noted earlier, very few American companies are organizing work for high performance. As a consequence, they provide very little training for non-college-educated frontline workers, who will constitute no less than 70 percent of the work force by the year 2000. Moreover, very few American companies provide much on-the-job education and training for their frontline workers. The main reason for this state of

affairs, as I have said, is because laissez-faire economic policies have neither imposed constraints on employers' tendency to pursue low-wage strategies nor provided incentives for high-wage strategies. The United States should therefore adopt wage, training, trade, industrial, and other incentives for companies to pursue high-wage strategies. These incentives might include requiring firms to help pay the social and environmental costs associated with plant closings; strengthening the right of workers to organize and bargain collectively; encouraging (or requiring, as in cases concerning occupational safety and health and control of trust funds) joint labor-management committees modeled after European works councils; raising minimum wage and income support levels; providing technical assistance to firms for reorganization, through an industrial extension service; stabilizing economic policy-making through better coordination and consensus processes; and greatly improving the education and training of frontline workers.

With respect to education and training, the CSAW recommended that all companies be required to invest at least 1 percent of payroll for the training of their workers. Those that did not invest this amount would be required to contribute 1 percent of payroll to a fund to be used by the states to upgrade workers' skills. The CSAW recommended, in addition, that governments provide technical assistance to companies, particularly small businesses, to help them organize for high performance.

6. A system of comprehensive human resource development and labor market policies should be created to provide general oversight and direction in the labor market. What policies we do have are fragmented, stigmatizing, and inefficient, and this is a major problem for workplace learning processes in the United States.

There are many labor market institutions in the United States, and some excellent programs — like the Job Corps discussed earlier, and the Summer Training and Education Program. What is needed is not more programs. We need a complete human resource infrastructure and mechanisms at the federal, state, and local levels to identify and help meet local labor market needs. The CSAW therefore recommends that a system of employment and training (E & T) boards be established by federal and state governments, together with local leadership, to organize and oversee the new school-to-work transition programs the commission proposes.

In addition to providing management and oversight to the youth centers, federal second chance programs, and the proposed system for awarding certificates for technical training at the local level, the E & T boards would manage a local labor market information system and oversee the operations of the job service. The E & T boards would be modeled after labor market mechanisms in other industrialized countries, where active labor market policies play important roles in improving labor market efficiency, making it possible to reduce unemployment to low levels along with lower inflation levels and to improve productivity by overcoming skill shortages while shifting workers and other resources to more productive sectors and enterprises. Much more than policies in other countries, the main U.S. labor market policies are either targeted almost exclusively to the disadvantaged, or they provide mainly unemployment compensation (rather than more active labor market services like training and relocation). U.S. labor market policies are therefore not very well organized in relation to overall economic strategies and contribute very little to improving economic performance.

7. Worker participation in the United States should be strengthened for reasons of efficiency and equity. Equity requires that workers have some way to balance power relationships within companies to protect and promote their interests. As noted earlier, there are direct, positive relationships between productivity and the degree of worker participation in company decisions. In general, worker participation will cause companies to make longer-term, more strategic decisions and to avoid low-wage competition. I have also noted, moreover, that workers are not likely to go all out to make high-performance systems most effective unless they have an independent source of power to protect their interests in the process.

U.S. policymakers should therefore be concerned about the fact that American workers have a weaker voice in the work place than their counterparts do in other major industrial countries. American unions now represent only about 12 percent of the private work force, compared with 17 percent in 1980 and about 35 percent in the 1950s. One reason for this decline is the inability of weak American labor law to protect the rights of workers to organize and bargain collectively. A major defect in the National Labor Relations Act is the weak penalties for employer violations of workers' rights. The only penalty for discharging workers who exercise their right to organize, for example, is the payment of back pay less anything the workers should have earned from other employment and reinstatement of the workers. In fact, the law has stiffer penalties against unions than against companies. The legal procedures provided for by U.S. labor law permit employers to mount campaigns to erode worker support during union organizing efforts. Indeed, U.S. law even permits companies to replace permanently workers who strike for economic reasons.

The United States should take action to strengthen penalties against employers for violating workers' rights and to speed up union representation elections. Other measures to strengthen worker participation should include prohibiting companies from permanently replacing workers during strikes and from deliberately destroying unions by refusing to bargain in good faith after workers have voted for union representation. Careful attention should be given to requiring arbitration or other measures to help workers attain first contracts after they opt for collective bargaining. Another option would include waiving the restriction on permitting unions to assist each other in strikes over first contracts.

U.S. policy also should encourage joint labor-management committees to protect workers' legal rights on the job. For example, labor-management committees could be required for safety and health, education and training, and other oversight activities. These committees could do much to improve the enforcement of labor laws as well as to give workers a greater voice in decisions that affect their rights and interests.

Adopting these recommendations for improving our learning systems would not be sufficient to improve the performance of the American economy, but we will not improve productivity and income very much without them. We also need to have much better coordination of economic policy based on consensus goals and strategies. If we do not make these changes, incomes will continue to polarize, social tensions will deepen and the United States will become a second-rate economic power, unable to protect and promote its interests in the global economy. Above all, we must realize that the status quo is not one of our options. We can either continue to drift toward becoming a country with low and more unequal wages or we can adopt a high-skills, high-wage strategy. It is hard to conceive of a choice with greater consequences for America's future.

Author's Note

This chapter is based in part on Ray Marshall and Marc Tucker, *Thinking for a Living: Education and the Wealth of Nations* (New York: Basic Books, 1992).

Notes

1. Although wages did not increase as much as productivity (which increased by 40 percent between 1920 and 1930) or profits (which rose by 80 percent), real wages nevertheless went up as a result of rising nominal wages and stable prices. In manufacturing, wages increased by only 8 percent between 1923 and 1929, while productivity rose by 32 percent and profits by 62 percent.

2. There are actually at least two basic quality concepts. Within a firm, internal quality refers to zero defects. But this is not as appropriate for competitiveness as it refers to meeting customers' needs. Timely delivery or convenience might be more useful to customers than zero defects. Some firms have extended the "meeting customers' needs" concept to include "customers" within the firm.

References

Adler, Paul. 1991. "Capitalizing on New Manufacturing Technologies: Current Problems and Emergent Trends in U.S. Industry." In National Academy of Engineering, and Commission on Behavioral and Social Sciences, Education, National Research Council, *People and Technology in the Workplace.* Washington, D.C.: National Academy Press.

American Association for the Advancement of Science (AAAS), Project 2061. 1989. *Science for All Americans.* Washington, D.C.: AAAS.

Aschauer, David A. 1990. *Public Investment and Private Sector Growth.* Washington, D.C.: Economic Policy Institute.

————. 1989a. "Is Public Expenditure Productive?" *Journal of Monetary Economics* 23: 177–200.

————. 1989b. "Public Investment and Productivity Growth in Seven Countries." *Economic Perspective* (September/October): 17–25.

————. 1988. "Rx for Productivity: Build Infrastructure." *Chicago Fed Letter* (September).

Baumol, W. J., S. A. Blackman, and E. N. Wolff. 1989. *Productivity and American Leadership: The Long View.* Cambridge, Mass.: MIT Press.

Bean, C., R. Layard, and S. Nickell. 1986. "The Rise in Unemployment: A Multi Country Study." *Economica* 53 (Supplement): 51–72.

Belman, Dale. 1992. "Unions, the Quality of Labor Relations, and Firm Performance." In Lawrence Mishel and Paula Voos (eds.), *Unions and Economic Competitiveness.* Armonk, N.Y.: M. E. Sharpe. pp. 41–107.

Berle, Adolf, Jr., and Gardiner Means. 1933. *The Modern Corporation and Private Prosperity.* New York: Macmillan.

Berlin, Gordon, and Andrew Sum. 1988. *Toward a More Perfect Union.* New York: Ford Foundation.

Blinder, Alan S. (ed.). 1990. *Paying for Productivity: A Look at the Evidence.* Washington, D.C.: Brookings Institution.

––––––. 1989/90. "Pay Participation and Productivity." *The Brookings Review* (Winter): 33–38.

Bound, John, and George Johnson. 1992. "Changes in the Structure of Wages in the 1980s: An Evaluation of Alternative Explanations." *American Economic Review* 82 (June).

Bruno, M., and Jeffrey Sachs. 1985. *Economics of Worldwide Stagflation.* Oxford: Blackwell.

Callahan, Raymond E. 1962. *Education and the Cult of Efficiency: A Study of the Social Forces that Have Shaped the Administration of the Public Schools.* Chicago: University of Chicago Press.

Carnevale, Anthony. 1983. *Human Capital: A High-Yield Corporate Investment.* Washington, D.C.: American Society for Training and Development.

Children's Defense Fund. 1989. *A Vision for America's Future/An Agenda for the 1990s: A Children's Defense Budget.* Washington, D.C.: Children's Defense Fund.

Chubb, John, and Terry Moe. 1990. *Politics, Markets, and America's Schools.* Washington, D.C.: Brookings Institution.

Coleman, James S., et al. 1966. *Equality of Educational Opportunity.* Washington, D.C.: U.S. Government Printing Office.

Coleman, James S., Thomas Hoffer, and Sally Kilgore. 1982. *Public, Catholic, and Private Schools Compared.* New York: Basic Books.

Comer, James. 1989. "Educating Poor Minority Children." *Scientific American* (November): 42–47.

––––––. 1988. "Is 'Parenting' Essential to Good Teaching?" *Families and Schools* (January): 34–40.

––––––. 1980. *School Power.* New York: The Free Press.

Commission on the Skills of the American Workforce (CSAW). 1990. *America's Choice: high skills or low wages.* Rochester, N.Y.: National Center on Education and the Economy.

Cortes, Ernie. 1990. "Reflections on the Catholic Tradition of Family Rights." Austin, Tex: TIAF (December 17).

Denison, E. F. 1985. *Trends in American Economic Growth 1929–1982.* Washington, D.C.: Brookings Institution.

Dertouzes, Michael L., Richard K. Lester, and Robert M. Solow. 1989. *Made in America: Regaining the Productive Edge.* Cambridge, Mass.: MIT Press.

Drucker, Peter. 1992. *Managing for the Future: The 1990s and Beyond.* New York: Dutton.

Duncan, Greg, and Saul Hoffner. 1985. "Economic Consequences of Marital Instability." In Martin David and Timothy Smeeding (eds.), *Horizontal Equity, Uncertainty and Economic Well-Being.* Chicago: University of Chicago Press.

Eaton, Adrienne and Paula Voos. 1992. "Unions and Contemporary Innovations in Work Organization, Compensation, and Employee Participation." In Lawrence Mishel and Paula Voos (eds.) *Unions and Economic Competitiveness.* Armonk, N.Y.: M. E. Sharpe. pp. 173–215.

Economic Policy Council. 1990. *The Common Interests of Employees and Employers in the 1990s.* New York: Economic Policy Council of the United Nations Association.

Edelman, Marion Wright. 1989. "Investing in Kids." *Union* (June/July).

Eurich, Nell. 1985. *Corporate Classrooms: The Learning Business.* Princeton, N.J.: Carnegie Foundation for the Advancement of Teaching.

Freeman, Richard, and James Medoff. 1984. *What Do Unions Do?* New York: Basic Books.

Galbraith, John K. 1961. *The Great Crash: 1929.* 2nd ed. Boston: Houghton Mifflin.

———. 1987. *Economics in Perspective: A Critical History.* Boston: Houghton Mifflin.

General Accounting Office (GAO). 1986. *Job Corps: Its Costs, Employment Outcomes and Service to the Public.* Washington, D.C.: General Accounting Office. GAO/HRD 86-121BR (July).

Glover, Robert, and Ray Marshall. 1993. "Improving the School-to-Work Transition of American Adolescents." *Teachers College Record* 94, no. 3 (Spring): 588–610.

Haber, S. 1944. *Efficiency and Uplift: Scientific Management in the Progressive Era, 1890–1920.* Chicago: University of Chicago Press.

Hamburg, David. 1987. "Early Interventions to Prevent Lifelong Damage: Lessons from Current Research." Testimony before the Senate Committee on Labor and Human Resources and the House Committee on Education and Labor. September 9.

Hession, Charles H., and Hyman Sardy. 1969. *Ascent to Affluence: A History of American Economic Development.* Boston: Allyn and Bacon.

Hoerr, John P. 1988. *And the Wolf Finally Came: The Decline of the American Steel Industry.* Pittsburgh: University of Pittsburgh Press.

Hofstadter, Richard. 1963. *Anti-Intellectualism in American Life.* New York: Alfred A. Knopf.

Jencks, Christopher, et al. 1972. *Inequality: A Reassessment of the Effect of Family and Schooling in America.* New York: Basic Books.

Keller, Maryann. 1989. *The Rude Awakening.* New York: Morrow.

Kelley, Maryellen, and Bennett Harrison. 1992. "Unions, Technology, and Labor-Management Cooperation." In Lawrence Mishel and Paula Voos (eds.), *Unions and Economic Competitiveness.* Armonk, N.Y.: M. E. Sharpe. pp. 247–286.

Kemmerer, E. W., and D. L. Kemmerer. 1950. *The ABC of the Federal Reserve System.* New York: Harper and Bros.

Kendrick, J. W. 1961. *Productivity Trends in the United States.* Princeton, N.J.: Princeton University Press.

Klein, Lawrence R. 1988. "Components of Competitiveness." *Science* 241 (July 15): 308–315.

Krafcik, John. 1988. "Triumph of the Lean Production System." *Sloan Management Review* (Fall): 41–52.

Kuznets, S. 1946. *National Income: A Summary of Findings.* New York: National Bureau of Economic Research.

Layton, E. T., Jr. 1971. *The Revolt of the Engineers: Social Responsibility and the American Engineering Profession.* Cleveland: Case Western Reserve University Press.

Levine, David I., and Laura D. Tyson. 1990. "Participation, Productivity, and the Firm's Environment." In Alan S. Blinder (ed.), *Paying for Productivity: A Look at the Evidence.* Washington, D.C.: Brookings Institution. pp. 183–243.

Levitan, Sar, and Frank Gallo. 1991. *Got to Learn to Earn: Preparing Americans for Work.* Washington, D.C.: George Washington University Center for Social Policy Studies.

Lillard, Lee A., and Hong W. Tan. 1986. *Private Sector Training: Who Gets It and What are Its Effects?* Santa Monica, Calif.: The Rand Corporation.

Lower, Milton. 1985. "The Industrial Economy and International Price Shocks." Presidential address to the Association for Evolutionary Economics, New York City (December 29).

Marshall, Ray. 1991. *Losing Direction: Families, Human Resource Development, and Economic Performance.* Vol. 3 of *State of Families.* Milwaukee: Family Service America.

———. 1990. "The Impact of Elementary and Secondary Education on State Economic Development." In Jurgen Schmandt and Robert Wilson (eds.), *Growth Policy in the Age of High Technology.* Boston: Unwin Hyman. pp. 211–253.

———. 1988. *Economics of Education.* Vol. 1. Austin, Tex.: LBJ School of Public Affairs and the Texas Education Agency.

———. 1987. *Unheard Voices: Labor and Economic Policy in a Competitive World.* New York: Basic Books.

———. 1967. *Labor in the South.* Cambridge, Mass.: Harvard University Press.

Mason, Geoff, and Bart van Ark. 1992. "Education, Training and Productivity: An Anglo-Dutch Comparison." Paper presented to the ESRC Study Group on the Economics of Education, London Business School, January 17.

Mathematica Policy Research. 1982. *Evaluation of the Economic Impact of the Job Corps: Third Follow-up Report.* Princeton, N.J.: Mathematica Policy Research.

———. 1983. *Relative Effectiveness of Job Corps Vocational Training by Occupational Grouping.* Princeton, N.J.: Mathematica Policy Research.

Metcalf, D. 1986. "Labour Market Flexibility and Jobs: A Survey of Evidence from OECD Countries with Special Reference to Great Britain and Europe." Working Paper no. 254. London School of Economics, Centre for Labour Economics.

Miller, Shelby. 1989. *Early Childhood Services: A National Challenge.* New York: Ford Foundation.

Mishel, Lawrence, and David Frankel. 1991. *The State of Working America.* Armonk, N.Y.: M. E. Sharpe.

Mishel, Lawrence, and Paula Voos. 1992. "Unions and American Economic Competitiveness." In Lawrence Mishel and Paula Voos (eds.), *Unions and Economic Competitiveness.* Armonk, N.Y.: M. E. Sharpe. pp. 1–12.

National Center on Education and the Economy (NCEE). 1989. *To Secure Our Future.* Rochester, N.Y.: NCEE.

National Commission on Children. 1991. *Beyond Rhetoric: A New American Agenda for Children and Families.* Washington, D.C.: U.S. Government Printing Office.

Neef, Arthur, and Christopher Kask. 1991. "Manufacturing Productivity and Labor Costs in 14 Economies." *Monthly Labor Review* (December): 24–37.

Nevins, A., and F. E. Hill. 1954. *Ford: The Times, the Man and the Company.* Vol. 1. New York: Scribner.

Newell, A., and J. Symon. 1986. "Corporatism, Laissez-Faire and the Rise of Unemployment." Working Paper no. 853. London School of Economics, Centre for Labour Economics.

Nielsen, Robert. 1990. "Anyone Can Learn Math: New Programs Show How." *American Educator* 14, no. 1 (Spring): 29–34.

Prais, S. J., and Karin Wagner. 1988. "Productivity and Management: The Training of Foremen in Britain and Germany." *National Institute Economic Review* (February).

Resnick, Laura. 1987a. *Education and Learning to Think.* Washington, D.C.: National Academy Press.

———. 1987b. "Learning in School and Out." Presidential address to American Educational Research Association, Washington, D.C. April 22.

Rogers, Mary Beth. 1990. *Cold Anger: A Story of Faith and Power Politics.* Denton, Tex.: University of North Texas Press.

Sachs, Jeffrey. 1989. "Social Conflict and Populist Policies in Latin America." Working Paper no. 2897. National Bureau of Economic Research. March.

Schultz, Theodore W. 1981. *Investing in People: The Economics of Population Quality.* Berkeley: University of California Press.

Sizer, Theodore. 1984. *Horace's Compromise.* Boston: Houghton Mifflin.

Tyack, David B. 1974. *The One Best System: A History of American Urban Education.* Cambridge, Mass.: Harvard University Press.

U.S. Department of the Census. 1948. *Historical Statistics of the U.S.: 1789–1945.* Washington, D.C.: U.S. Government Printing Office.

Zuboff, Shoshona. 1988. *In the Age of the Smart Machine.* New York: Basic Books.

23

Principles for a Post–New Deal Employment Policy

Thomas A. Kochan

One of the hallmarks of the previous generations of industrial relations researchers was their contributions to the development and analysis of public policies that regulate employment relationships.[1] The field of industrial relations was born out of the efforts of an early generation of institutional labor economists to find better ways to address the labor problems they observed in the early part of this century. Their work eventually provided the intellectual foundation for the New Deal labor policies and industrial relations system. This tradition was carried on by the next generation of institutional economists, who used their experiences with the War Labor Board to help develop and apply the principles guiding collective bargaining and labor policy in the postwar era. These two generations of scholars shared the view that government had an important role to play in protecting labor standards and regulating the rules of the game governing employee-employer relations.

Unfortunately, these views have been largely ignored in policy-making circles in recent years. Instead, the past decade saw a return to a laissez-faire labor and employment policy and a resurgence of neoclassical economics as the dominant intellectual framework for employment policy. Public policymakers were largely passive observers in the 1980s as management and labor in the private sector engaged in far-reaching trial-and-error efforts to update and transform their practices to accommodate changes in their product and labor markets. As a result, while significant innovations were initiated, they have yet to diffuse to the point where their potential benefits to the larger economy and society are realized.

While we in the research community have studied and debated the implications, for both theory and practice, of changes in private business practice (see, for example, Freeman and Medoff 1984; Piore and Sabel 1984; Kochan, Katz, and McKersie 1986; Derber 1982; Barbash 1980; Lewin 1987; Dunlop 1989; Freedman 1990; Chelius and Dworkin 1990), we have yet to fully explore the implications of these changes for the role of government as an actor in employment relationships. Although a number of us believe that the New Deal labor policies are no longer sufficient or adequate for today's economy and work force (see, for example, Weiler 1990; Kochan and McKersie 1988; Heckscher 1987; Marshall 1987; Lawler 1990), we have yet to articulate a convincing intellectual framework or a set of principles to replace the New Deal model.

This chapter sketches out a framework for a post–New Deal employment policy that builds on the institutionalists' view of the labor market. But it goes beyond that perspective by building on the lessons learned from the private experimentation of the past decade. The key extension of the New Deal approach is the suggestion that contemporary employment policy needs to support innovations in private practice that can create mutual or joint gains in employment relationships (Walton 1985). The central argument is that, if widely adopted, these innovations and others that will follow can contribute to the twin macroeconomic and social objectives of enhancing the competitiveness of the economy and promoting improvements in the standard of living. Achieving these twin objectives will, however, require breaking with the past decade's passive approach to employment policy.

The Need for a New Employment Policy

Over the course of the past decade, the recognition that changes in the international and domestic economy were challenging a host of traditional American policies and practices led to the formation of a large number of commissions and study groups focused on competitiveness, productivity, and similar issues. These groups covered the broad political spectrum ranging from President Reagan's Council on Competitiveness (now a private group), to New York governor Mario Cuomo's Commission on Trade and Competitiveness, to groups led by faculty members at universities such as Carnegie-Mellon, the University of California at Berkeley, Harvard, and MIT, to labor-management groups such as the Collective Bargaining Forum.[2] In addition to these broad-based commissions, five former secretaries of labor led or organized national commissions and studies aimed at identifying the implications of changes in the economy and the workforce for the future of labor and human resource policy and practice.[3]

A number of common rhetorical points can be found in each of these reports. First, there is a general recognition that the central economic and social policy challenge facing the United States today is to restore the competitiveness of U.S. industries and firms in world markets while simultaneously reversing the erosion in American standards of living experienced in the past decade. Second, there is an equally general recognition that to achieve these twin objectives U.S. firms must gain competitive advantage from the quality and utilization of their human resources. Moreover, most of these reports go on to argue that the key microeconomic strategy for achieving these objectives lies in improving the long-term rate of productivity growth, since productivity growth is a necessary condition for improving real wages and living standards. But these reports add new dimensions to the concept of productivity (cf. Cyert and Mowery 1986; Dertouzos, Solow, and Lester, 1989). In today's economy, productivity means more than simply output per work hour. It must also encompass the production of high-quality goods and services and the capacity to innovate and to adapt quickly to new technologies and market opportunities.

These reports also normally note that meeting these new productivity and quality imperatives will require significant investments in human resources and sustained cooperation and innovation in labor-management relations. Achieving world-class levels of quality and productivity requires organizations that achieve high levels of skill, motivation, participation, and trust from their work force. Here is where the lessons of the innovative side of private-sector labor and human resource practices of the past decade enter into the rhetoric. Although the specifics vary from industry to industry and firm to firm, the organizations capable of eliciting sustained mutual commitment to high levels of investment in human resources in return for high levels of trust and motivation usually involve some variation on the following principles:

• The firm competes on the basis of product quality and differentiation as well as price.
• Human resource considerations weigh heavily in corporate strategic decision making and governance processes. Employee interests are represented through the voice of human resource staff profes-

sionals, or employee representatives consult and participate with senior executives in decisions that affect human resource policies and employee interests. In either case, employees are treated as legitimate stakeholders in the corporation.

• Investments in new hardware or physical technology are combined with the investments in human resources and changes in organizational practices that are required to realize the full potential benefits of these investments.

• The firm sustains a high level of investment in training, skill development, and education, and personnel practices are designed to capture and utilize these skills fully.

• Compensation and reward systems are internally equitable, competitive, and linked to the long-term performance of the firm.

• Employment continuity and security are important priorities and values to be considered in all corporate decisions and policies.

• Workplace relations encourage flexibility in the organization of work, empowerment of employees to solve problems, and high levels of trust among workers, supervisors, and managers.

• Worker rights to representation are acknowledged and respected. Union or other employee representatives are treated as joint partners in designing and overseeing innovations in labor and human resource practices.

These principles are grounded in the innovations introduced by a number of leading firms and unions in the 1980s. The primary lesson to be learned from these experiments and the research that evaluated them is that it is possible to construct a mutual-gains employment relationship and that, when in place, employees respond favorably to it.

However, there is another side to the past decade's experience that the policy-making community has not been willing to face. These innovative practices and high rates of investment in human resources are limited to a small segment of the economy, they are difficult to sustain or institutionalize, and they are not diffusing. Instead, the majority of employment relationships are going in exactly the opposite direction called for by the conclusions and recommendations of these commissions and study groups.

Despite the calls for increased commitment to training, the levels of public and private-firm investment in human resources in the United States lags behind those in Germany and Japan (Kochan and Osterman 1991; MacDuffie and Kochan 1991). While U.S. firms have been estimated to spend more than $30 billion annually on training (Carnevale 1990), in reality this amounts to less than 2 percent of total private-sector compensation. The vast majority of these training dollars are spent by large firms on management development. The reality is that investments in training are not a widespread phenomenon but are concentrated on executives and managers in large, elite firms.

The same is true for sustained labor-management cooperation. While the 1980s were a decade of profound innovation in labor-management relations in some firms, the dominant labor relations trend of the 1980s was one of accelerated declines in union membership and escalating tensions and conflict between unions fighting for survival and legitimacy and employers intent on either avoiding or minimizing the influence of unions. By the end of the decade union membership in the private sector of the economy had fallen to less than 12 percent, the lowest point recorded since just prior to the Great Depression. Consequently the capacity of labor and management to work together in cooperative and innovative ways likewise declined.

Employment security also appears to have lost ground as a priority in corporate decision making in recent years. Firms such as IBM, Digital Equipment Corporation, Hewlett Packard, and others well known for their commitment to employment security were forced by shifts in their product markets to turn to layoffs or equivalent means of involuntary reductions in their work force.

Meanwhile the role and status of labor and human resource policy within the federal government also went in a direction opposite that called for by the rhetoric and recommendations of the commissions. Despite the demand for expanded training and innovation in labor-management relations, in 1990 the federal budget for training was less than half the level budgeted in 1980. In 1992, the only two (small) programs in the federal government devoted to promoting labor-management cooperation and innovation — the Bureau of Labor Management Relations and Cooperative Programs in the Department of Labor, and the Federal Mediation and Conciliation Service's grants to support innovative labor-management joint programs — were eliminated. (The grants program was reinstated by the Clinton Administration in 1993 and a new Office of the American Workplace was established to replace the former Bureau for Labor Management Cooperative Programs.)

Enforcement of safety and health policies weakened as well in the 1980s. The budgets and inspection staff of the Occupational Safety and Health Administration (OSHA) were reduced, and the process of setting new standards for exposure to toxic substances slowed considerably (Noble 1992). Even a bona fide crisis did not succeed in producing a shift in labor policy. In 1989 a major explosion in a petrochemical plant killed 23 workers and injured 232. As a result, the Congress requested that OSHA commission an independent study to determine the underlying cause of this and other recent accidents in petrochemical plants. A central issue to be studied was the claim that the increased use of poorly trained temporary contract workers to perform maintenance and related renovation work was increasing the risk of accidents in these plants. Although the study confirmed that the current regulatory and management systems in the industry were not effective in managing the risks associated with the use of contract labor, OSHA lacked the independent authority from higher levels of the executive branch (in this case, the Office of Management and Budget) to initiate any changes in the way it regulated these employment relationships (Kochan, Wells, and Smith 1992). While this is only one isolated example, it is symbolic of the general decline in the stature, independence, and influence of the Department of Labor in national economic, social, and employment policy debates. The Labor Department has lacked experienced and respected leadership by labor experts of the calibre of previous secretaries from the War Labor Board generation, such as George Shultz and John Dunlop, and it does not have the professional analytical staff necessary for it to play an effective role in policy-making discussions within the government.

Thus the current state of employment policy and practice is poorly matched to the needs of the economy and the work force. Indeed, I believe we are facing a crisis in labor policy and analysis at least as large as the challenge that faced scholars and policymakers in the years just prior to the beginning of the New Deal. If we are to carry on with the legacy left to us by earlier generations of industrial relations scholars, we will need to meet this crisis by providing the theoretically and empirically grounded principles that can serve as the intellectual framework for a new national employment policy. The next sections of this chapter are devoted to the development of such principles, starting with the enduring contributions of the institutional economists who provided the intellectual foundations and principles guiding the New Deal labor policy.

The Institutional Foundations to Labor Policy

The first generation of institutional economists proposed a view of the labor market that was an alternative to the prevailing classical economics model, a view that provided an important part of the intellectual justification for a more activist role for government policy in employment relations than prevailed at that time. The essence of the institutional view was (and remains) that the employment relationship is an ongoing economic and social relationship in which employees build up property rights that need to be balanced against the economic interests or property rights of employers. Employment transactions are not one-time exchanges of commodity goods but are ongoing bargains involving exchanges of human effort in return for current compensation and implicit promises of future economic security. Moreover, the institutionalists viewed these relationships as being what Walton and McKersie (1965) labeled as "mixed motive" in nature, that is, they involved a mixture of conflicting and common interests and thereby required both periodic, distributive negotiations and integrative efforts to pursue joint gains. Like any relationship involving conflicting interests, power plays a critical role in shaping the outcomes of these negotiations — thus the need to assure that power is reasonably "balanced." The early institutionalists believed government should balance the power between the parties in ways that promoted periodic negotiations and orderly resolution of the parties' conflicting interests.

The institutional model of labor markets further challenged a prevailing principle of classical economics, namely that perfect competition would provide the socially optimal outcomes for labor market transactions. Instead the institutionalists adopted a view first articulated by the Webbs in their discussion of the higgling of the market (Webb and Webb 1897). To the Webbs, competition meant price competition, which in turn translated into factor cost competition. Thus labor is treated like a commodity, a factor of production, and a cost to be minimized. Competitive market forces will serve to drive out any "rents" that labor power may create and thereby, if left unregulated by law or private institutions, will drive down labor standards.

Given this view of the labor market and the problems identified by the careful empirical research conducted by the first generation of institutional economists, it is not surprising that the New Deal labor policies focused on the distributive side of the employment relationship. Various labor standards (minimum wages, hours of work, unemployment insurance, workers' compensation insurance, social security, and so on) set a floor on working conditions, while collective bargaining legislation strengthened workers' ability to influence their conditions of employment. As such the New Deal policies reflected an effort to institutionalize and regulate conflicting interests at the workplace.

Since the institutionalists viewed conflicting interests between workers and employers as inherent and enduring features of employment relationships, the need for legislative protection of labor standards and the right to organize are seen as remaining equally necessary through time. Thus, the institutional legacy of industrial relations suggests a first principle for employment policy: government is responsible for creating an environment and a set of rules to redress imbalances in power in employment relationships and for ensuring that enduring conflicts of interest between workers and employers are resolved through negotiations and that basic worker rights are protected by labor standards.

While this remains an important first principle for employment policy, it is no longer sufficient. The early institutionalists and the New Deal labor policies had little to say about the integrative side of the employment relationship, that is, how public policy might encourage the pursuit of mutual gains in the workplace. In part this reflected the lack of an adequate theory of management, a weakness that continued to plague industrial relations theory for years to come. But if the view of the importance of managerial choices and actions posited in contemporary strategic choice models of industrial relations (Kochan, Katz, and McKersie 1986) is accurate, and if mutual gains' strategies are to be encouraged by policymakers, this weakness must be addressed. Mutual-gains strategies will only be chosen if human resource considerations and employee interests can influence the critical managerial choices and long-term strategies of the firm.

Organization Governance, Management, and Employment Policy

To the extent management was considered at all in early industrial relations research, it was in the context of how to limit management's potential abuse of its power in employment relationships. The institutionalists' traditional answer to this question was through collective bargaining that would specify worker and management rights and responsibilities. Beyond this, management retained its prerogatives to manage. Management retained the right to make strategic decisions affecting the enterprise; workers and their unions were to be given rights to negotiate or to file a grievance over management actions that affected wages, hours, and working conditions. Thus, to the extent there was an implicit theory of management in industrial relations, management was viewed through the eyes of its industrial relations representative.

Later industrial relations theorists clearly recognized and conceptualized the intraorganizational bargaining that occurs within management over labor policies (Slichter, Healy, and Livernash 1960; Walton and McKersie 1965; Dunlop 1967). But even they viewed the process through the eyes of the industrial relations manager preparing for or participating in collective bargaining. The burgeoning field of personnel management took a similar "functional" approach to its domain by focusing on the specific activities and techniques of recruitment, selection, compensation, performance appraisal, and so on. Little attention was given to conceptualizing the broader domain of strategic decision making regarding technology, investment, capital flows, or the governance structure of the firm, since these were perceived to lie well beyond the domain of labor policy. The essence of strategic choice theory is that this level of management must now be incorporated into labor and human resource theories and policies, because it is at this level of the firm that the key decisions are made that shape the outcomes of the employment relationship.

Research on these broader aspects of management fell to behavioral scientists who lacked both a deep understanding of the workings of labor markets and the values that guided the institutionalists' view of employment relations and public policy. Behavioralists either ignored or denied the distributive side of the employment relationship and took as their objective the search for managerial methods that integrated individual and organizational interests (Mayo 1933; McGregor 1960).

But some branches of modern organization theory (March and Simon 1958; Cyert and March 1963; Thompson 1967; Child 1972; Pfeffer 1992; Pettigrew 1973; Thomas 1992) as well as industrial relations theory (Kochan, Katz, and McKersie 1986) explicitly model management not as a monolithic actor but as a coalition of competing interests composed of multiple functional and hierarchical levels. While external markets, technologies, and social forces (including government) influence managerial actions, these external forces are not deterministic. Managers retain some discretion or range of choice in shaping an organization's long-term strategies and internal practices. Nor are top managers simply neutral coordinators of different functional interests. Instead, managers bring values and ideologies, functional interests, personal aspirations, and perceptual frames of reference to their decision-making roles, all of which needs to be taken into account in shaping government policy. Finally, the 1980s brought home a new empirical reality to students of management and employment relations, namely, that shareholder interests and external financial institutions affect managerial behavior and strategy, and outcomes of the employment relationship (Useem and Gottlieb 1992; Davis 1992). All of these emerging insights regarding managerial behavior and decision making need to be taken into account in shaping a modern approach to employment policy. The key question therefore is: How do human resource and labor issues fit into this structure and process of strategic decision making?

Human resources has historically ranked as one of the weakest components within the management structure of U.S. firms. The status of the personnel or human resources function has risen and fallen over time. As far back as 1919 Sumner Slichter and Paul Douglas noted that personnel managers were finally coming into their own and being viewed as important and influential within management as their colleagues in finance, marketing, and manufacturing (Slichter 1919; Douglas 1919). This same view again dominated the rhetoric in the personnel literature throughout the 1980s. Human resource executives were expected to become strategic partners with top executives and line managers. But the relative ranking of these executives has not fundamentally changed. In a recent small survey of high tech firms in New England I found that human resources still ranked fourth out of five managerial functions. Moreover, human resource executives continue to rely on their ability to establish "partnerships" with more powerful line executives or to gain the confidence and commitment of the top corporate executives to give voice and influence to human resource policies within the firm (Freedman 1990; Towers Perrin 1991). So long as this is the prevailing position of human resources in corporate governance and strategic decision making, this function will continue to occupy a relatively low or variable position of power and influence.

Historically, human resource innovations come in concentrated periods that coincide with wars, social crises, union threats, or major changes in government policy (Baron, Dobbin, and Jennings 1986; Jacoby 1985; Kochan and Cappelli 1984). As these external threats mount, so too does the power of those human resource, industrial relations, and other professionals within management who cope with the risks and potential threats to the organization that these external pressures entail. The more permanent the pressures, the more likely they are to result in lasting shifts in the influence of the professionals assigned to cope with them within the firm. These professionals are most successful, however, when they can translate the external pressures into mutual-gains strategies (Cebon 1992).

A counterpoint to this view of management dominated popular management research and writing in the 1980s. This alternative view sees top executives as the key group shaping the culture, values, and behavior of the firm, its managers, and its rank-and-file employees (Peters and Waterman 1982). What is known as the cultural school of management argues that modern executives have both learned and internalized the view that human resources are the firm's most important asset and therefore have become self-enlightened about the need to manage employees fairly and to provide them with opportunities to influence their jobs, work environment, and careers. According to this view, the values of managers have shifted from those of the robber barons of the past century to those of today's culture-conscious CEOs. Thus it is believed that union threats or government standards are no longer needed, because management will attend to employee interests.

This view of corporate governance and strategy making reflects an ahistorical and atheoretical view of the modern corporation. Corporate executives must function as coordinators of multiple interests, but ultimately they are agents of shareholders. The legal foundation of the American corporation rests on a premise that the fiduciary responsibility and primary function of management is to maximize the financial interests of shareholders. While since the writings of Berle and Means (1933) it has been recognized that managers develop interests of their own and a separation of ownership and control often occurs, more recently there was a resurgence in shareholder interest through the development in the 1980s of an active "market for corporate control." Shareholders, and outside bidders, became interested in asserting their short-term interests, because top executives were thought to have become complacent, to have stressed their own interests rather than the shareholders', and to have insulated the corporation from the market. This led to corporate restructuring with a vengeance in the 1980s (Doyle 1989). More recently, the two leading business periodicals, *Business Week* (1991) and the *Wall Street Journal* (1991), concluded that the culture building CEOs are being replaced by hard-driving cost-cutting executives who are not afraid to cut employment and clean house.

Underlying managerial behavior lies a set of capital markets and financial institutions that influence managerial time horizons and strategic decisions. Only recently, however, have we begun to examine the relationships between these markets and institutions and firm-level labor and human resource strategies (Levine and Tyson 1990; Porter 1992; Kochan and Osterman 1992, Wever and Allen 1992). The key hypothesis emerging out of this literature is that U.S.

capital markets and institutions constrain managerial time horizons to focus on short-term results. This in turn leads managers to under-invest in activities or projects that have clear short-term costs but only long-term payoffs. Investments in human resources and innovations in employment practices fit this description. This area of research is only in its infancy, but it needs to be pursued if we are to engage in a thoughtful and empirically grounded debate over the appropriate role of human resource strategies in organizational governance and the role that public policy plays in shaping that role.

Thus, a modern employment policy that seeks to encourage firms to pursue mutual-gains strategies must be based on a better-informed model of the role of decision making within corporations. If the real decisions that affect long-term employment relations are made at the top levels of the corporate hierarchy rather than through collective bargaining or within the personnel function of the corporation, if the human resource function continues to occupy a junior partnership position in most organizational hierarchies, and if, as some argue, U.S. financial markets and institutions bias decision making in favor of short time horizons and cost controls rather than long-term investments, human resource considerations and employee interests are not likely to be effectively taken into account at this level of decision making. The implication of research findings in this area is that one role for government would be to elevate and stabilize the otherwise weak and fluctuating influence that employee interests and human resource management concerns have in American corporations.

This suggests a second principle for a modern theory and perspective on the role of government in employment relations. The ability of human resource managers to influence corporate strategies is low, historically, in U.S. firms because of the legal doctrines governing the American corporations. Decision making regarding any functional group is a political process requiring significant influence. The influence of human resource professionals rises and falls over time in response to changes in the degree of external threat posed by the labor market, government, or unions and other employee representation institutions. Yet even within this range, the political influence of human resource and employee interests remains low relative to the competing interests of functions that are closer to the core concern of maximizing shareholder interests. Thus, one function of government policy should be to elevate and institutionalize the influence of human resource considerations and employee interests in the long-term strategic decisions and governance processes of the firm.

Government's Role in Diffusing
Mutual-Gains Innovations

While the preceding discussion suggests that there are systematic internal organizational barriers to sustained human resource innovations, a number of firms appear to have found exceptions to this rule. Over the course of the past two decades firms such as IBM, Polaroid, Digital Equipment Corporation, Xerox, and Hewlett Packard achieved reputations for giving a high priority to human resource considerations and employee interests. Their policies generally fit the principles of a mutual commitment organization that were summarized at the outset of this chapter. Yet despite the tremendous amount of favorable publicity these firms received in the 1980s, their approaches have not spread to large numbers of other firms. Instead, as their product markets became more competitive and the financial analysts became more vocal in their concerns over the high cost of these human resource policies, these firms experienced difficulties maintaining the policies. This suggests that the external environment may also be producing systematic market failures that limit diffusion of innovations across the economy and their sustainability within individual firms. As in other cases of market failure, only an active role by the government in changing the environment will produce widespread diffusion.

Levine and Tyson (1990) outline several factors that contribute to a market failure for human resource innovations: (1) volatility in product markets, (2) loose labor markets, and (3) impatient capital markets. The basic principle at work here is simple. If all employers cooperate and invest to upgrade and utilize the skills of the labor force and provide greater employment security, all firms, their employees, and the national economy will be better off. If one firm invests heavily and others do not, the investor loses and competitors that do not invest gain a cost advantage, because some portion of the benefits from the investment are lost to the external market. If no one invests, firms might be able to escape the problem in the short run by competing on the basis of labor costs, but employees and society eventually suffer, because productivity and living standards erode. Eventually more job-creating capital investment migrates to regions or countries with lower labor costs. As a result the overall economy suffers from an underinvestment problem.

U.S. firms are particularly prone to such market failures because of the strong tradition of firm independence and autonomy embedded in the American culture and ideology. Walton (1988) and Cole (1989) both identify as problematic the lack of either industrial or national infrastructures for diffusing human resource innovations. Commons recognized this problem more than 70 years ago in his analysis of the effects of the expansion of the market on the wages and labor standards of shoemakers (Commons 1919). What is needed now is the equivalent of the institutions that took wages out of competition in the post–New Deal system of collective bargaining. This then becomes an additional task for the government and therefore suggests another principle for contemporary employment policy. The ability of any individual firm to sustain high levels of investments in human resource policies and innovations depends on the extent to which other firms in their labor and product markets and supplier and customer network invest in similar practices. The role of the government is to encourage and support diffusion of human resource policies within individual firms that, if sustained and widely adopted, can produce benefits for the whole economy and for society.

The State as an Actor in Employment Policy

Any argument for a more activist role for government in employment policy must also be well grounded in an understanding of the policy-making and administrative processes within government. This, however, is another area of weakness in industrial relations theory and research. Too often researchers move directly to prescriptions for changes in national policies without first building a positive theory of the role of the American state in employment relations. Efforts to build a strategic choice model of industrial relations have been criticized for failing to fully conceptualize the role of the state as an actor in employment relations (Adams, 1992). While full development of such a theory is beyond the scope of this chapter, several points need to be made.

First, similar to its position within American firms, the priority or influence of labor and human resource policy is likewise rather low within the federal government. Thus, the politics of policy-making within the government must be taken into account in formulating a viable national employment policy. Second, again as is the case within individual firms, labor and human resource policies cannot stand alone. Instead these policies need to be integrated into and contribute to broader national economic and social policy objectives and strategies. A mutual-gains strategy is as essential for labor policy representatives in national policy-making as it is within individual firms. To succeed in achieving such a strategy requires both strong and respected advocates for employment policy within the economic policy-making community and deep technical and analytical support for these policy arguments. Third, policy-making influence within government requires the backing of a strong external constituency. Fourth, since researchers have described the United States as a weak government and one that is historically reluctant to initiate changes in labor policies (Hattam 1990; Stone 1988; Klare 1988), major changes in labor and employment policies only occur in rare political and economic circumstances. If the past is any guide, these circumstances arise in times of severe economic, national security, or social crises — wartime, periods of high inflation or unemployment, significant labor unrest, and so on. These were the conditions that were present both in the 1930s when the New Deal labor policies were enacted and in the 1960s when out of the urban crises emerged the state legislation granting collective bargaining rights to public employees. Finally, just as modern theories of management do not treat management as a monolithic actor, neither should the multiple interests and structure of decision making within government be ignored when formulating a theory of the role of the state.

Since its establishment in 1913 the U.S. Department of Labor has served as the central agency within the executive branch of government with responsibility for advising the president on labor and employment policy matters. Yet throughout its history, and especially in the past decade, the Labor Department has not been able to assert an independent voice in policy-making. Instead it has been subordinate to other cabinet-level agencies responsible for economic policy-making. In recent years the department has been relegated to an even more subordinate position by the collapse of its external constituency and by the degree of control over domestic and regulatory policy asserted by the Office of Management and Budget (OMB). All congressional testimony; administrative rules, regulations or standards; new legislative proposals; and even data collection instruments must be approved by OMB before the Labor Department (or other cabinet agencies) can act. This limits the freedom of the department to bring its own professional judgment to bear on policy issues within its substantive domain. Instead it must obtain approval for its initiatives from the keeper of the budget and the watchdog for limiting the number and scope of government regulations.

The decline in the status and influence of employment policy is both a cause and an effect of the decline in the influence of labor in society and at the level of the firm. As union membership declined, the political influence of labor likewise declined. When this decline crossed a threshold — perhaps with the defeat of the Labor Law Reform Bill in 1978 or perhaps with the firing of the striking air traffic controllers by President Reagan in 1981, perhaps when the nonunion sector became a sufficiently large and viable alternative for employers — employers and government officials outside the narrow domains of labor policy could deny labor policy-makers and representatives the legitimacy they need to participate in and influence issues of national policy. Political discourse could then label labor as a "special interest" with a narrow institutional agenda.

This suggests the following principle regarding government as an actor in employment policy. For employment policy to be effective it must achieve voice and be integrated into macroeconomic and social policy-making and administration. For it to achieve this status and influence requires that a broad and diverse set of external interests support and reinforce the efforts and influence of employment policy officials in the policy-making and administrative processes. Moreover, makers of employment policy must bring an independent and professional analytical capacity to bear in these policy debates, capable of identifying strategies for pursuing the joint objectives of effective macroeconomic performance and improvement in labor and living standards.

In summary, the contemporary challenge to government is to strengthen its internal analytical capacity to play a more active role in employment affairs. But it must do so with a substantive agenda and a strategy that is human resource or market enhancing — one that encourages firms and employees to focus on the joint outcomes of improving the competitiveness of the enterprise and the economy through a high-productivity and high-skills labor force. This means that within the firm, labor policy should serve to strengthen the role of human resources in corporate strategy and governance, encourage development of a long-term perspective that treats employees as valuable assets, and recognize the importance of a high-trust, cooperative culture for innovation and adaptation. Within the government itself, these same principles need to be applied to the development and administration of employment, economic, and social policies. That is, those responsible for labor or employment policy need to participate in the highest levels of macroeconomic and social decisions and policy-making and search for employment strategies and policy instruments that can achieve the joint goals of economic growth and competitiveness with high labor and living standards.

Labor standards and workers' right to effective representation must continue to be protected but should be embedded in a broader employment and economic policy and be responsive to a greater diversity in the work force than traditional regulatory and bargaining models have recognized.

Applying the Principles

At the outset of this chapter I noted that one of the legacies of prior generations of industrial relations scholars was their ability to translate the broad theoretical and normative principles guiding their work into practical policies. To be true to this legacy, I need to go beyond the broad principles I have outlined thus far to suggest how they might be applied.[4]

Specific policy initiatives

The policy initiatives proposed here start with a key labor and human resource component to macroeconomic policies designed to foster sustained improvements in productivity, move on to encourage mutual-gains strategies within individual firms, and support the diffusion of these strategies across the economy to the point that they produce macroeconomic and societal benefits. But consistent with the long-standing view in the field of industrial relations that effective employee representation is critical to both our democracy and our economy, embedded in these proposals are reforms of labor law that would allow employees to choose the forms of participation and representation that best allow them to influence the issues that affect their interests, contribute to the long-term performance of their employer, and, consistent with the forms of empowerment proposed, take more responsibility for their own long-term development, safety, and economic security. Thus, all of these recommendations have the effect of strengthening the influence of employees as stakeholders in corporate governance and strategic decision making.

Integrated Investment Strategies Most macroeconomic strategies for improving long-term rates of productivity growth call for some type of tax or depreciation incentives to encourage greater capital investment. This is the first point at which employment policy should be linked to macroeconomic policy. The evidence from the 1980s (MacDuffie and Krafcik 1991; MacDuffie and Kochan 1991) demonstrated that capital investments are more likely to pay off when combined with investments in human resources and integrated with changes in organizational practices designed to speed the implementation and utilization of the new equipment. Thus investment incentives should encourage enterprises to invest in both hardware and human resources and to put in place the governance and human resource practices required for these investments to reach their full potential. Specifically, any investment tax credit for hardware should be accompanied by evidence that employees have a voice in the technological choice and implementation process and by a human resource development plan for deploying the new equipment. Moreover, tax credits should also be available for investments in training and human resource development, provided that these are investments that build *general* human capital.

Human Resource Councils One way to ensure that these investments build general, transferable skills and serve to complement rather than substitute for the specific training needed to perform current jobs is to involve those who have the strongest direct interest in having general skills in the design and administration of the policies. Any tax credits for training or human resource investments should have an accompanying requirement that a representative cross section of the enterprise's work force participate in this fashion. In a previous paper Robert McKersie and I suggested that such human resource advisory councils should have a broad and open-ended mandate and agenda and therefore should be allowed to evolve in a way that is suitable to the diverse circumstances found in different enterprises and sectors of the economy. These councils could also take on responsibilities in other areas of employment policy, such as occupational safety and health, where employees have both the incentive and the potential to foster continuous improvements in practices and outcomes.

In some sectors enterprise-level human resource investment strategies will need to be supplemented by region- or occupation-based training and development strategies and institutions. Where there is heavy use of temporary or contract labor or where labor moves across firm boundaries, as in construction or clothing, investments in regional or industry consortia for training and human resource development should be eligible for the same tax credits made available for firm-sponsored training, again provided that employees are represented in the design and administration of the training program. These regional institutions could also develop occupational certifications and standards for the training provided in local educational institutions, and thereby support other initiatives to overcome the weaknesses that are now well documented and recognized in the

U.S. apprenticeship and related school-to-work transition processes (Batt and Osterman 1991).

Risk-Rewards Sharing and Governance The incentives to establish the new participatory and representative structures and processes called for in this plan should have the positive effect of upgrading employees' voice and human resource considerations in the operation of American firms. But there is room for further experimentation in organizational governance that flows from the evidence of the past decade. Federal tax policy has provided various incentives and inducements to encourage firms to establish employee stock ownership plans (ESOPs). The evidence suggests, however, that relatively few of these have given employees a voice in the governance of the corporation when ESOPs are introduced (Blasi and Kruse 1991). Therefore, tax incentives and other policies that encourage ESOPs and other forms of contingent compensation should provide for employee rights to nominate or elect representatives to their corporate board of directors. This would further encourage the transformation of American corporations from entities that focus on short-term shareholder interests to ones that give greater weight to long-run investments and growth opportunities. Specifically, tax credits for ESOPs or deferred profit sharing should only be provided if employees are given equivalent representation on corporate boards of directors, in a fashion that is consistent with the way other investors and financial stakeholders gain representation on corporate boards. This would further stimulate incentives for employees and firms to adopt contingent compensation programs that, if diffused broadly, would achieve some of the macroeconomic savings, growth, and stabilization objectives identified by Weitzman and others (Weitzman 1984; Weitzman and Kruse 1990).

Updating and Transforming Workers' Right to Representation While the preceding policy initiatives should help to create a climate that deepens trust at the workplace and encourages the parties to pursue integrative, mutual-gains strategies, employment policy cannot continue to ignore the need to provide employees with the basic right to join the employee organization of their choice. Not all employers will choose to compete in ways that are consistent with the types of institutional arrangements I have proposed. Distributive issues will remain a central part of employment relationships, even in those firms that do choose to embark on a mutual-gains strategy. Therefore labor law must provide employees with an effective right to join the type of labor organization that best suits their circumstances. Research conducted after the labor law reform debates of 1977–78 has demonstrated quite conclusively that current labor law no longer serves this function well (see Lawler 1990 and Weiler 1990 for reviews of this evidence). Minor reforms that simply encourage the parties to discover new tactics for escalating their rhetorical attacks on each other's motives and integrity will not serve anyone's long-term interests. Instead, union recognition procedures need to be transformed in ways that avoid starting the relationship off on a protracted and highly adversarial course. Effective reforms would include changes in the union recognition process that would encourage the parties to establish their own procedures for extending recognition voluntarily when new facilities or worksites are being planned, reduce delays in elections and certification decisions where elections are held, strengthen the penalties imposed on labor law violators so as to eliminate the economic incentives that now exist to violate the law, and provide for first contract arbitration in situations where the parties are unable to conclude these negotiations on their own following union certification.

The existence of human resource councils and effective procedures for establishing union representation will create a healthy environment of competition among existing and potentially new labor organizations and associations. In this type of policy environment union leaders will compete with other professional groups to train and offer technical assistance to human resource council representatives, much the same way that the Congress of Industrial Organizations (CIO) offered a competing model to the American Federation of Labor (AFL) organizing principles in the 1930s, and similar to the way unions and works councils in Germany relate to each other (Wever and Allen 1992). Whether out of this competition will arise a new national labor movement or a looser confederation of local, regional, and enterprise associations remains to be seen (Heckscher 1987; Kern and Sabel 1991). But, as has been seen in Germany, the representative organizations that will thrive in this environment are ones that develop skills and abilities to promote development, utilization, and mobility of the human capital embodied in the labor force of the future.

Deepening the Analytical Foundations of Employment Policy

Finally, a new comprehensive employment policy will require considerable strengthening of the analytical capacity of labor policy researchers within government and in the academic community. Here we come full circle and return to the basic traditions that gave rise to the field and that characterized the role of scholars from the days of the first generation of institutional economists to the post–War Labor Board generation of labor economists and industrial relations specialists. Those who featured prominently in the administration of New

Deal labor policies had prior training, research-based knowledge, and experience in the labor markets and organizational practices of their day. The same can be said of the War Labor Board generation, although some of that generation gained their knowledge of practice "on the job" and then deepened their experience through active involvement in the labor market and industrial relations affairs that followed in the postwar period.

A contemporary version of these generations of useful policy scholars and practitioners need not simply reincarnate the institutional economists of the past. Instead, the tools of modern theory and empirical techniques need to be blended with an appreciation of how modern labor markets and organizations work. Well-grounded and careful research of this type has proven useful in various state legislative debates over the effects of public-sector impasse resolution alternatives (Stevens 1966; Stern et al. 1975; Kochan et al. 1979). Similarly, careful studies of management and labor practices in key industries, such as automobiles, have helped to focus debates over the ways different production and human resource strategies work in practice (Katz 1985; Womack, Jones, and Roos 1990). In both the public-sector and the auto-industry examples, quantitative data and analysis were combined with analysis of the institutional issues involved. Unfortunately, there is all too little such research on national employment and labor policy issues.

The keys to producing this type of research lie in creating the data needed to support application of modern analytic techniques to policy analysis and in providing opportunities and incentives for scholars to participate in policy-making and analysis. This will require building national data bases capable of documenting and evaluating the contributions of human resource and labor market policies to economic performance. Currently we have labor cost, employment cost, and consumer price surveys, but we have no equivalent data base for tracking the payoffs from investments in skills training, education, and cooperative initiatives. A productivity, quality, and human resource innovations data base is needed to evaluate the effects of these policy initiatives and to convince skeptical managers, political leaders, and macroeconomic policymakers that these human resource investments and policies do pay off. Only by building a community of respected researchers who move in and out of various government or advisory roles, can employment policy have the analytical foundation and empirical justification needed to sustain the role envisioned for it here. Nothing would serve to carry on the traditions of prior generations of institutional labor economists in a more appropriate fashion.

Author's Note

The support for this research was provided by the MIT Leaders for Manufacturing Program and the MIT Industrial Performance Center. The views expressed in this chapter are solely those of the author.

Notes

1. To avoid confusion I will use the terms *employment policy* and *employment relations* to include what conventionally has been labeled labor, industrial relations, or human resource management or policy. In this chapter, as in all research in this tradition dating back to the origins of the field discussed here, the domain of interest is broad, encompassing all aspects of the employment relationship and the parties (workers, managers, labor representatives, government policymakers, and so on) who influence its institutions, policies, and outcomes.
2. See, for example, the various reports of the Berkeley Roundtable on International Trade; Cuomo Commission 1988; Dertouzos, Lester, and Solow 1989; Collective Bargaining Forum 1988 and 1991.
3. See, for example, Johnston and Packer 1987, a report by the Hudson Institute prepared for the U.S. Department of Labor; Commission on the Skills of the American Workforce 1990; U.S. Department of Labor 1989; and the recent report of the secretary of labor's National Commission on Work-Based Learning, U.S. Department of Labor 1992.
4. What follows is an updated and expanded version of the ideas in a paper written with my colleague Robert McKersie and first presented at the First Regional International Industrial Relations Association Congress of the Americas, Quebec City, August 1988 (Kochan and McKersie 1989).

References

Adams, Roy. 1992. "The Role of the State in Industrial Relations," in David Lewin, Peter Scherer, and Olivia Mitchell (eds.), *New Directions for Industrial Relations and Human Resource Management Research.* Madison, Wis.: Industrial Relations Research Association.

Barbash, Jack. 1980. "Values in Industrial Relations: The Case of the Adversary Principle," in *Proceedings of the Industrial Relations Research Association.* Madison, Wis.: Industrial Relations Research Association. 1–7.

Baron, James N., Frank R. Dobbin, and P. Devereaux Jennings. 1986. "War and Peace: The Evolution of Modern Personnel Administration in U.S. Industry," *American Journal of Sociology* 92, 350–384.

Batt, Rosemary, and Paul Osterman. 1991. *A National Framework for Employment and Training Policy.* Report prepared for the Economic Policy Institute, Washington, D.C.

Berle, Adolfe, and Gardiner Means. 1933. *The Modern Corporation and Private Property.* New York: Macmillan.

Blasi, Joseph, and Douglas Kruse. 1991. *The New Owners.* New York: Harper Business Press, 1991.

Business Week, 1991. "Tough Times, Tough Bosses," November 25, 174–184.

Carnevale, Anthony P. 1990. *America and the New Economy.* Washington, D.C.: U.S. Department of Labor.

Cebon, Peter. 1992. "Management at the Environmental Interface: Input-Output Functions in Organizations." Paper presented at the Academy of Management annual meeting.

Chelius, James, and James Dworkin (eds.). 1990. *Reflections on the Transformation of Industrial Relations.* Metuchen, N.J.: IMLR Press/Rutgers University.

Child, John. 1972. "Organizational Structure, Environment, and Performance: The Role of Strategic Choice," *Sociology* 6, 1–22.

Cole, Robert E. 1989. *Strategies for Learning.* Berkeley: University of California Press.

Collective Bargaining Forum. 1988. *New Directions for Labor and Management.* Washington, D.C.: U.S. Department of Labor, Bureau of Labor Management Relations and Cooperative Programs.

———. 1991. *Labor-Management Commitment: A Compact for Change.* Washington, D.C.: U.S. Department of Labor, Bureau of Labor Management Relations and Cooperative Programs.

Commission on the Skills of the American Workforce. 1990. *America's Choice: High Skills or Low Wages.* Rochester, N.Y.: National Center on Education and the Economy.

Commons, John R. 1919. "The American Shoemakers, 1648–1895: A Sketch of Industrial Evolution," *The Quarterly Journal of Economics.*

Cuomo Commission. 1988. *The Cuomo Commission Report on Trade and Competitiveness.* New York: Simon and Schuster.

Cyert, Richard M., and James G. March. 1963. *A Behavioral Theory of the Firm.* Englewood Cliffs, N.J.: Prentice Hall.

Cyert, Richard M., and David C. Mowery (eds). 1986. *Technology and Employment.* Washington, D.C.: National Academy Press.

Davis, Gerald. 1991. "Agents Without Principles? The Spread of the Poison Pill through the Intercorporate Network," *Administrative Science Quarterly* 36, no. 4, (December).

Derber, Milton. 1982. "Are We in a New Stage?" *Proceedings of the Industrial Relations Research Association.* Madison, Wis.: Industrial Relations Research Association. pp. 1–9.

Dertouzos, Michael, Robert Solow, and Richard Lester. 1989. *Made in America.* Cambridge, Mass.: MIT Press.

Douglas, Paul. 1919. "Plant Administration of Labor," *Journal of Political Economy* 27, 544–560.

Doyle, Frank P. 1989. "The Global Human Resource Challenge for the Nineties." Paper delivered to the World Management Congress, New York, September 23.

Dunlop, John T. 1967. "The Functions of the Strike," in Neil W. Chamberlain and John T. Dunlop (eds.), *Frontiers of Collective Bargaining.* New York: Harper & Row, 1967.

——, 1988. "Have the 1980's Changed the U.S. Industrial Relations," *Monthly Labor Review.* (May), 29–34.

Freeman, Richard E., and James L. Medoff. 1984. *What Do Unions Do?* New York: Basic Books.

Freedman, Audrey. 1990. *The Changing Human Resources Function.* New York: The Conference Board.

Hattam, Victoria. 1986. *Unions and Politics: The Courts and American Labor 1806–1896.* Ph.D. dissertation, MIT.

Heckscher, Charles. 1987. *The New Unionism.* New York: Basic Books.

Jacoby, Sanford. 1985. *Employing Bureaucracies.* New York: Columbia University Press.

Johnston, William, and Arnold Packer. 1987. *Workforce 2000.* Indianapolis: The Hudson Institute.

Katz, Harry C. 1985. *Shifting Gears.* Cambridge, Mass.: MIT Press.

Kern, Horst, and Charles F. Sabel. 1991. "Trade Unions and Decentralized Production: A Sketch of the Strategic Problems of the West German Labor Movement." Working paper, MIT Department of Political Science.

Klare, Karl. 1988. "Workplace Democracy and Market Reconstruction: An Agenda for Legal Reform," *Catholic University Law Review.* Fall, 1–68.

Kochan, Thomas A., and Peter Cappelli. 1983. "The Transformation of the Industrial Relations and Personnel Function," in Paul Osterman (ed.), *Internal Labor Markets.* Cambridge, Mass.: MIT Press.

Kochan, Thomas A., Harry C. Katz, and Robert McKersie. 1986. *The Transformation of American Industrial Relations.* New York: Basic Books.

Kochan, Thomas A., and Robert B. McKersie. 1992. "Human Resources, Organizational Governance, and Public Policy: Lessons from a Decade of Experimentation," in Thomas A. Kochan and Michael Useem (eds.), *Transforming Organizations.* New York: Oxford University Press.

Kochan, Thomas A., and Paul Osterman. 1992. "Human Resource Development and Utilization: Is There Too Little in the U.S.?" Paper prepared for the Time Horizons Project of the Council on Competitiveness, MIT.

Kochan, Thomas A., Paul Osterman, and John Paul MacDuffie. 1988. "Employment Security at DEC: Sustaining Values amid Environmental Change," *Human Resource Management Journal,* Fall.

Kochan, Thomas A., John H. Wells, and Michal Smith. 1992. "The Consequences of a Failed Industrial Relations System: Contract Workers in the Petrochemical Industry." Working paper, MIT Sloan School of Management.

Kochan, Thomas A., et al. 1979. *Dispute Resolution Under Factfinding and Arbitration.* New York: American Arbitration Association.

Lawler, John J. 1990. *Unionization and Deunionization.* Columbia: University of South Carolina Press.

Levine, David I., and Laura D' Andrea Tyson. 1990. "Participation, Productivity, and the Firm's Environment," in Alan S. Blinder (ed.), *Paying for Productivity.* Washington, D.C.: Brookings Institution, 183–236.

Lewin, David. 1987. "Industrial Relations as a Strategic Variable," in Morris M. Kleiner et al. (eds.), *Human Resources and the Performance of the Firm.* Madison, Wis.: Industrial Relations Research Association.

MacDuffie, John Paul, and Thomas A. Kochan. 1991. "Determinants of Training: A Cross-National Comparison in the Auto Industry." Paper presented at the annual meeting of the Academy of Management, August.

MacDuffie, John Paul, and John Krafcik. 1989. "Flexible Production Systems and Manufacturing Performance: The Role of Human Resources and Technology." Paper presented at the annual meeting of the Academy of Management, Washington, D.C., August 16.

March, James G., and Herbert Simon. 1958. *Organizations.* New York: Wiley.

Marshall, Ray. 1987. *Unheard Voices.* New York: Basic Books.

Mayo, Elton. 1933. *The Human Problems of Industrial Civilization.* New York: Macmillan.

McGregor, Douglas M. 1960. *The Human Side of the Enterprise.* New York: McGraw-Hill.

Noble, Charles. 1992. "Keeping OSHA's Feet to the Fire," *Technology Review.* February-March, 1–9.

Peters, Thomas, and Robert Waterman. 1982. *In Search of Excellence.* New York: Harper & Row.

Pettigrew, Andrew. 1973. *Politics of Organizational Decision Making.* London: Tavistock.

Pfeffer, Jeffrey. 1992. *Managing with Power.* Boston: Harvard Business School Press.

Piore, Michael, and Charles Sabel. 1984. *The Second Industrial Divide.* New York: Basic Books.

Porter, Michael (ed.). 1994. *Underinvestment in American Firms.* Cambridge, Mass.: Harvard Business School Press.

Slichter, Sumner. 1919. "The Management of Labor," *Journal of Political Economy* 27, 813–839.

Slichter, Sumner, James J. Healy, and E. Robert Livernash. 1960. *The Impact of Collective Bargaining on Management.* Washington, D.C.: Brookings Institution.

Stern, James L., et al. 1975. *Final Offer Arbitration.* Lexington, Mass.: D. C. Heath.

Stevens, Carl, M. 1966. "Is Compulsory Arbitration Compatible with Collective Bargaining?" *Industrial Relations* 5, 38–52.

Stone, Katherine Van Wezel. 1988. "Labor and the Corporate Structure: Changing Conceptions and Emerging Possibilities," *University of Chicago Law Review* 55, 73–173.

Thomas, Robert J. 1994. *What Machines Can't Do: Organizational Politics and Technological Change.* Berkeley: University of California Press.

Thompson, James D. 1967. *Organizations in Action.* New York: McGraw-Hill.

Towers, Perrin. 1991. *A 21st Century Vision: Priorities for Competitive Advantage.* New York: Towers Perrin Consulting Firm.

U.S. Department of Labor. 1989. *Investing in People.* Report of the Secretary of Labor's Commission on Workforce Quality and Labor Market Efficiency, Washington, D.C.: U.S. Department of Labor.

U.S. Department of Labor. 1992. *Final Report of the National Commission on Work-Based Learning.* Washington, D.C.: U.S. Department of Labor.

Useem, Michael, and Martin M. Gottlieb. 1992. "Corporate Restructuring, Ownership-Disciplined Alignment, and the Reorganization of Management," *Human Resource Management* 29, 285–306.

Wall Street Journal. 1991. "Torrent of Job Cuts Shows Human Toll of Recession Goes On," December 12, 1.

Walton, Richard E. 1985. "Toward a Strategy of Eliciting Employee Commitment Based on Policies of Mutuality," in Richard E. Walton and Paul R. Lawrence (eds) *HRM Trends & Challenges.* Boston: Harvard Business School Press, 1985, 35–65.

Walton, Richard E. 1987. *Innovating to Compete.* San Francisco: Jossey-Bass.

Walton, Richard E., and Robert B. McKersie. 1965. *A Behavioral Theory of Labor Negotiations.* New York: McGraw-Hill.

Webb, Sydney, and Beatrice Webb. 1897. *Industrial Democracy.* London: Longmans.

Weiler, Paul. 1990. *Governing the Workplace.* Cambridge, Mass.: Harvard University Press.

Weitzman, Martin L. 1984. *The Share Economy.* Cambridge, Mass.: Harvard University Press.

Weitzman, Martin L., and Douglas L. Kruse. 1990. "Profit Sharing and Productivity," in Alan S. Blinder (ed.), *Paying for Productivity.* Washington, D.C.: Brookings Institution, 95–139.

Wever, Kirsten, and Christopher Allen. 1992. "Change and Innovation in Germany and the U.S.: Internal versus External Flexibility." Working paper, Northeastern University.

Womack, James, J. Daniel Jones, and Daniel Roos. 1990. *The Machine That Changed the World.* New York: Rawson-Macmillan.

Index

Aaron, Benjamin, 422
Abraham, Katherine, 305, 320
Abrams, Roger I., 494
Absenteeism: research, 404–5; effect of hours worked, 558
Accelerationist model of unemployment, 260; natural rate version, 259, 262–63, 267; alternative, 260, 262–63
Adams, Roy, 659
Addison, J. T., 289, 291, 293
Adler, Paul, 316, 326–27, 622–23
Affirmative action programs: early development, 87, 582–87; competitive labor markets effect on, 145; legislation, 183, 478; compliance reviews, 575, 576–77, 582, 588, 591; provisions, 575, 576–77; executive orders, 575–76; goals, 576, 590, 591; mutual exclusivity with discrimination, 577–78; scope, 577–78; political support, 578–79; groups covered, 580; benefits, 581, 587; limitations, 581; measurable results, 581, 596–97; quotas, 581, 582, 590, 596; training components, 583; affected class relief provisions, 584; utilization aspects, 584; enforcement, 586, 587–88, 591; media attention, 586; sanctions, 586; maturation,

587–89; occupational advancement through, 589–90; as earnings redistribution program, 592; set-aside programs, 593; adverse impact claims, 596; impact on productivity, 596–97
Age Discrimination in Employment Act, 1967, 478
Agent-principle issues, 330
Airline Deregulation Act, 482
Air traffic controllers strike, 433, 443–44, 446, 481
Akerlof, George A., 177, 181, 321
Alchian, A. A., 239
Alexander v. *Gardner-Denver*, 496
Allen, Christopher, 656, 665
Allen, S., 290
Allen, Walter, 595
Althauser, Robert, 306
Altmeyer, Arthur J., 41, 53, 54–55
American Arbitration Association, 501
American Association for Labor Legislation, 41, 53–54, 352
American Capitalism: The Concept of Countervailing Power (Galbraith), 431
American Economic Association, 71
American economic system: influence of technology, 603; mass production emphasis, 603–

673